Cost Accounting
Principles and Practice

Cost Accounting
Principles and Practice

Alan Upchurch

FINANCIAL TIMES
Prentice Hall

An imprint of **Pearson Education**

Harlow, England · London · New York · Reading, Massachusetts · San Francisco · Toronto · Don Mills, Ontario · Sydney
Tokyo · Singapore · Hong Kong · Seoul · Taipei · Cape Town · Madrid · Mexico City · Amsterdam · Munich · Paris · Milan

Pearson Education Limited

Edinburgh Gate
Harlow
Essex CM20 2JE

and Associated Companies around the world

Visit us on the World Wide Web at:
www.pearsoneduc.com

_____

First published in Great Britain 2002

ISBN 0 273 64365 7

British Library Cataloguing-in-Publication Data
A catalogue record for this book can be obtained from the British Library.

Library of Congress Cataloging-in-Publication Data
Upchurch, Alan.
   Cost accounting / Alan Upchurch.
      p. cm.
   Includes index.
   ISBN 0-273-64365-7 (alk. paper)
     1. Cost accounting.   I. Title.

   HF5686.C8 U845 2001
   657'.42--dc21

                                    2001040544

10 9 8 7 6 5 4 3 2 1
08 07 06 05 04 03 02

Typeset in 10/12 Sabon by 25.
Printed by Ashford Colour Press Ltd., Gosport

BRIEF CONTENTS

CONTENTS

A Companion Website accompanies
COST ACCOUNTING

Visit the *Cost Accounting* Companion Website at
www.booksites.net/upchurch to find valuable teaching
and learning material including:

For Students
- Study material designed to help you improve your results
- Multiple choice and 'short form' questions to test your learning
- Links to relevant sites on the World Wide Web
- Extra coaching for chapters where there are common pitfalls

For Lecturers
- A secure, password-protected site with teaching material
- A downloadable version of the *Solutions Manual*
- Extra questions to use with your students
- Solutions to the extra questions
- PowerPoint slides that can be downloaded and used as OHTs
- A syllabus manager that will build and host your very own course web page

PREFACE

The purpose of this book is to provide an introduction to cost accounting. It is aimed principally at first- and second-year undergraduate courses and at non-degree courses such as higher national diploma. It is also suitable for Foundation and Intermediate professional examinations set by AAT, ACCA, CIMA and CIPFA. Although certain readers will have some knowledge of cost accounting, this is in no way an essential pre-requisite, as the book works from a base of zero prior knowledge. For those chapters that deal with double-entry bookkeeping, a very basic understanding of the subject will be helpful.

Use of the words 'principles' and 'practice' in the book's title indicates the general approach taken: we need to know both *why* things are (or should be) done in a particular way, and *how* we (should) do them. The problem is that the how and why cannot be understood in isolation – so principles and practice are dealt with in an integrated manner.

Techniques are an essential feature of cost accounting and a thorough understanding of these is clearly necessary for accounting practitioners. However, users of cost accounting information can also benefit greatly from technique-based knowledge. In particular, it should help to raise awareness of the fact that cost accounting does not offer some kind of organisational or managerial 'quick fix'. It is hard to imagine how any discipline's scope and (equally importantly) its limitations can be grasped without solid grounding in the methods that it employs in pursuit of its aims. Because cost accounting is such a pervasive element of the management process, understanding 'why' and 'how' acquires great significance.

Certain themes recur throughout the book:

- The need to provide different cost information for different purposes.
- The need for consistency between strategic, tactical and operational cost information.
- The likelihood that cost information, while important, provides only a partial picture of complex wholes.

Although stated separately here (and at various points in the book), these issues are almost inextricably linked. The potential danger of ignoring them should be much more apparent given an understanding of cost accounting principles and practice.

The implications for cost accounting of recent changes in organisational/managerial environment (such as increasing awareness of quality management) will be stressed early in the book. But a balance must be struck between 'new' and 'traditional'. On the one hand, emergence of philosophies like world-class manufacturing, of advanced manufacturing technologies and of just-in-time systems presents a vigorous challenge to many of the received (at least in a UK context) wisdoms of cost accounting. On the other hand, a book which purports to reflect 'principles and practice' cannot ignore how cost accounting still operates in very many organisations.

Cost accounting occurs in virtually every type of organisation: manufacturing, service, private and public sector, commercial and not-for-profit. Although details may differ between organisations, basic principles and methodologies are pretty much the same. For this reason, a wide variety of organisational settings has been used for in-chapter scenarios, questions, press and journal extracts. However, specialist knowledge of specific types of organisation is not required – the aim being to illustrate cost accounting's wide applicability.

The advance of semesterisation and modularisation has meant a move to 'short and fat' course provision, and a learning culture is now the major focus for instructional effort; all of which places added onus on students for taking charge of their own learning. For this reason, I felt that the book should be as reader-friendly as possible – hence the following features.

- *Chapter objectives and summaries* While these are fairly standard in most textbooks, chapter summaries are intended to be sufficiently detailed, not only to fulfil their role as summaries but also to provide quick reference, e.g. for revision purposes.
- *Newspaper and journal extracts* Quotations relevant to the topic under discussion are presented to underscore practical relevance and to add a 'real-world' dimension sometimes lacking in textbooks.
- *In-text activities* Each chapter contains a number of brief activities to be undertaken by the reader. These offer the chance to practise, consolidate or evaluate subjects as they are presented, and in 'bite-size' chunks. Activities are indicated by the symbol ✔ (check) and, in all cases, feedback is provided within the text immediately following.
- *Glossary* A separate glossary of technical terms is included at the end of the book; this should be useful in its own right and may also be valuable to readers dealing with chapters in a piecemeal way.
- *Chapter-end questions* Each chapter concludes with a section comprising several self-test questions plus several questions without answers. Answers to the former are provided at the end of the book; those to the latter in the accompanying *Solutions Manual*.
- *Chapter scenarios* Wherever practicable, a single example is used for illustrative purposes within each chapter, being progressively developed in line with the subject-matter. This avoids the distraction for readers of having to continually absorb new background information.

Lecturing colleagues have not been forgotten; the following supplementary material is available for use with the text:

- The *Solutions Manual* Including answers to chapter-end questions not provided within the text.
- *On-line facilities* A further large collection of questions not included in the book (along with solutions) is available to lecturers who adopt the text, in a password-protected area at http://www.booksites.net/upchurch.
- *PowerPoint™ disks* Key chapter points are presented on a series of 3.5-inch disks prepared using Microsoft PowerPoint™, offering the facility for computerised slide/OHP master generation and provision of handout materials.
- *OHP masters* A full set of 'conventional' OHP masters is available, based around chapter summaries.

ACKNOWLEDGEMENTS

Writing this book has involved the collaboration and support of numerous individuals and organisations. In acknowledging their contribution to that which is good in the book, I should also point out that any errors or omissions are entirely of my own making.

Not for the first time, Marion, Aileen, Gillian and Alba have suffered extended bouts of anti-social behaviour as writing has progressed; without their patience and calming influence, nothing would have been possible. As ever, Professor Alan Godfrey, Head of Division of Accounting and Finance at Glasgow Caledonian University, has been unstinting in his support and encouragement. At Pearson Education, my particular thanks are due to Pat Bond, for starting the ball rolling, and to Paula Harris, Catherine Newman and Liz Tarrant for dealing with my eccentricities on a regular basis. Thanks are due to Jim Shepherd who had the thankless task of sorting out the typescript. For their valued comment on draft material, I am grateful to Kim Arnold of Derby University, Eric Edwards of the University of Northumbria at Newcastle and Hywel Williams of Glamorgan University.

I am indebted to the following publications for their kind permission to print extracts from articles:

ACCA Students' Newsletter
CIMA Management Accounting
CIMA Student
The Economist Newspaper Limited, London
Financial Times Limited

The following examining bodies have been good enough to allow me to reproduce some of their questions:

The Association of Accounting Technicians (AAT)
The Association of Chartered Certified Accountants (ACCA)
The Chartered Institute of Bankers in Scotland (CIOBS)
The Chartered Institute of Management Accountants (CIMA)
The Chartered Institute of Public Finance and Accountancy (CIPFA)

In all cases, answers provided to these questions are my own.

If I have omitted anyone, please accept apologies and gratitude in equal measure.

Alan Upchurch

CHAPTER 1

Introduction

A critical view of product costing

... A famous quote made by Professor J. Maurice Clark in 1923 identified ten important functions for cost accounting.

1. To help determine a normal or satisfactory price for goods sold.
2. To help fix a minimum limit on price cutting.
3. To determine which goods are most profitable and which are unprofitable.
4. To control inventory.
5. To set a value on inventory.
6. To test the efficiency of different processes.
7. To test the efficiency of different departments.
8. To detect losses, waste and pilfering.
9. To separate the cost of idleness from the cost of producing goods.
10. To tie in with the financial accounts.

To this can be added, by way of comparison, the list produced by Bright *et al.* in 1992.

Uses of costing techniques

- Cost control
- Product pricing
- Investment justification
- Management performance
- Sourcing material/services
- New product introductions
- Market strategy
- Engineering process and product changes

Source: Bright *et al. Management Accounting Research*, 1992.

... It is essential that organisations have accurate and objective knowledge of the cost of providing a good or service ...

Clark's view of different costs for different purposes remains valid ...

Finally, product costing is not a closed system. Any product/service has to perform in the marketplace. It is here that the ultimate test will be undertaken. The costs are not just boring statistics. They are the basis of important attention-directing and decision-making information. The accurate cost of a product will dictate whether or not it is viable to stay in the market. Alternatively, the existence of known high costs may be a deterrent to competitors entering the market – high costs could be a barrier to entry. Still further, they are the basis for change and meaningful evaluation.

Source: M.L. Inman, *ACCA Students' Newsletter*, May 1994.

Exhibit 1.1 Purposes and importance of cost information

INTRODUCTION

Comparison of the two lists of uses for costing information presented in Exhibit 1.1 suggests that its importance is as great today as ever it was. Knowledge about the cost of organisational activities is vital – as is recognition of the fact that almost every activity has some kind of cost – or other financial – implication. What organisations do affects, or is of interest to, a wide range of individuals and groups, both within and outside the organisation. While these interested parties ('stakeholders') don't all need to be accountants, they do need to have appropriate information about the financial impact of an organisation's activities. It is exactly this sort of information that accounting as a general discipline is intended to convey. On the face of it, simple enough.

But closer inspection of Exhibit 1.1 sounds a warning about this apparent simplicity. Organisational activities are, after all, complex, and occur in a dynamic environment. Accounting information is not produced in a vacuum, and must reflect this complexity and dynamism – which raises a number of problems. In the first place, we need to know who are the users (or potential users) of accounting information and to have some idea of what their information needs might be. Although it's easy enough to draw up a list of users, and to suggest what they might need (or want) to know, it's questionable whether accounting, as a 'general-purpose' discipline, is capable of meeting the diverse information needs of a range of users.

Accounting has addressed this issue by distinguishing between users internal to the organisation and users external to the organisation, developing two forms of accounting aimed at meeting the needs of each of these broad user categories. Financial accounting is principally targeted at external users, while management accounting is mainly for internal users. But there are likely to be areas of overlap between external and internal information needs: for example, the pricing decision referred to in Exhibit 1.1. Financial and management accounting cannot, therefore, exist in glorious isolation from one another. Cost accounting can be seen as the common ground between the two. It provides information for stock valuation and profit measurement, which is of interest to both external and internal parties. It also provides information for the key (internal) management activities of decision making, planning and control. However, the distinction we are drawing, especially between cost accounting and management accounting, is extremely blurred in practice, and the two are often taken to mean the same thing, or we refer to 'cost and management accounting' as a single subset of accounting.

Perhaps the important point here is not the label we apply to different forms of accounting but the fact that we recognise the existence of a range of users of accounting information. This raises another problem: since different users have different needs, we need to use the same basic financial data for different purposes. As Exhibit 1.1 puts it 'different costs for different purposes'. This precept is arguably the fundamental from which cost accounting (and possibly a great deal of management accounting) flows. It is a principle that will be reiterated on many occasions in the pages and chapters that follow. We will also see ample evidence of the dangers of using the 'wrong' cost for the wrong purpose(s). What we will see is that 'cost' needs to be related to the situation and purpose – otherwise both the word and the figures it describes have little real meaning.

We have used the word 'information' several times in this introductory section, and before discussing the other issues raised here, we need to consider the difference between 'data' and 'information', along with the information system that organisations use to process the former into the latter. As a further important preliminary, we will also distinguish between different types of information.

OBJECTIVES

When you have completed this chapter, you will be able to:

- distinguish between data and information;
- appreciate that cost (and management) accounting form part of a wider, integrated management information system;
- distinguish between financial, non-financial, quantitative and qualitative information;
- use Anthony *et al.*'s strategic–tactical–operational 'hierarchy' to classify information;
- explain how problems relating to objectives may impinge on information provision;
- identify potential users of accounting information;
- outline the different roles of financial, cost and management accounting, their similarities and differences;
- define the purposes of cost accounting;
- state the main characteristics of useful information along with the significance of the cost/benefit criterion in this context;
- appreciate cost accounting's scorekeeping, attention-directing and problem-solving aspects and their interrelationship;
- suggest possible barriers to communication which may affect cost accounting information.

DATA, INFORMATION AND THE MANAGEMENT INFORMATION SYSTEM

Although we tend to use the words 'data' and 'information' interchangeably, there is an important difference in meaning: **data** are the 'raw' facts and figures that, once processed, become **information**. For example, a pile of supplier invoices (data), after passing through the accounting system, will provide information about such things as purchase costs, range of goods/services purchased and sources of purchase. The **management information system** (**MIS**) is a set of interrelated systems which filters and processes data from a variety of internal and external sources so as to produce usable information relating to an organisation's activities. Figure 1.1 illustrates.

 What 'other systems' might, along with accounting, form an organisation's MIS?

The precise constituents of an MIS will depend on the organisation concerned, but, in addition to accounting, we could see systems such as personnel, marketing, purchasing, production scheduling and quality control. The arrows with dotted lines in Figure 1.1 show that these 'subsystems' of an MIS do not exist in isolation: data (and possibly information) will frequently be shared between two or more of them. Employee data, for instance, will be input to both accounting and personnel systems, customer data to both marketing and accounting, supplier details to both purchasing

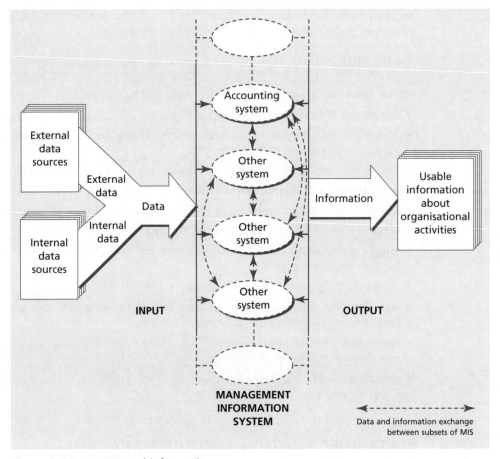

Figure 1.1 Data, MIS and information

and accounting. What should be clear from consideration of an MIS is the important role of accounting as a part of the wider management information system. Figure 1.1 also shows that data from sources external to the organisation (e.g. about the market conditions which it faces) are every bit as important as data from internal sources.

This, you may feel, is all very well and good for large organisations, but what about small ones? The general principles illustrated in Figure 1.1 are true for all organisations – large or small, private or public, commercial or non-profit – but the nature of an organisation will affect its MIS in the following ways:

1 *The degree of formality.* Generally, larger organisations will require a much more formal MIS than smaller organisations; but you should note that a certain minimum accounting system is necessary in all organisations.
2 *The precise subsystems.* The sophistication of the accounting system, along with what other subsystems exist within an MIS, will be determined by organisational circumstances (e.g. 'production' scheduling is irrelevant in a hospital, but a subsystem which schedules operating theatre usage is not).

The nature and complexity of an MIS is dictated not only by organisational circumstances but also by the system's cost. In the search for 'better' or more 'accurate' information, it might be easy to forget the cost of acquiring it. As a minimum, the cost of obtaining information should not be greater than the benefit of possessing it – a point we will return to later in the chapter.

Without an MIS to impose order on the mass of available data, organisational activity will at best be severely hampered, at worst will be quite impossible. One way in which the MIS imposes such order is by classifying information according to type: financial, non-financial, quantitative, qualitative.

FINANCIAL, NON-FINANCIAL, QUANTITATIVE AND QUALITATIVE INFORMATION

Financial information, like product cost or selling price, is merely a monetary expression of one or more aspects of organisational activity. Non-financial information (like the number of staff employed in different organisational departments) is stated in non-monetary terms. Information can be further split into:

- **quantitative information**: information expressed in numerical form;
- **qualitative information**: information which is not (or which cannot be) expressed in numerical form.

By its nature, accounting information will always be quantitative. Accounting's ability to describe a range of organisational activities using neat (and seemingly simple) figures like 'cost' or 'profit' is the reason for its popularity as a medium for communicating economic information. But look at Exhibit 1.2.

Peugot casts doubt over future of Ryton

PSA Peugeot Citroën, the French carmaker, has issued a further threat to manufacturing in Britain by casting doubt over the future of its Ryton plant in the West Midlands.

It said a £90.9m investment in its plant near Coventry could be jeopardised by Britain's wait-and-see approach to the Euro.

The disclosure comes the day after General Motors announced the closure of its Vauxhall plant in Luton with the loss of 2200 jobs.

Jean-Martin Folz, PSA chief executive, said plans for a new paint shop at the Ryton Peugot factory would be subject to an intensive review. Without a new paint shop, due in 2003, the future of the plant is uncertain ...

Source: Tim Burt, Robert Shrimsley and John Griffiths, *Financial Times*, 14 December 2000. Reprinted with permission.

Exhibit 1.2 Different types of information

The quantitative information in Exhibit 1.2 – both financial and non-financial – is easy to identify: '£90.9m investment', 'loss of 2200 jobs'. Information of this sort is routinely generated by an MIS, and by its accounting subsystem in particular.

✔ *Can you identify any qualitative information in Exhibit 1.2?*

There is really only one item of qualitative information in the exhibit, summarised by its last seven words: 'the future of the plant is uncertain'. And although it is not expressed in numbers, it is the most important piece of information provided.

The plant's 'uncertain future' may be based on analysis of quantitative evidence by its parent company, but it is essentially a matter of *judgement*, involving consideration of factors both internal and external to the organisation. What should be clear from Exhibit 1.2 – and this is a point that we shall return to on several occasions in subsequent chapters – is that financial/quantitative information may not present a complete picture. In fact, it could even give an impression that is at variance with the totality of a situation. What would happen to Exhibit 1.2 if we were to remove the crucial qualitative information? If we did this, we would be left with no information of any real value at all. Valuable as financial/quantitative information may be, it cannot (and should not) be used to the exclusion of qualitative. We might therefore define the role of accounting information as being:

> **provision of support for judgements about organisational activities past, present and future.**

STRATEGIC, TACTICAL AND OPERATIONAL INFORMATION

In addition to classification by type, an MIS may also classify information according to its scope and span. These two classifications are not mutually exclusive: that which we are about to describe cannot meaningfully be used in isolation from the last classification – a point that should become apparent as our discussion progresses. Anthony *et al*. (1965) identified the information 'hierarchy' set out in Figure 1.2, each level being roughly equated with the different strata of organisational management.

Strategic information

Strategic information will be employed mostly by senior management to determine organisational objectives, along with the resources and policies necessary to achieve them. Such information relates to the organisation as a whole, over a medium- or long-term time horizon, and in the context of the wider environment within which the organisation operates. The need for, and thrust of, strategic information often derives from an organisation's **mission statement** (or 'mission'), which specifies its intended economic/social role over the long term. Where it is explicitly stated, mission is most often expressed as a fairly generalised objective (e.g. 'provide high-quality domestic appliances to the retail market'). The purpose of strategic information can be seen as adding form and substance to such broad statements.

In Exhibit 1.2, any decision about the Ryton plant is strategic, and will be based on an analysis, by senior PSA executives, of strategic information.

 Suggest three examples of strategic information which PSA's management might consider when deciding the future of the Ryton plant.

One important area of strategic interest – and one entirely external to the company – is whether or not the UK decides to adopt the Euro, along with the time lapse before

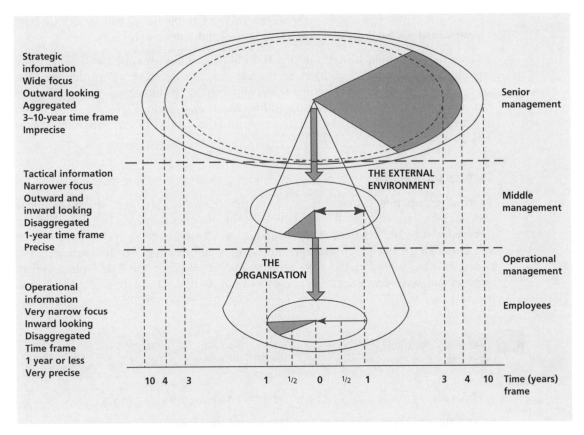

Strategic information
Wide focus
Outward looking
Aggregated
3–10-year time frame
Imprecise

Tactical information
Narrower focus
Outward and
inward looking
Disaggregated
1-year time frame
Precise

Operational information
Very narrow focus
Inward looking
Disaggregated
Time frame
1 year or less
Very precise

THE EXTERNAL
ENVIRONMENT

THE
ORGANISATION

Senior management

Middle management

Operational management

Employees

10 4 3   1 ½ 0 ½ 1   3 4 10 Time (years) frame

Figure 1.2 Anthony *et al.*'s hierarchy of information

such a decision is finally reached. Management would also be likely to consider factors such as:

- the extent to which closure/retention of the plant fits with the company's objectives/mission; criteria for assessing the desirability of closure may be developed in tandem;
- expected future demand for the company's cars;
- current and expected future developments both by PSA and by its competitors (e.g. new models of car);
- current and expected future cost trends at the Ryton plant and at the company's other plants;
- any other potential action by the UK government or by the European Community which might affect the company's market, its costs, or both;
- implications for the company of possible redundancies should the Ryton plant be closed (in terms of cost, industrial relations and company image).

Our list is far from being comprehensive, and you may well have made some different suggestions. Incomplete as it is, we can, however, use it to make two points about strategic, compared to tactical and operational information (which we discuss below):

1 Strategic information draws much more heavily on sources external to the organisation – 'environmental' sources.

2 It is considerably less precise – the whole tone of Exhibit 1.2 is redolent of this, with generalised phraseology like 'uncertain future' and 'intensive review'.

Gathering and using strategic information is vital to the continued well-being of an organisation, but there is evidence to suggest that this does not always happen. For example, a 1995 survey of 500 companies conducted by the Industrial Research Bureau concluded that there was 'a yawning gulf between organisations' growing recognition of the value of information as a strategic asset and their ability or inclination to manage it as an asset'.

Tactical information

Tactical information provides the conduit through which strategic objectives, plans and decisions are translated into action by middle management. The time horizon involved will be shorter than at the strategic level (commonly one year or less), there will be much greater precision, and the focus of information will be narrower. For example, management at PSA will prepare annual plans for the Ryton plant which, taken cumulatively over, say, 5 years, will add up to this plant's strategic plan for the period.

 Suggest three *items of tactical information which may be relevant to a decision by PSA regarding its Ryton plant.*

PSA's management may well be interested in tactical information such as:

- detailed annual cost and revenue estimates for the plant;
- productivity, manpower and output details;
- schedule of plant, equipment and premises giving, for example, sales values, adaptability for other internal uses;
- timetable for any closure plan that might be decided on, showing costs for each projected phase of closure.

Once again, our list is not exhaustive, but it is sufficient to illustrate the increased focus on internal factors, the narrower emphasis and need for greater precision characteristic of tactical (as opposed to strategic) information.

Operational information

Operational information is used by lower managerial echelons and employees to support the actions necessary to effect desired tactical outcomes (themselves aimed at achieving a given strategy). It can be defined as planning the economic, efficient and effective use of resources so as to achieve tactical plans.

British Steel's strategic plan in Exhibit 1.3 is to cut costs by shedding 1000 jobs per year over the next five years; the 400 job losses referred to in the article's title are part of the tactics deemed necessary to achieve this. The operational thread will stem from these tactics: e.g. estimating the costs/cost savings of the 150 jobs which 'are to go in the next 12 months', providing information to employees about voluntary redundancy or early retirement and assessing their potential take-up rate, deciding which categories of employee will be subject to compulsory redundancy (should this prove necessary).

British Steel sheds 400 jobs in cost-cutting drive

British Steel yesterday announced the loss of 400 jobs at its tinplate business in South Wales, as it took its first step towards implementing a company-wide cost-cutting programme launched earlier this month.

The group expects to announce further job cuts in the next few weeks as managers prepare detailed proposals to fulfil a plan to shed over 1000 posts a year over the next five years.

About 150 jobs are to go in the next 12 months at the tinplate plant at Ebbw Vale. A further 250 will be cut in the following year at Ebbw Vale and at a second plant at Trostre, Llanelli.

British Steel said the business, which employs 2750 people, was responding to overcapacity in the European tinplate market. 'We want to raise efficiency and improve services to customers,' said the company ...

Source: Stefan Wagstyl, *Financial Times*, 30 April 1997. Reprinted with permission.

Exhibit 1.3 Strategic–tactical–operational decision spectrum

Operational information is therefore much more narrowly focused, very largely internal and more precise and has a shorter time-frame than tactical or strategic.

The distinction between strategic–tactical–operational may be somewhat blurred in practice, as may be the users of each kind of information. In many small organisations, the same person(s) may use all three types, as may also happen in large organisations (particularly those where management 'delayering' has occurred). Nevertheless, Anthony *et al*'s 'hierarchy' emphasises two key issues:

1 Different information is required for different purposes.
2 Strategic, tactical and operational issues are inextricably linked.

Effective information provision should reflect these two points, and they will recur regularly in the chapters which follow. But if, as we have said, different information is required for different purposes, can we define an overall purpose for the output from an MIS?

ORGANISATIONAL OBJECTIVES

Information must be provided for a purpose and our discussion of strategic–tactical–operational information suggests that the ultimate purpose of all information is defined by its users' need to assess the organisation's progress towards achieving its strategic (or corporate) objectives. As Exhibit 1.3 makes clear, strategic objectives determine, in turn, tactical objectives, which themselves determine operational objectives.

 What strategic objective(s) might be applicable to a commercially operated passenger transport company?

Since we are dealing with a commercial concern, the most obvious answer is 'to earn sufficient profit to provide the company's shareholders with an acceptable return'. But there are plenty of other possibilities; for example:

- survival
- growth (e.g. increasing market share, diversification)
- provision of quality service at reasonable price
- company 'image'.

If we consider a public sector or non-profit organisation, such as a university, the same diversity of objectives is possible: for instance, growth in student numbers, increased flexibility in modes of attendance/study, academic reputation of the institution, and so on. We are not attempting here to provide a definitive statement about what precise objectives organisations may (or should) have – this will depend on the nature of the organisation concerned and the environment within which it operates. The intention is to consider certain features of objectives which have general relevance to information provision.

1 **Multiple objectives** As we have just seen, organisations may have several different objectives, and these may well conflict (e.g. 'quality' and 'profit'). This may be further complicated by different subunits within the organisation having different objectives, and by the possibility of individual managers' aims being at odds with those of the organisation.
2 **Change over time** Organisations operate in dynamic environments, which means that objectives are likely to change, or that the weighting attached to different objectives will change. In addition, objectives which may conflict in the short term, such as 'profit' and 'quality' may, in the longer term, prove to be complementary.
3 **Quantification** Many objectives are not readily quantifiable. This is particularly true of quality-related objectives and in relation to provision of many services. How, for example, do we quantify an objective such as 'provision of quality education'?

These three factors, together and in isolation, can have a major effect on information provision – even more so when distilled from strategic through tactical to operational levels. As a minimum, they serve to reinforce the points we have already made that different information will be required for different purposes, and that a range of financial, non-financial, quantitative and qualitative information should be employed by management. Unclear objectives can result in conflicting information 'signals' to management (e.g. the possibility of contradiction between quantitative and qualitative information).

Now that we have discussed the nature of information produced by an MIS, we can turn our attention to the key question of who the users of such information might be. Our main focus will be on users/potential users of output from the MIS's accounting subsystem, though the same groups and individuals may well use output from other MIS subsystems as well.

USERS OF ACCOUNTING INFORMATION

Because of its ability to provide a range of accessible, quantified, and comparatively simple indicators of organisational activity, accounting is an important element in every organisation's information system. Who are the users/potential users of accounting information? A short answer to this would be **stakeholders**: that is, those individuals, groups or other organisations who:

1 have an interest in the activities of the organisation producing the accounting information; and/or
2 are in some way affected by these activities.

Who are the likely stakeholders in a company which provides goods/services on a commercial basis?

Table 1.1 lists the potential stakeholders in such an organisation and suggests possible uses for which each might want accounting information.

Table 1.1 Organisational stakeholders and possible users of accounts

Stakeholder	Potential use(s) of accounting information
Owners/shareholders	Assessing their investment, e.g. dividends
Management	Running the business
Employees	Assessing security of employment, wage bargaining
Government (national/local)	Taxation: income, corporation and value added (VAT) economic statistics
Lenders	Assessing ability of borrower to repay
Suppliers	Likelihood, volume and value of future orders
Customers	Reliability of future supply
'Specialists'	Provision of investment advice
General public	Assessing impact on local economy

This is a wide-ranging list, with great diversity in the potential use(s) of accounting information; so much so that it is very debatable whether accounting can (or indeed should) address them all. What we can do with Table 1.1 is distinguish between *internal* users/uses of accounting information and *external*: management and employees comprise the former grouping, all other stakeholders the latter. The only possibly 'grey' area is that of owners/shareholders, since these may also manage the organisation (in which case they will be both internal and external users). Or there may be no 'owners' in the strict sense – as with charities or public sector organisations. Here there would be no such stakeholder group, but others (e.g. the general public) would assume greater significance as potential users of accounting information.

FINANCIAL ACCOUNTING, MANAGEMENT ACCOUNTING AND COST ACCOUNTING

The distinction which we have just drawn between internal and external users of accounting information can be extended to provide the basis for a distinction between different forms of accounting:

- **financial accounting** – primarily targeted at external users/uses
- **management accounting** – intended for internal users/uses, and management in particular.

Despite their different emphases, financial and management accounting have some common characteristics:

1 They reflect organisational activities in quantitative, and predominantly (but not exclusively) in financial terms.

2 They share certain data sources: for example, personnel data may be used by both financial and management accounting, albeit in different ways and for different purposes.

3 There is a limited area of common ground between the two as regards users/uses: for example, budgets prepared for internal use may form the basis of published profit forecasts.

4 They are key elements within the MIS, and a degree of integration between the two is often present: for example, budgetary control (management accounting) requires the input of actual costs and revenues which have been recorded in the financial accounts (see Chapter 18).

However, there is a danger that these surface similarities could obscure the very marked differences between financial and management accounting, and that this might result in the wrong type of accounting information being used for the wrong purpose (with possibly serious consequences for the organisation).

DTI asked to quiz William Cook on trading forecasts   **FT**

The Department of Trade and Industry has been asked to investigate discrepancies between a downbeat trading statement issued by William Cook, the steel castings group, and financial information it gave to its bankers a month earlier . . .

A document passed to the DTI entitled 'Confidential Information Memorandum' prepared by William Cook to help secure a £22.5m credit facility, appears to show the company forecasting increases in turnover and profits to March 29 1997. The letter [requesting the DTI to investigate] questions whether this is inconsistent with the information to shareholders on October 25 when William Cook published interim results . . .

Mr Cook [chairman of William Cook] said that the financial information prepared for the company's bankers, in September, was based on internal budgets, rather than profit forecasts . . .

Source: William Lewis and Richard Wolffe, *Financial Times*, 31 January 1997. Reprinted with permission.

Exhibit 1.4 Wrong information for the purpose?

The dispute described in Exhibit 1.4 may stem partly from the fact that the 'profit forecast' referred to is published by listed companies in compliance with Stock Exchange regulations (i.e. is financial accounting information), whereas figures provided to the company's bank are the product of its management accounting system. What should be clear from Exhibit 1.4 is that financial accounting and management accounting information (which presumably describe the same aspects of organisational activity) may differ quite markedly – hence the call for an investigation. We could take this further by suggesting that the root cause of the problem is provision to the bank (an external user) of accounting information meant for internal use. Table 1.2 summarises the main areas of difference between the two forms of accounting.

The differences shown in Table 1.2 are reflected in the definitions of financial and management accounting contained in the Chartered Institute of Management Accountants' (CIMA) *Official Terminology*.

1 **Financial accounting** 'The classification and recording of monetary transactions of an entity in accordance with established concepts, principles, accounting standards

Table 1.2 Main areas of difference between financial and management accounting

	Financial	**Management**
Users/uses	Mostly external	Mostly internal
Externally regulated/ published?	Yes: e.g. Companies' Act, Statements of Standard Accounting Practice, Financial Reporting Standards, external audit, Stock Exchange regulations	No
Time orientation	Predominantly historic	Predominantly future
Scope and span	Tactical and operational; routine recording of transactions	Strategic, tactical and operational; routine and *ad hoc* information

and legal requirements and presentation of a view of the effect of those transactions during and at the end of an accounting period.'

2 **Management accounting** 'An integral part of management concerned with identifying, presenting and interpreting information ...'

CIMA's definition of management accounting proceeds to list potential uses of management accounting information, which we shall consider in the next section. 'Integral' is an crucial part of the management accounting definition: not only is it a significant component of the management *process*, but it is also one constituent of a multidisciplinary management whole. It is for these reasons that an understanding of the subject is vital to managers whose principal expertise lies in areas other than finance and accounting.

 Do the differences listed in Table 1.2 and encapsulated in the CIMA definitions have any implications for the nature of the information provided by management accounting compared to that provided by financial accounting?

The nature of information produced differs in two important respects:

1 Management accounting information, will tend, on the whole, to incorporate more imprecision, as it largely concerns the future, rather than the past. Note, however, that this is a matter of degree – financial accounting is far from being a precise science. Exhibit 1.4 testifies to just how great this imprecision can sometimes be. The fact that accounting information contains imprecisions may occasionally cause difficulty, as some users may wrongly assume that quantitative information is accurate merely because it is quantitative.

2 Because of its lack of external regulation and its wider scope and span, management accounting information will tend to be much more organisation- and situation-specific.

The two points we have just made will recur frequently throughout our study of management accounting, and are worth bearing in mind.

Earlier in this section, we said that there is some limited common ground between financial accounting and management accounting. This common ground is largely the province of **cost accounting**, which CIMA's *Official Terminology* defines as 'the establishment of budgets, standard costs and actual costs of operations, processes, activities or products; and the analysis of variances, profitability or the social use of funds ... '

 From the definition above, can you distinguish between internal and external aspects of cost accounting?

Budgets, standard costs and variance analyses are almost exclusively internal matters, forming an intrinsic and important part of management accounting; actual costs are both internal and external, being integral to both financial and management accounting. But despite this commonality of actual costs between financial and management accounting, there exists between the two a very marked difference in the use of cost accounting information, and it is to this subject that we now turn.

PURPOSES OF COST ACCOUNTING

External use

Since cost accounting information is a constituent element of financial accounting, it will be useful if we present once more the CIMA definition of financial accounting:

'The classification and recording of monetary transactions of an entity in accordance with established concepts, principles, accounting standards and legal requirements and presentation of a view of the effect of those transactions during and at the end of an accounting period.'

(Official Terminology)

Determining the cost of what an organisation does fits comfortably within this definition.

 In the context of financial accounting, what purposes might cost accounting information serve?

We can identify two broad purposes:

1 *Profit determination* Profit is a very important external indicator of commercial success, and in accounting terms, is calculated as (sales revenue – expenses). To make this calculation, we need, in the words of Exhibit 1.1, an 'accurate and objective knowledge of the cost of providing a good or service'. For non-profit and public sector organisations, cost is reported so that external stakeholders know what use has been made of funds raised (for example, by charitable donations or by government taxation).

2 *Asset valuation* As a corollary to profit determination, we also need cost accounting information to enable us to value certain assets. Most commonly, we might need to place a value on stocks ('inventory' in Exhibit 1.1), which accounting convention requires us to value at the 'lower of cost and net realisable value'. 'Net realisable value' is simply what the stocks could be sold for in their current form. At the end of

an accounting period, for instance, we may have unused stocks of raw materials, of partly completed goods ('work-in-progress') and of finished goods. Since these have not yet been sold, we cannot deduct their cost from revenue in our profit calculation, and must carry it forward in the Balance Sheet as an asset. For manufacturing industries, the cost of stock – and, by implication, the cost of output sold during the period – has a major bearing on the amount of profit reported (hence on the external view of commercial success). For service organisations, stock valuation may be of less significance, though many such organisations do hold stocks. Hospitals, for example, carry significant stocks of drugs and other medical supplies. Occasionally, it may be necessary to cost other forms of asset – say, where an organisation constructs premises for its own use.

Cost accounting seeks to achieve the two purposes discussed above by application of cost classification and estimation techniques (see Chapters 2 and 3) which are then applied to the resources consumed in organisational activities (materials, labour and overhead – *see* Chapters 4, 5 and 6). Costs arrived at in this way are applied to organisational outputs using the costing methodology appropriate for the kind of output involved, and incorporated within the organisation's accounting records (see Chapters 7–12). However, this is not to say that the contents of Chapters 2–12 have an exclusively external orientation: many of the topics introduced there are used for internal purposes also – especially those dealing with cost classification and estimation.

Internal use

In addition to its external uses, cost accounting also forms an integral part of accounting information for internal use – i.e. of management accounting. We might make a 'broad-brush' statement of the objective of management accounting as being *provision of information which is useful in the management of an organisation*. To render this more precise, we need to consider how managers manage.

 In general terms, what do managers do in order to manage?

In order to fulfil its function, management must, as a minimum,

- **Plan and control**
- **Make decisions**

We can therefore redefine management accounting as *provision of useful information to help management plan, control and make decisions*. In addition, management accounting (and its cost accounting input) should mirror the facts that planning, control and decision making occur at strategic, tactical and operational levels and that they are essentially concerned with the future. Contrast this with the essentially short-term and historic nature of cost accounting information used for external purposes.

Planning and control

It is difficult to imagine how any organisation could survive for long without some form of planning and control. We will consider the detailed planning and control

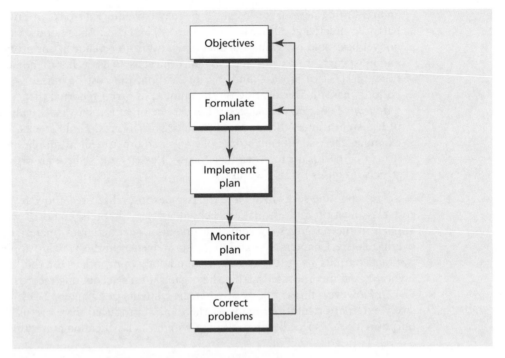

Figure 1.3 A simple planning and control cycle

process in Chapters 16, 17 and 18, but in outline form, the planning and control cycle might operate as illustrated in Figure 1.3.

The first aspect of Figure 1.3 worthy of note is the fact that plans stem from objectives, so that it is quite possible for difficulty with these to be transmitted into the planning and control process. The second feature is that planning and control cannot meaningfully exist in isolation – i.e. planning implies control and vice versa. Finally, control is not passive: when problems arise in the achievement of plans, *action* ('control action') is needed.

The CIMA definition quoted earlier contains cost accounting's most important contributions in the planning and control arena: **budgets** and **standard costs** (see Chapters 16, 17 and 18), and **variance analysis** (Chapter 19).

Decision making

Figure 1.4 illustrates the essential components of the 'alternative choice' decision-making process.

 At what stage(s) in the decision process will cost accounting provide inputs?

Cost accounting's principal inputs to the decision process occur at the evaluation and monitoring stages. As with planning and control, you will see that decisions stem from objectives – and again, we must bear in mind the potential difficulties with objectives. The need to make a decision may become apparent from financial information avail-

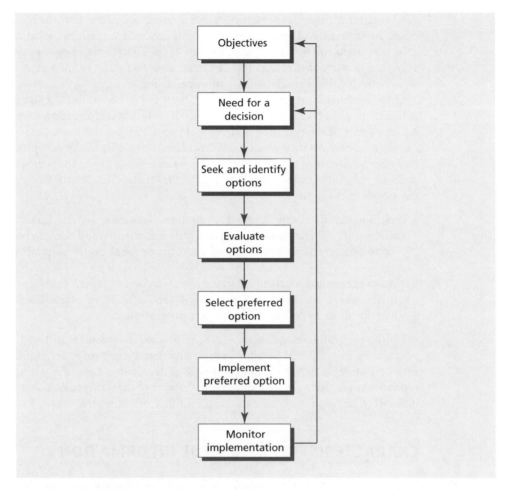

Figure 1.4 The 'alternative choice' decision process

able to management, but equally, it may stem from another source, either internal and/or external to the organisation.

The third stage in the decision process – 'seek and identify options' – appears simple on paper, but is likely to be much more problematic in practice. One particular difficulty is that identification of *all* feasible options is unlikely because of what is referred to as 'bounded rationality': that is, the inability of any single person or group to know everything. To the extent that this is true, we could say that the decision-making process is flawed. However, the effect of bounded rationality can be mitigated, if not removed, by pooling knowledge across a range of individual managers and managerial disciplines.

Virtually every decision has some kind of financial consequence: cost accounting, as we shall see in Chapters 12–15, offers a range of financial criteria against which strategic, tactical and operational decisions may be gauged. The attraction of such criteria is their ability to express complex realities concisely and comprehensibly. But there is the pitfall of over-reliance on financial evaluation, to the detriment (or even exclusion) of other criteria; and, as with planning and control, quantified financial decision criteria may suggest a precision which does not truly exist, given that decisions (like plans) relate to the future. There is also the possibility that certain financial criteria may be misunderstood, or be misapplied, or that their limitations could be overlooked: it is therefore important that managers have an understanding of the nature, strengths and weaknesses of the financial information presented to them.

Once a particular course of action has been embarked upon, the success with which it meets its objective(s) must be monitored; at this stage, decision making effectively becomes part of the planning and control cycle. In practical terms, many of an organisation's routine decisions will be encapsulated within its budgetary procedures. There will also be decisions of a 'one-off' (*ad hoc*) nature, required to meet specific, perhaps unusual, circumstances. We can make the following broad distinction between categories of decision:

- **Programmed decisions** These are routine decisions, where financial and other variables are subject to comparatively little uncertainty and the outcome(s) are fairly easy to predict. Many tactical, and most operational decisions tend to fall into this category.
- **Non-programmed decisions** Decisions of a non-routine, possibly non-recurrent nature, where variables and outcome(s) are subject to considerable uncertainty. Virtually all strategic decisions are non-programmed.

Unlike programmed decisions (such as placing a replenishment order with a supplier), non-programmed decisions require the exercise of managerial judgement, often to a considerable extent. Supporting such judgement is cost accounting's key role in organisational decision making. Note, however, that the role is one of *support* – ultimately, decision making is the responsibility of managers.

CHARACTERISTICS OF USEFUL INFORMATION

Regardless of whether it is used for internal or external purposes, cost accounting information must be useful: the extent to which it is (or is not) useful is the ultimate test of its value. In order to be useful, information should ideally possess certain characteristics.

 Suggest three *necessary features of useful information.*

You may have thought of a variety of features including: *relevance, understandability, timeliness, comparability, objectivity, reliability* and *completeness.* You should appreciate from the outset the potential for contradiction between these characteristics: for instance, the need for timely information may be at odds with its completeness or objectivity.

Relevance

Cost accounting information must be relevant to the purpose for which it is provided. This will be of particular importance in non-programmed situations where inclusion of irrelevant information may distort the financial 'signal', thereby exacerbating existing uncertainty and possibly resulting in an incorrect decision being taken. Cost accounting approaches the issue of relevance as primarily one of *classification* of costs and revenues, an issue which we will examine in the next chapter. Even in routine circumstances, care is needed – at the very least we must recognise that information which might be relevant to some/all external users is unlikely to be particularly relevant to management. Published accounts, for example, are typically based on historic transactions; management, as an essentially forward-looking activity, will be much more concerned with the future.

Understandability

Information will be of little use if it is incomprehensible to its user. This is a matter partly of explaining the nature of accounting information to managers in non-finance functions, and partly of accountants using appropriate, varied and imaginative methods of communication.

Timeliness

If it is received too late to be acted on, information has no value. For example, being published annually or bi-annually (and some time after the end of the relevant period as well), the published accounts of a limited company will be of little interest to management in their day-to-day activities. For tactical and operational purposes, management requires information much more quickly than this. A year-end comparison of budgeted cost with actual, for instance, and the discovery, at that point, of a significant overspend, will not help management – had budget and actual expenditure been monitored on an ongoing basis throughout the year (e.g. month by month), then the potential overspend might have been spotted sufficiently early to allow remedial action to be taken. Similarly, unforeseen circumstances may arise which require an almost instant response, with the accompanying requirement for support information.

Strategic information, however, is likely to be produced at less frequent intervals, since it relates to a longer time horizon. Progress towards a five-year strategic budget, for example, may be monitored on an annual basis.

Finally, the need for timely information may be so pressing as to override other considerations, such as completeness. The possible impact on information quality of extreme time pressure should be appreciated.

Comparability

Cost accounting information is frequently used to make comparisons: for example, of a department's performance over time, or of the performance of different departments within the same period. The success of such an exercise depends on our ability to compare like with like. This really means that cost accounting information should be prepared consistently, or, where it is not, the fact (and the reason why) should be made clear. It may be necessary to restate figures previously provided to show the effect of changing the basis of preparation. There are two difficulties here:

1 Restating figures previously provided may cause confusion and might detract from the credibility of future figures and of the cost accounting function; and
2 Consistency may be impossible: e.g. between programmed and non-programmed situations.

Objectivity

Users of cost accounting information need to be confident that it is as free from sub-jective elements as possible. Cost accounting information that is used for external pur-poses is almost exclusively historic in nature, and can usually be evidenced by means of transactions. To this extent, externally reported cost information is probably about as objective as we can reasonably expect.

There may, however, be more of a problem with cost information generated for internal use. Since the process of management is principally concerned with the future, and since this is inherently uncertain, it would be unrealistic to expect total objectivity in cost accounting information provided in support of this process. It is therefore important to specify (and be able to justify) any assumptions which have been employed to arrive at, say, an estimate of next year's labour cost. We need to remem-ber that management is not an impersonal process. If the people involved in, and affected by, planning, control and decision making feel that these are based on arbi-trary or indefensible information, then we may expect some sort of adverse behavioural consequences.

Reliability

Like objectivity, complete reliability is unlikely in information which relates mainly to the future, so this criterion could prove problematic in respect of cost information pro-vided for internal use. Again, statement of any underlying assumptions is important as is specification of any areas of particular uncertainty in the information being pro-vided. However, reliability does not necessarily mean 100% accuracy, nor does it require that every conceivable detail be included. The information should be suffi-ciently accurate for its purpose: strategic information, for example, will be consider-ably less detailed and accurate than tactical or operational – this does not nullify its value to management. A balance must be struck between too much detail (which can confuse) and too little (which may be insufficient for the purpose). One way in which this can be achieved is by reference to the cost/benefit criterion (see below).

Completeness

Subject to the 'bounded rationality' factor which we mentioned above, there should be no material omission from information. At the same time, it will generally not be neces-sary to include everything that is (or can be) known. Not only might this breach the concept of relevance, but it could prove counterproductive by clouding important issues.

The cost/benefit criterion

Information is a resource and, like all resources, has a cost, which can be either *explicit* or *implicit*. The explicit cost of information is exemplified by expenditure such as payment to an outside consultant to undertake a market survey, or acquisition of decision-support software. High as such costs may be, the implicit cost of information may be even higher.

✔ *What is the implicit cost of information?*

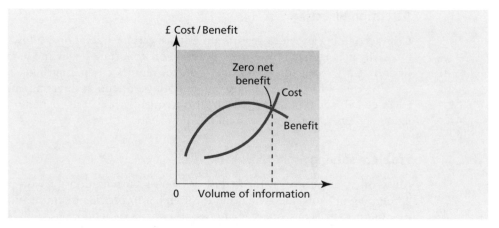

Figure 1.5 Costs and benefits of information

Management must spend time collecting, collating and interpreting information. Although this is one of management's primary functions, we need to be careful that time is not wasted with superfluous information, or in dealing with the wrong information at the wrong time in relation to events. A point will eventually be reached where the cost of obtaining additional information becomes disproportionate to the benefit derived from having it. In Figure 1.5, this occurs at all volumes of information greater than that indicated as yielding 'zero net benefit'.

It is not practicable to place precise monetary amounts on the costs and benefits of different volumes of information. As a 'rule of thumb', we could approximate the net benefit of information (i.e. its benefit *less* its cost) by assessing the extent to which users act upon it and whether those actions are preferable to what would have occurred without the information. If, for example, management complains about information overload and/or bypasses the formal MIS in favour of informal sources, then we can be reasonably confident that the cost/benefit criterion is not being met.

The desirable characteristics of useful information which we have just discussed must effectively be governed by the cost/benefit criterion. For example, complete information may be available – but may be too late to be useful, and have a cost that cannot be justified. Similarly, accuracy is desirable, but striving for total accuracy (especially in future-oriented information) is to pursue the unattainable at a cost likely to prove prohibitive.

COST ACCOUNTING FUNCTIONS

Cost accounting performs several identifiable, though not always clearly separable, functions in order to achieve its aim of providing useful information.

Scorekeeping

This is essentially an exercise in keeping tally of financial data. Arguably the most fundamental feature of cost accounting, scorekeeping involves activities such as calculating and recording the cost of resources acquired and consumed, and forms the principal subject matter of Chapters 4–11.

Attention directing

Cost accounting provides reports on key aspects of operations, allowing users (and especially managers) to focus their attention on important issues and to take action sufficiently early for it to be effective. Control reports comparing budgeted and actual costs/revenues for a period are an important attention-directing mechanism (see Chapter 18), and *ad hoc* reports are also frequently prepared – e.g. monitoring installation and operation of a new item of equipment.

Problem solving

Most often associated with analysis of non-recurrent decisions or problems, cost accounting in problem-solving 'mode' attempts to provide quantification of the positive and negative consequences of possible courses of action. Based on this quantification, a preferred course of action may be recommended to management (see, for example, Chapter 14, which deals with financial analysis of decisions).

The dividing-line between scorekeeping, attention directing and problem solving is often so fine as to defy definition. Typically, all three elements will be present in any given item of cost accounting information, but the balance between the three will depend on specific circumstances. Exhibit 1.5 provides a simple example to illustrate.

Bilton Primary School

The school, which has responsibility for managing its own budget, is considering replacement of some outdated computer hardware which has an excessively high operating cost of £1300 per unit per annum (there are 10 such units). Two mutually exclusive options are possible:
- purchase 10 desktop PCs with Internet connectivity built-in, cost £1200 each
- purchase 10 desktop PCs with no Internet facility, cost £900 each.

In every respect save Internet connectivity, the two options are identical. Because of its lower purchase cost, the second option has been recommended to the School governors as being financially preferable.

Exhibit 1.5 Scorekeeping, attention directing and problem solving

 From the information Exhibit 1.5, identify the scorekeeping, attention-directing and problem-solving elements.

The operating costs of existing equipment and purchase costs of proposed replacements represent scorekeeping; the 'excessive' operating cost of the present hardware is also attention directing, as reporting this figure has presumably led to the judgement that the amount is excessive. The problem-solving element consists of the comparison of the cost of proposed replacements and the recommendation that the second option is cheaper. Simple though our example is, it allows us to stress three points which we have already mentioned:

1 Scorekeeping, attention directing and problem solving are interrelated (i.e. financial information such as unit costs must be prepared for a purpose).

2 Financial considerations may not give the whole picture. For instance, if the cheaper hardware is purchased, what are the implications of inability to connect with the Internet? Can these units be upgraded to provide such connection? If so, at what cost?

3 There may be a conflict between objectives: is the purpose of the replacement to reduce costs *only*, or to reduce costs *and* improve the quality of pupils' hands-on experience? If the former, the recommendation in Exhibit 1.5 may be acceptable, if the latter, it is questionable.

And following from the last point:

4 There is often a need to compromise between objectives. In this case, the compromise is between maximum benefit to pupils and minimum cost. The school might achieve this by, for example, investigating the possibility of having *some* machines with Internet connectivity.

COST ACCOUNTING AS COMMUNICATION

We can summarise our discussion in this chapter under the single heading of 'communication'. This is the essence of an MIS and its cost accounting output. If cost accounting (or any other form of communication) is to be effective, we need to be clear about the following:

- Why are we providing information?
- To whom are we providing information?
- When are we providing information?
- What information are we providing?

The answers to these questions will define the 'how' of information provision. In a cost accounting context it will, for example, determine the critical issue of the most suitable cost classification (see Chapter 2). On paper, this appears to be straightforward, but, even if we can pinpoint the 'why–whom–when–what–how' of information, there are still difficulties in communicating effectively, often described as **barriers to communication**.

 Suggest three possible barriers to communication which might affect cost accounting.

There are many possibilities; some of the more commonly encountered are given below and are linked to certain of the characteristics of useful information which we discussed earlier.

1 *Bias* This could occur with either/both sender and receiver of information; hence the need for as much objectivity as possible in cost accounting information.

2 *Incomprehension* This relates not only to the recipient of information but also to the provider, who may fail to appreciate the needs or capabilities of the recipient. Information must therefore be understandable.

3 *Withholding information* This may be accidental, or may be by design (e.g. because of the 'knowledge = power' syndrome). Completeness is therefore desirable.

4 *'Noise'* This term describes the existence, within a system of communication, of irrelevance and/or inaccuracy which will cause distraction from the meaning of the information. Relevance is therefore critical.

5 *Lack of immediacy* Urgent information which is received after a time-lag may be viewed by its recipient as unimportant, or might be displaced by unimportant information which, by speedy transmission, may acquire the trappings of urgency and significance.

We could continue this list of potential barriers to communication for some time. However, even the fairly abbreviated version given should indicate that, regardless of an information *system's* complexity or sophistication, it is *people* who will ultimately determine the effectiveness (or otherwise) of that system. It would therefore be a grave error to think of cost accounting as a collection of mechanistic procedures, and you should bear this very much in mind as you progress through your study of the subject.

SUMMARY

In the course of this chapter we have refined and narrowed our initial, fairly broad discussion of information and an organisation's MIS to the point where we were able to identify and define a particular element of that output – cost accounting information. During the chapter, we have seen that:

- **Data** are unprocessed items of **information**.
- An organisation's **management information system** (MIS) consists of an integrated set of subsystems aimed at providing information about organisational activity.
- **Financial information** is stated in monetary terms; **non-financial information** is stated in non-monetary terms.
- **Quantitative information** is expressed in numerical form; **qualitative information** is not (or cannot be) expressed in numerical form.
- **Strategic information** is mainly the domain of senior managers, relating to organisational objectives and the policies/resources needed to achieve them.
- **Tactical information** is used principally by middle management and defines the resources/actions required to achieve, on a rolling basis, a given strategic objective.
- **Operational information** is the province of operational management and describes the specific actions needed to achieve desired tactical outcomes.
- **Organisational objectives** should be the ultimate determinant of information provision, but there may be problems in quantifying objectives, an organisation may have multiple objectives, and objectives may change over time.
- Potential users of accounting information are **stakeholders** – those individuals/ groups who have an interest in the activities of an organisation and/or who are affected by them.
- **Management accounting** is aimed at users internal to the organisation; **financial accounting** at users external to the organisation.

- Management accounting and financial accounting have certain broad similarities:
  - They are both predominantly quantitative
  - They share certain data sources
  - There is limited common usage
  - They are both key elements in the MIS and may be integrated
- There are major differences between management and financial accounting in the areas of:
  - External regulation
  - Time orientation
  - Scope and span
- **Cost accounting,** by establishing budgeted, standard and actual costs, represents the common ground between financial and management accounting.
- For external purposes, cost accounting information is used for profit determination and stock valuation; internally, it is used for planning, control and decision making.
- Cost accounting's contributions to planning and control include **budgets, standard costs** and **variance analysis.**
- Cost accounting's major inputs to decision making are at the option evaluation and post-implementation monitoring stages.
- The characteristics of useful information, which may conflict, are relevance, understandability, timeliness, comparability, reliability, completeness.
- The **cost/benefit criterion** stipulates that the cost (explicit and implicit) of obtaining information should not outweigh the benefit of possessing it.
- Cost accounting has three functions: **scorekeeping, attention directing** and **problem solving.**
- As a medium of communication, cost accounting may be affected by **barriers to communication** such as noise, bias, withholding of information, incomprehension and lack of immediacy.

In Chapter 2 we will discuss cost attribution, and describe developments in management philosophy and operational method, exploring the possible implications of these developments for cost and management accounting as a whole.

FURTHER READING

Anthony, R., Dearden, J. and Vancil, R., *Management Control Systems*, Irwin, 1965.

Chadwick, L. and Magin, M., *Creative Cost and Management Accounting*, Hutchinson Education, 1989: Chapter 1 provides some interesting introductory material.

Emmanuel, C., Otley, D. and Merchant, K., *Accounting for Management Control*, Chapman and Hall, 1990: Chapters 1 and 2 contain useful introductory material.

Inman, M. L., A critical review of product costing. *Students' Newsletter*, ACCA, May 1994.

Wilson, D. A., *Managing Information*, Butterworth-Heinemann, 1993: information management and the MIS is viewed from a wider managerial perspective in this text.

SELF-TEST QUESTIONS

1.1 For each of the statements which follow, place a tick in the appropriate box to indicate whether it is true or false.

	True	False
(a) Management accounting is not subject to external regulation; financial accounting is.	☐	☐
(b) In order to be useful, information should always be 100% accurate.	☐	☐
(c) Operational information should seek to achieve strategic aims.	☐	☐
(d) Management should be provided with all available information.	☐	☐
(e) A programmed decision requires the exercise of considerable managerial judgement because of the high level of uncertainty involved.	☐	☐
(f) Cost accounting information is predominantly qualitative.	☐	☐
(g) Because of its predominantly future-oriented nature, management accounting information will not be wholly objective.	☐	☐

1.2 A domestic television company plans to enter into a joint venture with an overseas partner in order to expand its range of productions. In the first year of the joint venture, two costume dramas and one major documentary will be co-produced; to this end, employees of both companies are presently seeking locations for the first costume drama.

Requirement

Identify the strategic, tactical and operational elements in the scenario outlined above.

1.3 Management of an organisation will make little use of published accounting information because:

I   it is not sufficiently objective
II it is not sufficiently reliable
III it is not sufficiently timely.

Which of the statements above is correct?

A I only
B II only
C III only
D I and III only.

1.4 TPO Ltd's computerised management information system is capable of producing, and regularly does produce, complex and detailed reports for managers. At a recent meeting, the following statements were made about these reports:

I   'As the company owns the computer hardware and software, they are produced at zero cost.'
II 'The reports incur a cost in respect of the stationery on which they are printed.'
III 'The reports incur costs which are not recorded in the accounts.'

Which of these statements is correct?

    A I only
    B II only
    C I and II only
    D II and III only

1.5   Telec plc, an electronic engineering business, is redesigning its accounting system. At a recent board meeting, the company chairman insisted that, to be of real value, the management accounting function of the new system 'must be able to tell managers everything they need to know to do their jobs properly'.

Requirement

Draft a memorandum to the chairman explaining the extent to which his desired criterion for a management accounting system is/is not achievable.

QUESTIONS WITHOUT ANSWERS

1.6   Which of the following correctly describes the existence of irrelevance within cost accounting information?

    A Bias
    B Incomprehension
    C Completeness
    D Noise

1.7   Which of the following is an *implicit* cost of information?

    A Stationery on which it is printed
    B Time spent interpreting its meaning
    C Overtime payments made to staff who prepare it
    D Computer disks on which it is stored

1.8   The board of TPN Ltd, which operates a country-wide chain of carpet retail stores, has been considering the possibility of diversifying the business, which at present is solely confined to sale of floor coverings.

Requirements

(a) Illustrate and explain the steps involved in the decision-making process, using the proposed diversification as an example.

(b) Assuming that diversification is to occur via take-over of another company, discuss the tactical and operational aims which might stem from this strategic objective and suggest what supporting information may be necessary at both tactical and operational levels.

(c) Explain the major areas of cost accounting input to (a) and (b).

1.9   At a recent meeting between senior officials of Saltoun County Council, discussion centred on user department dissatisfaction with the new management accounting system. The following exchanges are fairly typical:

Ms I. Conn (Director of Art Galleries and Museums): 'The system is worse than useless

– my staff and I can't make head nor tail of the reports we receive, which in any case, are usually too late to be of any value.'

Mr M. Pyre (Building Services Manager): 'The reports I receive seem to be full of information about Architectural Services, which is a different department, and detail of loan repayments and capital commitments; to make matters worse, I am constantly being hounded by staff from the Finance Department looking for information which I simply do not have and which the system seems to be incapable of providing me with.'

Mr R. E. Cumbent (Director of Leisure Services): 'Pounds and pence! Pounds and pence! What about the benefits our services offer? The quality of life?'

Ms I. M. Dunn (Deputy Director of Finance): 'I am surprised to hear your comments; the consultants employed by my department provided a detailed report which demonstrated beyond a shadow of a doubt that this system is at the cutting edge of technology and also represents the best possible value for the limited funds available.'

Requirement

Discuss the issues raised at the meeting relative to the effectiveness of the new system.

CHAPTER 2

The cost accounting framework

Overheads: the traditional whys and wherefores

Overheads are those costs (expense types) which cannot be economically attributed directly to a cost unit. Put another way, they are those costs incurred by a business which are not discretely associated with a particular product or service which that business provides for its customers.

Overheads may alternatively be termed 'indirect' costs (in relation to cost units) in contrast to 'direct' costs which *can* be discretely associated with a particular end product or service ...

This applies to each and every business, whatever the particular sector of industry in which the business operates, whether in the public or private sector and whether involved in manufacturing or service ...

Knowledge of the costs of different end products or services may be useful to a business:

- in providing information on their relative costs and efficiencies, which enables costs to be examined and challenged;
- in the valuation of stocks of work-in-progress and finished goods;
- in setting selling prices where cost plus applies, or in providing a guide to the selling prices that are required for a business to make a profit;
- in establishing the profitability of each product/service, which may be useful both for operational (tactical) and longer term (strategic) planning ...

Further benefits arise from the better control of costs that should be enabled at cost centre (as well as at cost unit) level ...

Source: N. Coulthurst, *ACCA Students' Newsletter*, September 1998.

Exhibit 2.1 Direct and indirect costs – a common classification

INTRODUCTION

In Chapter 1, we described the broad internal and external roles of cost accounting and we must now consider the basic mechanisms that cost accounting employs in order to fill these roles, how these mechanisms relate to organisational inputs and outputs, and how certain environmental developments could impact on the operation of a cost accounting system.

The foundation of all cost accounting lies in the key areas of cost attribution and classification. Attribution is the process of linking costs to particular objectives; this is so central to cost accounting that it would be virtually impossible to provide useful information without attribution having first taken place. Cost attribution is effected by means of cost classification – the grouping together of costs according to certain common characteristic(s). If attribution and classification are to be successful, we also need to know what we are attempting to determine the cost of, and why we wish to determine it.

The nature of an organisation's inputs, processes, procedures and outputs has a major bearing on cost attribution and classification. This is reflected in the costing methodologies that cost accounting employs in different organisational settings. In this chapter, we will provide an overview of these costing methodologies which will then be discussed in detail in later chapters. We also need to be aware that cost accounting's operational environment has been – and still is – changing. New approaches to organisational activity like world-class manufacturing and total quality management have developed; new production processes supported by technology (advanced manufacturing technologies) are becoming increasingly prevalent. These developments have major implications for cost accounting, both within specific organisations and in general. For example, the emergence of total quality management has been accompanied by the need for a whole new category of costs relating to various aspects of quality. We will discuss such issues later in this chapter.

OBJECTIVES

When you have completed this chapter, you will be able to:

- distinguish between subjective and objective classification;
- define and identify direct and indirect costs, along with their subdivisions into labour, materials and expenses;
- define and identify variable, fixed, step and semi-variable costs;
- explain the significance and meaning of the relevant range;
- describe the main characteristics specific order, continuous operation, job, contract, batch, process and service costing, citing examples of organisations/output where each would be appropriate;
- outline the principles of world-class manufacturing and total quality management;
- identify value-added and non-value-added activities;
- appreciate the benefits and potential problems of computerisation in the context of cost accounting, along with the potential impact of advanced manufacturing technologies.

WHY DO WE NEED TO ATTRIBUTE COSTS?

A short answer to the question 'why do we need to attribute costs?' is that it is necessary to permit effective scorekeeping (see Chapter 1), which in turn allows cost accounting to provide management with attention-directing and problem-solving information.

The key points to appreciate about cost attribution are first, that it is unavoidable and second, that the form which it takes should be governed by the reason for undertaking it. The starting-point for cost attribution is therefore identification of the **cost objective** – that is, the target or purpose at which such attribution is aimed: we need to know *what* is to be costed and *why* it is to be costed before we can proceed. Table 2.1 lists some common cost objectives, analysed into 'what' and 'why'.

Table 2.1 Common cost objectives

What is to be costed?	*Why* is it to be costed?
Cost units (i.e. units of product/service)	Stock valuation/profit measurement Basis of selling price Budgetary planning and control *Ad hoc* decisions (e.g. accept special order)
Cost centres (i.e. organisational subunits) to which costs traced	Departmental cost reporting Budgetary planning and control *Ad hoc* decisions (e.g. closure)
Profit centres/investment centres (i.e. organisational subunits to which costs + revenues/costs + revenues + capital investment traced)	Departmental profitability reporting Budgetary planning and control Performance evaluation *Ad hoc* decisions (e.g. disinvestment)
Competitive goods/services	Cost reduction, comparison with own costs
Other (e.g. specific capital investment proposal)	*Ad hoc* decisions (e.g. acquire/dispose of) Budgetary planning and control

Table 2.1 is not intended to be, nor can it be, exhaustive – but it should serve to illustrate that:

- Different cost objectives exist.
- A variety of reasons for attribution of costs to a given objective is possible.

Of the cost objectives illustrated in Table 2.1, one will occur in almost every organisation: the **cost unit**. This is a unit of the product or service which the organisation (or organisational subunit) produces. The cost unit – or units where more than one product/service is produced – must be an accurate reflection of the nature of the output to which costs are being attributed. For some organisations, selection of the cost unit will present little difficulty; for others, particularly those providing services rather than tangible goods, more care is required (see Chapter 11 for a more detailed discussion of this point). If the cost unit is wrongly (or inaccurately) defined, then there is every chance that the costs being attributed will also be wrong. Incorrect attribution could have serious consequences: e.g. for stock values and profit, or for selling prices where these are based on cost.

  Suggest an appropriate cost unit for each of the following organisations:

- *A manufacturer of computer printers.*
- *A passenger transport company.*

For the manufacturer of printers, the situation is fairly straightforward: if a single model of printer is produced, that will be the cost unit; if more than one model is involved, each different model will represent a cost unit. If the printers are produced in groups or batches, then each batch could be the cost unit. For the transport company, you may have suggested 'kilometres' as an appropriate cost unit; however, this fails to reflect the nature of the service being provided – namely *passenger* transport. Attributing costs to kilometres would therefore provide much less useful information than attribution to kilometres over which passengers are transported ('passenger/ kilometres'). In fact, using kilometres as the cost unit could provide seriously misleading cost information, e.g. for determining fare structures. (We will examine the costing of services like transport in Chapter 11.)

In this chapter, we will confine our cost attribution exercises to cost units. We will consider some of the other cost objectives in Table 2.1 in subsequent chapters: organisational subunits, for instance, in Chapters 5, 6, 16, 17 and 18, specific proposals in Chapters 13, 14 and 15. What this should underscore is the importance to cost accounting of attribution and classification.

Even from the limited variety in Table 2.1, we should appreciate that a uniform approach to cost attribution is inappropriate. Cost accounting links the 'what' and 'why' from Table 2.1 by means of *classification* – and in particular, classification of cost.

COST CLASSIFICATION

As with any kind of classification, the general objective of cost classification is to impose an ordered structure – in this case on an organisation's cost data. Without such a structure, effective recordkeeping and linkage of costs to cost objectives are impossible. Although cost classification is necessary for the production of financial accounting information, the classification used here will not always be relevant to management's information needs; it may even give managers exactly the *wrong* information (see, for example, Chapter 14).

Cost classification is essentially a matter of grouping together costs which share the same attribute(s) *relative to a stated cost objective*. The words in italics are vitally important because:

1 The cost objective should determine the classification to be used; and
2 Changing the cost objective may alter the categorisation of a specific cost within a given classification.

The statements above lead to a crucial conclusion: the classification(s) selected *must be appropriate to the purpose for which it is selected*. A large part of the discussion in subsequent chapters revolves around the issue of correct classification. In Chapter 14, for example, we will see that financial analysis of decisions requires that costs (and revenues) be classified into those which are relevant to the decision and those which are irrelevant; in Chapter 18, we will combine two classifications (into budgeted and actual and according to behaviour) to facilitate financial control. As a corollary to this, later chapters will illustrate the potential hazards attendant on misclassification, or use of an inappropriate classification.

Defining and grouping individual costs according to specified attributes (e.g. direct/indirect or fixed/variable) is termed **subjective classification**; linking a subjective classification to a stated cost objective is known as **objective classification**. You should note that neither type of classification can meaningfully exist in isolation: e.g. a statement that 'the foreman's salary is indirect' (subjective classification) immediately prompts the response 'indirect *relative to what*?' (objective classification).

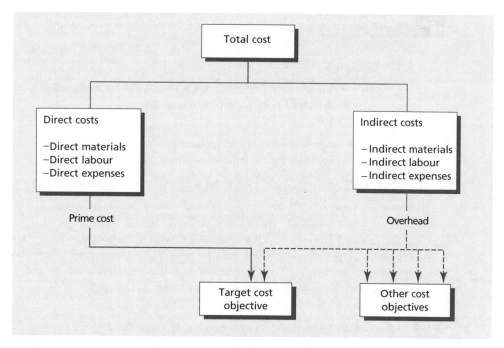

Figure 2.1 Classification of costs according to their nature

Classification into direct and indirect cost

This common classification makes a distinction between **direct costs** and **indirect costs**; direct costs can be unambiguously and quantifiably attributed to a single target cost objective, indirect costs cannot (see Figure 2.1).

The terms **prime cost** and **overhead** respectively describe total direct costs and total indirect costs. We shall use the information in Exhibit 2.2 to illustrate a direct/indirect classification of cost.

Cerma Ltd

This company, which produces ceramic mugs, has three production departments: Forming, Glazing & Painting and Firing. Some of the major costs incurred in running the business are listed below.

Supervisory salaries in each of Forming, Glazing & Painting and Firing.
Purchases of clay, glaze and paint.
Wages of potters, artists who paint and glaze the mugs and of kiln operatives.
Royalty paid by Cerma Ltd to the designer of a pattern used on one of its mugs.
Insurance of buildings and equipment.
Spare fireproof bricks used in maintenance of kilns.

Output is produced in batches of 200 mugs.

Exhibit 2.2 Cost classification

Classify the costs in Exhibit 2.2 into labour, materials and expenses.

The costs in each category are:

Labour   Supervisory salaries in each of Forming, Glazing & Painting and Firing
Wages of potters, artists who paint and glaze the mugs and of kiln operatives

Materials   Purchases of clay, glaze and paint
Spare fireproof bricks used in maintenance of kilns

Expenses   Royalty paid by Cerma Ltd to the designer of a pattern used on one of its mugs
Insurance of buildings and equipment

Materials and labour are self-explanatory, with 'expenses' referring to any cost which cannot be regarded as either of the first two. When dealing with cost classification and attribution, we use the term 'expenses' in this very narrow sense, and you should not confuse it with the wider, more everyday usage of the term.

 From Exhibit 2.2, suggest an appropriate cost unit for Cerma Ltd.

You may have suggested individual mugs as the cost unit, but, since output is produced in batches of 200, it is more likely that each batch would be the cost unit. As we shall see shortly, which of these cost units we choose to employ may affect the classification of certain costs.

In order to apply a direct/indirect classification to the costs in Exhibit 2.2, we must first specify the cost objective, which, for the moment, we will assume to be the cost unit of each batch of 200 mugs.

 Bearing in mind that direct costs can be unambiguously and quantifiably associated with a single target cost objective (batch of 200 mugs here), classify the costs from Exhibit 2.2 into direct and indirect, distinguishing between labour, materials and expenses.

The costs are classified as follows in relation to the cost unit:

Direct costs
Direct labour   Wages of potters, artists who paint and glaze the mugs and of kiln operatives
Direct materials   Purchases of clay, glaze and paint
Direct expenses   Royalty paid by Cerma Ltd to the designer of a pattern used on one of its mugs

Indirect costs
Indirect labour   Supervisory salaries in each of Forming, Glazing & Painting and Firing
Indirect materials   Spare fireproof bricks used in maintenance of kilns
Indirect expenses   Insurance of buildings and equipment

If you consider the direct costs listed above, you will see that it should be possible, for each batch of mugs, to state the number of hours of potters', artists' and kiln operatives' time required for production. Similarly, the quantity of clay, glaze and paint needed for each batch can be identified; and, for the relevant type of mug, the amount of royalty paid to the designer can be stated per batch. Since we can make a quantifiable link between these costs and a single target cost objective, we classify them as direct (prime cost in total).

For the indirect costs, on the other hand, such a quantifiable link to the target cost objective cannot be made. For instance, we cannot state the amount of buildings and equipment insurance required to produce each batch; nor is it likely that we can quantify the number of supervisory hours required per batch, as departmental supervisors will be concerned with all activities occurring within their department. Likewise, we cannot give the cost of replacement fireproof bricks per batch – unless these are replaced after firing each batch (which is unlikely). Since these costs are attributable to two or more cost units, they are classified as indirect (overhead in total). The best we can say about indirect costs is that they must be incurred in order to allow production to proceed. Attributing overhead to cost units needs special procedures which we shall discuss in Chapters 5 and 6.

The classification you produced may have been different to ours; you might, in particular, have treated supervisory salaries as direct labour. This would be correct had Exhibit 2.2 allowed us to establish a quantifiable link between supervisory salaries and batches of mugs. Since it does not, we cannot establish the kind of relationship necessary to support classification of this cost as direct. It might be possible to overcome this by using a sophisticated system for recording the resources consumed by batches of output – but you should bear in mind the cost/benefit criterion we discussed in the previous chapter.

 Suppose the cost objective were the three production departments of Forming, Painting and Glazing and Firing. Would this affect our classification of costs into direct/indirect? If so, in what way?

The cost objective has changed from cost unit to **cost centre** (department here) and we must be alert to the possibility of a change of designation for individual costs as a result:

Direct costs

Direct labour   Wages of potters, artists who paint and glaze the mugs and of kiln operatives

Supervisory salaries in each of Forming, Glazing & Painting and Firing

Direct materials   Purchases of clay, glaze and paint

Spare fireproof bricks used in maintenance of kilns

Indirect costs

Indirect expenses   Insurance of buildings and equipment

Royalty paid by Cerma Ltd to the designer of a pattern used on one of its mugs

As in the case of the individual job, more detailed information might allow us to quantify the equipment insurance cost in each production department, thereby permitting its classification as direct. You will see from the revised classification above that our treatment of three items has changed. Supervisory salaries and spare firebricks are now considered as direct costs: since each department presumably has its own supervisor and since spare firebricks will only be used in the Firing Department, these costs can be unambiguously and quantifiably associated with a single target cost objective (department in this case). The change in classification of the royalty payment is worthy of note. This is paid *per cost unit* – and, assuming that every batch of mugs on which the royalty is payable passes through all three production departments – cannot be unambiguously and quantifiably associated with a single cost centre (and is therefore indirect relative to this cost objective). Here again, additional information would be useful and again, the cost/benefit criterion needs to be borne in mind. As a final illustration of the relationship between objective and subjective classifications, think what would happen had the cost objective been the business as a whole: in this case, *all* costs would be direct. It is worth repeating our earlier statement at this stage: *if the cost objective changes, classification of individual costs may also change.*

A direct/indirect cost classification is the basis of costing methodology in virtually all UK organisations and underpins the absorption costing approach which we will describe in Chapters 5 and 6. Another common classification of cost is by behaviour in relation to some measure of volume; we will encounter this important classification on numerous occasions in later chapters, and it is to this classification that we now turn.

Classification according to the behaviour of costs

This approach classifies costs according to their behaviour in relation to changes in volume of activity (e.g. number of units produced). Although output is an important and commonly-used activity measure, we need to be aware that it is not the only possible measure: as we shall see, cost behaviour patterns are dependent on the specified cost objective in exactly the same way as was the direct/indirect nature of costs.

Figure 2.2 illustrates two basic cost behaviour patterns relative to volume of activity.

As Figure 2.2(a) shows, the total amount of a **variable cost** increases and decreases in line with increases/decreases in the volume of activity. However, the total amount of the **fixed cost** in Figure 2.2(b) is unaffected by increases/decreases in the volume of activity.

In relation to the number of batches of mugs produced, classify the costs listed in Exhibit 2.2 into those which are variable and those which are fixed.

Relative to the number of batches produced, cost behaviour in Exhibit 2.2 is as follows:

Variable costs
Purchases of clay, glaze and paint
Royalty paid by Cerma Ltd to the designer of a pattern used on one of its mugs

Fixed costs
Supervisory salaries in each of Forming, Glazing and Painting and Firing
Wages of potters, artists who paint and glaze the mugs and of kiln operatives

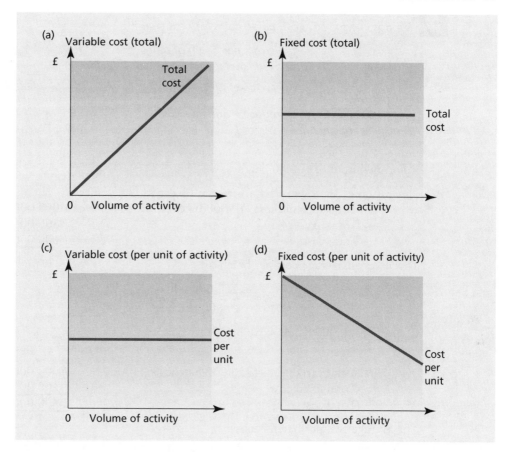

Figure 2.2 Variable and fixed costs

Spare fireproof bricks used in maintenance of kilns
Insurance of buildings and equipment

You may have treated wages of potters etc, spare fireproof bricks and possibly supervisory salaries as variable; if you look again at Figure 2.2(a), you will see that this is unlikely to be the case. Wages and salaries are generally paid at a fixed rate per month or week, regardless of volume of output; the cost of spare firebricks will likewise not conform to the behaviour pattern illustrated in Figure 2.2(a). We will return to this point shortly.

The costs illustrated in Figure 2.2 have a **linear relationship** with the volume of activity: i.e. the variable cost *per unit of activity* is constant at all volumes (as illustrated in Figure 2.2(c)), and the amount of total fixed cost is constant at all volumes, which results in a straight-line ('linear') plot for each cost when graphed against volume of activity. On a 'per unit' basis, fixed cost will decline (Figure 2.2(d)) as volume increases, since the same amount of total fixed cost is being spread over more and more units. If we combine the variable and fixed cost per unit, we have an average cost per unit which increases/decreases in an inverse relationship to increases/decreases in output in a manner not unlike the fixed cost per unit.

Suppose Cerma Ltd's estimated costs for next year are:

Variable cost per batch of mugs	*£100*
Total fixed costs for the year	*£600 000*

Determine the total cost (variable plus fixed), and the average cost per batch if

(i) 10 000 batches are produced; and
(ii) 20 000 batches are produced.

For an output of 10 000 batches, we get:

	£
Total variable cost (10 000 batches × £100)	1 000 000
Total fixed cost	600 000
Total cost	1 600 000

This gives an average cost per batch of:

$$\frac{£1\ 600\ 000}{10\ 000\ \text{batches}} = £160$$

If output is 20 000 batches, we have a total cost of:

	£
Total variable cost (20 000 batches × £100)	2 000 000
Total fixed cost	600 000
Total cost	2 600 000

The average cost per batch is now:

$$\frac{£2\ 600\ 000}{20\ 000\ \text{batches}} = £130$$

Awareness of these relationships may prevent incorrect decisions, e.g. about selling price if Cerma Ltd bases its selling prices on cost.

Although it is possible for unit variable costs to be constant, it is equally possible that they are not, as shown in Figure 2.3.

 What pattern of variable cost behaviour is suggested by Figure 2.3(a)?

The variable cost illustrated in Figure 2.3(a) is at a constant amount per unit of activity over each of the volume ranges 0–*a*, *a*–*b* and over *b*. However, the amount per unit differs between volume ranges, being higher over 0–*a* than *a*–*b*, and higher between *a*–*b* than at volumes greater than *b*. We can tell that this is the case by examining the slope of the total variable cost line within each volume range: the steeper the slope, the higher the variable cost per unit of activity. This sort of behaviour pattern might, for example, apply to materials where a differential discount was applied depending on the quantity purchased; in other words, a lower discount would apply to materials in the range 0–*a* than would apply within the range *a*–*b*, with the greatest discount applicable to quantities in excess of *b*. You should note, however, that the 'volume' measure here will more likely be the quantity of materials purchased than the volume of output

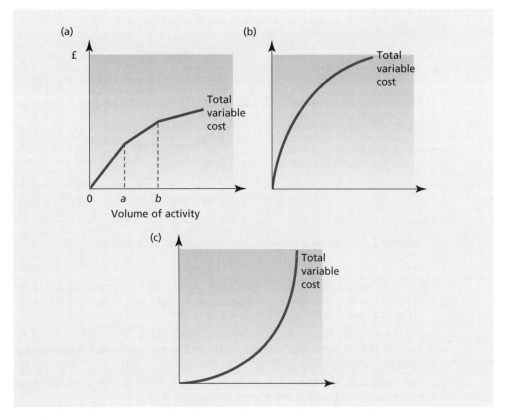

Figure 2.3 Non-linear variable costs

produced, as bulk discounts apply to purchases of material not to its usage in production.

Figures 2.3(b) and 2.3(c) illustrate **curvilinear cost functions**, meaning that there is a continuous change in the variable cost per unit of activity as volume increases/decreases. In Figure 2.3(b), the slope of the total cost curve is flattening as volume increases, indicating a decreasing unit variable cost, with the steadily steepening curve in Figure 2.3(c) indicating an increase in unit variable cost. You should note that, in both Figures 2.3(b) and 2.3(c), the *rate* of increase/decrease in variable cost per unit is not constant. One possible reason for curvilinear cost behaviour relates to direct labour and is termed the **learning curve**. What the learning curve suggests is that the more often a person performs a repetitive manual task, the more proficient that person becomes at performing it; as proficiency increases, so the time required to perform the task successively reduces; if the labour time for each repetition of a task reduces, so will the associated labour cost of that task. Figure 2.4 illustrates.

You will see from Figure 2.4 that, after volume of *a* has been achieved, the curve flattens and exhibits a constant labour cost per unit. This is known as the **steady state** and indicates that learning does not continue indefinitely – i.e. there is a limit to how proficiently any task can be performed. If a learning curve applies to labour operations, then total labour cost relative to volume of output will exhibit the sort of behaviour pattern illustrated in Figure 2.3(b).

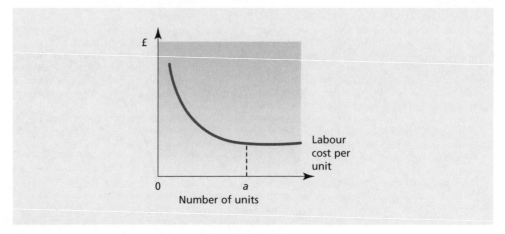

Figure 2.4 Effect of a learning curve on labour cost per unit

Cost behaviour of the kind shown in Figure 2.3(c) may be fairly uncommon, but might apply, say, where continued use of old equipment is increasingly uneconomic due to rapidly rising maintenance costs.

Let us now return to our earlier classification of the costs from Exhibit 2.2. We stated that supervisory salaries, wages of potters etc. and the cost of spare fireproof bricks were all fixed in relation to the number of batches of mugs produced. Is this strictly correct? Figure 2.5 presents what is likely to be a more plausible version of these costs' behaviour relative to volume of output.

A **step cost** is unchanged within a certain volume range (say *a*–*b* in Figure 2.5), falling by a lump sum to a reduced constant amount within a lower range (say 0–*a*) and increasing by a lump sum to a greater constant amount within a higher range (say *b*–*c*). The steps illustrated in Figure 2.5 are reasonably large and fairly uniform, but this need not necessarily be the case: consider supervision and property costs (e.g. rent and rates). Relative to the volume of output, supervision costs may follow the general pattern shown in Figure 2.5, but what about property costs? Look at Figure 2.6.

Because of the nature of the costs involved, the range of volumes over which prop-

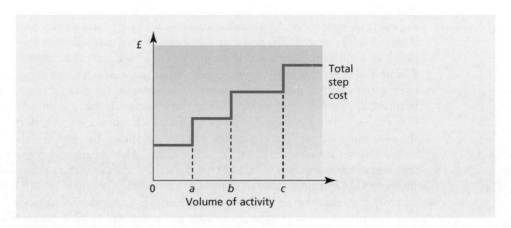

Figure 2.5 Step cost

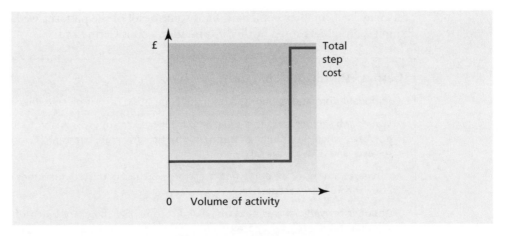

Figure 2.6 **Property costs relative to volume of activity**

erty costs remain fixed is very much larger than was the case for supervision and the size of step, when it occurs, is likewise much larger.

There remains one final pattern of cost behaviour to consider.

> ✔ *Relative to consumption of electricity, what behaviour pattern will be exhibited by the associated cost?*

The typical electricity bill consists of two elements – a standing charge (fixed regardless of consumption) plus a charge that depends explicitly on consumption – i.e. the cost is partly fixed and partly variable. Such a cost is referred to as **semi-variable, semi-fixed** or **mixed** (see Figure 2.7). In this context, 'semi' is slightly misleading, as it does not imply an even division of total cost between fixed and variable elements, merely that both are present in the composition of total cost – the exact proportion of each will differ depending on the cost concerned.

In practice, many costs exhibit step or semi-variable behaviour patterns and some

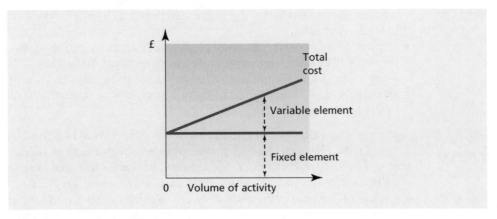

Figure 2.7 **Semi-variable cost**

costs may be a complex combination of some or all of the patterns we have described. Exhibit 2.3 presents some further information about Cerma Ltd.

Cerma Ltd: further cost data

Additional information about the business's operating costs is given below:

Wages and salaries: a fixed annual amount is paid to supervisors and to all employees; however, when the volume of business is particularly high, overtime is worked and paid for over and above basic salary.

Purchases of clay, glaze and paint: these are purchased in fixed quantities of 500 kg, 50 litres and 100 litres respectively.

Designer's royalty: this is paid at a fixed rate of £30 for every batch of mugs which incorporates the relevant pattern.

Insurance of buildings and equipment: the premium is fixed in advance each year, and only changes to reflect acquisitions/disposals of premises and equipment.

Spare fireproof bricks: these need to be replaced after every 50 batches of mugs are fired.

Exhibit 2.3 Cost behaviour

 If the number of batches of mugs produced is the cost objective, what is the likely behaviour pattern of each of the costs detailed in Exhibit 2.3?

Relative to the volume of output (i.e. number of batches), cost behaviour can be summarised as:

- *Variable*: designer's royalty – the higher the volume of output incorporating this pattern, the higher will be this cost in total; since the payment is a flat-rate amount per batch, the cost function is linear;
- *Fixed*: insurance of buildings and equipment – within certain fairly wide output limits, the amount of this cost is unlikely to be affected by the volume of work;
- *Semi-variable*: wages and salaries – the total amount of each of these costs comprises a fixed element (annual salary) plus an element which varies according to the volume of work (overtime);
- *Step*: purchases of clay, glaze and paint, cost of spare fireproof bricks – in both cases, the cost will be fixed over a given range of output (e.g. 50 batches in the case of spare fireproof bricks, or the number of batches that can be produced from 500 kg of clay) and will increase/decrease by a lump-sum amount when output exceeds/falls short of this output range.

We said that insurance of buildings and equipment would be fixed over fairly wide output limits. However, looked at over a wide enough range of output volumes, this cost will exhibit step behaviour. So, although we have succeeded in refining our initial classification of Cerma Ltd's costs, there may still be some 'grey' areas. But we need a classification which is sufficiently clear-cut to provide useful information; we can help achieve this by applying the concept of **relevant range** to our classification. The relevant range is the range of output volumes and/or time horizon over which a particular set of assumptions (e.g. about cost behaviour) is a reasonable approximation of reality. For example, if we consider insurance of buildings and equipment over an indefinite range of output volumes and time horizon, we undoubtedly have a step cost. However, if we examine the same cost over a limited output range and time period – say, likely volumes for the forthcoming year – then it is probably reasonable to suggest that the cost is fixed. The concept of relevant range has especial significance in the context of the strategic-tactical-operational information spectrum, as a cost which exhibits, say, variable behaviour in operational terms may behave differently in tactical terms and differently *again* in strategic terms.

We shall make particular reference to classification of costs according to their behaviour in Chapter 12 (marginal costing), Chapter 13 (cost/volume/profit analysis), and Chapter 18 (budgetary control).

Other classifications

In subsequent chapters, we will encounter and discuss other important classifications of cost and their use. Unlike the two classifications we have been describing (which are wide-ranging in their potential application), these other classifications tend to be used for specific purposes. For that reason, we will provide a summary here and describe them in detail in the chapter(s) that deal with the purpose(s) for which they are employed.

Classification into relevant and irrelevant costs

This classification is used in analysing the financial consequences of decisions (see Chapters 14 and 15). By classifying costs into relevant/irrelevant, we are attempting to reflect the nature of every decision:

1 Decisions involve choice between alternative courses of action; and
2 Decisions relate to the future.

Relevant costs (and benefits) are therefore future cash flows which differ between alternatives. Any cost (or benefit) which cannot be described in this way is irrelevant and should be excluded from the financial analysis of a decision.

Classification into standard/budgeted and actual costs

As we said in the previous chapter, planning and control are key management activities and one cannot meaningfully exist without the other. In cost accounting terms, planning and control commonly consist of estimating future costs and revenues (setting a **budget**), followed by periodic comparison of budgeted and actual figures; significant differences between budget and actual ('**variances**') should prompt some form of action by management.

As an aid to budgetary planning and control, many organisations also prepare estimates of resource usage and cost at the cost unit level (**standard costs**). Existence of standard costs can prove helpful not only in budget preparation, but will additionally allow management to analyse budget variances into their component elements.

We will discuss these important aspects of cost accounting in Chapters 16–19.

Classification into controllable and uncontrollable costs

As we shall see in Chapter 18, many budgetary planning and control systems operate on the basis of **responsibility accounting**, whereby individual managers are deemed to be responsible for achieving specific budgets. Within such a system, a vexed issue is the extent to which managers can (or cannot) control costs in the budget which they are responsible for achieving. When presenting budgetary control reports it may therefore be important to distinguish between controllable and uncontrollable costs to aid in judging performance against budget and to help alleviate perceptions of an 'unfair' system.

Classification according to organisational function or segment

In order to support an effective system of budgetary planning and control – especially in larger organisations, and where responsibility accounting is operating – it is necessary to attribute costs to individual departments, sections or functions. For cost accounting purposes, there are three fundamental types of organisational subunit:

1 **Cost centre**: budgeted and actual costs are attributed to cost centres;
2 **Profit centre**: budgeted and actual costs, revenues and profit are attributed to profit centres;
3 **Investment centre**: budgeted and actual costs, revenues, profit and capital investment (e.g. in equipment) are attributed to investment centres.

The most appropriate type of cost accounting subunit depends on organisational structure, the nature of outputs and associated processes and on management's information needs. Many organisations employ a mix of two or more types of centre, depending on circumstances. We will discuss this, and related issues, in Chapter 18.

Classification of cost by individual product/service

Management may wish to attribute costs – budgeted and actual – to individual products/services, or to groups of products/services. This may be done to assess product profitability, to help with decisions such as whether to discontinue a particular product, or for use in price-setting. We will encounter several instances of this approach in later chapters – e.g. in Chapters 10 and 12.

Classifications are sometimes combined – as in Chapter 10, where direct/indirect classification is combined with classification by individual product to obtain the cost of joint products emerging from the same production process; or in Chapter 18, where we suggest a combination of budgeted/actual with fixed/variable as an aid to financial control. However, the basic requirement remains: namely, that the classification(s) must be appropriate to the purpose, whether this be product/service costing, planning and control or decision making.

The usefulness of cost classification on its own is limited; we need to link cost attribution to the inputs, outputs, processes and procedures of the organisation. A number of costing methodologies have been developed in an attempt to achieve this, and we shall now provide a brief overview of the major approaches.

'TRADITIONAL' COSTING METHODOLOGIES

The nature of an organisation's output and associated procedures will be reflected in that organisation's method of attributing costs – e.g. by determination of the appropriate cost unit. Figure 2.8 illustrates 'traditional' approaches to this.

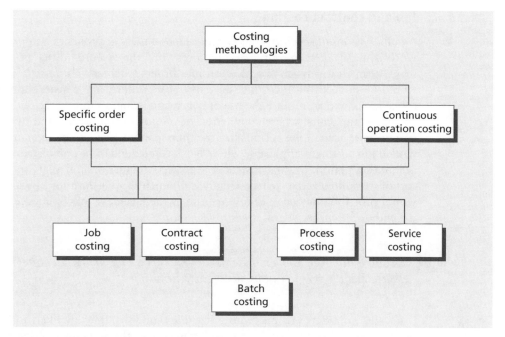

Figure 2.8 'Traditional' cost attribution

Specific order costing applies in situations where output is produced to customer order, whereas, under **continuous operation costing**, products/services result from a repeated procedure or series of procedures.

 Suggest two *types of output to which each of specific order and continuous operation costing might apply.*

Specific order costing would apply to output such as vehicle repairs in a garage, made-to-measure outfitting, or construction of buildings and roads. Continuous operation costing is relevant to provision of health-care, legal and accountancy services, or oil refining and chemical processing. However, some care is necessary in practice when assigning the most appropriate costing methodology to a given type of output, as the distinctions made in Figure 2.8 may be considerably less clear-cut in reality. An organisation's output may be such that more than one approach is necessary; or the method most suitable to the circumstances may be a hybrid of specific order and continuous operation costing. An engineering company, for example, might mass-produce a sub-assembly (continuous operation costing), which is then customised according to clients' specifications (specific order costing). The output of a legal firm consists of service to its clients, but the precise nature of the service provided will generally be subject to client instruction – so elements of both continuous operation and specific order costing can be seen here.

The need for a flexible approach to costing methodology is greater in face of factors like the increasingly 'globalised' market within which companies operate, development of advanced manufacturing technologies and emphasis on total quality (which we shall discuss later in the chapter).

Job and contract costing

As subdivisions of specific order costing, each of these approaches is appropriate where work is undertaken to customers' requirements, the essential difference being one of scale. Comparatively small-scale customer orders, such as vehicle repairs in a garage, would be subject to job costing, but large-scale orders, like construction of a road or office-block, would require the use of contract costing. In more precise terms, contract costing is applicable where completion of output substantively, and by design, spans two or more accounting periods (i.e. the time span involved is an inherent feature of the work). Job costing is applicable where work is intended to be completed within a single accounting period. Many construction projects require several years to complete; the sort of work involved in vehicle repairs is of much shorter duration and a particular job would probably only span two years due to the 'accident' of commencement towards the end of the earlier year.

 Cost units are likely to be much smaller in a job costing than in a contract costing environment. How might this affect cost attribution?

Because contracts are much more sizeable than jobs, they are likely to have a higher proportion of direct to total costs, which may have the advantage of reducing the need for arbitrary cost apportionments of the type we shall discuss in Chapters 5 and 6. We will examine job and contract costing in detail in Chapter 8.

Process costing

Process costing is appropriate to output of identical (or very nearly identical) units, often via a sequence of related processes. Oil refining and whisky distilling are typical examples, as are certain types of factory mass-production (e.g. food processing). Because of their mass-produced and identical nature, costs are not generally attributed to individual cost units, but to specific processes, from which point they are averaged over the number of units passing through the process concerned. In some cases, individual cost units may not be separately identifiable until the fairly late stages of production; in other instances, they may be so small as to render cost attribution to individual units unattractive in cost/benefit terms. It is also possible that two or more main products (**joint products**) may emerge from the same process (**joint process**). In process costing, it will almost always be true that rather less precision is possible in the attribution of costs to individual units of output than is the case with either contract or job costing. Process and joint product costing are dealt with in Chapters 9 and 10 respectively.

Batch costing

Here, output of identical items is produced in batches, with costs being traced initially to each batch and then being averaged over the number of units concerned (if a cost per unit is required). As Figure 2.8 suggests, batch costing has some of the characteristics of specific order, and some of continuous operation costing. Cerma Ltd (Exhibit 2.2) will almost certainly employ this costing methodology, as output is produced in batches of 200 mugs.

How will Cerma Ltd's costing methodology reflect both specific order and continuous operation costing?

Cerma Ltd's output may be based on customer requirements, and each batch will be separately identifiable throughout production, with costs being attributed to each batch (specific order costing). However, within each batch, mugs will be identical, are produced by a sequence of processes and a cost per unit within each batch may be obtained by averaging the batch cost over the number of mugs in the batch (continuous operation costing). We will have more to say about batch costing in Chapter 8.

Service costing

The output to which service costing applies is intangible, which distinguishes it from other forms of output outlined above. This is true regardless of whether the service concerned is provided on a commercial basis, by a public sector organisation, by a not-for-profit body or inter-departmentally within the same organisation. If we compare Cerma Ltd's output with that of, say, an investment advisor, we can see that not only is the latter's output intangible, but also that it cannot be stored, that each piece of advice is likely to differ markedly and that, once given, advice may be much less readily amended than might be the case for a batch of faulty mugs. When we discussed cost units earlier in this chapter, we saw that some form of composite cost unit is really needed for service organisations (passenger/kilometre in the case of the transport business). In Chapter 11 we will discuss this more fully, along with other features of service costing.

There is one final set of factors that plays an increasingly important role in the way organisations operate and which as a consequence can have major implications for cost accounting. We end our chapter with a brief overview and discussion of these.

COST ACCOUNTING'S DEVELOPING ENVIRONMENT

The increasing dynamism of organisations' environments has been reflected in development of managerial philosophies and of operational methods that may often 'challenge' accepted cost accounting wisdoms. For the moment, we will describe those developments which are of most significance, providing an indication of which later chapters discuss the potential challenge they may present.

Management accounting: financial accounting 'subset'?

In the previous chapter, we highlighted the different information needs of management and external users of accounting information: this suggests that cost and management accounting are (or should be) distinct from financial accounting. However, as Johnson and Kaplan (1987) have observed, management accounting – and by implication, cost accounting – may have become 'subservient' to financial accounting. Every organisation's financial accounting records are subject to some form of external regulation, such as the Companies' Acts in the case of limited companies or tax requirements in the case of small businesses. Since this is so, it seems reasonable to suggest that such regulation might easily come to dominate the form, content and output of an accounting system, to the possible prejudice of useful information for *internal* use.

The degree of integration which exists in many organisations between cost and management and financial accounting may provide evidence of Johnson and Kaplan's claim. Where cost accounting techniques form the basis of externally reported figures – stock values, for instance – such integration is understandable and justifiable. Unfortunately, in many circumstances, information extracted or derived from the financial accounts (or from a system that closely integrates cost and management with financial accounting) may provide management with precisely the *wrong* planning, control and decision making signals. In Chapter 14, for example, we shall see that the sort of historic cost data recorded by the financial accounting system is irrelevant to decision analysis and there is a very real danger that it might be wrongly included, with the consequent risk of incorrect decisions being made. Holzer and Norreklit (1991) have suggested that, in the past, provision of separate cost and management accounting information has failed the cost/benefit criterion, but that the reducing cost of information, coupled with the increasing cost of incorrect decisions (e.g. in highly competitive globalised markets), have persuaded organisations of the need to invest in sophisticated management accounting systems. Recognition of the need for decoupling of management from financial accounting is, hopefully, now a recognised fact.

World-class manufacturing (WCM)

Many organisations operate in markets which are not simply local or national, but global. One instance of this may be seen in the rapid growth of 'on-line' trading via the Internet. WCM attempts to respond to the added competitive pressure of a 'global marketplace'. The term 'world-class manufacturing' does not describe a single philosophy or method, but consists of a number of interrelated views and techniques each of which addresses specific areas of concern:

- *Quality* Quality of product/service (including after-sales service) is essential in order to maintain or improve market position.
- *Lead time* The length of time between receiving and completing an order may be a critical determinant of market standing.
- *Adaptability* Products/services which are flexible enough to meet different customer requirements are more likely to be successful in a global market.
- *Cost* Delivery of a quality product/service quickly *and* at lower cost than that supplied by competitors can provide a market advantage.

The overall aim of WCM might be summarised as producing output at the lowest possible cost consistent with quality and competitive considerations. WCM therefore advocates holding minimum stocks, training of personnel and their involvement in operational decisions (improving skill levels and possibly commitment to the organisation), effective product/service design and co-operation with suppliers. Emergence of WCM suggests the need for a shift of emphasis in cost and management accounting information; away from the predominantly internally-focused and cost-driven towards quality- and market-oriented. It also suggests that greater emphasis be placed on strategic information and on the need for operational and tactical information to conform with the dictates of strategy. The points we have just mentioned are reflected in several later chapters: e.g. the need for qualitative information in Chapter 14, and the central role of strategy in Chapter 15.

Value-added and non-value-added activities

One way in which costs may be reduced is to distinguish between **value-added activities** and **non-value-added activities**, attempting to reduce or eliminate the latter, along with their associated costs. Value added activities are those which increase the perceived worth of a product or service in the hands of its ultimate consumer; non-value added activities add no such worth and are therefore, arguably, unnecessary.

Exhibit 2.4 provides additional information about Cerma Ltd which we shall use to illustrate this distinction.

Cerma Ltd

Some of the activities involved in running the company's factory are given below:

potting (i.e. forming mugs)
painting and glazing mugs
firing mugs
inspection of raw materials on arrival at factory
movement of batches of mugs between production departments
inspection of batches of mugs after each of forming, painting and glazing and firing
storage of raw materials and finished batches of mugs

Exhibit 2.4 Value-added and non-value-added activities

 Which of the activities in Exhibit 2.4 can be classified as value-added and which as non-value-added?

Of the activities listed, only potting, painting and glazing and firing add worth to the output; all the others are non-value-added and might be the first to be scrutinised in an effort to reduce costs. For example, redesign of factory layout might reduce the need for movement of batches, better training of employees could reduce the degree of inspection required and negotiation with suppliers may lessen raw materials' stockholding. In each case, it might be possible, by contraction of non-value-added activities, to significantly reduce costs without any adverse effect on the quality of output.

The value-added concept can be extended into a **value chain**: this is essentially an interlinked sequence of value-creating activities starting with product/service development, moving through design, raw materials supply, production and marketing.

It is argued that recognition of the relationships between the value chain's different stages will promote cost-efficiency and end-user satisfaction, particularly when each successive stage is treated as its predecessor's 'client'. By adopting this approach, a consumer orientation should be uppermost at all stages of output/supply, with feedback from internal 'clients' and external end-users providing the basis for improvements.

It can therefore be argued that the cost accounting system should centre on the organisation's major activities (rather than on locations or sub-units), thereby permitting non-value-added activities to be highlighted and enhancing efforts at cost reduction. We shall discuss **activity based costing**, **activity based budgeting** and **activity based cost management** in Chapters 6, 17 and 18 respectively.

Total quality management (TQM)

One of the principal facets of world-class manufacturing is its emphasis on quality. In this context, 'quality' is all-embracing, covering not only outputs, but also inputs such as materials and labour. The TQM approach can be summarised as 'getting it right first time, all of the time'. The rationale is that, in the long run, the cost of 'getting it right first time, all of the time' will be less than that of rectifying quality failures after they have occurred. The benefits of TQM can be substantial, a fact borne out by Exhibit 2.5.

A leap out of the dark

Nobody could have associated Mortgage Express, one of TSB's mortgage subsidiaries, with excellence five years ago.

The business was losing £1m a week; a third of its customers were in arrears, and the staff, who had all been recruited during the housing boom of the late 1980s, had no experience of dealing with bad debts. Its prospects were so poor that in April 1991, TSB decided to wind it down over the following three years.

But after a remarkable revival, Mortgage Express yesterday became the joint winner of the 1996 UK Quality Award for business Excellence, a prize organised by the British Quality Foundation . . .

Mortgage Express's achievement was 'a real turnaround story', says the foundation. It transformed a £67m loss into a £38m profit inside three years 'during the deepest recession the market has seen and in the face of unprecedented competition'.

The company attributes much of this success to its adoption in 1992 of total quality management which requires continual improvement of all the main facets of the business, namely leadership, people management, policy and strategy, resources, processes, people satisfaction, customer satisfaction, impact on society and business results. Its enthusiasm is evident as soon as a visitor enters its offices in north London. The building's reception is adorned with a 'quality beacons' pennant, 'employee of the month' photographs, a 'process map', rosettes commemorating Investors in People targets and a huge photograph of the workforce . . .

Source: Vanessa Houlder, *Financial Times*, 4 December 1996. Reprinted with permission.

Exhibit 2.5 TQM and its benefits

 What implications does the TQM philosophy have for cost accounting?

Perhaps the simplest way to appreciate TQM's implications for cost accounting is to consider the prerequisites for effective quality management:

1 training/retraining of staff;
2 good product/service design;
3 sound and suitable information system.

The most obvious impact of these three requirements is in terms of cost, and we can classify quality-related costs as follows:

● **Prevention costs** costs incurred to prevent inferior quality, such as design and training
● **Appraisal costs** costs incurred to ensure achievement of the specified quality standard (e.g. inspection of inputs and outputs)

- **Internal failure costs** costs incurred as a result of quality failure before output is delivered to customers (e.g. scrap, reworks)
- **External failure costs** costs incurred as a result of quality failure after output is delivered to customers (e.g. replacement of customer returns).

In a TQM environment, it is important that the organisation's information system is capable of tracing and reporting quality-related costs. Similarly, the criteria applied to performance evaluation should recognise quality issues, which suggests the use of qualitative, as well as quantitative performance measures.

The importance of an adequate quality assurance system can be seen in the relevant standard set by the International Organisation for Standardisation (ISO 9000). In order to obtain accreditation under this standard, an organisation must submit its quality management system to external assessment; note, however, that accreditation does not guarantee quality of output, it merely approves the quality *system*.

TQM has another, possibly less obvious, implication for cost accounting: if the aim is to 'get it right first time, all of the time', then the relevance of the conventional approach to financial control can be questioned. In the previous chapter, we said that, in essence, this consisted of comparison between planned and actual outcomes (or between planned outcomes and objectives), with significant differences between the two triggering management action. But if we are trying to 'get it right first time', should there be any significant differences to act as a trigger for management action? Arguably not, as their existence suggests a failure to 'get it right'. We shall discuss this matter further in Chapters 18 and 19. Similarly, we will see in Chapter 9 that conventional process costing methodology makes allowance for 'normal losses' – in a TQM environment, no loss would be accepted as being 'normal'.

Just-in-time (JIT)

Originally developed by Toyota in the 1950s and 1960s, JIT has been increasingly adopted in the USA and, latterly, in the UK. The overarching aim of JIT is to eliminate waste at all stages of production, starting with product design, through production processes and stockholding to delivery. JIT is therefore an integral element of WCM and also relies heavily on the distinction between value-added and non-value-added activities. Hay (1988) highlights three key constituents of the overall JIT philosophy:

- *Quality* A TQM approach (see above) should be applied to inputs, processes, procedures and outputs.
- *Employee involvement* Hay argues that this is, perhaps the single most important aspect of JIT, and may require a major change in organisational culture. The workforce should be flexible, responsible and should participate in a process of continual improvement.
- *Production flow* JIT aims for a steady, uninterrupted flow of production. This may be achieved by a number of measures:
  - reducing (or even eliminating) non-value-added activities such as equipment set-ups
  - matching production with customer demand: this is known as a 'pull' system, whereby production is initiated by demand
  - matching material purchases with production requirements: that is, purchasing materials as close as possible to the time they are needed for production
  - reorganising production into 'cells' based on products/components, rather than on functions or procedures.

One implication of JIT is that unnecessary stockholdings will be eliminated. What sort of costs might be reduced/avoided as a result?

Stockholding incurs a variety of costs, some of which may be substantial: storage space may need to be rented or, if not used for storage, may be more profitably used in another way; the store will need heating and lighting, specialised facilities may be required for storing particular types of item (e.g. humidity control); insurance and security will be needed; there is the potential cost of obsolescence, deterioration and damage; staff will be needed to receive items into and issue items from store.

Possibly the greatest single cost attaching to stockholdings is *implicit*: holding large quantities of stock 'ties up' an organisation's capital in an unprofitable way – capital which, if invested differently, could earn a return. Decreasing the amount of stock held may therefore have a marked impact on an organisation's costs.

Operation of a JIT system effectively transfers much of the onus of stockholding (and control of the associated costs) from purchaser to provider, and it is in this respect that the WCM notion of co-operation between the two is vital. A breakdown in liaison at any point in the supply chain will very likely more than nullify the benefits of JIT. If stockholdings are reduced or even eliminated, then the need for many of the traditional material-related cost accounting procedures we will describe in Chapter 5 will be significantly reduced. For example, in a 'pull' system, where production and purchases are timed to coincide with demand, Economic Order and Economic Batch Quantities have no relevance. Similarly, since more flexible use is made of labour within a JIT environment, and since stocks of work-in-progress are likely to be negligible, attribution of labour times and costs to individual products (as described in Chapter 4) may be unnecessary. And, as we shall see in Chapter 12, JIT principles may conflict with the commonly-used technique of absorption costing, since the latter may encourage a build-up of stock.

Technological changes

The pace of technological advance – already great – is increasing. At a basic level, we can see its impact in the computerisation of cost accounting systems; e.g. many of the techniques we shall describe in subsequent chapters are ideally suited to, and are frequently performed on, computer spreadsheets. The general advantages to management accounting of computerisation can be summarised as follows:

- *Complexity* Techniques such as regression analysis (see Chapter 3), which may be unwieldy if performed manually, can be performed with comparative ease on appropriate software.
- *Speed* Response time should be shortened as a result of computers' ability to process large volumes of data quickly and accurately.
- *Job 'enrichment'* Computers can be used to perform tedious and repetitive tasks, thus freeing employees' time for more important and challenging activities.

Cost accounting's ability to respond adequately to a complex and dynamic environment may therefore be greatly aided by computers.

 Can you suggest any potential pitfalls in the use of computers?

There are two areas of danger with any computerised system.

1 *Over-reliance* management may, conceivably, substitute computer output for exercise of their own judgement, wrongly believing the machine to be infallible.
2 *Information overload* there is a possibility that we may provide information merely because a computer is capable of generating it, regardless of whether it is useful in a given situation.

Changes in production technology also have implications for cost accounting: the development of **advanced manufacturing technologies (AMTs)** such as computer-aided design and computer-aided manufacture (CAD/CAM), robotics (i.e. adaptable automation) and flexible manufacturing systems are all having a profound effect on operational practice and on the way in which cost accounting reflects this practice.

- *Automated information?* Although uncommon at present, it is possible to envisage a situation where certain cost accounting information is routinely produced as an integral part of the production process. Progress towards this can already be seen in some automated set-ups where material losses are recorded and reported by the production machinery itself. Greater computer integration of manufacturing is likely to lead to automatic production of an increasing amount of cost accounting information.
- *Labour-'free' production?* Improved technology has steadily reduced the significance of labour inputs in many organisations, with a corresponding decrease in the related cost. Conversely, capital costs (e.g. plant and machinery) have tended to assume greater significance. This may, for example, mean a higher proportion of fixed costs than might have previously been the case, coupled with much more substantial overheads. The result is that overheads may receive more managerial attention than in a labour-intensive environment.
- *'Instant' obsolescence?* The speed of technological advance, e.g. in computers, may require us to amend the way certain cost accounting techniques are applied. This is especially true of the capital investment appraisal criteria which we shall describe in Chapter 15.

The sort of changes we have been describing – to both managerial outlook and operational method – do not render cost accounting irrelevant or outdated. On the contrary, management's need for useful information has never been greater. However, cost accounting must be responsive to the changes taking place: development, flexibility and adaptability are needed. Moreover, there is a particular need for cost accounting information to be sensitive to the external environment within which organisations operate.

SUMMARY

In this chapter, we have described the key elements of the cost accounting framework – cost classification and costing methodology – describing the potential implications for cost accounting of developments in managerial philosophy and operational procedures. We have seen that:

- **Cost attribution** is necessary to permit effective **scorekeeping, attention directing** and **problem solving**.
- Cost attribution should be dictated by the **cost objective** – i.e. the target/purpose of the attribution.

- **Cost classification** groups together costs which share the same attribute(s) *relative to a stated cost objective*.
- The cost classification employed should be appropriate to the purpose for which it is used.
- **Subjective classification** groups individual costs according to specified attributes, **objective classification** links a subjective classification to the stated cost objective.
- **Direct costs** can be unambiguously and quantifiably attributed to a single target cost objective, **indirect costs** cannot.
- **Prime cost** is the total of direct labour, direct materials and direct expenses, **overhead** is the total of indirect labour, indirect materials and indirect expenses.
- The total amount of a **variable cost** increases/decreases in line with increases/decreases in the volume of activity, the total amount of a **fixed cost** is unaffected by the volume of activity.
- Cost behaviour is **linear** when the variable cost per unit is constant at all volumes of activity and/or where the total fixed cost is the same at all volumes.
- **Curvilinear cost functions** occur where the unit cost changes relative to volume of activity.
- A **step cost** is fixed within a given range of volumes, outside which, it increases/decreases by a lump-sum amount; a **semi-variable cost** is partly fixed, partly variable.
- The **relevant range** is the range of volumes and/or time horizon over which a particular set of assumptions is a reasonable approximation of reality.
- **Specific order costing** is applicable where output is produced to customer order, **continuous operation costing** where products/services result from a repeated procedure or series of procedures.
- **Job costing** applies where specific orders are small compared to those to which **contract costing** applies.
- **Process costing** is appropriate to output of identical (or very nearly identical) units, often via a sequence of related processes.
- **Batch costing** applies to output of identical units in batches, possibly to customer specification.
- **Service costing** applies to provision of intangible services.
- It is important to recognise the need to separate financial accounting from cost and management accounting information.
- **World-class manufacturing** recognises global competition by stressing quality, lead-time and adaptability of output.
- **Value-added activities** add worth to output in the perception of its final consumer; **non-value-added activities** do not.
- **Total quality management** advocates 'getting it right first time, all of the time'.
- Quality-related costs can be categorised as **prevention costs, appraisal costs, internal failure costs** or **external failure costs**.

- **Just-in-time** aims to eliminate waste at all stages in the production process.
- Computerised management accounting offers the benefits of complex analysis, speed and job 'enrichment', but may induce over-reliance and information overload.
- **Advanced manufacturing technologies** may have implications for management accounting:
  - automated information?
  - labour 'free' production?
  - 'instant' obsolescence.

In the next chapter, we will extend our discussion of the cost accounting framework to deal with cost estimation – a particularly important topic given the future's significance to managerial and organisational activity.

FURTHER READING

Bromwich, M. and Bhimani, A., *Management Accounting: Evolution not Revolution*, CIMA Publishing, 1993: this fairly short text discusses management accounting in the context of recent developments in managerial thinking and operational procedures.

Bromwich, M. and Bhimani, A., *Management Accounting: Pathways to Progress*, CIMA Publishing, 1994: Chapters 2 and 3 contain further discussion of the impact on management accounting of recent developments.

Chadwick, L. and Magin, M., *Creative Cost and Management Accounting*, Hutchinson Education, 1989: Chapters 2–6 explore the management accounting framework.

Cobb, I., *JIT and the Management Accountant*, CIMA Publishing, 1993: this short text examines current UK practice.

Gelinas, U., Oram, A. and Wiggins, W., *Accounting Information Systems* (2nd edition), South-Western Publishing Co., 1993: Part One discusses accounting systems from the information technology viewpoint.

Hay, E. J., *The Just-in-Time Breakthrough*, John Wiley, 1988.

Holzer, H. and Norreklit, H., Some thoughts on cost accounting developments in the United States. *Journal of Management Accounting Research*, March 1991.

Johnson, T. and Kaplan, R., *Relevance Lost: The Rise and Fall of Management Accounting*, Harvard University Press, 1987.

Upchurch, A., *Management Accounting Principles and Practice*, FT Management, 1998: see Chapter 3 for a discussion of the learning curve.

SELF-TEST QUESTIONS

2.1 TG Partnership, a recruitment agency, incurred the following costs last year:

Direct labour	£150 000
Direct expenses	£250 000
Indirect labour	£ 50 000
Indirect materials	£ 50 000

What was the total prime cost of operating the firm last year?

A £100 000
B £150 000
C £250 000
D £400 000

2.2 For each of the statements which follow, place a tick in the appropriate box to indicate whether it is true or false.

	True	False
(a) The cost of training employees is an internal failure cost.	☐	☐
(b) A variable cost function is linear when the cost per unit of activity decreases as volume increases.	☐	☐
(c) Service costing applies to intangible output.	☐	☐
(d) Cost reduction effort should concentrate first on value-added activities, thereafter on non-value-added activities.	☐	☐
(e) Just-in-time purchasing and production attempts to eliminate the costs associated with stockholding.	☐	☐
(f) If a given cost is direct with respect to one stated cost objective, it must be direct with respect to all other cost objectives.	☐	☐

2.3 What would be the most appropriate costing methodology for a firm of painters and decorators specialising in domestic work?

A Process costing
B Job costing
C Batch costing
D Contract costing

2.4 A direct cost is a cost which

A is incurred as a direct consequence of a decision.
B can be economically identified with the item being costed.
C cannot be economically identified with the item being costed.
D is immediately controllable.
E is the responsibility of the Board of Directors.

(CIMA, *Operational Cost Accounting*, November 1997)

2.5   Figure 2.9 illustrates three cost behaviour patterns relative to the volume of activity.

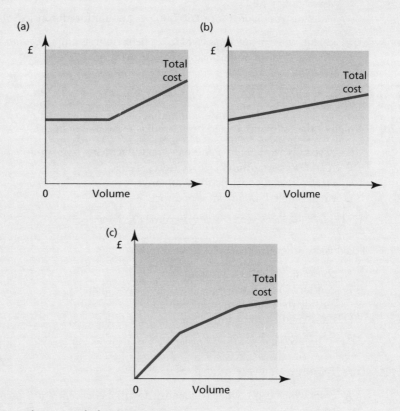

Figure 2.9 Three cost behaviour patterns

The costs described below are some of those incurred by PP Insurance Brokers:

1 *Payment to insurance company*: for each of the first 500 of a particular insurance company's policies which PP's agents sell, £5 is payable to that company; for sales of 501–1000 policies, £4 per policy is payable, and for sales in excess of 1000, £2 per policy is payable.

2 *Payments to sales staff*: all the firm's agents are paid an annual salary of £10 000; once an agent's sales of insurance policies exceed a stated target number, a commission of £20 per additional policy sold is paid.

3 *Administration costs*: £60 000 per annum is payable in respect of PP's offices and of the salaries of the full-time clerical staff employed there; in addition, each policy sold incurs an administration cost of £5 to cover items such as stationery.

Requirements

(a) Match the three costs described above to one of the behaviour patterns illustrated in Figure 2.9, providing a brief explanation of your choice in each case.

(b) Draw a sketch diagram illustrating the behaviour of each cost assuming the following:

  • Payment to the insurance company consists of a flat-rate £3 per policy for *all* policies sold.

- Sales staff are paid an annual salary of £8000 plus commission of £20 per policy for *every* policy sold.
- Administration costs are £60 000 per annum for all foreseeable sales volumes.

(c) Explain why an awareness of cost behaviour is important to management in their planning, control and decision-making activities.

QUESTIONS WITHOUT ANSWERS

2.6   Which of the following would be classed as indirect labour?

A   Assembly workers in a company manufacturing televisions;
B   A stores assistant in a factory store;
C   Plasterers in a construction company;
D   An audit clerk in a firm of auditors.

(CIMA, *Cost Accounting and Quantitative Methods*, November 1998)

2.7   Fixed costs are conventionally deemed to be

A   constant per unit of output.
B   constant in total when production volume changes.
C   outside the control of management.
D   those unaffected by inflation.

(CIMA, *Cost Accounting and Quantitative Methods*, November 1998)

2.8   Direct costs are

A   costs which can neither be identified with a cost centre nor identified with a single cost unit.
B   costs which can be identified with a single cost unit.
C   costs incurred as a direct result of a particular decision.
D   costs incurred which can be attributed to a particular accounting period.
E   none of the above.

(CIMA, *Operational Cost Accounting*, May 1999)

2.9   The Copying Centre operates a photocopying service in the centre of a local town. Sally Mullen, the business's owner, is worried about the number of complaints from customers and the cost of rectifying these. The problem is quality of copies, which is often so poor that they must be redone; Sally attributes this to a combination of three factors:

- Quality of paper used: to date, this has always been purchased in bulk from the cheapest source, requiring storage (often for a lengthy period) at the Copying Centre's premises.
- Photocopying equipment: this is all leased from the manufacturer and minimisation of lease costs guided selection of the machines leased.
- Work methods: although staff and photocopiers are sufficient in number to cope with the heaviest expected demand, particularly busy periods often result in staff using machines which they are not trained to operate.

Requirement

Draft a memorandum to Sally Mullen outlining the principles of total quality management, and explaining how these could be applied to operation of the Copying Centre; your memorandum should make mention of the relevance of the cost/benefit criterion in this context.

2.10   (a)   Discuss the contention that the classification of cost should be appropriate to the purpose for which it is to be used, providing relevant illustrations.

(b)   In the light of your answer to (a), outline the potential advantages and disadvantages of a computerised cost accounting system.

(c)   Distinguish between subjective and objective classification of cost, stating why one cannot meaningfully exist without the other.

(d)   Discuss the implications which developments such as world-class manufacturing and advanced manufacturing technologies may have for cost classification.

CHAPTER 3

Cost estimation

Underlying inflation rate drops below target

The fading effects of last year's Budget brought more good news in the fight against inflation for the government and the Bank of England yesterday.

The rate of underlying inflation slipped below the government's official target last month as the boost caused by last year's fuel duty increases dropped out of the annual rate. And the headline retail prices index rate slowed to 1.6%, the slowest annual increase for more than five years.

The government's favoured measure of inflation – RPIX, which excludes mortgage interest payments – slowed to an annual rate of 2.4% in April, 0.1 percentage point below the target set by Gordon Brown, the chancellor.

In March, the annual rate was 2.7%.

April's RPIX figure was only the second time since the Bank took control of interest rates the annual rate has dropped below the 2.5% target, which Mr Brown reaffirmed for a further year in a speech yesterday ... However, there was concern about signs of a rise in inflation once government taxes and housing costs were stripped out. RPIY, the index excluding tax changes and mortgage payments, increased at a monthly rate of 0.6% between March and April to an annual rate of 1.8% ...

Source: Richard Adams, *Financial Times*, 19 May 1999. Reprinted with permission.

Exhibit 3.1 Inflation – a key factor affecting cost estimates

INTRODUCTION

In the previous chapter, we discussed the issue of cost classification and said that the classification must be appropriate to the purpose for which it is used; we identified the main purpose of classification as the provision of useful information. However, on its own, classification of costs is of limited value. We also need to be aware of the *amount* of the costs concerned and, because a large part of cost accounting deals with the future, this inevitably involves estimation. As we shall see – and as Exhibit 3.1 suggests, with its reference to potentially conflicting indicators of inflation – cost estimation is not always a straightforward exercise. Yet it is an exercise with wide-ranging implications for organisations and their management (especially since a great deal of management activity centres on the future). It is also an exercise that affects perceptions about the cost of inputs such as raw materials, and of outputs (goods and services provided) and may also have a bearing on both the selling price and profitability of these goods and services. Cost estimates could raise issues of cost planning and control, sourcing of supplies and even production methods.

In this chapter, we will illustrate various methods which may be employed to estimate future costs, and discuss their strengths and weaknesses.

OBJECTIVES

When you have completed this chapter, you will be able to:

- appreciate the need for cost estimation and its importance to cost and management accounting;
- describe engineering and inspection of accounts approaches to cost estimation;
- use a scattergraph, high–low analysis and simple linear regression analysis to obtain estimates of cost;
- understand the application of multiple regression analysis to estimation problems;
- discuss the strengths and weaknesses of the different cost estimation techniques and the importance of relevant range in this context;
- adjust past costs for the effect of inflation.

THE NEED FOR COST ESTIMATION

In Chapter 1, we identified *decision making* and *planning and control* as major management activities which cost accounting aims to support by the provision of useful information.

 Why is cost estimation vital to cost accounting's support of both these areas of management activity?

As we observed in Chapter 1, much of the information generated by cost accounting must be future-oriented, since decisions and plans can only relate to the future. Financial control (see Chapter 18) requires comparison of like with like: if, for example, differences between budgeted and actual volume are partly the cause of differences between budgeted and actual cost, management should be aware of the fact and not wrongly attribute such differences to efficiency or price factors. It would be impossible to prepare next year's budget or to properly compare it with the actual outcomes without having some idea about:

1 *Which* costs may increase or decrease as the result of increases/decreases in volume and which may not (i.e. which costs/parts of costs are *variable* and which *fixed*);
2 *How much* variable costs are likely to vary with volume and whether volume changes are likely to have an effect on fixed costs;
3 The impact on all costs (fixed and variable) of *non-volume* factors such as inflation;
4 The appropriate *measure of activity* against which to gauge variable cost behaviour (i.e. the *cost unit*).

In effect, it is not possible for cost accounting to provide useful information in support of decision making and planning/control without a considerable element of estimation being present. Such estimates may be based on past experience, but, as we shall see, only to the extent that the past can be considered a reasonable guide to the future.

Given the crucial role of estimation in cost accounting, how can we obtain the required estimates and how much reliance can we place in the results of the different estimation techniques employed? In the discussion that follows, we shall concentrate on estimation of costs, but you should appreciate that some of the techniques can also be applied to estimation of revenues. In addition, it is important that you appreciate the collaborative aspect of cost estimation. To produce credible estimates, the cost and management accountant needs to liaise closely with other members of the management team, whose specialist knowledge about particular facets of the organisation is a necessary supplement to the estimation techniques themselves.

ENGINEERING APPROACHES TO ESTIMATION

These approaches to estimation typically stem from observation of the processes/procedures giving rise to costs, followed by some sort of engineering or operational research estimate of the input–output relationships involved – which can then be used as the basis for cost estimates. Techniques of this sort are not strictly 'cost accounting', but fall within the remit of specialists in operational research or of production engineers. We shall therefore confine ourselves to some general observations about the use of estimation methodologies which fall within the general 'engineering' category.

One major benefit of such techniques is that they will almost certainly provide more accurate cost predictions than anything produced by the techniques we shall describe shortly. This may be especially true where there is an identifiable relationship between inputs and outputs: e.g. in certain chemical processes it is possible to predict with considerable accuracy the outputs which will result from given inputs – and from this it may be a comparatively simple matter to estimate the associated costs.

A further advantage of engineering estimation is that, unlike the other methods which we shall describe below, they can generally be used even where no previous data exist. This may be useful where costs are being estimated for a new product/service or for a new version of an existing one where there are significant differences between the two versions.

 Can you suggest a potential disadvantage associated with use of engineering approaches to cost estimation?

The main disadvantage relating to engineering estimates relates to their very sophistication, which normally requires considerable expertise in operational research or production engineering methodology, and many organisations (especially smaller ones) may not possess such expertise. Although external consultants may be engaged, this could prove costly – so costly, in fact, that the cost/benefit criterion which we described in Chapter 1 may be breached. This may be exacerbated by the need to repeat the estimation exercise regularly (e.g. annually).

The sophisticated nature of engineering estimates may result in another problem: the detailed nature of engineering estimates may possibly mislead managers into believing these to be completely accurate; but no estimation technique will be totally accurate (except by luck) and over-reliance on the accuracy of estimates could conceivably result in dangerous overconfidence about the outcome of future events. If you look again at

Exhibit 3.1, you will see that the two measures of inflation mentioned appear to be giving contradictory signals about whether the rate is rising or falling – which clearly suggests the inaccuracy which in some measure may be an integral element of virtually every cost estimate.

Engineering estimates derive from specialised methodology; at almost the opposite extreme in terms of methodological rigour, is estimation by inspection of accounts.

ESTIMATION BY INSPECTION OF ACCOUNTS

This approach to cost estimation is also referred to as the *account classification* method. The accounts of previous periods are examined for each cost which it is desired to estimate; details of the volume of activity (e.g. output) relating to each of these past costs is also extracted from past records. Based on the pattern of the past costs and related activity levels, a judgement is made about the behaviour of each particular cost: is it wholly variable with activity? Wholly fixed? A mixture of the two? Once a decision about each cost's behaviour has been made, an estimate of the future amount can be made by adjusting for cumulative inflation, volume and other expected changes, so that the estimate produced reflects conditions in the future period to which it is to apply.

This sort of methodology, with some variation, is widely used in practice – many organisations base next year's budget on this year's, adjusted for anticipated changes (e.g. inflation and increases/decreases in volume) – and it can result in fairly reasonable estimates. Compared to engineering methods, it is inexpensive to operate as it does not require the same degree of specialised knowledge. In addition, the results of an account inspection may readily be adjusted to allow for all anticipated future changes in conditions, thereby providing some flexibility in response to what may be a volatile environment.

 What do you feel might be a major weakness of estimates based on an inspection of accounts?

One significant weakness in this estimation technique lies in its subjectivity: great reliance is placed on the judgement of the person(s) undertaking the inspection. How accurate is the estimate of underlying cost behaviour? Has adequate adjustment been made to allow for future changes in conditions? And, being based on past measures, there may be a danger of assuming that the past is an accurate predictor of the future: in a dynamic environment, this may be a dangerous assumption. For example, production technology may change very rapidly, or may be about to change, the *mix* of products/services being provided may have altered in response to changing market conditions, the type or source of raw materials may be different, and there is the impact of inflation to consider (an exercise we shall undertake later in the chapter). Any anticipated change which has cost implications must be incorporated into the estimation exercise. If it is not, the resulting estimates are likely to be, at best, misleading; at worst, they may have very serious consequences for the organisation.

One way of reducing the subjectivity of our estimates is to use past data in a more rigorous manner; the scattergraph, high–low analysis and linear regression all attempt to achieve this in varying degrees.

ESTIMATION USING A SCATTERGRAPH

This is a graphical approach to cost estimation whereby a number of past costs are plotted against their related volumes of activity, from which the plot of an estimated total cost function is derived. We will use the data in Exhibit 3.2 to illustrate the application of a scattergraph to cost estimation.

KTI Ltd: Production overhead

KTI Ltd, which produces and sells cheese, has recorded the following production overhead costs and associated volumes of output over the last six years:

Year	Production overhead £	Volume of output kg
19X1	820 000	360 000
19X2	1 040 000	510 000
19X3	720 000	310 000
19X4	920 000	390 000
19X5	1 060 000	470 000
19X6	1 220 000	560 000

In 19X7, it is anticipated that output will be 500 000 kg. It is known that some of the production overhead costs vary according to the number of kilograms produced, while some (like depreciation of production equipment) are incurred at a fixed amount per annum.

Exhibit 3.2 Basic data for cost-estimation exercise

The problem we are faced with here is determining to what extent production overhead is variable with volume of output and to what extent it is fixed irrespective of output. As a first step in our cost estimate for 19X7, we need to plot the past production overhead costs against their related output volumes; this is done in Figure 3.1.

In Chapter 2, we saw that a semi-variable cost has the general outline illustrated in Figure 3.2.

The points we have plotted in Figure 3.1 represent different measures of total cost relative to volume. What we must now try to do is to use these points as the basis of an estimate for a total cost 'line' of the pattern shown in Figure 3.2. This is achieved by visual estimate; that is, we 'place' our total cost line by examining the pattern of total costs previously plotted.

 By visual estimate, 'place' a straight line on Figure 3.1 which represents an estimate of total cost; extend this line to the left until it intersects the vertical axis. At approximately what value (in £s) does this intersection lie?

Figure 3.3 shows our estimate of the total cost line based on the six values of total cost plotted earlier in Figure 3.1.

You will see that our estimated total cost line in Figure 3.3 intersects the vertical axis at a value of £200 000. This may well be different from your own result – but such a difference is to be expected, since we have used visual estimate to 'place' the total cost line – and visual estimates of where best to place such a line will almost certainly differ

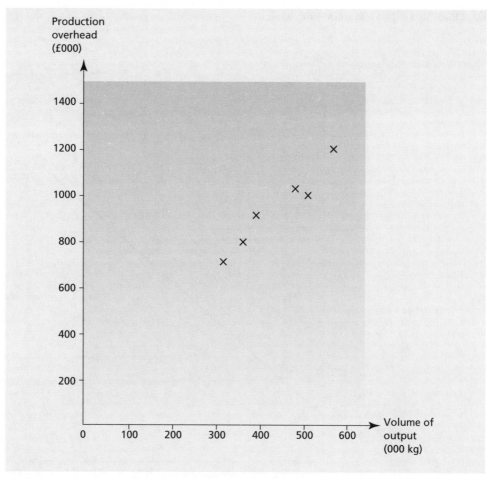

Figure 3.1 KTI Ltd – production overhead for past six years plotted against volume of output

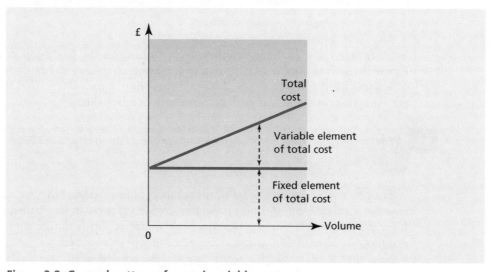

Figure 3.2 General pattern of a semi-variable cost

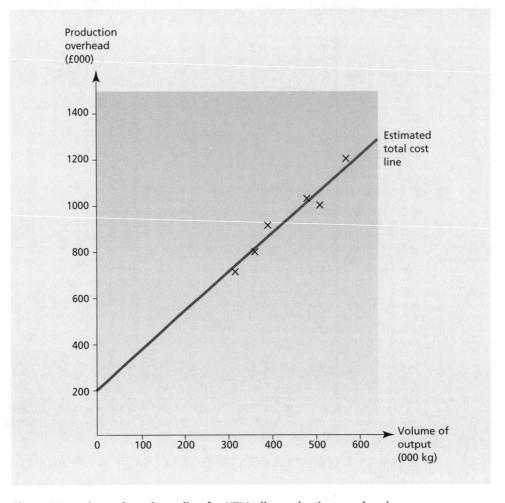

Figure 3.3 Estimated total cost line for KTI Ltd's production overhead

between one individual and another. In our example, the past total costs plotted in Figure 3.1 are fairly close to lying in a straight line, so the extent of differences in visual estimate is likely to be quite small. But this may not be the case, so that the accuracy of the estimated total cost line may be extremely questionable.

 What is the significance to our cost estimation exercise of the £200 000 intersection in Figure 3.3?

The point where our estimate of the total cost line intersects the vertical axis represents the fixed element of total production overhead; this can be verified by comparing Figures 3.2 and 3.3. The implication of this intersection is that, even if there is zero production, £200 000 in production overhead will be incurred.

Now that we have a value for the fixed cost, we can substitute this into one of the past costs to derive an estimate of the variable cost per kg of cheese produced:

	£
Total production overhead in 19X1 (from Exhibit 3.2)	820 000
Less fixed element	200 000
So the variable element =	620 000

We can now determine the estimated variable production overhead per kg:

$$\frac{\text{Variable element of 19X1 cost}}{\text{19X1 output}} = \frac{£620\,000}{360\,000\text{ kg}} = £1.72 \text{ (rounded)}$$

 Based on the estimates of fixed cost and variable cost per kg which we have just calculated, what is the estimated total production overhead for 19X7, when output will be 500 000 kg?

Estimated total production overhead for 19X7 will be:

	£
Fixed element	200 000
Variable element (500 000 kg @ £1.72)	860 000
Total cost	1 060 000

This is a very straightforward approach to cost estimation, but it does suffer from certain weaknesses. The first is the subjectivity involved in placement of the estimated total cost line which we referred to above. Another problem is that, like the account inspection method (and indeed the other methods we shall describe below), the scattergraph assumes that the past can be taken as a reasonable guide to the future. Looking again at Figure 3.3, we might argue that one way to help reduce the subjective element in our placement of the estimated total cost line would be to plot a greater number of previous total overhead costs and related output volumes.

Suppose we had plotted total production overhead costs from the last 20 years. Would this really have improved the quality of our estimate? Highly unlikely, as the further into the past we go, the less relevant is the information likely to be for the present or the immediate future, and the harder it will be to make adjustment for changes, both over the time span involved (e.g. the effect of inflation over such a long period) and anticipated for the future (e.g. working methods next year relative to those of 20 years ago). In fact, rapid change in organisational environment and methods may render even fairly recent data suspect as a basis for estimation.

In addition, the scattergraph assumes linear cost behaviour: i.e. that the fixed element of total cost is unchanged at all volumes and that the variable cost per unit is constant, thereby ignoring the possibility of step fixed costs and curvilinear variable costs, of the sort described in the previous chapter.

One final weakness of the scattergraph is that the estimate of variable cost may depend on which past cost is selected for the fixed cost substitution procedure.

 Substitute the £200 000 estimated fixed cost into the 19X5 total production overhead cost given in Exhibit 3.2 and recalculate the estimated variable cost per kg and the estimated total production overhead cost for 19X7.

Using 19X5's total production overhead cost for the substitution gives:

	£
19X5 total cost	1 060 000
Less Fixed element	200 000
Variable element	860 000

So the estimated variable cost per kg is:

$$\frac{£860\ 000}{470\ 000} = £1.83 \text{ (rounded)}$$

Although this is fairly close to our previous estimate (£1.72), the difference is more substantial when a revised total cost estimate for 19X7 is produced:

	£
Fixed element	200 000
Variable element (500 000 @ £1.83)	915 000
Estimated total cost	1 115 000

which is £55 000 more than our first estimate. Which should we accept? If the original £1 060 000 is used, we may be understating the cost, whereas the second estimate may overstate it. An inaccuracy of this kind exaggerates the inaccuracy inherent to any estimation technique. In some situations, the resulting margin of error could be so great that the credibility of estimates produced is seriously affected. Moreover, if our estimates are inaccurate to this extent, then the value of the information to management may be greatly reduced.

As an alternative to graphing a number of past costs and activity levels, we can simplify procedures by using high-low analysis, which employs only two past observations.

HIGH–LOW ANALYSIS

The scattergraph used a number of previous costs and activity levels as the basis of an estimate of total cost; high–low analysis uses only two:

- the highest activity level and its associated total cost; along with
- the lowest activity level and its associated total cost.

From Exhibit 3.2, we can see that the highest and lowest outputs occurred in 19X6 and 19X3 respectively. Figure 3.4 plots these values along with their associated production overhead costs, joins the plots and, like the scattergraph, extends the plot to obtain a value for estimated fixed production overhead.

From Figure 3.4, we obtain an estimate of £100 000 for the fixed element of production overhead. Substituting this into the overhead cost of the high activity allows us to derive an estimate of the variable cost per kg:

	£
Total cost for 19X6 (from Exhibit 3.2)	1 220 000
Less Fixed element	100 000
Variable element	1 120 000

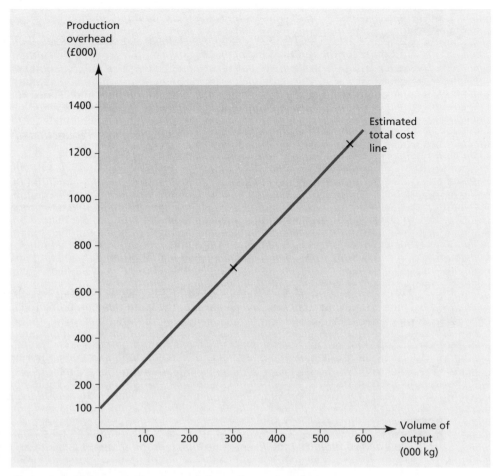

Figure 3.4 Highest and lowest activity and associated costs

Variable overhead per kg:

$$\frac{£1\ 120\ 000}{560\ 000\ \text{kg}} = £2.00$$

Unlike the scattergraph, high–low analysis will give us the same estimate of variable overhead per kg regardless of whether we use the high volume total cost or the low volume total cost in the substitution process – you may wish to check that this is the case.

However, drawing graphs can be somewhat cumbersome, and it is possible to obtain the same result by arithmetic means. If we assume a linear cost behaviour pattern, then we are assuming that the fixed element of each of the high and low volume total overhead costs is the same. We are also assuming that the variable cost per kg is constant, so the difference in total cost between the two output levels will be attributable to the variable cost of the difference in activity. We can therefore produce an estimated variable cost per unit:

$$\frac{\text{Difference in total cost}}{\text{Difference in activity}}$$

From Exhibit 3.2, extract the highest and lowest total outputs along with their related total production overhead costs, and use the formula above to obtain an estimate for the variable cost per kg.

A comparison of the highest and lowest total outputs and related total production overhead costs reveals the following:

	Output	*Production overhead*
		£
Highest volume (19X6)	560 000	1 220 000
Lowest volume (19X3)	310 000	720 000
Difference	250 000	500 000

The estimated variable overhead per kg is:

$$\frac{£500\ 000}{250\ 000} = £2.00$$

This value can now be substituted into *either* the highest volume total cost *or* the lowest volume total cost to obtain an estimate for the fixed element. Using the highest volume total cost, we get:

	£
Total cost	1 220 000
Less Variable element (560 000 @ £2.00)	1 120 000
So the fixed element =	100 000

 Substitute the £2.00 per kg variable overhead estimate into the lowest volume total cost and confirm that the fixed cost estimate is the same.

Using the lowest volume total cost gives:

	£
Total cost	720 000
Less Variable element (310 000 @ £2.00)	620 000
So fixed element =	100 000

Based on our high–low analysis, estimated total production overhead for 19X7 is:

	£
Fixed element	100 000
Variable element (500 000 @ £2.00)	1 000 000
Total cost	1 100 000

This is another very simple estimation technique but it, too, suffers from certain weaknesses. Like the scattergraph, it assumes linear cost behaviour and that the past is a reasonable guide to the future. A particular weakness of high–low analysis lies in the two activity levels used in the estimation process. If these extreme volumes are significantly different from more 'normal' volumes, then there is every chance that the associated cost behaviour could be significantly different. For example, if the difference between high and low volumes is large, then the fixed element of total cost could well contain at least one 'step' at some intermediate volume.

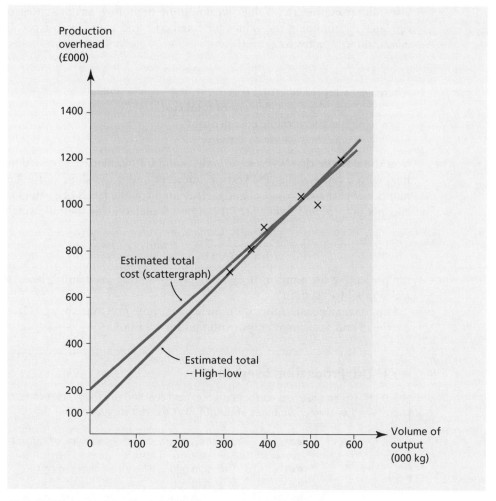

Figure 3.5 Scattergraph and high–low total cost estimates

Figure 3.5 compares the estimated total cost functions resulting from scattergraph and high–low analysis.

The reason for the difference in our fixed cost estimate is clear – the scattergraph has attempted to incorporate *all* the past observations, whereas high–low uses only two. Figure 3.5 should also point up our earlier comment about potential distortion of cost estimates caused by using only two extreme values – and remember, here, the past observations of total cost are very close to exhibiting a linear relationship with volume.

The final estimation technique we will illustrate uses mathematical analysis, and is the most rigorous in its use of past data.

LINEAR REGRESSION ANALYSIS

This technique overcomes the subjectivity inherent in the scattergraph by calculating a precise placement for the estimated total cost line; by using a number of past values, it also addresses the 'two-value' weakness of high–low analysis. Regression analysis operates by obtaining the values for fixed cost and variable cost per unit in a mathematical formula for total cost:

$$y = a + bx$$

where y represents total cost
               a is the fixed element of total cost
               b is the variable cost per unit
               x is the volume of activity.

You should note that '$y = a + bx$' is the standard mathematical equation for a straight line, with a representing the vertical intercept and b the slope of the line. Based on a number of past total costs (y) and their related volume levels (x), values for the variable cost per unit (b) and fixed cost (a) can be calculated using the following formulae:

$$b = \frac{n \sum xy - \sum x \sum y}{n \sum x^2 - (\sum x)^2} \quad \text{and} \quad a = \frac{\sum y}{n} - \frac{b \sum x}{n}$$

n representing the number of past observations being used and $\sum$ being the mathematical symbol for 'sum of'.

For convenience, Exhibit 3.3 presents again the previous six years' total production overhead and associated output volumes for KTI Ltd.

KTI Ltd: Production overhead

KTI Ltd, which produces and sells cheese, has recorded the following production overhead costs and associated volumes of output over the last six years:

Year	Production overhead £	Volume of output kg
19X1	820 000	360 000
19X2	1 040 000	510 000
19X3	720 000	310 000
19X4	920 000	390 000
19X5	1 060 000	470 000
19X6	1 220 000	560 000

In 19X7, it is anticipated that output will be 500 000 kg. It is known that some of the production overhead costs vary according to the number of kilograms produced, while some (like depreciation of production equipment) are incurred at a fixed amount per annum.

Exhibit 3.3 KTI Ltd production overhead

There are six past costs and volume levels, so here, $n = 6$. Although the formulae above appear very daunting, a simple tabulation will provide us with the other values we need to enable us to obtain values for a (fixed cost) and b (variable cost per kg). For ease of calculation, all the values for x (output) and y (total production overhead) in the table which follows have been stated in thousands (kg and £).

x	y	xy	x^2
360	820	295 200	129 600
510	1 040	530 400	260 100
310	720	223 200	96 100
390	920	358 800	152 100
470	1 060	498 200	220 900
560	1 220	683 200	313 600
$\Sigma\,2\,600$	$\Sigma\,5\,780$	$\Sigma\,2\,589\,000$	$\Sigma\,1\,172\,400$

Inserting the appropriate values into the formula for b gives:

$$b = \frac{n\sum xy - \sum x\sum y}{n\sum x^2 - (\sum x)^2} = \frac{6(2\,589\,000) - (2600 \times 5780)}{6(1\,172\,400) - 2600^2} = \frac{15\,534\,000 - 15\,028\,000}{7\,034\,400 - 6\,760\,000}$$

$$= \frac{506\,000}{274\,400} = 1.84 \text{ (rounded)}$$

In other words, our estimate of the variable overhead per kg is £1.84. This value can now be used to obtain a value for a (the fixed cost):

$$a = \frac{\sum y}{n} - \frac{b\sum x}{n} = \frac{5780}{6} - \frac{(1.84 \times 2600)}{6} = 963.33 - 797.33 = 166.00$$

Bearing in mind that the figures for x and y are stated in thousands, our estimate of the fixed production overhead is £166 000. Estimated total production overhead for 19X7 will be:

	£
Fixed element	166 000
Variable element (500 000 kg @ £1.84)	920 000
Total cost	1 086 000

This approach is undoubtedly more *mathematically* precise than the scattergraph or high–low analysis: but does it provide a more accurate prediction of total cost? Like both of these methods, linear regression analysis assumes linear cost behaviour. (Remember that the mathematical expression for total cost which we gave above ($y = a + bx$) is the standard formula for a straight line). In addition, we are still taking the past to be a reasonable indicator of the future; in mathematical terms, the more past observations which we include in our regression analysis, the more mathematically valid the result. However, as we have already observed, inclusion of a large number of past figures may have exactly the opposite effect on our cost estimation exercise.

One important consideration in cost estimation is what causes variability in costs. Is it a single factor (and if so, have we correctly identified it?) or is more than one factor involved (in which case, how do we recognise the fact?).

THE 'SINGLE-FACTOR' ASSUMPTION

So far, our cost estimation exercise relating to KTI Ltd has assumed that the variable element of production overhead varies in relation to increases/decreases in the volume of output.

What other factors may affect the variability of production overhead?

Production overhead may vary relative to several factors – for example, the number of machine or direct labour hours needed for a given volume of output, the age of production equipment, or the number of times equipment needs to be set up for production. None of these additional factors has been included in our scattergraph, high–low or regression estimates – nor can they be. These techniques assume that cost variability arises because of a single factor (the number of kg in this case), so we need to be confident that the measure of activity we are using is the main cause of variability in cost.

We can assess the relationship between a particular activity measure and cost variability by means of two statistical indicators: the **correlation coefficient** and the **coefficient of determination**.

The correlation coefficient

More correctly termed the *product moment correlation coefficient*, this assesses the strength of linear relationship between two variables. The correlation coefficient's value can range between –1 and +1, indicating, respectively, perfect negative and perfect positive correlation. A correlation coefficient of zero (or close to zero) normally suggests that there is no correlation between the variables being examined. Negative correlation occurs where variables are inversely related – i.e. the value of y (total cost) reduces as the value of x (activity) increases and vice versa. A relationship of this sort would be unrealistic in the context of total cost and activity level; here, we would expect to see evidence of positive correlation (a correlation coefficient close to +1), indicating that, as activity increases, total cost also increases and vice versa.

 Look again at Figure 3.1. Does the pattern of total costs plotted suggest positive or negative correlation with the number of kg produced?

Since total overhead cost in Figure 3.1 is generally increasing as the number of kg increases, correlation appears to be positive. To determine just how strong is the degree of correlation, we can calculate the correlation coefficient – r – using the following formula:

$$r = \frac{\Sigma (x - \bar{x})(y - \bar{y})}{\sqrt{\Sigma (x - \bar{x})^2 \, \Sigma (y - \bar{y})^2}}$$

where $\bar{x}$ and $\bar{y}$ represent the average values of x and y.

Using KTI Ltd's data from Exhibit 3.3, the average values for x (kg of output) and y (total production overhead) are:

$$\bar{x} = \frac{(360\,000 + 510\,000 + 310\,000 + 390\,000 + 470\,000 + 560\,000)}{6}$$

$$= 433\,333$$

$$\bar{y} = \frac{(820\,000 + 1\,040\,000 + 720\,000 + 920\,000 + 1\,060\,000 + 1\,220\,000)}{6}$$

$$= 963\,333$$

A tabulation will provide the values we need for the correlation coefficient formula. For convenience, we have again stated the values of x and y in thousands.

x	$(x - \bar{x})$	$(x - \bar{x})^2$	y	$(y - \bar{y})$	$(y - \bar{y})^2$	$(x - \bar{x})(y - \bar{y})$
360	(73.333)	5 377.729	820	(143.333)	20 544.349	10 511.039
510	76.667	5 877.829	1 040	76.667	5 877.829	5 877.829
310	(123.333)	15 211.029	720	(243.333)	59 210.949	30 010.989
390	(43.333)	1 877.749	920	(43.333)	1 877.749	1 877.749
470	36.667	1 344.469	1 060	96.667	9 344.509	3 544.489
560	126.667	16 044.528	1 220	256.667	65 877.949	32 511.238
		Σ 45 733.333			Σ 162 733.334	84 333.333

Inserting the appropriate figures from our tabulation into the correlation coefficient formula, we get:

$$r = \frac{\Sigma (x - \bar{x})(y - \bar{y})}{\sqrt{\Sigma (x - \bar{x})^2 \, \Sigma (y - \bar{y})^2}} = \frac{84\ 333.333}{\sqrt{(45\ 733.333)(162\ 733.334)}} = \frac{84\ 333.333}{86\ 268.985} = 0.978$$

Since the correlation coefficient has a value very close to +1, we have a high degree of positive correlation between the number of kg produced and total production overhead. This suggests that volume of output may well be the factor causing total production overhead to vary. But we must be careful in our interpretation of the correlation coefficient: the best we can say here is that it is strongly indicative of volume of output causing variability in total production overhead. High positive correlation does not, of itself, prove that there is a *causal* link between the number of kg and total production overhead – some further investigation will be required.

The coefficient of determination

This statistical measure – r^2 (the square of the correlation coefficient) – indicates the proportion of variation in actual past costs which may be predicted with reference to changes in the selected activity measure. For KTI Ltd's production overhead relative to the number of kg produced, the coefficient of determination is:

$$0.978^2 = 0.956$$

A coefficient of determination with a value close to 1 (i.e. 100%) would suggest that the correct activity measure has been chosen; if the coefficient of determination is significantly lower than 1, the implication is that the relationship between activity measure and variability in total cost is weak. But, like the correlation coefficient, the coefficient of determination does not necessarily provide an accurate reflection of the *causal* relationship between activity and variability in cost. So although 95.6% of variability in KTI Ltd's past production overhead may be predicted in terms of variations in the number of kg produced, we do not know for sure that variation in the volume of output is *causing* variation in total production overhead.

Multiple and non-linear regression

It is also possible to deal with the single-factor problem by using a **multiple regression**

model. This allows for the impact on cost variability of a range of different factors, so that the total cost formula given above ($y = a + bx$) would appear as follows:

$$y = a + b_1 x_1 + b_2 x_2 + b_3 x_3 + \cdots b_n x_n$$

x_1, x_2, etc. representing the different factors having a bearing on cost behaviour. However, including additional factors in the analysis will not automatically improve the accuracy of the resulting predictions. In addition, it might be difficult or even impossible to identify all the factors affecting cost behaviour. And, even where they can be identified, quantification could be problematic: for example, linking the age of production machinery with variability of production overhead in KTI Ltd's case.

In addition to allowing cost estimates to incorporate more complex – possibly more realistic – cause/effect patterns, a multiple regression model might help to alleviate the danger of cost estimation focusing solely or unduly on factors internal to the organisation: inflation is one important external consideration. However, even this may not be enough, as there may be other critical external influences – e.g. how do our costs compare with those of our competitors?

As we saw in the previous chapter, cost behaviour need not necessarily be linear, and it is possible to employ more sophisticated mathematical techniques to obtain estimates where non-linear cost functions are involved. Although the calculations involved in multiple and non-linear regression models can appear daunting if undertaken manually, proprietary software packages are readily available for such purposes.

When estimating costs, we also need to bear in mind the concept of **relevant range**, otherwise our estimates may lack credibility.

THE RELEVANT RANGE AND COST ESTIMATION

We introduced this important concept in the previous chapter; the relevant range is the range of activity volumes and/or the time horizon over which a particular set of assumptions can be taken to be reasonable approximations of reality. If we apply this to cost estimation, we can say that our estimates are likely to be reasonable only within a particular volume range and time period. The importance of a limited volume range is particularly evident if we consider high–low analysis. We have said that the major problem with this approach is that the volumes are extremes and so the associated cost behaviour may not be typical of more 'normal' levels of activity – another way of stating the same problem is to say that these extreme volumes breach the relevant range.

In more general terms, the assumption of linear cost behaviour – constant variable cost per unit and unchanging total fixed cost – may *only* be reasonable within the relevant range. Look again at our scattergraph and regression analysis. Is extrapolation of the estimated total cost line as far as the vertical intercept (i.e. zero volume) reasonable? Or is the range of volumes covered by the cost function thus extrapolated so wide that the relevant range is seriously compromised (and with it, our assumption of linear cost behaviour)?

Turning to the issue of time period, we can see the effect of failing to place a limit on this if we look at scattergraphs or regression analysis: these techniques both use a number of past costs and activity levels. It is possible that using a large number of past figures will improve our estimates, but it may also be true that the older the data, the less its relevance to the future: that is, there is a danger that the time aspect of the relevant range may be breached.

If we are to produce acceptable cost estimates, we must recognise the limitations imposed by the relevant range and adapt our calculations accordingly – e.g. by limiting the number of past figures used, or by using more measures within the relevant time-span (e.g. monthly or quarterly figures, rather than annual), or by limiting the extent of extrapolation. One final – and potentially crucial – factor to consider in cost estimation is inflation.

INFLATION AND COST ESTIMATION

Even with comparatively low rates of inflation, the cumulative effect over time can be marked. Therefore, when we are estimating future costs, allowance must be made for inflation. This raises two potential difficulties:

1 providing a credible estimate of future inflation;
2 adjusting past costs for the effect of inflation where these are being used as the basis of our estimate.

We shall discuss each of these issues below.

Assessing future inflation

The problem here lies in producing reasonable estimates of how inflation will affect a particular organisation, and this may be difficult, as Exhibit 3.4 suggests.

Static factory gate prices underline slowdown

... Official figures published on Thursday are expected to show that the annual rate of retail price inflation fell below 3% last month for the first time in more than a year.

Output prices, including the more volatile components, rose by a non-seasonally adjusted 0.4% between December and January and by 3.8% in the year to January – the lowest annual increase since March last year.

Industry was hit by higher oil prices, which rose 5.5% last month, due partly to unusually cold weather, particularly in the US.

But this was more than offset by declines in the prices of other raw materials. The price of fuels other than crude oil fell by 1.9% in January.

Manufacturers' overall fuel and raw material costs declined by 0.3% last month, following a rise of 1.8% in December. Input price inflation peaked at about 12% in the first half of last year but it has slowed sharply since. In the year to January input costs rose 4%, the lowest annual increase since July 1994 ...

Source: Graham Bowley, *Financial Times*, 13 February 1996. Reprinted with permission.

Exhibit 3.4 Inflationary pressure is not uniform

Exhibit 3.4 illustrates the potential volatility of inflation, depending on the specific resources being considered. For example, 'manufacturers' overall fuel and raw material costs declined by 0.3% last month, following a rise of 1.8% in December' – and these are previous *monthly* figures. Imagine how difficult it may be to produce estimated rates of price increase covering, say, a one-year period and relating to the *specific* input resources required by an organisation. In some instances, it may be possible to use published sources for estimates of inflation: e.g. the Bank of England's quarterly *Inflation Report*, which contains both historic inflation figures and projections; or figures produced by the Office for National Statistics, such as *Industrial Trends*, showing past and anticipated price movements in various categories of resources. In some economic sectors, such as building, organisations can obtain information from specialist trade journals. However, even with these sources, care is necessary:

> Management at KTI Ltd intends to utilise the published Retail Price Index to adjust its past and estimated future production overhead costs for inflation. Is there a possible weakness in this approach?

The weakness in the proposed use of the Retail Price Index is that this index is a general indicator of inflation and is measured with reference to a 'basket' of goods and services as diverse as muesli and mortgage interest. It is thus unlikely that such an index would provide a particularly relevant measure in terms of the price changes affecting the *specific* resources used by KTI Ltd. More specific indices such as those contained in the Office for National Statistics' *Industrial Trends* may have greater relevance. Even here, some imprecision may exist, as the measures tend to be expressed in terms of categories of goods/services.

Alternatively, an organisation may develop its own measures of inflation based on past experience and expectations about future changes in costs. In situations where changes in cost are particularly volatile, it may be advisable to limit the scope of a detailed estimate to, say, the forthcoming month or quarter, rather than attempting to encompass a full year with a single estimated inflation rate.

Adjusting past costs for inflation

The key fact to bear in mind when adjusting past costs for inflation is that inflation is a *cumulative* phenomenon. Exhibit 3.5 gives some additional information about KTI Ltd's maintenance costs.

Before we can undertake any estimation exercise based on the data in Exhibit 3.5, we need to adjust the costs for the effect of inflation, so that they are stated on a common basis. If we fail to do this, our resulting estimate will be distorted by the cumulative effect of inflation over time. In other words, part of the differences between the past costs we used for our earlier estimates is due to inflation, rather than to changes in the volume of activity – and it is the impact of this which we are seeking to neutralise.

It is possible to make such an adjustment in one of two ways: by *removing* the cumulative effect of inflation from all the past costs (known as **deflating**), or by *adding* the cumulative effect of inflation to all the past costs (i.e. **inflating** them). If we deflated the costs in Exhibit 3.5, we would effectively need to state each cost in terms of 19X1 price levels. Since the object of the exercise is to obtain an estimate for 19X7, this approach seems rather cumbersome, as we would then need to inflate the resulting estimate to 19X7 price levels. It is therefore much simpler to inflate all the past costs to 19X7 price levels, although, as we shall see in Chapter 18, deflation may be useful in the context of financial control.

KTI Ltd: Production overhead and inflation

Total production overhead over the last six years along with the associated volume of output and annual inflation rates, have been as follows:

Year	Total production overhead £	Volume of output kg	Annual inflation rate %
19X1	820 000	360 000	4.5
19X2	1 040 000	510 000	5.0
19X3	720 000	310 000	4.0
19X4	920 000	390 000	3.5
19X5	1 060 000	470 000	3.0
19X6	1 220 000	560 000	3.0

From trade and technical journals relating to the company's industrial sector, management has estimated that an annual inflation rate 2.5% is appropriate for next year.

Exhibit 3.5 Impact of inflation on KTI Ltd's production overhead

To inflate the 19X1 overhead cost in Exhibit 3.5 to 19X7 price levels, we need to increase it in line with cumulative inflation in 19X2, 19X3, 19X4, 19X5, 19X6 and also with the estimated inflation rate for 19X7:

$$(£820\ 000 \times 1.05 \times 1.04 \times 1.035 \times 1.03 \times 1.03 \times 1.025)$$
$$= £1\ 007\ 802 \text{ (rounded to the nearest whole £1)}$$

Note that the 19X1 cost is not adjusted for 19X1 inflation – this will already be included in the stated £820 000.

 Working to the nearest whole £1, inflate the 19X2 production overhead from Exhibit 3.5 to 19X7 price levels.

The 19X2 cost will need to be uplifted to reflect cumulative inflation in 19X3, 19X4, 19X5, 19X6, and the estimated rate for 19X7:

$$(£1\ 040\ 000 \times 1.04 \times 1.035 \times 1.03 \times 1.03 \times 1.025)$$
$$= £1\ 217\ 322 \text{ (to the nearest whole £1)}$$

Applying similar adjustments to the other past costs in Exhibit 3.5 gives the full list of inflated past costs:

Year	Cost inflated to 19X7 price levels £	Volume of output kg
19X1	1 007 802	360 000
19X2	1 217 322	510 000
19X3	810 347	310 000
19X4	1 000 429	390 000
19X5	1 119 095	470 000
19X6	1 250 500	560 000

It is worth noting that, despite the comparatively low rates of inflation quoted in

Exhibit 3.5, their cumulative effect over a period of seven years is substantial, particularly on the earlier costs.

Now that inflationary discrepancies between past data have been removed, we can apply any of the quantitative estimation techniques described earlier to obtain our cost estimate for 19X7.

 Apply high–low analysis to the inflated past costs given above to obtain an estimate of the variable production overhead per kg and the total annual fixed cost. State the variable cost per kg to the nearest £0.01.

The high and low output volumes and associated total production overhead costs are:

	Volume of output	Total production overhead
		£
High volume	560 000	1 250 500
Low volume	310 000	810 347
Difference	250 000	440 153

The variable cost per kg is:

$$\frac{\text{Difference in total cost}}{\text{Difference in activity}} = \frac{£440\ 153}{250\ 000} = £1.76$$

Substituting into the high volume total cost:

	£
Total cost	1 250 500
Less Variable element (560 000 kg @ £1.76)	985 600
So the fixed element is	264 900

 Use the results of the high–low analysis to provide an estimate of total production overhead for 19X7, when output will be 500 000 kg.

Using our inflation-adjusted high–low analysis, the 19X7 estimate will be:

	£
Fixed element	264 900
Variable element (500 000 kg @ £1.76)	880 000
Total maintenance cost	1 144 900

Our original high–low estimate for 19X7, which was not adjusted for inflation, was £1 100 000 – an underestimate of roughly 4% due solely to our failure to adjust the original data for inflation. This difference is an unnecessary inaccuracy, easily corrected and which, if not remedied, strikes at the credibility of our cost estimate. In addition, had the applicable inflation rates been higher, and/or had the high and low volumes been further in the past, the difference between the adjusted and unadjusted estimates would have been greater.

However, inflating the cost figures in the way we have done poses one problem: the estimated inflation rate given for 19X7 relates to the *year* – so it could be argued that, by applying the full year's inflation of 2.5%, we have overinflated our cost estimate. It will take a full year for all of the 2.5% to feed through into costs and it is unlikely that the costs will be incurred at the end of the year – i.e. at a point in time when all of the annual inflation will have occurred. We might combat this by using a mid-year average value for inflation, but even here, there may be some distortion in the estimate, depending on when costs are incurred during the year. In particularly volatile situations, estimates may be updated, e.g. on a monthly basis (see Chapter 17 for a description of rolling budgets); but additional accuracy may be gained at the expense of extra cost and effort involved in preparing estimates. However, compared to the potential distortion caused by ignoring inflation altogether, inaccuracy stemming from how we incorporate its effect is probably less significant and need not destroy the credibility of our estimates.

In Exhibit 3.5, the inflation rates were stated as percentages; such information may also be expressed in the form of *index numbers*. If, in Exhibit 3.5, 19X1 is taken as the *base year* (index number 100), and if inflation in 19X2 is 5%, then the 19X2 inflation index is 105 – i.e. (100×1.05); the 19X3 index will be:

$$100 \times (1.05 \times 1.04) = 109.2$$

indicating that, over the two years from the end of 19X1, cumulative inflation has been 9.2%.

This approach is useful where factors such as inflation need to be expressed relative to a common basis, and could be of especial relevance to financial control, a topic we will discuss in Chapter 18.

SUMMARY

In this chapter, we have discussed techniques which may be used to estimate future costs; cost estimation is vital to cost accounting and we shall encounter its use in later chapters dealing with cost/volume/profit analysis, decision making, capital investment appraisal, budgeting and control. Possibly the most important points that emerge from our discussion are that the figures resulting from a cost estimation exercise are just that – estimates, and that these estimates are heavily influenced by the technique used to obtain them. This may be why a study by Drury *et al.* (1993) found that formal analytical techniques such as multiple regression analysis were not widely employed, with 35% of respondents 'never' using this particular approach; similarly, 59% of respondents classified costs (into fixed/variable) on the basis of managerial judgement.

We have seen that:

- **Engineering techniques** such as work study or input/output analysis may be used, and may yield very accurate predictions. These are, however, very specialised techniques.

- Estimates may be derived from inspection of past accounting records; although this is a simple approach, its success is heavily reliant on the judgement of the person inspecting the accounts.

- A **scattergraph** plots a number of past costs against their related activity levels; the total cost line is placed on the graph by visual estimate, the point where this intersects the vertical axis being the estimated fixed cost. The estimated fixed cost can then be substituted into one of the past costs to obtain an estimate of variable cost; another simple method, but placement of the total cost line is subjective.

- **High–low analysis** uses only two past measures – the high and low volume activity levels and associated total costs; based on the difference between these two activity levels and total costs, the variable cost can be calculated as:

$$\frac{\text{Difference in total cost}}{\text{Difference in activity}}$$

the result being substituted into either the high volume or low volume total cost to obtain an estimate of fixed cost. Again, it is simple to use, but based on two activity levels at which cost behaviour may be different from that at more 'normal' levels.

- **Linear regression analysis** is a mathematical technique used to formulate the equation of the total cost line $y = a + bx$ from a number of past costs and activity levels

where y is the total cost
  a is the fixed cost
  b is the variable cost per unit of activity
  x is the volume of activity

The values of a and b are derived from the following formulae:

$$b = \frac{n \sum xy - \sum x \sum y}{n \sum x^2 - (\sum x)^2} \quad \text{and} \quad a = \frac{\sum y}{n} - \frac{b \sum x}{n}$$

- Linear regression analysis is more mathematically precise than account inspection, scattergraph and high–low analysis, but, like the two latter, assumes linear cost behaviour and its mathematical precision does not necessarily result in more accurate cost predictions.

- Implicit in most estimation techniques is an assumption that a single factor causes variability in cost, but such variability may be the result of several factors; it is possible to recognise this by using **multiple regression analysis**.

- The **correlation coefficient** measures the strength of linear relationship between two variables (cost and activity measure), and is calculated as:

$$r = \frac{\sum (x - \bar{x})(y - \bar{y})}{\sqrt{\sum (x - \bar{x})^2 \sum (y - \bar{y})^2}}$$

- The **coefficient of determination** (r^2) measures the proportion of variation in past costs that can be predicted relative to variation in a selected activity measure.

- The implications of the **relevant range** should be borne in mind when estimating costs.

- The effect of inflation should be incorporated into cost estimates; the source of inflation statistics may be external (e.g. publications of the Office for National Statistics), or may be generated internally; in either case, care should be taken that the inflation figure to be applied is representative of an organisation's specific input costs.

- Where past costs are the basis for an estimate of future cost, they should be inflated cumulatively so that they are stated in terms of the price level which will apply in the period to which the estimate relates.

In the next chapter, we shall commence our discussion of the treatment of individual elements of cost with an examination of materials and labour.

FURTHER READING

Daniel, W. and Terrell, J., *Business Statistics for Management and Economics* (7th edition), Houghton Mifflin Co., 1995: Chapter 10 deals with multiple regression analysis.

Drury, C., Braund, S., Osborne, P. and Tayles, M., *A Survey of Management Accounting Practices in UK Manufacturing Businesses*, ACCA, 1993.

SELF-TEST QUESTIONS

3.1 The following extract is taken from the production cost budget for S Limited:

Production (units)	4 000	6 000
Production cost (£)	11 100	12 900

The budget cost allowance for an activity level of 8000 units is

A £7200
B £14 700
C £17 200
D £22 200
E none of these values.

(CIMA, *Operational Cost Accounting*, May 1999)

3.2 For each of the statements which follows, place a tick in the appropriate box to indicate whether it is true or false.

	True	False
(a) In a linear regression analysis of past costs, the value calculated for *a* represents the variable cost per unit of activity.	☐	☐
(b) Linear regression analysis gives equal weight to all past costs used in the estimation process.	☐	☐
(c) High–low analysis assumes linear cost behaviour.	☐	☐
(d) The scattergraph is more mathematically precise than regression analysis.	☐	☐
(e) The Retail Price Index is a measure of general inflation.	☐	☐
(f) The linearity assumption suggests that variable cost per unit increases in line with increases in volume of activity	☐	☐
(g) The coefficient of determination measures the proportion of variation in cost that is caused by variation in a particular measure of activity.	☐	☐

3.3 A local college's total actual costs and applicable inflation rates over the last three years have been:

	Total cost £	Inflation rate %
19X6	4 000 000	3.5
19X5	3 400 000	4.7
19X4	3 200 000	5.9

The estimated inflation rate for 19X7 is 2.8%.

Working to the nearest whole £1, inflate each of the three costs above to 19X7 price levels.

3.4 Krystal Manufacturing make one product. For budgeting purposes an estimate of costs over the next three months is needed. The direct costs of production have been estimated at £12

per unit. General overheads have been assessed at £70 000 per month. However, there have been problems estimating the production overhead cost due to the difficulty in establishing the relationship of costs to activity. To assist, the last six months' activity in terms of units and production overhead costs have been identified as shown below.

	Units 000	Costs £000
January	21	380
February	40	462
March	50	558
April	60	580
May	42	486
June	33	396
Total	246	2862

Expected production in the next three months is 180 000 units in total (70 000, 45 000 and 65 000 respectively).

Requirements

(a) Using both the least squares (single regression) method by formula, and the high–low method, estimate the fixed cost per month and variable cost per unit for production overheads. **(10 marks)**

(b) Using the figures you have calculated in part (a), estimate for both methods the total cost for the three months July to September. **(4 marks)**

(c) Comment on the results of your calculations. **(6 marks)**
(Total: 20 marks)

(CIPFA, *Management Accounting*, June 1997)

3.5 Over the last five years, Weston Council's Computer Services Department has undertaken the following volumes of work and has incurred the following total costs:

Year	Volume of work (hours' processing time)	Total cost £
19X3	38 146	133 000
19X4	48 170	150 000
19X5	32 000	120 000
19X6	54 138	163 000
19X7	63 680	170 000

The inflation rates which applied to the Computer Services Department's costs each year have been:

19X3 8%   19X4 7%   19X5 5%   19X6 6%   19X7 4%

Estimates for 19X8 are that 68 000 hours of processing time will be worked and that the applicable inflation rate will be 5%. In 19X8, the council intends to charge other departments for use of the Computer Services Department's time and facilities; this charge is to be based on:

1/10 of the Computer Services Department's estimated annual fixed cost
plus
a charge per hour of each department's usage based on the estimated variable cost per processing hour.

Requirements

(a) Inflate the costs for each of the years 19X3–19X7 to 19X8 price levels; work to the nearest whole £1.

(b) Using your inflation-adjusted costs from (a), perform a high–low analysis to provide an estimate for the Computer Services Department's fixed cost and variable cost per processing hour (to two decimal places) for 19X8.

(c) Based on your estimates in (b), calculate the Computer Services Department's estimated total cost for 19X8 and determine the charge to be made to each user department.

(d) State and briefly discuss *two* factors not included in your estimates which could have a bearing on the Computer Services Department's costs in 19X8.

QUESTIONS WITHOUT ANSWERS

3.6 The Valuation Department of a large firm of surveyors wishes to develop a method of predicting its total costs in a period. The following past costs have been recorded at two activity levels:

	Number of valuations (V)	Total cost (TC) £
Period 1	420	82 200
Period 2	515	90 275

The total cost model for a period could be represented thus:

A $TC = £46\,500 + 85V$

B $TC = £42\,000 + 95V$

C $TC = £46\,500 - 85V$

D $TC = £51\,500 - 95V$

(CIMA, *Cost Accounting and Quantitative Methods*, May 1998)

3.7 A firm buys a material on a long-term contract which stipulates a price increase per annum of 6% compound. If the current price is £100 per kg, the price in 5 years, to the nearest penny, will be

A £106.00

B £130.00

C £133.82

D £136.10

(CIMA, *Cost Accounting and Quantitative Methods*, November 1998)

3.8 The following extract is taken from the production cost budget of W Limited:

Production units	2 000	3 000
Production cost	£17 760	£20 640

The budget cost allowance for an activity level of 4000 units is

A £11 520

B £23 520

C £27 520

D £35 520

E none of these values.

(CIMA, *Operational Cost Accounting*, November 1998)

3.9 The following data have been extracted from the budget working papers of BL Limited:

Production volume	1000	2000
	£/unit	£/unit
Direct materials	4.00	4.00
Direct labour	3.50	3.50
Production overhead – department 1	6.00	4.20
Production overhead – department 2	4.00	2.00

The total fixed cost and variable cost per unit is

	Total fixed cost £	Variable cost per unit £
A	3600	7.50
B	3600	9.90
C	4000	11.70
D	7600	7.50
E	7600	9.90

(CIMA, *Operational Cost Accounting*, November 1995)

3.10 TL & Co produces an executive laptop computer. As part of next year's budget preparation process, an estimate of production overhead costs is required. Relevant data for the last four years are given below:

Year	Total production overhead cost (adjusted for inflation) £	Output (units)
19X5	1 200 000	38 000
19X6	1 400 000	40 000
19X7	1 100 000	36 000
19X8	1 700 000	60 000

It is estimated that, in 19X9, production will be 50 000 units.

Requirements

(a) Use linear regression analysis to produce an estimate of the firm's fixed production overhead and variable production overhead per unit.

(b) Using your answer to (a), provide an estimate of total production overhead for 19X9.

(c) TL & Co's General Manager has suggested that the accuracy of the cost estimates would be improved if the past ten years' data were incorporated. The Production Manager has countered this with a claim that the nature of the firm's product, market and production processes renders extensive use of past data for estimation purposes questionable. Discuss the validity of each of these points of view.

CHAPTER 4

Costing materials and labour

Skill shortage 'holds back' technology companies

A persistent shortage of skilled staff is holding back the growth of European technology companies, according to research published today.

More than half of all the privately owned European technology companies surveyed by PwC, the professional services group, said a shortage of quality staff was the main barrier to planned growth ...

Pressure to attract and retain staff is forcing companies to offer above-average salary increases. Half of those taking part in the survey had increased average salaries for permanent staff by between 6 and 15% in the past year, while some had awarded increases of more than 20%.

Yet staff turnover rates are still running at about 17%. 'This is a major expense because organisations must offer higher salaries to attract new recruits, bear the added cost of training new staff, and pay large fees to recruitment agencies,' the report finds.

The authors advocate the wider introduction of share option schemes as a means of locking in staff, and offering more training. The report found that successful companies placed more emphasis on interpersonal and management skills when training staff ...

Source: Peter Thal Larsen, *Financial Times*, 24 May 1999. Reprinted with permission.

Exhibit 4.1 The importance of labour, labour turnover, remuneration and incentives

INTRODUCTION

In Chapter 2, we made the distinction between three broad categories of cost: labour, materials and overhead. In the present chapter, we will examine the costing of labour and materials; approaches to costing overhead form the subject of Chapters 5 and 6. As Exhibit 4.1 makes clear, labour costs can be very significant, including as they do the cost of obtaining, training and retaining suitable staff. And although most manufacturing industries are now much less labour-intensive than they once were, many service sector businesses continue to rely heavily on labour. Materials can likewise form a major part of total cost and in recent years, much effort has been devoted both to minimising material costs and to optimising the physical flow of materials into and within the business. Just as labour costs involve more than merely wages and salaries, so material costs involve more than just their purchase cost. For example, there are costs involved in holding stocks of material, in placing orders with suppliers of material, and in checking the quantity of stocks on hand. We will consider all these issues in the course of the current chapter.

OBJECTIVES

When you have completed this chapter, you will be able to:

- explain the factors affecting the complexity and formality of materials' and labour costing procedures;
- describe the documentation that might be found in typical materials' and labour costing situations;
- calculate the economic order quantity and discuss its underlying assumptions;
- distinguish between periodic stocktaking, continuous stocktaking and ABC classification;
- calculate reorder level, minimum level, maximum level and free stock;
- apply LIFO, FIFO and AVCO to cost issues from stores and appreciate the advantages and disadvantages of these approaches;
- describe MRPI and MRPII;
- calculate labour turnover and explain the associated costs;
- define, and explain the costing treatment of idle time, overtime and employers' NI contributions;
- differentiate between output- and time-based remuneration systems, and between output-based and other types of incentive;
- provide an overview of payroll procedures.

COSTING MATERIALS

Although precise details and documentation may vary between different organisations and situations, transactions and other events involving materials follow the general pattern illustrated in Figure 4.1.

The administrative effort and formality attaching to the materials' 'cycle' illustrated in Figure 4.1 depends on a number of factors:

1 *The nature of the business.*

 Can you suggest how manufacturing and service businesses might differ in their treatment of materials?

For manufacturing businesses, materials are likely to be a significant part of total cost, and may therefore be subject to rigorous procedural control. However, in many service organisations, materials' costs form a smaller part of total cost, and therefore do not warrant so much administrative effort.

2 *The organisation's size and structure.*
Larger organisations – simply because of their size – tend to have more formalised procedures for virtually every aspect of operations than smaller ones. In larger organisations, we might, for example, expect to find a Central Stores Department with its own staff (and possibly premises), and there could be a Purchasing Section that specialises in dealing with the supplier aspects of the materials' 'cycle' in Figure 4.1.

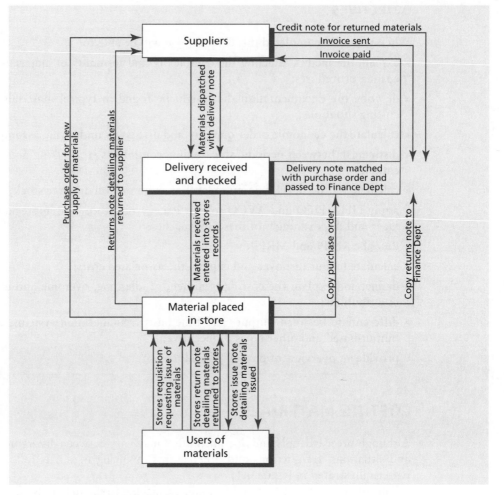

Figure 4.1 The materials 'cycle'

3 *The volume, range and cost of materials.*
   Where a high volume and/or a wide range and/or high-cost materials are involved, procedures must allow management to exercise adequate control over both physical and financial aspects of the materials' 'cycle'.

4 *The cost/benefit criterion.*
   A complex system is potentially expensive to operate, and the cost involved must not outweigh the benefit in terms of improved information for planning, control and decision making.

Bearing in mind that the precise detail of the materials' 'cycle' will differ between organisations, we can now discuss the key elements of Figure 4.1 in more detail.

Ordering materials

Depending on circumstances, the need to place an order for materials could be triggered by a variety of events. In a just-in-time (JIT) environment (see Chapter 2), receipt of a customer order will typically cause materials to be ordered – here, the materials will be those required to fulfil the specific customer order received. Alternatively, the need for a materials order may be suggested by the fact that stocks have reached their **reorder level** (a stock control indicator that we will discuss later in the chapter). Or management may be aware of the need for an order to be placed simply from their own observation of materials' usage and current stock levels. Sometimes, the details of a materials order which needs to be placed are recorded on a **purchase requisition**. Where used, this is an internal document, which might be completed by Stores or Production personnel, then passed to the Purchasing Department as a signal that materials need to be ordered from suppliers.

In virtually every organisation, orders to suppliers of materials are made (or confirmed) in writing using a **purchase order**. This document should detail the type and quantity of materials to be supplied, and may also specify their price and delivery date/method. One copy of the purchase order is forwarded to the supplier (perhaps electronically) and the originator retains at least one copy.

 Sometimes, more than one copy of a purchase order is retained. To what departments might multiple copies of a purchase order be distributed?

The Purchasing Department might retain one copy, with others being forwarded to Stores (to warn of an incoming delivery) and to the Finance Department (for eventual matching with the supplier's invoice).

For security, purchase orders need to be numbered sequentially, with a limited number of staff being authorised to sign them. There may likewise be a list of authorised suppliers for different types of material; this would be especially important in a JIT situation, where a close working relationship with reliable suppliers is essential. It is also advisable – though not always possible in smaller organisations – to separate staff duties so that the person placing orders is not the same person who receives/stores them when delivered. The purchase order is an important document, as it provides evidence not only of what has been ordered but also of when orders were placed. The latter is useful if it proves necessary to 'chase' late orders.

In a JIT system, the quantity of materials to be ordered will be dictated by the requirements of the customer order that initiated the purchase. In some cases, purchase quantities could depend on management experience and expectations about future usage. There is also a mathematically derived approach to this problem: the **economic order quantity** (EOQ).

Economic order quantity

EOQ is the size of purchase order that achieves the optimum 'trade-off' between the cost of placing orders and the cost of holding materials in stock – in other words, EOQ is the order size that minimises the total of these two costs. Figure 4.2 illustrates the general principle.

What Figure 4.2 shows is that, as the order size increases, so the number of orders that need to be placed falls, with a consequent reduction in ordering costs. But as order size increases, so does the amount of material held in stock, resulting in higher holding costs. The minimum total of these two costs occurs at their point of intersection: the economic order quantity, which has total holding plus ordering costs of $£y$.

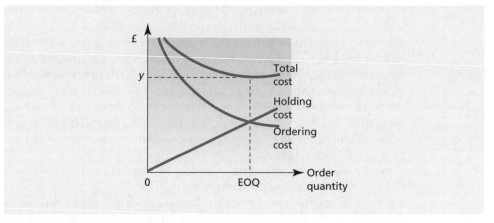

Figure 4.2 The economic order quantity

 Suggest examples of ordering and holding costs.

Ordering costs might include staff time, stationery, postage and telephone calls. Holding costs could consist of wages of stores staff, rental of storage space, insurance of stock, lighting, heating and the cost of damage, loss or obsolescence. There may also be an element of **opportunity cost**: for example, where space used for storage could be rented to a third party – here, rental income is lost because the space is being used to hold stock. (See Chapter 14 for more detailed discussion of opportunity cost.) We will use Exhibit 4.2 to illustrate the EOQ.

Donside Health Trust

The Trust, which provides hospital and other health services, operates a central store. One item regularly ordered by and held in the central store is paper. This is purchased in boxes, each of which contains 5 reams of blank A4 size sheets. Trust management has made the following estimates for this material in respect of next year:

Usage	4000 boxes
Cost of placing an order	£2.25
Cost of holding 1 box in stock for a year	£5

The Trust's supplier of paper will accept orders of any size above a minimum of 20 boxes.

Exhibit 4.2 EOQ illustrative data

We could attempt to determine the EOQ by tabulating ordering plus holding costs for different order sizes.

 For the year under consideration in Exhibit 4.2, determine the number of orders required and the related ordering cost if Trust management is considering order sizes of:

50, 100, 200 and 250 boxes

The number of orders to be placed in the year is:

$$\frac{\text{Annual usage (boxes)}}{\text{Order size (boxes)}}$$

We know from Exhibit 4.2 that annual usage is 4000 boxes, giving 80, 40, 20 and 16 orders for order sizes of 50, 100, 200 and 250 boxes respectively. Related ordering costs for the year (at £2.25 per order) are thus £180, £90, £45 and £36.

To determine the holding cost, we need to make two assumptions:

1 Usage occurs evenly over the year; and
2 No stocks exist when each order is received (or any stocks held are maintained at a constant level throughout the year).

Given these assumptions, average stock held at any point during the year (or the amount of such stock that is relevant to the EOQ calculation) is:

$$\frac{\text{Order quantity}}{2}$$

It is this average stock figure which determines the holding cost. Table 4.1 shows the annual ordering, holding and total costs for each of the specified order sizes.

Table 4.1 Ordering, holding and total costs for different order sizes

Order size	50 boxes	100 boxes	200 boxes	250 boxes
Number of orders	80	40	20	16
Average stock	25 boxes	50 boxes	100 boxes	125 boxes
Ordering cost	£180	£ 90	£ 45	£ 36
Holding cost	£125	£250	£500	£625
Total cost	£305	£340	£545	£661

From Table 4.1, it would appear that the EOQ occurs at an order size of 50. However, we cannot be sure whether this is correct, or whether the EOQ is an order size not shown on the table – i.e. below 50 boxes, or between 50 and 100 boxes. We could graph the results in Table 4.1 as illustrated in Figure 4.2 and obtain a value for EOQ. But there is a more direct, formulaic, approach:

$$\text{EOQ} = \sqrt{\frac{2DO}{H}}$$

where D represents annual usage
O is the cost of placing an order
H is the annual holding cost/unit.

Applying this formula to our example, we get:

$$\text{EOQ} = \sqrt{\frac{2(4000 \times £2.25)}{£5}} = 60$$

Total ordering plus holding cost is therefore minimised if the order size is 60 boxes – a value not immediately apparent from Table 4.1.

When undertaking EOQ calculations, you should be careful that the time periods applied to usage and holding cost are consistent. For instance, if a monthly usage figure is combined with an annual holding cost, we need to restate either usage (on an annual basis) or holding cost (on a monthly basis).

The results of our EOQ calculation can also be used to indicate when orders should be placed. If we assume that boxes of paper are used evenly over a 50-week, 5-day-per-week-year, then usage per day is:

$$\frac{\text{Annual usage}}{\text{Number of days}} = \frac{4000}{(50 \times 5)} = 16 \text{ boxes}$$

If orders are delivered on the same day as the order is placed, then an order for 60 further boxes must be placed every 60/16 = 3.75 days. If – as is more likely – there is a delay between placing and receiving an order (**lead time**), then the reorder timing should be adjusted accordingly. If, say, there is lead time of 1 day, orders will need to be placed every 2.75 days to ensure stocks of paper do not run out.

The EOQ can be adapted to determine the optimum production batch size – the **economic batch quantity** (EBQ). Here, the trade-off is between the cost of production set-ups and the cost of holding stocks. The larger the batch size, the fewer production set-ups that are needed, so total set-up costs are lower; however, larger batches mean more units in stock, incurring higher total holding costs. The EBQ formula is:

$$\sqrt{\frac{2DS}{H}}$$

where D is annual demand for the product
S is the cost of setting up one production run
H is the annual holding cost per unit.

However, the EOQ is based on a number of key assumptions. We have already mentioned that usage (demand in the EBQ) is assumed to be constant. This may be rather unrealistic: usage can exhibit seasonal or cyclical variation and could even have some random variations. We also mentioned the assumption of zero (or constant) stocks independent of those created by the EOQ. But stocks may also be subject to seasonal and cyclical variation, and purchasing policy could be determined more by market conditions for particular materials than by internal considerations. The EOQ/EBQ model further assumes certainty – about usage, holding and ordering costs; in a volatile environment such certainty may not exist.

You may have noticed that our EOQ calculations do not consider the purchase cost itself. This is because we assume the purchase cost to be constant. But purchase cost may be a major (or even the only) determinant of order sizes. Consider Exhibit 4.3.

Donshire Health Trust – quantity discount

The Trust's supplier of paper has offered a discount of £0.05 per box if orders of 100 boxes are placed. Management is uncertain whether it would be financially beneficial to order in multiples of 100 boxes, rather than using the EOQ of 60 boxes.

Exhibit 4.3 Quantity discount

✔ *Determine the total annual cost of ordering and holding if the Trust uses the EOQ of 60 boxes.*

Ordering plus holding costs for the EOQ are:

$$\text{Ordering } \frac{4000}{60} \times £2.25 \qquad £150.00$$

$$\text{Holding } \frac{60}{2} \times £5 \qquad \underline{£150.00}$$

$$\underline{£300.00}$$

If the order size is 100 boxes, the financial implications are:

	£
Ordering plus holding cost (from Table 4.1)	304
Less Discount (4000 boxes × £0.05)	200
Net cost	104

Changing from the EOQ to a 100-box order size thus offers a financial benefit of (£300 – £104) = £196 to the Trust.

So, if the EOQ/EBQ is applied in a mechanical way, without due consideration being given to its assumptions, there is a danger of financial or other disadvantage. For instance, ignoring the real pattern of usage could easily result in over- or understocking – both of which incur unnecessary and potentially heavy costs (e.g. increased likelihood of damage/obsolescence if stocks are too high). And although the basic EOQ/EBQ model can be adapted to incorporate more 'realistic' assumptions, this comes at the cost of additional complexity in the model.

Once materials have been ordered – however the order quantity is determined – the next step in the 'cycle' is their receipt and storage.

Receipt and storage of materials

Some organisations may have a dedicated Goods Inward Department, others may not. But regardless of where or by whom performed, supplier deliveries should be checked on receipt. Deliveries are usually accompanied by a **delivery note** (or **advice note**). This document details delivery contents along with the order to which the delivery relates and is used as the basis of a physical check on quantities and specifications. Once the contents of the delivery have been verified against the delivery note (and possibly against the relevant purchase order as well), the materials are either placed in store or distributed for use. The delivery note is forwarded to the Finance Department, and signals impending receipt of the associated invoice; assuming no discrepancies between delivery and order, it also signals that the invoice may be paid. In some cases, organisations will produce a **goods received note** when materials are received, containing the same basic information as the supplier's advice note, but in a standard format suited to the organisation's information needs. A goods received note is also useful when no advice note accompanies the delivery.

Where a wide range of materials is used or held in stock, it is essential that they can be correctly identified.

What can an organisation do to aid correct identification of materials?

Providing a full description of materials on each document that refers to them can be unwieldy and time-consuming. Abbreviating such descriptions in the form of material codes is therefore common. An organisation may choose to adopt suppliers' codes which has the benefits of simplicity and consistency with ordering. However, where many different suppliers are involved, this approach could also cause confusion, as individual suppliers will employ different coding formats. In these circumstances, an internal coding system may be developed. If this is done, the code should allow each material to be uniquely identified, should be simple to use (in particular it should not be too long), and should offer scope for expansion sufficient to cope with new materials.

Details of material receipts are entered in the **stores ledger** (also called the stock ledger, or materials ledger). This ledger contains a separate account for each material used by the organisation. Entries in the individual stores ledger accounts are summarised in the Stores Ledger Control Account (see Chapter 7). A materials stores ledger account might look like the one illustrated in Exhibit 4.4, listing receipts, issues and balance on hand, along with the associated costs.

Material code					Description:				
	Receipts				Issues			Balance	
Date	Goods received/ Advice note	Quantity	Cost per unit £	Amount £	Stores requisition No.	Quantity	Amount £	Quantity	Amount £

Exhibit 4.4 A stores ledger account

The **stores requisition** referred to in Exhibit 4.4 is a document which users of materials send to stores requesting that issue of the specified materials be made. We will have more to say about issue of materials shortly. Information about dates, quantities received, issued and balance on hand that is recorded in a material's stores ledger account is sometimes also recorded on a **bin card** which is kept at the location where the material concerned is stored and is updated after every receipt/issue of that material.

Stock control

Stocks of material can be extremely valuable, so it makes sense to exercise effective control – both financial and physical – over them. One way in which this can be done is by **stocktaking** – i.e. physically counting stocks on hand and verifying that this count tallies with what is recorded in the stores ledger. There are two basic approaches to stocktaking. **Periodic stocktaking** involves checking all stocks once per period – say, once a year. This has the merit of providing a comprehensive 'snap-shot' of stock at a particular point in time.

> ✔ *Can you see any disadvantages of periodic stocktaking?*

Where large stocks are held, periodic stocktaking may involve considerable time, effort and possible disruption to operations. Associated costs may also be high: for example, overtime working may be needed in order to minimise disruption. In addition, if the period between stocktakes is too long, problems may go uncorrected for longer and could even worsen as a consequence.

As an alternative, organisations may use **continuous stocktaking**. Here, stock is checked on a rolling basis, so that, over a period (a year, say), all stock items have been checked at least once. This should markedly reduce the disruption that periodic stock-taking might cause, but for large stores, it could involve employing specialist 'stock audit clerks'. **ABC classification** is a variant of continuous stocktaking, whereby stocks are grouped according to their annual purchase cost. 'Category A' items have the highest annual purchase cost, 'Category B' have medium annual purchase cost, with 'Category C' items having low annual purchase cost. The idea is that the greatest control effort is concentrated on 'Category A' items, which might be physically verified several times over the course of the year. Less time and effort is devoted to stocks falling into Categories B and C – which might be checked only once. Not only should ABC classification ensure that control is directed at the correct materials, but it should also reduce the administrative burden, as it is likely that the majority of annual material purchase costs will relate to a comparatively low proportion of the total number of materials held in stock. This is sometimes referred to as Pareto Analysis, which suggests that 80% of total materials' cost will be accounted for by only 20% of the range of materials. Although precise percentages may vary between organisations, the general principle is certainly consistent with their experience of material costs.

When stocktaking reveals a discrepancy between the stores ledger account/bin card and physical quantities, stores documentation must be amended to reflect what is actually in stock. Stock losses represent a cost to the organisation, and it may be worth while keeping track of these in a Stock Loss Account (see Chapter 7). Stock losses are then either charged to the Profit and Loss Account as a cost, or are included in the period's overhead. There are also a number of stock control indicators that can be calculated and which we will use Exhibit 4.5 to illustrate.

The **reorder level** is the stock level at which a new order should be placed with suppliers, and is calculated as:

$$(\text{maximum usage} \times \text{maximum lead time})$$

> ✔ *Calculate Donshire Health Trust's reorder level for paper. Comment on your answer.*

Donshire Health Trust

The following estimated data relate to the Trust's use of paper next year:

EOQ (adjusted to allow for quantity discount) 100 boxes
Lead time   1–3 days
Maximum usage   60 boxes per day
Minimum usage   30 boxes per day.

Exhibit 4.5 Stock control indicators

The Trust's reorder level is (60 boxes × 3 days) = 180 boxes. Unless the Trust maintains a reasonable **safety stock**, there is every chance that the store will run out of supplies of paper if usage tends towards the heavy and/or lead times are long. Safety stock (or **buffer stock**) is held as contingency cover in the event of error in estimates of usage or lead time, and will generally be maintained at a fairly constant level. Alternatively, if usage tends more towards light, and if lead times are short, there is a danger that stocks may build up – although this may only be temporary, being remedied when usage and/or lead times increase.

The **minimum level** acts as a warning that usage may be higher than anticipated, with resultant use of safety stocks. It is calculated as:

(reorder level – [average usage × average lead time])

From Exhibit 4.5, average usage and average lead time are, respectively,

$$\frac{(60 + 30)}{2} = 45 \text{ boxes}$$

and

$$\frac{(1 + 3)}{2} = 2 \text{ days}$$

The minimum level is therefore (180 boxes – [45 boxes × 2 days]) = 90 boxes.

The **maximum level** also acts as a warning to management: in this case of lower-than anticipated usage, with the attendant danger of a costly stock build-up. Maximum level is:

(reorder level + EOQ) – (minimum usage × minimum lead time).

 From Exhibit 4.5, and from our calculations above, determine the Trust's maximum level for stocks of paper.

The maximum level is: (180 + 100) – (30 boxes × 1 day) = 250 boxes.

Where they are used, values for these stock control indicators are frequently shown on the stores ledger account/bin card for the material to which they relate. However, as with the EOQ/EBQ, reorder, minimum and maximum levels need to be applied with care. In particular, you should remember that they are based on estimates of usage and lead time. If either/both of these estimates is seriously wrong, stocks could build up unnecessarily or could run out unexpectedly.

One final stock control measure is **free stock**. This notional stock figure indicates the amount of stock that is potentially available to users at a given point in time:

(quantity on hand + quantity currently on order with suppliers)
less
quantity allocated to users but not yet issued

Tracking increases/decreases in free stock can give early warning of dangerous stock build-ups or declines.

Issue of materials

Materials' issues will be requested by various users, often on a **stores requisition** which identifies the department submitting the requisition and states the material(s) and quantity required. The requisition may also specify which particular job the materials are needed for. As well as providing evidence to support an issue from stores, the requisition is used to update the stores ledger (and bin cards, if these are used).

Costing materials' issues

The appropriate materials' cost and costing methodology to use depends on a combination of factors:

1 The nature of the materials, and the purchasing/storage policy in operation; and
2 The purpose for which materials' costs are required.

 How might procedures for costing high-value materials differ from those applied to low-value materials?

For high-value materials (and possibly also for those which are used in small quantities), it should be possible – and advisable – to match the invoice cost with the specific materials in each issue. The same is true in a Just-in-Time system: since materials are only ordered in response to receipt of a customer order, matching material costs with orders should be relatively straightforward. However, for low-value or high-volume items (and in a non-JIT environment), this specific identification of cost with physical issue may not be possible in a cost-effective way.

If the purpose of costing materials is to provide information for planning, then **standard cost** should be used. Standard cost is an estimated cost applicable to the relevant planning period (see Chapter 16). If we need materials' costs for decision-making purposes, we should use **relevant cost** (see Chapter 14 for definition and discussion). For financial accounting – and in particular for external reporting – we need to use actual cost.

This raises the question of what do we mean by actual cost? Table 4.2 lists some commonly-encountered items of potential difficulty, along with their suggested treatment in determination of actual cost.

Where specific identification is not possible (or is not cost-effective), and where actual cost varies from delivery to delivery, we need to adopt one of the costing methodologies described below. At the outset, you should note that these methodologies do not attempt to reflect the physical pattern of material issues from stores.

Table 4.2 Some problem areas in determination of purchase cost

Item	Suggested treatment
Transport/delivery charges	Include as part of purchase cost if possible; otherwise treat as overhead.
Discounts for prompt payment of invoices	Generally considered as separate matter from purchase cost, and not allowed for in its determination.
Quantity discounts	Reduce purchase cost to reflect these.
Value Added Tax (VAT)	If organisation is VAT-registered, exclude from purchase cost, as VAT suffered on purchases can be set against VAT collected on sales. Otherwise include in purchase cost.

First-In–First-Out (FIFO)

In conformance with what would be considered normal storekeeping procedure, FIFO uses the oldest cost applicable to available stocks first. When the number of units issued equals the number in stock at this cost, then the next oldest cost is used for subsequent units, until units issued equal units in stock at this later cost – and so on. We will use Exhibit 4.6 to illustrate.

Donshire Health Trust: material purchases and issues

On 1 November, the Trust's store held a stock of 120 boxes of paper, each of which cost £6.80 to purchase. During the first week of November, the following receipts and issues occurred:

2 November	Issued	70 boxes
3 November	Received	100 boxes, cost £6.90 each
4 November	Issued	80 boxes
5 November	Issued	40 boxes
6 November	Received	100 boxes, cost £6.95 each
7 November	Issued	50 boxes
8 November	Issued	40 boxes.

Exhibit 4.6 Costing materials' issues

 Apply FIFO principles to obtain the cost assigned to the issues made on 2 and 4 November.

On 2 November, the oldest available cost is £6.80, so the cost assigned to the issue made on that date is: (70 boxes × £6.80) = £476. Since 120 boxes were in stock at this cost, we are able to issue a further (120 – 70) = 50 boxes at £6.80. Which means that the cost assigned to the 4 November issue will be a composite of £6.80 and the next oldest cost:

	£
50 boxes × £6.80	340
30 boxes × £6.90	207
80 boxes	547

A further (100 − 30) = 70 boxes can therefore be issued at a cost of £6.90; thus, the issue made on 5 November will have a cost of (40 boxes × £6.90) = £276 − leaving £6.90 available to cost a further (70 − 40) = 30 boxes, after which, the next oldest cost (£6.95) will come into force.

Exhibit 4.7 shows the stores ledger account for paper in respect of the first week in November. This has been prepared using a **perpetual inventory** (or continuous inventory) approach: i.e. the account is updated after each receipt and issue, so that the balance should accurately reflect stock on hand.

Material code					Description: A4 paper				
	Receipts				**Issues**			**Balance**	
Date	Goods received/ Advice note	Quantity	Cost per unit £	Amount £	Stores requisition No.	Quantity	Amount £	Quantity	Amount £
1 Nov								120	816
2 Nov						70	476	50	340
3 Nov		100	6.90	690				150	1030
4 Nov						80	547	70	483
5 Nov						40	276	30	207
6 Nov		100	6.95	695				130	902
7 Nov						50	346	80	556
8 Nov						40	278	40	278

Exhibit 4.7 Stores ledger account based on FIFO

For simplicity, we have not made any entries in the 'goods received note' or 'stores requisition' columns − but remember that this documentation forms an integral part of many systems.

Balances in Exhibit 4.7 are obtained by adding quantities received (and their cost) to the previous balance, or by deducting quantities issued (and their cost) from the previous balance.

 Show the composition of the £346 issue cost recorded for 7 November.

Like that on 4 November, the 7 November issue is a composite of two purchase costs. On 7 November, the oldest available cost was £6.90, which we have already determined could be applied to issues of a further 30 boxes, after which £6.95 is the applicable cost. The 7 November issue is therefore costed at:

	£
30 boxes × £6.90	207
20 boxes × £6.95	139
50 boxes	346

Not only is FIFO consistent with normal stores issue procedure, but, by using the oldest prices first, it ensures that, when costs are rising, stocks are valued at the most up-to-date price. However, this also means that issues are costed at out-of-date prices; if profit were to be calculated based on these issue costs, the result is arguably overstated (since cost of sales is based on out-dated material costs).

Last-In First-Out (LIFO)

This approach operates in exactly the opposite manner to FIFO, taking the most recent cost applicable to stock available, and working backward. Using LIFO, the issue made on 4 November will be costed at (80 boxes × £6.90) = £552 – £6.90 being the most recent price on the issue date. Since a total of 100 boxes may be costed at £6.90, we can use this cost for a further (100 – 80) = 20 boxes.

 Apply LIFO principles to determine the cost assigned to the 5 November issue.

Since this issue consists of 40 boxes, and since the most recent price of £6.90 can be applied to a further 20 boxes only, we need to cost 20 boxes at the next most recent price available on 5 November (£6.80):

	£
20 boxes × £6.90	138
20 boxes × £6.80	136
40 boxes	274

 After the 5 November issue, how many boxes can still be priced at £6.80?

Bearing in mind that both the 2 November issue and 20 boxes of the 5 November issue will have been costed at £6.80, then we can still price (120 – 70 – 20) = 30 boxes at £6.80. Exhibit 4.8 shows the stores ledger account prepared using LIFO principles.

 Show the breakdown, in boxes and cost per box, of the balance recorded on 8 November.

The most recent price on 8 November is £6.95, applicable to 100 boxes; this has been applied to issues of (50 + 40) boxes on 7 and 8 November; so 10 boxes of stock at 8 November are costed at £6.95. From our earlier discussion, we know that a cost of £6.80 can be applied to a further 30 boxes, and this represents the remainder of the 8 November balance:

	£
10 boxes × £6.95	69.50
30 boxes × £6.80	204.00
40 boxes	273.50

Material code			Description: A4 paper						
	Receipts				Issues			Balance	
Date	Goods received/ Advice note	Quantity	Cost per unit £	Amount £	Stores requisition No.	Quantity	Amount £	Quantity	Amount £
1 Nov								120	816
2 Nov						70	476	50	340
3 Nov		100	6.90	690				150	1030
4 Nov						80	552	70	478
5 Nov						40	274	30	204
6 Nov		100	6.95	695				130	899
7 Nov						50	347.5	80	551.5
8 Nov						40	278	40	273.5

Exhibit 4.8 Stores ledger account based on LIFO

By using the most recent cost first, LIFO ensures that materials are issued at up-to-date cost. However, when material costs are rising, this has the effect of understating both stock values and profit. In the UK, LIFO is not normally accepted by the Inland Revenue for the tax purposes; similarly, Statement of Standard Accounting Practice No 9 (dealing with stock valuation in published accounts) does not recommend the method. In addition, LIFO may be confusing, as it operates in a manner exactly opposite to normal stores issue procedure, whereby older items tend to be issued first.

Weighted Average Cost (AVCO)

As the name suggests, AVCO costs materials' issues at an average cost which is recalculated after each receipt into stores.

 Use the 'Balance' column from Exhibit 4.8 to obtain an average cost (correct to three decimal places of £1) per box on 3 November. Use this to determine the cost of issues on 4 November.

The average cost per box on 3 November is

$$\frac{£1030}{150 \text{ boxes}} = £6.867$$

giving a cost of $(80 \times £6.867) = £549.36$ for the 4 November issue. The average cost of £6.867 will remain in force until 6 November, when it is recalculated following receipt of a further 100 boxes. Exhibit 4.9 presents the stores ledger account prepared using AVCO.

 From Exhibit 4.9, determine (to three decimal places of £1) the average cost after the 6 November receipt.

Material code					Description: A4 paper				
	Receipts				Issues			Balance	
Date	Goods received/ Advice note	Quantity	Cost per unit £	Amount £	Stores requisition No.	Quantity	Amount £	Quantity	Amount £
1 Nov								120	816
2 Nov						70	476	50	340
3 Nov		100	6.90	690				150	1030
4 Nov						80	549.36	70	480.64
5 Nov						40	274.68	30	205.96
6 Nov		100	6.95	695				130	900.96
7 Nov						50	346.50	80	554.46
8 Nov						40	277.20	40	277.26

Exhibit 4.9 Stores ledger account based on AVCO

We can obtain the average cost from the 'Balance' column of Exhibit 4.9:

$$\frac{£900.96}{130 \text{ boxes}} = £6.930 \text{ per box}$$

This revised average cost is used to cost the 7 and 8 November issues.

Where purchase costs are subject to fluctuation, AVCO will prove rather more satisfactory than FIFO or LIFO, as the effect of these fluctuations on issue costs, stock values and profit will be somewhat smoothed by the averaging process. However, average cost will not correspond with actual purchase cost, except by accident.

While our example has not produced major differences in issue costs and stock values between FIFO, LIFO and AVCO, it should not be hard to imagine that, with greater volatility in purchase cost, such differences could be very significant.

Materials requirement planning (MRPI)

Inherent in the EOQ/EBQ model and the stock control indicators we discussed earlier is an assumption that planning and control of purchases and stocks occurs independently of other activities (like production scheduling). Similarly, independence between individual materials is also assumed. At best, these models and techniques treat material usage as a sort of passive corollary to stock ordering and control. **Materials requirement planning (MRPI)** explicitly recognises that, in complex manufacturing environments, it is the pattern and volume of output which should drive material purchasing and stock levels. The starting-point for MRPI is therefore a master production schedule that gives both volumes and timings for finished output. Supporting the master production schedule are a bill of materials showing the composition of each finished product in terms of materials, components and subassemblies and a master parts file detailing lead times of purchased materials and internally produced components. Finally, there is an inventory file, which shows, for each material, component and subassembly, the balance on hand, quantities ordered and amounts allocated to production.

The basic idea of MRPI is to start with the production schedule for finished goods and to work backwards from this to determine the quantities of subassemblies, components and materials needed for each of the earlier stages of production. In this way, MRPI aims to minimise stock levels, minimise disruption of production and eliminate the extra cost of rush orders for materials.

MRPI has developed into **manufacturing resource planning** (**MRPII**), which seeks to provide a comprehensive manufacturing control system. MRPII involves the integration of material requirement planning, capacity planning, production scheduling and cost accounting into a complex (normally computerised) model of operations. By taking this more holistic view, it is argued that MRPII can provide a link between strategic planning and manufacturing control, as well as forming a basis for the plans of different functions within an organisation (e.g. finance, purchasing and production). And there can be little question that both MRPI and MRPII are more flexible in the face of a dynamic environment than 'traditional' models like EOQ. However, viewed from a World–Class Manufacturing perspective (see Chapter 2), MRPI and MRPII could be argued to be failures. This is because, however accurate they may be as models of what happens, they *are* models of what happens. In other words, they will include existing production inefficiencies, rather than encouraging the continuous improvement central to a world–class philosophy.

Electronic systems

Almost every organisation that uses materials to any degree will use computers to deal with certain procedures relating to purchase, storage and issue. The general benefits of this are the same as we described in Chapter 2 in the context of cost accounting as a whole. Computers are particularly useful – virtually essential – in handling the sort of complex analyses required by MRPI and MRPII.

In other situations, the extent of computer use in the materials' 'cycle' varies widely. At one end of the spectrum, material records (e.g. stores ledger accounts, bin cards) may be held on computer, but with manual involvement in the system still being significant. At the other extreme, manual involvement may be all but non-existent. An example of this can be seen in how large supermarkets operate. Sales are recorded by scanning the bar codes on goods ('usage' of materials), and the resulting information is transferred by electronic data interchange to an in-house store (eventually signalling the need to refill shelves). From the in-house store, data is transferred to central warehouses, triggering deliveries to the supermarket's in-house store. It may even happen that orders from central warehouses to suppliers are transmitted electronically, based on data about deliveries to supermarkets. Similar sophistication is emerging in manufacturing business, with the use of automated material handling systems, computer-integrated manufacturing and automated storage and retrieval systems.

While computers can greatly reduce the administrative burden attendant on potentially complex material 'cycles', the basic principles which we have been describing nevertheless still apply. Only by operating a strict just-in-time purchasing policy can they be significantly modified or avoided.

COSTING LABOUR

As for materials, there is a labour 'cycle'. But here, there are two related 'cycles' in operation: clearly, there is the recurring cycle of work performed/wages and salaries paid. Overlying this, however, is the broader, and possibly less regular cycle of recruitment–training–staff turnover. Figure 4.3 illustrates.

What Figure 4.3 suggests is that labour costs comprise much more than simply wages and salaries. Costs – often substantial – are associated with each of the stages illustrated. Like the materials' 'cycle', the degree of formality attaching to the labour 'cycle' depends on factors like organisation size and structure, the number of employees and the range of different employee grades or types. Thus, for example, in a large organisation, employees may be assigned a works (or employee) number so that they can be individually identified in personnel and payroll records. This is analogous to

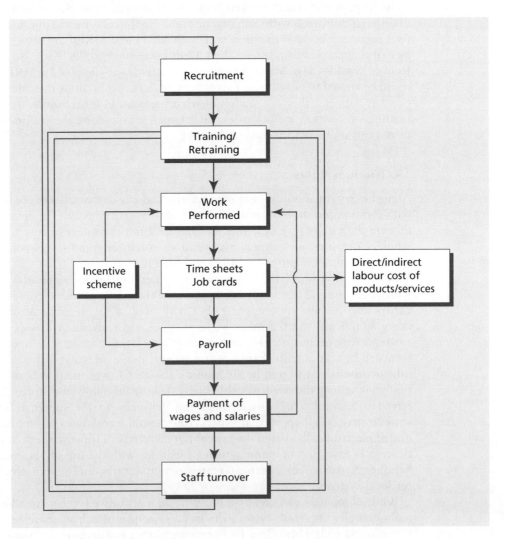

Figure 4.3 Dual labour 'cycles'

assigning code numbers to materials. In smaller organisations, however, employees can easily be identified by name, rendering a system of works numbers unnecessary.

Staff turnover, recruitment and human resources

Staff turnover is the proportion of total employees who leave and are replaced in a period. While a certain level of staff turnover is unavoidable (due, for example, to retirement), too high a turnover rate can be expensive, and can adversely affect both the morale of remaining workers and their productivity.

 What sort of costs are incurred by staff turnover?

Staff turnover can incur a potentially wide range of costs: advertising for replacements, interviewing applicants, induction/training of new employees and disruption to operations. We can express staff turnover as a ratio:

$$\frac{\text{Number of staff replaced during period}}{\text{Total number of staff employed during period}}$$

Given the widespread employment of part-time workers, it is common to express staff numbers in terms of **full-time equivalents** (or **whole-time equivalents**). This provides us with a single measure of staff numbers. Exhibit 4.10 illustrates.

PP Insurance Ltd

PP Insurance employs 10 full-time sales staff, who each work a 40-hour week. In addition, the firm employs some part-time sales staff, whose details follow:

2 employees, each working a 10-hour week
4 employees, each working a 20-hour week
6 employees, each working a 30-hour week

Exhibit 4.10 Full-time equivalents

Each of the employees working for 10 hours per week represents 10/40 – i.e. 0.25 of a full-time employee (who works 40 hours per week). Since there are two employees in this category, we have $(2 \times 0.25) = 0.5$ full-time equivalents.

 From Exhibit 4.10, determine the number of full-time equivalent sales staff employed by PP Insurance. (Don't forget about the 10 full-time employees.)

Full-time equivalents (FTEs):

10×1 FTE	10.0
2×0.25 FTE	0.5
$4 \times \dfrac{20}{40} = 0.5$ FTE	2.0
$6 \times \dfrac{30}{40} = 0.75$ FTE	4.5
	17.0

Thus, if two of the sales staff working a 30-hour week were to leave and be replaced during a period, PP Insurance's staff turnover would be

$$\frac{(2 \times 0.75 \text{ FTE})}{17 \text{ FTE}} = 0.09$$

Such are the potential costs of high staff turnover, that the rate and reasons for leaving should be monitored. If dissatisfaction emerges as a major contributory to staff turnover, then perhaps a change in the organisation's human resources policy needs to be considered.

In larger organisations, monitoring staff turnover would be one important function of the Human Resources (or Personnel) Department. Other typical duties of this department include placing job advertisements, arranging interviews for applicants and maintaining a personnel record for each employee. This latter includes employees' personal details, tax status and other information relevant to their employment.

Recording work performed

In many situations, it is necessary to record the amount of time employees have spent on various tasks and types of work. This has two purposes:

1 It allows for calculation of the labour cost of units of product/service.
2 In some cases, it may form the basis for payment of wages.

Where employees are required to detail their working time, they will usually do so on a **time sheet**, which distinguishes between productive time (split into different jobs or tasks), non-productive time (like time spent travelling to jobs) and any idle time (due, perhaps, to machine breakdown). It is also likely that the time sheet will separate normal working time from overtime (*see* later), and will contain whatever other information is appropriate to the nature of the work performed. Once authorised by employees' superiors, time sheets provide one input to the process of wages payment.

Employee times may also be entered onto **job cost cards** (or **job sheets**) so that the labour cost of units of product/service can be determined. We will have more to say about job costing in Chapter 8. However, you should note that this process of recording employee times is not confined to manufacturing organisations – it is also common in those providing services.

Idle time, overtime, direct and indirect labour costs

Idle time occurs when an employee cannot perform any kind of task, whether directly or indirectly related to output. This might happen, for example, if machinery unexpectedly breaks down. Idle time could even be a necessary element of the output process – PP Insurance's sales staff may spend a fair amount of time travelling and possibly calling on clients who do not purchase an insurance policy; they will also be entitled to paid holidays. It is thus possible to make a distinction between *expected* idle time and *unexpected*: the cost accounting treatment of each is different. Consider Exhibit 4.11.

The six days' work lost due to adverse weather conditions is unexpected idle time: as such, it is treated as an overhead. However, the non-productive time each week is expected, and should therefore be included in direct labour cost.

PP Insurance: Idle time

The firm's full-time sales staff are paid a basic wage of £400 for a 40-hour week. Management anticipates that 20% of each working week will be spent travelling and in other non-productive activity. During November, two of the sales team were unable to work at all for 6 days; this was due to severe gales and flooding across their sales territory.

Exhibit 4.11 Idle time

From Exhibit 4.11, determine the following:

> *the labour cost per hour; and*
> *the labour cost per productive hour*

for the firm's full-time sales staff.

Labour cost per hour: £400/40 hours = £10. To obtain the labour cost per productive hour, we need to eliminate expected idle time from the denominator, which we therefore reduce by 20% – i.e. to 32 hours: £400/32 hours = £12.50. So, if management wished to know the direct labour cost of selling a policy, and if that sale occupied two hours of sales staff's time, the calculation would be (2 hours × £12.50) = £25. This process of 'grossing up' labour charges is common – especially in job costing situations, where labour and other costs are being traced to individual units of product/service. It is also essential to make allowance for anticipated idle time when preparing labour budgets. Failure to do so could result in a significant understatement of manpower requirements, with consequent disruption to the planned volume of output. We will return to this subject when we discuss budgeting in Chapter 17.

Overtime occurs where work is performed outwith normal working hours. Sometimes, overtime is 'paid' for by allowing 'time off in lieu'; e.g. if an employee works four hours' overtime, then she may be allowed to take (say) six hours off during what would otherwise be normal working time. To avoid the possible operational problems which this might cause, many employers will make an extra wage/salary payment in respect of overtime.

PP Insurance: overtime working

During November, one of the firm's full-time sales staff worked 20 hours' overtime at management's request. Overtime is paid for at a rate of time and one half. The weekly wage is £400 for normal time of 40 hours – i.e. £10 per hour.

Exhibit 4.12 Overtime payment

From Exhibit 4.12, determine the total amount paid to this employee in respect of overtime working.

The overtime payment is (20 hours × [£10 × 1.5]) = £300. The overtime payment has two elements: 20 hours are paid for at the rate for normal time (£10), to which is added an **overtime premium** of (0.5 × £10) = £5 per hour. This split determines the cost accounting treatment, with the normal time element of overtime being treated as direct labour and the overtime premium being overhead. (A similar treatment is accorded to **shift premiums** – i.e. an extra payment sometimes made to employees whose work involves a changing pattern of shifts.) The rationale is that charging overtime (and shift) premiums to work that just happens to have been performed at a particular point in time would give an artificially inflated view of its labour cost when compared to other, possibly similar, work performed at different points in time. In some cases, the overtime premium may be treated as a direct cost: e.g. if the overtime is worked at a customer's request to achieve early completion of a job.

Treatment of UK National Insurance (NI) contributions can also cause some confusion. NI contributions consist of two elements: an employee's contribution and an employer's contribution. The former is a deduction from gross wages/salaries that employers collect on behalf of government – it is thus part of employers' gross wages cost. The latter is a cost borne entirely by employers and, while based on the amount of gross wages/salaries, is not part of them. The costing problem arises when computing the amount of direct wages, with two treatments being possible:

1 The cost of gross direct wages/salaries can be increased to allow for employers' NI contributions – i.e. we can apply the same sort of 'grossing up' procedure that was used for expected idle time. Thus, employers' NI contributions applicable to the wages/salaries of direct workers would be incorporated into the direct labour cost of units of product/service.
2 Employers' NI contributions can be viewed as a labour-related overhead, like the costs associated with operating a personnel function. Using this approach, we exclude employers' NI contributions from gross direct wages/salaries (hence from the direct labour cost of output) and treat them as, say, production overhead.

Employers' NI contributions relating to indirect wages/salaries such as production management, administration, selling and distribution are always dealt with as production, administration or selling and distribution overheads.

Labour records should thus be sufficiently detailed to allow direct labour to be separated from indirect. This is important because it permits the correct accounting treatment to be applied to different elements of labour cost, thereby facilitating the costing of outputs.

Remuneration and incentive schemes

There are two fundamental approaches to remuneration: time-based and output-based. At its simplest, a time-based wage would be (hours worked × wage rate per hour) – in the UK, the statutory minimum wage is expressed as an hourly rate. There is now, however, an increasing tendency towards payment of salaries – i.e. fixed annual amounts – which means that many labour costs are fixed relative to the volume of output. The most basic form of output-related pay is 'straight piecework', where the gross wage is (units produced × rate per unit). This kind of payment system – which would result in a labour cost that is wholly variable relative to output – is comparatively rare, and is more normally combined with some form of guaranteed minimum wage. PP Insurance's sales staff, for instance, are likely to be paid a salary plus a commission based on the value of policies sold.

As Exhibit 4.1 indicates, many organisations seek to improve labour productivity, and possibly improve morale, commitment and loyalty by means of some kind of bonus or incentive scheme. The forms which these take are many and varied, and can be complex to administer – but this seems to be a price that some organisations are prepared to pay in order to obtain the associated benefits. As Exhibit 4.1 also observes, this could be especially true where labour (or labour possessed of particular skills) is in short supply. Many incentive schemes are explicitly linked to output – the higher the volume of output produced in a given time, the higher the bonus received. This has the obvious advantage of encouraging more output.

> ✔ *Can you see a potential disadvantage with output-related incentive schemes?*

Although they may encourage volume of output, quality might suffer as a consequence, resulting in higher costs for rejects, reworks and inspection. And, for some functions (e.g. administrative), 'output' may be difficult to measure in a completely objective manner. Possibly to counter these weaknesses, many organisations have introduced profit-based incentives: profit-sharing schemes, profit-related pay and employee share option schemes being the most common. This kind of approach has the advantage of focusing attention on wider and longer-term company issues, rather than simply considering the volume of output. Here, however, may be the weakness of such schemes: long term and company-wide issues could be viewed by some employees (especially at 'shopfloor' level) as too far removed from the day-to-day reality of their work to act as an effective incentive. Some organisations may offer more indirect incentives: a firm like PP Insurance might provide its sales staff with company cars, or pay their travelling expenses; benefits like a subsidised canteen or loans at preferential interest rates might be available to staff.

Payroll procedures

'Payroll procedures' describes the process of calculating and paying wages and salaries. Figure 4.4 illustrates the general procedures that might be involved.

In many situations, the procedures illustrated in Figure 4.4 will be handled by computer with only minimal manual inputs. Payment may also be dealt with electronically, by credit transfer from employer's to employees' bank accounts – which is both administratively straightforward and avoids the security problems associated with handling large cash sums. Small organisations are likely to operate a simplified version of Figure 4.4; but even here, a certain minimum amount of record-keeping is required – in particular, details of gross wages/salaries and deductions therefrom in respect of tax and National Insurance.

We will examine the bookkeeping entries for wages and salaries in Chapter 7. For the moment, you should note that this is a two-stage process. The first stage consists of recording gross wages for the period – gross wages consisting of net amounts paid plus all wage deductions. The second stage involves charging gross wages to different cost objectives (cost centres, for example) – which, in turn, requires us to be able to distinguish between direct and indirect wages/salaries.

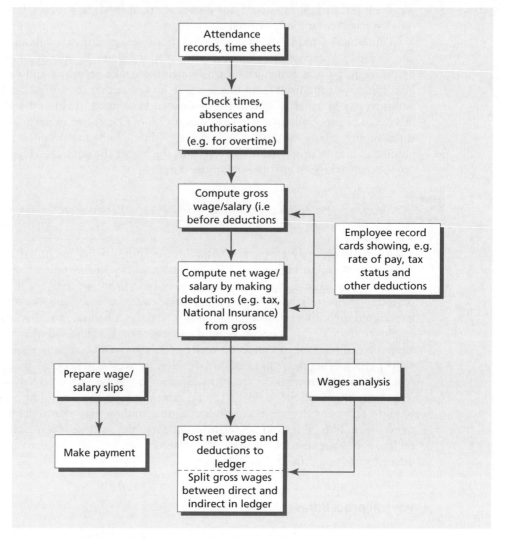

Figure 4.4 Payroll procedures

SUMMARY

In this chapter we have discussed the costing of two important resources – materials and labour. Like so many other aspects of cost accounting, there is no universally-applicable 'rule' or approach; organisational and operational circumstance must dictate what is most appropriate. We have seen that:

- The administrative effort and formality of materials' and labour costing systems depends on:
  - the nature of the business
  - the organisation's size and structure

- the volume, range and cost of materials/number of employees and different grade of employee
  - the cost/benefit criterion.

- Key documents that might be associated with the materials 'cycle' are: **purchase requisition, purchase order, delivery note, goods received note, stores requisition, bin card**.

- The **economic order quantity** (EOQ) attempts to minimise the total cost of holding plus ordering materials, and is calculated as:

$$\sqrt{\frac{2DO}{H}}$$

where D = annual usage
O = cost of placing an order
H = annual holding cost/unit

- The EOQ rests on a number of key assumptions:

  - constant usage
  - zero/constant stocks independent of any created by use of the EOQ
  - certainty about ordering and holding costs, and about usage
  - constant purchase price of materials.

- The **stores ledger** contains a separate account for each material, detailing receipts, issues, balance on hand, and associated costs. Where the stores ledger is updated after each receipt or issue, **perpetual inventory** is in operation.

- **Stocktaking** involves physical verification of stock quantities and reconciliation of these with recorded quantities. **Periodic stocktaking** occurs once per period, **continuous stocktaking** occurs on a rolling basis.

- **ABC classification** concentrates control effort on those materials that represent the majority of annual purchase cost ('category A' items).

- **Safety stock (buffer stock)** is held as a contingency against incorrect estimation of usage and/or lead times.

- **Reorder level** the stock level at which a new order should be placed with suppliers, and is calculated as (maximum usage × maximum lead time).

- **Minimum level** warns that usage may be higher than expected, with resulting use of safety stock; minimum level is (reorder level – [average usage × average lead time]).

- **Maximum level** warns of lower-than-expected usage, with resultant stock build-up; it is determined as (reorder level + EOQ) – (minimum usage in minimum lead time).

- **Free stock** is the amount of stock notionally available to users:

(quantity on hand + quantity currently on order with suppliers)
less
quantity allocated to users but not yet issued

- In defining materials' 'purchase cost', the following items may cause difficulty: transport/delivery charges, quantity and early payment discounts, VAT.

▶

- **First-In–First-Out** (FIFO) uses the oldest cost applicable to stocks for issues from stores; stocks will thus be valued at their most up-to-date cost, but issues may be under-stated if costs are rising, leading to potential over-statement of profit.

- **Last-In–First-Out** (LIFO) uses the most recent cost applicable to stocks for issues from stores; issues will therefore be valued at their most up-to-date cost, but stocks (and profit) may be understated if costs are rising.

- **Weighted average cost** (AVCO) costs stores' issues at an average cost that is recalculated after each receipt. While this may even out fluctuations caused by FIFO and LIFO, average cost is not the same as actual purchase cost.

- **Materials requirement planning** (MRPI) explicitly recognises the link between materials' requirements and the pattern of production, working backwards from production to determine materials' requirements.

- **Manufacturing resource planning** (MRPII) combines material requirement planning, production scheduling and cost accounting into a single system.

- The **staff turnover** ratio is:

$$\frac{\text{Number of staff replaced during period}}{\text{Total number of staff employed during period}}$$

- In order to arrive at a single figure for the number of employees, part-time employees are converted to **full-time equivalents** (**whole-time equivalents**).

- Labour times may be recorded on **time sheets** and **job cards**.

- **Idle time** should be split into expected and unexpected idle time: the former is included in the 'normal' labour charge by a process of 'grossing up', the latter is treated as overhead.

- **Overtime premium** is payment above the normal rate of pay made in respect of overtime working. It is usually treated as an overhead.

- A distinction must be made between employees' National Insurance and employers' National Insurance contributions. Employees' contributions are part of gross wages; employers' contributions may either be included in wages costs or treated as overhead.

- Remuneration systems may be time- or output-based ('piecework').

- Incentive schemes can reward output but possibly at the expense of quality; or they can focus on wider, longer-term issues like company profitability.

- 'Payroll procedures' describes the process of calculating and paying wages/salaries. Detail from the payroll forms the basis labour cost postings to the ledger.

In the next two chapters, we will discuss the problematic issue of overhead, and in particular, how we might determine an overhead cost per unit of product/service.

FURTHER READING

Maskell, B. Why MRPII hasn't created world class manufacturing ... where do we go from here? *Management Accounting*, November 1993 (CIMA).

SELF-TEST QUESTIONS

The *following information should be used for Questions 4.1 and 4.2*

A large retailer with multiple outlets maintains a central warehouse from which the outlets are supplied. The following information is available for Part Number SF525.

Average usage	350 per day
Minimum usage	180 per day
Maximum usage	420 per day
Lead time for replenishment	11–15 days
Reorder quantity	6500 units
Reorder level	6300

4.1 Based on the data above, what is the maximum level of stock?

A 5250
B 6500
C 10 820
D 12 800

(CIMA, *Cost Accounting and Quantitative Methods*, May 1998)

4.2 Based on the data above, what is the approximate number of Part SF525 carried as buffer stock?

A 200
B 720
C 1680
D 1750

(CIMA, *Cost Accounting and Quantitative Methods*, May 1998)

4.3 Place a tick in the appropriate box to indicate whether each statement is true or false.

	True	False
(a) The EOQ attempts to minimise the purchase cost of materials.	☐	☐
(b) Employee entitlement to paid holidays is a form of expected idle time.	☐	☐
(c) Employers' National Insurance contributions are a deduction from gross wages.	☐	☐
(d) FIFO is consistent with normal stores' issue procedure.	☐	☐
(e) The minimum stock level is that at which a new order should be placed with suppliers.	☐	☐
(f) Quantity discounts are ignored when determining the purchase cost of materials.	☐	☐
(g) For planning purposes, materials should be costed at standard cost.	☐	☐
(h) Continuous stocktaking and perpetual inventory both refer to physical verification of stocks on an on-going basis.	☐	☐

4.4 Bunker plc stock one raw material item, Drum 4, which forms the raw material content for their sole product, and the information below relates to this stock item for May 1997.

Opening stock

80 units   Price £20 per unit

Receipts of Stock Item

2.5.97	100 units	Price £22 per unit
13.5.97	300 units	Price £25 per unit
21.5.97	120 units	Price £30 per unit

Issues to production

6.5.97	150 units
19.5.97	200 units
30.5.97	150 units

Requirements

(a) For Drum 4, calculate the value of closing stock as at 31 May 1997, and the cost of materials issued to production for the month of May, using perpetual methods of valuation for:

FIFO;
LIFO; and
Weighted average cost.   **(16 marks)**

(b) List four advantages of perpetual inventory compared to periodic inventory.

(4 marks)
(Total: 20 marks)

(CIPFA, *Management Accounting*, June 1997)

4.5 Kilminser plc employ 20 staff in their production department which makes a number of products.

The staff are paid 52 weeks per year.

Staff are entitled to 5 weeks' annual paid leave as well as 2 weeks' paid statutory holidays, and work 40 hours per week. They are paid £4 per hour.

Overtime is not normally worked. However, a special job has been requested which will require 2000 hours of overtime.

Eighty per cent of the overtime will be paid at time and a half. The balance will be paid at double time.

Requirements

(a) (i) Calculate the direct labour pay cost to be charged to a 2-labour-hour job under the normal time.
    (ii) Calculate the direct labour pay cost of the special job.   **(4 marks)**

(b) The company are considering the introduction of a bonus system. Using both the Halsey and Rowan systems for calculating bonus payments, calculate the full pay of a worker who produces 184 units in a week with a standard time of $\frac{1}{4}$ hour per unit. Assume for this part of the question that 2 hours a week are normally idle time.

(6 marks)

[Author's note. The Halsey system calculates bonus as: ($\frac{1}{2}$ time saved against standard × standard rate per hour). The Rowan scheme calculates bonus as (time taken/time allowed × time saved × standard rate per hour).]

(b) Explain the advantages and disadvantages of a time-based system for remunerating staff. **(5 marks)**

(Total: 15 marks)

(CIPFA, *Management Accounting*, December 1997)

QUESTIONS WITHOUT ANSWERS

4.6 A firm uses the First-In–First-Out (FIFO) system for pricing stocks. During a period, product costs were overstated and profits understated. This meant that during the period, prices were

A falling
B unchanged
C rising slowly
D rising rapidly

(CIMA, *Cost Accounting and Quantitative Methods*, November 1999)

4.7 A wholesaler has 8450 units outstanding for Part X100 on existing customers' orders; there are 3925 units in stock and the calculated free stock is 5525 units.

How many units does the wholesaler have on order with his supplier?

A 9450
B 10 050
C 13 975
D 17 900

(CIMA, *Cost Accounting and Quantitative Methods*, November 1997)

4.8 A small manufacturing company produces a range of small tools. The tools are only sold in composite sets. The sets are packed in a plastic storage box which is 'bought in' from another company.

The information and data below relates to the storage box:

Estimated usage for the forthcoming year	1000 boxes
Basic purchase price of box	£10 each
Delivery charges	£20 per order
Storage costs	£1.00 per box per year

The company is trying to decide the size of order to place with the supplier of the storage boxes and is considering order sizes of 50, 100, 200, 250, 500 or 1000 boxes.

Requirements

(a) Produce a table that shows the total annual:

   (i) delivery costs;
   (ii) storage costs; and
   (iii) delivery plus storage costs,

for each of the six order sizes mentioned above. **(6 marks)**

(b) Use the economic order quantity formula to determine an appropriate order size and compare your results with that seen in (a).

The economic order quantity formula is given as:

$$EOQ = \sqrt{\frac{2CoD}{Ch}}$$

where D = annual demand, Co = delivery (ordering) costs and Ch = annual holding costs/unit. **(3 marks)**

(c) The supplier of the storage boxes now says that it is prepared to offer bulk discount at the following levels:

Less than 250 boxes	No discount
250–499 boxes	2% discount
500–999 boxes	4% discount
1000 boxes or more	6% discount

Determine whether any of these levels of discount is worth taking. **(7 marks)**

(d) The sales of the tool sets for the last year were as follows:

January	100	July	100
February	120	August	80
March	80	September	100
April	140	October	40
May	60	November	60
June	80	December	40

Draw a bar chart detailing the monthly sales for last year.
Marks will be awarded for presentation. **(9 marks)**
(Total: 25 marks)

(ACCA, *Cost Accounting Systems*, June 1998)

4.9 You have been asked to assist a customer, who has recently started trading, with their stock valuation. In order to explain alternative methods and their effect on profit you decide to provide calculations using transactions from the first month of trading.

Requirements

(a) Using the information below calculate the closing stock valuation using LIFO and FIFO methods showing stock valuations after each transaction. **(12 marks)**

(b) For each method, calculate gross profit for the period assuming a selling price of £7 per unit. **(4 marks)**

(c) Provide advice for your customer on the costs involved in maintaining stock at too high a level. **(4 marks)**
(Total: 20 marks)

Date 1999	Receipts units	£	Issues units
2 March	210	5.00	
8 March	80	5.10	
9 March			190
14 March			50
22 March	60	5.40	
23 March	70	5.50	
28 March			80

(CIOBS, *Business Accounting*, March 2000)

4.10 Most textbooks consider that the optimal reorder quantity for materials occurs when 'the cost of storage is equated with the cost of ordering'. If one assumes that this statement is acceptable and also, in attempting to construct a simple formula for an optimal reorder quantity, that a number of basic assumptions must be made, then a recognised formula can be produced using the following symbols:

C_0 = cost of placing an order
C_h = cost of storage per annum, expressed as a percentage of stock value
D = demand in units for a material, per annum
Q = reorder quantity, in units
$Q/2$ = average stock level, in units
p = price per unit

Requirements

(a) To present formulae, using the symbols given above, representing:

    (i)   total cost of ordering;
    (ii) total cost of storage;
    (iii) total cost of ordering and storage;
    (iv) optimal reorder quantity.   **(4 marks)**

(b) State the limitations experienced in practice which affect the user of the formula for optimal reorder quantity as expressed in (a)(iv) above.   **(4 marks)**

(c) Calculate the optimal reorder quantity from the following data:

    Cost of storage is 20% per annum of stock value
    Cost of placing an order is £30 each
    Demand for material is 2000 units per annum
    Price of material is £70 per unit   **(3 marks)**

(c) Explain a system of stock usage which renders economic order quantity reordering obsolete.   **(4 marks)**
         (Total: 15 marks)

(CIMA, *Cost Accounting*, November 1993)

CHAPTER 5

Absorption of overhead

Exhibit 5.1 Overhead costs

INTRODUCTION

When we discussed cost classification in Chapter 2, we made the distinction between costs which are unambiguously and quantifiably attributable to individual cost objectives (**direct costs**) and costs which are common to two or more cost objectives (**overheads**). However, in some circumstances, it may be necessary or desirable to treat overheads 'as if' they were direct relative to units of output. Procedures for determining costs such as the manufacturing overhead per case of whisky referred to in Exhibit 5.1 – **overhead absorption** (alternatively, overhead *recovery* or *application*) – form the subject matter of this chapter. The second quotation in Exhibit 5.1 indicates just how significant an expenditure overhead can be. The proportion of overhead to total cost has been (and is likely to continue) increasing for most organisations; one of the principal causes of this is the ongoing shift from labour-intensive to technology-intensive operations. So treatment of overhead relative to cost units merits careful consideration.

Because overheads are indirect costs, their absorption involves a more complex methodology than that used for attribution of direct costs. Overhead absorption may follow the 'traditional' route or may employ a more recent (arguably more sophisticated) technique – activity based costing (ABC). In this chapter, we shall describe and illustrate the 'traditional' approach to overhead absorption; activity based costing is discussed in Chapter 6. Regardless of the mechanics employed, we can view the process of overhead absorption as a series of cost attributions, each moving closer to the ultimate cost objective – the cost unit. We should also stress that, irrespective of methodology, overhead absorption will always be subject to a certain element of imprecision. The aim is to devise a set of absorption procedures that minimise such imprecision.

Although we shall use a manufacturing business to illustrate overhead absorption procedures, you should note that these procedures are equally applicable to service, non-profit and public sector organisations (see Chapter 11).

OBJECTIVES

When you have completed this chapter, you will be able to:

- explain the rationale underlying absorption of overheads;
- distinguish between allocation and apportionment of overheads;
- develop and apply apportionment and reapportionment bases;
- appreciate the potential subjectivity inherent in the apportionment exercise;
- distinguish between production ('front-line') and service ('support') cost centres and understand the need for secondary distribution of service cost centres' overheads to production cost centres;
- develop overhead absorption rates using different bases and apply them to cost units;
- understand the relative merits of plantwide, departmental, actual and predetermined absorption rates;
- appreciate the significance of normal volume, practical capacity and annual budgeted volume to calculation of absorption rates;
- explain the meaning of over- and underabsorption and calculate their amount in given circumstances.

RATIONALE FOR ABSORPTION OF OVERHEADS

If, as we have said, overheads are not directly attributable to cost units, why is it necessary to undertake the sort of attribution exercise which we will describe below?

RPG Ltd

This light engineering company manufactures precision alloy castings. Among the company's costs are rent and rates, insurance of machinery and lighting and heating.

Exhibit 5.2 RPG Ltd – overheads

Why can it be argued that the cost of each casting produced should include a charge in respect of the overhead costs mentioned?

We can take the view that overhead costs such as those mentioned in Exhibit 5.2 are necessarily incurred because of the company's output. This argument can be expanded by suggesting that whereas direct costs are attributable to a single cost unit, overhead is attributable to *all* cost units – cost units being the cost objective in this instance. If we accept this view, then it is a short step to the conclusion that each unit produced should receive a charge for overheads in addition to its direct costs.

Organisations may absorb overhead to determine a 'full' cost per unit. This could, for example, be important if selling price is to be based on cost. Omission of some or all overheads from unit costs may result in underpricing and consequent failure to cover *all* costs – a situation which might have serious implications for the organisation if it is allowed to continue for any length of time. Inclusion of overheads in unit costs for purposes such as price setting could be viewed as an attempt to approximate the long-run average cost of output since, in the long run, all costs must be covered to ensure continued profitability and even survival. But you should note that cost is not the only consideration in setting selling prices; competition within a firm's market and the extent to which demand reacts to price changes are two examples of other important influences on selling price. In addition, even where cost is highly significant, e.g. for planning and control purposes, overhead absorption may yield unit costs which are inappropriate, and could result in incorrect financial analysis of a particular situation – a potential weakness which we shall examine in later chapters. For the moment, we will confine our discussion of overhead absorption to determination of unit costs.

Another reason for absorbing overheads (at least in the UK) is given in Statement of Standard Accounting Practice No. 9 (Stocks and Long Term Contracts): '... "costs" of stocks should comprise that expenditure which has been incurred in the normal course of business in bringing the product or service to its present location and condition. Such costs will include all related production overheads ...' In effect, this means that all accounts subject to the provisions of the standard – principally the *published* accounts of limited companies – are required to employ absorption costing for stock valuation – and hence profit reporting – purposes. We shall examine the precise implications for profit of inclusion or non-inclusion of overheads in stock values in Chapter 12. However, our discussion in Chapters 1 and 2 of financial and management accounting would suggest that unit costs calculated to meet the requirements of published accounts are unlikely to have much relevance for internal users of financial information.

ABSORPTION COSTING: 'TRADITIONAL' METHODOLOGY

Overview of absorption procedures

Figure 5.1 provides a diagrammatic overview of the 'traditional' overhead absorption methodology.

Primary distribution of overhead

The first step in overhead absorption is to *allocate* and *apportion* overheads to cost centres, which are typically (but not invariably) organisational departments.

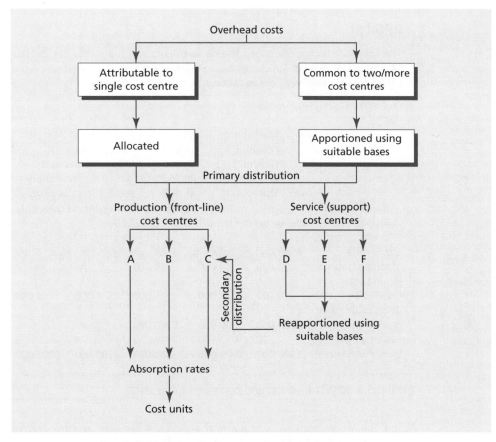

Figure 5.1 Overview of 'traditional' absorption methodology

Exhibit 5.3 provides further cost and other data relating to RPG Ltd. In this example, the amounts have been kept small for simplicity; but you should appreciate that, for an organisation of any size, overhead costs can be considerable.

 Of the overhead costs listed in Exhibit 5.3, which can be related to a specific department and which relate to two or more departments?

From Exhibit 5.3, only supervisory salaries can be unambiguously associated with a single department; all the other overheads are common to two or more. Overheads which relate to a single cost centre can be **allocated** to that cost centre; however, common costs require to be **apportioned** (i.e. shared) between the cost centres concerned. In order to undertake this apportionment, we need to develop an **apportionment basis** suitable to each common overhead cost. As a general 'rule of thumb', apportionment bases should derive from the underlying cause of the cost concerned, termed the **cost driver**. In addition to reflecting the cost driver, apportionment bases should:

1 be readily quantifiable; and
2 meet the cost/benefit criterion.

RPG Ltd

The company is organised into five departments which are also designated cost centres: Machining, Polishing, Finishing, Maintenance and Stores. Estimated overhead costs and other data for next year are as follows:

Overhead costs

		£		£
Supervisory salaries:	Machining	50 000	Lighting and heating	12 000
	Polishing	56 000	Rent and rates	64 000
	Finishing	60 000	Insurance: property	6 000
	Maintenance	40 000	machinery	8 000
	Stores	46 000	Production planning	80 000
Canteen costs		60 000	Power for machines	24 000
Employers' National Insurance contributions £150 000				

Other data	*Machining*	*Polishing*	*Finishing*	*Maintenance*	*Stores*	*Total*
Machine hours	200 000	40 000	10 000	nil	nil	250 000
Floor area (metres^2)	16 000	12 000	8 000	1 000	3 000	40 000
Book value of machinery	£700 000	£200 000	£100 000	nil	nil	£1 000 000
No. of employees	10	30	50	4	6	100
Direct wages cost	£300 000	£900 000	£1 500 000	£100 000	£200 000	£3 000 000

Exhibit 5.3 RPG Ltd – overhead costs and other data

What this may mean in practice is that, even where the true underlying cause of an overhead cost can be identified and precisely quantified, its use as an apportionment basis may be prohibitively expensive. For example, it may be possible to meter usage of power by individual machines, which should reduce (or possibly eliminate) the need to apportion power costs. However, the cost of purchasing and installing a sufficiently sophisticated metering system may be disproportionately high relative to the benefit of a more precise absorption of overheads.

This, of course, assumes that the cost driver is identifiable and quantifiable. Consider the cost of business rates for an organisation's premises. It is a simple matter to identify the underlying cause of this overhead (the premises' rateable value) and to quantify its incidence (£x of rates paid per £1 of rateable value). But how do we use this information to apportion the rates cost to individual cost centres within the premises? In such cases, where it is not practicable, or cost effective, to employ the cost driver as an apportionment basis, we need to use a *proxy* measure, having regard to the nature of the cost and the information which is available or readily obtainable.

 From the information available in Exhibit 5.3, what is the most appropriate apportionment basis to use for RPG Ltd's property costs (rent and rates, lighting and heating, insurance)?

Given the nature of these costs (related to occupancy of premises) and the available information, floor area would be the most appropriate apportionment basis. Having selected the apportionment basis, it is now a straightforward matter to split the property-related costs according to each department's share of the total floor area:

	m^2	%
Machining	16 000	40.0
Polishing	12 000	30.0
Finishing	8 000	20.0
Maintenance	1 000	2.5
Stores	3 000	7.5
	40 000	100.0

Applying these percentages to the lighting and heating cost in Exhibit 5.3 provides the required apportionment:

	£		£
Machining	4800	Polishing	3600
Finishing	2400	Maintenance	300
Stores	900		

The full allocations and apportionments to cost centres can be shown on an **overhead analysis sheet,** such as Table 5.1.

Although this sort of tabulation is cumbersome to prepare manually, use of a computer spreadsheet can greatly reduce the time and effort involved.

 Bearing in mind the nature of each cost involved and the information available in Exhibit 5.3, complete the apportionments in Table 5.1 and determine the total overhead for each department.

Table 5.1 Partially completed overhead analysis sheet for RPG Ltd

Overhead cost	Amount £	Apportionment basis	Percentages	Machining £	Polishing £	Finishing £	Maintenance £	Stores £
Supervisory salaries	252 000	Allocated	Not applicable	50 000	56 000	60 000	40 000	46 000
Lighting and heating	12 000	Floor area	40%; 30%; 20% 2.5%; 7.5%	4 800	3 600	2 400	300	900
Rent and rates	64 000							
Insurance: property	6 000							
Insurance: machinery	8 000							
Production planning	80 000							
Canteen costs	60 000	Number of employees	10%; 30%; 50% 4%; 6%	6 000	18 000	30 000	2 400	3 600
Power costs	24 000							
Employers' Nat. Insur.	150 000							
Totals	656 000							

Table 5.2 Completed overhead analysis sheet for RPG Ltd

Overhead cost	Amount £	Apportionment basis	Percentages	Machining £	Polishing £	Finishing £	Maintenance £	Stores £
Supervisory salaries	252 000	Allocated	Not applicable	50 000	56 000	60 000	40 000	46 000
Lighting and heating	12 000	Floor area	40%; 30%; 20% 2.5%; 7.5%	4 800	3 600	2 400	300	900
Rent and rates	64 000	Floor area	40%; 30%; 20% 2.5%; 7.5%	25 600	19 200	12 800	1 600	4 800
Insurance: property	6 000	Floor area	40%; 30%; 20% 2.5%; 7.5%	2 400	1 800	1 200	150	450
Insurance: machinery	8 000	Book value of machinery	70%; 20%; 10% nil; nil	5 600	1 600	800	Nil	Nil
Production planning	80 000	Number of employees	10%; 30%; 50% 4%; 6%	8 000	24 000	40 000	3 200	4 800
Canteen costs	60 000	Number of employees	10%; 30%; 50% 4%; 6%	6 000	18 000	30 000	2 400	3 600
Power costs	24 000	Machine Hours	80%; 16%; 4% Nil; Nil	19 200	3 840	960	Nil	Nil
Employers' Nat. Insur.	150 000	Direct wages Cost	10%; 30%; 50% 3.33%; 6.67%	15 000	45 000	75 000	4 995	10 005
Totals	656 000			136 600	173 040	223 160	52 645	70 555

Table 5.2 is the completed overhead analysis sheet showing the allocations and apportionments of overhead costs to each of RPG Ltd's five departments.

Note that the direct labour costs referred to in Exhibit 5.3 appear *only* as an apportionment basis for Employers' National Insurance contributions in Table 5.2. Since *direct* labour is not an overhead, its allocation to cost centres along with overheads on the analysis sheet would be a serious error of principle. In addition, if we were to treat direct labour in this way, we would almost certainly end by double-counting it, as it will already have been charged directly to cost units.

The apportionment bases employed in Table 5.2 are all subjective to some extent, so it is important that they are at least defensible in terms of the nature of the cost which is being apportioned and of the cost/benefit criterion. Take RPG Ltd's Production Planning cost: in the absence of more detailed information, it seems reasonable to use the number of employees as an apportionment basis – the greater the number of a cost centre's employees, the larger the department, and so the greater is likely to be that cost centre's involvement in Production Planning processes or its usage of Production Planning facilities. Heating and lighting relates to occupancy of premises, and, although volume (rather than area) might be more accurate, area is at least an acceptable approximation of the cause of this cost.

Secondary distribution of overhead

Table 5.2 completed the first stage in the 'traditional' overhead absorption process, but we are not yet in a position to calculate an overhead cost per unit of output.

Why would the departmental overhead totals in Table 5.2 provide an unsuitable basis for determination of an overhead cost per unit of output?

Two of the departments in Table 5.2 – Maintenance and Stores – provide internal *support services*. A distinction must be made between *production cost centres* and *service cost centres*. In a service organisation, we might term these, respectively, 'front-line' and 'support' cost centres.

Since it is only production cost centres that deal with cost units – the ultimate target of our absorption procedures – we need a mechanism for incorporating service cost centres' overheads into the totals for production cost centres (i.e. Machining, Polishing and Finishing in RPG Ltd's case). A **secondary distribution** is required, whereby service cost centres' overheads are *re*apportioned to production cost centres.

We therefore need to develop **reapportionment bases**, which must reflect the underlying cause of each service cost centre's overhead (i.e. the cost driver relating to the service being provided) if it is readily identifiable and quantifiable, failing which we should use the best available proxy. Exhibit 5.4 summarises the results of the primary distribution and presents some additional information relating to RPG Ltd.

RPG Ltd: Additional information

Cost centre	Machining	Polishing	Finishing	Maintenance	Stores
Departmental overhead from primary distribution (see Table 5.2)	£136 600	£173 040	£223 160	£52 645	£70 555
Number of stores requisitions	2 000	1 000	600	400	nil
Number of maintenance call-outs	120	50	20	nil	10

Exhibit 5.4 RPG Ltd – information for secondary distribution

From the information in Exhibit 5.4, we can use number of stores requisitions to reapportion Stores overhead and number of maintenance call-outs for Maintenance.

There is one final issue to consider before undertaking the secondary distribution: to what extent should we recognise **reciprocal services** (i.e. services performed by one service cost centre for another service cost centre)? We can ignore them totally (**direct reapportionment**), we can partially recognise them (**step reapportionment**), or we can recognise them fully (**repeated distribution/algebraic reapportionment**). You should note, however, that even full recognition of reciprocal services may still result in inaccurate departmental totals, as it does not allow for services performed by a service cost centre on its own behalf.

Direct reapportionment

This approach to secondary distribution reapportions service cost centres' overheads to production cost centres *only*.

 Use the data in Exhibit 5.4 to determine appropriate percentages for reapportioning Stores and Maintenance to each of the three production cost centres.

For RPG Ltd, Maintenance and Stores overheads (£52 645 and £70 555 from Exhibit 5.4) will be reapportioned to Machining, Polishing and Finishing on the basis of maintenance call-outs and stores requisitions in those two departments *only*; i.e. we ignore the stores requisitions raised by Maintenance and the maintenance call-outs made by Stores.

From Exhibit 5.4, the number and percentage (to the nearest whole per cent) of stores requisitions for each production cost centre is:

Machining	2000	56%
Polishing	1000	28%
Finishing	600	16%
	3600	100%

For maintenance call-outs, we get:

Machining	120	63%
Polishing	50	26%
Finishing	20	11%
	190	100%

The departmental overhead resulting from primary distribution is the starting-point for our secondary distribution, shown in Table 5.3. (Note that reapportionments to production cost centres have been rounded to the nearest whole £1.)

Table 5.3 Direct reapportionment

	Amount £	Reapportionment basis	Percentages	Machining £	Polishing £	Finishing £	Maintenance £	Stores £
Totals	656 000			136 600	173 040	223 160	52 645	70 555
Stores overhead reapportioned	70 555	No. of stores requisitions	56%; 28%; 16%	39 511	19 755	11 289		(70 555)
Maintenance overhead reapportioned	52 645	No. of maintenance call-outs	63%; 26%; 11%	33 166	13 688	5 791	(52 645)	
Totals				209 277	206 483	240 240		

Step reapportionment

Also termed **specified order of closing**, step reapportionment starts either with the service cost centre having the highest departmental overhead total after primary distribution or with that providing the greatest service to other cost centres. This cost centre's overhead is reapportioned to *all* other departments (including other service cost centres), and the relevant column in the overhead analysis sheet is then 'closed off'. Moving to the next service cost centre in sequence (as determined by departmental overhead or extent of services provided), we reapportion this department's overhead to all other departments, excluding the service cost centre whose column has already been closed off. This procedure is repeated until all columns relating to service cost centres have been closed off.

When performing step reapportionments, two computational requirements should be borne in mind:

1 the percentages used to make the reapportionments should relate only to those cost centres receiving a share of the reapportioned cost;

2 for all service cost centres subsequent to the first, the amount of overhead being reapportioned will consist of that centre's total from the primary distribution *plus* a share of previously, reapportioned service centres' overhead.

We shall begin our step reapportionment with Stores, since this centre has the higher of the two service departments' overhead totals; stores requisitions is still the reapportionment basis, but we are now including those raised by Maintenance.

 Use the data in Exhibit 5.4 to determine appropriate percentages for reapportioning Stores overheads to the other four cost centres.

The number of stores requisitions and reapportionment percentages are:

Machining	2000	50%
Polishing	1000	25%
Finishing	600	15%
Maintenance	400	10%
	4000	100%

For reapportionment of Maintenance, the percentages used are the same as for the direct method; this is because, having closed off the Stores column in the analysis sheet, only the three production cost centres receive a share of Maintenance overhead *plus* Maintenance's share of Stores. Table 5.4 shows the step reapportionment.

Table 5.4 Step reapportionment

	Amount £	Reapportionment basis	Percentages	Machining £	Polishing £	Finishing £	Maintenance £	Stores £
Totals	656 000			136 600	173 040	223 160	52 645	70 555
Stores overhead reapportioned	70 555	No. of stores requisitions	50%; 25%; 15%; 10%	35 278	17 639	10 583	7 055 59 700	(70 555)
Maintenance overhead reapportioned	59 700	No. of maintenance call-outs	63%; 26%; 11%	37 611	15 522	6 567	(59 700)	
Totals	656 000			209 489	206 201	240 310		

Reapportionment by repeated distribution

The **repeated distribution** (or **continuous allotment**) method gives full recognition to reciprocal services. Service cost centres' overhead is reapportioned in sequence to all other departments, including other support departments. Using this method, the sequence in which the service cost centres are reapportioned is unimportant, providing it is applied consistently to every 'repeated distribution'. Once this first 'round' of reapportionments has been completed, the column for the service cost centre which started the sequence will contain a figure which is used as the basis for a second 'round' of reapportionments; at the end of this 'round', another (smaller) figure will remain in the first service centre's column, which serves as the basis for another 'round' of reapportionments – and so on until the amount remaining in one of the service centre columns is too small to warrant detailed reapportionment, being split arbitrarily between the production cost centres.

The reapportionment bases are still stores requisitions and maintenance call-outs for Stores and Maintenance respectively; the percentages used should, as always, relate to those cost centres which are to receive part of the reapportioned service centres' overhead.

 Use the data in Exhibit 5.4 to determine appropriate percentages for reapportioning Stores and Maintenance to the other four cost centres.

In this example, Machining, Polishing, Finishing and Maintenance will receive a reapportionment of Stores overhead, so the relevant percentages derived from those centres' stores requisitions are 50%, 25%, 15% and 10% (as calculated for the step reapportionment above). For Maintenance overhead, Machining, Polishing, Finishing and Stores receive a reapportionment, so the relevant percentages based on call-outs (from Exhibit 5.4) are:

Machining	120	60%
Polishing	50	25%
Finishing	20	10%
Stores	10	5%
	200	100%

Table 5.5 shows the resulting secondary distribution.

Table 5.5 Reapportionment using repeated distribution

	Amount £	Reapportionment basis	Percentages	Machining £	Polishing £	Finishing £	Maintenance £	Stores £
Totals	656 000			136 600	173 040	223 160	52 645	75 555
Stores overhead reapportioned	70 555	No. of stores requisitions	50%, 25% 15%, 10%	35 278	17 639	10 583	7 055 59 700	(70 555)
Maintenance overhead reapportioned	59 700	No. of maintenance call-outs	60%, 25% 10%, 5%	35 820	14 925	5 970	(59 700)	2 985
Stores overhead reapportioned	2 985	No. of stores requisitions	50%, 25% 15%, 10%	1 493	746	448	298	(2 985)
Maintenance overhead reapportioned	298	No. of maintenance call-outs	60%, 25% 10%, 5%	179	75	30	(298)	14
Stores overhead reapportioned	14	Arbitrary split	Not applicable	5	5	4		(14)
Totals				209 375	206 430	240 195		

Algebraic reapportionment

Repeated distribution, while fully reflecting reciprocal services, can be unwieldy, as Table 5.5 suggests. This may be avoided by adopting an algebraic approach to reapportionment. The first step is to express each service cost centre's overhead as an equation; using RPG Ltd's data, we get:

$$M = £52\ 645 + 10\%S \qquad (5.1)$$

$$S = £70\ 555 + 5\%M \qquad (5.2)$$

where M is total Maintenance overhead (including share of Stores overhead)
S is total Stores overhead (including share of Maintenance overhead).

Note that the 10% and 5% included in the expressions for M and S represent the proportion of stores requisitions and maintenance call-outs requests calculated for Maintenance and Stores as a preliminary to repeated distribution. We must now solve equations (5.1) and (5.2) to obtain a value for each of M and S:

$$\text{Rearranging gives: } M - 10\%S = £52\ 645 \qquad (5.3)$$

$$\text{and } S - 5\%M = £70\ 555 \qquad (5.4)$$

$$\text{Equation (5.3) multiplied by 10 is: } 10M - S = £526\ 450 \qquad (5.5)$$

Adding equations (5.4) and (5.5) we get:

$$S - 5\%M = £\ \ 70\ 555$$

$$10M - S = £526\ 450$$

$$\overline{9.95M = £597\ 005}$$

M is therefore (£597 005 ÷ 9.95) = £60 001. Substituting this value into equation (5.2):

$$S = £70\ 555 + 5\%(£60\ 001)$$

$$\Rightarrow S = £70\ 555 + £3000$$

$$\Rightarrow S = £73\ 555.$$

Finally, we apportion these values for M and S to Machining, Polishing and Finishing (Table 5.6).

Table 5.6 Reapportionment of algebraically determined support centre overhead

	Amount £	Reapportionment basis	Percentages	Machining £	Polishing £	Finishing £
Totals				136 600	173 040	223 160
Maintenance overhead reapportioned	60 001	No. of maintenance call-outs	60%, 25%, 10%	36 001	15 000	6 000
Dispatch overhead reapportioned	73 555	No. of stores requisitions	50%, 25%, 15%	36 778	18 389	11 033
Total				209 379	206 429	240 193

Comparison of the departmental totals in Table 5.6 with those obtained using repeated distribution in Table 5.5 shows that, allowing for small rounding differences, they are the same. Although the algebraic approach may be less cumbersome than repeated distribution, the calculations involved can become complex where it is necessary to solve more than two simultaneous equations in order to obtain departmental overhead totals for support cost centres (i.e. where there are more than two support centres).

Secondary distribution: which method?

The overhead figures for each of Machining, Polishing and Finishing which result from the different methods of secondary distribution are:

	Machining £	Polishing £	Finishing £
Direct reapportionment	209 277	206 483	240 240
Step reapportionment	209 489	206 201	240 310
Repeated distribution	209 375	206 430	240 195
Algebraic reapportionment	209 379	206 429	240 193

The differences in this particular case are extremely small and there would appear to be little justification for use of a more involved methodology where a simpler one produces substantively the same result. Additionally, it can be argued that, because of the subjectivity inherent to certain apportionment/reapportionment bases, the degree of accuracy implied by the repeated distribution or algebraic methods is misleading. As a general guide, the sophistication of secondary distribution should be governed by:

1 the extent of reciprocal servicing: if negligible, complex secondary distribution is not warranted;
2 the nature of reciprocal servicing: some services may readily be translated into reapportionment bases, possibly rendering a more thorough approach viable;
3 the cost/benefit criterion: the cost of obtaining additional information about reciprocal servicing sufficient to support its recognition in secondary distribution should not outweigh the benefit to be derived from more 'accurate' methodology.

However, it may be the case that increasing accessibility of suitable computer software (and spreadsheets in particular) will enhance recognition of reciprocal servicing where this may breach the cost/benefit criterion if done manually.

The overhead absorption rate

The **overhead absorption rate** (also termed '**recovery**' or '**application**' rate) is the detailed means whereby the departmental overhead for production/front-line cost centres is translated into a cost per unit of output. In general terms, an absorption rate can be defined as:

$$\frac{\text{Overhead cost}}{\text{Volume measure}}$$

There are three important considerations in developing an absorption rate:

1 choice of volume measure;
2 choice between a plantwide or a departmental absorption rate; and
3 choice between an actual or a predetermined absorption rate.

Choice of volume measure

The most appropriate measure of volume (i.e. of output) depends on the precise circumstances; in particular it depends on the nature of the output (e.g. are all cost units identical?) and on the nature of the processes by which this output is produced (e.g. what mix of labour and machine?). In the same way as we did with apportionment/reapportionment bases, we are trying, in the overhead absorption rate, to reflect the underlying cause of the overheads being absorbed.

Exhibit 5.5 contains some further information about RPG Ltd:

RPG Ltd

Estimated overhead costs and other information for the company's three production cost centres is as follows:

	Machining	Polishing	Finishing	Total
Estimated departmental overhead after primary and secondary distribution	£209 375	£206 430	£240 195	£656 000
Estimated machine hours	200 000	40 000	10 000	
Estimated direct labour hours	14 000	42 000	70 000	
Estimated direct labour cost	£300 000	£900 000	£1 500 000	

For the year to which the above estimates apply, management reckons that RPG Ltd's total output will be 220 000 castings, comprising the company's five basic designs plus modifications to these as per customer specification.

Estimated data per unit for one of the company's basic castings are given below:

Catalogue number		C4U
Estimated machine hours:	Machining	50
	Polishing	–
	Finishing	2
Estimated direct labour hours:	Machining	–
	Polishing	5
	Finishing	15
Estimated direct labour cost:	Machining	–
	Polishing	£40
	Finishing	£90

Exhibit 5.5 RPG Ltd – information for absorption rate calculation

At its most basic, 'volume' may be defined in terms of the number of cost units produced:

$$\text{Cost unit absorption rate: } \frac{\text{Overhead cost}}{\text{Number of cost units}}$$

 Using RPG Ltd's total overhead and total output from Exhibit 5.5, calculate a cost unit absorption rate. (Work to two decimal places of £1.)

The absorption rate is:

$$\frac{£656\ 000}{220\ 000\ \text{castings}} = £2.98 \text{ per casting}$$

Therefore every casting produced by RPG Ltd will receive a charge of £2.98 for production overheads *in addition* to its direct costs.

 Study the data in Exhibit 5.5 again. How appropriate is a cost unit absorption rate for RPG Ltd?

As we have just seen, a cost unit absorption rate will charge each cost unit the same amount in respect of production overhead; so every casting will be charged £2.98. The implication of this is that all castings are identical in terms of resource inputs, since they all receive the same charge for overhead. Since RPG Ltd produces five different castings and also customises castings to customer specification, this is extremely unlikely. Using a unit absorption rate in such circumstances may result in a significant distortion of unit costs, particularly where there are major differences in resource inputs between units. A cost unit absorption rate is therefore only appropriate where the units concerned are identical, or very nearly so.

Alternatively, the activity measure used may be machine hours:

$$\text{Machine hour absorption rate: } \frac{\text{Overhead cost}}{\text{Number of machine hours}}$$

Using the data for RPG Ltd's Machining cost centre:

$$\frac{£209\ 375}{200\ 000 \text{ machine hours}} = £1.05 \text{ per machine hour}$$

 Apply the formula above to the data in Exhibit 5.5 and determine an absorption rate per machine hour for the Polishing and Finishing cost centres. (Work to two decimal places of £1.)

For Polishing, we have:

$$\frac{£206\ 430}{40\ 000 \text{ machine hours}} = £5.16 \text{ per machine hour}$$

For Finishing:

$$\frac{£240\ 195}{10\ 000} = £24.02 \text{ per machine hour}$$

Thus, every casting requiring machine-hours in the Polishing and Finishing cost centres will receive, in addition to its direct costs, a charge of £5.16 and £24.02 for each such hour it needs in those departments. From Exhibit 5.5, each C4U casting will receive the following charge for overhead:

	£
Machining overhead (50 machine hours @ £1.05)	52.50
Polishing overhead (0 machine hours @ £5.16)	nil
Finishing overhead (2 machine hours @ £24.02)	48.04
Total overhead charged	100.54

Use of a machine hour absorption rate overcomes the problem of the unit rate discussed above since it can reflect differences in input resources via the overhead charged to cost units. This is important to organisations such as RPG Ltd, where cost units are not uniform. However, using a machine-hour rate for *every* cost centre may be inappropriate: look again at the overhead charged to each C4U using this method: there is a zero charge in respect of Polishing overhead, yet we know from Exhibit 5.5 that this product does pass through that cost centre (but uses only labour hours). The resulting cost could hardly be said to be a reasonable representation of the production resources needed to produce one C4U.

If we use a machine hour absorption rate, we assume that the number of machine hours is the most appropriate measure of activity – i.e. that the output process is predominantly machine-intensive (so that the overhead cost being absorbed is principally incurred in relation to machine operations). While this may be true of RPG Ltd's Machining cost centre, and *may* be true of Polishing, it is manifestly untrue of the Finishing cost centre. Exhibit 5.5 shows that this cost centre is predominantly labour-intensive (70 000 labour hours, compared to 10 000 machine hours).

If a production cost centre's activity is mostly labour-intensive, the overhead absorption rate may use either direct labour hours or direct labour cost as the measure of activity:

$$\text{Direct labour–hour absorption rate: } \frac{\text{Overhead cost}}{\text{Number of direct labour hours}}$$

$$\text{Direct labour–cost absorption rate: } \frac{\text{Overhead cost}}{\text{Direct labour cost}} \times 100\%$$

 Use the formulae given above in conjunction with Exhibit 5.5 to determine, for the Machining cost centre:

an absorption rate per direct labour hour; and
a percentage of direct labour cost absorption rate.

(Work to two decimal places.)

The two labour-based absorption rates are:

Per direct labour hour:

$$\frac{£209\ 375}{14\ 000 \text{ direct labour-hours}} = £14.96 \text{ per direct labour-hour.}$$

$$\text{As a percentage of direct labour cost: } \frac{£209\ 375}{£300\ 000} \times 100\% = 70\%$$

For Polishing and Finishing, the rates are:

	Polishing	Finishing
Per direct labour hour	$\dfrac{£206\ 430}{42\ 000}$	$\dfrac{£240\ 195}{70\ 000}$
	= £4.92	= £3.43
Percentage of labour cost	$\dfrac{£206\ 430}{£900\ 000} \times 100\%$	$\dfrac{£240\ 195}{£1\ 500\ 000} \times 100\%$
	= 23%	= 16%

> ✔ *Apply each of the three absorption rates calculated above to the data for a C4U casting in Exhibit 5.5 to determine each unit's overhead charge.*

The direct labour-hour absorption rate will charge:

	£
Machining (0 hours × £14.96) =	nil
Polishing (5 hours × £4.92) =	24.60
Finishing (15 hours × £3.43) =	51.45
Total overhead charged	76.05

Applying the direct labour cost percentage rate:

	£
Machining (£0 × 70%) =	nil
Polishing (£40 × 23%) =	9.20
Finishing (£90 × 16%) =	14.40
Total overhead charged	23.60

You will see that using a labour-based rate causes the same kind of problem with Machining overhead that we experienced when applying a machine hour rate to Polishing overhead. Each C4U clearly passes through Machining, but uses no labour hours and incurs no labour cost, thereby incurring a zero charge for overhead.

In choosing between the two labour-based absorption rates, we must be guided in the first instance by the nature of the overhead costs which we are trying to absorb. If overhead is predominantly related to the number of labour hours (as supervision may be), then a labour-hour absorption rate is appropriate. If, however, overhead mainly relates to direct labour cost (as would employers' National Insurance contributions in the UK), then the labour cost percentage rate is suitable. Where such relationships cannot be established with reasonable assurance, then choice of absorption rate may be of less significance in terms of the accuracy with which it reflects resource consumption.

It is also possible to base the overhead absorption rate on direct materials' cost or on prime cost (i.e. the sum of all direct costs):

Percentage of direct materials' cost: $\dfrac{\text{Overhead cost}}{\text{Direct materials' cost}} \times 100\%$

Percentage of prime cost: $\dfrac{\text{Overhead cost}}{\text{Prime cost}} \times 100\%$

The problem with use of both of these rates is the same as it is with use of a percentage of direct labour cost rate, namely that situations in which direct materials' *cost* or prime *cost* is the underlying cause of overheads being incurred are somewhat hard to imagine.

What our discussion and calculations above should highlight is the importance of selecting a volume measure which is appropriate to the particular circumstances; an error in this respect may have serious consequences for unit costs, for stock values, for profit and for selling price (if it is based to any extent on cost). Consider two possible overhead charges to the C4U casting:

> £2.98 per unit using a cost unit rate
> £100.54 per unit using a machine hour rate.

This is such a large difference that management's perception of the product's profitability will inevitably be affected by the absorption rate employed. If the wrong rate has been used, incorrect decisions might be made about pricing and, conceivably, whether the product should continue to be produced.

Departmental versus plantwide absorption rate

Our discussion of absorption rates has not, so far, made any distinction between **departmental** and **plantwide** (or **blanket**) rates. The former are developed for individual production cost centres, whereas the latter apply to the whole factory. The cost unit absorption rate we calculated earlier is a plantwide rate, being based on total production overhead and total cost units. A similar approach can be taken with any other measure of activity volume.

 From the data in Exhibit 5.5, obtain RPG Ltd's plantwide machine hour absorption rate. (Work to two decimal places.)

The plantwide rates using machine hours is:

$$\text{Machine hour rate:} \quad \frac{£656\,000}{250\,000} = £2.62 \text{ per machine-hour}$$

The advantage of using plantwide absorption rates lies in their simplicity of calculation. All we need do is determine the total overhead cost and divide by an appropriate activity measure in total for the production cost centres. Because we do not need departmental figures, there is no necessity for primary and secondary apportionments, which undoubtedly represents a considerable saving in time and effort, and possibly an improvement in the 'objectivity' of the absorption rate, since potentially arbitrary apportionment/reapportionment bases are not involved.

 Can you suggest why a plantwide absorption rate may be unsuitable for a company such as RPG Ltd?

The weakness of a plantwide absorption rate is also related to its simplicity; we suggested earlier that RPG's cost units are not uniform – and this is true in terms of both the pattern and extent of their resource consumption. Added to this is the possibility that output procedures may differ from cost centre to cost centre: e.g. may be labour-intensive in one and machine-intensive in another (compare Machining to Finishing, for example). How can we adequately reflect such differences in a single absorption rate?

A plantwide absorption rate is only really workable where there is considerable uniformity of output method and of cost units. In any other circumstances, departmental absorption rates are preferable, since these will enable differences between cost centre output procedures and between cost units to be better reflected in the overhead absorbed.

Actual versus predetermined absorption rate

All our absorption rate calculations have used estimates – of overhead costs and of volume measure: i.e. they are **predetermined absorption rates**. Absorption rates which use actual overhead costs and activity measures are also possible, but could suffer from two very serious limitations:

1 actual costs and activity may not be known until the end of the relevant period; and
2 actual costs and activity may fluctuate within a particular period.

The extent to which these limitations render actual absorption rates impractical will depend on specific circumstances. If there are unlikely to be significant differences between estimated and actual cost and volume of activity (e.g. because they are largely fixed by contract) and if costs/activity occur reasonably evenly throughout the period, then an actual absorption rate is possible.

Where an organisation's situation is more volatile (involving, say, a seasonal pattern of costs and output levels), then use of an actual absorption rate may be inadvisable or impractical. For example, it will not be possible to produce meaningful forecasts of the profit to be reported in published accounts (bearing in mind that absorption costing is required for the published accounts of many organisations). Selling prices which use cost as their basis effectively cannot be set in advance, which could cause difficulties for companies such as RPG Ltd in preparing quotations for castings being made to customer specifications. Unit costs, stock values, profit and perhaps selling prices may fluctuate from month to month within a year merely because of the time of year at which unit costs are calculated. In practical terms, therefore, use of predetermined absorption rates may be a necessity, but these give rise to problems of their own.

Estimation of overhead costs

We examined the topic of cost estimation at length in Chapter 3 and you will recall from our discussion that it is far from straightforward. In the case of overhead, the position may be complicated by the fact that 'overhead' is a generic term, describing the total of a number of different costs. Thus it may be necessary to undertake several estimation exercises for the component elements of a 'global' overhead estimate.

Estimation of volume

The denominator in our overhead absorption rate must also be estimated: that is, we need an estimate of the number of units to be produced, or of machine hours to be worked. The volume selected for the absorption rate calculation can have a major effect on the overhead cost per unit of output, and hence on unit costs; this will be particularly true in organisations with predominantly fixed overheads.

 Why might the selection of a volume measure be of especial significance to absorption of fixed overheads?

The significance lies in the fact that the cost being absorbed is fixed relative to volume of output: e.g. estimated fixed overhead of £500 000 absorbed over a volume of 10 000 units yields £50 per unit whereas the same amount of fixed overhead absorbed over 15 000 units results in a charge of £33.33 per unit. And if, say, the volume is wrongly set at 10 000 units rather than at 15 000, the result will be a unit cost which is overstated by £16.67, which in turn may mean overstated stock values and possibly selling price (and this latter may have an effect on demand).

Note, however, that this problem does not affect variable overhead, since, by definition, the amount of variable overhead will react to changes in volume.

Three broad views of activity level can be taken:

1 **Normal volume** This is a medium-term average volume, allowing for demand over, say, a five-year period and allowing for seasonal and cyclical fluctuations and is the measure which is recommended for use in Statement of Standard Accounting Practice No. 9, which deals with the question of stock valuation in published accounts. The argument in favour of using normal volume is that fluctuations in absorption rate caused by seasonal and cyclical factors are smoothed out, and that, by attempting to approximate longer-term costs in this way, there may be less danger of overemphasising short-term considerations at the expense of the longer-term view.

 Can you see a possible problem with use of normal volume?

The difficulty with using normal volume lies in arriving at a credible estimate spanning the sort of time horizon involved – a problem which may be exacerbated if an organisation's activities are subject to significant cyclical fluctuations.

2 **Practical capacity** Practical capacity is effectively maximum operational capacity. It can be argued that, given the drive for optimum efficiency which exists in almost all organisations, practical capacity provides a reasonable measure of volume. It is also suggested that the underabsorption of overhead which will almost invariably result from use of practical capacity provides management with some measure of the 'cost' of failing to achieve maximum operational capacity; we shall discuss over- and underabsorption of overhead shortly. However, because it is based on maximum volume, practical capacity will yield a lower overhead cost per unit than other volume measures and this may result in under-statement of unit costs. In addition, assuming maximum capacity may have behavioural implications – may, e.g. be viewed as unachievable and therefore not worth striving for.

3 **Annual budgeted volume** This is the expected activity level during the forthcoming year, upon which the organisation's annual budget is based. Unlike normal volume and practical capacity, it reflects current operating conditions and this is the main argument put forward in favour of its use. However, being an annual estimate, it will be subject to cyclical fluctuations from year to year and may fail to reflect the 'cost' of failure to achieve maximum capacity.

Estimation – of both costs and activity – is therefore of crucial importance to determination of an overhead absorption rate, but this leads to the final problem associated with predetermined absorption rates: over- and underabsorption of overhead.

Over- and underabsorption of overhead

It is extremely unlikely that estimates of overhead cost or of activity volume will be wholly accurate predictions of what actually happens.

 If an organisation uses a predetermined absorption rate to charge overheads to cost units, what will be the result if actual overhead and/or volume of activity differ from the estimates used for the absorption rate?

Where the estimates used in producing an absorption rate differ from actual costs and/or volume of activity, the result will be that the overhead absorbed by cost units will differ from the actual amount of overhead incurred:

- If the overhead absorbed *exceeds* the actual overhead, an **overabsorption** of overhead has occurred.
- If the overhead absorbed is *less than* the actual overhead, an **underabsorption** of overhead has occurred.

In either case, the overhead charged to cost units differs from the actual amount, so a correcting adjustment is required in the accounts.

Exhibit 5.6 provides additional information about RPG Ltd:

RPG Ltd

During the year under consideration, the company has used predetermined departmental absorption rates as follows:

Machining: £1.05 per machine-hour. Polishing: £5.16 per machine-hour. Finishing: £3.43 per direct labour-hour.

At the end of the year, actual results were discovered to be:

Actual production overhead incurred: Machining £204 000, Polishing £210 000, Finishing £245 000.

Actual machine-hours worked: Machining 210 000, Polishing 42 000.

Actual direct-labour hours worked: Finishing 68 000.

Exhibit 5.6 RPG Ltd – determination of over/underabsorption of overhead

In order to determine whether RPG Ltd has over- or underabsorbed, we need to compute the total amount of overhead absorbed (based on *actual* volume) and compare this to the overhead incurred.

 From Exhibit 5.6, determine the amount of overhead absorbed by each production cost centre. Compare this to the actual overhead and state the amount of over- or underabsorbed overhead.

The amount of overhead absorbed in each department is calculated as (actual hours × departmental absorption rate):

	£
Machining (210 000 machine-hours × £1.05)	220 500
Polishing (42 000 machine-hours × £5.16)	216 720
Finishing (68 000 direct-labour hours × £3.43)	233 240

Comparison of the absorbed amount with actual gives the over-/underabsorption:

	Actual £	*Absorbed* £	*(Over)/underabsorption* £
Machining	204 000	220 500	(16 500)
Polishing	210 000	216 720	(6 720)
Finishing	245 000	233 240	11 760
Total	659 000	670 460	(11 460)

The overabsorption will be credited to RPG Ltd's profit and loss account for the year in order to reduce the cost charged there (an underabsorption would increase the cost charged to the profit and loss account). We shall illustrate the mechanics of this in Chapter 7 when we examine cost bookkeeping systems.

The overabsorption might be interpreted as a measure of the 'benefit' of bettering estimated volume of activity. But use of overabsorptions (or underabsorptions) in this way may be misleading: remember that there are *two* estimates involved in the predetermined absorption rate – volume and cost – so that an over/underabsorption may have as much (or more) to do with differences between estimated and actual cost as with over/underachievement of estimated volume.

ADMINISTRATION, SELLING AND DISTRIBUTION OVERHEADS

For the purposes of certain organisations' published accounts (in the UK), Statement of Standard Accounting Practice No. 9 requires that stock values reflect the cost of bringing goods to their 'present location and condition'. This effectively means that, for the valuation of stocks in the published accounts of organisations subject to the Standard's provisions, selling and distribution overheads should be excluded. Administration overhead may likewise need to be excluded, though an element may be included as being necessary to bring goods 'to their present location and condition'. Since service organisations cannot keep stocks of their output (see Chapter 11), the problem principally affects manufacturing businesses, where a distinction needs to be drawn between *production overheads* (included in published stock values) and *non-production overheads* (excluded from published stock values). Organisations subject to the requirements of SSAP No. 9 may choose, for *internal* purposes, to include a charge for non-production overheads in unit costs; this might, for example, be done as part of the price-setting exercise to help ensure coverage of all costs by selling price. The problem with absorbing overheads which are not incurred in direct support of output is that the rate used is likely to be merely indicative of the cost being absorbed and the related cost driver. Thus, for example, selling and distribution costs could be absorbed on the basis of sales value (as they are incurred because of sales-related activity):

$$\text{Absorption rate} = \frac{\text{Estimated overhead cost}}{\text{Estimated sales revenue}} \times 100\%$$

 Suggest a possible absorption rate for administration overhead.

Sales revenue could be used as the absorption basis, or alternatively, we could use total production cost (i.e. direct cost + production overhead):

$$\text{Absorption rate} = \frac{\text{Estimated overhead cost}}{\text{Estimated total production cost}} \times 100\%$$

Neither sales revenue nor total production cost is entirely satisfactory, since use of the former could suggest that administration is primarily linked to sales and use of the latter that it is principally production-related; in most cases, administration is likely to be concerned with all organisational activities. It may therefore be preferable to absorb administration overhead on the basis of total cost:

Absorption rate =

$$\frac{\text{Estimated overhead cost}}{\text{(Estimated total production cost} + \text{estimated total non-production cost)}} \times 100\%$$

Absorption rates for non-production overheads (where they are used) are unlikely to improve the 'accuracy' of overhead absorption since the link between overhead cost and volume measure is likely to be tenuous.

SUMMARY

Absorption of overheads can be a complex and even contentious affair but, as the quotations in Exhibit 5.1 make clear, overhead costs are an important item of expenditure in many organisations and their treatment can have significant implications for unit costs, stock values, reported profit and possibly selling prices.

We have seen that:

- Absorption costing takes the view that overheads are necessarily incurred to support output and should therefore be included in unit costs.

- Stock values reported in the published accounts of many organisations must include a charge for appropriate overheads.

- The procedures involved in overhead absorption are summarised in Figure 5.2.

- Apportionment (and reapportionment) bases should use, wherever practicable, an overhead's **cost driver** – i.e. its underlying cause.

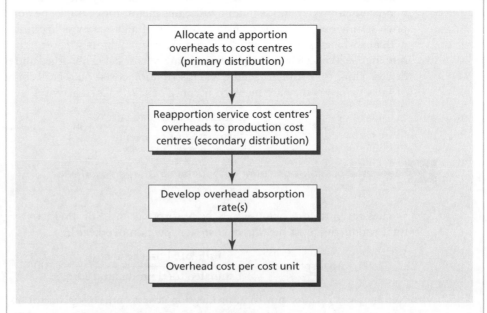

Figure 5.2 Overhead absorption procedures

- Service cost centres' overhead may be reapportioned to production cost centres using:
  - **direct reapportionment** which ignores reciprocal services
  - **step reapportionment** which gives limited recognition to reciprocal services
  - **repeated distribution** or **algebraic reapportionment,** both of which give full recognition to reciprocal services
- In general terms, the absorption rate may be calculated as:

$$\frac{\text{Estimated overhead cost}}{\text{Estimated volume measure}}$$

- Predetermined absorption rates are preferable to actual when actual costs and activity fluctuate within a period and will not be known until the period end.
- Use of predetermined rates requires both cost and volume to be estimated, the latter being based on:
  - **normal volume** *or*
  - **practical capacity** *or*
  - **annual budgeted volume**
- Since the estimates involved in a predetermined absorption rate will differ from actuals, overhead absorbed will not equal overhead incurred:
  - absorbed amount > amount incurred termed **overabsorption**
  - absorbed amount < amount incurred termed **underabsorption**
- Non-production overheads are not absorbed in the published accounts of organisations subject to SSAP9, but may be for internal purposes such as price-setting.

In the next chapter, we will describe and discuss an alternative approach to the absorption of overheads: activity-based costing, which, it is argued, provides unit costs that are a more accurate reflection of the resources consumed in order to achieve output.

FURTHER READING

Elliott, B. and Elliott, J., *Financial Accounting and Reporting* (6th edition), Financial Times Prentice Hall, 2001: Chapter 17 provides detailed coverage of SSAP 9 and stock valuation in published accounts.

SELF-TEST QUESTIONS

5.1 A firm of barristers charges £50 per client/hour for overhead; during the year just ended, the firm underabsorbed by £50 000 on an actual work volume of 11 000 client/hours. Budgeted overhead was £500 000 for the year.
What was the firm's actual overhead for the year?

    A £450 000

    B £500 000

    C £550 000

    D £600 000

5.2 For each of the following statements, tick the appropriate box to indicate whether it is true or false.

	True	False
(a) Normal volume is the estimated output volume for the forthcoming year.	☐	☐
(b) A cost driver is the main underlying cause of an overhead.	☐	☐
(c) Use of a plantwide absorption rate avoids the need for primary and secondary apportionment of overheads.	☐	☐
(d) Overheads which are common to two or more cost centres are allocated to those cost centres.	☐	☐
(e) An underabsorption of overhead requires to be charged to the accounts as an additional cost.	☐	☐

5.3 PT Ltd manufactures and installs a range of commercial and domestic satellite decoders. The company is split into two cost centres, Production and Installation, details of which are as follows:

		Production	*Installation*
Estimated:	Departmental overhead	£240 000	£330 000
	Machine hours	48 000	1 000
	Direct labour hours	2 000	15 000
	No. of units produced/installed	10 000	7 500

Requirement

Compute an appropriate departmental absorption rate for each of Production and Installation, providing a brief justification of the volume measure you have selected in each case.

5.4 A company reapportions the costs incurred by two service cost centres, materials handling and inspection, to the three production cost centres of machining, finishing and assembly. The following are the overhead costs which have been allocated and apportioned to the five cost centres:

	£000
Machining	400
Finishing	200
Assembly	100
Materials handling	100
Inspection	50

Estimates of the benefits received by each cost centre are as follows:

	Machining	Finishing	Assembly	Materials handling	Inspection
	%	%	%	%	%
Materials Handling	30	25	35	–	10
Inspection	20	30	45	5	–

You are required to

(a) calculate the charge for overhead to **each** of the **three** production cost centres, including the amounts reapportioned from the two service centres, using

   (i)   the continuous allotment (or repeated distribution) method, and
   (ii) the algebraic method;   **(15 marks)**

(b) comment on whether re-apportioning service cost centre costs is generally worth while and suggest an alternative treatment for such costs.   **(4 marks)**

(CIMA, *Cost Accounting*, November 1989)

5.5 A manufacturing company uses predetermined rates for absorbing overheads based on the budgeted level of activity. A rate of £22 per labour hour has been calculated for the Assembly Department for which the following overhead expenditure at various activity levels have been estimated:

Total overheads £	Number of labour hours
338 875	14 500
347 625	15 500
356 375	16 500

Requirements

(a) Calculate the variable overhead absorption rate per labour-hour.   **(2 marks)**

(b) Calculate the estimated total fixed overheads.   **(3 marks)**

(c) Calculate the budgeted level of activity in labour hours.   **(3 marks)**

(d) Calculate the amount of under/over recovery of overheads if the actual labour hours were 15 850 and actual overheads were £355 050.   **(2 marks)**

(e) State the arguments for and against using departmental absorption rates as opposed to a single factory-wide rate.   **(5 marks)**

                                                      (Total marks: 15)

(CIMA, *Cost Accounting and Quantitative Methods*, May 1998)

QUESTIONS WITHOUT ANSWERS

5.6 Budgeted overheads for a period were £340 000. In the event, actual labour hours and overheads were 21 050 hours and £343 825 respectively.

If there was overabsorption of £14 025, how many labour-hours were budgeted?

A 20 000
B 20 225
C 20 816
D 21 050

(CIMA, *Cost Accounting and Quantitative Methods*, May 1998)

5.7 Overhead apportionment is used to

A charge whole items of costs to cost centres.
B charge cost units with an appropriate share of overheads.
C spread common costs over cost centres.
D ensure budgeted overheads are not exceeded.

(CIMA, *Cost Accounting and Quantitative Methods*, May 1999)

The following information is to used for questions 5.8 and 5.9:

Budgeted overheads	£493 200
Budgeted machine hours	10 960
Actual machine hours	10 493
Actual overheads	£514 157

5.8 Based on the data above, what is the machine-hour absorption rate?

A £45.00
B £46.91
C £47.00
D £49.00

(CIMA, *Cost Accounting and Quantitative Methods*, November 1998)

5.9 Based on the data above, what is the amount of the overhead under/overabsorbed?

A £20 957 underabsorbed.
B £21 015 overabsorbed.
C £21 015 underabsorbed.
D £41 972 underabsorbed.

(CIMA, *Cost Accounting and Quantitative Methods*, November 1998)

5.10 Hillage Contracting produces a variety of products, one of which is the EOW1. EOW1s are produced in batches of 1000 units.

The company has two production departments and two service departments, all of which contribute to the production of EOW1s.

In a period 3000 EOW1s are produced and the costs detailed below are the total costs and activity in the period for the company.

Total costs for the period

	Production Department 1	Production Department 2	Service Department 1	Service Department 2
	£000	£000	£000	£000
Direct labour	500	300		
Direct materials	170	250		
Direct expenses	50	40		
Indirect labour	80	60	100	150
Indirect materials	3	3	50	70
Indirect expenses	17	40	10	20
	820	693	160	240

Service department 1 charges its costs using a cost estimate. The relevant percentages are 30% to production department 1, 60% to production department 2 and 10% service department 2.

Service department 2 charges its costs using a time estimate. The estimates of time are 1000 hours for production department 1, 3500 hours for production department 2 and 500 hours for service department 1.

Reciprocal charges between the service departments are made.

The total hours forecast in the time period are (in thousands):

	Production departments	
	1	2
Direct labour-hours	40	30
Machine-hours	10	50

The direct costs and hours spent producing EOW1s in the period has been established using labour, stock and accounting systems as follows:

	Production Department 1	Production Department 2
	£000	£000
Direct labour	20.3	11.5
Direct materials	12.5	12.2
Direct expenses	4.3	10.4
Total direct costs	37.1	34.1
Direct labour hours	500 hours	200 hours
Machine hours	300 hours	450 hours

Requirement

(a) Calculate the full absorption cost of a single batch of EOW1s in the period.

(12 marks)

(b) Explain the advantages and disadvantages of using a single rate for absorbing overheads compared to departmental rates. (4 marks)

(c) Outline the arguments for and against the use of absorption costing for internal reporting. (4 marks)

(Total: 20 marks)

(CIPFA, *Management Accounting*, June 1997)

5.11 A company has two production departments (A and B), and two service departments (Y and Z), in its factory. The four departments are each treated as cost centres.

Certain production overhead cost elements are collected directly at cost centre level, while others are collected on a factory-wide basis and apportioned to cost centres using a single key driver for each cost element.

It is estimated that the benefit derived from the service departments is as follows:

Department Y:
Department A	65%
Department B	30%
Department Z	5%

Department Z:
Department A	50%
Department B	40%
Department Y	10%

Cost centre overhead absorption rates are determined using key cost driver(s) for each department. Sixty per cent of the overheads for Department A are particularly influenced by the direct labour costs of the department, and the remainder by machine hours. In Department B, the key cost driver is direct labour hours.

Budgeted production overheads, by cost element/department for a period, and key cost driver data are as follows:

	Total	Department			
		A	**B**	**Y**	**Z**
Cost element (£000)					
Indirect labour	582.6	186.2	235.2	74.1	87.1
Indirect materials	125.6	53.5	38.6	28.2	5.3
Machine depreciation	165.1	108.0	30.7	14.0	12.4
Space costs (rent, rates, heat, light, power, buildings insurance)	207.0				
Machinery insurance	41.5				
Management and supervision	204.6				
Cost driver					
Floor space (m²)	110	55	33	15	7
Capital value of machinery (£000)	1025	580	201	125	119
Machine-hours (000)	566	410	156		
Direct labour-hours (000)	670	310	360		
Direct labour costs (£000)	4126	1772	2354		

Required

(a) Explain the rationale for establishing the production overhead cost of a product.

(2 marks)

(b) Establish the total budgeted production overhead costs for each of the two production departments, using the algebraic method to apportion service department costs. (Show workings clearly and round to one decimal place of £000 throughout). **(12 marks)**

(c) Determine the production overhead absorption rates to be applied in each production department.

(6 marks)

(Total: 20 marks)

(ACCA, *Management Information*, June 1998)

CHAPTER 6

Activity-based costing

Activity-based costing for beginners

Most businesses today use standard costing techniques for their product or service costing. While easy to understand and apply, with the exception of factory or operational direct costs, they fail to apportion or allocate other business costs on a realistic basis – costs such as manufacturing indirect, sales and marketing, customer service, R & D, purchasing, supply, IT support and personnel. Standard costing apportions these on an arbitrary basis – direct labour hours, square metres, number of units produced or sold, number of customers etc. In a non-manufacturing or service business, the problem is understandably more acute, with very little cost being allocated on a true basis.

ABC takes a rational approach to product, service and customer costing, identifying what major activities are performed in each function across the business. An assessment is made of how much company resource is actually consumed by each activity, 'resource' meaning anything that is a cost to the business, i.e. employee time, assets, money etc. These are allocated to activities using appropriate methods dependent on the type of resource to be allocated ... the aim being to establish a true cost for each activity, based on the consumption of all resources.

The next step establishes what causes or 'drives' each activity and the relationship between the driver and a product, service or customer, if such relationship exists ...

Source: John McKenzie, *Management Accounting*, March 1999.

Exhibit 6.1 An overview of activity-based costing

INTRODUCTION

In the previous chapter, we illustrated the 'traditional' approach to absorption of overheads. The methodology we described was developed in manufacturing industry around the beginning of the twentieth century. At that time, product ranges were much smaller and production processes much simpler than they are today. Direct costs – and direct labour in particular – formed a much more significant percentage of total cost than they presently do. Against this sort of background, inaccuracies in overhead costing brought about by the rather arbitrary nature of some of the procedures we described in the previous chapter were probably not a major problem. However, today's economic and operational environment is markedly different. Manufactured output no longer predominates, with service industries and organisations (see Chapter 11) accounting for a large proportion of economic activity in many countries. The ranges of products and services being offered are wide and diverse – and, moreover, are being offered within an increasingly competitive global market. Production processes are complex and increasingly capital-intensive. In many organisations, overhead may represent a higher percentage of total cost than direct costs.

It is therefore argued (as, for example, in Exhibit 6.1) that the kind of overhead cost distortions that could be caused by the procedures we described in Chapter 5 are unacceptable. Activity-based costing (ABC) was developed in the late 1980s to remedy perceived defects in the 'traditional' approach to dealing with overheads. In this chapter, we describe and illustrate ABC, before discussing the extent to which the newer methodology improves upon its more established counterpart.

OBJECTIVES

When you have completed this chapter, you will be able to:

- appreciate the factors which led to dissatisfaction with 'traditional' absorption methodology;
- explain the rationale underlying ABC;
- distinguish between activities, cost pools and cost drivers;
- develop cost driver absorption rates and apply these to cost units;
- compare and contrast ABC and 'traditional' systems of overhead absorption.

FACTORS LEADING TO DISSATISFACTION WITH 'TRADITIONAL' METHODOLOGY

ABC developed from a feeling (see Cooper, 1990; Cooper and Kaplan 1988) that the 'traditional' approach to absorption of overheads not only inadequately reflected increasingly complex products, services and processes within many organisations but also failed to deliver cost information that was useful and relevant in a dynamic operating environment. We can identify two linked sets of arguments supporting the perceived inadequacy of 'traditional' absorption methods.

Processes and cost structure

As we suggested in the Introduction, the processes by which output is produced are much more complex than they once were. In manufacturing businesses, we have seen the emergence and rapid growth of advanced manufacturing technologies (AMTs): robotics, computer-aided design and manufacture (CAD-CAM), for instance. As production processes have become more capital-intensive, cost structures have changed. For many businesses, direct costs now represent a smaller proportion of total cost than overheads – and in absolute amount, overhead costs are often very large. At the same time, the manufacturing base in many economies has been shrinking, with service organisations assuming increasing importance. As we shall see in Chapter 11, one of the hallmarks of many service organisations is the high incidence of overhead costs. In these circumstances, it can be argued that an approach to overhead absorption that is (or is believed to be) arbitrary, is inadequate. The need for more accurate cost information is reinforced by the fact that many businesses now operate in global markets characterised by fierce international competition. In localised markets, competition may have been less intense, competitors were probably using pretty much the same costing methods, and the consequences of inaccurate unit costs may not have had particularly serious implications.

Complexity versus volume

A further characteristic of most organisations' operational environment is the complexity of output processes. If you review the absorption rates we developed in the previous chapter, you will appreciate that they are all derived from the volume of output. In some cases, 'traditional' absorption rates reflect volume directly – the cost unit, machine hour and direct labour hour rates fall into this category. Other 'traditional' rates, based on direct cost percentages, reflect output volume indirectly; for example, direct labour cost may be assumed to increase/decrease roughly in line with increases/decreases in volume of output. Such an approach may be appropriate to production processes that are fairly uniform across different products, or to limited product ranges; it may, however, be too simplistic a representation of complex output processes and diverse product ranges. This problem becomes even more evident when we consider service organisations, where input–output relationships generally have little to do with volume, but derive from factors like the nature and complexity of the service being provided, or even from the knowledge required to provide it. (See Chapter 11 for further discussion of service costing.)

In addition, many overhead costs will bear little relationship to volume of output: building occupancy costs and material receipt and inspection costs, for example, have only the most tenuous link with output volume. Absorbing such costs as if they are linked with volume could give a completely misleading view of cost behaviour patterns, resulting not only in inaccurate unit costs but also possibly in incorrect decisions by management.

We will use the information in Exhibit 6.2 to demonstrate the potential inapplicability of a volume-based absorption rate to a service organisation.

 From the information in Exhibit 6.2, calculate the company's existing departmental overhead absorption rates. (Work to two decimal places of £1.)

The departmental absorption rates are:

$$\frac{\text{Estimated overhead cost}}{\text{Estimated tutor hours}}$$

For Bookkeeping, we get

$$\frac{£170\,710}{15\,000} = £11.38 \text{ per tutor hour}$$

and for Secretarial

$$\frac{£263\,290}{19\,000} = £13.86 \text{ per tutor hour}$$

 Use these absorption rates to obtain an overhead charge to each Introduction to spreadsheets *and* Advanced shorthand *course.*

Success Direct Ltd

This company provides correspondence courses on a variety of business-related subjects, and is presently organised into four departments that are also designated cost centres: Bookkeeping Courses, Secretarial Courses, Reprographic Services and Dispatch. Bookkeeping Courses and Secretarial Courses are the front-line cost centres, with Reprographic Services and Dispatch providing support services.

Estimated overhead costs and other information for the two front-line cost centres are as follows:

	Bookkeeping	Secretarial	Total
Estimated departmental overhead after primary and secondary distribution	£170 710	£263 290	£434 000
Estimated computer hours	60 000	100 000	160 000
Estimated tutor (direct labour) hours	15 000	19 000	34 000
Estimated tutor salary (direct labour) cost	£178 000	£234 000	£412 000
Number of different courses offered	10	5	15
Estimated total number of courses offered (i.e. cost units)	4 000	12 000	16 000

Estimated data per student for two specific courses are given below:

	Introduction to spreadsheets	Advanced shorthand
Estimated computer hours:		
Bookkeeping	195	nil
Secretarial	5	nil
Estimated tutor (direct labour) hours:		
Bookkeeping	10	nil
Secretarial	1	30
Estimated tutor (direct labour) cost:		
Bookkeeping	£120	nil
Secretarial	£ 12	£360
Estimated direct material cost (course manuals)	£ 50	£ 20

At present, Success Direct Ltd absorbs overhead on the basis of predetermined departmental tutor hour rates.

Exhibit 6.2 Correspondence school – overhead absorption

Each *Introduction to spreadsheets* course will absorb:

	£
Bookkeeping (10 tutor hours × £11.38)	113.80
Secretarial (1 tutor hour × £13.86)	13.86
	127.66

The amount absorbed by each *Advanced shorthand* course is:

	£
Bookkeeping (nil tutor hours × £11.38)	nil
Secretarial (30 tutor hours × £13.86)	415.80
	415.80

A quick glance at Exhibit 6.2 suggests that the overhead costs per course that we have just calculated are, at best, only a rough indication of the resources required to produce each course (i.e. of the complexity of output processes). For example, the heavy use of computer time on *Introduction to spreadsheets* is ignored in the absorption calculation for that course, as is use of course manuals on both *Introduction to spreadsheets* and *Advanced shorthand*. The potential distortion to unit costs caused by this approach to overhead absorption is compounded if we consider the estimated total overhead absorbed by each cost centre:

Bookkeeping (15 000 tutor hours × £11.38)	£170 700
Secretarial (19 000 tutor hours × £13.86)	£263 340

(Note that the departmental totals above do not tally exactly with those in Exhibit 6.2 because the absorption rates have been rounded to two decimal places.)

What should be obvious from the departmental totals for overhead absorbed is that the cost centre with the higher volume of output (Secretarial) absorbs a markedly higher percentage of overhead than the cost centre with the lower volume of output. This ignores not only major resource inputs (computer hours and course manuals), but also the range of different courses being offered in each cost centre – 10 in Bookkeeping as opposed to only five in Secretarial. It can be argued that the low-volume courses place as great a demand (perhaps even a greater demand) on support services as high-volume courses; the same might also be said of a wider (as opposed to a narrower) range of courses. A traditional approach to overhead absorption masks – or might even completely reverse – very real differences of this sort, tending to absorb too little overhead into the cost of low-volume products/services while absorbing too much into the cost of high-volume products/services.

The assumptions of our tutor-hour absorption rate are therefore:

1 that overhead costs are principally linked with tutor hours; and
2 that volume of output – as measured by the number of tutor hours – is the main determinant of overhead.

In Success Direct Ltd's circumstances, both assumptions are questionable. If this is so, how can we develop a more rational approach to overhead absorption?

THE RATIONALE FOR ABC

The fundamental principle upon which ABC is based is understanding cost behaviour in relation to products/services, coupled with recognition of the fact that, in the long term, all costs are variable. When we discussed cost estimation in Chapter 3, we made the point that estimation techniques were somewhat limited by their assumption that cost behaviour was influenced by a single factor (typically volume of output). ABC, with its recognition of different activities, each having its own cost driver, may go some way towards remedying this shortcoming.

The view of cost taken by ABC is essentially different from that taken by 'traditional' methods; the latter tend to reflect *acquisition* of the resources required to support output, whereas ABC attempts to reflect *consumption* of resources to support output. ABC views the organisation as a collection of activities that incur costs; products/services consume activities in their production. The key to ABC is therefore identifying

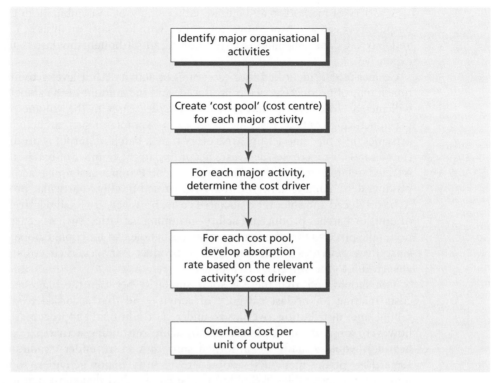

Figure 6.1 ABC system in outline

how units of product/service consume activities – i.e. identifying each activity's **cost driver** (see Chapter 5 and below) and using this to absorb overhead into cost units.

Figure 6.1 illustrates an ABC system in outline. We now need to examine the various elements of Figure 6.1 in more detail.

DESIGN AND OPERATION OF AN ABC SYSTEM

Identification of major activities

Identification of major activities requires a balance to be struck between the desire for accurate cost data and the cost/benefit criterion. On the one hand, we could take a broad view of the word 'major', ending up with dozens of activities (plus related cost pools and absorption rates). This, however, is unlikely to be cost effective, and it is doubtful whether the resulting cost data will be sufficiently accurate to justify the time, cost and effort involved. Alternatively, we could take a more pragmatic view and pool related, but on their own comparatively insignificant, activities to form a single major activity. For example, in some organisations, material receipt/inspection and material handling could be of sufficient importance to be designated separate activities; in others, they might be combined into a single activity.

✔ *How might an organisation set about identifying its major activities?*

A variety of methods may be used, either singly or in combination: examination of output processes and procedures, interviews with key staff, analysis of job descriptions and payroll data, engaging external consultants (though this last is likely to prove expensive).

Cooper (1990) identified four categories of activity. **Unit-level activities** occur every time a unit of product/service is produced, and the amount of the associated total cost will increase/decrease in line with increases/decreases in the volume of output; in a manufacturing context, machine usage is an example of such an activity. **Batch-level activities**, like machine set-up, arise every time a batch of output is produced; the associated total cost increases/decreases according to the number of batches produced, but is fixed relative to units within each batch. **Product-sustaining activities**, such as product design and enhancement, are performed to allow particular products/services to be produced and sold; the associated costs, however, are fixed relative to the number of units or batches produced. **Facility-sustaining activities**, such as general administration, take place so that the organisation as a whole can function; Cooper suggests that, since these activities are common to all products/services, their costs should not be absorbed into the unit cost of output.

You should note that there is some similarity between the suggested treatment of costs relating to the last category of activity and that accorded to administration, selling and distribution overheads under a 'traditional' approach (see Chapter 5); however, some of the costs relating to facility-sustaining activities (e.g. lighting and heating) would usually be absorbed into unit costs under 'traditional' methods. Regardless of the method(s) adopted to identify major activities, some element of judgement is inevitable. It should also be emphasised that most major activities will cross traditional departmental boundaries. In general terms, there are probably three criteria that should be borne in mind when defining major activities:

1 Is the activity significant in terms of cost?
2 Is the activity a key element of output processes and procedures?
3 Is it possible to identify a single cost driver (see below) that adequately explains how most of an activity's costs arise?

If activities are defined too narrowly, criteria 1 and 2 above are unlikely to be satisfied; too broadly, and criterion 3 may not be met.

Create a cost pool for each major activity

For each major activity identified, we create an **overhead cost pool** to collect the associated costs. In other words, we are designating each activity a **cost centre**. Although the two terms are therefore pretty much synonymous, we will use 'cost pool' in an ABC context to help avoid the departmental connotation of 'cost centre'.

Allocate and apportion overhead costs to cost pools

Exhibit 6.3 contains further information about Success Direct Ltd.

 Using the data in Exhibit 6.3, complete the overhead analysis sheet in Table 6.1 by allocating and apportioning Success Direct Ltd's overheads to each of the company's main activities.

Success Direct Ltd: Overhead costs, activities and cost pools

The company is considering the use of ABC to absorb overheads. Investigation has revealed four major activities: tutoring, computer-related, course materials and communication. The following overhead costs have been extracted from next year's budget working papers:

	£		£
Computer consumables	34 000	Printing costs	35 000
Insurance: computers	2 000	Phone/fax/e-mail	48 000
printing equipment	3 000	Postage and stationery	16 000
Supervising tutor's salary	40 000	Tutoring indirect labour costs	48 000
Travel and subsistence for tutors	30 000	Software	26 000
Maintenance: computers	18 000	Sundry tutoring overhead	30 000
printing equipment	22 000	Print room supervision	20 700
fax	3 000	Lease of digital communication line	20 300

In addition to the overheads above, which can be allocated to the appropriate activity's cost pool, £38 000 requires to be apportioned across tutoring, computer-related, course materials and communication in the proportions 20 : 8 : 6 : 4.

Exhibit 6.3 Allocation and apportionment of overhead to cost pools

Table 6.1 Incomplete ABC overhead analysis sheet

Overhead cost	Tutoring cost pool	Computer-related cost pool	Course materials cost pool	Communication cost pool
Computer consumables		£34 000		
Printing costs			£35 000	
Insurance				
Phone/fax/e-mail				
Postage and stationery				
Supervising tutor's salary				
Tutoring indirect labour costs				
Travel and subsistence for tutors				
Software				
Maintenance				
Sundry tutoring overhead				
Print room supervision				
Lease of digital communication line				
Other				
TOTALS				

Table 6.2 is the completed overhead analysis sheet showing allocations and apportionments to each of the four main activities.

If you compare the allocation and apportionment procedures we have just completed with those described in the last chapter, you will see that:

1 secondary distribution is unnecessary; and
2 the proportion of allocations (as opposed to apportionments) is greater, which ought to reduce the subjectivity of the absorption exercise – a point we shall return to later in the chapter.

Identifying the cost driver for each activity

Before we can develop absorption rates for each cost pool, we need to identify each activity's **cost driver**. As we saw in the previous chapter, a cost driver is the main underlying cause of the cost associated with an activity.

 Suggest a suitable cost driver for each of Success Direct Ltd's main activities: tutoring, computer-related, course materials and communication.

A suitable cost driver for each activity might be:

- tutoring   number of tutor hours
- computer-related   number of computer hours
- course materials   number of course manuals
- communication   number of course assignments

Table 6.2 Completed ABC overhead analysis sheet

Overhead cost	Tutoring cost pool	Computer-related cost pool	Course materials cost pool	Communication cost pool
Computer consumables		£34 000		
Printing costs			£35 000	
Insurance		£2 000	£3 000	
Phone/fax/e-mail				£48 000
Postage and stationery				£16 000
Supervising tutor's salary	£40 000			
Tutoring indirect labour costs	£48 000			
Travel and subsistence for tutors	£30 000			
Software		£26 000		
Maintenance		£18 000	£22 000	£3 000
Sundry tutoring overhead	£30 000			
Print room supervision			£20 700	
Lease of digital communication line				£20 300
Other	£20 000	£8 000	£6 000	£4 000
TOTALS	£168 000	£88 000	£86 700	£91 300

You may have suggested different cost drivers from those above. As with identification of major activities, some judgement will be involved, and it may be necessary to interview key staff, utilise operational research techniques, or employ external consultants in order to obtain a satisfactory result. In our example, all the cost drivers relate to the number of times a particular event occurs. While this might be suitable for Success Direct Ltd's activities, it may be unsuitable in other circumstances.

Machine set-up costs, for instance, *may* be driven by the number of machine set-ups that occur – but it could equally well be that the time required for different set-ups is the main determinant of the associated cost. We therefore need to be careful not to leap to the wrong conclusion about cost drivers. In some situations, it may be impossible (or too costly) to quantify a cost driver directly; suppose material handling costs are driven by the relative fragility of different materials – here, we might apply weightings to indicate the cost driver, with the most fragile materials receiving the highest weightings.

Broadly speaking, selection of cost drivers should be guided by the following considerations:

1 they should be readily measurable;
2 they should provide a link between overhead costs and outputs;
3 they should represent a reasonably accurate measure of how most (not necessarily all) costs associated with an activity are incurred – if they do not, then the resulting absorption rates will be every bit as arbitrary as those derived from 'traditional' methodology;
4 their identification, quantification and use should conform with the cost/benefit criterion.

Developing cost driver absorption rates

The final stage in ABC procedures is to combine the amount in each overhead cost pool with the related cost driver to obtain an absorption rate. Exhibit 6.4 presents relevant information about Success Direct Ltd.

Success Direct Ltd

Based on the company's usual absorption methods, departmental absorption rates for next year are:

Bookkeeping   £11.38 per tutor hour   Secretarial   £13.86 per tutor hour

The company is considering the use of ABC to absorb overheads, and investigation has revealed the following:

Activity	Estimated overhead cost pool £	Cost driver
Tutoring	168 000	34 000 tutor hours
Computer-related	88 000	160 000 computer hours
Course materials	86 700	9 000 course manuals
Communication	91 300	100 000 course assignments
	434 000	

▶

The following estimated information relates to two specific courses:

		Introduction to Spreadsheets	Advanced shorthand
Computer hours		200	nil
Course manuals		5	2
Tutor hours:	Bookkeeping	10	nil
	Secretarial	1	30
Assignments		6	20

Exhibit 6.4 Success Direct Ltd – cost pools and cost drivers

 Using the data in Exhibit 6.4, determine, for each activity, the absorption rate per unit of cost driver. (Work to two decimal places of £1.)

On an activity basis, the absorption rates are:

Tutoring: $\dfrac{\text{Overhead cost pool}}{\text{Tutor-hours}} = \dfrac{£168\,000}{34\,000} = £4.94$ per tutor hour

Computer-related: $\dfrac{\text{Overhead cost pool}}{\text{Computer-hours}} = \dfrac{£88\,000}{160\,000} = £0.55$ per computer hour

Course materials: $\dfrac{\text{Overhead cost pool}}{\text{Course manuals}} = \dfrac{£86\,700}{9000} = £9.63$ per manual

Communication: $\dfrac{\text{Overhead cost pool}}{\text{Course assignments}} = \dfrac{£91\,300}{100\,000} = £0.91$ per assignment

We can now compare the overhead absorbed by each of the courses in Exhibit 6.4 under each approach. Using the 'traditional' departmental absorption rates, we get:

	Introduction to spreadsheets £	Advanced shorthand £
Bookkeeping overhead: 10/nil tutor hours @ £11.38	113.80	nil
Secretarial overhead: 1/30 tutor hours @ £13.86	13.86	415.80
Total overhead charged to course	127.66	415.80

Determine the total overhead charged to each course using the ABC absorption rates calculated above.

Applying the ABC absorption rates to each job gives:

	Introduction to spreadsheets £	Advanced shorthand £
Tutoring overhead: 11/30 tutor hours @ £4.94	54.34	148.20
Computer-related overhead: 200/nil computer hours @ £0.55	110.00	nil
Course materials: 5/2 course manuals @ £9.63	48.15	19.26
Communication: 6/20 assignments @ £0.91	5.46	18.20
Total overhead charged to course	217.95	185.66

As you can see, there is a substantial difference in the total overhead charged to each course under the 'traditional' and ABC methods: an increase of roughly 71% for the 'spreadsheet' course, compared to a decrease of about 55% for 'shorthand'. Differences will likewise occur across Success Direct Ltd's entire range of courses. Changing the method of absorbing overhead will alter the comparative cost and profitability of different courses – and may also cause changes in their selling prices. Since choice of absorption method could have a material effect on management perceptions about cost and related issues, we need to consider which approach (if either) is 'superior'.

'TRADITIONAL' ABSORPTION COSTING AND ABC COMPARED

There are several areas where comparison of the two systems is worthwhile, and we discuss these below.

Reflection of resource inputs to support outputs

We have already said that absorption rates based on 'simple' activity measures such as direct labour or machine hours may be unrepresentative of complex relationships between support activities and outputs. Closer inspection of the two sets of overhead figures calculated above might suggest why ABC could be superior in this respect. Assuming tolerable accuracy in identification and quantification of activities, cost drivers and overhead costs, the very calculation of a greater range of absorption rates should allow ABC to more accurately reflect consumption of support resources by output. For example, ABC gives overhead charges which explicitly show the two courses' differing requirements for tutor *and* computer hours; under the 'traditional' approach, this difference is not apparent in the overhead charged to each job because computer-related costs (and the reason for their being incurred) are 'hidden' within the single-activity departmental absorption rates. What this means is that:

1 we cannot determine the charge made to each course in respect of computer-related costs; and
2 the 'Advanced shorthand' course has received some charge for computer-related costs, even although no computer hours are actually required to provide the course.

In circumstances such as those we have just described, unit overhead costs derived from ABC will give a more accurate picture of input/output relationships.

The subjectivity 'problem'

In the previous chapter, we described the potential subjectivity of apportionment/re-apportionment bases in the context of the 'traditional' absorption methodology. It is possible that ABC might improve this aspect of overhead absorption. Looking at Success Direct Ltd, we can see from Exhibit 6.2 that, under the 'traditional' methodology, the company has two front-line cost centres (Bookkeeping Courses and Secretarial Courses), along with two support cost centres (Reprographic Services and Dispatch). Before overhead can be absorbed into cost units, primary and secondary distribution of overheads must occur. ABC, however, removes the need for secondary distribution, allocating and apportioning overhead to the four cost pools from which overhead is to be absorbed. For Success Direct Ltd, only £38 000 of total overhead (£434 000) requires apportionment under ABC – i.e. less than 10%. Elimination of secondary distribution ought, therefore, to reduce subjectivity in treatment of overheads.

Apart from removing secondary distribution, does ABC reduce subjectivity? This really depends on specific circumstances – in particular on an organisation's cost structure and definition of major activities. If, for example, activities are defined very narrowly, it is possible that apportionment could still play a large part in treatment of overhead; but such narrow definition of activities could be beneficial in terms of more rational absorption rates. If, on the other hand, activities are defined fairly broadly, less apportionment is likely to be needed – but at the potential expense of less objectivity in absorption rates.

What might happen in many cases is that, by changing the cost objective from departmentally based cost centres to activity-based cost pools, different costs require to be allocated and apportioned under each approach. Consider the cost of departmental supervision: using the 'traditional' method, this cost would typically be allocated to the appropriate cost centre. In an ABC environment, and in view of the fact that many activities will cross departmental boundaries, departmental supervision costs may well need to be apportioned across a number of different cost pools. Conversely, costs that may require apportionment under the 'traditional' approach (e.g. machine maintenance) may be allocated under ABC.

Regardless of absorption methodology, there are likely to be costs which will have to be dealt with somewhat arbitrarily. Costs associated with product-sustaining activities could present this sort of problem; research and development costs, for example. Even if research and development is treated as a separate activity in ABC (allowing allocation of R&D costs to the related cost pool), there remains the problem of devising an objective absorption rate.

Thus we should be careful about making unrealistic claims for ABC. As Ahmed and Scapens (1991) observe, ABC is unlikely to be able to relate all overhead to activities.

Cost drivers as absorption rates

Where possible, using the cost driver as absorption rate makes sense, given that it is the underlying cause of the cost being absorbed, which is preferable to employing a more general activity measure, such as machine hours. But using cost drivers in this way may pose problems:

1 It may be difficult to identify the cost driver; e.g. the cost driver for Success Direct Ltd's communication cost was stated to be the number of assignments – it could also be the number of students, number of courses, relative complexity of courses, or a combination of all four.

2 It may be difficult to quantify the cost driver once identified: e.g. 'relative complexity of courses'.

3 Where there are problems identifying/quantifying cost drivers, any related absorption rate must be open to question.

4 Once identified, quantified and related to output, it will almost certainly be true that the cost driver is, at best, the *main* underlying cause of the costs within a particular pool: e.g. each of Success Direct Ltd's overhead cost pools contains an apportionment (albeit a small one) of overhead costs, which are not driven by any of the factors identified in Exhibit 6.4; if one/more separate cost pools were to be set up to deal with the cost which presently requires apportionment, problems 2 and 3 above may be very much in evidence.

However, what we have just said does not mean that cost drivers cannot or should not be used as absorption rates, but that complete causal accuracy may need to be traded off against practicality and the cost/benefit criterion.

More accurate unit costs

Assuming major activities have been well defined and cost drivers correctly identified and quantified, then, as we saw with Success Direct Ltd's two courses earlier in the chapter, ABC will produce unit costs which better reflect the pattern of resource consumption required for output than 'traditional' absorption methods. But we are not claiming 100% accuracy for ABC-generated costs. In the right circumstances, ABC may improve the quality of cost information; subjectivity, although potentially reduced in comparison with the 'traditional' approach, still exists – and to the extent that it does, unit costs under ABC retain an element of inaccuracy.

Identifying activities

Traditional absorption costing systems tend, on the whole, to attribute overheads to departments, which at least has the merit of simplicity, but which may result in a rather inflexible approach in the context of a dynamic environment. But although there is greater potential flexibility in an activity basis, this may itself create a difficulty. Many activities (such as computing at Success Direct Ltd) cross departmental boundaries, which may make them difficult to define with reasonable precision, especially where there are differences in the exact nature of apparently identical activities being carried on in (or on behalf of) several departments. This could, in turn, affect the cost driver: e.g. in Success Direct Ltd, communication costs for Bookkeeping may be driven by the complexity of courses provided, whereas for Secretarial, the same cost might be driven by the number of assignments. In such circumstances, we may either need to develop a cost driver rate for each department, which raises the problem of apportioning computing costs between departments, or may require to revert to a 'traditional' departmental absorption rate.

Cost of setting up and operating absorption systems

Whether it be 'traditional' or ABC, there are costs involved in installing and operating an absorption costing system: estimates of costs and activity measure(s) need to be made, actual costs and activity measure(s) must be recorded and data for apportionment (and possibly reapportionment) bases must be found. Some of this information will be available as a matter of routine (e.g. budgeted and actual costs) and some may be readily obtained – but it must be recognised that there is nevertheless a cost involved, and the significance of the cost/benefit criterion should be borne in mind. It might be that the more complex analysis required by ABC could impose additional costs for information-gathering and updating such that the associated benefit is outweighed. In many cases, adoption of ABC necessitates the use of external consultants to identify activities/cost drivers, which could be prohibitively expensive.

ABC as a control aid

One important argument advanced in support of ABC is its use as an aid to cost control: if the major activities and related cost drivers can be identified then any action to reduce the incidence of either or both should have the effect of reducing the related costs. However, it may also be argued that, where some dubiety attaches to the definition of activities and/or cost drivers, this is a questionable benefit of ABC. It is also argued that identification of an organisation's major activities should help management distinguish between those which are 'value-added' and those which are 'non-value-added', thereby allowing cost reduction effort to be targeted at the latter type of activity. We shall discuss these aspects of ABC in Chapters 17 and 18.

'Traditional' versus ABC approaches: a final word

Our discussion of the two broad approaches to absorption costing suggests that each has its strengths and weaknesses – this is not to say that they are mutually exclusive. It is possible to incorporate the 'best' elements of each within a single system: for example, trying to use cost drivers to define apportionment bases, using multiple absorption rates rather than plantwide or 'simple' departmental ones, and avoiding nebulous definitions of activities and cost drivers. In addition, several features of absorption costing are common to both approaches: e.g. the need for care in selection of a volume measure is every bit as important in ABC as in the 'traditional' method; predetermined absorption rates are a practical necessity whether these are based on 'simple' measures such as machine hours or on the relevant cost driver. Possibly, as we shall see in Chapter 12, the debate should not be about which method of absorption costing is better, but whether absorption costing is itself of limited value in many situations.

Friedman and Lyne (1997) suggest an interesting advantage to adoption of ABC:

> ... where activity-based techniques have been implemented [by companies interviewed], management accounting information will be considered more useful, and the bean counter image of management accountants will be dispelled or seriously weakened.

The authors believe that current interest in activity-based techniques will continue in the short term, but are 'less sanguine' about their long-term effectiveness due to factors such as rapid environmental change.

Perhaps the final word on the matter should rest with two surveys (Innes and Mitchell, 1990, 1994) of the extent to which ABC has been adopted by UK organisations. In the 1990 study, it was found that 6% of respondents had implemented ABC; the 1994 survey was a follow-up of respondents to the earlier survey and found that

16% were now using some form of ABC; interestingly, the later survey found that about 57% of respondents *not* using ABC were considering it. Of the companies which had considered using ABC but had rejected the idea, cost of implementation was commonly cited as the reason. Although the authors of these two studies concede that their direct comparison should be viewed with care, it would appear to be the case that use of ABC is spreading and is likely to spread further.

SUMMARY

In this chapter, we have discussed and illustrated activity-based costing, an alternative to the 'traditional' overhead absorption methodology.

We have seen that:

- Two broad approaches to absorption costing are possible – 'traditional' and activity-based costing (ABC); the procedures involved in each of these are summarised in Figure 6.2.

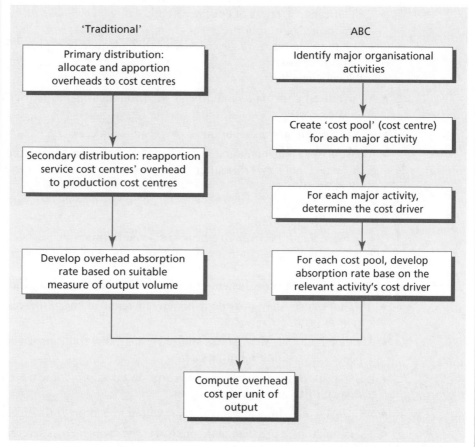

Figure 6.2 'Traditional' and ABC approaches to overhead absorption

- Dissatisfaction with 'traditional' absorption methodology has arisen because:
  - output processes are now more complex
  - wider ranges of products/services are now produced
  - direct costs are less significant as a proportion of total cost
  - 'traditional' absorption rates are based on output volume, but many overheads are unrelated to output.
- ABC attempts to reflect consumption, rather than acquisition of resources.
- ABC is based on the principle that activities incur costs and outputs consume activities.
- Major organisational activities can be classified as:
  - **unit-level activities** which occur every time a cost unit is produced
  - **batch-level activities** which are performed every time a batch of units is produced
  - **product-sustaining activities** which are undertaken to allow particular products/services to be produced/sold
  - **facility-sustaining activities** which occur so that the organisation as a whole can function; the associated costs are not absorbed into unit costs.
- Identification of major activities should be guided by:
  - significance in terms of cost incurred
  - importance to output processes
  - ability to identify a single cost driver that adequately explains the majority of associated costs
  - the cost/benefit criterion.
- An **overhead cost pool** should be created for each major activity to collect the associated costs.
- In ABC, secondary distribution of overhead is unnecessary.
- A **cost driver** is the main underlying cause of a cost, and should be identified for each major activity, thereafter being used as the basis for the overhead absorption rate.
- Cost drivers should:
  - be readily measurable
  - provide a link between overhead costs and outputs
  - be a reasonably accurate representation of how most of an activity's costs are incurred
  - conform to the cost/benefit criterion in identification, quantification and use.
- ABC unit costs may provide a better reflection of the resources consumed in output of products/services.
- ABC methodology may be less subjective than the 'traditional' method, but this depends on specific circumstances.
- It is logical to use cost drivers as absorption rates, providing these can be identified, quantified and linked to output.
- While ABC may improve cost data, it will not result in 100% accurate costs.
- There might be a problem in defining activities which cross several departmental boundaries.

- Identification of activities and cost drivers may aid management in cost control and cost reduction exercises.

In the next chapter, we will describe and discuss cost bookkeeping systems and illustrate the accounting disposition of the type of figures we have been obtaining in this and the previous three chapters.

FURTHER READING

Ahmed, N. and Scapens, R., Cost allocation theory and practice: the continuing debate. In *Issues in Management Accounting* (Ashton, D., Hopper, T. and Scapens, R., eds), Prentice Hall, 1991.

Cooper, R., Explicating the logic of ABC. *Management Accounting*, November 1990, CIMA.

Cooper, R. and Kaplan, R., Measure costs right: make the right decision. *Harvard Business Review*, September–October 1988.

Friedman, A. and Lyne, S., Activity based techniques and the death of the bean counter. *The European Accounting Review*, 6: 1, 1997.

Innes, J. and Mitchell, F., *Activity Based Costing: A Review with Case Studies*, CIMA, 1990.

Innes, J. and Mitchell, F., ABC: a follow-up survey of CIMA members. *Management Accounting*, July/August 1994, CIMA.

McKenzie, J., Activity based costing for beginners. *Management Accounting*, March 1999, CIMA.

Tanaka, M., Yoshikawa, T., Innes, J. and Mitchell, F., *Contemporary Cost Management*, Chapman & Hall, 1993: Chapter 8 contains an interesting discussion of ABC, along with a useful numerical comparison of ABC and the 'traditional' approach.

SELF-TEST QUESTIONS

6.1 In ABC systems, costs are accumulated by activity using

A   cost drivers
B   cost centres
C   cost pools
D   cost/benefit analysis.

(CIMA, *Cost Accounting and Quantitative Methods*, May 1997)

6.2 For each of the following statements, tick the appropriate box to indicate whether it is true or false.

	True	False
(a) ABC does not require secondary distribution of overheads.	☐	☐
(b) A cost driver is the main underlying cause of an overhead.	☐	☐
(c) The terms 'cost pool' and 'cost unit' are synonymous.	☐	☐
(d) The total cost associated with a facility-sustaining activity increases/decreases in line with increases/decreases in volume of output.	☐	☐
(e) ABC uses cost drivers as the basis for absorption rates.	☐	☐
(f) Use of activity-based cost pools eliminates the need for apportionment of overheads.	☐	☐
(g) Cost drivers should reflect the number of times an activity occurs.	☐	☐

6.3 Hensau Ltd has a single production process for which the following costs have been estimated for the period ending 31 December 1991:

	£
Material receipt and inspection cost	15 600
Power cost	19 500
Material handling cost	13 650

Three products – X, Y and Z – are produced by workers who perform a number of operations on material blanks using hand-held electrically powered drills. The workers have a wage rate of £4 per hour.

The following budgeted information has been obtained for the period ending 31 December 1991:

	Product X	Product Y	Product Z
Production quantity (units)	2000	1500	800
Batches of material	10	5	16
Data per product unit:			
Direct material (square metres)	4	6	3
Direct material (£)	5	3	6
Direct labour (minutes)	24	40	60
Number of power drill operations	6	3	2

Overhead costs for material receipt and inspection, process power and material handling are presently each absorbed by product units using rates per direct labour hour.

An ABC investigation has revealed that the cost drivers for the overhead costs are as follows:

Material receipt and inspection: number of batches of material.
Process power: number of power drill operations.
Material handling: quantity of material (square metres) handled.

Requirements

(a) Prepare a summary which shows the budgeted product cost per unit for each of products X, Y and Z for the period ending 31 December 1991 detailing the unit costs for each cost element:
   (i) using the existing method for the absorption of overhead costs and
   (ii) using an approach which recognises the cost drivers revealed in the ABC investigation.
   (22 marks)

(b) Explain the relevance of cost drivers in activity-based costing. Make use of figures from the summary statement prepared in (a) to illustrate your answer. **(8 marks)**
   (Total: 30 marks)

(ACCA, *Cost and Management Accounting II*, June 1991)

6.4 Trimake Limited makes three main products, using broadly the same production methods and equipment for each. A conventional product costing system is used at present, although an ABC system is being considered. Details of the three products for a typical period are:

	Hours per unit		*Materials*	*Volumes*
	Labour hours	*Machine hours*	*per unit £*	*(units)*
Product X	$\frac{1}{2}$	$1\frac{1}{2}$	20	750
Product Y	$1\frac{1}{2}$	1	12	1250
Product Z	1	3	25	7000

Direct labour costs £6 per hour and production overheads are absorbed on a machine hour basis. The rate for the period is £28 per machine hour.

Requirements

(a) Calculate the cost per unit for each product using conventional methods. **(4 marks)**

Further analysis shows that the total of production overheads can be divided as follows:

	%
Costs relating to set-ups	35
Costs relating to machinery	20
Costs relating to materials handling	15
Costs relating to inspection	30
	100%

The following activity volumes are associated with the product line for the period as a whole.

Total activities for the period

	Number of set-ups	Number of movements of materials	Number of inspections
Product X	75	12	150
Product Y	115	21	180
Product Z	480	87	670
	670	120	1000

(b) Calculate the cost per unit for each product using ABC principles;   **(15 marks)**

(c) Comment on the reasons for any differences in the costs in your answers to (a) and (b).

(3 marks)

(Total: 22 marks)

(CIMA, *Management Accounting Techniques*, May 1994)

6.5 Repak Ltd is a warehousing and distribution company which receives products from customers, stores the products and then repacks them for distribution as required. There are three customers for whom the service is provided – John Ltd, George Ltd and Paul Ltd. The products from all three customers are similar in nature but of varying degrees of fragility. Basic budget information has been gathered for the year to 30 June 1993 and is shown in the following table:

	Products handled (cubic metres)
John Ltd	30 000
George Ltd	45 000
Paul Ltd	25 000
	Costs
	£000
Packing materials (see note)	1950
Labour – Basic	350
Overtime	30
Occupancy	500
Administration and management	60

Note: Packaging materials are used in repacking each cubic metre of product for John Ltd, George Ltd and Paul Ltd in the ratio 1 : 2 : 3 respectively. This ratio is linked to the relative fragility of the goods for each customer.

Additional information has been obtained in order to enable unit costs to be prepared for each of the three customers using an ABC approach. The additional information for the year to 30 June 1993 has been estimated as follows:

(i) Labour and overhead costs have been identified as attributable to each of three work centres – receipt and inspection, storage and packing as follows:

	Cost allocation proportions		
	Receipt and inspection	Storage	Packing
	%	%	%
Labour – basic	15	10	75
overtime	50	15	35
Occupancy	20	60	20
Administration and management	40	10	50

(ii) Studies have revealed that the fragility of different goods affects the receipt and inspection time needed for the products for each customer. Storage required is related to the average size of the basic incoming product units from each customer. The repacking of goods for distribution is related to the complexity of packaging required by each customer. The relevant requirements per cubic metre of product for each customer have been evaluated as follows:

	John Ltd	George Ltd	Paul Ltd
Receipt and inspection (minutes)	5	9	15
Storage (square metres)	0.3	0.3	0.2
Packing (minutes)	36	45	60

Requirements

(a) Calculate the budgeted average cost per cubic metre of packaged products for each customer for each of the following two circumstances:
  (i) where only the basic budget information is to be used **(6 marks)**
  (ii) where the additional information enables an activity based costing approach to be applied. **(14 marks)**

(b) Comment on the activities and cost drivers which have been identified as relevant for the implementation of activity based costing by Repak Ltd and discuss ways in which activity based costing might improve product costing and cost control in Repak Ltd. Make reference to your answer to part (a) of the question, as appropriate.

(10 marks)
(Total: 30 marks)

(ACCA, *Cost and Management Accounting II*, June 1992)

QUESTIONS WITHOUT ANSWERS

6.6 Omega Limited manufactures many engineering products. Details are set out below for two products and the plant as a whole.

	Delta	Deltaplus	Total for plant for the year
Production volume	20 000 units	5000 units	180 000 units
Size of production run	4000 units	500 units	–
Number of production runs	–	–	280
Materials cost	£10 per unit	£18 per unit	£4m
Direct labour hours (DLH)	1 DLH per unit	1.5 DLH per unit	200 000
Overheads:			
Machine hours	2 per unit	5 per unit	400 000
Set-ups per production run	1 per run	4 per run	500 production runs
Handling costs per production run	£4000	£10 000	£900 000
Other overheads	–	–	£1.5m

Notes
1 Direct labour hours are charged at £9 per hour.
2 Machine hours are charged at £5 per hour.
3 Each set-up costs £250.

Requirements

(a) Calculate unit costs for Delta and Deltaplus using the traditional absorption costing method based on direct labour hours. **(5 marks)**

(b) Calculate activity-based unit costs for Delta and Deltaplus using the data set out above, assuming that 'other overheads' are allocated using machine hours. **(12 marks)**

(c) Discuss the usefulness of results from (a) and (b) above for decision making and control within Omega Limited. **(8 marks)**
(Total: 25 marks)

(ACCA, *Management Accounting*, June 1998)

6.7 Having attended a CIMA course on ABC you decide to experiment by applying the principles of ABC to the four products currently made and sold by your company. Details of the four products and relevant information are given below for one period:

Product	A	B	C	D
Output in units	120	100	80	120
Costs per unit:	£	£	£	£
Direct material	40	50	30	60
Direct labour	28	21	14	21
Machine hours (per unit)	4	3	2	3

The four products are similar and are usually produced in production runs of 20 units and sold in batches of 10 units.

The production overhead is currently absorbed by using a machine hour rate, and the total of the production overhead for the period has been analysed as follows:

	£
Machine department costs (rent, business rates, depreciation and supervision)	10 430
Set-up costs	5 250
Stores receiving	3 600
Inspection/Quality control	2 100
Materials handling and dispatch	4 620

You have ascertained that the 'cost drivers' to be used are as listed below for the overhead costs shown:

Cost	Cost driver
Set-up costs	Number of production runs
Stores receiving	Requisitions raised
Inspection/Quality control	Number of production runs
Materials handling and dispatch	Orders executed

The number of requisitions raised on the stores was 20 for each product and the number of orders executed was 42, each order being for a batch of 10 of a product.

Requirements

(a) Calculate the total costs for each product if all overhead costs are absorbed on a machine-hour basis. **(4 marks)**

(b) Calculate the total costs for each product, using ABC. **(7 marks)**

(c) Calculate and list the unit product costs from your figures in (a) and (b) above, to show the differences and to comment briefly on any conclusions which may be drawn which could have pricing and profit implications. **(4 marks)**
(Total: 15 marks)

(CIMA, *Cost Accounting*, November 1991)

6.8 Ditton Cooperage Ltd manufactures four sizes of aluminium kegs for draught beer. The following budgeted information is available for next year:

	Keg sizes (litres)			
	50	100	150	200
Prime cost per unit	£10	£20	£30	£40
Production overhead per unit	£12	£15	£21	£24
Production cost per unit	£22	£35	£51	£64
Machine operations per unit	2	3	5	8
Batch size (units)	500	350	250	25
Number of batches	10	8	6	15
Material movements per batch	4	6	6	8

Production overhead is presently absorbed at a predetermined rate of £60 per machine hour. The production manager has suggested that this rate results in overhead charges per unit which are unrepresentative of resource consumption and believes that ABC would yield more accurate figures. Investigation has revealed the following:

Activity	Cost driver	% of total overhead attributable to activity
Machine calibration	Number of batches	15
Machine power	Number of machine operations	30
Machine maintenance	Number of machine hours	20
Material handling	Number of material movements	20
Internal transport	Number of completed units	15

Requirements

(a) Compute the unit production cost of each keg size using the existing absorption rate **and** using ABC.

(b) Discuss the production manager's contention.

6.9 The Haematology Laboratory within a large local hospital is currently reviewing its costing and charging methodology. Because of the nature of the work undertaken, by far the majority of the laboratory's costs (budgeted at £1.3 million next year), are indirect relative to 'output' and it is the treatment of these costs which is to be reviewed. At present, laboratory overheads are absorbed at a 'flat rate' of 120% of the total direct cost of a specimen or investigation.

For administrative purposes, the laboratory is split into four departments: Blood Transfusion, Routine Investigation, Special Investigation & Coagulation and Unit Administration. Each department is run by a consultant haematologist, with a senior consultant, based in Unit Administration, having overall charge of the laboratory.

With the exception of Unit Administration, each department is divided into a number of workstations. Some of these workstations are capable only of highly specialised work associated with the specific department within which they are located, while the remainder can undertake work of a more general nature which is common to all departments.

Although medical staff and technicians are assigned to a particular department, they are not assigned to a particular workstation and it is frequently necessary for staff to perform work in departments other than that to which they are assigned. Similarly, roughly 30% of the laboratory's work requires the use of facilities in two or more departments and, at times of peak demand for the laboratory's services, all suitable facilities and staff are utilised, irrespective of the department within which they are located.

Requirements

Draft a report to the hospital's Board of Management explaining why overheads may need to be included in unit costs and why the existing system of charging the Haematology Laboratory's overheads to cost units is unsatisfactory; suggest *two* alternative systems which might be adopted, detail the strengths and weaknesses of each in relation to the laboratory's circumstances and on this basis, recommend the most suitable approach.

6.10 (a) In the context of ABC, it was stated in *Management Accounting – Evolution not Revolution* by Bromwich and Bhimani that 'cost drivers attempt to link costs to the scope of output rather than the scale of output thereby generating less arbitrary product costs for decision making'.

Requirement

Explain the terms 'activity based costing' and 'cost drivers'. **(13 marks)**

(b) XYZ plc manufactures four products, namely A, B, C and D, using the same plant and processes. The following information relates to a production period:

Product	Volume	Material cost per unit	Direct labour per unit	Machine time per unit	Labour cost per unit
A	500	£5	$\frac{1}{2}$ hour	$\frac{1}{4}$ hour	£3
B	5000	£5	$\frac{1}{2}$ hour	$\frac{1}{4}$ hour	£3
C	600	£16	2 hours	1 hour	£12
D	7000	£17	$1\frac{1}{2}$ hours	$1\frac{1}{2}$ hours	£9

Total production overhead recorded by the cost accounting system is analysed under the following headings:

Factory overhead applicable to machine-oriented activity is £37 424.
Set-up costs are £4355.
The cost of ordering materials is £1920.
Handling materials – £7580.
Administration for spare parts – £8600.

These overhead costs are absorbed by products on a machine-hour rate of £4.80 per hour, giving an overhead cost per product of:

$$A = £1.20 \qquad B = £1.20 \qquad C = £4.80 \qquad D = £7.20$$

However, investigation into the production overhead activities for the period reveals the following totals:

Product	Number of set-ups	Number of material orders	Number of times material was handled	Number of spare parts
A	1	1	2	2
B	6	4	10	5
C	2	1	3	1
D	8	4	12	4

Requirements

(i) Compute an overhead cost per product using activity-based costing, tracing overheads to production units by means of cost drivers. **(6 marks)**

(ii) Comment briefly on the differences disclosed between overheads traced by the present system and those traced by ABC. **(6 marks)**

(Total: 25 marks)

(CIMA, *Management Accounting – Control and Audit*, November 1990)

CHAPTER 7

Cost bookkeeping

Double-entry bookkeeping

Double-entry rules

To record entries in a double-entry system there are three rules to learn ...

Rule 1. The duality rule

Every transaction has two effects, one of which will be recorded as a debit in one account and the other which will be recorded as a credit in another account. If this rule is broken, the trial balance will not agree ...

Rule 2. The when to DR and CR rule

The rules as to when to debit a T account and when to credit a T account can be summarised in the following table.

The DR/CR table

	Increase	Decrease
Asset Expense Purchases Drawings	Debit	Credit
Liability Income Sales Capital Provisions	Credit	Debit

Rule 3. Debit is on the left and credit is on the right!

Living in the UK where cars always drive on the left-hand side of the road, I can remember this rule by the phrase 'DRive on the left and CRash on the right'.

Source: Tom Clendon, *ACCA Students' Newsletter*, July 2000.

Exhibit 7.1 A reminder of the basics of double-entry

INTRODUCTION

In the previous three chapters, we have discussed and illustrated the costing of resources: labour, materials and overhead. What we must now do is examine how these costs are incorporated into an organisation's bookkeeping system. Although the majority of accounting systems are computerised, it is nevertheless essential that you understand the relationships between the various accounts that comprise these systems. For example, we must be able to check the accuracy of accounting data and to trace errors should they arise. To do so, we need to appreciate the principles involved – a need that is all the more pressing where output from the accounting system is not only used by management but also forms the basis for organisations' published accounts. In this chapter, we concentrate on cost bookkeeping, but you should realise two things. First, the general rules of double-entry described in Exhibit 7.1 apply equally to cost and financial accounting. Second, there are many common areas between the two – debtors, creditors and wages in particular. Such is the extent of this bookkeeping commonality that, in many organisations, there is little or no distinction between cost accounting and financial accounting.

OBJECTIVES

When you have completed this chapter, you will be able to:
- explain the nature of control accounts;
- distinguish between integrated and interlocking (non-integrated) accounting systems and appreciate their relative strengths and weaknesses;
- post cost bookkeeping entries to both integrated and interlocking systems;
- explain why cost accounting and financial accounting profit may differ in an interlocking system and effect a reconciliation between the two.

CONTROL ACCOUNTS

Before we can look at a detailed example of cost bookkeeping, we must discuss a key feature of all but the most rudimentary bookkeeping systems: **control accounts**. Examination questions on cost bookkeeping make extensive use of them (mostly as a convenience to reduce the number of accounts that need to be posted); so it is important for us to understand the nature of these accounts. A control account reflects the total of a number of similar (but individual) items – i.e. it is a summary account. They are commonly used in respect of creditors, debtors, wages, stores (raw materials), work-in-progress (WIP) and finished goods. (A cash control account is sometimes also employed.) If you look at the areas of a business's financial activity dealt with by control accounts, you will see that all these activities are vitally important – a clear indication of the significance attached to control accounts. A simple example will illustrate how control accounts operate.

The sales transactions shown in Exhibit 7.2 will, in the first instance, be recorded in the Sales Day Book and in the personal account of each individual debtor. At some point in time, the information will be summarised and posted to the Debtor Control Account. Thus, the control account will show a single debit entry of £5000 for sales made during the week – i.e. the total of the three separate sales shown in Exhibit 7.2.

Unicorn Ltd

The company, which specialises in manufacture of commercial signs, had the following debtor and sales-related transactions last week:

Amounts owed at start of week	Sales (all credit)	Payments received (by cheque)
£4000 by JY & Co	£2500 to AC Ltd	£3000 from HM Ltd
£900 by FG Ltd	£1400 to KL & Co	£2200 from GF Ltd
£1200 by GKL Ltd	£1100 to Newsfayre	£700 from RT Ltd
£1800 by SDF Ltd		
£2200 by GF Ltd		
£2300 by SDG Ltd		

Exhibit 7.2 Debtor Control Account

 Determine the following entries for the Debtor Control Account: opening balance, credit for payments received and closing balance.

The opening balance and credit for payments received are, respectively, £12 400 and £5900; again, these are the totals of the individual debtor figures from Exhibit 7.2. The closing balance is:

	£
Opening balance	12 400
Add Sales for the week	5 000
	17 400
Less Cash received	5 900
Closing balance	11 500

At the end of the week, Unicorn Ltd's Debtor Control Account will look like this:

Debtor Control Account

	£		£
Opening balance b/fwd	12 400	Bank	5 900
Sales	5 000	Closing balance c/fwd	11 500
	17 400		17 400
Opening balance b/fwd	11 500		

When undertaking a bookkeeping exercise, you should make sure that you bring forward any opening balance on accounts and carry forward any closing balance.

Control accounts serve two main purposes:

- They provide a single source of information; in this case, a debtor figure for Unicorn Ltd's Balance Sheet.
- They act as a check on the arithmetic accuracy of entries in individual debtors' personal accounts, since the balance on the control account should equal the sum of the balances on the individual accounts.

Control accounts for creditors, raw materials (or stores), work-in-progress, finished goods, various categories of overhead and wages perform similar functions for their respective area of operations.

INTEGRATED ACCOUNTING SYSTEMS

In an **integrated system,** cost and financial bookkeeping functions are performed within the same ledger. Consider Exhibit 7.3 which provides summarised information about Unicorn Ltd's operations for January.

Unicorn Ltd: January operations

The following balances existed as at 1 January:

	£000		£000
Land & buildings	80	Finished goods control account	8
Plant & machinery	30	Bank account (DR balance)	24
Other fixed assets	20	Debtor control account	12
Provision for depreciation:		Creditor control account	10
land & buildings	15	Creditor for PAYE tax and	
plant & machinery	5	National Insurance	6
other fixed assets	2	Share capital issued & fully-paid	100
Stores control account	8	Retained profit (CR balance)	48
Work-in-progress (WIP) control			
account	4		

During the month of January, the following transactions occurred:

	£000		£000
Gross wages:		Materials received and invoiced	17
direct production	18	Overhead expenses (all credit):	
indirect production	3	production overhead	7
administration	9	administration overhead	10
selling & distribution	6	Depreciation:	
PAYE tax & employees'		land & buildings	1
National Insurance	8	plant & machinery	0.5
Employer's National Insurance:		other fixed assets	0.4
production wages	1	Production overhead absorbed	16
administration wages	0.5	Production cost of goods sold	47
selling & distribution wages	0.3	Cash paid to creditors:	
Sales (all on credit)	87	general	10
Material issued to production	14	PAYE/NI	7
Material issued to production		Material issued to administration	2
support departments	5	Cash received from debtors	61
Cost of completed production			
transferred to finished goods	46		

▶

Notes
1 60% of depreciation on land & buildings is considered to be production-related, with the remainder being administration overhead.
2 Depreciation of 'other fixed assets' relates to delivery vans.
3 No fixed assets were purchased or sold during the month.
4 Corporation Tax and Value Added Tax are to be ignored.
5 The company treats employers' national insurance contributions in respect of direct wages as production overhead.

Exhibit 7.3 A month's transactions

Even in a simplified and control account-level example like that in Exhibit 7.3, there are still quite a few accounts to be posted, so we shall proceed in stages, before preparing the company's profit and loss account and balance sheet.

The Creditor Control Account

In our example, purchase of materials and overhead expenses are both posted to the Creditor Control Account. Sometimes, credit purchases of goods/services other than materials may be dealt with using a separate 'Expense Creditors' Account.

 Purchases are credited to the Creditor Control Account; what item(s) from Exhibit 7.3 will be debited?

The Creditor Control Account is debited with £10 000 payment to general creditors.

Creditor Control Account

	£000		£000
Bank account	10	Opening balance b/fwd	10
Closing balance c/fwd	34	Stores Control Account	17
		Production Overhead Control Account	7
		Administration Overhead Control	
		Account	10
	44		44
		Opening balance b/fwd	34

If the company used cash to purchase materials or to pay for overhead expenses, then the Creditor Control Account is not involved. The ledger entries are:

> *DR* Stores Control (or appropriate Overhead) Account
> *CR* Bank Account

The other creditor account mentioned in Exhibit 7.3 is that for PAYE tax and National Insurance, which is credited with the month's wage deductions for these items and with the employer's NI contributions:

PAYE/NI Creditor Account

	£000		£000
Bank account	7	Opening balance b/fwd	6
Closing balance c/fwd	8.8	Wages Control Account	8
		Production Overhead Control Account	1
		Administration Overhead Control Account	0.5
		Selling & Distribution Overhead Control Account	0.3
	15.8		15.8
		Opening balance b/fwd	8.8

You will see that employees' NI contributions are extracted from the Wages Control Account; this reflects the fact that they represent a deduction from gross wages. Employers' NI contributions for all categories of wages/salaries are treated as overhead, and are therefore dealt with in the appropriate overhead accounts.

Debtor Control Account

As we saw earlier, this account is debited with credit sales for the month and credited with payments received from debtors:

Debtor Control Account

	£000		£000
Opening balance b/fwd	12	Bank account	61
Sales	87	Closing balance c/fwd	38
	99		99
Opening balance b/fwd	38		

 Suppose, in addition to £87 000 of credit sales, Unicorn Ltd also had £4000 of cash sales in January. How would this affect the Debtor Control Account?

Cash sales do not affect the Debtor Control Account in any way; had the company made £4000 of cash sales during the month, the appropriate bookkeeping entries would be:

> *DR* Bank Account £4000
> *CR* Sales £4000

Wages Control Account

The Wages Control Account serves two important purposes:

- It draws together detail for individual employees contained in the payroll (see Chapter 4): gross wages, wage deductions like PAYE tax, employees' National Insurance contributions, and net wages paid.
- It shows the organisational functions/departments to which gross wages are charged.

The account is debited with net wages paid and with all wage deductions; taken together these amount to gross wages for the period. Credits to the account show the disposition of gross wages between different organisational departments/functions.

 From Exhibit 7.3, determine the amount of net wages paid in January.

Net wages are (gross wages *less* wage deductions):

		£000
Gross wages	Direct production	18
	Indirect production	3
	Administration	9
	Selling & distribution	6
		36
Deductions	PAYE tax & employees' NI	8
	Net Wages	28

Wages Control Account

	£000		£000
Bank account (net wages)	28	WIP Control Account	18
PAYE/NI creditor	8	Production Overhead Control Account	3
		Administration Overhead Control Account	9
		Selling & Distribution Overhead Control Account	6
	36		36

In addition to the information given in Exhibit 7.3, you are aware that direct production workers undertook 200 hours of overtime during January. The hourly rate for normal-time work is £8, with a premium of 50% for overtime. State the bookkeeping entries used to reflect this overtime. (Ignore PAYE tax and NI contributions.)

As we saw in Chapter 4, the *premium* element of overtime pay must be separated from the normal-time element. The former is treated as production overhead, the latter as part of gross direct wages. The postings would be:

	£	£
DR Wages Control Account (200 hours @ [£8 + 50%])	2400	
CR Bank account		2400
– net wages paid (equal to gross as we are ignoring tax and NI)		
DR WIP Control Account (200 hours @ £8)	1600	
CR Wages Control Account		1600
– normal time element of overtime payment		
DR Production overhead control account		
(200 hours @ [£8 × 50%])	800	
CR Wages Control Account		800
– overtime premium		

The same kind of treatment is accorded to shift premiums (i.e. a special payment for working a rotating shift pattern and/or for working unsocial hours).

When idle (or non-productive) time occurs, its treatment depends on whether it is unexpected or expected under normal conditions. The cost of unexpected idle time is credited to the Wages Control Account and debited to the appropriate overhead account. Expected idle time is included in the normal labour cost, effected by 'grossing up' the cost of productive time to allow for idle time (see Chapter 4 for details).

As was also discussed in Chapter 4, employers' NI contributions in respect of direct wages may be included as part of the direct labour cost, rather than being treated as a production overhead. Such treatment necessitates a slight rearrangement in the book-keeping. An additional debit (employers' NI contributions for direct and indirect production wages) is made to the Wages Control Account, with the credit entries for the direct wages charge to WIP and indirect wages to production overhead being increased accordingly. This amendment will have a 'knock-on' effect on the cost of work completed, the closing stock of WIP and finished goods, cost of sales and the amount of overabsorbed production overhead. The overall effect on profit for the month is, however, negligible. Employers' NI contributions for administration, selling and distribution overhead could likewise be debited to the Wages Control Account, with the labour charges to each of these overhead accounts being increased by the relevant amount (the overall amount of these costs is not affected by this alteration in book-keeping).

In an exam situation, the deciding factor in treatment of employers' NI is the information provided. Exhibit 7.3, for instance, does not show the split between direct/indirect of employers' NI for production wages, so it is not possible to treat the direct portion of employers' NI as part of the direct labour cost. In practical terms, book-keeping treatment of employers' NI is likely to depend on whether management views it as an overhead cost (like the cost of running a personnel department), or as an integral element of direct labour cost.

Overhead accounts

Because 'overhead' is a generic term describing a diverse range of different costs, control accounts are generally created for each category of overhead (production, administration and selling/distribution), the purpose being to collect in summary form all the detail relating to the individual costs that comprise overhead. We shall look first at the control accounts for administration and selling & distribution overhead.

Administration Overhead Control Account

	£000		£000
Provision for depreciation:			
land & buildings	0.4	Profit and Loss Account	21.9
Wages Control Account	9		
PAYE/NI creditor	0.5		
Creditor Control Account	10		
Stores Control Account	2		
	21.9		21.9

Selling & Distribution Overhead Control Account

	£000		£000
Wages Control Account	6	Profit and Loss Account	6.7
PAYE/NI creditor	0.3		
Provision for depreciation: other fixed assets	0.4		
	6.7		6.7

The amount debited to each of these accounts in respect of the PAYE/NI creditor is the employer's NI contribution detailed in Exhibit 7.3. This exhibit states that 60% of depreciation of land and buildings is to be treated as production overhead, the remainder being administration; the amount to be debited to the administration overhead account is thus (0.4 × £1000). As we saw in Chapter 5, non-production overheads are not usually absorbed into unit costs; this is why we have transferred the costs directly to January's Profit and Loss Account.

However, in the Production Overhead Control Account, we must make a posting to show the amount of overhead absorbed (£16 000 from Exhibit 7.3). This amount is credited to the Production Overhead Control Account and debited to the WIP Control Account.

 If there is a balance on the Production Overhead Control Account at the end of January, what does this represent?

Any balance on the Production Overhead Control Account represents over- or underabsorption of overhead. If the balancing figure appears on the credit side of the account, we have an underabsorption; a balancing figure on the debit side is therefore an overabsorption. Exhibit 7.3 makes no mention of any opening balance on the Production Overhead Control Account, which can mean one of three things:

• that there has been no over- or underabsorption in previous months of the accounting year (which is somewhat unlikely);
• that January is the first month of the company's accounting year;
• that any over- or underabsorption is transferred to the profit and loss account each month.

In this example, we will adopt the last view, though you should be aware that, in some systems, a balance on the Production Overhead Control Account is carried forward from month to month for eventual transfer to the Profit and Loss Account at the year-end. The reason for taking a year-end approach is to smooth out any fluctuations in overhead absorption which may occur due to variations in actual cost and/or volume of output over the year. Unicorn Ltd's Production Overhead Control Account is presented below.

Production Overhead Control Account

	£000		£000
Wages Control Account	3	WIP Control Account	
PAYE/NI creditor	1	(overhead absorbed)	16
Creditor Control Account	7	Profit and Loss Account (balance)	
Stores Control Account	5	(underabsorption)	1.1
Provision for depreciation:			
land & buildings	0.6		
Provision for depreciation:			
plant & machinery	0.5		
	17.1		17.1

Stores (or Raw Material) Control Account

This account summarises purchases and issues of raw materials – i.e. reflects the total of all transactions recorded on the individual stores ledger accounts we described in Chapter 4. Purchases are debited, issues credited:

Stores Control Account

	£000		£000
Opening balance b/fwd	8	WIP Control Account	14
Creditor control account	17	Production Overhead Control Account	5
		Administration Overhead Control	
		Account	2
		Closing balance c/fwd	4
	25		25
Opening balance b/fwd	4		

Direct materials are debited to work-in-progress, with indirect materials being debited to the relevant overhead account. Materials returned to store from production are recorded as follows:

> *DR* Stores Control Account
> *CR* WIP Control Account

In the event that materials must be returned to the supplier, the postings are:

> *DR* Creditor Control Account
> *CR* Stores Control Account

 Following a physical stock-take, management discovers that stock has a value £200 less than that recorded in the stores ledger. What are the accounting entries for this discrepancy?

The bookkeeping entries are:

DR Stock Discrepancy (or Stock Loss) Account   £200
       CR Stores Control Account   £200

At the end of the accounting period, the balance on the Stock discrepancy cost is transferred to the Profit and Loss Account. It could alternatively be debited to production overhead.

WIP Control Account

This account records production activity, being debited with production costs (including overhead absorbed) and credited with the cost of completed output transferred to finished goods stock during the month.

Work-in-progress Control Account

	£000		£000
Opening balance b/fwd	4	Finished Goods Control Account	46
Stores Control Account	14	Closing balance c/fwd	6
Wages Control Account	18		
Production Overhead Control Account	16		
	52		52
Opening balance b/fwd	6		

Finished Goods Control, Cost of Sales and Sales Accounts

The finished goods control account is debited with the cost of output completed during the period and credited with the production cost of goods sold. This latter amount is transferred to the cost of sales account, whence it passes to the profit and loss account. Sales are credited to the sales account and then to the profit and loss account.

Finished Goods Control Account

	£000		£000
Opening balance b/fwd	8	Cost of Sales Account	47
WIP Control Account	46	Closing balance c/fwd	7
	54		54
Opening balance b/fwd	7		

Cost of Sales Account

	£000		£000
Finished Goods Control Account	47	Profit and Loss Account	47

Sales Account

	£000		£000
Profit and Loss Account	87	Debtor Control Account	87

Other accounts

Before we can prepare the profit and loss account and balance sheet, we must post the remaining accounts: Bank, Provision for Depreciation, Fixed Asset and Share Capital Accounts. Of these, only the Bank and Depreciation accounts record any activity for January; in the others, we need only carry forward January's opening balance to February. (There have been no purchases/disposals of fixed assets and no issues/redemptions of share capital.)

The Bank Account is debited with cash receipts and credited with cash payments. When dealing with Bank Account double-entries, we need to pay particular attention to the rules of double-entry set out in Exhibit 7.1. This is because, in everyday speech, 'debiting' and 'crediting' a bank account mean exactly the opposite of what they mean in bookkeeping terms.

Unicorn Ltd's remaining accounts for January are presented below.

Bank Account

	£000		£000
Opening balance b/fwd	24	Wages Control Account (net wages)	28
Debtor Control Account	61	Creditor Control Account	10
		PAYE/NI creditor	7
		Closing balance c/fwd	40
	85		85
Opening balance b/fwd	40		

Provision for Depreciation: Land & Buildings

	£000		£000
Closing balance c/fwd	16	Opening balance c/fwd	15
		Production Overhead Control Account (60% × 1)	0.6
		Administration Overhead Control Account (40% × 1)	0.4
	16		16.0
		Opening balance b/fwd	16.0

Provision for Depreciation: Plant & Machinery

	£000		£000
Closing balance c/fwd	5.5	Opening balance b/fwd	5.0
		Production Overhead Control Account	0.5
	5.5		5.5
		Opening balance b/fwd	5.5

Provision for Depreciation: Other Fixed Assets

	£000		£000
Closing balance c/fwd	2.4	Opening balance b/fwd	2.0
		Selling & Distribution Overhead	
		Account	0.4
	2.4		2.4
		Opening balance b/fwd	2.4

Land & Buildings Account

	£000		£000
Opening balance b/fwd	80	Closing balance c/fwd	80
Opening balance b/fwd	80		

Plant & Machinery Account

	£000		£000
Opening balance b/fwd	30	Closing balance c/fwd	30
Opening balance b/fwd	30		

Other Fixed Assets Account

	£000		£000
Opening balance b/fwd	20	Closing balance c/fwd	20
Opening balance b/fwd	20		

Share Capital Account

	£000		£000
Closing balance c/fwd	100	Opening balance b/fwd	100
		Opening balance b/fwd	100

The only remaining account is the profit and loss account, which we will now prepare, along with a balance sheet as at the end of January.

Profit and Loss Account and Balance Sheet

For these statements, we will adopt a columnar (vertical) format, as this is the approach most commonly used. A horizontal (i.e. double-entry) layout may be used, but is now comparatively uncommon. Unicorn Ltd's Profit and Loss Account for January is presented in Exhibit 7.4.

Unicorn Ltd: Profit and Loss Account for the month ending 31 January

	£000	£000
Sales		87.0
Production cost of sales		47.0
Gross profit		40.0
Administration overhead	21.9	
Selling & distribution overhead	6.7	
Underabsorbed production overhead	1.1	29.7
Net profit for the month		10.3
Retained profit brought forward		48.0
Retained profit carried forward		58.3

Exhibit 7.4 Profit and Loss Account for January

You will see that the underabsorbed overhead is simply treated as an additional cost; an overabsorption would have the effect of reducing cost.

 Why is the underabsorption treated as a cost?

As we saw in Chapter 5, an underabsorption arises when the amount of overhead absorbed using a predetermined absorption rate is less than the amount actually incurred. In other words, we have not absorbed a sufficient amount into production cost, and must therefore increase the cost to bring absorbed overhead into line with overhead incurred. If we fail to adjust for the underabsorption, the consequences would be that:

- the accounts understate actual overhead cost for the period; and
- the ledger will not balance.

The same reasoning applies to the reduction in cost made in respect of an overabsorption. The company's Balance Sheet as at 31 January is shown in Exhibit 7.5.

The balance sheet has been prepared by listing all the balances remaining on accounts after preparation of the Profit and Loss Account. The balance on each of the Provision for Depreciation Accounts (representing accumulated depreciation) has been set off against the cost of the related asset(s) to give net book value.

Since the Profit and Loss Account and Balance Sheet are for internal use, we do not need to concern ourselves with any format requirements that may apply to published accounts.

Journal entries

The **journal** may be thought of as a 'diary' providing narrative details of certain book-keeping entries before these are entered in the accounts. Although in practice the journal tends to be used mostly for unusual transactions (e.g. correction of errors), you may still be faced with an examination question that requires you to produce journal

Unicorn Ltd: Balance Sheet as at 31 January

	£000 Cost	£000 Accum. Depr'n	£000 Net Book Value
Fixed assets			
Land & buildings	80.0	16.0	64.0
Plant & machinery	30.0	5.5	24.5
Other	20.0	2.4	17.6
	130.0	23.9	106.1
Current assets			
Stock: Raw materials	4.0		
WIP	6.0		
Finished goods	7.0		
Debtors	38.0		
Bank	40.0	95.0	
Current liabilities			
Creditors	34.0		
PAYE/NI creditor	8.8	42.8	52.2
			158.3
Share capital			100.0
Retained profit			58.3
			158.3

Exhibit 7.5 Balance Sheet as at 31 January

entries in respect of cost bookkeeping situations. Note, however, that the journal is not itself part of an organisation's double-entry system.

Using Unicorn's issue of materials to production, production support and administration as an example, we have the following journal entries:

	DR £000	CR £000
WIP Control Account	14	
Production Overhead Control Account	5	
Administration Overhead Control Account	2	
Stores Control Account		21
Issue of materials to production, production support and administration		

Credit entries in the journal are usually inset, both to distinguish them from debits and to help ensure that both 'legs' of each transaction are recorded. An important feature of the journal is the short narrative attached to the record of transactions. This provides an explanation of the nature of the transaction being recorded and also of the related double-entries in the ledger, which can aid in the audit process and act as a check on fraudulent bookkeeping activity.

INTERLOCKING ACCOUNTING SYSTEMS

In an **interlocking** (or **non-integrated**) system, the financial and cost accounts are maintained in separate ledgers. The cost accounting ledger is used to record detail of the cost attribution exercise: e.g. how the cost of WIP is built up. Figure 7.1 provides a schematic overview of an interlocking system.

As you can see from the diagram, the cost accounting ledger contains most of the control (and subsidiary) accounts that we have already encountered in an integrated system.

 Certain accounts do not appear in the cost ledger in Figure 7.1. What are these accounts?

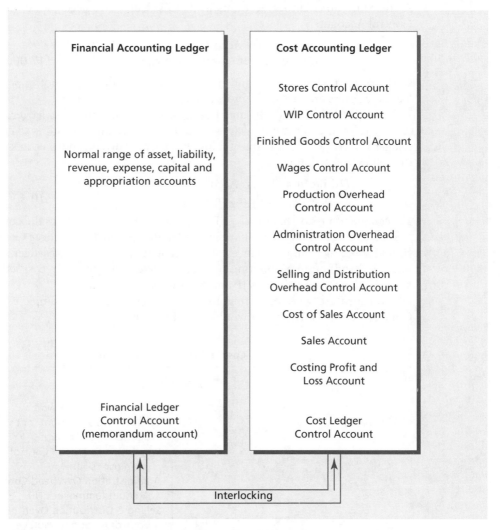

Figure 7.1 Overview of an interlocking accounting system

The cost ledger contains no accounts for debtors, bank, creditors, fixed assets or appropriations (e.g. dividends), nor is there a separate cost accounting Balance Sheet. So how do we maintain the double-entry 'balance' within the cost ledger when transactions like credit sales involve debtors? This is the purpose of the **Cost Ledger** (or **General Ledger**) **Control Account** shown in Figure 7.1: to record one 'leg' of all double-entries involving an account that does not exist within the cost ledger. Unicorn had £87 000 of credit sales during January; since this transaction involves debtors, for whom there are no accounts within the cost ledger, the entries are:

> *DR* Cost Ledger Control Account   £87 000
>   *CR* Sales Account   £87 000

 The company purchased £17 000 of raw materials on credit during January. What are the entries in the cost ledger of an interlocking system?

As there are no creditors' accounts in the cost ledger, we need to use the Cost Ledger Control Account:

> *DR* Stores Control Account   £17 000
>   *CR* Cost Ledger Control Account   £17 000

Cash received from debtors and paid to creditors will simply not appear in the cost ledger (as there are neither Debtor, Bank nor Creditor Accounts).

Although there is a Profit and Loss Account within the cost ledger, there are no capital accounts, so the only way we can deal with retained profit is to credit the Cost Ledger Control Account (debit if a loss has been incurred). In Unicorn's case, we have the following for January:

> *DR* Profit and Loss Account   £10 300
>   *CR* Cost Ledger Control Account   £10 300

We can therefore say that the Cost Ledger Control Account allows the cost ledger to be 'self-balancing'. At any point in time, the balance on the Cost Ledger Control Account should equal the sum of balances on all accounts within the cost ledger. At the beginning (and end) of an accounting period, it is likely that the only cost ledger accounts having balances are Stores, WIP and Finished Goods Control.

If Unicorn Ltd were operating an interlocking system, the completed Cost Ledger Control Account for January would be as follows:

Cost Ledger Control Account

	£000		£000
Sales	87	Opening balance b/fwd	20
Closing balance c/fwd	17	Wages Control Account (net wages)	28
		Wages Control Account (PAYE/NI)	8
		Production Overhead Control Account (employer's NI)	1
		Administration Overhead Control Account (employer's NI)	0.5
		Selling & Distribution Overhead Control Account (employer's NI)	0.3
		Stores Control Account	17

£000		£000
	Production Overhead Control	
	Account (overhead expenses)	7
	Administration Overhead Control	
	Account (overhead expenses)	10
	Production Overhead Control	
	Account (depreciation, land	
	& buildings)	0.6
	Administration Overhead Control	
	Account (depreciation, land	
	& buildings)	0.4
	Production Overhead Control	
	Account (depreciation, plant	
	& machinery)	0.5
	Selling & Distribution Overhead	
	Control Account (depreciation,	
	'other')	0.4
	Profit and Loss Account	10.3
104		104.0
	Opening balance b/fwd	17.0

The opening balance on the Cost Ledger Control Account is the sum of the opening balances on the three stock accounts (given in Exhibit 7.3):

	£000
Stores Control Account	8
WIP Control Account	4
Finished Goods Control Account	8
	20

 Verify from Exhibit 7.5 that the closing balance on the Cost Ledger Control Account represents the sum of the closing balances on the company's three stock accounts.

In the Balance Sheet presented in Exhibit 7.5, closing stock balances are given as:

	£000
Raw materials	4
WIP	6
Finished goods	7
	17

which agrees with the closing balance on the Cost Ledger Control Account.

All other entries for January are exactly the same as they were in the integrated ledger we posted earlier. For example, the Stores Control Account will now look like this:

Stores Control Account

	£000		£000
Opening balance b/fwd	8	WIP Control Account	14
Cost Ledger Control Account	17	Production Overhead Control Account	5
		Administration Overhead Control Account	2
		Closing balance c/fwd	4
	25		25
Opening balance b/fwd	4		

The only difference from the integrated version is that 'cost ledger control' replaces 'creditor control' for the second debit entry.

Besides allowing self-balancing of the cost ledger, the Cost Ledger Control Account fulfils another important function: it provides the mechanism for interlocking the cost ledger with the financial ledger. If you look again at Figure 7.1, you will see that the financial ledger contains a Financial Ledger Control Account. For each entry appearing in the Cost Ledger Control Account, the Financial Ledger Control Account will contain an equal, but opposite entry. Take, for instance, Unicorn Ltd's credit sales for January; the postings in the financial ledger are:

DR Debtor Control Account	£87 000	
CR Sales Account		£87 000
CR Financial Ledger Control Account		£87 000

The credit of £87 000 to the Financial Ledger Control Account is thus equal and opposite to the £87 000 debited to the Cost Ledger Control Account.

It may seem odd to make three entries in respect of a single transaction. But the Financial Ledger Control Account is a **memorandum account** – i.e. it does not form part of the financial ledger's double-entry system – existing merely to link the financial ledger with the cost ledger. Contrast this with the Cost Ledger Control Account, which is integral to the cost ledger's double-entry system. At the end of January, the Financial Ledger Control Account will present a bookkeeping mirror image of the Cost Ledger Control Account, with a debit to one account being matched by a credit to the other (and vice versa). This, of course, assumes that there are no errors in the ledgers; it further assumes that the profit figure recorded in both ledgers is the same. However, as we are about to discover, there may be perfectly good reasons for cost accounting and financial accounting profit to differ.

Reconciling differences in profit

Where differences (other than errors) arise between the financial and cost accounting ledgers, the Cost Ledger and Financial Ledger Control Accounts will not 'interlock' in the manner described above (i.e. will not be equal but opposite), so we need to effect a reconciliation between the two. Since any such differences will be reflected in the profit reported by each of the cost and financial accounting ledgers, reconciliation inevitably involves the two profit figures.

There are three general reasons why profit differences may arise.

1 *Different treatment of the same item* Stock valuations may differ between the cost and financial accounting ledgers. For internal reporting purposes (i.e. in the cost accounting ledger), stocks may be valued at standard cost (*see* Chapter 20); whereas in the financial accounting ledger, the same asset is valued at actual cost (standard cost is not a permissible valuation base for published accounts). It is possible that other items could be valued differently – depreciation for example, where the cost ledger might aim to show a depreciation charge more closely related to usage than is often the case with the equivalent financial accounting charge.

2 *Items appearing only in the financial accounting ledger* Certain revenue and expense items will only be recorded in the financial accounting ledger. The most common of these are dividends and interest (paid/received) and taxation.

3 *Items appearing only in the cost accounting ledger* There are two costs that an organisation might choose to record in its cost accounting ledger. Both of these are **notional costs**: i.e. they do not involve payment in cash or kind, and are included to reflect 'loss of benefit'. **Interest on capital** would be charged to the cost ledger to approximate the **opportunity cost** of 'tying up' capital, say, in stock. In other words, any capital tied up in stock cannot be used for another purpose, which could involve some loss of benefit. **Notional rent** might be charged in respect of premises the organisation owns – either to render the cost of owned property compatible with the cost of rented property (where an organisation has both) or to reflect the loss incurred as a result of occupying the premises rather than renting them to a third party.

Exhibit 7.6 provides some additional information about Unicorn Ltd, which we will use to illustrate the profit reconciliation process.

Unicorn Ltd: Profit reconciliation

For January, the company's costing ledger recorded profit of £10 300, while the financial ledger showed profit of £6300. Investigation reveals the following differences between the two ledgers:

Stock valuations	Financial Ledger		Cost Ledger	
	Opening stock	Closing stock	Opening stock	Closing stock
	£	£	£	£
Raw materials	10 000	5 000	8 000	£4 000
WIP	3 000	5 000	4 000	6 000
Finished goods	9 000	6 000	8 000	7 000
	22 000	16 000	20 000	17 000

Dividends & Interest

The financial accounts recorded interest paid of £2000 and dividends received of £1000 in January. Neither amount Is recorded in the costing ledger.

Exhibit 7.6 Interlocking accounts – profit reconciliation

Before we can prepare our reconciliation, we need to be clear about the profit implications of the information in Exhibit 7.6 – and of the different stock valuations in particular.

 Opening stock of finished goods has a higher value in the financial than cost ledger. What is the impact of this difference on each ledger's profit?

A higher value for opening stock results in a lower profit in the financial ledger. If you are in any doubt about this, or about the effect of the other stock differences, you can prepare a brief trading account (using simple imaginary figures) to verify the relationship between stock values and profit. Confining ourselves to opening stock value, we might get something like this:

	£	£	£	£
Sales		10 000		10 000
Cost of sales				
Opening stock	2000		3000	
Cost of production	5000		5000	
	7000		8000	
Closing stock	nil	7 000	nil	8 000
Profit		3 000		2 000

By holding all other values constant and changing only opening stock, we can clearly see that the effect of a higher opening stock value is lower profit (and conversely that a lower opening stock value results in higher profit).

 What is the profit impact of higher and lower closing stock values?

Higher closing stock value results in higher profit; lower closing stock value results in lower profit. You can verify this by changing the closing stock from nil to (say) £1000 in one of the trading accounts above.

The profit effects we have just described apply irrespective of the category of stock under consideration (i.e. raw materials, WIP or finished goods). This allows us to simplify our reconciliation by using the total opening and closing stocks in each of the cost and financial ledgers. Total opening stocks in the financial ledger are £2000 higher than in the cost ledger, so profit in the financial ledger is £2000 lower as a consequence. Total closing stocks are £1000 lower in the financial than in the cost ledger, so financial ledger profit is £1000 lower.

Starting from the financial ledger profit, differences causing this to be lower are added back while those differences giving rise to a higher financial ledger profit are deducted. Following this procedure, dividends received and interest paid – which are recorded in the financial, but not in the cost ledger – are respectively deducted and added back to the financial ledger profit. (In relation to cost ledger profit, dividends received increase financial ledger profit; interest paid reduces financial ledger profit.)

Unicorn Ltd: Profit reconciliation, January

		£	£
Profit recorded in the financial ledger			6 300
Less	Dividends received	(1000)	
Add	Interest paid	2000	
	Difference in opening stock valuations	2000	
	Difference in closing stock valuations	1000	4 000
Profit recorded in the costing ledger			10 300

We could equally well have chosen to start with the cost ledger profit, working back to the financial ledger profit. Had we done this, items added in the statement above would be deducted, whilst items deducted would be added.

INTEGRATED VERSUS INTERLOCKING SYSTEMS

In practice, integrated accounting systems are by far the more common. The main reason is probably ease of use. Integrated accounts do not require two separate sets of double-entries for many transactions (with a third 'leg' in the Financial Ledger Control Account). Nor is there a need for periodic reconciliation of cost and financial accounting ledgers. This should make bookkeeping procedures simpler, quicker and could reduce the likelihood of error. It might also ease the auditor's job, which could be complicated by the existence of two separate ledgers – ledgers which may quite validly contain significantly different entries.

 Can you see a potential problem with integrated accounts?

It is possible that an integrated system will suffer from 'accounting schizophrenia' – i.e. a single set of accounts trying to satisfy two distinct sets of information needs: those of internal and external users of accounts. And because the form and content of published financial statements is subject to various kinds of statutory and professional regulation (like UK Financial Reporting Standards), it is very likely that an integrated system will largely conform with these regulations. The problem here is that what is appropriate for external users is unlikely to be appropriate for internal. To take one example, absorption of fixed production overhead into unit costs is required in the published accounts of many organisations. But, as we shall see in Chapters 12, 13 and 14, unit costs calculated in this way are wholly unsuitable for most decision-making purposes. Similarly, financial accounting records are based principally on a historic cost approach: e.g. material purchases are recorded at their actual purchase cost. However, for decision making, historic cost is irrelevant (see Chapter 14). So there is a danger that an integrated system could (perhaps from convenient availability of figures) result in management basing decisions on incorrect cost data. There is thus an increased risk of incorrect decisions, maybe even serious financial loss.

SUMMARY

In this chapter, we have discussed cost bookkeeping systems, and have seen that:

- **Control accounts** are summary accounts.
- The **journal** provides a narrative record of transactions.
- In an **integrated system**, financial and cost accounts are kept within the same ledger.
- In an **interlocking system**, financial and cost accounts are maintained in separate ledgers.
- The cost ledger in an interlocking system will contain a **Cost Ledger Control Account**, which contains one 'leg' of every double-entry involving accounts that do not exist within the cost ledger.
- Profit in the cost and financial ledgers may validly differ because of:
  - differing treatment of the same item
  - items appearing only in the financial ledger
  - items appearing only in the cost ledger
- In profit reconciliation exercises, higher opening stocks mean lower profit, lower

▶

opening stocks mean higher profit; higher closing stocks mean higher profit, lower closing stocks mean lower profit.

- Integrated systems offer the benefit of ease of use, but may suffer from the drawback of trying to provide information for both internal and external uses.

In the next four chapters, we will describe in more detail how cost accounting may be applied to specific order and continuous operation situations.

FURTHER READING

Clendon, T., Double-entry bookkeeping. *Students' Newsletter*, ACCA, July 2000.

Wood, F. and Sangster, A., *Business Accounting 1*, Financial Times Management, 1999: see Chapters 1–5 (basic double-entry), 17 (the journal) and 30 (control accounts).

SELF-TEST QUESTIONS

7.1 A firm operates an integrated cost and financial accounting system. The accounting entries for Absorbed Manufacturing Overhead would be:

    A DR Overhead control account
        CR Work-in-progress control account
    B DR Finished goods control account
        CR Overhead control account
    C DR Overhead control account
        CR Finished goods control account
    D DR Work-in-progress control account
        CR Overhead control account

(CIMA, *Cost Accounting and Quantitative Methods*, November 1999)

7.2 Place a tick in the appropriate box to indicate whether each statement is true or false.

	True	False
(a) The Memorandum Control Account held within the financial ledger of an interlocking system does not form part of that ledger's double-entry system.	☐	☐
(b) The Wages Control Account is credited with employers' National Insurance contributions.	☐	☐
(c) Interest on capital attempts to reflect opportunity cost.	☐	☐
(d) In a profit reconciliation, lower closing stock is reflected in lower profit.	☐	☐
(e) The Creditor Control Account is credited with cash paid to creditors.	☐	☐
(f) In an interlocking system, the cost ledger does not have a Debtor Control Account.	☐	☐
(g) The balance on a Debtor Control Account will be equal but opposite to the sum of balances on all individual debtors' accounts.	☐	☐

7.3 The following data have been taken from the books of CB plc, which uses a non-integrated accounting system:

	Financial accounts £	Cost accounts £
Opening stock of materials	5000	6400
Closing stock of materials	4000	5200
Opening stock of finished goods	9800	9600
Closing stock of finished goods	7900	7600

The effect of these stock valuation differences on the profit reported by the financial and cost accounting ledgers is that

    A the financial accounting profit is £300 greater than the cost accounting profit.
    B the financial accounting profit is £2100 greater than the cost accounting profit.

  C the cost accounting profit is £300 greater than the financial accounting profit.
  D the cost accounting profit is £900 greater than the financial accounting profit.
  E the cost accounting profit is £2100 greater than the financial accounting profit.

(CIMA, *Operational Cost Accounting*, May 2000)

7.4 WYZ Limited has separate accounting systems for the cost and financial ledgers which are interlocked by means of control accounts in the two ledgers. The following information was available for period 7:

	£
Cost of goods sold	1 310 750
Cost of finished goods produced	1 241 500
Direct wages	173 400
Direct material issues	598 050
Direct material purchases	617 300
Production overheads (actual expenditure as per the financial accounts)	392 525

At the beginning of the period, the various account balances in the Cost Ledger were:

Account	£
Work-in-progress control	125 750
Finished goods control	94 500
Direct material stores control	48 250

In the Cost Accounts, additional production depreciation of £35 000 is charged, and production overheads were overabsorbed by £63 775 for the period.

Requirements

  (i) Prepare the following Control Accounts in the Cost Ledger showing clearly the double entries between the accounts and the closing balances:
  Accounts required: Work-in-progress control
                        Direct material stores control
                        Finished goods control
                        Production overhead control.   **(11 marks)**
  (ii) Calculate the number of hours worked if production overheads are absorbed at the rate of £17 per labour hour AND give possible reasons for the overabsorption of overheads in the period.   **(4 marks)**
                                                          (Total: 15 marks)

(CIMA, *Cost Accounting and Quantitative Methods*, November 1999)

7.5 Rontree plc operate an integrated accounting system. At the beginning of the financial period on 1 December 1996 the following balances are included in the accounts:

	£
Stock of raw materials	72 000
Work in progress	132 000
Finished goods	82 000

Production overheads are absorbed using pre-determined machine hour rates. Production overheads were budgeted at £500 000 for the period, with machine hours totalling 50 000. Rontree manufacture a variety of products.

Raw materials issues during the six months were as follows:

	£
From stock to direct production	392 000
Other issues from stock to indirect production	15 000

Returns for the same period were:

	£
From production to stock	4 000
To suppliers as faulty	24 000

Actual sales in the six months were £1 800 000. Actual machine hours were 44 000, and the following costs were incurred:

	£
Direct labour	425 000
Raw materials purchased	450 000
Production overheads	465 000
General overheads	375 000

The following stock valuations have been made at 31 May 1997:

	£
Work in progress	180 000
Finished goods	252 000

Requirements

(a) Prepare the following accounts for the six months ended 31 May 1997:
Raw materials control account
Production overheads control account
Work in progress control account
Finished goods control account
Profit and loss account **(16 marks)**

(b) Explain why a company might use pre-determined overhead recovery rates rather than rates calculated on actuals. **(4 marks)**

(c) Explain the distinction between the direct cost of production and production overheads. **(5 marks)**
(Total: 25 marks)

(CIPFA, *Management Accounting*, December 1997)

QUESTIONS WITHOUT ANSWERS

7.6 In a non-integrated accounting system, the balance shown on the cost ledger control account at the beginning of a financial year is
  A equal to the value of accumulated reserves shown in the financial accounts
  B equal to the value of stocks and work-in-progress shown in the financial accounts
  C equal to the value of stocks and work-in-progress shown in the cost accounts
  D equal but opposite to the value of stocks and work-in-progress shown in the financial accounts
  E equal but opposite to the value of the stocks and work-in-progress shown in the cost accounts

(CIMA, *Operational Cost Accounting*, November 1995)

7.7 At the end of a period, in an integrated cost and financial accounting system, the accounting entries for £18 000 overheads underabsorbed would be

    A Debit work-in-progress control account
       Credit overhead control account
    B Debit profit and loss account
       Credit work-in-progress control account
    C Debit profit and loss account
       Credit overhead control account
    D Debit overhead control account
       Credit profit and loss account

(CIMA, *Cost Accounting and Quantitative Methods*, May 1998)

7.8 The profit shown in the cost accounts was £211 250 but the financial accounts showed a different figure. The following stock valuations were used, which were the only differences between the accounts except for the profits.

	Cost accounts £	Financial accounts £
Opening stock	48 750	53 920
Closing stock	65 010	59 200

What was the profit in the financial accounts?

    A £200 270
    B £211 250
    C £211 890
    D £222 230

(CIMA, *Cost Accounting and Quantitative Methods*, November 1998)

7.9 Lonestar plc manufactures a variety of products. The company operates a non-integrated accounting system. The following information relates to the transactions in a three-month period 1 August to 31 October 1996.

(i)   Opening balances consisted of stocks of

Raw materials	£75 000
Work in progress	£50 000
Finished goods	£70 000

      With the corresponding balance on the General Ledger Adjustment account.

(ii)   Raw materials of £200 000 were purchased on credit.

(iii) Issues of raw materials to production for the period totalled £160 000.

(iv) The total of indirect materials issues to production in the period was £10 000.

(v)   Raw materials sent back to the suppliers due to defects were £2000.

(vi) The cost of wages paid to employees was £256 000. Payment was by cheque.

(vii) £76 000 of the wages cost related to indirect production labour. The balance of wages costs was direct.

(viii) Additional indirect production expenses of £26 000 were incurred in this period.

(ix) Overhead expenses charged to jobs by means of factory overhead absorption rates totalled £116 000 for the period.

(x)   Non-manufacturing overhead incurred and paid was £35 000.

(xi) The cost of jobs completed and transferred to the stock of finished goods was £400 000.

(xii) The cost of goods withdrawn from stock and delivered to customers was £380 000.

(xiii) Sales in the period were £500 000.

Requirements

(a) Open and complete the necessary cost accounts for the period. **(15 marks)**

(b) Compile a costing profit and loss account for the period. **(5 marks)**

(c) Explain the advantages of the alternative of operating an integrated accounting system.
(5 marks)
(Total: 25 marks)

Note: ignore employers' national insurance contributions and taxation.

(CIPFA, *Management Accounting*, December 1996)

7.10 (a) A company uses 2600 units of a component per annum in the manufacture of one of its products. The bought-in cost of the component is £4.00 per unit. Each purchase order costs £65. The cost of carrying stock is 20% of the bought-in cost per annum.

Requirement

Calculate the Economic Order Quantity of the component. **(4 marks)**

(b) In the previous month, stock movements of another component used by the company were:

Purchase:	320 units at £1.778/unit	Working Day 4
Purchase:	275 units at £1.785/unit	Working Day 15
Usage:	494 units	Throughout month

Opening stock was 228 units (£401.81)

Calculate:
(i) the amount charged to production in the month for component usage, using a weighted average price calculated to three decimal places of £;
(ii) the value of the closing stock of the component, using FIFO. **(6 marks)**

(c) Summary transactions for all materials/components for the month were:

	£000
Credit purchases	2176.2
Issues to production	2024.6
Write-offs	3.9
Returns to suppliers	52.5
Returns from production	32.7
Stock adjustment (excess revealed by physical count)	1.8

The value of materials in stock at the beginning of the month was £1 563 700.

Prepare the Materials Control Account for the month in the company's integrated accounting system. **(5 marks)**

(d) Explain the term 'materials coding system' and list the advantages of materials coding.
(5 marks)
(Total: 20 marks)

(ACCA, *Management Information*, December 1998)

CHAPTER 8

Specific order costing

Specific order costing

Specific order costing is the name given to the group of costing methods used when goods are manufactured or services are provided which are specific to the needs of their customer. Each cost unit is therefore likely to be different, and should relate to a specific customer order.

The starting point for any specific order costing system is the receipt of a customer specification. This may be in the form of a technical drawing, a detailed request or a formal customer order. At this point the supplier must decide if it is interested in undertaking the work. If the supplier wishes to proceed then an estimate must be prepared based on the customer's specification. If this is accepted by the customer then the work begins. Each cost unit is represented by a number, often called a works order number or a job number. This is used to reference the costs incurred in completing the work required by the customer. These costs are collected from material requisitions, labour time sheets and invoices and recorded on a cost sheet ...

Source: Examiner, Operational cost accounting, *CIMA Student*, February 1996.

Exhibit 8.1 Overview of specific order costing

INTRODUCTION

In the previous chapter, we illustrated the operation of cost bookkeeping systems, and we made the point that the Work-in-Progress (WIP) Control Account represents the sum of all transactions passing through individual work-in-progress accounts. It is to these individual accounts that we now turn. In this chapter, we will consider WIP accounts where specific order costing is in operation. Specific order costing has two variants: job costing and contract costing. Batch costing, which we will also discuss, has some characteristics of specific order costing and some of continuous operation costing.

Emergence of the Just-in-Time (JIT) philosophy, with its emphasis on reduction/ elimination of the non-value-added costs associated with stockholding, means that specific order costing – which responds to customers' specific requirements – is of particular importance to many manufacturing businesses. But specific order costing is not limited merely to manufactured output: as the quotation in Exhibit 8.1 makes clear, the method is also relevant to businesses in the service sector. Accountants, for instance, operate a recognisable job costing system when attributing costs to work performed on clients' behalf.

OBJECTIVES

When you have completed this chapter, you will be able to:

- identify the distinguishing characteristics of specific order costing, and of job, batch and contract costing;
- prepare job and batch cost cards showing estimated and actual data;
- use estimated cost data as the basis for specific order price quotations;
- post job, batch and contract ledger accounts;
- deal with retentions within a contract cost bookkeeping system;
- calculate an appropriate amount of profit to be recognised on contracts in progress;
- show extracts from a published balance sheet in respect of contracts in progress.

SPECIFIC ORDER COSTING

The key word here is 'specific': procedures are almost invariably initiated by receipt of either a firm order, a request for a quotation, or an enquiry from an existing or potential customer. Further, regardless of whether job, batch or contract costing is in operation, the order can be separately identified as work progresses. This is reflected (as Exhibit 8.1 says) in the fact that each order (quotation or enquiry) is assigned a unique code or number. The works/job/batch or contract number is then used to attribute costs, to monitor progress and to assess profitability. Thus, the job, batch or contract is the cost unit, quite different from the mass-production scenarios we will describe in the next two chapters, where it is unlikely to be cost effective to trace costs to individual units of output (and where, in fact, it may be extremely difficult to do so prior to their completion).

Another feature of the type of work suited to specific order costing is that it need not occur exclusively at the company's own premises. It might also take place at the client's premises, at a mix of company/client premises (see illustrative example in Exhibit 8.2), or could be performed at a separate location entirely.

JOB COSTING

The orders to which job costing is applied are smaller and of shorter duration than those for which contract costing is used. If a job spans two accounting periods, this is not so much a characteristic of the work as an accidental consequence of when that job happens to have started.

 Can you suggest three *types of work where job costing might be suitable?*

Job costing is very widely applicable. Garages may use it for costing vehicle repairs; tradesmen like plumbers, electricians and decorators can employ it for work carried out in customers' houses; accountants and solicitors may cost clients' work in this way; the hospitality industry can determine the cost of special functions and conferences to be held in hotels on a job basis. Doubtless you can think of other relevant examples. We will use Exhibit 8.2 for illustration.

PJ & Co. – client enquiry

PJ & Co., a firm of accountants and management consultants, has been invited to provide a quotation for the design and installation of a new budget system for DEW Ltd, a client company for whom PJ & Co. already undertakes audit work. One of PJ & Co.'s Managing Partners has prepared a specification or the new budget system after consultation with management at DEW Ltd. The potential job has been assigned the number DEW00/14 and the following estimates have been prepared based on the Managing Partner's specification.

		£
Direct materials		500
Direct labour:	accounting staff 100 hours @ £15	1500
	IT staff 80 hours @ £12	960
	support staff 20 hours @ £8	160
Direct expenses		1180

Overhead is absorbed at the following rates:
  £6 per hour for accounting staff time
  £4 per hour for IT staff time
  £5 per hour for support staff time.

PJ & Co. has a target profit margin of 20% of sales revenue for this kind of work.

Exhibit 8.2 Basic job cost data

The estimated data in Exhibit 8.2 are entered onto a **job cost sheet** (or **job cost card**), which will also be used to record actual costs and resources should PJ & Co. obtain the work. In many cases, the job cost sheet also shows selling price and job profit. These last items may be important because management will wish to monitor the profitability of individual jobs. Such a monitoring exercise might be significant where, for example, unforeseen additional work needs to be carried out subsequent to completion of the job. Monitoring job profitability also provides a check on the accuracy of the original estimates: if these prove to be significantly different from actual, improvement in estimation procedures might be required.

A partly completed job cost sheet – which, until the work is obtained or definitely lost, shows only estimates – might look like that illustrated in Exhibit 8.3.

There is no standard format for the job cost sheet; the information included should be relevant to the specific type of work being performed and should also be adequate for management's information needs. Many proprietary accounting software packages include a job cost sheet that is linked with the accounting ledger and which can be customised to suit the user's requirements.

You may be wondering how we determined the selling price and estimated profit for the job. We are told in Exhibit 8.2 that PJ & Co. seeks a profit margin of 20% of sales revenue, but Exhibit 8.2 only provides us with cost data for the job.

PJ & Co. Job cost sheet			Ref: DEW00/14	

Specification prepared by .... Date ....

Date submitted to client .... Date accepted by client ....

Start date: estimated ....   Finish date: estimated ....

      actual ....   actual ....

	Estimated	£	Actual	
Direct materials		500		XX
Direct labour:				
Accounting staff time	100 hours @ £15	1500		XX
IT staff time	80 hours @ £12	960		XX
Support staff time	20 hours @ £8	160		XX
Direct expenses		1180		
PRIME COST		4300		XX
Overhead:				
Accounting staff time	100 hours @ £6	600		XX
IT staff time	80 hours @ £4	320		XX
Support staff time	20 hours @ £5	100		XX
TOTAL OVERHEAD		1020		XX
TOTAL COST		5320		XX
SELLING PRICE		6650		XX
PROFIT		1330		XX

Comments
Design and installation of budget system.

Exhibit 8.3 Partly completed job cost sheet

 If profit is 20% of revenue, what percentage of revenue is the total job cost?

Total job cost (*TC*) represents (100 − 20) = 80% of revenue (*R*); from this, we can obtain an expression for revenue:

$$TC = 0.8R, \text{ therefore } R = \frac{TC}{0.8}, \text{ giving } \frac{£5320}{0.8} = £6650$$

Estimated profit on the job is thus (£6650 − £5320) = £1330, which equals 20% of revenue. Had the firm employed a profit mark-up (i.e. expressed profit as a percentage of cost), then this particular problem would not arise.

We have taken a rigidly cost-based approach to price determination. In practice, such rigidity could be unwise, and management may well amend the £6650 quotation to take account of competitive pressure within the business's market. For example, a lower quotation might be offered if PJ & Co. is particularly anxious to obtain the work, or if management feels that competition is likely to be especially fierce. But you should also bear in mind that price is not the only factor affecting the quotation's success. Prospective clients will consider aspects like the quality of work, potential disruption to their operations caused by installation of the new system and the timescale involved. The fact that PJ & Co. already undertake audit work for DEW Ltd may (but only may) give the firm some advantage in quoting for new work.

We will assume that a quotation of £6650 is accepted, that the job proceeds, and that the actual job costs and resources were as set out in Exhibit 8.4.

PJ & Co. – actual data for Job DEW00/14

Having been successful with their quotation of £6650, and having completed the job, the following were the actual resources consumed and costs incurred:

		£
Direct materials		540
Direct labour:	accounting staff 90 hours @ 15	1350
	IT staff 104 hours @ £12	1248
	support staff 25 hours @ £8	200
Direct expenses		1175

Overhead is absorbed at the rates set out in Exhibit 8.2.

Exhibit 8.4 Actual job data

 Using the format set out in Exhibit 8.3, prepare a job cost sheet for Job DEW 00/14 showing both estimated and actual costs and profit. Comment on your results.

A completed job cost sheet is presented in Exhibit 8.5.

You will see from Exhibit 8.5 that the job's selling price has not been adjusted to reflect inaccuracies in estimated cost. Having quoted a price of £6650, PJ & Co. is obliged to charge this amount, unless there is a clear understanding that the price can be increased to reflect unforeseen events. Such an understanding is much more likely to exist for contracts than for jobs. In this case, the overall effect of estimation errors is that actual profit is lower than estimated profit. Management will need to decide whether the scale of error is sufficient to warrant investigation.

 What are the likely sources of information about actual materials, labour and expenses for the job?

Typical sources of actual job data include creditor invoices and material requisitions in the case of direct materials, time sheets and possibly payroll for direct labour (see Chapter 4); creditor invoices and cash receipts for direct expenses.

Job cost double-entry

In a job costing system, a separate ledger account is maintained for each job. Postings to the job account follow the same pattern as that illustrated in the previous chapter for the WIP Control Account (always remembering that the control account summarises the transactions posted to all the individual WIP accounts). For PJ & Co., the account for Job DEW00/14 would be as follows.

PJ & Co. Job cost sheet **Ref: DEW00/14**

Specification prepared by .... Date ....

Date submitted to client .... Date accepted by client ....

Start date: estimated ....   Finish date: estimated ....

       actual ....   actual ....

	Estimated	£	Actual	£
Direct materials		500		540
Direct labour:				
Accounting staff time	100 hours @ £15	1500	90 hours @ £15	1350
IT staff time	80 hours @ £12	960	104 hours @ £12	1248
Support staff time	20 hours @ £8	160	25 hours @ £8	200
Direct expenses		1180		1175
PRIME COST		4300		4513
Overhead:				
Accounting staff time	100 hours @ £6	600	90 hours @ £6	540
IT staff time	80 hours @ £4	320	104 hours @ £4	416
Support staff time	20 hours @ £5	100	25 hours @ £5	125
TOTAL OVERHEAD		1020		1081
TOTAL COST		5320		5594
SELLING PRICE		6650		6650
PROFIT		1330		1056

Comments
Design and installation of budget system.

Exhibit 8.5 Fully completed job cost sheet

Job DEW00/14 Account

	£		£
Creditors/stores Control:		Cost of sales	5594
Direct materials	540		
Wages Control:			
Accounting staff	1350		
IT staff	1248		
Support staff	200		
Expense creditor/bank/cash:			
Direct expenses	1175		
Overhead Control:			
Accounting staff	540		
IT staff	416		
Support staff	125		
	5594		5594

The cost of completed WIP has been transferred to Cost of Sales in contrast to the previous chapter, where it was transferred to Finished Goods. Why is this?

The transfer to Cost of Sales rather than Finished Goods occurs for two reasons. First, it is not possible for a firm like PJ & Co. which provides services (as opposed to manufactured output) to hold stock of finished 'goods'; we will discuss service costing further in Chapter 11. Second, even if we were dealing with manufactured output, job costing is initiated by customer orders: once the job is complete, the order has been fulfilled, and the customer is invoiced. To match sales revenue with the related cost of sales, we must therefore transfer job costs to the Cost of Sales Account.

If desired, profit on individual jobs could be shown in the Job Account. Had PJ & Co. adopted this approach, Job DEW00/14 Account would have been credited with the £6650 revenue, with the balance on the account representing profit (which would be transferred direct to the profit and loss account).

BATCH COSTING

As the name suggests, batch costing applies where output consists of batches of identical items. Batch costing is a hybrid: it has some of the characteristics of specific order costing (batches are produced to customer specification) combined with some of the characteristics of continuous operation costing (costs are attributed to the batch, rather than to individual units within the batch). This type of costing is very common in certain sectors of the clothing industry, where clothes are produced in batches in response to orders from retail outlets. The attraction of batch production is the potential for achieving cost savings as a result of high-volume (typically mechanised) production: such cost savings are referred to as **economies of scale**.

You should distinguish this sort of production method from mass production which occurs in batches and where production is not triggered by a customer order. The latter is strictly speaking a form of continuous operation costing, although costing and accounting procedures are very similar to those employed in batch costing. The major accounting difference is that output mass-produced in batches, but not the subject of a customer order, will be transferred to Finished Goods on completion. Further, because of the nature of mass batch-production (and in particular its capital-intensity), many of the costs attributed to batches of output relate to a given time period, or to an overall production volume – i.e. they are related much more to the fact of having a mechanised production facility than to the output of specific batches.

Apart from the fact that we are dealing with a batch of output, costing and accounting procedures are virtually identical to those adopted for job costing:

• The batch is the cost unit.
• A **batch cost sheet** (or **batch cost card**) is prepared showing essentially the same information in respect of the batch that a job cost card shows in respect of a job.
• A Batch Account is opened for each batch, is debited with batch costs and once complete, batch cost (like job cost) is transferred to Cost of Sales.

If management wishes to ascertain the cost of individual units within a batch, this can be obtained by a simple averaging process:

$$\frac{\text{Total batch cost}}{\text{Number of units in the batch}}$$

As we will see in the next chapter, this calculation bears a strong resemblance to that which is used in simple process costing scenarios.

CONTRACT COSTING

Both job and batch costing relate to work that is comparatively small-scale. Contract costing, on the other hand, applies to large-scale operations.

 Suggest two examples of work to which contract costing may be applied.

Contract costing is often used on large construction projects: building roads, ships, office blocks etc. Unlike jobs and batches, which may span two accounting periods as an accidental consequence of when work happened to start, contract costing operations will span two/more accounting periods because of their long-term nature. However, UK Statement of Standard Accounting Practice (SSAP) No. 9, which deals with stocks and long-term contracts, suggests that contract costing may also be applied to work of a shorter timescale (i.e. falling within a single accounting period), providing it is sufficiently 'material to the activity of the period'.

In a contract costing system, the individual contracts are the cost units, and a separate Contract Account will be maintained for each contract. Because cost units tend to be large, overhead as a proportion of total cost is likely to be lower for contracts than for jobs or batches. Many contracts are almost like self-contained businesses, with their own sites, fixed assets (in the form of plant and machinery) and management teams; quite often the only overhead charged to a contract is a share of the contractor's Head Office costs. The scale and geographical dispersion of contracts can also give rise to cost and operational control problems. For example, there may be variation in the cost of resources like labour and materials, which could be affected by differences in local conditions. These variations and control difficulties are exacerbated where contracts are undertaken on an international basis.

A further difficulty with long-term contracts is how, and when, to recognise profit on contracts-in-progress – an issue we will explore in detail shortly. Initially, however, we will consider the Contract Account and certain related subsidiary accounts.

The Contract Account

The basic bookkeeping for contract costing is fairly straightforward, and we will use Exhibit 8.6 to illustrate.

One feature of the information in Exhibit 8.6 with which you may be unfamiliar is the certification of work. On virtually every contract of any significance, the client engages the services of surveyors, architects, or others suitably qualified, whose duty it is to periodically inspect work as it progresses. Work subjected to survey will be 'certified' as being satisfactorily completed, whereupon the client makes a **progress payment** to the contractor in respect of work certified in this way. Precise arrangements

CPG Construction Group – reservoir contract

One of the Group's contracts currently underway involves construction of a dam and reservoir for South Western Water Authority. Work started 14 months ago, with completion scheduled for completion in a further 12 months. Work completed to date spans two of CPG Group's accounting years; of the work completed to date, two months occurred during accounting year ending 31 March 20X1, with the remaining 12 taking place in the accounting year ending 31 March 20X2. The following are the details for each of these accounting years.

Year ending 31 March 20X1	Year ending 31 March 20X2
Plant and machinery sent to site (cost) £600 000	Additional plant and machinery sent to site (cost) £100 000
Plant hire charges £20 000	Plant hire charges £70 000
Direct labour £30 000 (of which £3 000 was accrued at the year-end)	Direct labour £160 000 (of which £12 000 was accrued at the year-end)
Materials sent to site £140 000	Materials sent to site £86 000
Materials returned to supplier from site £14 000	Materials transferred to Contract C17/6 £30 000
Site supervision £12 000	Site supervision £68 000
Site expenses £8000	Site expenses £94 000
Sub-contract costs £3000	Sub-contract costs £110 000
Charge for Head Office costs £4000	Charge for Head Office costs £60 000
Materials on site at 31 March £90 000	Materials on site at 31 March £36 000

Notes
1   None of the work completed as at 31 March 20X1 had been certified; at 31 March 20X2, the value of work certified was £700 000, with an associated cost of £480 000.
2   Plant and machinery is depreciated at 12% per annum on cost.

Exhibit 8.6 Contract costing

governing certification of work and progress payments will be set out in the contract (or other agreement) between client and contractor which is drawn up prior to commencement of work. Note that the 'value' of work certified relates to the *sales* value – i.e. is stated from the client perspective. Determining the *cost* of work which has been certified is a matter for the contractor's own surveyors.

 Use the data in Exhibit 8.6 to determine the depreciation on plant and machinery for each of the two accounting years.

We need to exercise a degree of care with time-based calculations; in this instance, work on the reservoir contract for the year to 31 March 20X1 lasts only two months, so only two months' depreciation should be charged to the contract. No such problem applies to the year ending 31 March 20X2, as a full year's work (hence depreciation) is involved.
Depreciation for year ending 31 March 20X1:

$$\left(12\% \text{ per year} \times \frac{2}{12} \text{ year}\right) \times £600\,000 = £12\,000$$

So the book value of plant and machinery carried forward from 20X1 to 20X2 is (£600 000 – £12 000) = £588 000.

Depreciation for year ending 31 March 19X2:

$$12\% \times (\pounds600\ 000 + \pounds100\ 000) = \pounds84\ 000$$

Remember that Exhibit 8.6 specifies that depreciation is based on the cost of assets, and that additional plant and machinery is used on the site during the second year. The book value of plant and machinery carried forward from 20X2 to 20X3 is:

	£	£
Cost of plant sent to site in 20X1		600 000
Cost of plant sent to site in 20X2		100 000
		700 000
Less Depreciation for 20X1	12 000	
Depreciation for 20X2	84 000	96 000
Book value of plant carried forward to 20X3		604 000

Depreciation is typically not shown on the face of the Contract Account; instead, the account is debited with the book value (cost in 20X1) of plant on site at the start of the period, and credited with the book value carried forward to next period. The difference between these two entries represents the depreciation charge. The contract account covering the two accounting periods is shown below.

Reservoir Contract Account

Year ending 31 March 20X1	£		£
Plant and machinery	600 000	Materials returned to supplier	14 000
Plant hire charges	20 000	Materials on site c/fwd	90 000
Direct labour: paid	27 000	Plant and machinery on site c/fwd	588 000
accrued c/fwd	3 000	Cost of work not certified c/fwd	
Materials	140 000	(balance)	125 000
Site supervision	12 000		
Site expenses	8 000		
Sub-contract costs	3 000		
Head Office costs	4 000		
	817 000		817 000
Year ending 31 March 20X2			
Materials on site b/fwd	90 000	Accrued wages b/fwd	3 000
Plant and machinery on site b/fwd	588 000	Materials transferred to	
Cost of work not certified b/fwd	125 000	Contract C17/6	30 000
		Materials on site c/fwd	36 000
Additional plant and machinery	100 000	Plant and machinery on site c/fwd	604 000
Plant hire charges	70 000	Cost of work certified c/fwd	480 000
Direct labour: paid	148 000	Cost of work not certified c/fwd	
accrued c/fwd	12 000	(balance)	398 000
Materials sent to site	86 000		
Site supervision	68 000		
Site expenses	94 000		
Sub-contract costs	110 000		
Charge for Head Office costs	60,000		
	1 551 000		1 551 000
Cost of work certified b/fwd	480 000	Cost of sales	480 000

Year ending 31 March 20X3

Materials on site b/fwd	36 000	Accrued wages b/fwd	12 000
Plant and machinery on site b/fwd	604 000		
Cost of work not certified b/fwd	398 000		

As with every WIP account, the Contract Account is debited with resources used on the contract. The difference here is that, when contracts are incomplete at the end of an accounting period, the balance carried forward is split into several distinct elements: the book value of plant and machinery, materials on site, cost of work not certified plus accruals and prepayments. These balances have a bearing on how contract details are disclosed in the Balance Sheet (see later). You will see that the cost of work certified has been separately carried down and transferred to Cost of Sales at the end of the second year, so that the account for 20X2 has two sections. This is principally a matter of tidy bookkeeping – highlighting the fact that it is the cost of work certified that is transferred to Cost of Sales. It will also be useful when we must adjust the amount transferred to Cost of Sales, as we will need to do shortly.

Progress payments and retentions

As well as making progress payments, is also normal for the client to withhold an agreed percentage of the contract value; payments withheld in this way are termed **retentions**. The main purpose of retentions is to provide the client with a measure of protection in the event that problems arise after work has been completed. At the end of a stipulated period following final completion of the contract, the client will pay the retention monies to the contractor. Relevant data for the reservoir contract's first two accounting years is given in Exhibit 8.7.

CPG Construction Group: progress payments and retentions

Progress payments for the reservoir contract are based on the value of work certified in a given accounting year. In the year ending 31 March 20X1, no work was certified as complete, but South Western Water Authority made an unscheduled payment on account of £50 000. During the year ending 31 March 20X2, the sales value of work certified was £700 000, with the client paying £610 000; the contract governing construction of the reservoir stipulates that the client is entitled to retain 5% of each progress payment.

Exhibit 8.7 Contract progress payments and retentions

 Bearing in mind the payment made in 20X1 and the retentions for 20X2, determine the amount owing (or paid in advance) by South Western Water Authority at 31 March 20X2.

The client's indebtedness as at 31 March 20X2 is:

	£
Value of work certified	700 000
Less Payment made in 20X1	50 000
Payment made in 20X2	610 000
Retentions (5% × £700 000)	35 000
Still to pay	5 000

Therefore £5000 will be the balance on the relevant Contract Debtor Account (sometimes termed the 'Contractee Account') as at 31 March 20X2. It is possible to leave the retentions within the Contract Debtor Account (as part of the balance carried forward), but this could give a misleading impression of the amount the client is immediately liable to pay. It might therefore be preferable to isolate retentions in a separate account. For CPG Construction, the relevant accounts would be:

Reservoir Contract Debtor Account

	£		£
Year ending 31 March 20X1			
Balance c/fwd	50 000	Bank	50 000
Year ending 31 March 20X2			
Sales (value of work certified)	700 000	Balance b/fwd	50 000
		Bank	610 000
		Retentions	35 000
		Balance c/fwd	5 000
	700 000		700 000
Year ending 31 March 20X3			
Balance b/fwd	5 000		

Reservoir Contract Retentions Account

	£		£
Year Ending 31 March 20X2			
Reservoir Contract Debtor Account	35 000	Balance c/fwd	35 000
Year ending 31 March 20X3			
Balance b/fwd	35 000		

Having a credit balance on the Contract Debtor Account for 20X1 may seem odd, but it merely indicates that the client has made an advance payment. In effect, the client is a 'creditor' of CPG Group until the first progress payment is due. As the contract advances, further progress payments will be made and additional retentions will be held by the contract debtor, so that the balance on the Retentions Account will increase. This balance is likely to remain for some time after final completion of the contract; at the end of the agreed period following contract completion, South Western Water Authority will pay the retentions to CPG Group, at which point the bookkeeping entries are:

> DR   Bank Account (payment received)
> CR Retentions Account

If (as here) the Retentions Account relates to a single client/contract only, then the above entries will serve to close it. However, it is possible for a single Retentions Account to cover several clients/contracts, in which case the account may well continue to show a balance.

Recognising profit on contracts-in-progress

Two basic accounting principles apply to profit recognition. The **matching concept** states that revenue should be recognised in the period in which it arises, and should be matched with related costs to obtain that period's profit. The implication being that profit should be recognised on an ongoing basis as a contract progresses. The **prudence concept** states that revenue should not be anticipated and that costs (and losses) should be recognised in full as soon as they occur (or are 'reasonably foreseeable'). The implication of this is that it might be imprudent to recognise profit on contracts (especially lengthy ones) while they are in progress, because their outcome cannot be 'reasonably foreseen'. So we might be better waiting until a contract is complete before taking any profit on the work.

This conflict of principles is resolved by compromise: profit should be recognised on contracts-in-progress, but on a prudent basis. The rationale is one of 'substance over form' – i.e. a desire for accounts to reflect economic reality. If we waited until contracts were complete before showing the related profit, then contractors' accounts would arguably be unrealistic, reflecting the value of contracts that happened to have finished during the year, rather than economic activity during the year.

Calculating recognised profit

The diversity of possible approach to this problem is very great. However, the basic principle that profit on contracts-in-progress should be recognised on a prudent basis has three general effects.

- *Contracts in their early stages* If contracts are in their very early stages, it can be argued that their final outcome is not 'reasonably foreseeable'. It is therefore imprudent to recognise any profit on such contracts. Management needs to decide at what point in a contract's life it is prudent to start recognising profit. An oft-quoted 'rule-of thumb' is not to recognise profit on any contract which is less than one-third complete. But contractors will develop their own policy about this – indeed the requisite degree of completion could well vary from contract to contract, depending on their precise nature.
- *Recognise profit in relation to completion* For contracts that are sufficiently advanced to permit profit to be taken, the amount of profit recognised should be linked to the degree of completion.
- *Full recognition of anticipated losses* If it becomes apparent (while work is in progress) that a contract will incur a loss, then that loss should be recognised immediately and in full; we should not wait until completion, nor should we attempt to apportion the loss over the contract's lifespan.

We shall now deal with each of these situations in turn.

Contract in its early stages

If you look again at Exhibit 8.6, you will see that the reservoir contract has a total duration of 36 months. At 31 March 19X1, the contract was only two months advanced; it would therefore be imprudent to recognise any profit. In the circumstances given in Exhibit 8.6, this presents no problem as none of the work has been certified at 31 March 20X1. The balances carried forward on the contract account that year in respect of cost of work not certified, plant and machinery, materials on site and accrued wages would simply appear on the Balance Sheet.

> ✔ *Under what Balance Sheet heading or headings would each of the contract account balances for 19X1 appear?*

The appropriate Balance Sheet headings are:

Plant and machinery	Fixed Assets
Cost of work not certified and materials on site	Stocks and WIP
Accrued wages	Creditors

The £50 000 credit balance on the Contract Debtor Account would appear on the Balance Sheet under 'Creditors' (since the client has paid in advance).

Suppose, however, that the information in Exhibit 8.8 applies.

CPG Group: reservoir contract

For the two months' work on the contract carried out in the year ending 31 March 20X1, the value of work certified was £80 000 with CPG's surveyors estimating the associated cost at £70 000

Exhibit 8.8 **Contract in early stages**

Since some of the work performed in 20X1 has been certified, we effectively have a sales figure for the reservoir contract for that year, with which we need to match a cost of sales figure.

 What is the appropriate amount for cost of sales to match with the value of work certified for the year ending 31 March 20X1?

If we wish to show no profit on the contract for the year ending 31 March 20X1, we need to set cost of sales equal to sales (i.e. equal to the value of work certified):

	£
Value of work certified	80 000
Cost of work certified	80 000
Profit	nil

However, according to CPG's surveyors, the cost of work certified was £70 000, giving an apparent profit of (£80 000 − £70 000) = £10 000. So we need to increase cost of sales by this amount. Had no surveyor's valuation of the cost of work certified been given, we could simply credit the Contract Account and debit the Cost of Sales Account with cost of work certified £80 000. It is possible to adopt the same approach even when we have the surveyor's figure for cost of work certified. The relevant section of the Contract Account would then be:

Reservoir Contract Account

Year ending 31 March 20X1	£		£
Plant and machinery	600 000	Materials returned to supplier	14 000
Plant hire charges	20 000	Materials on site c/fwd	90 000
Direct labour: paid	27 000	Plant and machinery on site c/fwd	588 000
accrued c/fwd	3 000	Cost of work certified c/fwd	80 000
Materials	140 000	Cost of work not certified c/fwd	
Site supervision	12 000	(balance)	45 000

Site expenses	8 000		
Sub-contract costs	3 000		
Head Office costs	4 000		
	817 000		817 000
Cost of work certified b/fwd	80 000	Cost of sales	80 000

Year ending 31 March 20X2

Materials on site b/fwd	90 000	Accrued wages b/fwd	3 000
Plant and machinery on site b/fwd	588 000		
Cost of work not certified b/fwd	45 000		

> ✔ *Why might the approach adopted above for cost of work certified not be advisable?*

It might not be advisable to alter the cost of work certified in this way because it could then be argued that the Contract Account fails to reflect economic reality – i.e. it has ignored a technical valuation of work performed in favour of a somewhat artificial accounting interpretation. Since we are adjusting cost of sales as a matter of prudence (because the contract's outcome cannot be reasonably foreseen at 31 March 20X1), we can create a **Contract Provision Account** to deal with this kind of prudence-based adjustment. By doing so, we are withholding a proportion of contract profit to reflect our uncertainty about the contract's outcome – and in particular about unforeseen future events that might lead to additional costs and/or a loss on the contract. In this case, the cost of work certified recorded in the Contract Account and transferred to Cost of Sales would be the surveyor's valuation of £70 000 plus a contract provision of £10 000. An extract from the Contract Account, along with the Contract Provision and Cost of Sales Accounts would be as follows:

Reservoir Contract Account (extract)

	£		£
Cost of work certified b/fwd	70 000	Cost of sales	80 000
Contract provision	10 000		
	80 000		80 000

Contract Provision Account

	£		£
Balance c/fwd	10 000	Reservoir contract	10 000
		Balance b/fwd	10 000

Cost of Sales Account

	£		£
Reservoir Contract Account	80 000	Profit and Loss Account	80 000

The balance on the Contract Provision Account will appear in the Balance Sheet under 'provisions for liabilities and charges'.

Profit recognised relative to degree of completion

At the end of 20X2, CPG's reservoir contract is 14 months underway, with estimated completion being 36 months. It is probably acceptable for the contractor to recognise some profit in 20X2, but, as ever, bearing in mind the need for prudence. Some additional data is presented in Exhibit 8.9.

CPG Construction Group: reservoir contract

For the year ending 31 March 20X2, the value of work certified on the Group's reservoir contract was £700 000, with associated costs of £480 000; the cost of work not certified at the year end was £398 000. The contract's total value is £2 800 000 and estimated cost to complete the contract is £1 400 000.

Exhibit 8.9 Contract profit recognition

As a first step, we need to obtain a notional figure for contract profit. This profit figure is 'notional' because it is unlikely that we will actually recognise all of it (as a matter of prudence). We could determine notional profit on work to date: (value of work certified *less* cost of work certified), which gives (£700 000 – £480 000) = £220 000. Although this figure does reflect the degree of contract completion, it might nevertheless be considered imprudent to recognise the entire amount. At this point in time, the contract is only 14 months into its 36-month duration, so we could argue that the final outcome cannot yet be foreseen with sufficient certainty to justify taking the entire £220 000. If so, we may scale this amount down, say by $\frac{2}{3}$ or $\frac{3}{4}$, or by some other factor depending on management's view of the degree of prudence required for this particular contract. Suppose management decides that a factor of $\frac{3}{4}$ should be applied to the year's notional profit; profit recognised for 20X2 is ($\frac{3}{4} \times$ £220 000) = £165 000. We therefore have:

	£
Sales (value of work certified)	700 000
Profit recognised	165 000
Cost of sales (balance)	535 000

 We know from Exhibit 8.9 that the cost of work certified was £480 000, yet the cost of sales shown above is £535 000. How do we account for the £55 000 difference?

As this is a prudence-based adjustment, we debit the Reservoir Contract Account with £55 000 and credit the Contract Provision Account.

As an alternative to the current year's notional profit, we could work with total notional contract profit. This is possible because Exhibit 8.9 presents both the costs to date and the estimated cost to complete the contract.

 Use the data in Exhibit 8.9 to determine total notional contract profit.

Total notional contract profit:

	£	£
Total contract sales value		2 800 000
Less Costs incurred to date:		
Cost of work certified	480 000	
Cost of work not certified	398 000	
Estimated cost to complete	1 400 000	2 278 000
Notional profit		522 000

There is a wide variety of possible methods we can take to scaling down the £522 000 to reflect the contract's degree of completion. One, possibly rough and ready way, might be to say that, as the contract is 14 months advanced out of 36 months' duration, we can recognise $\frac{14}{36}$ of total notional profit (which is £203 000). We could also approximate degree of completion in terms of sales value or cost, calculating profit to be recognised as either:

$$\frac{\text{Value of work certified}}{\text{Total contract value}} \times \text{notional profit}$$

or:

$$\frac{\text{Cost to date}}{\text{Estimated total contract cost}} \times \text{notional profit}$$

 Apply each of the proportions above to the contract's total notional profit to obtain a figure for profit to be recognised in 20X2.

Using a value-based approach, recognised profit would be:

$$\frac{£700\,000}{£2\,800\,000} \times £522\,000 = £130\,500$$

The cost-based proportion yields:

$$\frac{(£480\,000 + £398\,000)}{£2\,278\,000} \times £522\,000 = £201\,192$$

If we wish to be especially prudent, we might further reduce these profit figures (say by $\frac{2}{3}$ or $\frac{3}{4}$).

We therefore have a wide range of possible figures for profit, and this diversity of approach is reflected in practice. Perhaps the key point is that, regardless of the method used, it should be applied consistently. Exactly how prudent we should be largely depends on management's assessment of the risk associated with particular projects. In an examination context, you may be limited by the information presented in the question. For example, if you are not provided with a figure for estimated cost to complete the contract, you need to use notional profit on work to date in your answer.

Anticipated contract losses

When it is anticipated that a contract will incur a loss, prudence requires that we recognise this loss immediately and in full. Consider Exhibit 8.10.

CPG Group – contract loss

As the reservoir contract has progressed, unforeseen problems with the site have emerged, and, towards the end of accounting year ending 31 March 20X2, management revised their estimate of the cost to complete the work; the revised estimate is £2 000 000. Total contract value is £2 800 000 and costs incurred to date amount to £878 000. During the year ending 31 March 20X2, the value of work certified was £700 000, with associated cost of £480 000.

Exhibit 8.10 Anticipated contract loss

 From Exhibit 8.10, determine the anticipated loss on the reservoir contract.

The anticipated loss is:

	£	£
Total contract value		2 800 000
Less Costs to date	878 000	
Estimated cost to complete	2 000 000	2 878 000
Anticipated loss		78 000

In order to reflect a loss of £81 000 in the 20X2 accounts, we must increase the cost of sales by an appropriate amount. Notional contract profit on work certified is:

	£
Value of work certified	700 000
Cost of work certified	480 000
Notional profit	220 000

To convert notional profit of £220 000 into a loss of £78 000, we need to increase cost of sales by (£220 000 + £78 000) = £298 000:

	£	£
Value of work certified		700 000
Cost of work certified	480 000	
Additional cost	298 000	778 000
Loss		78 000

 What is the bookkeeping disposition of the additional £298 000 charged to the 20X2 accounts?

Since we are making a prudence-based adjustment, the £298 000 is treated as a contract provision. Once again, we debit the Reservoir Contract Account and credit the Contract Provision Account. An extract from the Reservoir Contract Account is given below.

Reservoir Contract Account (extract)

Year ending 31 March 20X2	£		£
Cost of work certified b/fwd	480 000	Cost of sales	778 000
Contract provision	298 000		
	778 000		778 000

Disclosure in published accounts

In the UK, treatment of long-term contracts-in-progress in published accounts is dealt with in Statement of Standard Accounting Practice (SSAP) No. 9. The procedures we have been describing are consistent with its requirements. The standard prescribes certain disclosure requirements in published accounts, particularly the Balance Sheet. The main provisions are set out in Table 8.1.

Table 8.1 Balance Sheet disclosure and SSAP 9

Item	Balance Sheet disclosure
Book value of plant on site	Fixed assets
Materials on site	Stocks and WIP
Contract debtor	Debtors: 'amounts recoverable on long-term contracts' or, if the contractee has paid in advance, disclose under creditors
Cost of work not certified	Stocks and WIP: 'long-term contract balances'
Contract provision	Creditors: provisions for liabilities and charges

The standard specifies that the contract provision should be set off against contract balances. If the provision exceeds contract balances, then the excess provision should appear under Creditors ('provisions for liabilities and charges'). Where there is a credit balance on the Contract Debtor Account (i.e. the contractee has made advance payment), this should be set off against contract balances. Any credit balance on the Contract Debtor Account remaining after set-off against contract balances should be disclosed as Creditors ('payments on account').

CPG Group: Balance Sheet extracts as at 31 March 20X2

At 31 March 20X2, the Group's accounts revealed the following in respect of the reservoir contract:

Contract Debtor £5000 (debit balance)   Retentions £35 000 (debit balance)
Contract provision £55 000 (credit balance)   Cost of work not certified £398 000
Plant and machinery on site £604 000   Materials on site £36 000
Accrued wages £12 000

Exhibit 8.11 Balance Sheet disclosure

 Use Exhibit 8.11 to prepare extracts from CPG Group's Balance Sheet as at 31 March 20X2 in conformity with SSAP 9.

Following the requirements of SSAP 9, we offset the contract provision against 'contract balances' (i.e. against the cost of work not certified):

Cost of work not certified	398
Less Contract provision	55
	343

'Amounts recoverable on contracts' (debtors) comprises two elements: the contract debtor of £5000, plus retentions of £35 000 = £40 000. Relevant Balance Sheet extracts are:

			£000
Fixed Assets	Plant and machinery on site		604
Current Assets	Stocks: materials on site	36	
	contract balances	343	379
	Debtors: amounts recoverable		
	on contracts		40
Creditors: Amounts falling due within one year			
	Provisions for liabilities and charges: accrued wages		(12)

The amount of accrued wages is shown in parentheses to indicate that, unlike the other figures, it is a credit balance.

SUMMARY

In this chapter, we have looked at three forms of specific order costing: job costing, batch costing and contract costing. We have seen that:

- Specific order costing procedures originate with a customer order/enquiry, with the work to which it relates being identifiable as a separate cost unit.

- **Job costing** applies to relatively small jobs compared to contract costing.

- A **job cost sheet** (or **job cost card**) is prepared for each job, typically specifying estimated and actual resources and costs, perhaps also selling price and profit.

- A ledger account is maintained for each job, being debited with the cost of resources used; when a job is complete, its cost is transferred to cost of sales, rather than to finished goods.

- **Batch costing** is used when output consists of batches of identical items; the batch is the cost unit here.

- The batch cost card and batch account contain the same information as their counterparts in job costing, except that costs and resources relate to the batch.

- We can calculate a cost per unit for units within a batch as:

$$\frac{\text{Total batch cost}}{\text{Number of units in the batch}}$$

- **Contract costing** applies to large projects which typically span two/more accounting periods because of their nature.

- The contract forms the cost unit, each having a separate contract account in the ledger.

- The contract account is debited with the cost of resources consumed (including the book value of plant sent to the site); credit balances consist of the closing book value of plant and machinery, materials on site, the cost of work certified and the cost of work not certified.

- Work that has been **certified** by the client's surveyor represents contract sales for the period, and forms the basis of **progress payments**.

▶

- **Retentions** are monies withheld by the client by agreement with the contractor in case problems arise with the work; retentions will be paid to the contractor after the contract has been accepted as having been successfully completed.
- Profit on contracts-in-progress should be recognised on an ongoing basis, but having regard to prudence:
  - profit should not be recognised on contracts in their early stages
  - profit should be recognised relative to a contract's degree of completion
  - anticipated losses should be recognised in full as soon as they are foreseen
- **Notional contract profit** can be calculated as (value of work certified *less* cost of work certified) or as (total contract value *less* costs to date + estimated cost to complete).
- Notional profit can be scaled down in a number of ways; fractions commonly applied are:

$$\frac{\text{Value of work certified}}{\text{Total contract value}} \quad \text{and} \quad \frac{\text{Cost to date}}{\text{Estimated total contract cost}}$$

As a matter of additional prudence, these may be further reduced, say by $\frac{2}{3}$ or $\frac{3}{4}$.

- A **contract provision** is used for prudence-based adjustments to notional contract profit.
- In the UK, Statement of Standard Accounting Practice (SSAP) No. 9 deals with contract costing as it affects published accounts.

In the next two chapters, we move from specific order to continuous operation costing, looking at process and joint product costing.

FURTHER READING

Blake, J. *Accounting Standards* (7th edition), Financial Times Prentice Hall, 2001.

Examiner for Operational Cost Accounting, Specific order costing, *CIMA Student*, CIMA, February 1996.

SELF-TEST QUESTIONS

8.1 State which of the following are characteristics of contract costing:
  (i) identical products
  (ii) customer-driven production
  (iii) short timescale from commencement to completion of the cost unit.

  A None of them
  B (i) and (ii) only
  C (ii) and (iii) only
  D (i) and (iii) only
  E (ii) only.

  (CIMA, *Operational Cost Accounting*, November 1999)

8.2 Place a tick in the appropriate box to indicate whether a particular statement is true or false.

	True	False
(a) Anticipated contract losses should be recognised gradually over the remaining years of the contract's life.	☐	☐
(b) The cost of completed jobs is usually debited to the Cost of Sales Account rather than to Finished Goods.	☐	☐
(c) Notional contract profit is (contract sales value *less* [costs to date + estimated cost to complete]).	☐	☐
(d) Prudence suggests that profit should not be recognised on contracts in their very early stages.	☐	☐
(e) Work on both jobs and contracts may span two accounting periods.	☐	☐
(f) Client retentions are credited to the Contract Account.	☐	☐
(g) Depreciation on equipment used on a contract is credited to the Contract Provision Account.	☐	☐

8.3 Indricar Limited manufacture carpets for the hotel trade. They do not carry any stock of finished goods as they only manufacture specifically to customers' orders. They do, however, hold a range of raw materials in their storeroom.

At 30 November 1998 they had two incomplete jobs in progress. The details of this work and the costs incurred up to and including the 30 November 1998 were as follows:

	Job X123 £	Job X124 £
Direct material	1250	722
Direct labour	820 (164 hours)	600 (120 hours)
Factory overhead	1640	1200

For the period from 1 December 1998 to 31 December 1998 the company accepted three more jobs, X125, X126 and X127 and incurred additional costs as follows:

	Job X123 £	Job X124 £	Job X125 £	Job X126 £	Job X127 £
Direct material issued from stores	420	698	1900	1221	516
Direct material returned to stores	(120)	Nil	(70)	(217)	Nil
Direct material transfers	(100)	Nil	100	Nil	Nil
Direct labour hours	52	78	312	151	58

Direct labour is paid at a rate of £5.00 per hour and factory production overhead is absorbed at the rate of 200% of labour cost.

During the month of December Jobs X123, X124 and X125 were completed, but Jobs X126 and X127 would not be completed until January 1999. On completion of a job the company adds 20% to the total factory production cost in order to recover its selling, distribution and administration costs. The amounts invoiced to customers during December for the completed jobs were:

Job X123	Job X124	Job X125
£6250	£6000	£7900

Requirements

(a) Calculate the total production cost for Jobs X123, X124, X125, X126 and X127, taking into account the recovery of selling, distribution and administration overhead as appropriate. **(15 marks)**

(b) Calculate the profit or loss arising on those Jobs completed and invoiced to customers during December 1998. **(5 marks)**

(c) The company have received an enquiry from a new customer. The cost of the materials for this job have been estimated at £4500. It is also expected that the job will take 125 hours to complete. Taking into account the company's normal method of recovering Production Overhead and its normal method of recovering Selling, Distribution and Administration Overhead, calculate

(i) the total cost of the job, and

(ii) the amount that should be quoted to the customer for this new job if the company wishes to add 30% to its total costs to allow for profit. **(5 marks)**

(Total: 25 marks)

(ACCA, *Cost Accounting Systems*, December 1998)

8.4 (a) PZ plc undertakes work to repair, maintain and construct roads. When a customer requests the company to do work, PZ plc supplies a fixed price to the customer, and allocates a works order number to the customer's request. This works order number is used as a reference number on material requisitions and timesheets to enable the costs of doing the work to be collected.

PZ plc's financial year ends on 30 April. At the end of April 1997, the data shown against four of PZ plc's works orders were:

Works order number	488	517	518	519
Date started	1/3/96	1/2/97	14/3/97	18/3/97
Estimated completion date	31/5/97	30/7/97	31/5/97	15/5/97
	£000	£000	£000	£000
Direct labour costs	105	10	5	2
Direct material costs	86	7	4	2
Selling price	450	135	18	9
Estimated direct costs to complete orders:				
Direct labour	40	60	2	2
Direct materials	10	15	1	1
Independent valuation of work done up to 30 April 1997	350	30	15	5

Overhead costs are allocated to orders at the rate of 40% of direct labour costs. It is company policy not to recognise profit on long-term contracts until they are at least 50% complete.

Requirements

(i)   State, with reasons, whether the above works orders should be accounted for using contract costing or job costing.   (**4 marks**)

(ii) Based on your classification at (i) above, prepare a statement showing *clearly* the profit to be recognised and balance sheet work-in-progress valuation of *each* of the above works orders in respect of the financial year ended 30 April 1997.
                                                                                        (**10 marks**)

(iii) Comment critically on the policy of attributing overhead costs to works orders on the basis of direct labour cost.   (**6 marks**)

(b) Explain the main features of process costing. Describe what determines the choice between using process costing or specific order costing in a manufacturing organisation.
                                                                                        (**10 marks**)
                                                                                   (**Total: 30 marks**)

(CIMA, *Operational Cost Accounting*, May 1997)

8.5 M Pyre (Builders) Ltd has a contract to construct a large refrigerated store for S K Mow Ltd. The following data relate to the contract:

Date commenced:	3 January 19X2
Scheduled completion:	15 March 19X3

Accounting year ending 30 September 19X2

	£
Wages paid	140 660
Materials purchased and sent to site	166 320
Materials issued from stores to site	5 780
Materials returned to stores from site	630
Materials transferred from site to other contracts	1 580
Book value of plant sent to site on 15 January 19X2	49 000
Subcontract work	64 000
Site expenses	22 000
Architects' fees	40 000
Wages accrued at 30 September 19X2	2 300
Prepaid expenses at 30 September 19X2	1 500
Materials on site at 30 September 19X2	16 200
Cost of work not certified at 30 September 19X2	31 000
Invoice value of work certified at 30 September 19X2	520 000
Cash received from S K Mow Ltd	410 000
Estimated cost to complete	414 000

The total contract price is £1 million and amounts invoiced to the client are based on the value of work certified less agreed retentions of 15% thereof. Depreciation on the plant is £20 000 per annum.

Requirements

(a) Prepare the refrigerated store contract account for accounting year ending 30

September 19X2; calculate the profit (if any) to be recognised for the year, showing any transfer to the contract provision in the contract account.

(b) In respect of the contract, show relevant extracts from the company's profit and loss account and balance sheet for the period.

QUESTIONS WITHOUT ANSWERS

8.6 Which of the following characteristics are associated with the use of contract costing?

    (i) A range of items is produced and made available for sale: the customer chooses which item he or she requires.

    (ii) The work is undertaken at the customer's request.

    (iii) Work usually takes a long time to complete, often spanning the contractor's financial year-end.

    A (i) and (iii) only

    B (ii) and (iii) only

    C (iii) only

    D (i) only

    E (ii) only

(CIMA, *Operational Cost Accounting*, May 1998)

8.7 HR Construction plc makes up its accounts to 31 March each year. The following details have been extracted in relation to two of its contracts:

	Contract A	Contract B
Commencement date	1 April 1994	1 December 1994
Target completion date	31 May 1995	30 June 1995
Retention %	4	3
	£000	*£000*
Contract price	2000	550
Materials sent to site	700	150
Materials returned to stores	80	30
Plant sent to site	1000	150
Materials transferred	(40)	40
Materials on site 31 March 1995	75	15
Plant hire charges	200	30
Labour cost incurred	300	270
Central overhead cost	75	18
Direct expenses incurred	25	4
Value certified	1500	500
Cost of work not certified	160	20
Cash received from client	1440	460
Estimated cost of completion	135	110

Depreciation is charged on plant using the straight-line method at the rate of 12% per annum.

Requirements

(a) Prepare contract accounts, in columnar format, for *each* of the contracts A and B, showing clearly the amounts to be transferred to profit and loss in respect of each contract.

    (20 marks)

(b) Show balance sheet extracts in respect of *each* contract for fixed assets, debtors and work-in-progress. **(4 marks)**

(c) Distinguish between job, batch and contract costing.
Explain clearly the reasons why these methods are different. **(6 marks)**

(Total: 30 marks)

(CIMA, *Operational Cost Accounting*, May 1996)

8.8 Knowing that you are studying for the CIMA qualification, a friend who manages a small business has sought your advice about how to produce quotations in response to the enquiries which her business receives. Her business is sheet metal fabrication – supplying ducting for dust extraction and air-conditioning installations. She believes that she has lost orders recently through the use of a job cost estimating system which was introduced, on the advice of her auditors, seven years ago. You are invited to review this system. Upon investigation, you find that a plant-wide percentage of 125% is added to prime costs in order to arrive at a selling price. The percentage added is intended to cover all overheads for the three production departments (Departments P, Q and R), all the selling, distribution and administration costs, and the profit.

You also discover that the selling, distribution and administration costs equate to roughly 20% of total production costs, and that to achieve the desired return on capital employed, a margin of 20% of sales value is necessary.

You recommend an analysis of overhead cost items be undertaken with the objective of determining a direct labour hour rate of overhead absorption for each of the three departments work passes through. (You think about activity based costing but feel this would be too sophisticated and difficult to introduce at the present time.) There are 50 direct workers in the business plus 5 indirect production people. From the books, records and some measuring, you ascertain the following information which will enable you to compile an overhead analysis spreadsheet, and to determine overhead absorption rates per direct labour hour for departmental overhead purposes:

Cost/expense	Annual amount £	Basis for apportionment where allocation not given
Repairs and maintenance	62 000	Technical assessment: P £42 000, Q £10 000, R £10 000
Depreciation	40 000	Cost of plant and equipment
Consumable supplies	9 000	Direct labour hours
Wage-related costs	87 000	$12\frac{1}{2}$% of direct wages costs
Indirect labour	90 000	Direct labour hours
Canteen/rest/smoke room	30 000	Number of direct workers
Business rates and insurance	26 000	Floor area

Other estimates/information

	Department P	Department Q	Department R
Estimated direct labour hours	50 000	30 000	20 000
Direct wages costs	£386 000	£210 000	£100 000
Number of direct workers	25	15	10
Floor area in square metres	5 000	4 000	1 000
Plant and equipment, at cost	£170 000	£140 000	£90 000

Requirements

(a) Calculate the overhead absorption rate for each department, based on direct labour hours. **(9 marks)**

(b) Prepare a sample quotation for Job 976, utilising information given in the question, your answer to (a) above, and the following additional information:

Estimated direct material cost	£800
Estimated direct labour hours:	30 in Department P
	10 in Department Q
	5 in Department R **(3 marks)**

(c) Calculate what would have been quoted for Job 976 under the 'auditors' system' and to comment on whether your friend's suspicions about lost business could be correct.

(3 marks)

(Total: 15 marks)

(CIMA, *Cost Accounting*, November 1994)

CHAPTER 9

Process costing

Process costing – part one

Process costing is the continuous operation costing method that is applied within manufacturing, where there is a continuous flow of homogeneous product resulting from a sequence of repetitive operations ...

The establishment of product unit costs in a process costing system may, in many practical situations, be calculated very straightforwardly, by dividing the total costs (direct materials, direct labour, and overheads) for an accounting period by the total number of units of product completed in that period.

However, the establishment of product unit costs may also have to deal with the following:

- a desire to establish whether any losses of material/product occurring in the process are normal or abnormal, and to reflect these appropriately in product costs ...
- the incidence of partly completed production at the end of an accounting period, and thus the need to establish a valuation for the incomplete units that reflects the degree of completion ...

Particular complexity arises where both normal/abnormal losses and part-completed production occur simultaneously within the same process ...

Source: Nigel Coulthurst, *ACCA Students' Newsletter*, January 2000.

Exhibit 9.1 Process costing defined and some of its complexities identified

INTRODUCTION

In the previous chapter, we examined job, batch and contract costing. Here, output was being produced to customers' specific requirements, individual units (or batches) were separately identifiable during production and were normally different from each other. It was thus fairly easy to trace costs to individual jobs, contracts or batches. Process costing, on the other hand, relates to mass production of identical (or very similar) items, and would be appropriate for industries like oil and chemical refining, brewing and distilling. In these circumstances, attributing costs to individual cost units is unlikely to meet the cost/benefit criterion. It is therefore more practical and cost-effective to attribute costs to processes in the first instance and then average these costs over the units in the process. This procedure is similar to the one stated in the previous chapter to obtain the cost for each unit within a batch of output. It will now be apparent why, in Figure 2.8, we showed batch costing as having some of the characteristics of both specific order and continuous operation costing. However, process costing is more likely than batch costing to possess the kind of complexities described in Exhibit 9.1 – all of which we shall encounter as the current chapter progresses.

OBJECTIVES

When you have completed this chapter, you will be able to:

- appreciate the costing implications of the sequential nature of many process costing situations;
- prepare process accounts for basic scenarios and incorporating losses, gains and equivalent units;
- distinguish between scrap, waste, normal losses, abnormal losses and abnormal gains and undertake the appropriate accounting treatment of each;
- distinguish between main products and by-products and undertake the appropriate accounting treatment of by-products;
- understand and apply the concept of equivalent units;
- value closing work-in-progress on both an average cost and a First-In–First-Out basis.

BASIC ACCOUNTING PROCEDURES

We will use the information from Exhibit 9.2 to illustrate the basic process cost accounting procedures.

NKF Ltd

The company produces a chemical reagent by means of two sequential processes, Blending and Purification. The information given below relates to these processes for the accounting period just ended.

Blending Process
Direct labour (1000 hours @ £10) £10 000
Direct materials: X (40 000 litres @ £2) £80 000
                 Y (60 000 litres @ £3) £180 000

Purification Process
Direct labour (400 hours @ £10) £4000
Direct materials: Z £20 000

The company uses a plantwide absorption rate of £30 per direct labour hour for production overheads. During the period, 100 000 litres were transferred from the Blending to the Purification Process and the same quantity was also transferred from the Purification Process to Finished Goods. There was no work-in-progress in either process during the period.

Exhibit 9.2 Process costing – basic accounting procedures

Output from the Blending Process is transferred to the Purification Process. What is the implication of this for the cost of transfers from the Purification Process to Finished Goods?

If physical output is transferred from Blending to Purification, then the associated costs are also transferred – which means that the cost of transfers from Purification to Finished Goods will include that of transfers from Blending to Purification. Total process cost and cost per unit will therefore accumulate as production progresses through the sequence of processes. This is highlighted in the process accounts illustrated below.

Blending Process Account

	Litres	£		Litres	£
Direct labour			Purification Process	100 000	300 000
(1000 hours @ £10)		10 000			
Direct materials: X	40 000	80 000			
Y	60 000	180 000			
Overhead					
(1000 hours @ £30)		30 000			
	100 000	300 000		100 000	300 000

Purification Process Account

	Litres	£		Litres	£
Blending Process	100 000	300 000	Finished Goods	100 000	336 000
Direct labour					
(400 hours @ £10)		4 000			
Direct materials: Z		20 000			
Overhead					
(400 hours @ £30)		12 000			
	100 000	336 000		100 000	336 000

The basic accounting entries are thus the same as those for job, batch and contract accounts (illustrated in the previous chapter): inputs are debited to the account, outputs are credited. You will see that the process accounts have an additional column for litres on each of the debit and credit sides. This allows us to check that inputs and outputs balance in monetary *and* physical terms – which could be important in the more complex scenarios we shall encounter shortly.

Following the methodology suggested in Exhibit 9.1, we can obtain the cost per unit for the two processes with the following simple calculation:

$$\frac{\text{Total process cost}}{\text{Units produced}}$$

This yields unit costs of:

$$\text{Blending Process } \frac{\text{£300 000}}{\text{100 000 litres}} = \text{£3 per litre}$$

$$\text{Purification Process } \frac{£336\,000}{100\,000 \text{ litres}} = £3.36 \text{ per litre}$$

If you look at the Purification Process Account, you will see that, although £20 000 worth of Material Z has been added as part of this process, no entry appears in the 'litres' column. This is not an omission: although more material has been added, it need not necessarily increase the volume of *output* (which is the basis of our unit cost calculations). Material Z may, for instance, be a powder that is mixed with previously blended materials in order to effect their purification before they are saleable. Another example of an added material that does not increase the volume of output is packaging.

Now that we have illustrated the basic accounting procedures for process costing, we can introduce the first of a number of features of most process costing situations: normal losses.

NORMAL LOSS, WASTE AND SCRAP

An important characteristic of almost every process is the existence of **normal loss**. This is a loss which is expected to arise under normal circumstances as a consequence of the nature of the process. It may arise, for example, because of evaporation or due to the way certain process inputs react with each other.

When accounting for normal losses, we need to distinguish between **waste** and **scrap**. Waste comprises discarded substances of no value – evaporation for instance. Scrap, on the other hand, has some value; although it is discarded from the process, scrap may be saleable or may have some value in use – e.g. as a material input – possibly after some further work in both cases. When accounting for process losses (and gains, which we shall discuss shortly), it is vital not to confuse production cost with any scrap value these units may have – the two values are quite distinct and are almost invariably different.

We shall use the additional data about NKF Ltd in Exhibit 9.3 to illustrate accounting procedures for normal losses.

NKF Ltd: Normal losses

Due to the nature of the chemical reactions involved, management expects a normal loss to arise in each process; details are as follows.

Blending Process
Normal loss is 4% of inputs to the process; this loss is caused by condensation and has no scrap value.

Purification Process
Normal loss is 6.25% of inputs to the process; each litre lost from the Purification Process can be sold as scrap for £0.50 per litre.
During the accounting period under review, only the normal loss arose in each process.

Exhibit 9.3 NKF Ltd – normal losses

In Exhibit 9.3, normal losses are expressed as a percentage of inputs to each process; they may also be expressed in terms of outputs or of throughput (opening work-in-progress + materials introduced – closing work-in-progress).

> ✔ *From Exhibits 9.2 and 9.3, determine, in litres, the normal loss and output for each process.*

We can obtain the inputs to each process from Exhibit 9.2; applying the normal loss percentages specified in Exhibit 9.3 gives the required result.

			litres
Blending Process	Inputs:	Material X	40 000
		Material Y	60 000
			100 000
		Normal loss @ 4%	4 000
		Output	96 000
Purification Process	Inputs:	Transfers from Blending	96 000
		Normal loss @ 6.25%	6 000
		Output	90 000

Note again the effect of the sequence of processing: the input to Purification is the output from Blending. Where materials added in a later process increase the volume of output, inputs to the later process will consist of

(output from the previous process + materials added in the later process)

The cost accounting treatment of normal losses is based on the fact that they are *expected* under normal operating conditions: the cost of units lost in this way (reduced to reflect any scrap value they may have) is therefore borne by all other units in the process.

Where the normal loss is waste, we merely credit the process account with the units of normal loss, thus showing that total output comprises good units plus normal losses, thereby balancing physical inputs with physical outputs. Since there is no monetary value attaching to the normal loss, there is no need for a corresponding debit entry.

Blending Process Account

	Litres	£		Litres	£
Direct labour			**Normal loss**	**4 000**	–
(1000 hours @ £10)		10 000	Purification Process	96 000	300 000
Direct materials: X	40 000	80 000			
Y	60 000	180 000			
Overhead					
(1000 hours @ £30)		30 000			
	100 000	300 000		100 000	300 000

When the normal loss is allowed for, we have a cost per litre of output of:

$$\frac{£300\,000}{96\,000\ litres} = £3.125$$

which is higher than our previous calculation (£3 per litre), as we now have the same cost (£300 000), but spread over fewer litres of output.

Where the normal loss is scrap, we credit the process account with the units lost and their scrap value, as shown in the Purification Process Account below.

Purification Process Account

	Litres	£		Litres	£
Blending Process	96 000	300 000	Normal loss @ £0.50 per litre	6 000	3 000
Direct labour					
(400 hours @ £10)		4 000	Finished Goods	90 000	333 000
Direct materials: Z		20 000			
Overhead					
(400 hours @ £30)		12 000			
	96 000	336 000		96 000	336 000

The £333 000 cost of transfers to Finished Goods is simply the balancing figure on the process account.

> ✔ **What is the cost per litre of output from the Purification Process?**

The cost per litre transferred from Purification to Finished Goods is:

$$\frac{£333\ 000}{90\ 000\ \text{litres}} = £3.70 \text{ per litre}$$

Although this is higher than our original cost per litre (£3.36), the cost of the normal loss has been mitigated somewhat by its scrap value. The *net* process cost (i.e. after adjustment to reflect the normal loss's scrap value) is £333 000, and this is the amount to be charged to completed output.

Because the normal loss has a monetary as well as a physical value, we need to complete the accounting double entry by debiting a Normal Loss Account:

Normal Loss Account

	£	
Purification Process	3000	

We record sale of the scrap by crediting the Normal Loss Account with the sales proceeds and debiting the Bank Account (if the sale is for cash) or the appropriate Debtor Account (if the sale is on credit). NFK Ltd's completed Normal Loss Account is:

Normal Loss Account

	£		£
Purification Process	3000	Bank (or debtor)	3000

For some types of scrap, selling prices may be volatile. Where there is a timing difference between debiting the Normal loss Account with the scrap value and its actual sale, it is possible the selling price could change. Suppose such price volatility affects scrap from the Purification Process; after the Normal Loss Account has been debited with the £6000 scrap value, it is discovered that the best selling price that can be obtained at present is £0.40 per litre. The Normal Loss Account will be:

Normal Loss Account

	£		£
Purification Process	3000	Bank (or debtor)	
		6000 litres @ £0.40	2400
		Profit & Loss (balance)	600
	3000		3000

The £600 debited to the Profit and Loss Account represents the 'cost' of over-estimating the scrap value by £0.10 per litre. (Had the scrap value been under-estimated, a credit to the Profit and Loss Account would result, reflecting the 'benefit' of underestimation.)

Occasionally, normal losses may incur a cost (rather than having a sales value) – e.g. disposal costs; such costs are debited to the process account. However, events do not always conform to plan, and it is likely that the actual process loss will differ from the normal loss, giving rise either to abnormal losses or abnormal gains.

ABNORMAL LOSSES AND ABNORMAL GAINS

Abnormal losses

An **abnormal loss** occurs where the actual process loss exceeds the normal loss, being the difference between actual loss and normal loss. It is important that we keep this category of process loss separate from normal losses, so that management is made aware of the extent to which actual losses are deviating from what was expected along with the associated cost. Exhibit 9.4 provides some additional information about NKF Ltd's Blending Process.

NKF Ltd: Blending Process abnormal loss

For the accounting period under review, the following information relates to the company's Blending Process:

Direct labour (1000 hours @ £10)	£10 000
Direct matrials : X (40 000 litres @ £2)	£80 000
Y (60 000 litres @ £3)	£180 000

Production overhead: £30 per direct labour hour.
Normal loss: 4% of input
Complete output transferred to Purification Process: 94 000 litres

---

Exhibit 9.4 Blending Process abnormal loss

> ✔ Compare the Blending Process's physical inputs and outputs from Exhibit 9.4 and established the extent of the period's abnormal loss.

Bearing in mind that normal loss forms part of the process's output, we have (in litres):

Inputs Direct materials	X		40 000
	Y		60 000
			100 000
Outputs Normal loss			
(4% × 100 000)		4 000	
Transfer to Purification Process		94 000	98 000
Therefore abnormal loss is			2 000

In other words, actual output (94 000 litres) is 2000 litres less than what we would expect from inputs of 100 000 litres given a normal loss of 4% of inputs. Because it is an unexpected loss, the abnormal loss is credited to the process account at its production cost. Per litre, this will be the same as for completed output:

$$\frac{\text{Net process cost}}{\text{Expected output}} = \frac{£300\ 000}{(100\% - 4\%) \times 100\ 000\ \text{litres}} = £3.125$$

The cost of the period's abnormal loss is therefore (2000 litres × £3.125) = £6250, which is the amount we credit to the Blending Process Account, as shown below.

Blending Process Account

	Litres	£		Litres	£
Direct labour			Normal loss	4 000	–
(1000 hours @ £10)		10 000	**Abnormal loss**	**2 000**	**6 250**
Direct materials: X	40 000	80 000	Purification Process	94 000	293 750
Y	60 000	180 000			
Overhead					
(1000 hours @ £30)		30 000			
	100 000	300 000		100 000	300 000

The value of transfers to the Purification Process is (as before) simply the balancing figure on the account. We can verify its accuracy:

(94 000 litres × £3.125 per litre) = £293 750

The cost of the abnormal loss is debited to an Abnormal Loss Account:

Abnormal Loss Account

	£		£
		Profit and Loss	
Blending Process	6250	Account	6250

As you can see, the balance on the Abnormal Loss Account is transferred to Profit and Loss, indicating to management the cost of the period's additional loss in the Blending

Process. If the size/cost of abnormal loss is considered unacceptable, the reasons may be investigated with a view to rectification in future periods.

In this particular example, losses from the Blending Process are waste. If they were scrap, we would need to slightly amend our earlier procedures. Suppose all losses from the Blending Process have a scrap value of £0.60 per litre.

 Using the net process cost (i.e. after deduction of the scrap value of the normal loss), recalculate the cost per litre for transfers to Purification and for abnormal loss.

The recalculated cost per litre is:

$$\frac{\text{Net process cost}}{\text{Expected output}} = \frac{£300\ 000 - (4000 \times £0.60)}{100\ 000 \times (100\% - 4\%)} = £3.10$$

Total cost of the abnormal loss is now (2000 litres × £3.10) = £6200. A revised Blending Process Account is presented below. Note that the cost of transfers to Purification is now (94 000 litres × £3.10) = £291 400, i.e. the balance on the account.

Blending Process Account

	Litres	£		Litres	£
Direct labour			**Normal loss**	4 000	**2 400**
(1000 hours @ £10)		10 000	**Abnormal loss**	2 000	**6 200**
Direct materials: X	40 000	80 000	**Purification Process**	94 000	**291 400**
Y	60 000	180 000			
Overhead					
(1000 hours @ £30)		30 000			
	100 000	300 000		100 000	300 000

You should ensure that the scrap value attaching to an abnormal loss is dealt with in the Abnormal Loss Account – *not* the process account:

Abnormal Loss Account

	£		£
Blending Process	6200	**Bank (or debtor)**	
		2000 litres @ £0.60	1200
		Profit & Loss (balance)	5000
	6200		6200

In the Abnormal Loss Account above, the £5000 debited to Profit and Loss represents the *net* cost of the extra process loss in the period. Had the abnormal loss incurred a cost (say, for disposal), this would be debited to the Abnormal Loss Account.

Abnormal gains

An **abnormal gain** arises when the actual process loss is lower than the normal loss, the extent of abnormal gain being the difference between the two. Like abnormal losses, abnormal gains should be reported separately, again so that their quantity and cost can be highlighted to management. Exhibit 9.5 contains some further information about NKF Ltd's Purification Process.

NKF Ltd – Purification Process abnormal gain

Details of the Purification process for the period are:

Transferred from Blending Process:	94 000 litres, total cost £293 750.
Direct labour (400 hours @ £10)	£4 000
Direct materials: Z	£20 000

Production overhead: £30 per direct labour hour
Normal loss: 6.25% of inputs.
Completed output transferred to Finished Goods: 88 800 litres.
Losses may be sold as scrap for £0.50 per litre.

Exhibit 9.5 Purification Process abnormal gain

 Compare the Purification Process's physical inputs and outputs in Exhibit 9.5 to determine the quantity of abnormal gain for the period.

Inputs	Transfers from Blending Process		94 000 litres
Outputs	Normal loss (6.25% × 94 000)	5 875	
	Transfer to Finished Goods	88 800	94 675 litres
	Therefore abnormal gain is		675 litres

While the normal loss from an input of 94 000 litres is 5875, the actual loss for the period was only 5200 litres – hence we have an abnormal gain of 675 litres. The abnormal gain – in physical and financial terms – is debited to the Process Account. Before we can do this, we must obtain a cost for the abnormal gain (and for the outputs transferred to Finished Goods). As before, this is calculated as:

$$\frac{\text{Net process cost}}{\text{Expected output}}$$

 Using the data in Exhibit 9.5, along with the formula above, determine the cost per litre of abnormal gain and transfers to Finished Goods. (Work to two decimal places of £1.)

The cost per litre is:

$$\frac{(\text{Transfers from Blending} + \text{Material Z} + \text{Labour} + \text{Overhead}) - \text{Scrap value of normal loss}}{\text{Expected output}}$$

$$= \frac{(£293\,750 + £20\,000 + £4000 + £12\,000) - (5875 × £0.50)}{(100\% - 6.25\%) × 94\,000} = £3.71$$

Total cost of the abnormal gain is thus (675 litres × £3.71) = £2504, and the completed Purification Process Account is:

Purification Process Account

	Litres	£		Litres	£
Blending Process	94 000	293 750	Normal loss @		
Direct labour			£0.50 per litre	5 875	2 938
(400 hours @ £10)		4 000	Finished Goods		
Direct materials: Z		20 000	(balance)	88 800	329 316
Overhead					
(400 hours @ £30)		12 000			
Abnormal gain	**675**	**2 504**			
	94 675	332 254		94 675	332 254

If you seek to verify the value of transfers to Finished Goods (88 800 litres × £3.71), you will discover a rounding difference of £132: not only has the cost per litre of £3.71 been rounded, but the scrap value of normal loss has also been stated to the nearest whole £1. Given the amounts involved, this is not a material difference.

The cost of the abnormal gain is credited to the Abnormal Gain Account; but this isn't quite the end of the accounting procedures for abnormal gains.

 Consider the Normal Loss Account as it presently stands, and which is presented below. If the actual loss was only 5200 litres, what is the implication for the amount stated in this account?

Normal Loss Account

	£		£
Purification Process	2938		

The scrap value of the normal loss is £2938 (5875 litres @ £0.50); since the actual loss was 5200 litres, this amount is effectively overstated by (675 litres @ £0.50). In other words, it is overstated by the scrap value of the number of litres constituting the abnormal gain. We must therefore make a compensating entry between the Normal Loss and Abnormal Gain Accounts to remedy this overstatement. (This adjustment is unnecessary where the normal loss is waste.) The completed Normal Loss and Abnormal Gain Accounts are shown below.

Normal Loss Account

	£		£
Purification Process	2938	Abnormal gain	
		(675 litres @ £0.50)	338
		Bank (or debtor)	
		5200 litres @ £0.50	2600
	2938		2938

Abnormal Gain Account

	£		£
Normal Loss	338	Purification Process	2504
Profit and Loss			
Account (balance)	2166		
	2504		2504

At the end of the period, the balance transferred from Abnormal Gain to Profit and Loss represents the net financial benefit of output in excess of what was expected from inputs to the process.

In addition to scrap, processes may also give rise to by-products, which we will now consider.

BY-PRODUCTS

A **by-product** occurs as the incidental consequence of the process – i.e. it is not the process's principal output, which is termed the **main product**. (In the next chapter, we will discuss the situation where a process produces several main products: **joint products**.) In practice, the distinction between scrap and by-products may be rather blurred. For example, the offal that is the incidental result of fish processing may be treated as scrap or as a by-product; the latter treatment could be justified since, after some further processing, fish offal may be used as fertiliser. As a general rule, it is probably true to say that by-products will have a higher resale value than scrap, but will be of relatively low value compared to main products.

We will use the data in Exhibit 9.6 to illustrate the accounting treatment of by-products.

NKF Ltd – Blending Process by-product

The following information relates to the company's Blending Process during the last accounting period:

Direct labour (1000 hours @ £10)	£10 000
Direct materials: X (40 000 litres)	£80 000
Y (60 000 litres)	£180 000

Production overhead: £30 per direct labour hour
Normal loss (waste): 4% of input   Abnormal loss (waste): 2000 litres
Completed output transferred to Purification Process: 90 000 litres.
In addition to completed output, the Blending Process produced 4000 litres of By-product F during the period. This can be sold for £1.50 per litre after incurring further processing costs of £0.10 per litre.

Exhibit 9.6 By-product in Blending Process

There are two possible methods of accounting for By-product F:

(a) Credit the process account with the by-product's **net realisable value** (i.e. its sales value less further processing costs); or
(b) Credit the profit and loss account with the by-product's net realisable value.

In either case, it is important to appreciate that *units* of by-product (like units of normal loss) are excluded from the 'expected output' figure used in determining the cost per unit of output. You should see that the effect on the process account of treatment (a) above is similar to that of a normal loss with scrap value; the effect of treatment (b) is similar to that of a normal loss which is waste.

Regardless of where its net realisable value is to be credited, we need a by-product account. The first version shown below assumes that the by-product's net realisable value is credited to the Profit and Loss Account.

By-product F Account

	£		£
Bank (or creditor) – further processing costs [4000 litres @ £0.10]	400	Bank (or debtor) – sales proceeds [4000 litres @ £1.50]	6000
Profit and Loss Account (balance) – net realisable value	5600		
	6000		6000

We now need to look at the effect on the Blending Process Account of this treatment of the by-product.

 Use the data in Exhibit 9.6 to determine the expected output from the Blending Process.

Expected output is:

Inputs Materials	X		40 000 litres
	Y		60 000 litres
			100 000 litres
Less Normal loss (4% of inputs)		4 000	
By-product		4 000	8 000 litres
Expected output			92 000 litres

This yields a cost per litre for completed output and abnormal loss of:

$$\frac{\text{Net process cost}}{\text{Expected output}} = \frac{£300\ 000}{92\ 000\ \text{litres}} = £3.261\ (\text{rounded})$$

(The net process cost used here is the sum of direct materials, direct labour and production overhead costs from Exhibit 9.6.)

If the by-product's net realisable value is credited direct to the profit and loss account, the blending Process Account is as shown below.

Blending Process Account

	Litres	£		Litres	£
Direct labour			Normal loss	4 000	–
(1000 hours @ £10)		10 000	Abnormal loss (2000 @		
Direct materials: X	40 000	80 000	£3.261)	2000	6 522
Y	60 000	180 000	**By-product**	**4 000**	–
Overhead			Purification Process		
(1000 hours @ £30)		30 000	(balance)	90 000	293 478
	100 000	300 000		100 000	300 000

The cost of the by-product is therefore carried by the abnormal loss and transfers to Purification in exactly the same way as is the cost of the normal loss.

Had we credited the by-product's net realisable value to the Blending Process Account, this would be debited to the By-product Account in place of the 'profit and loss account' entry in the version above:

By-product F Account

	£		£
Bank (or creditor) –		Bank (or debtor) – sales	
further processing costs		proceeds (4000 litres	
(4000 litres @ £0.10)	400	@ £1.50)	6000
Blending Process			
Account (balance) –			
net realisable value	5600		
	6000		6000

 Using the data from Exhibit 9.6 and incorporating the by-product's net realisable value, determine the cost per litre of completed output and abnormal loss in the Blending Process.

Cost per litre:

$$\frac{\text{Net process cost}}{\text{Expected output}} = \frac{(£300\,000 - £5600)}{92\,000 \text{ litres}} = £3.20$$

The Blending Process Account is now:

Blending Process Account

	Litres	£		Litres	£
Direct labour			Normal loss	4 000	–
(1000 hours @ £10)		10 000	Abnormal loss		
Direct materials: X	40 000	80 000	(2000 litres @ £3.20)	2000	6400
Y	60 000	180 000	**By-product**		
Overhead			**(net realisable value)**	**4 000**	**5 600**
(1000 hours @ £30)		30 000	Purification Process		
			(balance)	90 000	288 000
	100 000	300 000		100 000	300 000

Treating the by-product in this way thus has the same effect as scrap value attaching to normal loss – i.e. the process cost is reduced to the extent of the by-product's net realisable value.

So far, our example has covered only units that are fully completed; what we must now consider is how to deal with incomplete units.

INCOMPLETE UNITS

The basic problem and its solution

The existence of incomplete units in process costing gives rise to two problems: calculation of an 'output' figure and the fact that different categories of unit may have achieved different degrees of completion for different elements of cost. We will consider each of these difficulties and their solution, before bringing the two together in a process account.

Calculation of an 'output' figure

We need a measure of process output to enable us to determine the cost per unit for the process. Until now, this has been straightforward (net process cost divided by expected output). However, if expected output comprises fully *and* partly-completed units – i.e. is not stated on a single basis – we cannot undertake this simple unit cost calculation. The problem is solved by use of **equivalent units** (or **equivalent production**). Equivalent units are notional units of fully complete output: partly completed units are converted to an equivalent number of fully completed units by applying the estimated degree of completion to the number of units concerned.

In addition to 20 000 kg of completed output, a process also has 6000 units of work-in-progress at the end of the period. It is estimated that the work-in-progress is 60% complete. Net process cost for the period was £118 000.
How many equivalent units does the work-in-progress represent and what is the process's total output in equivalent units for the period? Determine the cost per equivalent unit.

The work-in-progress consists of $(6000 \times 60\%) = 3600$ equivalent units; i.e. 6000 units 60% complete is equivalent to 3600 units 100% complete. Total output from the process for the period is therefore:

Work-in-progress	3 600 equivalent units
Completed output	20 000 equivalent units
	23 600 equivalent units

Note that completed output in equivalent unit terms is $(20\,000 \times 100\%)$. The cost per equivalent unit is therefore:

$$\frac{\text{Net process cost}}{\text{Process equivalent units}} = \frac{£118\,000}{23\,600} = £5$$

We are now in a position to value completed output and work-in-progress:

	£
Completed output (20 000 × £5)	100 000
Work-in-progress (3600 × £5)	18 000
	118 000

It is important you appreciate that the £5 is the cost per *equivalent unit* – i.e. per fully complete unit. This is why we have used 3600 *equivalent units* to value the work-in-progress.

Different units, different costs, different degrees of completion

It will often happen that different categories of unit (work-in-progress, normal losses, abnormal losses, abnormal gains) have achieved different degrees of completion for various elements of cost (materials, labour and overhead). This problem is overcome by calculating equivalent units for each separate category of unit; for each category of unit, we further determine the number of equivalent units for individual elements of cost. We shall use the information in Exhibit 9.7 to illustrate.

NKF Ltd: Purification Process work-in-progress

The following information relates to the company's Purification Process for last period.

Transfers from blending Process	100 000 litres, cost £300 000
Direct labour (400 hours @ £10)	£4000
Direct materials: Z	£20 000
Production overhead (400 hours @ £30)	£12 000
Transfers to Finished Goods	75 000 litres
Closing work-in-progress	25 000 litres, 20% complete

Materials are input at the start of the process, whilst labour and overheads are incurred evenly.

Exhibit 9.7 Purification Process work-in-progress

Table 9.1 shows the degree of completion achieved by the Purification Process's completed output and closing work-in-progress in respect of each element of cost.

 Although Exhibit 9.7 states that closing WIP is only 20% complete, Table 9.1 shows it to be 100% complete in respect of both transfers from Blending and direct materials. Can you suggest a reason for this apparent anomaly?

Table 9.1 Purification Process – degrees of completion

	Transfers from Blending Process	Direct labour	Direct materials	Production overhead
Completed output: % complete	100	100	100	100
Closing WIP: % complete	100	20	100	20

Common sense indicates that every litre in Purification must be 100% complete in respect of transfers from the earlier process – otherwise such transfers would not occur (except perhaps by accident). As for direct materials, Exhibit 9.7 says that these are input at the start of the process: i.e. every litre that has passed beyond the start of the process will have all the direct materials it will *ever* have.

In Table 9.2, we combine degrees of completion from Table 9.1 with the appropriate number of litres from Exhibit 9.7 to obtain equivalent units for each category of unit and cost element.

Table 9.2 Purification Process – degrees of completion and equivalent units

	Transfers from Blending Process	Direct labour	Direct materials	Production overhead
Completed output	(100% × 75 000) 75 000	(100% × 75 000) 75 000	(100% × 75 000) 75 000	(100% × 75 000) 75 000
Closing WIP	(100% × 25 000) 25 000	(20% × 25 000) 5 000	(100% × 25 000) 25 000	(20% × 25 000) 5 000
Total equivalent units	100 000	80 000	100 000	80 000

The process account

We are now in a position to 'pull together' the preceding illustration and prepare the Purification Process Account incorporating closing work-in-progress.

 Using the cost data from Exhibit 9.7 in conjunction with the total equivalent units from Table 9.2, determine a cost per equivalent unit for each of the four cost elements listed in Table 9.2.

Table 9.3 shows the calculation of the cost per equivalent unit for each element of cost. (For a method of reducing the size of presentations like Table 9.3 and those that follow, you should refer to Appendix 9A. For consistency and ease of explanation, we will continue to use the unabridged version for the remainder of this chapter.)

Table 9.3 Purification Process – cost per equivalent unit

	Transfers from Blending Process	Direct labour	Direct materials	Production overhead
Completed output	(100% × 75 000) 75 000	(100% × 75 000) 75 000	(100% × 75 000) 75 000	(100% × 75 000) 75 000
Closing WIP	(100% × 25 000) 25 000	(20% × 25 000) 5000	(100% × 25 000) 25 000	(20% × 25 000) 5000
Total equivalent units	100 000	80 000	100 000	80 000
Cost (from Exhibit 9.7)	£300 000	£4000	£20 000	£12 000
Cost/equivalent unit	£3.00	£0.05	£0.20	£0.15

Using the cost per equivalent unit in conjunction with the appropriate number of equivalent units from Table 9.3, determine the cost of the Purification Process's completed output.

The cost of completed output is:

> 75 000 equivalent units × (£3 [transfers] + £0.05 [direct labour] + £0.20 [direct materials] + £0.15 [production overhead])
> = £255 000

The Purification Process Account incorporating closing WIP is presented below.

Purification Process Account

	Litres	£		Litres	£
Blending Process	100 000	300 000	**Finished Goods**	75 000	255 000
Direct labour			**Closing WIP c/d**		
(400 hours @ £10)		4 000	**(balance)**	25 000	81 000
Direct materials: Z		20 000			
Overhead					
(400 hours @ £30)		12 000			
	100 000	336 000		100 000	336 000
WIP b/d	25 000	81 000			

We can verify the cost of closing WIP using the equivalent units and cost per equivalent unit from Table 9.3:

	£
Transfers from Blending (25 000 equivalent units × £3)	75 000
Direct labour (5000 equivalent units × £0.05)	250
Direct materials (25 000 equivalent units × £0.20)	5 000
Production overhead (5000 equivalent units × £0.15)	750
	81 000

Note once again that we need to cost the closing WIP on the basis of *equivalent units* for each element of cost. Verifying the value of closing WIP in this way is not necessary for the purpose of posting the process account, but it does provide some check on the arithmetic accuracy of equivalent unit costing calculations.

Now that we have illustrated the procedural mechanics for dealing with incomplete units, we need to look once more at normal and abnormal losses and abnormal gains.

Normal losses and equivalent units

Earlier in the chapter, we said that the accounting treatment of normal losses is based on their being expected under normal conditions – i.e. their cost (net of any scrap value) should be borne by other units in the process. This is still the guiding principle. Exhibit 9.8 provides information about NFK Ltd's Blending Process.

The easiest way of dealing with the normal loss is simply to omit the units concerned from our unit cost tabulation. By doing this, the cost of these 'omitted' units is automatically apportioned between all the units that remain in the tabulation. (For an alternative treatment, see Appendix 9B.)

NFK Ltd: Blending Process

Details of the company's Blending Process for the last accounting period are:

Direct labour (1000 hours @ £10) £10 000
Direct materials: X (40 000 litres @ £2) £80 000
           Y (60 000 litres @ £3) £180 000
Production overhead (1000 hours @ £30) £30 000
A normal loss of 4% of inputs arises during the process; this is caused by condensation and has no scrap value.
Completed output transferred to Purification Process: 65 000 litres
Closing WIP: 31 000 litres, 50% complete.

Materials X and Y are both input at the start of the process, whilst labour and overheads are incurred evenly throughout the process.

Exhibit 9.8 Blending Process – equivalent units and normal losses

 Using the data from Exhibit 9.8 and Table 9.3 as a guide, complete Table 9.4 to show (correct to three decimal places) the cost per equivalent unit for each cost element.

Table 9.4 Blending Process – cost per equivalent unit

	Direct labour	Direct material X	Direct material Y	Production overhead
Completed output	(100% × 65 000) 65 000			
Closing WIP				(50% × 31 000) 15 500
Total equivalent units	80 500	96 000		
Cost (from Exhibit 9.8)				
Cost/equivalent unit				

Table 9.5 Blending Process – cost per equivalent unit

	Direct labour	Direct material X	Direct material Y	Production overhead
Completed output	(100% × 65 000) 65 000	(100% × 65 000) 65 000	(100% × 65 000) 65 000	(100% × 65 000) 65 000
Closing WIP	(50% × 31 000) 15 500	(100% × 31 000) 31 000	(100% × 31 000) 31 000	(50% × 31 000) 15 500
Total equivalent units	80 500	96 000	96 000	80 500
Cost (from Exhibit 9.8)	£10 000	£80 000	£180 000	£30 000
Cost/equivalent unit	£0.124	£0.833	£1.875	£0.373

Table 9.5 is the completed tabulation. (Remember that when materials are input at the start of a process, every unit in the process is 100% complete for this cost element.)

 Use the cost per equivalent unit figures from Table 9.5 to determine the cost of completed output in the Blending Process for the period.

Cost of completed output:

65 000 equivalent units × (£0.124 [direct labour] + £0.833 [material X] + £1.875 [material Y] + £0.373 [production overhead])

= £208 325

The completed Blending Process Account is thus:

Blending Process Account

	Litres	£		Litres	£
Direct labour			Normal loss	4 000	–
(1000 hours @ £10)		10 000	Purification Process	65 000	208 325
Direct materials: X	40 000	80 000	**Closing WIP**		
Y	60 000	180 000	c/d (balance)	31 000	91 675
Overhead					
(1,000 hours @ £30)		30 000			
	100 000	300 000		100 000	300 000
WIP b/d	31 000	91 675			

If you verify the closing WIP cost using the equivalent units and costs per equivalent unit from Table 9.5, you will obtain a value of £91 651.5 – the £24.50 difference is due to the effect of rounding the costs per equivalent unit.

The Blending Process's normal loss was waste; had it been scrap, we would need to allow for the scrap value in our tabulation. This is usually effected by reducing the direct material cost by the amount of scrap value attaching to the normal loss. We shall see how this works in the next section of the chapter where we also consider abnormal losses and abnormal gains.

Abnormal losses, abnormal gains and equivalent units

Exhibit 9.9 contains the information we will use to illustrate the treatment of abnormal losses and gains.

NFK Ltd: blending and purification processes

Information in respect of the company's two processes for the last accounting period is as follows.

Blending Process
  Direct labour (1000 hours @ £10) £10 000
  Direct materials: X (40 000 litres) £80 000
                    Y (60 000 litres) £180 000
  Production overhead (1000 hours @ £30) £30 000

A normal loss of 4% of input arises during processing; this is caused by condensation and has no scrap value.
  During the period, 63 000 litres were transferred to the Purification Process; there were 31 000 litres of closing WIP, estimated to be 50% complete.

▶

> *Purification Process*
> Direct labour (400 hours @ £10) £4000
> Direct materials: Z £20 000
> Production overhead: (400 hours @ £30) £12 000
> Normal loss for the period was 3937 litres and had a total scrap value of £1969; 35 063 litres were transferred to Finished Goods, with 25 000 litres of closing WIP (estimated to be 20% complete).
> In both processes, materials are input at the start of processing, whilst labour and overheads are incurred evenly. Should any abnormal loss/gain arise in either process, it is detected at the 75% degree of completion.

Exhibit 9.9 Equivalent units, abnormal losses and abnormal gains

 Compare inputs and outputs for both processes and determine the extent of any abnormal loss/gain.

Blending Process

Inputs	Materials:	X		40 000 litres
		Y		60 000 litres
				100 000 litres
Outputs	Normal loss (4% of inputs)		4 000	
	Completed output		63 000	
	Closing WIP		31 000	98 000 litres
Therefore abnormal loss =				2 000 litres

Purification Process

Inputs	Transfers from Blending		63 000 litres
Outputs	Normal loss (from Exhibit 9.8)		
		3 937	
	Transfers to Finished Goods	35 063	
	Closing WIP	25 000	64 000 litres
Therefore abnormal gain =			1 000 litres

Because output from Blending forms the input to Purification, we need to cost the earlier process first. The abnormal loss units are included in our equivalent unit table, from which we obtain the cost to be credited to the process account, as shown in Table 9.6.

Remember that materials are input at the start of the process, so all units are 100% complete for this cost.

 Use the data from Table 9.6 to obtain the cost of completed output and abnormal loss for the Blending Process.

Table 9.6 Blending Process – cost per equivalent unit

	Direct labour	Direct material X	Direct material Y	Production overhead
Abnormal loss	(75% × 2000) 1500	(100% × 2000) 2000	(100% × 2000) 2000	(75% × 2000) 1500
Completed output	(100% × 63 000) 63 000	(100% × 63 000) 63 000	(100% × 63 000) 63 000	(100% × 63 000) 63 000
Closing WIP	(50% × 31 000) 15 500	(100% × 31 000) 31 000	(100% × 31 000) 31 000	(50% × 31 000) 15 500
Total equivalent units	80 000	96 000	96 000	80 000
Cost (from Exhibit 9.9)	£10 000	£80 000	£180 000	£30 000
Cost/equivalent unit	£0.125	£0.833	£1.875	£0.375

Cost of completed output

$$63\ 000 \text{ equivalent units} \times (£0.125 + £0.833 + £1.875 + £0.375)$$
$$= £202\ 104$$

Cost of abnormal loss

	£
Direct labour and production overhead:	
1500 equivalent units × (£0.125 + £0.375)	750
Materials X and Y:	
2000 equivalent units × (£0.833 + £1.875)	5416
	6166

Only when we have a cost for output from Blending can we determine the output costs for Purification. But before we do, we must consider our treatment of the abnormal gain in the later process. You will recall from our earlier discussion that an abnormal gain represents, in effect, an unexpected increase in good output produced (i.e. actual loss is lower than expected). In the case of NFK Ltd's Purification Process, the abnormal gain is detected at the 75% completion stage – i.e. after the degree of completion reached by closing WIP. What this means is that the abnormal gain forms part of the Purification Process's completed output.

You will also remember that we do not adjust the normal loss to reflect an abnormal gain, meaning that the normal loss is overstated to the extent of the abnormal gain. Bearing in mind that we have already dealt with the equivalent unit implications of the normal loss (by omitting the units concerned from our table), and that the abnormal gain is included in completed output, we must *deduct* the abnormal gain in our equivalent unit calculations. If we fail to do so (or if we add abnormal gain units) we will double-count the units concerned (triple-count if we add), and the process account will not balance. To enable us to post the process account, the abnormal gain is costed using the results from our equivalent unit calculations.

> ✔ *In our equivalent unit tabulation, what is the correct treatment of the £1969 scrap value attaching to normal loss?*

Table 9.7 Purification Process – cost per equivalent unit

	Transfers from Blending Process	Direct labour	Direct materials	Production overhead
Abnormal gain	(100% × (1000)) (1000)	(75% × (1000)) (750)	(100% × (1000)) (1000)	(75% × (1000)) (750)
Completed output	(100% × 35 063) 35 063	(100% × 35 063) 35 063	(100% × 35 063) 35 063	(100% × 35 063) 35 063
Closing WIP	(100% × 25 000) 25 000	(20% × 25000) 5000	(100% × 25 000) 25 000	(20% × 25000) 5000
Total equivalent units	59 063	39 313	59 063	39 313
Cost	£202 104[1]	£4000	(£20 000 – £1969) £18 031[2]	£12 000
Cost/equivalent unit	£3.422	£0.102	£0.305	£0.305

Notes
1 We calculated this cost earlier when we dealt with the Blending Process.
2 Cost of material Z less the scrap value of normal loss.

The normal loss's scrap value (which represents a monetary credit to the process account) should be deducted from input cost. Typically, this is effected by reducing the material cost in the cost/equivalent unit calculation. Table 9.7 shows the appropriate figures for the Purification Process.

Cost of transfers to Finished Goods

$$35\ 063 \text{ equivalent units} \times (£3.422 + £0.102 + £0.305 + £0.305)$$
$$= £144\ 950$$

Cost of abnormal gain

	£
Transfers from Blending and material Z:	
1000 equivalent units × (£3.422 + £0.305)	3727
Direct labour and production overhead:	
750 equivalent units × (£0.102 + £0.305)	305
	4032

Finally, we can prepare the process accounts, which are given below.

Blending Process Account

	Litres	£		Litres	£
Direct labour			Normal loss	4 000	–
(1000 hours @ £10)		10 000	**Abnormal loss**	**2 000**	**6 166**
Direct materials: X	40 000	80 000	**Purification Process**	**63 000**	**202 104**
Y	60 000	180 000	**Closing WIP c/d (balance)**	**31 000**	**91 730**
Overhead					
(1000 hours @ £30)		30 000			
	100 000	300 000		100 000	300 000
WIP b/d	**31 000**	**91 730**			

Purification Process Account

	Litres	£		Litres	£
Blending Process	63 000	202 104	Normal loss	3 937	1 969
Direct labour			Finished Goods	35 063	144 950
(400 hours @ £10)		4 000	Closing WIP		
Direct materials: Z		20 000	c/d (balance)	25 000	95 217
Overhead					
(400 hours @ £30)		12 000			
Abnormal Gain	1 000	4 032			
	64 000	242 136		64 000	242 136
WIP b/d	25 000	95 217			

 Use the data from Table 9.7 to confirm the value of closing WIP in the Purification Process. (Allow for a £7 rounding difference.)

Value of closing WIP:
Transfers from Blending and material Z:

	£
25 000 equivalent units × (£3.422 + £0.305)	93 175
Direct labour and production overhead:	
5000 equivalent units × (£0.102 + £0.305)	2 035
	95 210
Rounding difference	7
Value per process account	95 217

The last aspect of process costing we need to examine is the impact of opening WIP.

Opening work-in-progress

The existence of opening WIP presents us with something of a dilemma. We have to decide whether the opening WIP is indistinguishable from the current period's production or whether it is completed first in the current period. If we take the first view, we will adopt an **average cost (AVCO)** approach to stock valuation. If we take the second view, we will adopt a **First-In-First-Out (FIFO)** approach. (You should be familiar with these terms from our discussion of materials' stock valuation in Chapter 4.)

Average cost (AVCO) method

Since we are assuming that the opening WIP is physically indistinguishable from the current period's production, we are assuming the same about the related cost. This being so, the cost of opening WIP, which must be subdivided into its separate cost elements, is added to the cost of the current period's inputs in the equivalent unit tabulation. We shall use Exhibit 9.10 to illustrate.

 Compare the process's inputs and outputs, and obtain the amount of any abnormal loss/gain in litres.

NFK Ltd: Blending Process opening WIP

Information in respect of the Blending Process for last accounting period is as follows.

Opening WIP (30% complete): 20 000 litres, total cost £60 000. The total cost comprises direct labour £2000, Material X £20 000, Material Y £30 000 and production overhead £8000.
Direct labour (1000 hours @ £10) £10 000
Direct materials: X (40 000 litres) £80 000
                  Y (60 000 litres) £180 000
Production overhead (1000 hours @ £30) £30 000

A normal loss of 4% of input arises during processing; this is caused by condensation and has no scrap value. During the period, 83 000 litres were transferred to the Purification Process; there were 31 000 litres of closing WIP, estimated to be 50% complete. Any abnormal losses/gains are detected at the 75% completion stage.
Materials are input at the start of processing, while labour and overheads are incurred evenly.

Exhibit 9.10 Opening WIP

What we need to remember here is that opening WIP now forms part of the process inputs, which, by increasing inputs, will affect the amount of normal loss (which is 4% of inputs):

			Litres
Inputs	Opening WIP		20 000
	Direct materials: X		40 000
	Y		60 000
			120 000
Outputs	Normal loss (4% × 120 000)	4 800	
	Closing WIP	31 000	
	Completed output	83 000	118 800
Therefore abnormal loss =			1 200

Dealing with the cost of opening WIP requires only a minor insertion in our equivalent units calculation, as illustrated in Table 9.8 on page 256.

 Opening WIP units *are not shown in Table 9.8. Why is this?*

The average cost method of stock valuation assumes that opening WIP is indistinguishable from current period's production. Therefore opening WIP units will form part of the period's completed output and/or closing WIP and/or abnormal loss – which are shown in Table 9.8. The cost of completed output is:

83 000 equivalent units × (£0.121 + £0.868 + £1.823 + £0.382)
= £265 102.

Table 9.8 Blending Process – cost/equivalent unit with opening WIP (AVCO)

	Direct labour	Direct material X	Direct material Y	Production overhead
Abnormal loss	(75% × 1200) 900	(100% × 1200) 1200	(100% × 1200) 1200	(75% × 1200) 900
Completed output	(100% × 83 000) 83 000	(100% × 83 000) 83 000	(100% × 83 000) 83 000	(100% × 83 000) 83 000
Closing WIP	(50% × 31 000) 15 500	(100% × 31 000) 31 000	(100% × 31 000) 31 000	(50% × 31 000) 15 500
Total equivalent units	99 400	115 200	115 200	99 400
Cost (from Exhibit 9.10): opening WIP current inputs total	**£2 000** **£10 000** **£12 000**	**£20 000** **£80 000** **£100 000**	**£30 000** **£180 000** **£210 000**	**£8 000** **£30 000** **£38 000**
Cost/equivalent unit	£0.121	£0.868	£1.823	£0.382

Abnormal loss is costed as:

	£
Direct materials X and Y	
1200 equivalent units × (£0.868 + £1.823)	3229
Direct labour and production overhead:	
900 equivalent units × (£0.121 + £0.382)	453
	3682

We can now post the process account:

Blending Process Account

	Litres	£		Litres	£
Opening WIP	**20 000**	**60 000**	Normal loss	4 800	–
Direct labour			**Abnormal loss**	**1 200**	**3 682**
(1000 hours @ £10)	40 000	10 000	**Purification Process**	**83 000**	**265 102**
Direct materials: X	60 000	80 000	**Closing WIP**		
Y		180 000	c/d (balance)	31 000	91 216
Overhead					
(1000 hours @ £30)		30 000			
	120 000	360 000		120 000	360 000
WIP b/d	**31 000**	**91 216**			

First-In–First-Out (FIFO) method

If we use this method to value WIP, we take the view that opening WIP is distinguishable from the current period's production, being completed first during the current period. Opening WIP will therefore be included in the process's completed output for the period. Equivalent unit calculations should thus exclude (in both physical and monetary terms) opening WIP to the extent that it is complete at the start of the present period. The cost of opening WIP is added to the cost of the period's completed output. Table 9.9 applies FIFO principles to the Blending Process data from Exhibit 9.10; as with the AVCO method, a simple amendment to the basic equivalent units table is all that is needed.

 Use the data from Table 9.9 to determine the cost of abnormal loss and completed output from the Blending Process.

Cost of abnormal loss

	£
Materials X and Y:	
1200 equivalent units × (£0.840 + £1.891)	3277
Direct labour and production overhead:	
900 equivalent units × (£0.107 + £0.321)	385
	3662

Some care is needed in determination of the cost of completed output. First, we must remember to add the cost of opening WIP; secondly, we need to extract the correct number of equivalent units for each cost element from Table 9.9.

Cost of completed output

	£
Opening WIP (from Exhibit 9.10)	60 000
Materials X and Y:	
63 000 equivalent units × (£0.840 + £1.891)	172 053
Direct labour and production overhead:	
77 000 equivalent units × (£0.107 + £0.321)	32 956
	265 009

Table 9.9 Blending Process – cost/equivalent unit with opening WIP (FIFO)

	Direct labour	Direct material X	Direct material Y	Production overhead
Abnormal loss	(75% × 1200)	(100% × 1200)	(100% × 1200)	(75% × 1200)
	900	1200	1200	900
Completed output	(100% × 83 000)	(100% × 83 000)	(100% × 83 000)	(100% × 83 000)
less **Opening WIP**	–(30% × 20 000)	–(100% × 20 000)	–(100% × 20 000)	–(30% × 20 000)
equivalent units	77 000	63 000	63 000	77 000
Closing WIP	(50% × 31 000)	(100% × 31 000)	(100% × 31 000)	(50% × 31 000)
	15 500	31 000	31 000	15 000
Total equivalent units	93 400	95 200	95 200	93 400
Cost (from Exhibit 9.10): current inputs	**£10 000**	**£80 000**	**£180 000**	**£30 000**
Cost/equivalent unit	£0.107	£0.840	£1.891	£0.321

When FIFO is employed, the Blending Process Account is:

Blending Process Account

	Litres	£		Litres	£
Opening WIP	**20 000**	**60 000**	Normal loss	4 800	–
Direct labour			**Abnormal loss**	**1 200**	**3 662**
(1000 hours @ £10)	40 000	10 000	**Purification Process**	83 000	265 009
Direct materials: X	60 000	80 000	**Closing WIP**		
Y		180 000	c/d (balance)	31 000	91 329
Overhead					
(1000 hours @ £30)		30 000			
	120 000	360 000		120 000	360 000
WIP b/d	**31 000**	**91 329**			

AVCO and FIFO: final thoughts

The choice of which method to adopt really depends on the nature of the process(es) concerned: i.e. can opening WIP be separately identified or not? And you should remember that equivalent unit calculations which can appear quite intimidating to undertake manually are ideally suited to computer spreadsheets. On rare occasions, you may be faced with an examination question which does not specify whether AVCO or FIFO is to be used. Assuming only one method is permissible, you should apply the following guidelines to opening WIP:

1 AVCO can *only* be used when the cost of opening WIP is subdivided into its separate constituent cost elements.
2 FIFO can *only* be used when opening WIP's degree of completion is given for each element of cost.

SUMMARY

In this chapter, we have discussed and illustrated process costing, a form of continuous operation costing applicable to mass-production of items which are identical (or very nearly so). We have seen that:

- Many process-costing situations involve a series of sequential processes; this has implications for the costs of subsequent processes.
- **Normal losses** are expected under normal operating conditions with the associated cost being borne by other output from the process.
- **Waste** is discarded substances that have no value.
- **Scrap** is discarded substances that have some value – either sales value or re-use value.
- **By-products** are the incidental outcome of producing main products, and have a relatively low sales value compared to main products.
- **Abnormal losses** arise where the actual process loss exceeds that which was expected.

- **Abnormal gains** arise where actual process loss is lower than that which was expected.
- Abnormal losses and abnormal gains are treated separately from normal losses in order to enhance production control.
- Process costing double-entries are as set out in Table 9.10:

Table 9.10 Process costing double-entries

	Account debited	Account credited
Process inputs (direct materials, labour and overhead)	Process	Stores, Wages Control, Overhead as appropriate
Normal loss: waste **Normal loss: scrap**	None Normal Loss	Process (units lost *only*) Process (units and scrap value)
Abnormal loss: cost **Abnormal loss: scrap value**	Abnormal Loss Bank/Debtor	Process (units and *cost*) Abnormal Loss
Abnormal gain: cost **Abnormal gain: scrap value**	Process Abnormal Gain	Abnormal Gain Normal Loss
By-product	By-product	Process *or* Profit and loss (net realisable value)

- When there are no incomplete units, cost per unit of completed output and of abnormal gain/abnormal loss is:

$$\frac{\text{Net process cost}}{\text{Expected output}}$$

- **Equivalent units** (**equivalent production**) convert incomplete output into notional units of complete output by the following conversion:

$$(\text{incomplete units} \times \text{degree of completion})$$

- Because their cost is borne by other process output, normal losses are omitted from cost/equivalent unit calculations (but see Appendix 9B).
- Abnormal losses are included in the cost/equivalent unit calculation as 'output'.
- To prevent double-counting, abnormal gains are *deducted* in determining the number of equivalent units produced.
- The **average cost** (**AVCO**) method assumes that opening WIP is indistinguishable from the current period's output. The cost of opening WIP is therefore added to that of the current period's inputs and averaged over all outputs in determination of the cost/equivalent unit.
- The **First-In–First-Out** (**FIFO**) approach assumes that opening WIP is completed first in the current period. The cost of opening WIP and the related equivalent units are excluded from the cost/equivalent unit calculation, with the cost of opening WIP being added to that of the current period's completed output.

In the next chapter, we will develop our discussion of process costing to examine production of two or more main products from the same process.

FURTHER READING

Coulthurst, N., Process costing – part one. *Students' Newsletter*, January 2000 (ACCA).

Coulthurst, N., Process costing – part two. *Students' Newsletter*, February 2000 (ACCA).

APPENDIX 9A: ABRIDGING THE UNIT COST TABULATION

The tabulations needed to determine unit costs may take a little time to prepare. Under examination conditions, time is at a premium, so it might be desirable to reduce the amount of work involved. One way in which we can achieve this is to group certain cost elements together. Consider Table 9A.1, which is a reproduction of Table 9.3 from the body of the chapter.

From Exhibit 9.7, we know that transfers from Blending and direct materials are both input at the start of the process; we could therefore combine their separate columns under the heading 'Materials'. Similarly, direct labour and production overhead are both incurred evenly and could thus be combined under the heading **Conversion cost**. (Some examination questions make this last combination for you). An abridged version of the unit cost tabulation based on these combinations of cost elements is presented in Table 9A.2.

The costs of completed output and closing WIP are, respectively,

$$75\ 000 \text{ equivalent units} \times (£3.20 \text{ [materials]} + £0.20 \text{ [conversion cost]})$$
$$= £255\ 000$$

and

	£
25 000 equivalent units × £3.20 [materials]	80 000
5000 equivalent units × £0.20 [conversion cost]	1 000
	81 000

These are precisely the same values we obtained in the body of the chapter using the longer methodology. The Purification Process Account will also be exactly the same as the one presented on page 248.

Table 9A.1 Purification Process – cost per equivalent unit

	Transfers from Blending Process	Direct labour	Direct materials	Production Blending Process
Completed output	(100% × 75 000) 75 000	(100% × 75 000) 75 000	(100% × 75 000) 75 000	(100% × 75 000) 75 000
Closing WIP	(100% × 25 000) 25 000	(20% × 25 000) 5000	(100% × 25 000) 25 000	(20% × 25 000) 5000
Total equivalent units	100 000	80 000	100 000	80 000
Cost (from Exhibit 9.7)	£300 000	£4000	£20 000	£12 000
Cost/equivalent unit	£3.00	£0.05	£0.20	£0.15

Table 9A.2 Purification Process – abridged unit cost tabulation

	Materials	Conversion cost
Completed output	(100% × 75 000) 75 000	(100% × 75 000) 75 000
Closing WIP	(100% × 25 000) 25 000	(20% × 25 000) 5000
Total equivalent units	100 000	80 000
Cost*	£320 000	£16 000
Cost/equivalent unit	£3.20	£0.20

* The cost is merely the sum of the individual cost elements comprising each combined category:

Materials	£
Transfers from Blending	300 000
Direct materials	20 000
	320 000

Conversion cost	
Direct labour	4 000
Production overhead	12 000
	16 000

You should note, however, that you can *only* combine cost elements that are incurred on the same basis. In this case we have two costs that arise at the start of the process (and which we can therefore combine) plus two costs that arise evenly throughout the process (which we can also combine). It would not be possible to combine, say, direct materials with direct labour. If we had made such a combination, how many equivalent units should we show for closing WIP?

APPENDIX 9B: NORMAL LOSSES AND EQUIVALENT UNITS

Apportioning the cost of normal losses

When we calculated the cost per equivalent unit during this chapter, we omitted normal loss units from our tabulation. Although this is the easiest way of dealing with such units, it is not the only approach; nor, in certain circumstances, is it the most technically correct method. As an alternative, we could include the normal loss units in our tabulation, determine a cost for the normal loss, then apportion this cost between completed output, closing WIP and abnormal loss (if relevant). For convenience Exhibit 9.8 from the chapter is reproduced below as Exhibit 9B.1.

If we are to assign a cost to the normal loss and apportion it between completed output and closing WIP, the cost/equivalent unit tabulation will be as shown in Table 9B.1. Compare this with Table 9.5 within the chapter.

NFK Ltd: Blending Process

Details of the company's Blending Process for the last accounting period are:

Direct labour (1000 hours @ £10) £10 000
Direct materials: X (40 000 litres @ £2) £80 000
Y (60 000 litres @ £3) £180 000
Production overhead (1000 hours @ £30) £30 000

A normal loss of 4% of inputs arises during the process; this is caused by condensation and has no scrap value.

Completed output transferred to Purification Process: 65 000 litres
Closing WIP: 31 000 litres, 50% complete.

Materials X and Y are both input at the start of the process, while labour and overheads are incurred evenly throughout the process.

Exhibit 9B.1 Blending Process – equivalent units and normal losses

Table 9B.1 Blending Process – cost per equivalent unit

	Direct labour	Direct material X	Direct material Y	Production overhead
Normal loss	(100% × 4000) 4000	(100% × 4000) 4000	(100% × 4000) 4000	(100% × 4000) 4000
Completed output	(100% × 65 000) 65 000	(100% × 65 000) 65 000	(100% × 65 000) 65 000	(100% × 65 000) 65 000
Closing WIP	(50% × 31 000) 15 500	(100% × 31 000) 31 000	(100% × 31 000) 31 000	(50% × 31 000) 15 500
Total equivalent units	84 500	100 000	100 000	84 500
Cost (from Exhibit 9B.1)	£10 000	£80 000	£180 000	£30 000
Cost/equivalent unit	£0.118	£0.800	£1.800	£0.355

In the table, we have assumed that the normal loss is 100% complete for every element of cost. We will alter this shortly.

Cost of normal loss:

4000 equivalent units × (£0.118 + £0.800 + £1.800 + £0.355)
= £12 292

Cost of completed output:

65 000 equivalent units × (£0.118 + £0.800 + £1.800 + £0.355)
= £199 745

Total units produced = 65 000 (completed output) + 31 000 (closing WIP) = 96 000. Completed output represents 65 000/96 000 of total units, so completed output will receive this proportion of the cost of the normal loss (in addition to the £199 745 calculated above):

$$\frac{65\ 000}{96\ 000} \times £12\ 292 = £8323 \text{ (rounded)}$$

The full cost of completed output is thus (£199 745 + £8,323) = £208 068.
The completed Blending Process Account is now:

Blending Process Account

	Litres	£		Litres	£
Direct labour			Normal loss	4 000	–
(1000 hours @ £10)		10 000	Purification Process	65 000	208 068
Direct materials: X	40 000	80 000	**Closing WIP**		
Y	60 000	180 000	**c/d (balance)**	31 000	91 932
Overhead					
(1000 hours @ £30)		30 000			
	100 000	300 000		100 000	300 000
WIP b/d	**31 000**	**91 932**			

The difference between the values in bold type for completed output and closing WIP in the account above and those we obtained in the chapter (£208 325 and £91 675 respectively) is due solely to the effect of rounding. Therefore, if we can reasonably assume that the normal loss is 100% complete, then the treatment adopted in the chapter is both simpler and technically correct.

Normal loss not 100% complete

It is possible that losses may arise at a discrete point in processing. Suppose, in Exhibit 9B.1, that normal losses arise at the 60% completion stage. This is a later stage of processing than that achieved by the closing WIP, and we could argue that, to be technically correct, only units which have passed 60% completion should receive an apportionment of this cost. In our example closing WIP is only 50% complete, so it may be inappropriate to charge these units with a share of a loss that is still to occur. Thus, only completed output would be charged with the cost of the normal loss.
A revised unit cost tabulation for this situation is shown in Table 9B.2.

Cost of normal loss:

	£
Direct labour and production overhead	
2400 equivalent units × (£0.121 + £0.362)	1 159
Direct materials X and Y	
4000 equivalent units × (£0.800 + £1.800)	10 400
	11 559

Cost of completed output:

	£
65 000 equivalent units × (£0.121 + £0.800 + £1.800 + £0.362)	
	200 395
Add Cost of normal loss	11 559
	211 954

Table 9B.2 Blending Process – cost per equivalent unit

	Direct labour	Direct material X	Direct material Y	Production overhead
Normal loss	(60% × 4000) 2400	(100% × 4000) 4000	(100% × 4000) 4000	(60% × 4000) 2400
Completed output	(100% × 65 000) 65 000	(100% × 65 000) 65 000	(100% × 65 000) 65 000	(100% × 65 000) 65 000
Closing WIP	(50% × 31 000) 15 500	(100% × 31 000) 31 000	(100% × 31 000) 31 000	(50% × 31 000) 15 500
Total equivalent units	82 900	100 000	100 000	82 900
Cost (from Exhibit 9B.1)	£10 000	£80 000	£180 000	£30 000
Cost/equivalent unit	£0.121	£0.800	£1.800	£0.362

The Blending Process Account is now:

Blending Process Account

	Litres	£		Litres	£
Direct labour			Normal loss	4 000	–
(1000 hours @ £10)		10 000	Purification Process	65 000	211 954
Direct materials: X	40 000	80 000	**Closing WIP**		
Y	60 000	180 000	c/d (balance)	31 000	88 046
Overhead					
(1000 hours @ £30)		30 000			
	100 000	300 000		100 000	300 000
WIP b/d	**31 000**	**88 046**			

Although technically correct, the additional work involved might not be justified. Justification is essentially a matter of how significantly relevant valuations are affected by our choice of method. If you compare the values for completed output and closing WIP in the account immediately above with those in the previous version (and hence – allowing for rounding differences – with the version in the chapter itself), you will see that the differences are roughly 2% and 4% for completed output and closing WIP respectively. In the circumstances, we might therefore reasonably conclude that our original approach produced figures of acceptable accuracy.

SELF-TEST QUESTIONS

9.1 For each of the statements that follows, place a tick in the appropriate box to indicate whether it is true or false.

	True	False
(a) A FIFO approach to work-in-progress valuation assumes that opening work-in-progress is completed first in the current period.	☐	☐
(b) In an equivalent units calculation, abnormal gain units should be added to good units produced.	☐	☐
(c) In a process with no work-in-progress, the cost per unit of good production is $\dfrac{\text{Net process cost}}{\text{Good output produced}}$	☐	☐
(d) In a process account, normal loss should be netted off against any abnormal gain that may arise.	☐	☐
(e) The accounting treatment of waste differs from that of scrap.	☐	☐
(f) In a process where an abnormal gain arises, the normal loss's scrap value must be reduced to reflect the scrap value of that gain.	☐	☐
(g) In an equivalent units calculation, units transferred from a previous process will be 100% complete in respect of that process's costs.	☐	☐

9.2 XYZ plc manufactures its product through a series of processes. The FIFO method of valuing opening work in process is used and the following details relate to April 1999.

- Opening work in process was 300 units, each unit being 80% processed as to materials and 60% processed as to conversion costs.
- Normal loss was 250 units, fully completed.
- Finished output was 7250 units; there were no abnormal losses or gains.
- Closing work in process was 400 units, each unit being 70% processed as to materials and 40% processed as to conversion costs.

When calculating the costs per equivalent unit, the number of equivalent units to be used is:

	Materials	Conversion
A	7290	7230
B	7470	7290
C	7590	7530
D	7770	7590
E	8020	7480

(CIMA, *Operational Cost Accounting*, May 1999)

9.3 The following details relate to the main process of W Limited, a chemical manufacturer:

Opening work-in-progress	2000 litres, fully complete as to materials and 40% complete as to conversion
Material input	24 000 litres
Normal loss is 10% of input	
Output to Process 2	19 500 litres

Closing work-in-progress   3000 litres, fully complete as to materials and 45% complete as to conversion

The number of equivalent units to be included in W Limited's calculation of the cost per equivalent unit using a **FIFO basis** of valuation are:

	Materials	Conversion
A	19 400	18 950
B	20 500	20 050
C	21 600	21 150
D	23 600	20 750
E	23 600	21 950

(CIMA, *Operational Cost Accounting*, November 1996)

9.4 A chemical producer manufactures Product XK by means of two successive processes, Process 1 and Process 2. The information provided below relates to the most recent accounting period, period 10.

	Process 1	Process 2
Opening work in progress	Nil	Nil
Material input during period	2400 units – cost £5280	2200 units (from Process 1)
Added material		£9460
Direct labour	£2260	£10 560
Factory overhead	100% of labour cost	2/3 of labour cost
Transfer to Process 2	2200 units	
Transfer to finished goods		2200 units
Closing work in progress	200 units 100% complete with respect to materials and 30% complete with respect to labour and production overhead	Nil

Requirements:

(a) Calculate the value of the goods transferred from Process 1 to Process 2 during period 10 and the value of the closing work in progress left in Process 1 at the end of period 10. **(12 marks)**

(b) Calculate the value of the goods transferred from Process 2 to finished goods during period 10, and the value of 1 unit of production. **(7 marks)**

(c) Describe, using no more than one or two sentences, the accounting treatment of scrap proceeds in process costing. **(2 marks)**

(d) Describe, using no more than one or two sentences, the accounting treatment of abnormal losses in process costing. **(2 marks)**

(e) Describe, using no more than one or two sentences, the accounting treatment of abnormal gains in process costing. **(2 marks)**

(Total: 25 marks)

(ACCA, *Cost Accounting Systems*, June 1998)

9.5 Chemical Processors manufacture Wonderchem using two processes – Mixing and Distillation. The following details relate to the Distillation process for a period.

	£
No opening work-in-progress (WIP)	
Input from mixing 36 000 kg at a cost of	166 000
Labour for period	43 800
Overheads for period	29 200

Closing WIP of 8000 kg, which was 100% complete for materials and 50% complete for labour and overheads.

The normal loss in Distillation is 10% of fully complete production. Actual loss in the period was 3600 kg, fully complete, which were scrapped.

Requirements:

(a) Calculate whether there was a Normal or Abnormal loss or Abnormal gain for the period. **(2 marks)**

(b) Prepare the Distillation Process account for the period, showing clearly weights and values. **(10 marks)**

(c) Explain what changes would be required in the accounts if the scrapped production had a resale value *and* give the accounting entries. **(3 marks)**

(Total: 15 marks)

(CIMA, *Cost Accounting and Quantitative Methods*, November 1997)

QUESTIONS WITHOUT ANSWERS

9.6 A chemical process has a normal wastage of 10% of input. In a period, 2500 kg of material were input and there was an abnormal loss of 75 kg. What quantity (kg) of good production was achieved?

    A 2175
    B 2250
    C 2325
    D 2475

(CIMA, *Cost Accounting and Quantitative Methods*, November 1998)

9.7 The following details relate to the main process of X Limited, a chemical manufacturer:

Opening work-in-progress	2000 litres, fully complete as to materials and 40% complete as to conversion
Material input	24 000 litres
Normal loss is 10% of input	
Losses arise at the end of processing.	
Output to process 2	19 500 litres
Closing work-in-progress	3000 litres, fully complete as to materials and 45% complete as to conversion

The number of equivalent units to be included in X Limited's calculation of the cost per equivalent unit, using a **weighted average basis** of valuation are:

	Materials	Conversion
A	21 400	19 750
B	21 400	20 850
C	22 500	21 950
D	22 500	20 850
E	23 600	21 950

(CIMA, *Operational Cost Accounting*, November 1999)

9.8 A company manufactures a product which passes through two processes before completion. The following data relates to the manufacture of the product during the period just ended when 100 000 units were input to Process 1:

	Process 1	Process 2
Basic raw material (£)	143 969	(from Process 1)
Materials added in process (£)	–	76 023
Direct labour costs (£)	47 104	34 337
Production overhead (% of direct labour cost)	125	108
Normal loss (% of input units)	4.1	3.0
Scrap value of process losses (£/unit)	0.36	0.52
Output (units)	95 725	92 984

There was no work in progress at the beginning or end of the period. Lost units are fully complete.

Requirements:

(a) Prepare the process cost accounts for the period. (Loss/gain accounts are *not* required.)

(13 marks)

(b) Describe how process accounts are prepared where work remains in progress at the end of each period and the FIFO valuation method is used. (Assume no process losses.)

(7 marks)
(Total: 20 marks)

(ACCA, *Management Information*, June 1998)

9.9 Industrial Solvents Limited mixes together three chemicals – A, B and C – in the ratio 3 : 2 : 1 to produce Allklean, a specialised anti-static fluid. The chemicals cost £8, £6 and £3.90 per litre respectively.

In a period, 12 000 litres in total were input to the mixing process. The normal process loss is 5% of input and in the period there was an abnormal loss of 100 litres whilst the completed production was 9500 litres.

There was no opening work-in-progress (WIP) and the closing WIP was 100% complete for materials and 40% complete for labour and overheads. Labour and overheads were £41 280 in total for the period. Materials lost in production are scrapped.

Requirements:

(a) Calculate the volume of closing WIP. **(3 marks)**

(b) Prepare the Mixing process account for the period, showing clearly volumes and values. **(9 marks)**

(c) Briefly explain what changes would be necessary in your account if an abnormal gain were achieved in a period. **(3 marks)**

(Total: 15 marks)

(CIMA, *Cost Accounting and Quantitative Methods*, May 1999)

9.10 C Limited manufactures a range of products and the data below refer to one product which goes through one process only. The company operates a thirteen four-weekly reporting system for process and product costs and the data given below relate to Period 10.

There was no opening work-in-progress stock.
5000 units of materials input at £2.94 per unit entered the process.

	£
Further direct materials added	13 830
Direct wages incurred	6 555
Production overhead	7 470

Normal loss is 3% of input.

Closing work-in-progress was 800 units but these were incomplete, having reached the following percentages of completion for each of the elements of cost listed:

	%
Direct materials added	75
Direct wages	50
Production overhead	25

270 units were scrapped after a quality control check when the units were at the following degrees of completion:

	%
Direct materials added	$66\frac{2}{3}$
Direct wages	$33\frac{1}{3}$
Production overhead	$16\frac{2}{3}$

Units scrapped, regardless of the degree of completion, are sold for £1 each and it is company policy to credit the process account with the scrap value of normal loss units.

Requirements:

(a) Prepare the Period 10 accounts for the
  (i) process account; and
  (ii) abnormal gain or loss **(23 marks)**

(b) Suggest **two** possible reasons to explain the gain or loss shown in (a)(ii) above.

(2 marks)

(Total: 25 marks)

(CIMA, *Cost Accounting*, November 1990)

CHAPTER 10

Joint product costing

Are your joint costs out of joint?

... Common costs are shared costs between different products or services. These may be regarded as 'joint' products or services as a common material or expense has been used in their provision ... The problem arises in determining how these common costs are to be shared out amongst the products. Whether the common costs are derived from the ingredients in a witches' cauldron, a vat in a distillery or supervision of direct operatives carrying out a public service, there is still the need to apportion them in some way across the joint products or services.

    The main reasons for sharing out the common cost may be to facilitate an absorption costing system and to ascertain the profitability of the joint products. However, if an arbitrary method of apportionment is used there is a danger of distortion ...

Source: Richard Smith, *CIMA Student*, August 1994.

Exhibit 10.1 The rationale for joint product costing

INTRODUCTION

In the previous chapter, we considered the treatment of by-products in a process-costing scenario. As an incidental outcome of processing, and of comparatively low sales value, by-products do not warrant the same detailed costing treatment as main products. However, this changes when two or more *main* products emerge from the same process. Since main products are the purpose of the process, we must – as Exhibit 10.1 makes clear – apportion process costs to these main products. But, as the Exhibit also points out, joint cost apportionments may lead to distortions – a point we shall return to later in the chapter. You will remember from our discussion of overhead in Chapters 5 and 6 that cost apportionment is not a precise science, and is always likely to contain a certain element of subjectivitiy. Exactly the same may be said of apportioning joint process costs to main products.

OBJECTIVES

When you have completed this chapter, you will be able to:

- distinguish between joint process costs and further processing costs;
- explain the meaning and significance of the split-off point (point of separation);

- apportion joint process costs to main products on the basis of output, final, intermediate and notional sales values;
- apportion joint process costs so as to achieve a uniform profit margin;
- apply a profit centre approach to the joint process;
- explain the strengths and weaknesses of different methods of dealing with joint process costs;
- evaluate the financial viability of 'sell or process further' decisions;
- appreciate the limitation of joint cost apportionments for decision making, planning and control;
- prepare joint process accounts for a variety of situations, including those involving losses, gains and incomplete units.

THE COSTING PROBLEM

Figure 10.1 illustrates a typical joint product costing situation: a set of common inputs to the process (materials, labour and overhead) result in three main products plus a by-product. If we are to measure profit and value stocks of the main products, we need some method of attributing an appropriate share of the joint process's cost to them.

The initial costing 'problem' in Exhibit 10.1 is how to apportion the cost of common inputs to the process (**common costs** or **joint costs**) between the three main products

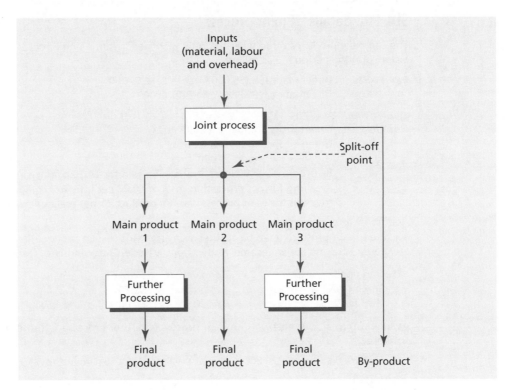

Figure 10.1 A typical joint process situation

(**joint products**). Note that by-products, being an incidental outcome of the process, do *not* receive an apportionment of joint costs.

The **split-off point** (or **point of separation**) indicated in Figure 10.1 refers to that stage of processing at which the common inputs become identifiable as three separate main products. In many situations, this will occur at the end of the joint process, although the split-off point may also arise during processing.

A second potential problem deriving from Figure 10.1 is that some (or all) joint products may be subjected to further processing after the split-off point. In some cases, further processing is a necessity if joint products are to be made saleable. In other cases, management may be free to decide whether or not to further process beyond the split-off point – so we need to provide an analysis of the costs and benefits of doing so.

Initially, we shall consider the cost apportionment exercise.

APPORTIONING JOINT PROCESS COST

We will use the information from Exhibit 10.2 to illustrate the different apportionment bases that can be applied to joint process costs.

 Use the data in Exhibit 10.2 to determine the total amount of the joint process cost that is to be apportioned.

SDL Ltd: details of joint process

The company produces three types of liquid plant feed from a single process. Details for last accounting period are as follows:

Input costs   Direct materials (55 000 litres @ £1) £55 000
Direct labour (500 hours @ £12) £6000
Production overhead: 140% of direct labour cost.

Outputs   Green-Grow Standard: 25 000 litres
Green-Grow Extra: 15 000 litres
Green-Grow Super: 10 000 litres
By-product Z: 5000 litres. This can be sold for £0.50 per litre after incurring further processing costs of £0.22 per litre. It is company policy to credit the joint process with By-product Z's net realisable value.

Additional information
All three main products may be further processed; after such processing, Green-Grow Standard, Extra and Super become, respectively, Miracle-Grow Standard, Extra and Super.

Selling price per litre:	Standard	Extra	Super
Green-Grow	£1.30	£2.20	£2.40
Miracle-Grow	£2.20	£4.00	£4.50

Assuming that all output from the joint process is further processed, further processing costs are:

Green-Grow Standard £20 000; Green-Grow Extra £30 000; Green-Grow Super £15 000.

Exhibit 10.2 Joint process data

Joint process cost:

	£	£
Direct materials		55 000
Direct labour		6 000
Production overhead (140% × direct labour cost)		8 400
		69 400
less Net realisable value of By-product Z:		
Sales value (5000 litres × £0.50)	2 500	
Processing cost (5000 litres × £0.22)	1 100	1 400
		68 000

We therefore need to apportion £68 000 between the three 'Green-Grow' products.

Apportionment on the basis of output

Probably the simplest approach is to apportion the joint process cost in proportion to each 'Green-Grow' product's share of total output (Table 10.1).

Table 10.1 Output basis of apportionment

Product	Output (litres)	% of total output	Joint cost apportioned
Green-Grow Standard	25 000	50	£34 000 (50%)
Green-Grow Extra	15 000	30	£20 400 (30%)
Green-Grow Super	10 000	20	£13 600 (20%)
	50 000	100	£68 000

 Can you see any problems with using output as the basis for apportionment of joint costs?

Although output is undoubtedly a straightforward apportionment basis, its use may give rise to problems.

Joint products with different physical characteristics

In our example, all three joint products are liquids. Suppose, however, one had been a liquid, one a gas and one a solid: it would not be possible to determine percentages of total output because output is in different physical states. Thus, apportionment using output simply would not work – unless we were to express output in much more technical terms (atomic weight, say). Doing this would almost certainly destroy the cost/benefit advantage of using output as the apportionment basis.

Lower of cost and net realisable value rule

In Chapter 4, we stated that the fundamental principle governing stock valuation is that stock should be valued at the lower of cost and net realisable value.

Determine the cost per litre of Green-Grow Standard and comment on this in light of the product's net realisable value per litre.

Cost per litre of Green-Grow Standard:

$$\frac{\text{Joint cost apportioned}}{\text{Output}} = \frac{£34\,000}{25\,000 \text{ litres}} = £1.36 \text{ per litre}$$

From Exhibit 10.1 we know the net realisable value of Green-Grow Standard is only £1.30. So there could be a danger that use of output as the apportionment basis might result in stock values that breach a fundamental rule of accounting. In fact, if you check the figures in Table 10.1, you will see that the cost per litre for *all three* 'Green-Grow' products is £1.36, which might be taken to imply that the three products are the same. Is this reasonable in light of their markedly different selling prices per litre?

In order to overcome the difficulties of using output as the apportionment basis, we may choose to employ sales value as an alternative. The problem here lies in defining what we mean by 'sales value'. There are three major possible definitions, each of which we will consider below.

Apportionment on the basis of final sales value

Using this approach, we apportion joint process cost on the basis of each joint product's proportionate share of total final sales value. 'Final' in this context means sales value after any further processing. Table 10.2 gives the results of this approach.

You will see that the calculations in Table 10.2 are based on sales value *not* selling price. And, for the purpose of determining the cost of joint products, we use the sales value of output from the joint process – regardless of what actual or budgeted sales volumes might be.

Sales value (unlike output) can be used as the apportionment basis irrespective of the physical characteristics of joint products, so mixes of gas, solid and liquid outputs present no problem. In our example, the potential problem of breaching the 'lower of cost and net realisable value' rule for stocks of Green-Grow Standard is also

Table 10.2 Final sales value as basis of apportionment

Product	Output (litres)	Final sales value of output	% of total sales value	Joint cost apportioned
Green-Grow Standard	25 000	(25 000 × £2.20)		
		£55 000	34.375	£23 375 (34.375%)
Green-Grow Extra	15 000	(15 000 × £4.00)		
		£60 000	37.500	£25 500 (37.500%)
Green-Grow Super	10 000	(10 000 × £4.50)		
		£ 45 000	28.125	£19 125 (28.125%)
		£160 000	100.000	£68 000

solved:

$$\text{Cost per litre} = \frac{£23\,375}{25\,000 \text{ litres}} = £0.935 \text{ per litre}$$

Since the net realisable value is £1.30 per litre, a stock value of £0.935 per litre would not breach this fundamental accounting rule. However, using sales value as the apportionment basis does not automatically resolve this particular difficulty, although there may be less likelihood of its arising since the method explicitly considers the revenue-earning potential of products (which an output basis does not). But net realisable value is principally governed by market conditions for the product concerned, not by how we apportion costs to that product.

 Might it be argued that final sales value is inappropriate in circumstances such as SDL Ltd's? If so, why?

Using final sales values could be argued to distort product costs: we are attempting to attribute cost to output as it emerges from the joint process. Yet we have used sales value after further processing to do this. But final sales value may be as much (or more) a function of further processing as of joint processing. SDL Ltd's three products clearly change markedly as a result of further processing, with different brand names and selling prices per litre. If this potential distortion is felt to be unacceptable, we can use intermediate sales value as the basis.

Apportionment on the basis of intermediate sales value

Rather than using final sales value, we can apportion joint costs on the basis of each product's share of **intermediate sales value** – i.e. sales value at split-off point. Table 10.3 applies this approach to SDL Ltd's joint process.

By using sales values applicable to output from the joint process at that stage of production, this approach removes the possible distortion that a final sales value basis may cause.

 Can you think of any circumstances where intermediate sales value cannot be used?

Table 10.3 Intermediate sales value as basis of apportionment

Product	Output (litres)	Intermediate sales value of output	% of total sales value	Joint cost apportioned
Green-Grow Standard	25 000	(25 000 × £1.30) £32 500	36.313	£24 693 (36.313%)
Green-Grow Extra	15 000	(15 000 × £2.20) £33 000	36.872	£25 073 (36.872%)
Green-Grow Super	10 000	(10 000 × £2.40) £24 000	26.815	£18 234 (26.815%)
		£89 500	100.000	£68 000

Joint products might require to be further processed before they are capable of sale, so would not have any sales value at the split-off point. Here, we might use notional sales value.

Apportionment on the basis of notional sales value

Notional sales value (also referred to as **net sales value** or, somewhat inaccurately, as **net realisable value**) is calculated as:

(final sales value *less* further processing costs)

Applying this approach to SDL Ltd, we obtain the result shown in Table 10.4.

Table 10.4 Notional sales value as basis of apportionment

Product	Output (litres)	Final sales value of output (from Table 10.2) £	Further processing cost £	Notional sales value £	% of total sales value	Joint cost apportioned £
Green-Grow Standard	25 000	55 000	20 000	35 000	36.842	25 052 (36.842%)
Green-Grow Extra	15 000	60 000	30 000	30 000	31.579	21 474 (31.579%)
Green-Grow Super	10 000	45 000	15 000	30 000	31.579	21 474 (31.579%)
		160 000		95 000	100.000	68 000

Although this approach overcomes the problem of joint products that cannot be sold at the split-off point, there might be a danger of notional sales value being confused with actual sales value at the split-off point (which may very well be zero). This danger could be exacerbated if notional sales value is incorrectly referred to as net realisable value. The concept might therefore give rise to some confusion, and even cause management to make incorrect decisions.

Apportionment on the basis of uniform profit margin

It could be argued that, as joint products represent output from the same process, then they ought to have the same profit margin. It is possible to apportion joint process costs so as to obtain this result. In order to use this approach, we need to decide at the outset whether we are using final, intermediate or notional sales value to determine profit margin. Derivation of the profit margin from each of these sales values has the same strengths and weaknesses as use of the sales values themselves to apportion cost. We shall use intermediate sales values for illustration.

From Table 10.3, overall profit (based on sale of all three joint products at split-off point) is:

	£
Revenue	
Green-Grow Standard (25 000 litres × £1.30)	32 500
Green-Grow Extra (15 000 litres × £2.20)	33 000
Green-Grow Super (10 000 litres × £2.40)	24 000
	89 500
Less Joint process net cost	68 000
Overall profit	21 500

The overall profit margin is:

$$\frac{£21\ 500}{£89\ 500} \times 100\% = 24\%$$

Table 10.5 apportions the joint process cost so as to achieve a profit margin of 24% for each product.

Table 10.5 Apportionment to achieve uniform profit margin

	Green-Grow Standard £	Green-Grow Extra £	Green-Grow Super £	Total £
Revenue	32 500	33 000	24 000	89 500
Less **Profit @ 24% of revenue**	7 800	7 920	5 780	21 500
Joint cost (balance)	24 700	25 080	18 220	68 000

Using this method, the joint cost apportionment is a residual amount after deduction of the required profit margin from sales revenue. Although it is fairly straightforward to apply, the desire to obtain a uniform margin may well have the effect of distorting relative joint product costs by masking even further very real differences in the nature of the products concerned. In other words, the joint cost apportionments might bear little relationship to the relative worth of the products, being principally a function of the uniform margin being applied.

What we have seen is that for joint process cost apportionment – as for every apportionment exercise – there is no 'best' or universally applicable method. The most appropriate basis will be dictated by cost/benefit considerations and the specific nature of the products/processes concerned, e.g. are joint products actually saleable at the split-off point and if so, can a selling price be readily obtained?

THE 'SELL OR PROCESS FURTHER' DECISION

As we suggested in Figure 10.1, a feature of many joint products is the possibility of further processing after the split-off point. Where management can choose whether or not to undertake such further processing, we need to be able to assess its financial viability. Exhibit 10.3 presents a summary of certain key information about SDL Ltd's joint process.

What is the significance of the £68 000 joint process cost to the financial analysis of a decision about whether or not to further process the joint products?

The short answer is 'none'. The joint process cost is irrelevant to financial analysis of this particular decision, as it must be incurred regardless of whether joint products are further processed. This type of cost is termed a **sunk cost**: i.e. a cost which the organisation is committed to paying because of a different decision from the one under consideration. Here, management has obviously decided that a joint process will exist – in which case, the business is committed to incurring joint process costs – unless a

---

SDL Ltd: sell or process further?

Last accounting period, the company's joint process yielded the following output of main products:

    Green-Grow Standard: 25 000 litres   Green-Grow Extra: 15 000 litres
    Green-Grow Super: 10 000 litres

    The joint process's net cost was £68 000.

    Each of the joint products may be further processed should management so desire. After such processing Green-Grow Standard, Extra and super become, respectively, Miracle-Grow Standard, Extra and Super. Details are:

	Standard	Extra	Super
	£	£	£
Selling price per litre: Green-Grow	1.30	2.20	2.40
Further processing cost of output volume given above	20 000	30 000	15 000
Selling price per litre: Miracle-Grow	2.20	4.00	4.50

Exhibit 10.3 Sell or process further

decision about the financial viability of the joint process itself is needed. We shall have more to say about sunk costs in Chapter 14.

In order to assess the financial viability of the sell or process further decision, we need to compare the additional revenue gained as a result of further processing with the additional cost incurred. These additional costs and revenues are referred to as **incremental costs** and **incremental revenues**. Comparison of the two yields **incremental profit** (or loss).

Looking at Green-Grow Standard in Exhibit 10.3, and assuming that all output from the joint process is further processed into Miracle-Grow Standard and sold, we have:

	£
Incremental revenue 25 000 litres × (£2.20 – £1.30)	22 500
Incremental cost (i.e. further processing cost)	20 000
Incremental profit from further processing	2 500

Incremental revenue is simply the difference between the product's intermediate and final selling prices multiplied by the appropriate output volume. Since further processing yields an incremental profit, it is financially worth while. (Assuming all output is further processed and sold. If this assumption does not hold, we compare only the incremental revenues and incremental costs for that portion of joint product to be further processed – which might result in a different financial outcome.)

 Determine the incremental profit or incremental loss from further processing all the output of Green-Grow Extra and Green-Grow Super and advise management.

Further processing Green-Grow Extra:

	£
Incremental revenue: 15 000 litres × (£4.00 – £2.20)	27 000
Incremental cost	30 000
Incremental loss from further processing	3 000

As further processing incurs an incremental loss, this product should be sold at the split-off point.

Further processing Green-Grow Super:

	£
Incremental revenue: 10 000 litres × (£4.50 – £2.40)	21 000
Incremental cost	15 000
Incremental profit from further processing	6 000

We should therefore further process this product.

The total profit resulting from this production plan is:

		£
Revenue:	Miracle-Grow Standard (25 000 litres × £2.20)	55 000
	Green-Grow Extra (15 000 litres × £2.20)	33 000
	Miracle-Grow Super (10 000 litres × £4.50)	45 000
	£	133 000
Joint process cost	68 000	
Further processing costs:		
Green-Grow Standard	20 000	
Green-Grow Super	15 000	103 000
Profit		30 000

The profit calculation assumes that the further processing cost associated with Green-Grow Extra is wholly avoided if this product is sold at the split-off point.

 What would overall profit be if all three joint products were to be processed further?

Further processing all three joint products would result in a profit of £27 000:

	£
Profit as above	30 000
Less Incremental loss from further processing	
Green-Grow Extra	3 000
Revised profit	27 000

(You might like to confirm the revised profit figure by preparing a full profit statement based on further processing all three joint products.)

Although our analysis indicates that further processing Green-Grow Extra is not financially viable, there may be compelling non-financial reasons for doing so. For example, the effect on customer perception or on competitor action of not producing Miracle-Grow Extra.

If you look at our profit calculations, you should see that how we apportion the joint process cost will make no difference to the overall profit, although it *will* affect the relative profitability of individual products – a point we will now examine in more detail.

JOINT COST APPORTIONMENTS, PLANNING, CONTROL AND DECISION MAKING

We said earlier that the main purpose of joint cost apportionments is to permit assessment of the profitability of individual joint products. But exactly how useful are such apportionments for this purpose? We will use the data in Exhibit 10.4 to illustrate.

SDL Ltd: joint product profitability

Output and selling price per litre at the split-off point, along with each product's apportionment of the joint process cost (based on output) is:

	Green-Grow Standard	Green-Grow Extra	Green-Grow Super
Output (litres)	25 000	15 000	10 000
Selling price	£1.30	£2.20	£2.40
Apportionment of joint process cost	£34 000	£20 400	£13 600

Exhibit 10.4 Assessing joint product profitability

 Assuming total output of all three products is sold at the split-off point, use Exhibit 10.4 to determine the profit from each product and in total for the period.

	Standard £	Extra £	Super £	Total £
Revenue	32 500	33 000	24 000	89 500
Less Joint process cost	34 000	20 400	13 600	68 000
Profit/(Loss)	(1 500)	12 600	10 400	21 500

But is Green-Grow Standard genuinely a loss-making product? Consider Table 10.6,

Table 10.6 Product profit using different apportionment bases

	Standard	Extra	Super	Total
Apportionment basis:				
Final sales value	£	£	£	£
Revenue	32 500	33 000	24 000	89 500
Less: Joint process cost (Table 10.2)	23 375	25 500	19 125	68 000
Profit	9 125	7 500	4 875	21 500
Apportionment basis:				
Intermediate sales value	£	£	£	£
Revenue	32 500	33 000	24 000	89 500
Less: Joint process cost (Table 10.3)	24 693	25 073	18 234	68 000
Profit	7 807	7 927	5 766	21 500
Apportionment basis:				
Notional sales value	£	£	£	£
Revenue	32 500	33 000	24 000	89 500
Less: Joint process cost (Table 10.4)	25 052	21 474	21 474	68 000
Profit	7 448	11 526	2 526	21 500

which restates product profits using each of the other three apportionment bases we have discussed.

Since the profitability of individual joint products is dependent on the apportionment basis, management would be ill-advised to make decisions about relative profitability based on figures that include apportionments – particularly when no apportionment method is clearly superior in every situation. And, even if we are confident that (say) Green-Grow Standard is a genuine loss-maker, is it practical to suggest that it no longer be produced? The nature of the joint process could very well render such a suggestion physically impossible.

 Because of the £1500 loss reported under the output basis of apportionment, management decides that Green-Grow Standard will be produced (as this cannot physically be avoided) but should not be sold. Will this improve overall profit?

If sale of Green-Grow Standard is discontinued, overall profit is:

		£
Revenue:	Extra (15 000 litres × £2.20)	33 000
	Super (10 000 litres × £2.40)	24 000
		57 000
Less: Joint process cost		68 000
Loss		11 000

Admittedly, this is a very simplistic illustration, but it serves to highlight the potential danger of using apportioned costs as the basis for decision making. If the nature of the joint process precludes a reduction in joint cost by discontinuing production of a particular product and if management is concerned about profitability, then profitability of the joint process as a whole should be the object of their concern. And what Table 10.6 makes clear is that joint cost *apportionments* are irrelevant to the overall profitability of the process. What is relevant is the amount of joint cost *incurred*. In Chapter 14, we will give detailed consideration to the issue of identifying relevant costs for decision making.

Everything we have just said about joint cost apportionments in the context of decision making applies equally to planning and control. In setting budgets, we do not budget for apportionments, but for the estimated amount of expenditure (which we may then apportion). Similarly, cost control is based on expenditure rather than on apportionments of that expenditure. When we discuss financial control in Chapter 18, we will see that there are arguments for and against use of apportionments for planning and control purposes. Suffice it to say at present that this can be a very contentious area in many budget systems.

THE JOINT PROCESS ACCOUNT

Posting the Joint Process Account follows the same pattern as that illustrated in the previous chapter. The difference here is that we have several outputs. Using the data from Exhibit 10.2 and assuming joint process costs are apportioned on the basis of notional sales value (Table 10.4), the Joint Process Account is:

Joint Process Account

	Litres	£		Litres	£
Direct materials	55 000	55 000	By-product Z net		
Direct labour		6 000	realisable value:		
Overhead (140%			5000 × (£0.50 – £0.22)	5 000	1 400
of direct labour cost)		8 400	Completed output:		
			Green-Grow Standard	25 000	25 052
			Green-Grow Extra	15 000	21 474
			Green-Grow Super	10 000	21 474
	55 000	69 400		55 000	69 400

If there are incomplete units, we need to add an additional stage to our procedures. Exhibit 10.5 contains relevant details.

SDL Ltd: joint process incomplete units

Input and output data for the company's joint process last period are given below.

Opening WIP   5000 litres, cost £3200; 100% complete for materials, 40% complete for labour and overhead.

Input costs   Direct materials (61 000 litres @ £1) £61 000
Direct labour (500 hours @ £12) £6000
Production overhead (140% of direct labour cost) £8400

Outputs   Green-Grow Standard: 25 000 litres
Green-Grow Extra: 15 000 litres
Green-Grow Super: 10 000 litres
By-product Z: 5000 litres. This can be sold for £0.50 per litre after incurring further processing costs of £0.22 per litre. It is company policy to credit the joint process with By-product Z's net realisable value.

Closing WIP   6000 litres, 100% complete for materials, 30% complete for labour and overhead.

A normal loss of 5% of input is expected during the process, having a scrap value of £0.20 per litre. Any abnormal losses/abnormal gains are detected when output is 100% complete for materials, 50% complete for labour and overhead. The company uses a First-In–First-Out (FIFO) approach to stock valuation. Joint process costs are apportioned on the basis of notional sales value.

Exhibit 10.5 Joint process incomplete units

Before we can apportion joint process costs to the main products, we need to determine the amount of cost involved (just as we did earlier in the chapter). But now, we have to calculate the cost attributable to completed output using an equivalent units tabulation of the sort introduced in the previous chapter.

 From Exhibit 10.5, compare the process's inputs and outputs so as to determine the amount of any abnormal loss or abnormal gain.

The joint process has an abnormal loss for the period:

			Litres
Inputs	Opening WIP		5 000
	Direct materials		61 000
			66 000
Outputs	Normal loss (5% × 66 000 litres)	3 300	
	Closing WIP	6 000	
	Completed output:		
	Green-Grow Standard	25 000	
	Green-Grow Extra	15 000	
	Green-Grow Super	10 000	
	By-product Z	5 000	64 300
	Therefore abnormal loss =		1 700

 In the equivalent unit tabulation, what is the correct treatment of by-product Z's net realisable value and of the normal loss's scrap value?

As we saw in Chapter 9, the by-product's net realisable value and the normal loss scrap value should both be deducted from input cost. This is usually effected by reducing the cost of direct materials; from Exhibit 10.5, the adjusted materials' cost is:

	£	£
Material inputs: 61 000 litres × £1		61 000
Less: Net realisable value of By-product Z		
5000 litres × (£0.50 – £0.22)	1 400	
Scrap value of normal loss 3300 litres × £0.20	660	2 060
		58 940

This is the value used in the FIFO equivalent unit tabulation shown in Table 10.7.

You will see from Table 10.7 that the by-product units (like the normal loss) are not

Table 10.7 FIFO equivalent unit tabulation for joint process

	Direct labour	Direct material	Production overhead
Abnormal loss	(50% × 1700) 850	(100% × 1700) 1700	(50% × 1700) 850
Completed output *less* **Opening WIP equivalent units**	(100% × 55 000) −(40% × 5000) 53 000	(100% × 55 000) −(100% × 5000) 50 000	(100% × 55 000) −(40% × 5000) 53 000
Closing WIP	(30% × 6000) 1800	(100% × 6000) 6000	(30% × 6000) 1800
Total equivalent units	55 650	57 700	55 650
Cost: current inputs	£6000	£58 940	£8400
Cost/equivalent unit	£0.108	£1.021	£0.151

shown. The cost of the abnormal loss is:

	£
Direct materials (1700 equivalent units × £1.021)	1736
Direct labour and production overhead:	
850 equivalent units × (£0.108 + £0.151)	220
	1956

> ✔ *Use Table 10.7 and Exhibit 10.5 to obtain the cost of completed output for the period.*

Cost of completed output:

	£
Opening WIP	3 200
Direct materials (50 000 equivalent units × £1.021)	51 050
Direct labour and production overhead:	
53 000 equivalent units × (£0.108 + £0.151)	13 727
	67 977

Remember that when FIFO is in use, we assume that opening WIP is completed first during the current period, so that its cost will be included with that of completed output.

Now that we have the overall cost attributed to completed output, we can apportion it to each of the three joint products on the basis of their net realisable value. This is done in Table 10.8.

Table 10.8 Cost of completed output apportioned on notional sales value basis

Product	Output (litres)	Final sales value of output (from Table 10.2) £	Further processing cost £	Notional sales value £	% of total sales value	Joint cost apportioned £
Green-Grow Standard	25 000	55 000	20 000	35 000	36.842	25 045 (36.842%)
Green-Grow Extra	15 000	60 000	30 000	30 000	31.579	21 466 (31.579%)
Green-Grow Super	10 000	45 000	15 000	30 000	31 579	21 466 (31.579%)
		160 000		95 000	100.000	67 977

Joint process cost is apportioned *only* to the joint products; although abnormal loss and WIP receive a share of the joint process cost, they do so via the equivalent unit valuation undertaken above. The Joint Process Account is presented below.

Allowing for a rounding difference, we can confirm the closing WIP value from the cost per equivalent unit figures in Table 10.7:

	£
Direct materials (6000 equivalent units × £1.021)	6126
Direct labour and production overhead:	
1800 equivalent units × (£0.108 + £0.151)	466
	6592
Value per process account	6607
Rounding difference	15

Joint Process Account

	Litres	£		Litres	£
Opening WIP	5 000	3 200	Normal loss	3 300	660
Direct materials	61 000	61 000	Abnormal loss	1 700	1 956
Direct labour		6 000	By-product Z net		
Overhead (140% of			realisable value:		
direct labour cost)		8 400	5000 × (£0.50 – £0.22)	5 000	1 400
			Completed output:		
			Green-Grow Standard	25 000	25 045
			Green-Grow Extra	15 000	21 466
			Green-Grow Super	10 000	21 466
			Closing WIP c/d (balance)	6 000	6 607
	66 000	78 600		66 000	78 600
WIP b/d	6 000	6 607			

Had the company employed the average cost method of WIP valuation, the sequence of calculations would have been exactly the same, but with the AVCO equivalent units tabulation.

THE JOINT PROCESS AS A PROFIT CENTRE

What we have seen is an apportionment exercise where the results can be flawed regardless of the basis applied, and where these results are of doubtful value for decision making, planning and control. It may therefore be preferable to avoid apportioning joint costs. This can be achieved if we treat the joint process as a **profit centre**. Instead of crediting the joint process with the *cost* of joint products, we credit the process with their *sales value*. The sales value employed should be that applicable to joint products when they emerge from the joint process: intermediate where products are (or are capable of being) further processed, final sales value where they are not.

From Table 10.3, we know that Green-Grow Standard, Extra and Super have intermediate sales values of £32 500, £33 000 and £24 000 respectively. Substituting these values into the preceding version of the joint process account, we get:

Joint Process Account

	Litres	£		Litres	£
Opening WIP	5 000	3 200	Normal loss	3 300	660
Direct materials	61 000	61 000	Abnormal loss	1 700	1 956
Direct labour		6 000	By-product Z net		
Overhead (140% of direct			realisable value:		
labour cost)		8 400	5000 × (£0.50 – £0.22)	5 000	1 400
Profit & Loss Account			Completed output:		
(balance)		**21 523**	Green-Grow Standard	25 000	**32 500**
			Green-Grow Extra	15 000	**33 000**
			Green-Grow Super	10 000	**24 000**
			Closing WIP c/d*	6 000	6 607
	66 000	100 123		66 000	100 123
WIP b/d	6 000	6 607			

> ✔ *Does the £21 523 balance represent profit or loss?*

Because the balance is a debit, revenues exceed costs, so £21 523 is the joint process's profit for the period.

Adopting a profit centre approach to the joint process offers three advantages:

1 *It avoids the need for apportionment of joint costs* Since every apportionment basis suffers from some weakness, avoiding the need for apportionment precludes criticism of the method used.

2 *It is consistent with the principles of responsibility accounting* **Responsibility accounting** is a commonly employed framework for budgetary planning and control, where individual managers are deemed to be responsible for achieving (and possibly setting) the budget for a designated area of organisational activity (**responsibility centre**). Since apportionment bases are open to criticism, it is arguable whether there is any benefit in reporting cost apportionments within such a system of personal responsibility and their inclusion might even have undesirable consequences. We will discuss this matter in greater detail in Chapter 18.

3 *It is consistent with assessment of the 'sell/process further' decision* We saw earlier that the financial viability of this decision should be assessed on the basis of its incremental profit – i.e. the difference between extra ('incremental') cost and extra revenue resulting from further processing. If we treat both joint and further processes as profit centres, then the further processing account will automatically reflect this information, as transfers from joint to further process will be made at intermediate sales value.

Consider Green-Grow Extra: output of this product can be further processed at a total cost of £30 000, then sold as Miracle-Grow Extra for £4.00 per litre. If both processes are treated as profit centres, the relevant further processing account will be as follows:

Further Processing Account

	Litres	£		Litres	£
Joint process (Green-Grow Extra @ intermediate sales value)	15 000	33 000	Completed output (Miracle-Grow Extra @ £4 per litre sales value)	15 000	60 000
Further processing cost		30 000	Profit and Loss Account		3 000
	15 000	63 000		15 000	63 000

The £3000 transferred to Profit and Loss represents the incremental loss incurred by further processing. If you look back at our earlier discussion of the sell/process further decision, you will see that this is the same as the result obtained at that point.

Although having much to recommend it, the profit centre approach also has two drawbacks:

1 *Actual sales value necessary* If the method is to overcome the somewhat arbitrary nature of joint cost apportionments, we must have an *actual* sales value. Where joint products are not subject to (or capable of) further processing, this presents no

problem, as final sales value will be used. However, where joint products cannot be sold at the split-off point, we have no actual sales value for them and are therefore forced to fall back on notional sales value – which completely negates the benefit of avoiding cost apportionment.

2 *Unsuitable for valuing stock of completed output* Unless it is lower than cost, sales value (i.e. net realisable value) cannot be used for valuation of finished goods stock. Where stock of completed joint products exists, we will need to use some form of apportionment to obtain a stock value for profit reporting purposes. The profit centre approach is thus only appropriate for internal management purposes.

SUMMARY

In this chapter, we have extended our discussion of process costing to include joint products. We have seen that:

- **Joint products** are two or more main products produced from the same process (**joint process**).

- **Split-off point** (**point of separation**) is the stage of production at which joint products become separately identifiable.

- For stock valuation and profit measurement, it is necessary to apportion joint process cost to joint products.

- Joint process costs are not apportioned to by-products.

- Apportionment can be based on each joint product's proportion of total output from the joint process. While simple, this method may breach the lower of cost and net realisable value rule and cannot be used for joint products having different physical states.

- Apportionment can be based on each joint product's proportion of **final sales value** (i.e. sales value after further processing). This approach can deal with any mixture of physical states and may be less likely to breach the lower of cost and net realisable value rule; but product costs could be distorted because sales values may relate to quite different products to those emerging from the joint process.

- Apportionment can be based on **intermediate sales value** (i.e. sales value at the split-off point). Although this relates sales value specifically to the output as it emerges from the joint process, it is inapplicable where products cannot be sold at the split-off point.

- Apportionment can be based on **notional sales value** (**net realisable value** or **net sales value**). Notional sales value is (final sales value *less* any further processing cost). This can be applied to products that cannot actually be sold at the split-off point, but could be confused with products' true net realisable value.

- Joint process costs may be apportioned as a residual after deduction of a uniform profit margin from the sales value of joint products.

- The financial viability of the 'sell or process further' decision is assessed on the basis of **incremental profit/incremental loss**: i.e. the difference between the extra

▶

revenue (**incremental revenue**) and extra cost (**incremental cost**) resulting from further processing. Joint process cost (and its apportionment) is irrelevant to this decision.

- The apportionment basis does not affect overall profit from the joint process – merely how this is distributed between joint products.

- Joint cost apportionments may have little value for decision making, planning and control.

- Where there are incomplete units in a joint process, we need to calculate the cost of completed output using an equivalent unit tabulation, thereafter apportioning this cost on an appropriate basis.

- If we treat the joint process as a **profit centre**, we credit the account with joint products' sales value at the split-off point rather than their cost.

- The profit centre approach avoids the need for apportionments, and is consistent with both sell/process further appraisal and with the principles of responsibility accounting. But the approach cannot be used except with actual sales values and does not provide an acceptable basis for valuation of finished goods' stock.

Perhaps the last word on the subject should be left with the results of a 1984 study by Slater and Wootton, which found that intermediate sales value and estimated net realisable value were the most common bases in the petrochemical sector, while output was most frequently used in coal-related processing. Perhaps most interestingly, the report found that most respondent oil refining businesses did not employ any form of joint cost apportionment. The reasons cited for this were the complex nature of production processes, coupled with the large number of different products involved.

In the next chapter, we will move away from manufacturing organisations to consider those which provide services.

FURTHER READING

Slater, K. and Wootton, C., *Joint and By-product Costing in the UK*, CIMA, 1984.

Smith, R., Are your joint costs out of joint? *CIMA Student*, August 1994 (CIMA).

10.1 Place a tick in the appropriate box to indicate whether each of the following statements is true or false.

	True	False
(a) A profit centre treatment of the joint process is consistent with requirements for finished goods stock valuation.	☐	☐
(b) Reported product profitability can alter if the apportionment basis is changed.	☐	☐
(c) Notional sales value is (final sales value *less* further processing cost).	☐	☐
(d) Final sales value is the most appropriate apportionment basis where joint products undergo significant further processing.	☐	☐
(e) Joint process cost is not apportioned to by-products.	☐	☐
(f) Split-off point generally occurs at the end of further processing.	☐	☐
(g) A uniform profit margin approach treats joint cost apportionment as a residual after deduction of a uniform margin from joint products' sales value.	☐	☐
(h) If joint costs are apportioned on an output basis, every unit of all joint products has the same joint process cost.	☐	☐

10.2 Chemicals X, Y and Z are produced from a single joint process. The information below relates to the month of November 1998:

Input into process:	Direct materials 3200 litres, cost £24 000
	Direct labour £48 000
	Factory overheads are absorbed at 120% of prime cost
Output from process:	Scrap normally accounts for 10% of input and can be sold for £16.20 per litre.
	Actual scrap in November was 10% of input. Proceeds from the sale of scrap is credited to the process account.
	Chemical X – 1440 litres
	Chemical Y – 864 litres
	Chemical Z – 576 litres
The selling prices of the three chemicals are:	Chemical X – £100 per litre
	Chemical Y – £80 per litre
	Chemical Z – £60 per litre

Requirements

(a) Calculate the total cost of each of Chemicals X, Y and Z using the following methods for splitting joint costs.
  (i) Relative sales value. **(7 marks)**
  (ii) Volume. **(7 marks)**
  All workings should be to the nearest £.

(b) Write up the process account as it would appear in the cost accounts, assuming the company uses the relative sales value method of valuing joint products. Your account should record volumes as well as monetary amounts. **(6 marks)**

(c) Chemical Z can be converted to Chemical Z2. The costs of converting Chemical Z into Chemical Z2 are £50 per litre input for direct labour and £40 per litre input for factory

overheads. No additional materials are required but there is a 10% loss in process. The loss has no saleable value. Calculate the conversion cost incurred to produce 200 litres of good output of Chemical Z2.   **(5 marks)**
                                                                              (Total: 25 marks)

(ACCA, *Cost Accounting Systems*, December 1998)

10.3 BK Chemicals produces three joint products in one common process but each product is capable of being further processed separately after the split-off point. The estimated data given below relate to June:

	Product B	Product K	Product C
Selling price at split-off point (per litre)	£6	£8	£9
Selling price after further processing (per litre)	£10	£20	£30
Post-separation point costs	£20 000	£10 000	£22 500
Output in litres	3 500	2 500	2 000

Pre-separation point joint costs are estimated to be £40 000 and it is current practice to apportion these to the three products according to litres produced.

Requirements

(a) (i) Prepare a statement of estimated profit or loss for each product and in total for June if all three products are processed further, and
   (ii) Advise how profits could be maximised if one or more products are sold at the split-off point. Your advice should be supported by a profit statement.
                                                                              (11 marks)

(b) It has been suggested that responsibility accounting would be more relevant in BK Chemicals with the process incurring the common cost being treated as a profit centre.
   (i) Explain briefly how this could best be achieved,
   (ii) State the resulting profit to be shown for the common process, and
   (iii) State **two** advantages of this approach.   **(5 marks)**

(c) Discuss the problems associated with joint cost apportionments in relation to
   (i) planning,
   (ii) control, and
   (iii) decision making.   **(9 marks)**
                                                                              (Total: 25 marks)

(CIMA, *Cost Accounting*, May 1992)

10.4 PQR Limited produces two joint products – P and Q – together with a by-product R, from a single main process (process 1). Product P is sold at the point of separation for £5 per kg whereas product Q is sold for £7 per kg after further processing into product Q2. By-product R is sold without further processing for £1.75 per kg.

Process 1 is closely monitored by a team of chemists who planned the output per 1000 kg of input materials to be as follows:

Product P	500 kg
Product Q	350 kg
Product R	100 kg
Toxic waste	50 kg

The toxic waste is disposed of at a cost of £1.50 per kg, and arises at the end of processing.

Process 2, which is used for further processing of product Q into product Q2, has the following cost structure:

Fixed costs	£6000 per week
Variable costs	£1.50 per kg processed

The following actual data relate to the first week of accounting period 10:

Process 1		£
Opening work in process		Nil
Materials input	10 000 kg costing	15 000
Direct labour		10 000
Variable overhead		4 000
Fixed overhead		6 000

Outputs:	kg
Product P	4800
Product Q	3600
Product R	1000
Toxic waste	600
Closing work in process	Nil

Process 2		kg
Opening work in process		Nil
Input of product Q		3600
Output of product Q2		3300
Closing work in process	300 kg, 50% converted	

Conversion costs were incurred in accordance with the planned cost structure.

Requirements

(a) Prepare the main process account for the first week of period 10 using the final sales value method to attribute pre-separation costs to joint products. **(12 marks)**

(b) Prepare the toxic waste accounts and process 2 account for the first week of period 10. **(9 marks)**

(c) Comment on the method used by PQR Limited to attribute pre-separation costs to its joint products. **(4 marks)**

(d) Advise the management of PQR Limited whether or not, on purely financial grounds, it should continue to process product Q into product Q2

    (i)   if product Q could be sold at the point of separation for £4.30 per kg and

    (ii) if 60% of the weekly fixed costs of process 2 were avoided by not processing product Q further. **(5 marks)**

(Total 30 marks)

(CIMA, *Operational Cost Accounting*, May 1995)

10.5 QR Limited operates a chemical process which produces four different products Q, R, S and T from the input of one raw material plus water. Budget information for the forthcoming financial year is as follows:

	£000
Raw materials cost	268
Initial processing cost	464

Product	Output in litres	Sales	Additional processing cost
		£000	£000
Q	400 000	768	160
R	90 000	232	128
S	5 000	32	–
T	9 000	240	8

The company policy is to apportion the costs prior to the split-off point on a method based on net sales value.

Currently, the intention is to sell product S without further processing but to process the other three products after the split-off point. However, it has been proposed that an alternative strategy would be to sell all four products at the split-off point without further processing. If this were done the selling prices obtainable would be as follows:

	Per litre £
Q	1.28
R	1.60
S	6.40
T	20.00

Requirements

(a) Prepare a budgeted profit statement showing the profit or loss for each product, and in total, if the current intention is proceeded with. **(10 marks)**

(b) Show the profit or loss by product, and in total, if the alternative strategy were to be adopted. **(6 marks)**

(c) Recommend what should be done and why, assuming that there is no more profitable alternative use for the plant. **(4 marks)**

(Total: 20 marks)

(CIMA, *Cost Accounting*, May 1990)

CHAPTER 11

Service costing

Costing in the service sector

Britain has a powerful service economy but nonetheless costing has only become a talking point in the service sector in the last decade. The service sector is wide-ranging. It not only covers a whole variety of business areas but also includes the head office administrative element of manufacturing companies ...

In theory costing should be easier in the service sector: there are no stocks or work-in-progress to be valued, while, secondly, being a Johnny-come-lately in costing, it has been possible to take account of the cost management issues in manufacturing, avoid the pitfalls and take advantage of the new concepts such as life-time costing and the time element in cost determination. Not a few new businesses in the service sector have been able to introduce ABC or incorporate ABC concepts, right from the start without going through the trauma and expense of dismantling their previous costing systems.

But there are disadvantages too. The products are so subjective. Simultaneity and perishability are also key factors. One cannot build for stock. A lawyer without clients loses billable time for ever; a hotel with rooms unoccupied or an airline with seats unsold cannot recoup the costs after the event ...

If management's bottom-line objective is – as it usually is – cost management through cost understanding and traceability, the task is not made any easier because in most service industries one is dealing with intangibles. Everything is intangible. You cannot touch the product as you can in manufacturing. So, how do you measure it? How does one define a product or service? How does one cost IT? Everything seems to be an overhead and therefore, try as one will, one cannot get away from that bugbear of the management accountant's life – allocations ...

Source: Tom Sheridan, *Management Accounting*, May 1996.

Exhibit 11.1 A broad overview of service sector costing

INTRODUCTION

The quotation contained in Exhibit 11.1 encapsulates much of what we will say in this chapter. Service industries form a very significant element of both the UK and other economies. In the UK, service organisations may generate as much as four times the economic activity of 'traditional' manufacturing industries. The range of services provided is vast, covering both commercial services such as banking, leisure and tourism as well as public sector services like health care and education. Clearly, no single approach to costing will apply to all of these. However, what we will see is that many of the techniques we have discussed in earlier – and will discuss in later – chapters are as relevant to service organisations as they are to manufacturing. As Exhibit 11.1

suggests, this could be especially true of overhead allocation and apportionment (see Chapters 5 and 6).

Because of the service sector's diversity, we will confine our discussion to the nature of service 'output' and the way in which this might impact on cost accounting in service environments. We will also distinguish between commercial and internal service provision, discussing whether the latter should be charged for and if so, on what basis.

OBJECTIVES

When you have completed this chapter, you will be able to:

- explain the characteristics that distinguish service output from manufactured output;
- appreciate the costing implications that these characteristics may have – and in particular with respect to the cost unit employed;
- discuss different approaches to charging users for internally provided services.

CHARACTERISTICS OF SERVICE OUTPUT

Regardless of whether it is provided in-house, on a commercial basis, by the public or private sector, service output possesses certain characteristics which are either unique or are much more marked than is the case with manufactured output. These characteristics have a major bearing on both the physical provision of services and on certain key aspects of their costing. We will use the example in Exhibit 11.2 to effect a comparison between service and manufactured output.

Two companies

Digipic Ltd manufactures digital cameras that produce computer-ready images, while KD & Co is a firm of management consultants specialising in design of staff performance evaluation and review systems on behalf of clients.

Exhibit 11.2 Manufactured and service output

 Can you suggest four ways in which KD & Co's output differs from that of Digipic Ltd?

Perhaps the most obvious difference between the two types of output is that of **intangibility**. Services do not have a physical form that allows them to be touched, held or seen – unlike manufactured output, which always exists in a physical form (even when units are not fully complete). Some service output, like the air flights referred to in Exhibit 11.1, may be more in the nature of an 'experience' than an object.

A second major difference is the degree of **heterogeneity** of output. Digipic Ltd's output is likely to be fairly uniform, with one unit being the same (or very nearly the same) as another (**homogeneous** output). The precise services that KD & Co provides will differ – possibly very significantly – between one client and another. Not only that, but the service provided may also vary from one consultant/group of consultants to another, possibly in terms of quality or in the amount of time needed for the work. Further, the standard of work performed by the same consultant/group of consultants – or the time required to perform it – could differ between different clients. However, you should note that heterogeneity/homogeneity of output is a matter of degree and that heterogeneity is not a unique feature of services. For example, KD & Co may have a standard evaluation and review package which is 'tweaked' to meet specific clients' needs. To the extent that this is true, output is homogeneous. Conversely, Digipic Ltd could produce a range of cameras, thereby introducing a degree of heterogeneity into its output.

A third distinguishing characteristic of service output is its **perishability**. Unlike tangible manufactured goods, it cannot be produced in advance of demand and held in stock.

 What operational difficulty might result from the perishability of services?

Perishability can cause difficulties when service organisations are planning operational capacity, particularly in industries where demand is seasonal or volatile. This is highlighted in Exhibit 11.1, when the author states that 'A lawyer without clients loses billable time forever; a hotel with rooms unoccupied or an airline with seats unsold cannot recoup the costs after the event ...'

Finally, service output tends to have a much greater degree of **simultaneity** than manufactured goods. In other words, services are generally consumed at (or very close to) the point in time at which they are provided. Given its intangible and perishable nature, this is only to be expected of service output. For manufactured goods, there is a time-lag between production and supply to customers (although it might be of fairly short duration, especially in a Just-In-Time system). Manufactured goods can therefore be inspected for quality prior to delivery and may be returned if they are not what the customer requires. This is likely to be much more difficult in the case of services. KD & Co may be able to undertake a fair amount of work and consultation with clients in advance of finally installing their evaluation and review systems – but such advance work/consultation effectively constitutes part of the service itself. For other services, simultaneity can be much greater. Consider hairdressing, where the service is consumed, quite literally, at the point of supply.

Now that we have considered the distinguishing characteristics of service provision, we need to study how these might affect cost accounting.

SERVICES AND COST ACCOUNTING

The nature of service provision has a number of effects on how cost accounting is applied. We discuss these below.

The cost unit

We introduced the concept of the cost unit in Chapter 2, defining it as a unit of the product or service which the organisation provides and to which we wish to attribute costs. At that point, we also said that a cost unit should be an accurate reflection of the nature of the output to which costs are being attributed. Because of the heterogeneous and intangible nature of their output, this can create difficulties for many service organisations.

 Suggest an appropriate cost unit for a hotel that provides accommodation on bed and breakfast, half-board and full-board bases. The hotel's restaurant and bar are used by both guests and non-residents.

You may have been tempted to suggest 'guests' as the cost unit. However, this does not provide an accurate reflection of the nature of the service being provided. In the first place, guests will stay for varying lengths of time; moreover, some will stay on a bed and breakfast, some on a half-board and some on a full-board basis. We can deal with the first of these complications by using a **composite cost unit** – that is, a cost unit which reflects the key variables involved in provision of the service. In this case, we need to consider both guests and the length of their stay, so an appropriate cost unit might be *guest/night*: in other words, the cost per guest per night. This could be calculated for different categories of guest – bed and breakfast, full- and half-board – and also for different types of room (single, double, twin).

However, using a composite cost unit doesn't completely solve our problem: we still have to consider the restaurant and bar, and the fact that these are used by both guests and by non-residents. A guest/night cost unit – even one that is split between different categories of guest – will not allow for use of restaurant and bar by non-residents. A separate cost unit is thus needed for these areas of operation. We might use 'covers' (i.e. meals) as the restaurant cost unit, and customers for the bar. Further refinement may be applied if required: e.g. separation of 'covers' between set meals and 'à la carte'.

A similar approach – using composite cost units in conjunction with a range of other cost units – is required in other service organisations. Hospitals, for example, might calculate a cost per patient bed/day for in-patient wards, a cost per patient for an out-patient department, and a cost per procedure for various kinds of surgical operation.

But this degree of complexity in selecting an appropriate cost unit need not apply to all service output.

 Consider KD & Co's management consultancy business in Exhibit 11.2. What might be an appropriate cost unit for this sort of service?

Although the firm's output is heterogeneous, being based on client requirements, it has a narrower focus than was the case for the hotel above. We could therefore adopt the client/hour or chargeable client/hour as the cost unit. The cost of service provided to individual clients will thus depend on the number of hours' work involved, which is almost certainly adequate to reflect the nature of this particular service. You should note, though, that 'client/hour' is still a composite cost unit; there will be a difference between the number of hours the firm (or its employees) works and the number of these hours devoted specifically to dealing with clients. (We shall return to this issue shortly.)

Like so many other aspects of cost accounting, the choice of service cost unit is situation-specific, and depends on the following critical considerations:

- *Nature of the service involved* As we have seen, certain services (like our hotel and hospital examples) may – because they are particularly heterogeneous – require the use of several cost units. For others (like KD & Co's management consultancy), a single cost unit may be sufficient.

- *Internal and external information needs* The information needed by management to make decisions, plan and control depends largely on the nature of the service and the market within which it operates. For example, in a seasonal business such as that run by hotels, a range of cost unit data could be invaluable as an aid to deciding about things like tariffs for peak and off-peak periods. For some service organisations – particularly those operating in the public sector – external reporting requirements may be a key determinant of the cost unit. In the UK, for example, council Roads Departments are required to report maintenance cost per carriageway/kilometre.

- *The cost/benefit criterion* Providing more accurate cost information in the form of a more representative cost unit itself incurs a cost. Where management is free to exercise discretion in the matter (i.e. where it is not dictated by external requirements), care is needed to ensure that the benefits of a more sophisticated costing system are not outweighed by the costs of operating it.

The nature of service provision has a major bearing not only on choice of cost unit, but also on the cost structure of service organisations.

Service organisation cost structure

Organisations that produce manufactured output are often characterised by high investment in fixed assets (equipment, for example) coupled with comparatively low labour inputs. In addition, they may carry significant stocks of raw materials, work-in-progress and finished goods. Service organisations may be markedly different in these respects, and it to areas of such potential difference that we now turn.

Capital- versus labour-intensive

In manufacturing industry, the trend in recent years has been for increased mechanisation and automation. The importance of labour, both as an input resource and as an element of total cost, has therefore reduced – in some cases very dramatically.

 Can you suggest an example of a service organisation where labour is significant both as an input resource and as a proportion of total cost?

Labour is a major resource and cost in a wide variety of service organisations. Hotels and restaurants, for example, are very labour-intensive. The same is true of consultancy businesses such as KD & Co; in fact, for a small business of this kind, labour may be easily the largest single type of cost. Similarly in hospitals and education, labour forms a very significant input, with the associated costs representing a high proportion of total cost.

What this means is that the kind of procedures we described in Chapter 4 for recording labour times, determining labour cost and processing payroll are likely to be more important to many service providers than to their manufacturing counterparts. In some service situations (such as small consultancies), labour may predominate to such an extent that it is the organisation's most valuable asset – an asset, moreover, that is not shown in the accounts (except very imperfectly by means of wages, salaries and related costs).

Overhead

The quotation in Exhibit 11.1 states that, for service providers, 'everything seems to be an overhead'. Although this is something of a generalisation, it nevertheless indicates a potential difficulty in service costing. We have already seen that service industries often need to use composite cost units (or even several different cost units). This may make it difficult to determine accurately (or within the bounds of the cost/benefit criterion) which costs are direct and which indirect in relation to the cost unit(s). Consider the summary cost data for KD & Co presented in Exhibit 11.3.

KD & Co: summary cost data

A summary of the firm's budgeted cost and other data for next year is as follows:

	£		£
Consultants' salaries	176 400	Telephone & fax	10 000
Travelling costs	20 000	Stationery	8 000
Administrative costs	111 000	General expenses	40 000

Each of the firm's five consultants works for 35 hours per week, and there are 36 working weeks in the year.

Exhibit 11.3 Service costing overhead

For many firms like KD & Co, the most straightforward approach is to treat labour (the consultants here) as the only direct cost, with all other costs being overhead.

 Assuming that consultants' salaries are the only cost treated as direct, determine an overhead rate per hour.

Total budgeted hours for the year:

$$5 \text{ consultants} \times 35 \text{ hours} \times 36 \text{ weeks} = 6300$$

Total budgeted overhead:

	£
Telephone & fax	10 000
Travelling costs	20 000
Stationery	8 000
Administrative costs	111 000
General expenses	40 000
	189 000

This gives an overhead rate per hour of:

$$\frac{\text{Total budgeted overhead}}{\text{Total budgeted hours}} = \frac{£189\,000}{6300} = £30$$

 Use the data in Exhibit 11.3 to determine the direct cost per hour, and thereafter, the total cost per hour.

Since the only direct cost is the consultants' salaries, we obtain a direct cost per hour of:

$$\frac{\text{Budgeted consultants' salaries}}{\text{Budgeted hours}} = \frac{\pounds 176\,400}{6300} = \pounds 28$$

Total cost per hour is therefore:

	£
Direct cost	28
Overhead	30
	58

In effect, our £30 per hour overhead is a **blanket** (or **plantwide**) **absorption rate** of the kind we encountered in Chapter 5. (You may wish to review our discussion of overhead absorption in the earlier chapter.) As we said at that point, such an approach has the merit of simplicity, but, by its 'broad-brush' nature, might distort unit costs by masking differences between cost units and the resources needed to produce them. These arguments are equally applicable to service organisations.

 Suggest two *ways in which KD & Co might refine its approach to unit costing.*

KD & Co might consider refining its treatment of overheads and/or of direct costs. Overhead could be analysed along departmental lines, and departmental absorption rates obtained (just as we did with a manufacturing business in Chapter 5). Alternatively, the firm could implement an activity-based system of the sort illustrated in Chapter 6. More rigorous analysis of the firm's cost structure could reveal that some costs treated as overhead under the blanket approach should more properly be considered as direct. For example, some (or even all) travelling costs may be directly related to work on behalf of clients and are thus direct. However, you should bear in mind that additional refinement comes at a cost – in both financial terms and in relation to the costing system's complexity – and this cost should not outweigh the benefits derived from a more sophisticated system. For service organisations, this cost/benefit assessment may well be complicated by the nature of their output.

In this respect, KD & Co has output that is readily translatable into a single cost unit to which we can attribute costs. But note that it would be something like 'client/hours' or 'chargeable client hours', rather than 'consultant hours' (which we have used); we shall return to this point shortly. Compare this with, say, a passenger transport business. In this case, we might have a fairly obvious cost unit – the passenger/kilometre – but what proportion of total cost can be considered direct in relation to this cost objective? Without seriously breaching the cost/benefit criterion and without producing figures that are subjective to the point of lacking credibility, very few costs (possibly none at all) are likely to be classified as direct in relation to the passenger/kilometre. Yet there can be little doubt that the passenger/kilometre is a reasonable reflection of output produced.

 How might such a problem be overcome?

One solution is to treat as direct only those costs that can indisputably and easily be classified as direct in relation to the cost unit – all other costs (probably a very high proportion of the total) being considered overhead. This was the approach we took with KD & Co's data in Exhibit 11.3. Although it is very rough-and-ready, we can justify such a method on grounds of cost/benefit and objectivity. In principle, there is no reason why the passenger transport business cannot do the same. However, as the outcome of a series of apportionments, the resultant unit cost may be of questionable value for the purposes of management planning, control and decision making. (Remember that the process of apportionment always contains a certain element of subjectivity; see Chapter 5.)

Alternatively, more than one cost unit can be employed. Thus, for example, the passenger transport business could attribute costs to journeys or routes in the first instance, thereafter averaging these costs over the number of passenger/kilometres on each route. Although 'routes' is one step removed from the sharp end of providing passenger transport, it has the merit of allowing a higher proportion of total cost to be allocated (i.e. treated as direct) than is the case with 'passenger/kilometre'. By reducing subjectivity in this way, a more aggregated cost unit might be of greater use to management, though a cost per passenger/kilometre can still be calculated, perhaps for external reporting purposes.

What this discussion highlights is the need for care in selection of a cost unit, along with the importance of the factors governing this choice which we discussed earlier:

- the nature of the service being provided;
- internal and external information needs; and
- the cost/benefit criterion.

Service capacity

We have said that services possess the characteristics of perishability and simultaneity. We cannot therefore produce for stock when capacity exceeds demand, so planning capacity levels is clearly of the utmost importance for service providers. But this is not just a planning issue – there are cost implications as well, as Exhibit 11.4 illustrates.

KD & Co: summary cost and capacity data

A summary of the firm's budgeted cost and other data for next year is as follows:

Consultants' salaries	£176 400	Telephone & fax	£10 000
Travelling costs	£20 000	Stationery	£8 000
Administrative costs	£111 000	General expenses	£40 000

Each of the firm's five consultants works for a maximum of 35 hours per week, and there are 36 working weeks in the year. Management estimates that 4000 chargeable client/ hours will be worked next year; it further estimates that, for every chargeable client/hour, an additional 0.2 hours will be spent by consultants on client-related but unproductive activities (e.g. travelling to and from clients' premises). In addition, management reckons that, given the expected level of demand, 20% of maximum consultant hours will be devoted to general administrative duties.

Exhibit 11.4 Service costs and capacity

 Use the data in Exhibit 11.4 to determine KD & Co's spare capacity in terms of consultants' hours.

Total number of consultant hours available in the year:

5 consultants × 35 hours × 36 weeks		6300
Less Chargeable client hours	4000	
Non-productive client-related activities (20% × 4000)	800	
General administrative duties (20% × 6300)	1260	6060
Spare capacity		240

At just under 4% of maximum consultant hours, management may decide that spare capacity is not likely to be a major issue next year and that accordingly, no action is needed. However, the existence of non-productive and spare hours does raise a question over the cost of £58 per hour we calculated earlier.

 Do you feel that £58 should be used as the cost per chargeable client/hour? Explain your reasoning.

The short answer is 'no' – £58 is based on maximum available hours; if we use this as the cost per chargeable client/hour, we assume that maximum available and chargeable client hours are the same. But this is not the case, as it fails to allow for non-productive client-related and administrative time. In other words, the 6300 hours we used to arrive at a cost of £58 is overstated, with a resulting understatement in the cost per hour. What we can do with our £58 is to use it as a basis for determination of the total cost of 4000 chargeable client hours:

	£
Chargeable client hours (4000 × £58)	232 000
Non-productive client-related time (800 × £58)	46 400
General administrative time (1260 × £58)	73 080
	351 480

The cost per chargeable client/hour is thus:

$$\frac{£351\ 480}{4000 \text{ chargeable client/hours}} = £87.87$$

Management must now decide whether or not to include the cost of spare capacity within the cost per chargeable client/hour. Inclusion gives a revised cost per chargeable client hour of:

	£
Total cost of chargeable client/hours (as above)	351 480
Add Cost of spare capacity (240 × £58)	13 920
	365 400

Cost per chargeable client/hour is now:

$$\frac{£365\ 400}{4000 \text{ chargeable hours}} = £91.35$$

We could achieve the same result by using chargeable client/hours in our calculation of unit cost. Direct cost per hour is:

$$\frac{\text{Consultants' salaries}}{\text{Chargeable client/hours}} = \frac{£176\ 400}{4000} = £44.10$$

and the overhead per hour becomes:

$$\frac{\text{Total overhead}}{\text{Chargeable client hours}} = \frac{£189\,000}{4000} = £47.25$$

The cost per chargeable client/hour is thus:

	£
Direct cost	44.10
Overhead	47.25
	91.35

Regardless of the mechanics of calculation, we can see that adjusting for unproductive time, time spent on general administration duties, and possibly for spare capacity has a very marked effect on unit cost:

If no allowance made for unproductive etc. hours	£58.00
If unproductive and administrative hours allowed for	£87.87
If unproductive, administrative hours and spare capacity allowed for	£91.35

In such circumstances, management should, as a minimum, make allowance for the unproductive client-related hours along with those hours spent on general administration. The justification for this is that these hours are lost in the normal course of business and can be expected under normal operating conditions. Their cost should therefore be borne by productive hours. We can view them as analogous to the normal losses we described in the context of process costing (see Chapter 9). The case regarding spare capacity is less clear-cut. On the one hand, we could view its cost as a form of abnormal loss – i.e. as lost hours in excess of what is expected and acceptable under normal operating conditions.

The cost of spare capacity would not be included as part of the cost per chargeable client/hour. On the other hand, we could argue that, given the nature of service provision, it is not practicable to match capacity precisely with demand, so a certain amount of spare capacity might be expected under normal conditions. So we might include this as an element of the cost per chargeable client/hour.

The sort of capacity-to-demand consideration we have been discussing is common to a wide range of service providers. Hotels and hospitals, for example, need to consider, respectively, room and bed occupancy ratios; schools must take account of pupil : teacher ratios; and transport organisations must look at passenger utilisation rates. Ultimately, the extent to which spare capacity is/is not included within service unit costs is likely to depend on a number of factors:

1 *Significance* Where significant overcapacity exists, inclusion within unit cost will result in unit costs that are markedly overstated and unrepresentative of what is being provided. Less significant overcapacity may be less of a problem in this respect. (KD & Co's unit cost increases by only about 5% as a result of including spare capacity, so there may not be a serious issue here).

2 *Commercial practice* In certain service sectors (transport, for example), allowance may be made for an expected level of spare capacity as a matter of commercial practice within the sector. This treatment would therefore treat some spare capacity as 'normal' (and include as part of unit cost); spare capacity over and above this expected level would be treated as 'abnormal' and dealt with separately.

3 *Use of unit cost* If unit costs are to be used for planning, control and decision making, it may be preferable not to cause potential distortion by including a

significant element of spare capacity cost. This would be especially true where unit costs were being used as the basis for selling price, with any unnatural distortion to unit cost resulting in an uneconomic and uncompetitive selling price. Similarly, it may be important for management to be aware of both the extent and the cost of spare capacity, rather than having such costs 'hidden' within unit cost.

4 *Cost/benefit criterion* While there is always likely to be some benefit for management in being aware of the cost of spare capacity, it may not always be cost-effective to determine such a cost. For example, in KD & Co, the dividing line between genuinely spare capacity and unproductive client-related hours/general administration time may be extremely difficult to draw with any precision. The time and effort required to do so will probably be disproportionate to any resulting benefit.

Stocks

Since services cannot be stored, it follows that stocks and their valuation are much less important to service than manufacturing organisations. However, this is not to say that stocks simply do not exist in such organisations.

 Would any kind of stock exist within KD & Co? If so, what?

Although stocks are not a major element of KD & Co's operations, they will nevertheless exist. You may have suggested stocks of stationery, or of consumables like computer disks. It is also possible that the firm could have stock of work-in-progress (unlikely as this might seem). If, at the end of its accounting year, the firm is engaged on work for clients that is unfinished, then we effectively have work-in-progress which would need to be costed for the purposes of the firm's annual accounts. Exhibit 11.5 provides some details.

KD & Co: work-in-progress at accounting year-end

At the end of its current accounting year, the firm was working on two projects, which were incomplete at that point in time. Details are as follows:

Client XY Ltd: this project is of 250 hours' duration and management has estimated that it is 40% complete at the year-end.
Client AB Ltd: this project is of 400 hours' duration and is estimated to be 80% complete at the year-end.

KD & Co's cost per chargeable client hour is £87.87.

Exhibit 11.5 Service WIP

 Use the data in Exhibit 11.5 to obtain the cost of KD & Co's work-in-progress at the accounting year-end.

Just as we did in Chapter 9 for process costing, we need to adjust WIP units to reflect their degree of completion – i.e. convert partly complete output to its fully complete equivalent. You will recall from the earlier chapter that to do this, we multiply partly completed units by their degree of completion. In this case, 'hours' are the units concerned.

	£
Client XY Ltd: (250 hours × 40%) × £87.87 per hour	8 787.00
Client AB Ltd: (400 hours × 80%) × £87.87 per hour	28 118.40
WIP at year-end	36 905.40

In addition to the work-in-progress above, the firm's balance sheet will show the cost of any unused materials like stationery and computer consumables. For KD & Co, this latter category of stock is unlikely to be a particularly large amount. However, in other service organisations, 'material' stocks may be very much more important. For example, large stocks of drugs and other medical supplies will exist in a hospital; hotels need to carry stocks of food and drink. But although material and work-in-progress stocks may exist to varying degrees of magnitude in different service sectors, what is true of all sectors is the absence of finished goods stock.

For those service providers which carry very little stock, it follows that determination of stock values is a much less crucial activity than for their manufacturing counterparts. It may therefore be the case that unit cost calculations can be tailored much more specifically to management needs. Where unit costs must meet both internal and external requirements, tailoring of information in this way could be difficult, if not impossible.

Adoption/adaptation of costing methodologies

In the foregoing discussion, we have seen some examples of how costing methodologies intended originally for other forms of output can be applied to services. For instance, we discussed the use of normal and abnormal losses in determination of service unit costs, and used equivalent units to value the firm's work-in-progress stock. We first encountered these techniques in Chapter 9 when we discussed process costing.

 Can you suggest any other cost accounting techniques or methodologies discussed in the last few chapters that we might apply to service output?

To a greater or lesser extent almost every technique discussed in Chapters 1–10 could be applied to service output. For example, KD & Co might apply job costing principles to the work it does for clients (see Chapter 8), with each client project being treated as a job. If projects are especially large and of long duration, the firm might even use contract costing, with clients making progress payments and the firm reporting profit on incomplete contracts. Overhead absorption techniques – either 'traditional' or activity-based – can just as easily be applied to service as to manufactured output. Even the joint product costing methods introduced in Chapter 10 could have their use: KD & Co's consultants may, for example, undertake different forms of work for clients, which the firm might treat as joint products, apportioning joint costs like consultants' salaries between them.

As we progress through later chapters in this book, we will see many more instances of cost accounting techniques that are equally applicable to service and manufactured output.

INTERNALLY PROVIDED SERVICES

Not only can services be provided on a commercial basis, but they may also be provided by one sub-unit of an organisation to another sub-unit within the same organisation. Some of these internal services – IT, for example – can incur high levels of cost, so their treatment merits careful consideration. The general costing issues we have been discussing so far apply equally to internal as to commercial provision. However, internal service provision raises another problem: should a charge be made by providers to users?

 Can you suggest a danger in not charging users for internal provision of high-cost services like IT?

While there might be circumstances where no charge is appropriate (e.g. to encourage use of an underutilised facility, or where determination of a charge would breach the cost/benefit criterion), there is a danger that users might come to believe that they are somehow 'free', and make unnecessary and even wasteful use of them. By making a charge, users are made aware of the cost of supporting their activities, and the likelihood of unnecessary usage may therefore be reduced. Charging for internal services might improve not only efficiency of usage but also of provision. If, for example, the cost of internal provision is viewed by users as too high (say, relative to the cost of similar services obtained from an external source), then internal providers could be forced to reduce their costs, or to control them more effectively. Creating charges for internal services could also improve perceptions about the costing system's 'fairness', as fewer costs would be subject to what might be fairly arbitrary treatment in the process of overhead absorption. And, as a corollary, unit costs of the end product/service may present a more accurate picture of the resources consumed in producing it.

Where charges are set for internal services, it is crucial that they are neutral – i.e. they are not seen as favouring either provider or user. The charge basis must therefore be as objective as possible, and we discuss the main approaches below.

Charge on the basis of external market value

We can charge for internally provided services at the price charged for similar services on the external market. This means that the department/sub-unit providing service is treated as a **profit centre** (see Chapter 2), being credited with 'revenue' in the form of charges for services provided and reporting 'profit' thereon. We illustrated such an approach in the previous chapter when we credited a joint process account with the intermediate sales value of joint products.

 What do you see as the main advantage(s) of this charging basis?

The main advantage of using external market price is its objectivity: external price is a fact, easily verified by providers and users. It is thus a straightforward approach, and, because of its objectivity, can reduce the possibility of dispute between providers and users. It could also encourage innovation and effective cost control/reduction by treating both provider and user as if they were parties to a genuine 'arms' length' commercial transaction.

However, there are some drawbacks. First, the service being provided internally may not be available on the outside market, or may be available in a form that is markedly different. Second, users may object because they are not purchasing services on the open market, but from another department within the same organisation. Faced with this kind of objection, the provider might consider discounting the external price to reflect the fact that costs like selling and distribution do not attach to internally provided services.

Charge on the basis of cost

At the outset, we need to decide whether to use actual cost or budgeted/standard cost. A **standard cost** is a predetermined cost per unit of product/service (see Chapter 16 for detailed discussion).

 Why would actual cost generally be inappropriate as the basis for internal service charges?

As we observed in Chapter 5 in relation to overhead absorption rates, actual cost will not be known until after the event; it will also fluctuate – e.g. from month to month. This is unsatisfactory from the service users' standpoint, as the amount of charge will not be known in advance, and will fluctuate in line with fluctuations in the providers' cost. Planning by the service recipient – for instance about the amount of service to use – will thus be seriously hampered. But there is another, possibly more serious, problem with use of actual cost: the service provider has no reason to control cost, as any inefficiencies and cost overspends are automatically passed to users of the service. Similarly, if service providers are operating at low volume, the actual cost per unit of service will almost certainly be greater than at higher volumes. This might discourage use of expensive internal services, and may have the effect of artificially inflating the unit cost of output from service recipients. But although standard (or budgeted) cost is generally preferable, problems still exist; for example, standards need to be kept up to date (see Chapter 16 for a discussion of the problems associated with standard costing).

We still have the difficulty of deciding which specific costs to include in the charge. Inclusion of fixed plus variable costs causes the receiver to treat the provider's fixed costs as if they were variable, possibly leading to the perception of 'overcharging' by the receiver, with consequent unwillingness to use the service. If, on the other hand, we include only the variable cost of provision, we run exactly the opposite risk of users perceiving service cost as unrealistically low, with the attendant risk of unnecessary or wasteful usage.

In broad terms, management should therefore address the following questions in setting a charge for internal service provision:

1 *Effect on usage of service.* Will the proposed charge encourage or discourage use? What is management's aim in this respect?
2 *Efficiency of provision.* Is a charge likely to improve the efficiency and quality of internal provision? Are cost reductions likely to be achievable?
3 *Effect on unit costs.* What effect is a service charge likely to have on the unit cost of the organisation's final product/service? Will this cost become more representative of resources consumed, or is there a danger of its being artificially inflated/deflated?

4 *Behavioural implications.* What is the probability of disputes arising as a result of the charging system? Is it possible that managers of provider/user departments might act in a manner which is not in the wider organisational interest (e.g. by reducing service demand to such a degree that quality of final output is prejudiced)?

SUMMARY

In this chapter, we have discussed some general issues involved with service costing. In particular, we have seen that:

- Service output possesses the following characteristics:
  - **Intangibility**
  - **Heterogeneity**
  - **Perishability**
  - **Simultaneity**
- Because of their nature, many service outputs require the use of a **composite cost unit** or of more than one cost unit.
- Choice of the most appropriate cost unit depends on:
  - The nature of the service
  - Internal and external information needs
  - The cost/benefit criterion
- Unlike their manufacturing counterparts, many service organisations are labour-intensive.
- Overhead tends to represent a high proportion of the total cost of service provision.
- Because of service output's perishability and simultaneity, costing spare or unproductive capacity may be an important issue. Expected unproductive capacity could be treated as a normal loss and included in unit cost; unexpected spare capacity may be treated as an abnormal loss and reported separately.
- Costing treatment of spare capacity can depend on a number of factors:
  - Significance
  - Commercial practice
  - Use of the cost unit
  - Cost/benefit criterion
- Stocks of finished goods will not exist in service organisations, though work-in-progress and materials' stocks may be encountered and may sometimes be significant in amount.
- Service costing may adopt or adapt costing methodologies originally developed for other forms of output.
- Making a charge for internally provided services might improve efficiency of both usage and provision.
- Charges for internal services could be based on:
  - External market price
  - Cost

▶

Where cost is the basis, budgeted/standard is generally preferable to actual, as the latter permits inefficiencies and overspends to be passed to users.

In the next chapter, we will discuss two alternative treatments of unit cost determination and profit measurement: absorption costing and marginal costing.

FURTHER READING

Kotas, R., *Management Accounting for Hospitality and Tourism*, International Thomson Business Press, 2000.

Sheridan, T., Costing in the service sector. *Management Accounting*, May 1996 (CIMA).

SELF-TEST QUESTIONS

11.1 State which of the following are characteristics of service costing:

  (i)   high levels of indirect costs as a proportion of total costs
  (ii) use of composite cost units
  (iii) use of equivalent units

    A (i) only
    B (i) and (ii) only
    C (ii) only
    D (ii) and (iii) only
    E All of them

(CIMA, *Operational Cost Accounting*, May 1995)

11.2 Place a tick in the appropriate box to indicate whether each statement is true or false.

	True	False
(a) Service output is generally more homogeneous than manufactured output.	☐	☐
(b) Charging for internally provided services at actual cost gives the provider no incentive to control cost.	☐	☐
(c) A composite cost unit should reflect the key variables involved in service provision.	☐	☐
(d) Service organisations are principally capital-intensive.	☐	☐
(e) The perishability and simultaneity of services suggests that output can be tailored very closely to demand.	☐	☐
(f) Unproductive capacity that arises under normal operating conditions should be excluded from a service's unit cost.	☐	☐
(g) Stock of WIP may exist in certain service situations.	☐	☐

11.3 An accountant is to set up in private practice. She anticipates working a 35-hour week and taking four weeks' holiday per year. General expenses of the practice are expected to be £20 000 per year, and she has set herself a target of £30 000 a year salary. Assuming that only 75% of her time worked will be chargeable to clients, what should she quote (to the nearest £) for a job anticipated to take 50 hours?

    A £794
    B £1831
    C £1984
    D £2172

(CIMA, *Cost Accounting and Quantitative Methods*, May 1997)

11.4 The following estimated costs relate to Druminch Hospital's next financial year:

	Surgical wards	Medical wards	Out-patients
	£000	£000	£000
Doctors' salaries	1000	1500	450
Nurses' salaries	1650	2100	900
Renewal of equipment	400	–	–
Ward maintenance	120	200	–
Operating theatre costs	800	–	–
Medicine & drugs	600	820	450
Reception staff	–	–	90

The hospital's support departments along with the related cost estimates are:

	£000
Laundry	300
Porterage & cleaning	410
X-ray department	900
Surgical supplies	880
Laboratories	1200

The hospital's policy is to charge the cost of these support departments direct to wards and out-patients using the fairest available basis. The following additional information is available:

	Surgical wards	Medical wards	Out-patients
Number of patients	–	–	86 000
Bed occupancy	90%	85%	–
Number of wards	10	12	–
Beds per ward	25	25	–
Out-patient beds	–	–	20
Number of supply requisitions	3300	3600	2 100
Area (square metres)	4000	6000	5 000
Average patient stay (days)	10	7	–

General hospital running costs for the year are estimated to be:

	£000
Building occupancy	1300
Administration	1200
Canteen	500

Technical studies suggest that these general costs should be apportioned as follows:

	Building occupancy	Administration	Canteen
	%	%	%
Surgical wards	30	30	30
Medical wards	40	30	45
Out-patients	10	20	5
Laundry	5	5	5
Porterage & cleaning	5	5	5
Surgical supplies	2	2	2
X-ray department	3	3	3
Laboratory	5	5	5

Requirement

Determine the following:
(i) cost per patient bed-day for surgical wards
(ii) cost per patient bed-day for medical wards and
(iii) cost per patient for out-patients.

11.5 Mr G and Mrs H have recently formed a consultancy business, and have sought your advice concerning costs and fees. Mr G and Mrs H each wishes to receive a salary of £20 000 in the first year of trading. They have purchased two cars at a cost of £13 000 each and expect to use them for three years. At the end of this time each of the cars has an expected resale value of £4000. Straight-line depreciation is to be applied.

Mr G and Mrs H each expect to work for 8 hours per day, 5 days per week for 45 weeks per year. They refer to this as *available time*. Twenty-five per cent of the available time is expected to be used dealing with administrative matters relating to their own business, and in the first year it is expected that there will be idle time which will average 22.5% of the available time. The remainder of the available time is expected to be chargeable to clients.

Mr G and Mrs H agreed that their fee structure should comprise:

• an hourly rate for productive client work;
• an hourly rate for travelling to/from clients; and
• a rate per mile travelled to/from clients.

They expect that the travelling time will equal 25% of their chargeable time, and will amount to a total of 18 000 miles. They have agreed that this time should be charged at one-third of their normal hourly rate.

Apart from the costs referred to above, Mr G and Mrs H have estimated their other costs for the first twelve months as follows:

	£
Electricity	1200
Fuel for vehicles	1800
Insurance – professional liability and office	600
Insurance – vehicles	800
Mobile telephones	1200
Office rent and rates	8400
Office telephone/facsimile	1800
Postage and stationery	500
Secretarial costs	8400
Servicing and repairs of vehicles	1200
Vehicle road tax	280

Requirements

(a) In order that the consultancy business breaks even after paying the required salaries, classify the costs between professional services and vehicle costs, and then, using the above costs and data, calculate the following:

   • an hourly rate for productive client work
   • an hourly rate for travelling to/from clients and
   • a rate per mile travelled to/from clients. **(15 marks)**

(b) Explain how Mr G and Mrs H may monitor their income and costs during the year to see if they are achieving their objectives. **(5 marks)**

(c) Explain the method of cost accounting which should be used by Mr G and Mrs H in order to ensure that each of their clients is charged correctly for the services provided.

(5 marks)

(Total: 25 marks)

(CIMA, *Operational Cost Accounting*, November 1995)

QUESTIONS WITHOUT ANSWERS

11.6 A management consultancy recovers overheads on chargeable consulting hours. Budgeted overheads were £615 000 and actual consulting hours were 32 150. Overheads were under-recovered by £35 000.

If actual overheads were £694 075 what was the budgeted overhead absorption rate per hour?

A £19.13
B £20.50
C £21.59
D £22.68

(CIMA, *Cost Accounting and Quantitative Methods*, May 1997)

11.7 Speedee Ltd has three main divisions – a motor-cycle courier service; a domestic parcel delivery service; and a bulk parcel service for industry. The following information is available for a period:

	Courier service	Domestic parcels	Bulk parcels
Sales (£000)	205	316	262
Number of vehicles	45	15	9
Distance travelled (000 km)	168	82	54
Identifiable fixed costs (£000)	25	32	25

Variable costs vary both with the distance travelled and also the type of vehicle used, and are £307 800 for the company as a whole. A technical estimate shows that the various vehicles used for the three services incur variable costs per kilometre in the ratio of 1 : 3 : 5, respectively for the courier service, domestic parcels and bulk parcels.

The general fixed costs for the business, which are not directly identifiable, total £76 000 for the period.

Requirements

(a) Calculate, for each service,

(i) the contribution (5 marks)
(ii) the contribution per kilometre (2 marks)
(iii) the net profit. (3 marks)

(Author's note: contribution is (sales revenue – variable costs) or (revenue per kilometre – variable cost per kilometre)

(b) Describe briefly how a spreadsheet can assist in the budgeting process. (5 marks)

(Total: 15 marks)

(CIMA, *Cost Accounting and Quantitative Methods*, November 1998)

11.8 The Northshire Hospital Trust operates two types of specialist X-ray scanning machines, XR1 and XR50. Details for the next period are estimated as follows:

Machine	XR1	XR50
Running hours	1100	2000
	£	£
Variable running costs (excluding plates)	27 500	64 000
Fixed costs	20 000	97 500

A brain scan is normally carried out on machine type XR1: this task uses special X-ray plates costing £40 each and takes 4 hours of machine time. Because of the nature of the process, around 10% of the scans produce blurred and therefore useless results.

Requirements

(a) Calculate the cost of a satisfactory brain scan on machine type XR1. **(7 marks)**

(b) Brain scans can also be done on machine type XR50 and would take only 1.8 hours per scan with a reduced reject rate of 6%. However, the cost of the X-ray plates would be £55 per scan.
Advise which type should be used, assuming sufficient capacity is available on both types of machine. **(8 marks)**
(Total: 15 marks)

(CIMA, *Cost Accounting and Quantitative Methods*, November 1997)

11.9 A supermarket which sells numerous food and grocery items has eight check-out points. There is also a separate wines and spirits section which operates as a 'shop within a shop' and has its own check-out point. Each check-out has electronic point-of-sale terminals.

The manager is not satisfied that she is being given all the information that she ought to receive in order to manage and control the supermarket efficiently. She seeks your advice.

Requirement

As the management accountant, write a report which contains lists of the information you think should be provided for her on

(i)   a daily basis
(ii) a weekly basis
(iii) a monthly basis.

You may assume that computer facilities are available to assist with the provision of the information. **(15 marks)**

(CIMA, *Cost Accounting*, November 1993)

11.10 A polytechnic offers a range of degree courses. The polytechnic organisation structure consists of three faculties each with a number of teaching departments. In addition, there is a polytechnic administrative/management function and a central services function.

The following cost information is available for the year ended 30 June 1987:

(i) *Occupancy costs:* Total: £1 500 000. Such costs are apportioned on the basis of area used which is:

	Square feet
Faculties	7 500
Teaching departments	20 000
Administration/management	7 000
Central services	3 000

(ii) *Administration/management costs:* Direct costs £1 775 000. Indirect costs: an apportionment of occupancy costs. Direct and indirect costs are charged to degree courses on a percentage basis.

(iii) *Faculty costs:* Direct costs: £700 000. Indirect costs: an apportionment of occupancy costs and central service costs. Direct and indirect costs are charged to teaching departments.

(iv) *Teaching departments:* Direct costs: £5 525 000. Indirect costs: an apportionment of occupancy costs and central service costs plus all faculty costs. Direct and indirect costs are charged to degree courses on a percentage basis.

(v) *Central services:* Direct costs: £1 000 000. Indirect costs: an apportionment of occupancy costs.

Direct and indirect costs of central services have, in previous years, been charged to users on a percentage basis. A study has now been completed which has estimated what user areas would have paid external suppliers for the same services on an individual basis. For the year ended 30 June 1987, the apportionment of the central services cost is to be recalculated in a manner which recognises the cost savings achieved by using the central services facilities instead of using external service companies. This is to be done by apportioning the overall savings to user areas in proportion to their share of the estimated external costs.

The estimated external costs of service provision are as follows:

	£000
Faculties	240
Teaching departments	800
Degree courses:	
Business studies	32
Mechanical engineering	48
Catering studies	32
All other degrees	448
	1600

(vi) Additional data relating to the degree courses is as follows:

	Degree course		
	Business Studies	*Mechanical Engineering*	*Catering Studies*
Number of graduates	80	50	120
Apportioned costs (as % of totals)			
Teaching departments	3%	2.5%	7%
Administration/management	2.5%	5%	4%

Central services are to be apportioned as detailed in (v) above.

The total number of graduates from the polytechnic in the year to 30 June 1987 was 2500.

Requirements

(a) Prepare a flow diagram which shows the apportionment of costs to user areas. No values need be shown. **(3 marks)**

(b) Calculate the average cost per graduate, for the year ended 30 June 1987, for the polytechnic and for each of the degrees in business studies, mechanical engineering and catering studies, showing all relevant cost analysis. **(14 marks)**

(c) Suggest reasons for any differences in the average cost per graduate from one degree to another, and discuss briefly the relevance of such information to the polytechnic management. **(5 marks)**
(Total: 22 marks)

(ACCA, *Paper 2.4*, June 1988)

CHAPTER 12

Absorption costing and marginal costing

Towards a better understanding of the absorption and marginal costing methods

... The controversy concerning which of these two costing methods is the better has existed for a considerable time, there being no overriding argument in favour of either. The fundamental argument relates to whether fixed production overhead should be treated as a product or a period cost.

Proponents of the absorption costing method take the view that the elements that make up fixed production overhead are product costs, that is to say that such costs are necessarily incurred in the production of a finished product ... Although such fixed costs are not directly traceable to the production of a unit of product, without their incurrence, the business would not be in a position to produce ...

This appears to be a very strong argument in favour of the use of the absorption costing method. Strong enough, in fact, for the method to be incorporated into SSAP 9.

One of the more obvious arguments put forward in favour of the use of the marginal costing method is that production fixed overheads are, in most instances, related to a time function. Rent is based on a time period, as are salaries paid to supervisors ...

For this reason alone, therefore, the proponents of marginal costing consider that production fixed overhead should be regarded as a period cost rather than a cost related to product ...

Source: J.D. Lane, *ACCA Students' Newsletter*, December 1990.

Exhibit 12.1 The fundamental difference between absorption and marginal costing

INTRODUCTION

When we examined overhead absorption in Chapters 5 and 6, we saw that all output-related costs (direct and indirect) were included in unit costs and said that this approach was necessary for the published accounts of many organisations. What this means is that absorption costing effectively ignores cost *behaviour*. In this chapter we will describe and illustrate an alternative view – **marginal** (or **variable**) **costing**, which attributes only variable costs to cost units, and which may be more useful for *internal* purposes, although not permissible for published accounts (in the UK). We will compare and contrast profit statements prepared under both approaches and show how the different profit figures may be reconciled. In addition, we will see how marginal costing principles may be useful to management: for example, we will demonstrate a marginal costing approach to determining the contribution of different business segments, products or services and illustrate how this might be used to aid decision making. Finally, we will compare absorption and marginal costing, discussing their relative strengths and weaknesses.

OBJECTIVES

When you have completed this chapter, you will be able to:

- appreciate the difference in rationale and cost classification underlying absorption and marginal costing;
- prepare profit statements using both marginal and absorption costing;
- explain the reason for differences in profit resulting from application of each of the two systems and reconcile such differences;
- adjust an absorption costing profit statement for over/underabsorbed overhead;
- apply marginal costing principles to decision-making scenarios;
- assess the relative strengths and weaknesses of marginal costing and absorption costing.

MARGINAL AND ABSORPTION COSTING: DIFFERENT RATIONALES

Absorption costing stems from the view that certain overheads are necessarily incurred to allow output to occur and should therefore be included in unit costs. In effect, absorption costing is based on a *functional* classification of costs: i.e. all output-related (or production) costs are attributed to cost units with non-production costs being excluded from unit costs (at least for stock valuation and profit measurement purposes). Marginal costing, however, is based on a distinction between variable and fixed costs (see Chapter 2), with the former being attributed to cost units and the latter being dealt with in total for a particular period. The justification for this treatment of fixed costs is that, in general, costs such as rent, rates and insurance relate to a *period of time*, rather than to volume of output and their accounting treatment should reflect this fact.

Not only can absorption of fixed costs be viewed as illogical in light of their predominantly time-based nature, but it may also cause confusion about their behaviour and even amount. Under absorption costing, increases/decreases in the volume of output will result in increases/decreases in the amount of fixed overhead absorbed, which might give the misleading impression that the amount of the underlying costs *incurred* is increasing/decreasing in line with output – i.e. that we are dealing with variable costs. Consider Figure 12.1 which compares fixed overhead absorbed with fixed overhead incurred over the relevant range.

✔ *Which line in Figure 12.1 represents fixed overhead incurred and which the absorbed amount?*

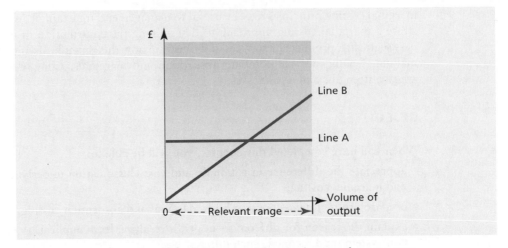

Figure 12.1 Fixed overhead incurred versus absorbed over relevant range

Line A represents fixed overhead incurred while Line B represents the absorbed amount and it is possible that use of absorption costing could result in a misunderstanding of cost behaviour: e.g. if the 'absorbed' line in Figure 12.1 were erroneously thought to depict the behaviour of the costs concerned, then zero fixed overhead would be predicted at the lowest volume within the relevant range – which is very unlikely to be the case. Potential misconceptions of this sort may, as we shall see, suggest adoption of courses of action which are financially inadvisable. (You should note that this difficulty does not arise in the case of *variable* overheads: by definition, total variable overhead increases/decreases in line with increases/decreases in output.)

A final problem with absorption of fixed costs is that it may give rise to some anomalies in reported profit relative to sales and production volume; we will illustrate this shortly.

Marginal costing seeks to remove any potential difficulty which might be caused by treating fixed costs 'as if' they were variable, attributing only variable costs to units of output and treating *all* fixed costs on a total basis for the period to which they relate. The unit output cost as calculated for each of marginal and absorption costing is as follows:

		£
Marginal costing: unit output cost		
Variable costs:	direct materials	x
	direct labour	x
	direct expenses	x
	variable production overhead	x
Cost per unit		x

		£
Absorption costing: unit output cost		
Direct costs:	direct materials	x
	direct labour	x
	direct expenses	x
Prime cost		x
Indirect costs:	variable production overhead	x
	fixed production overhead	x
Cost per unit		x

You will see that the only difference between the two unit costs lies in the treatment of fixed output-related overhead: this is important to our later discussion of how to reconcile profit differences and should be borne in mind. The marginal version of unit output cost treats direct costs as also being variable. While this is a useful simplifying assumption for the illustrative profit statements which follow, you will recall from Chapter 2 that direct costs (and in particular labour) are not necessarily variable in nature.

ABSORPTION AND MARGINAL COSTING PROFIT STATEMENTS

The different treatment of fixed output-related overhead and the difference in the underlying cost classification are reflected in the profit statement produced by each system. In absorption costing, all output-related costs (direct and indirect, fixed and variable) are included in the cost of sales calculation, hence in determination of **gross profit**. In a marginal costing system, all variable costs (direct and indirect, output-related and otherwise) are included in the cost of sales calculation, hence in determination of **contribution**. In the first instance (sales less all variable costs) provides contribution towards covering fixed costs, thereafter providing contribution to profit. The concept of contribution is central to marginal costing: we shall use it later in the chapter, and also extensively in Chapter 13 so it is important to distinguish it clearly from absorption costing's gross profit:

> Contribution = sales less all variable costs incurred to generate sales
> Gross profit = sales less all output-related costs incurred to generate sales.

We shall use the data in Exhibit 12.2 to illustrate the basic construction of profit statements using absorption and marginal costing. We will use a manufacturing business for this, so that we can demonstrate the impact on profit of stock movements; but the marginal versus absorption costing debate is equally applicable to service organisations.

PLW Ltd

PLW Ltd manufactures a single type of digital camera at one of its factories and estimated figures for next year are:

			£
Per unit	Selling price		250
	Variable costs:	direct materials	120
		direct labour	40
		production overhead	20
		selling overhead	10

Production/sales will be 20 000 units and there will be no stocks at the start or end of the year.

			£
Fixed costs for the year:	production overhead		800 000
	selling & distribution overhead		70 000
	administration overhead		120 000

PLW Ltd absorbs fixed production overhead using a cost unit rate derived from annual budgeted volume.

Exhibit 12.2 Basic data for absorption and marginal costing profit statements

> ✔ *From Exhibit 12.2, determine the production cost per unit using:*
>
> 1 *absorption costing; and*
> 2 *marginal costing.*

Before we can calculate the absorption costing unit cost, we must obtain an absorption rate for fixed production overhead:

$$\frac{\text{Fixed production overhead cost}}{\text{Units of output}} = \frac{£800\ 000}{20\ 000} = £40 \text{ per unit}$$

The cost per unit is thus:

	£	£
Direct materials		120
Direct labour		40
Prime cost		160
Variable production overhead	20	
Fixed production overhead	40	60
Production cost per unit		220

Applying marginal costing principles gives:

Direct materials	120
Direct labour	40
Variable production overhead	20
Production cost per unit	180

Note that the variable selling overhead is not included in *production* cost. Bearing in mind the definition we gave above, contribution per unit is:

	£	£
Selling price per unit		250
Less marginal production cost	180	
Variable selling overhead	10	190
Contribution per unit		60

You will see that *all* variable costs – production and non-production – have been deducted from selling price in order to determine contribution. Total contribution is therefore

(units sales × contribution per unit) = (20 000 × £60) = £1 200 000

If £1 200 000 is sufficient to cover all PLW Ltd's fixed costs, the company will earn a profit equal to the excess of total contribution over total fixed costs; to the extent that £1 200 000 does not cover total fixed costs, a loss will be incurred. We can confirm the total contribution and the company's profit/loss position from the marginal costing profit statement presented below.

PLW Ltd: Marginal costing profit statement for the year

	£	£
Sales (20 000 @ £250)		£5 000 000
Cost of sales		
Opening stock	nil	
Add Marginal cost of production		
(20 000 @ £180)	3 600 000	
	3 600 000	
Less Closing stock	nil	
	3 600 000	
Variable selling overhead (20 000 @ £10)	200 000	3 800 000
Contribution (20 000 @ £60 – see above)		1 200 000
Fixed costs: production overhead	800 000	
selling & distribution overhead	70 000	
administration overhead	120 000	990 000
Net profit		210 000

From the profit statement, you will once again note that *all* variable costs are deducted from sales to determine contribution. You will also see that we have shown a stock adjustment in the profit statement, even though there was no opening of closing stock. Its inclusion here, and in the absorption costing statement immediately following, is merely to allow consistency of presentation with later statements, where stocks are present.

PLW Ltd's profit statement based on absorption costing is as follows:

PLW Ltd: Absorption costing profit statement for the year

	£	£
Sales (20 000 @ £250)		£5 000 000
Cost of sales		
Opening stock	nil	
Add Cost of production (20 000 @ £220)	4 400 000	
	4 400 000	
Less Closing stock	nil	4 400 000
Gross profit		600 000
Selling & distribution overhead:		
fixed	70 000	
variable (20 000 @ £10)	200 000	
Administration overhead	120 000	390 000
Net profit		210 000

Since both of our profit statements reveal the same net profit, does it really make any difference which approach we use? Let us examine the impact on the two systems' relative profit of stock changes.

Impact on relative profit of stock increase

Our first set of profit statements were based on production equalling sales; suppose now that the year's production is estimated at 25 000 units, rather than the 20 000 in Exhibit 12.2. If sales and opening stock remain, respectively, at 20 000 units and nil, stock increases by (25 000 – 20 000) = 5000 units during the year. How will this affect our profit calculations?

For ease of illustration, we will assume that the increased production volume will have no effect on PLW Ltd's cost structure – i.e. that the amount of fixed costs is unaffected and that the variable costs per unit are as given in Exhibit 12.2. Given this assumption, a change in estimated production volume will alter the absorption rate for fixed production overhead, this being derived from annual budgeted volume:

$$\frac{\text{Fixed production overhead cost}}{\text{Units of output}} = \frac{£800\ 000}{25\ 000} = £32 \text{ per unit}$$

Production cost per unit is now:

	£	£
Direct materials		120
Direct labour		40
Prime cost		160
Variable production overhead	20	
Fixed production overhead	32	52
Production cost per unit		212

 Insert the missing figures in the profit statement below to determine the absorption costing profit under the revised circumstances.

PLW Ltd: Absorption costing profit statement for the year

Sales (.........@ £250)   £.........
Cost of sales
Opening stock (.........@ £212)   £.........
Add Cost of production (.........@ £212)   £.........
                                                         £.........
Less Closing stock (.........@ £212)   £.........   £.........
Gross profit   £.........
Selling & distribution overhead:
                                   fixed   £.........
                 variable (.........@ £10)   £.........
Administration overhead   £.........   £.........
Net profit   £.........

The completed absorption costing profit statement is:

PLW Ltd: Absorption costing profit statement for the year

	£	£
Sales (20 000 @ £250)		5 000 000
Cost of sales		
Opening stock (0 @ £212)	nil	
Add Cost of production (25 000 @ £212)	5 300 000	
	5 300 000	
Less Closing stock (5000 @ £212)	1 060 000	4 240 000
Gross profit		760 000

	£	£
Selling & distribution overhead:		
fixed	70 000	
variable (20 000 @ £10)	200 000	
Administration overhead	120 000	390 000
Net profit		370 000

Note that the variable selling & distribution overhead varies with the volume of *sales*, not production. Simply by increasing stocks, PLW Ltd has improved net profit by (£370 000 – £210 000) = £160 000; we shall return to this point later.

 Look again at the original marginal costing profit statement. Will the 5000-unit stock increase have any effect on the profit of £210 000?

The short answer is 'no': although the volume of production has increased, *sales* volume is unchanged, which means that revenue, cost of sales and fixed costs are also unchanged, so that net profit remains at the £210 000 originally calculated. For sceptics, a revised marginal costing profit statement is given below.

PLW Ltd: Marginal costing profit statement for the year

	£	£
Sales (20 000 @ £250)		5 000 000
Cost of sales		
Opening stock (0 @ £180)	nil	
Add Marginal cost of production		
(25 000 @ £180)	4 500 000	
	4 500 000	
Less Closing stock (5000 @ £180)	900 000	
	3 600 000	
Variable selling & distribution overhead		
(20 000 @ £10)	200 000	3 800 000
Contribution		1 200 000
Fixed costs: production overhead	800 000	
selling & distribution overhead	70 000	
administration overhead	120 000	990 000
Net profit		210 000

We could argue that this unchanged profit figure is a better reflection of what has actually happened – i.e. no change in sales volume (or any factors other than production volume/stock) – than the £160 000 increase in net profit recorded in the absorption costing statement.

Impact on relative profit of stock reduction

Assume now that PLW Ltd will have opening stock of 6000 units and that estimated production during the year is 16 000 units – all other factors being the same as those set out in Exhibit 12.2. How will this change in circumstances affect the net profit reported under each system? We will deal with absorption costing first.

Compute the cost unit absorption rate for fixed overheads based on output of 16 000 units and use this to determine the production cost per unit using absorption costing principles.

Using a denominator of 16 000 units, the fixed overhead absorption rate is:

$$\frac{£800\,000}{16\,000\text{ units}} = £50\text{ per unit}$$

which gives a production cost per unit of:

	£
Prime cost (as before)	160
Variable production overhead (as before)	20
Fixed production overhead	50
	230

Assuming that a production cost of £230 per unit is also applicable to the opening stock, then the absorption costing profit statement is:

PLW Ltd: Absorption costing profit statement for the year

	£	£
Sales (20 000 @ £250)		5 000 000
Cost of sales		
Opening stock (6000 @ £230)	1 380 000	
Add Cost of production (16 000 @ £230)	3 680 000	
	5 060 000	
less Closing stock (2000 @ £230)	460 000	4 600 000
Gross profit		400 000
Selling & distribution overhead:		
fixed	70 000	
variable (20 000 @ £10)	200 000	
Administration overhead	120 000	390 000
Net profit		10 000

Units of closing stock are calculated as:

	units
Opening stock	6 000
Add Production	16 000
	22 000
Less Sales	20 000
= Closing stock	2 000

The effect of the stock reduction has therefore been a reduction of £200 000 in net profit initially calculated (£210 000).

 What will be the effect on marginal costing net profit of the 4000-unit reduction in stock?

Once again, the answer is 'none' – marginal costing will report a net profit of £210 000 irrespective of changes in volume of *stock*. Only if sales volume were to change from the original 20 000 units would marginal costing net profit react, increasing if sales volume increases, decreasing if it decreases.

Summary of relative net profit reported

We can summarise the relative net profit reported under each of absorption and marginal costing for PLW Ltd as follows:

Sales volume	20 000	20 000	20 000
Stock change	none	+5 000	−4 000
	£	£	£
Absorption costing net profit	210 000	370 000	10 000
Marginal costing net profit	210 000	210 000	210 000

In other words, assuming other factors to be unchanged – and in particular that none of the production volumes lie outside the relevant range – absorption costing net profit reacts to changes in both sales *and* stock volumes; whereas marginal costing net profit reacts to changes in sales *only*. A set of general relationships between relative net profit, production and sales volumes can be derived:

1 where production = sales (i.e. no stock increase), both systems yield the same net profit;
2 where production > sales (i.e. stock increases), absorption costing yields the higher net profit;
3 where production < sales (i.e. stock decreases), marginal costing yields the higher net profit.

However, in the long term (i.e. over the life of the organisation) both systems will report the same total profit, as the same total costs will be incurred over that lifespan, irrespective of how we attribute them to cost units.

Reason for profit differences and their reconciliation

If you review our earlier description of unit production costs for each of absorption and marginal costing, you will see that the only cost which is treated differently under the two systems is *fixed production overhead*. Since this is the only difference in unit production cost under the two approaches, it follows that this is the reason for profit differences between the two systems. Looking at the statement of comparative profit above, we can also see that the situations in which profit differs are those where there are stock movements during the period.

The link between these two factors is stock valuation: because of the different unit costs, stock values will differ between absorption costing and marginal costing. Absorption costing stocks will include fixed production overhead, marginal costing stocks will not. We can therefore effect a reconciliation between the different profit figures by examining the increase or decrease in stocks and determining the amount of fixed production overhead absorbed by that increase or decrease.

PLW Ltd: Summary of key figures for 'stock change' situations

	Scenario 1	Scenario 2
Opening stock (units)	nil	6 000
Closing stock (units)	5 000	2 000
Production (units)	25 000	16 000
Sales (units)	20 000	20 000
Fixed overhead absorption rate per unit	£32	£50
Absorption costing net profit	£370 000	£ 10 000
Marginal costing net profit	£210 000	£210 000

Exhibit 12.3 Key data for reconciliation of absorption and marginal costing profit

Using the data for Scenario 1 in Exhibit 12.3, the profit reconciliation is:

	£
Absorption costing net profit	370 000
Marginal costing net profit	210 000
Difference	160 000
Fixed production overhead absorbed in stock increase: (5000 units @ £32)	160 000

 Using the Scenario 2 data from Exhibit 12.3, reconcile absorption and marginal costing profit.

The Scenario 2 reconciliation is:

	£
Absorption costing net profit	10 000
Marginal costing net profit	210 000
Difference	(200 000)
Fixed production overhead absorbed in stock decrease (6000 – 2000 units @ £50)	(200 000)

We are now in a position to see why absorption costing net profit reacts the way it does to stock increases/decreases. Because the absorption unit cost is higher than the marginal, absorption stock values will be higher for the same volume of stock; this means that when there is a stock increase, absorption costing will carry forward for charging as a future cost (when the stock is sold) a higher amount of the current period's cost than marginal costing. Conversely, when there is a stock decrease, absorption costing will charge in the current period a higher amount of previous periods' cost than marginal costing. This is why PLW Ltd's absorption costing net profit increased by £160 000 when production exceeded an unchanged sales volume – i.e. under absorption costing £160 000 more of the current period's cost was deferred than under marginal costing; and when sales exceeded production, £200 000 more of a previous period's cost was charged in the current period.

Absorption costing: treatment of over- and underabsorption

In Chapter 5, we saw that one of the problems associated with using a predetermined overhead absorption rate is that the estimates of volume and overhead cost employed in its calculation can differ from actual volume and/or cost – giving rise to over- and underabsorption. Exhibit 13.3 presents PLW Ltd's actual results for the year under consideration. For simplicity, we have assumed that the only differences between estimate and actual have arisen in respect of production volume and fixed production overhead cost.

PLW Ltd: Actual information for the year

The company's predetermined absorption rate for fixed production overhead (£40) during the year in question was based on production volume of 20 000 units and overhead cost of £800 000. At the end of the year, it is known that actual production was 21 000 units and fixed production overhead incurred £890 000. In all other respects, actual results were in line with estimates, i.e.

Sales: 20 000 units @ £250 each
Prime cost per unit: £160

Variable selling overhead: £10 per unit

Opening stock: nil
Variable production overhead per unit: £20
Fixed selling & distribution overhead for the year: £70 000
Fixed administration overhead for the year: £120 000

Exhibit 12.4 PLW Ltd – over/underabsorption of overhead

 From Exhibit 12.4, determine the amount of over- or underabsorbed fixed production overhead for the year.

In Chapter 5, we saw that determination of over- or underabsorption involves comparison of the amount absorbed using a predetermined rate with the amount incurred; remembering that the amount absorbed is based on actual *production* (not sales), we get:

	£
Fixed production overhead absorbed (21 000 @ £40)	840 000
Fixed production overhead incurred	890 000
Underabsorption	50 000

Because overhead incurred exceeds that absorbed, we have an underabsorption; in other words, use of the predetermined rate of £40 per unit has resulted in £50 000 too little overhead being charged, and we need to adjust the absorption costing profit statement accordingly:

OSN Ltd: Absorption costing profit statement for the year

	£	£
Sales (20 000 @ £250)		5 000 000
Cost of sales		
Opening stock	nil	
Add Cost of production (21 000 @ £220)	4 620 000	
	4 620 000	
Less Closing stock (1000 @ £220)	220 000	
	4 400 000	
Add Underabsorbed overhead	50 000	4 450 000
Gross profit		550 000
Selling & distribution costs:		
variable (20 000 @ £10)	200 000	
fixed	70 000	
Administration overhead	120 000	390 000
Net profit		160 000

You will see that the underabsorption does not affect *unit* production cost, which is calculated as before:

	£
Prime cost	160
Variable production overhead	20
Fixed production overhead	40
	220

 Suppose OSN Ltd had had an overabsorption *of £50 000 for the year. How would the absorption costing profit statement be adjusted to reflect this?*

If an overabsorption had arisen, the overhead absorbed would be more than that incurred and it would be necessary to *deduct* £50 000 from the cost of sales (as opposed to adding in the case of the underabsorption illustrated above). Adjusting for over- and underabsorption means that the profit statement reflects actual overhead incurred. Such an adjustment is not necessary in the marginal costing profit statement, nor does it have any impact on the difference in profit reported (which, as we have seen, is a function of fixed production overhead absorbed in stock changes). You will also realise that the adjustment we have been discussing here is simply the vertical-format equivalent of the double-entry adjustment illustrated in Chapter 7.

MARGINAL AND ABSORPTION COSTING: DECISION MAKING

Having examined the profit implications of the two systems, we will now look at their use in decision-making situations. Exhibit 12.5 provides some information about a special order which PLW Ltd has the opportunity to undertake.

 Should the special order be accepted on financial grounds?

PLW Ltd: special order

A large wholesale customer has asked PLW Ltd to supply, as a 'special' order, 2000 of its standard model of digital camera at a reduced price of £200. The unit production cost and normal selling price of this model are as follows:

Per unit		
Selling price		£250
Production costs: variable	£180	
fixed	£ 40	£220

(No variable selling cost would be incurred if the order were accepted.)

The company has sufficient idle capacity to undertake the order and other sales will be unaffected; management is keen to accept the order, as there is a good chance of substantial repeat business in future, but at the same time does not wish to incur a loss on the 2000 units involved.

Exhibit 12.5 PLW Ltd – special order

Superficial examination of the figures in Exhibit 12.5 suggests rejection of the order:

Revenue from accepting (2000 units @ £200)	£400 000
Production costs of order (2000 units @ £220)	£440 000
Loss from accepting	£ (40 000)

This, however, is exactly the sort of incorrect analysis we referred to earlier when discussing Figure 12.1 and the danger inherent in treating fixed costs (via the overhead absorption rate) 'as if' they were variable. The £440 000 production 'cost' above consists of additional variable production costs (which will presumably only be incurred if the extra units are produced) plus fixed production overhead *absorbed* at £40 per unit. Inclusion of £40 per unit for fixed production overhead implies that the overhead *incurred* will increase as a result of accepting the order, but there is nothing to suggest any such increase. Assuming that the amount of fixed production overhead *incurred* will be unaffected by the order, we can restate our financial analysis:

	£
Revenue from accepting	£400 000
Additional costs *incurred* (variable production costs)	
(2000 @ £180)	360 000
Contribution from accepting	40 000

It now appears that acceptance, even at the heavily discounted selling price, is financially worth while.

If we are reasonably confident that fixed costs will not be affected, we can take a short-cut approach to determination of the profit resulting from acceptance of the order. You will recall that contribution is (sales – all variable costs); given this, an increase/decrease in sales will cause a corresponding increase/decrease in contribution and, assuming no change in fixed costs, this increase/decrease in contribution will be the same as the increase/decrease in net profit.

✔ *Determine the contribution per unit for PLW Ltd's special order and confirm the total contribution from acceptance calculated above.*

The unit contribution for the special order is:

	£
Selling price	200
Variable costs	180
Contribution	20

If the order is undertaken, total contribution will be (2000 units @ £20) = £40 000, which is the same as the figure we calculated above.

Although marginal costing contribution can provide a useful 'ready reckoner' for the profit impact of certain decisions, its use in this way depends on the assumption that fixed costs incurred will be unaffected by the decision in question. As we shall see below (and also in Chapters 13 and 14), this is not always true. It is particularly important that you appreciate the *short-term* and *ad hoc* nature of the financial analysis we have just performed. In the short term, PLW Ltd's fixed costs are unaffected by the decision and can be safely ignored – but in the *long term*, and for *routine* decisions, this would be foolhardy – a point we shall return to shortly.

Contribution analysis

In our 'special' order scenario above, PLW Ltd's fixed costs were assumed to be unaffected by acceptance. Is it possible to employ marginal costing in situations where fixed costs *are* affected by a decision? Consider Exhibit 12.6, which gives details of both product lines produced by PLW Ltd.

PLW Ltd: two product lines

In addition to a digital camera, the company produces a document/image scanner, separate statements being prepared in order to assess the profitability of each. Next year's estimated profit statement for each product and for the company as a whole is given below.

	Camera	Scanner	Total
Production/sales (units)	20 000	12 000	
	£	£	£
Sales revenue	5 000 000	1 200 000	6 200 000
Cost of sales	4 400 000	1 100 000	5 500 000
Gross profit	600 000	100 000	700 000
Selling & distribution costs	270 000	70 000	340 000
Administration costs	120 000	50 000	170 000
Net profit/(loss)	210 000	(20 000)	190 000

Management is concerned at the loss being incurred by production/sale of the scanner and it has been suggested that this product line be discontinued next year in order to improve overall profitability. The following additional information is available:

- *Cost of sales*: 80% of this is variable and the balance fixed. Of the fixed element, 60% is an apportionment of general production overheads which will not be avoided should a product line be discontinued; the remaining 40%, being product-specific, will be avoided on discontinuance.

- *Selling & distribution costs*: 30% of these costs are product-specific and will be avoided should a product line be discontinued, the remainder being an apportionment of company-wide cost.
- *Administration costs*: these are general company costs.

Exhibit 12.6 PLW Ltd – two-product output/sales

 Would discontinuing production and sale of scanners next year improve the company's overall profit?

At first glance, the answer might seem to be 'yes', since production/sale of scanners appears to incur an estimated loss of £20 000 next year. But, as with the 'special' order scenario above, we need to remember that the £20 000 'loss' is based on absorption costing principles; if we claim that discontinuing the product line will avoid the £20 000 loss, what we are also claiming is that *all* the costs associated with scanners in Exhibit 12.6 will be avoided – and the additional information makes clear that this will not happen. We therefore need to restructure the product and company profit statements in such a way that we are able to distinguish between avoidable and unavoidable (or product-specific and general) costs; only by doing this can we properly assess the profit impact of the proposed discontinuance.

PLW Ltd: Revised profit statement

	Camera £	Scanner £	Total £
Sales revenue	5 000 000	1 200 000	6 200 000
Marginal cost of sales (80% of Exhibit 12.6)	3 520 000	880 000	4 400 000
Contribution	1 480 000	320 000	1 800 000
Other product-specific costs:			
Cost of sales (40% × 20% of Exhibit 12.6)	352 000	88 000	440 000
Selling & distribution costs (30% of Exhibit 12.6)	81 000	21 000	102 000
Product contribution to general costs	1 047 000	211 000	1 258 000
General costs:			
Cost of sales (60% × 20% of Exhibit 12.6)			660 000
Selling & distribution costs (70% of Exhibit 12.6)			238 000
Administration costs			170 000
Net profit			190 000

 Based on PLW Ltd's revised profit statement above, will discontinuing production/sale of scanners improve overall profit next year?

The revised profit statement indicates that discontinuing production/sale of scanners next year will worsen overall profitability: company net profit will fall by £211 000 (i.e. the scanners' contribution to general costs). General costs are *assumed* (in the absence of information to the contrary) to be unaffected by the discontinuance and will still require to be covered, but by the product contribution from cameras only.

Revising profit statements to determine product (or department/division) contributions to general costs is termed **contribution analysis**. It might be more accurate to place 'contribution' in inverted commas in this context, since, to arrive at the product contributions above, we have deducted from sales revenue *all* product-specific costs, fixed and variable, whereas contribution in a strict definition is sales less variable costs only. However, what we have demonstrated is that the concept of contribution can be adapted to suit different circumstances. We shall extend our discussion of marginal costing's application to decision analysis in the next chapter.

ABSORPTION AND MARGINAL COSTING: A COMPARISON

Now that we have described the principles and operation of absorption and marginal costing systems, it is necessary to evaluate their relative strengths and weaknesses.

External versus internal reporting

In Chapter 5, we said that Statement of Standard Accounting Practice No. 9 requires many organisations (in the UK) to use absorption costing to value stocks in their published accounts; for such organisations and for this purpose, marginal costing cannot be used. However, for *internal* purposes – decision making, planning and control – marginal costing may be more appropriate.

Decision making

Our analysis of the 'special' order and product discontinuation decisions faced by PLW Ltd provides a good illustration of the applicability of marginal costing to decision making. Since marginal costing distinguishes between variable and fixed costs and since many (but not necessarily all) fixed costs will be unaffected by decisions, the resulting cost classification may be roughly analogous to the relevant/irrelevant classification which should underpin the financial analysis of all decisions (and which we shall discuss in Chapter 14). If absorption costing is applied to financial analysis of a decision, there is a danger (as we have seen) that incorrect decisions may result because:

1 the fixed overhead absorption rate treats fixed costs 'as if' they were variable; and
2 some, or even all, of the underlying amount of the fixed costs being absorbed will be unaffected by a decision and is therefore irrelevant.

However, marginal costing should be used with care in decision analysis. We have already mentioned the possibility of making a simplistic assumption about the reaction of all fixed costs to a decision and there are other potential difficulties. We used marginal costing as an aid in two different decisions accept/reject a special order and discontinue/retain a product line. For the special order, which is likely to be a 'one-off' decision with short-term implications, our financial analysis may be adequate (although non-financial considerations will also have a bearing). The product line decision, however, is different, having longer-term and strategic implications. Our contribution analysis of this situation is inadequate, as it is based solely on a single year's figures and therefore imposes a short-term outlook on a decision which has more than a short-term impact. For example, general costs may not be affected in the short term, but, over a period of (say) five years, may well reduce if the product line is discontinued. Next year's healthy product contribution from scanners may be totally unrepresentative of the longer-term position to such an extent that immediate discontinuation could save substantial future costs arising as a consequence of continuing production/sale for another year. If marginal costing is to be used in the financial analysis of decisions which have significant effect beyond the short term, then it must be used in a way which recognises this effect – i.e. by incorporating estimates for a number of years and in conjunction with the sort of techniques which we will encounter in Chapter 15.

In addition, marginal costing is based on a fixed/variable cost classification which may itself pose problems:

1 Making a reasonably accurate split between fixed and variable costs may not be possible for many organisations.
2 Marginal costing may have little relevance in situations where only a small proportion of total cost is variable – this might, for example, be the case with advanced manufacturing technologies.

Planning and control

When budgets are being prepared, or when they are being compared with actual results, an appreciation of cost behaviour is necessary: for example, if budgeted and actual volumes are different, which costs will react to this difference and which will not? As we shall see in Chapter 18, failure to allow for the impact of volume changes on budgeted and actual costs may undermine the value of a budget/actual comparison because like is not being compared with like. If a budget based on one estimated volume is compared to actual results based on a different volume then the differences between the two will result partly from the volume difference and partly from efficiency and price differences. For effective control, it is desirable to separate these influences on budget/actual variation as far as possible. Marginal costing should help clarify these issues by segregating fixed and variable costs. Absorption costing, however, may make differentiation between volume, price and efficiency factors less clear because of the 'unitisation' of fixed costs via the absorption rate.

Absorption costing may suffer from another weakness. In Chapter 5 we saw that an element of subjectivity is inevitable for apportionment and reapportionment bases. To the extent that such apportionments and reapportionments exist, control may be hampered. If, for example, a cost centre's budgeted and actual costs contain significant apportionments/reapportionments, we can ask to what extent these are genuinely controllable by the cost centre concerned; and the fact that there are apportionments/ reapportionments may not be obvious from absorption costing profit or cost statements. Marginal costing, e.g. by using a contribution analysis format, may help to highlight those costs which are specific to a cost centre (and therefore presumably controllable by it) and apportionments of general costs (which are unlikely to be directly controllable by the cost centre).

What we have, then, is a situation where many organisations must use absorption costing for external purposes, but where marginal costing may be superior for internal purposes. It might be possible to use marginal costing for internal and absorption costing for external reporting – either by running the two systems in parallel or by employing marginal costing and making year-end adjustments in order to comply with the requirements of published accounts.

 Can you see any problems in operating a 'dual' absorption/marginal system either in whole or in part?

The drawbacks to use of any form of 'dual' system are the cost of operation and the potential for confusion and error, which may be so great that the cost/benefit criterion is not met.

Variability of profit

Earlier in the chapter, we used PLW Ltd's data to demonstrate that, under absorption costing, net profit varies with both sales and stock changes, whereas marginal costing net profit varies with sales volume only. This facet of absorption costing may cause serious confusion: e.g. does the higher absorption costing net profit in the 'stock increase' situation indicate better performance than the lower corresponding marginal costing net profit? A rather cynical view of this would suggest that absorption costing profit could be manipulated up or down as circumstances dictate merely by increasing/decreasing the volume of output (regardless of the sales volume).

But marginal costing may also be problematic with respect to variability of profit. In highly seasonal businesses – toy manufacturing, for example – stocks may be deliberately built up during the 'off-peak' season, in order to cope with peak demand. In this sort of situation, marginal costing profit is likely to fluctuate widely; by reacting to stock changes as well as to sales, absorption costing profit will somewhat smooth (but not eliminate) these fluctuations, giving, perhaps, a more balanced picture of the business over the entire period.

Marginal costing and price-setting

In Chapter 5, we suggested that inclusion of fixed overheads in unit costs could be seen as an attempt to approximate longer-term cost. Extending this argument, it might be said that, by using only variable costs, marginal costing takes a particularly short-term view of cost and that this may cause problems where selling price is based to any extent on cost. To ensure long-term profitability, revenue must cover *all* costs, whether direct, indirect, fixed or variable; marginal costing, by excluding fixed costs from the cost per unit, may run the risk of understating unit costs with an associated risk of failure to set a price high enough to cover all costs. We saw, for example, that PLW Ltd would earn a profit of £40 000 on its special order at a selling price of £200; if this selling price were set for the company's *regular* sales, contribution would be insufficient to cover fixed costs and a loss would result:

Unit selling price	200
Unit variable cost (including variable selling cost)	190
Unit contribution	£ 10
Regular sales (from Exhibit 12.2)	20 000 units

Total contribution	200 000
Total fixed costs (from Exhibit 12.2)	990 000
Loss	£(790 000)

However, this assumes that prices are mainly cost-driven. Although cost can have an important bearing on selling price, there may be other factors with equal (or greater) significance: competitive pressure within the market, for example, or consumer taste.

'Marginal' versus 'variable' cost

So far in this chapter, we have implied that the terms 'marginal' and 'variable' are synonymous, but this is not strictly true. A marginal cost is the additional cost incurred to provide one extra unit. Within the relevant range of output volumes and time horizon, this may be the same as a unit's variable cost – but outside the relevant range, this correlation becomes suspect. Consider, for example, the impact of step costs: as output increases, a volume will eventually be reached where the 'true' marginal cost of the next unit will consist of that unit's variable cost plus the amount of increase in step cost resulting. Although this may appear to be largely a problem of terminology, it does have a more practical aspect, as evidenced in PLW Ltd's decision about discontinuation of a product line: namely that it is dangerously unrealistic to assume that general fixed costs remain immutably fixed. In addition, it is unlikely that variable/marginal cost per unit is constant at all volumes (due to the sort of factors we discussed in Chapter 2).

Even if marginal and variable cost are roughly equivalent, marginal costing is dependent on our ability to separate costs into their fixed and variable elements with tolerable precision. Although problems of cost estimation and behaviour also affect absorption costing, it is possible to claim that, because of the different emphasis of the underlying cost classification (i.e. direct/indirect), simplistic assumptions such as 'marginal = variable' or 'fixed costs stay fixed' are less likely with absorption costing. On the other hand, a direct/indirect classification may divert attention from important issues of cost behaviour.

The overall picture is distinctly fuzzy: neither absorption nor marginal costing is clearly superior in all circumstances. In practice, absorption costing is the most common approach: for many organisations, its use is dictated by the requirements of published accounts, and for the rest, a desire to be aware of the 'full' unit cost of products/services provided is the governing consideration. However, this does not preclude the use of marginal costing on an *ad hoc* basis. For example, recent UK National Health Service guidelines on costing and pricing of contracts within the NHS 'internal market' recommend that full (i.e. absorption) costing should normally be used, as marginal costing would result in under-recovery of costs, but go on to say that marginal costing might be appropriate for costing the use of any spare capacity. A similar type of approach can be seen in the sale of deep-discounted airline tickets by 'bucket shops' and of reduced-cost 'off-peak' rail travel. In both cases, the fixed costs associated with operating the flight/train are irrelevant as these would presumably still run regardless of the number of passengers. Thus any price in excess of the variable cost per passenger will generate additional profit in the same way as occurred earlier with PLW Ltd's special order.

SUMMARY

In this chapter, we have described and illustrated marginal costing, comparing and contrasting this approach with absorption costing. We have seen that:

- Marginal costing is based on the principle that, since many fixed overheads are time-, rather than volume-related, they should be treated as costs in their entirety within the period to which they relate.

- Under marginal costing, the production cost per unit will exclude fixed production overhead but this is the only difference between marginal and absorption unit costs.

- In an absorption costing profit statement, all output-related costs (direct and indirect, fixed and variable) are deducted from sales to determine **gross profit**. In a marginal costing profit statement all variable costs (output- and non-output-related, direct and indirect) are deducted from sales to determine **contribution** – in the first instance to meeting fixed costs and thereafter, to profit.

- Marginal costing net profit reacts to changes in sales volume only; absorption costing net profit reacts to changes both in sales and in stock volumes.

- The pattern of relative net profit reported by the two systems is:
  production = sales: same under both approaches
  production > sales: absorption costing higher
  production < sales: marginal costing higher

- Where the two systems report a different profit, this difference is solely attributable to the fixed production overhead absorbed in the stock increase/decrease during the period.

- Because many fixed costs are unaffected by decisions (and are therefore irrelevant), marginal costing may provide a useful aid to the financial analysis of decisions.

- Contribution analysis extends marginal costing to encompass situations where fixed costs are affected by a decision.

- Marginal and absorption costing may be compared in a number of ways, with the results being summarised as:

  - absorption costing is necessary for many organisations' published accounts
  - marginal costing may be more appropriate for many internal purposes
  - absorption costing may be seen as an attempt to approximate longer-term unit costs, whereas marginal costing concentrates on short-term costs
  - the variability of absorption costing net profit with both sales and production volume may cause confusion
  - marginal and variable cost are not synonymous

In the next chapter, we will extend our discussion of marginal costing to illustrate its use in determination of such key indicators as breakeven point and margin of safety along with its use in further decision scenarios.

FURTHER READING

Bromwich, M. and Bhimani, A., *Management Accounting Pathways to Progress*, CIMA, 1994: Chapter 4 contains an interesting discussion of the problem of fixed overheads and a suggested accounting report format based on the characteristics of cost.

Chadwick, L., *The Essence of Management Accounting* (2nd edition), Prentice Hall, 1997: see Chapter 6 for a concise summary of the 'absorption versus marginal' costing debate.

Lane, J. D., Towards a better understanding of the absorption and marginal costing methods. *ACCA Students' Newsletter*, December 1990.

SELF-TEST QUESTIONS

12.1 For each of the statements below, tick the appropriate box to indicate whether that statement is true or false:

	True	False
(a) Absorption of fixed overhead into unit costs may give the impression that the underlying cost is variable.	☐	☐
(b) Marginal costing net profit varies with both sales and production volumes.	☐	☐
(c) Unit costs as calculated using marginal principles are approximations of long-term unit costs.	☐	☐
(d) Marginal costing cannot be used for the published accounts of organisations subject to the requirements of Statement of Standard Accounting Practice No. 9.	☐	☐
(e) Variable selling, distribution and administration costs are excluded in calculation of marginal costing contribution.	☐	☐
(f) Changes in the amount of fixed costs can readily be accommodated in a marginal costing analysis of a decision.	☐	☐

12.2 When comparing the profits reported using marginal costing with those reported using absorption costing in a period when closing stock was 1400 units, opening stock was 2000 units, and the actual production was 11 200 units at a total cost of £4.50 per unit compared to a target cost of £5.00 per unit, which of the following statements is correct?

    A Absorption costing reports profits £2700 higher.
    B Absorption costing reports profits £2700 lower.
    C Absorption costing reports profits £3000 higher.
    D Absorption costing reports profits £3000 lower.
    E There are insufficient data to calculate the difference between the reported profits.

(CIMA, *Operational Cost Accounting, Specimen Exam*)

12.3 Dougal plc is a small manufacturing company situated in the city of Magicville. They produce a single product which is used in the production of playground equipment. The cost of this product is as follows:

Direct materials	£7 per unit
Direct wages	£10 per unit
Fixed production overheads	£3 per unit (based on normal production level of 20 000 units per period)

The selling price of the product is £30 each.
Production and sales quantities for Periods I and II are as follows:

	Period I	Period II
Production	20 000 units	20 000 units
Sales	18 000 units	22 000 units

(*Note:* There were no opening stocks at the start of Period I.)

Requirements

(a) Prepare operating statements for each of the two periods using:

    (i)   Marginal costing
    (ii) Absorption costing.   **(8 marks)**

(b) Prepare a statement that reconciles the difference between the annual profits reported in the operating statements in (a).   **(3 marks)**

(c) Describe the advantages and disadvantages of each approach.   **(4 marks)**
                                                  (Total: 15 marks)

(CIPFA, *Foundation Stage Management Accounting*, June 1999)

12.4 Your client, J Docherty Ltd, is facing a severe cash flow problem and is in danger of exceeding its banking agreements. The directors wish to reduce production quickly to make cost savings. They supply the following information and request that you prepare a marginal costing statement identifying the contribution of each product and the total profit for all products. Also state which product line, if any, should be cut.

	Product X £	Product Y £	Product Z £
Revenue	262 400	140 800	295 000
Expenses			
Direct material	37 200	45 100	69 000
Direct wages	82 400	94 600	110 000
Sales & admin expenses	23 400	29 000	33 200
Production overhead	44 300	56 200	61 900

Of the sales and admin expenses, 80% is fixed, 20% variable; production overhead is 60% fixed and 40% variable.   **(20 marks)**

(CIOBS, *Business Accounting*, December 1997)

12.5 MP & Co, an insurance agent, sells three broad categories of insurance: house, car and commercial and the following estimates are available for next year:

	Revenue £	Variable costs £	Wages £	Selling costs £	Admin costs £
House insurance	80 000	16 000	28 000	12 000	6 000
Car insurance	220 000	90 000	50 000	30 000	10 000
Commercial insurance	105 000	40 000	34 000	14 000	8 000
Totals	405 000	146 000	112 000	56 000	24 000

Additional information
1 Forty per cent of the total wages cost is a fixed general company cost, representing the salaries of sales and office staff, and is apportioned to each of the three areas of operation; the balance represents sales commission which, being variable with revenue, is specifically attributable to the different types of insurance.
2 Selling costs are wholly fixed, with 30 per cent being specific to the particular type of insurance and the remainder being an apportionment of general costs.
3 Admin. costs are general costs which are apportioned to each category of insurance.

Requirements

(a) Prepare a marginal costing statement showing the contribution of each type of insurance to the firm's general costs, the firm's total contribution and profit.

(b) It has been suggested that a sales campaign be undertaken next year in order to improve the profitability of house insurance. It is estimated that this campaign would result in the following increases in next year's estimates:

> revenue 30%   variable costs 15%   specific selling costs £10 000.

On the basis of house insurance's contribution to the firm's general costs, advise whether the sales campaign is financially worth while.

QUESTIONS WITHOUT ANSWERS

12.6 Exe Limited makes a single product whose total cost per unit is budgeted to be £45. This includes fixed cost of £8 per unit based on a volume of 10 000 units per period. In a period, sales volume was 9000 units, and production volume was 11 500 units. The actual profit for the same period, calculated using absorption costing, was £42 000.

If the profit statement were prepared using marginal costing, the profit for the period

A would be £10 000

B would be £22 000

C would be £50 000

D would be £62 000

E cannot be calculated without more information.

(CIMA, *Operational Cost Accounting*, May 1998)

12.7 RH Limited makes and sells one product, the standard production cost of which is as follows for one unit:

		£
Direct labour	3 hours at £6 per hour	18
Direct materials	4 kg at £7 per kg	28
Production overhead:	Variable	3
	Fixed	20
Standard production cost		69

Normal output is 16 000 units per annum and this figure is used for the fixed production overhead calculation.

Costs relating to selling, distribution and administration are

Variable	20 per cent of sales value
Fixed	£180 000 per annum.

The only variance is a fixed production overhead volume variance. There are no units in finished goods stock at 1 October 1992. The fixed overhead expenditure is spread evenly throughout the year. The selling price per unit is £140.

For the two six-monthly periods detailed below, the number of units to be produced and sold are budgeted as:

	Six months ending 31 March 1993	Six months ending 30 September 1993
Production	8500	7000
Sales	7000	8000

Requirements

(a) Prepare statements for management showing sales, costs and profits for **each** of the six monthly periods, using
   (i)   marginal costing   **(6 marks)**
   (ii) absorption costing.   **(9 marks)**

(b) Prepare an explanatory statement reconciling for **each** six-monthly period the profit using marginal costing with the profit using absorption costing.   **(4 marks)**

(c) State and explain **three** business situations where the use of marginal costing may be beneficial to management in making a decision.   **(6 marks)**
                                                              (Total: 25 marks)

(CIMA, *Cost Accounting*, November 1992)

12.8 PM Ltd sells three models of mobile phone; on the basis of last year's results, which are given below, management feels that all three products are equally profitable and should continue to be sold.

Results for last year	Model XX/3l £	Model YY/7k £	Model ZZ/4t £
Sales	180 000	360 000	228 000
Cost of sales	100 000	170 000	104 000
Gross profit	80 000	190 000	124 000
Selling & distribution overhead	30 000	96 000	48 000
Administration overhead	30 000	30 000	30 000
Net profit	20 000	64 000	46 000

In the profit statement above, selling & distribution and administration overheads, being wholly fixed, have both been apportioned fairly arbitrarily to the three products but further investigation reveals the following:

1 *Cost of sales*: 80% is variable, the balance being an apportionment of general costs.
2 *Selling & distribution overhead*: of the total incurred, 20% is an apportionment of general costs, 40% is specific to Model XX/3l, and 20% is specific to each of Models YY/7k and ZZ/4t.
3 *Administration overhead*: of the total incurred, 40% is specific to Model XX/3l, 10% is specific to each of the other models, and the remainder is a general cost.

Requirements

(a) Prepare a profit statement based on marginal costing which shows, for each product, the contribution to general costs; your statement should also show aggregated figures for the company overall.

(b) Using your answer to (a), advise on the possibility of changing the sales mix in order to maximise profit and quantify the effect that making such a change would have had on the company's profit last year.

(c) Explain *two* assumptions which underlie your analysis in (b).

12.9 FDS Ltd manufactures and sells computer monitors; data for last year in respect of this company's 14-inch SVGA model were:

Sales	24 000 units	Production	26 000 units
Opening stock	2 000 units	Closing stock	4 000 units
Selling price per unit	£90		

		£
Variable costs per unit:	direct materials	20
	direct labour	10
	direct expenses	6
	selling overhead	4

		£
Fixed costs for the year:	production overhead – incurred	324 000
	production overhead – estimated	300 000
	selling overhead	110 000
	administration overhead	80 000

The company absorbs fixed production overhead on the basis of the annual budgeted volume of cost units, which was 25 000 for the year just ended.

Requirements

(a) Prepare FDS Ltd's profit statement for the year just ended based on:

    1 absorption costing principles; and
    2 marginal costing principles.

(b) Explain the reason for any difference in net profit reported in the two statements in (a) and reconcile any such difference.

(c) Comment on a claim by FDS Ltd's Operations Manager that, when production fluctuates but sales remain constant, marginal costing net profit will likewise fluctuate.

12.10 PPF Ltd is a publishing house whose output falls into three broad categories: Children's, Fiction and Non-fiction. The company aims, over the next five years, to increase its share of the market for both Children's and Non-fiction publications. At a recent board meeting to discuss the projected expansion, the following figures were produced:

	Children's	Fiction	Non-fiction	Total
	£000	£000	£000	£000
Sales revenue	8 900	11 400	5 800	26 100
Cost of sales	3 700	6 200	2 100	12 000
Gross profit	5 200	5 200	3 700	14 100
Administration costs				6 300
Selling & distribution costs				5 100
Net profit				2 700

In the course of the board meeting, a heated dispute arose between PPF Ltd's Managing Director and Sales Director, details of which are summarised below.

Managing Director's contention
On the basis of the figures above, the Managing Director has claimed that doubling sales of Children's and Non-fiction titles over the next five years will double the gross profit

associated with each of these lines of business (i.e. to £10.4 and £7.4 million respectively). He further claimed that the effect of this would be to increase PPF Ltd's net profit to £11.6 million.

Sales Director's contention
The Sales Director's view is that the figures used by the Managing Director, along with the related conclusion, are questionable and she has urged that further analysis be undertaken before any firm decision is taken.

PPF Ltd's Chairman, concerned at the dispute, adjourned the meeting and requested that you, as Development Director, prepare an urgent report on the situation.

Requirement

Prepare a report for the Chairman which addresses the following issues:
1 the suitability or otherwise of the figures provided as a basis for the Board's decision and the possible impact of this on the Managing Director's conclusion;
2 an explanation of how (if at all) the figures could be made more useful, with supporting rationale for, and reservations about, your suggestions;
3 a statement of any additional information or improvements to available information which would aid the board's deliberations.

CHAPTER 13

Cost/volume/profit analysis

Freeserve online to break even

Dixons, Britain's biggest high street electrical and electronic retailer, expects its free internet service to break even this autumn – only a year after its September launch.

The company, chaired by Sir Stanley Kahns, said yesterday that, in the first 16 weeks, Freeserve attracted 900 000 registered accounts, of whom 700 000 were active users.

Customers are not charged a subscription but pay local call charges.

John Clare, group chief executive, said more new customers and greater usage by existing customers meant that Dixons thought the service would break even sooner than expected ...

Source: Alison Smith, *Financial Times*, 14 January 1999. Reprinted with permission.

Exhibit 13.1 Breakeven – an important indicator in cost/volume/profit analysis

INTRODUCTION

A set of relationships vital to the success of any business is that which exists between cost, volume and profit. For example, it may be of great importance for management to be aware of the volume of sales which must be achieved in order to cover costs and avoid a loss being made – as it was for Dixons in Exhibit 13.1. Or it may be important to have an idea of the vulnerability of a business's profit to reductions in demand, or to know what volume of sales will yield a particular target profit.

In this chapter, we will discuss and illustrate the use of cost/volume/profit analysis – which attempts to address these issues – along with its underlying assumptions and the extent to which these can be reconciled with reality.

OBJECTIVES

When you have completed this chapter, you will be able to:

- explain the concepts of breakeven point, margin of safety and sensitivity analysis;
- use a formulaic approach to calculate breakeven point, margin of safety and sales required to earn a target profit;
- present cost/volume/profit relationships graphically in the form of breakeven charts, contribution charts and profit/volume charts;

- use sensitivity analysis to assess the impact of changes to one or more variables within the cost/volume/profit model;

- appreciate the assumptions on which the model rests and the importance of relevant range in this context.

BREAKEVEN POINT

Central to cost/volume/profit analysis is the concept of **breakeven point**. This is the sales volume – expressed either in units or in revenue – at which costs are exactly covered by revenue: i.e. at breakeven point, profit is zero. Cost/volume/profit analysis is a marginal costing technique and all the calculations we are about to describe derive from the principles introduced in the previous chapter. Exhibit 13.2 contains the basic data we shall use to illustrate the cost/volume/profit model.

KD & Co Accountancy Services

Bookkeeping is one of the services this firm provides to clients, for which it is proposed to charge £50 per hour next year. The variable cost per hour and total fixed cost relating to KD & Co's bookkeeping service have been respectively estimated at £10 per hour and £120 000 for the year.

Exhibit 13.2 Information for breakeven calculation

Complete the abbreviated marginal costing profit statement below to determine the total contribution which must be earned if KD & Co's bookkeeping service is to break even next year (i.e. if profit is to be zero).

	£
Total contribution	....
Less Total fixed costs	....
Profit	zero

Working backwards from profit, the completed statement reads:

	£
Total contribution	120 000
Less Total fixed costs	120 000
Profit	zero

Thus, at breakeven point, total contribution = total fixed costs.

From Exhibit 13.2, determine the contribution per hour of bookkeeping work. How many hours need to be worked at this contribution per hour in order to earn total contribution of £120 000 (i.e. in order to attain breakeven point)?

The contribution per hour of bookkeeping work is:

$$(\text{unit selling price} - \text{unit variable cost}) = (£50 - £10) = £40$$

The issue of determining breakeven point now resolves itself into 'how many hours at a contribution of £40 must be worked in order to earn total contribution of £120 000?' The required number is:

$$\frac{\text{Total fixed cost}}{\text{Contribution per hour}} = \frac{£120\,000}{£40} = 3\,000 \text{ hours}$$

We now have a general formula for obtaining breakeven point in terms of unit sales:

$$\frac{\text{Total fixed cost}}{\text{Contribution per unit}}$$

We can check that a volume of 3000 hours does result in profit of zero if we insert the data from Exhibit 13.2 into a marginal costing profit statement:

	£
Sales revenue (3000 @ £50)	150 000
Less Marginal cost of sales (3000 @ £10)	30 000
Total contribution	120 000
Less Total fixed cost	120 000
Profit	zero

If we want breakeven point in terms of revenue rather than unit sales, we can simply multiply the breakeven volume by the selling price per unit:

$$(3000 \times £50) = £150\,000$$

Suppose, however, that no unit data are available; here we need to amend the breakeven formula by using the **contribution/sales (CS) ratio** as the denominator. The CS ratio is simply contribution expressed as a proportion of sales – either unit contribution and unit selling price or total contribution and total sales revenue.

 What is the contribution/sales ratio for KD & Co's bookkeeping service?

Based on the unit data in Exhibit 13.2, the CS ratio is:

$$\frac{\text{Contribution per hour}}{\text{Selling price per hour}} = \frac{£40}{£50} = 0.8$$

The same ratio results from use of total contribution and total sales revenue from the marginal costing profit statement above:

$$\frac{\text{Total contribution}}{\text{Total sales revenue}} = \frac{£120\,000}{£150\,000} = 0.8$$

Rearranging the CS ratio calculation, we can say that:

$$\text{Contribution} = (\text{CS ratio} \times \text{sales})$$

At breakeven point,

$$\text{Total contribution} = \text{total fixed cost}$$

so:

$$(\text{CS ratio} \times \text{sales}) = \text{total fixed cost}$$

 The data for KD & Co's bookkeeping service has been inserted into the last formula to give the following:

$$(0.8 \times sales) = £120\ 000$$

What is the breakeven point in sales revenue?

To determine the value of sales we need one final rearrangement to the formula:

$$\text{Breakeven sales} = \frac{£120\ 000}{0.8} = £150\ 000$$

This is the same revenue figure we obtained in our marginal costing profit statement for the breakeven volume of 3000 hours: (3000 @ £50). In general terms, breakeven point in revenue is:

$$\frac{\text{Total fixed cost}}{\text{CS ratio}}$$

SALES REQUIRED TO EARN A TARGET PROFIT

Achieving a breakeven position is unquestionably better than incurring a loss, but a positive profit would be even better:

KD & Co: target profit for bookkeeping service

For next year, KD & Co aims to earn a target profit of £85 000 from its bookkeeping service. All other information is as set out in Exhibit 13.2.

Exhibit 13.3 Sales required to earn a target profit

 Complete the statement below to determine the total contribution required to yield target profit of £85 000.

	£
Total contribution	....
Less Total fixed cost	....
Profit	85 000

The completed statement reads:

	£
Total contribution	205 000
Less Total fixed cost	120 000
Profit	85 000

How many hours' bookkeeping work must be performed in order to earn total contribution of £205 000?

At a contribution per hour of £40, £205 000/£40 = 5125 hours need to be worked to earn the desired target profit. From this, we can derive a formula for sales volume in units required to earn a specified target profit:

$$\text{Sales units to earn target profit} = \frac{\text{Total fixed cost} + \text{Target profit}}{\text{Contribution per unit}}$$

This is really just an extension of the breakeven formula, the difference here being that there is a positive target profit (whereas the target profit was zero in the breakeven formula).

 What sales revenue is required to provide the target profit of £85 000?

All that is needed is to change the denominator to the CS ratio:

$$\frac{\text{Total fixed cost} + \text{Target profit}}{\text{CS ratio}} = \frac{£205\,000}{0.8} = £256\,250$$

 Confirm that a volume of 5125 hours yields a profit of £85 000.

We can use a marginal costing profit statement to confirm our result:

	£
Sales revenue (5125 @ £50)	256 250
Less Marginal cost of sales (5125 @ £10)	51 250
Total contribution	205 000
Less Total fixed cost	120 000
Profit	85 000

At volumes in excess of breakeven point, increased/decreased total contribution will correspond with increased/decreased profit. This provides an alternative route to the required sales:

profit/contribution required *above* breakeven point	£85 000
÷ contribution per hour	£40
= units required *above* breakeven point	2 125

Since we know the breakeven point to be 3000 hours, (3000 + 2125) = 5125 hours will give the desired profit.

THE MARGIN OF SAFETY

Cost/volume/profit analysis can help management assess the vulnerability of profit to reductions in demand.

> ## KD & Co: estimated volume of bookkeeping work
>
> KD & Co reckons that 5000 hours of bookkeeping work will be performed next year. Breakeven volume is 3000 hours and 5125 hours must be worked to earn the firm's target profit of £85 000 for the year.

Exhibit 13.4 Margin of safety

 If sales volume is 5,000 hours' bookkeeping work, by how much will profit fall short of the £85 000 target?

We could prepare a marginal costing profit statement based on sales of 5000 units:

	£
Sales revenue (5000 @ £50)	250 000
Less Marginal cost of sales (5000 @ £10)	50 000
Total contribution	200 000
Less Total fixed cost	120 000
Profit	80 000

The estimated volume thus falls short of target by (£85 000 − £80 000) = £5000.

Alternatively, we can take a short-cut approach, derived from the fact that, above breakeven point, total contribution and profit are the same:

Hours below target sales (5125 − 5000)	125
Contribution per hour	£40
Shortfall in total contribution/profit	£5000

Being aware that the estimated sales volume is unlikely to achieve the target profit allows management to consider some form of action. Steps could be taken to boost sales volume, or to reduce costs; the target might be amended as being too optimistic; or all three areas could be examined.

 By how many hours must estimated volume fall before the bookkeeping service incurs a loss?

At any volume lower than breakeven point, losses will be incurred, so estimated sales will need to fall by more than (5000 − 3000) = 2000 hours or (£250 000 − £150 000) = £100 000 in revenue terms.

To facilitate comparisons (e.g. between different years' operations), this volume difference can be expressed as a percentage of estimated sales (occasionally actual sales are used instead of estimated):

$$\frac{\text{(Estimated or actual sales} - \text{breakeven sales)}}{\text{Estimated or actual sales}} \times 100\%$$

 What is this percentage figure for KD & Co's bookkeeping service and what does it indicate?

The relevant percentage is:

$$\frac{(5000 - 3000)}{5000} \times 100\% = 40\%$$

This tells us that sales of bookkeeping services must fall by an amount in excess of 40% of their estimated volume before losses are incurred. Using revenue in the formula yields the same result:

$$\frac{(£250\ 000 - 150\ 000)}{£250\ 000} \times 100\% = 40\%$$

The difference between estimated (or actual) sales volume and breakeven sales volume is termed the **margin of safety**. This provides management with a measure of the vulnerability of profit to reductions in sales volume; the higher the margin of safety, the better, since profit will be less vulnerable to demand drops than with a lower margin of safety. However, in KD & Co's case, we cannot definitely say whether 40% is 'good' or 'bad': it appears to be quite healthy, but we need to have some sort of yardstick – e.g. data from comparable businesses, or from previous years' trading – before we can be more certain. We also need to have reasonable confidence in the accuracy of the estimated sales volume before too much significance can be attached to the margin of safety. *If* the estimate is reasonable then the margin of safety may be more than adequate. Another way of looking at the same thing is to ask 'how likely is it that estimated sales volume is overstated by more than 40%?'

GRAPHICAL PRESENTATIONS

Graphical representations of cost/volume/profit relationships can have much greater immediacy and impact on the reader than their formula-based counterparts. This could be especially beneficial to those users of accounting information with little or no training in its meaning or use. For example, the bald statement that KD & Co has a margin of safety of 40% may have considerably less effect and meaning than a graphical illustration of the same fact; a well-designed chart can highlight the significance of a large or small margin of safety without the necessity of a complex-looking formula. However, graphical presentations may suffer the drawback of being somewhat inaccurate, as figures may be difficult to plot with absolute precision. But this need not be a major deterrent to their use: in most cases, the data being plotted will relate to estimates, which will themselves be subject to error, and use of computers can greatly reduce inaccuracy of plots.

Graphical presentations: scaling the axes

Selection of an appropriate scale for the axes of a graphical presentation may occasionally be problematic. You may find the following general guidelines useful:

1 What is the breakeven point? It may be worth determining this by formula before preparing your chart.
2 What is the maximum volume? If none is specified, select one which is high enough to accommodate both the breakeven and estimated sales volumes; this will permit the margin of safety to be illustrated if required.

3 What is the maximum monetary amount involved? This can be determined by reference to the sales revenue associated with the maximum volume in 2 above.

In the graphical presentations of KD & Co's bookkeeping service which follow, a maximum volume of 8000 hours has been used. This is sufficiently high to cover both the breakeven and the estimated sales volumes for the period under consideration.

1 The breakeven chart

To construct a breakeven chart, we need to plot the following against volume:

- total fixed cost
- total cost
- sales revenue

 Figure 13.1 is a breakeven chart for the bookkeeping service, but with labels missing from all of its lines. Indicate the total fixed cost, total cost and sales revenue lines on Figure 13.1, along with the breakeven point. (The two cost lines should be familiar to you from Chapter 2, and we have already calculated the breakeven point.)

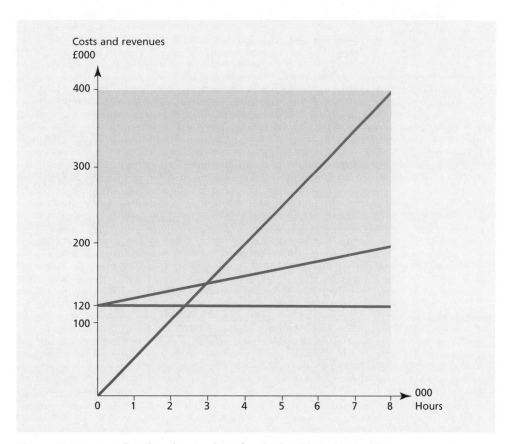

Figure 13.1 Incomplete breakeven chart for the bookkeeping service

Figure 13.2 is the completed breakeven chart. The total fixed cost line will run parallel to the horizontal axis at a height of £120 000. Total cost at any volume will comprise (total variable cost + total fixed cost); bearing in mind (from Chapter 3) that we need total costs for only two volumes to enable us to plot this line, we select two volumes:

		£
zero volume	total variable costs	nil
	total fixed costs	120 000
	total cost	120 000
8000 hours	total variable cost (8000 @ £10)	80 000
	total fixed cost	120 000
	total cost	200 000

Joining the total cost plots for these two volumes provides the total cost line on our breakeven chart. We have taken the assumed maximum volume in addition to zero: any volume in excess of zero will serve, although it helps if the associated total cost is easy to plot.

The sales revenue line can be plotted in a similar manner by selecting revenue at two volumes (zero and any volume greater than zero):

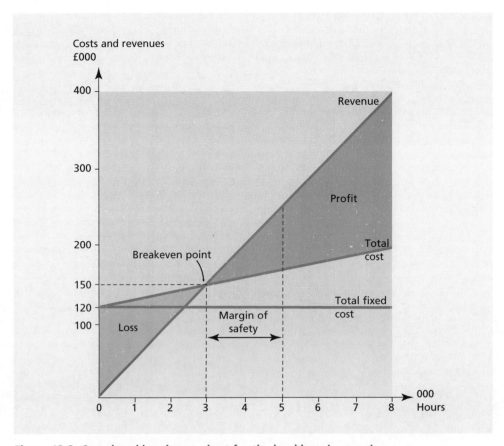

Figure 13.2 Completed breakeven chart for the bookkeeping service

		£
Zero volume	revenue	nil
8000 hours	revenue (8000 @ £50)	400 000

Joining these plots in a straight line gives the sales revenue function.

The breakeven point in Figure 13.2 occurs where the sales revenue and total cost lines intersect: i.e. where revenue = total cost. Profit will be zero at this point. We can then read down to the horizontal axis to obtain the breakeven point in units or across to the vertical axis to obtain the revenue equivalent. At all volumes to the left of the breakeven point, the total cost line lies above the revenue line (i.e. total cost exceeds revenue), so losses are incurred; whereas at all volumes to the right of breakeven point, sales revenue exceeds total cost, so profits are earned.

The breakeven chart is a clear representation of the key variables in the cost/volume/profit model. However, it does not show total variable cost, total contribution or profit at different volumes; these can certainly be determined from the breakeven chart – but not *directly*. For example, profit at different volumes can be determined by calculating the vertical distance between the revenue and total cost lines, or total variable cost as the vertical distance between the total cost and total fixed cost lines. An alternative presentation may therefore be desirable in order to highlight elements of the model not directly revealed by this approach.

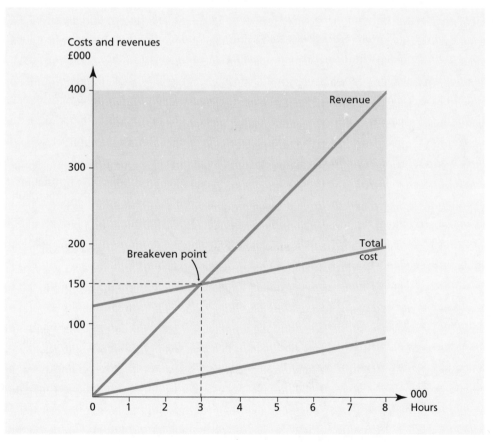

Figure 13.3 Incomplete contribution chart for the bookkeeping service

2 The contribution chart

Figure 13.3 is an incomplete contribution chart for the franchise.

 Only two of the lines in Figure 13.3 are labelled: what does the third line represent? Is total fixed cost shown on this chart? If so, where? What about total contribution?

This type of presentation differs from the breakeven chart in that total variable costs are plotted against volume – this is what the third line in Figure 13.3 represents. This line is plotted like the revenue line, using zero and some volume greater than zero:

Zero volume	total variable cost	zero
Maximum volume	total variable cost (8000 @ £10)	£80 000

Plotting and joining these two values gives the required cost function. Total fixed cost is not shown separately, but is the vertical distance between the total variable cost and the total cost lines; since total fixed cost is the same at all volumes, these lines are parallel, and we can read the fixed cost value from the vertical axis (£120 000). The sales revenue and total cost plots are exactly the same as they were in Figures 13.1 and 13.2. The completed contribution chart is shown in Figure 13.4.

Despite its name, this sort of chart does not show total contribution directly: instead,

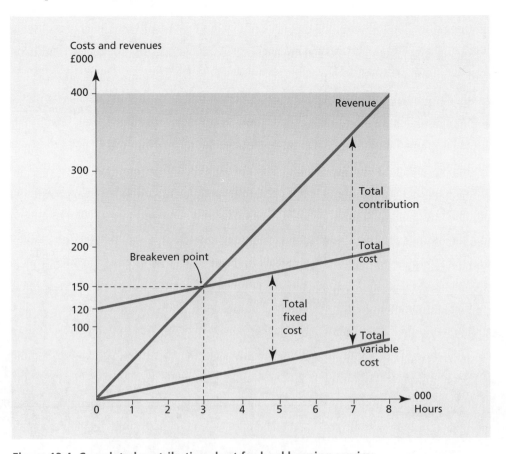

Figure 13.4 Completed contribution chart for bookkeeping service

total contribution can be determined by calculating the vertical distance between the sales revenue and total variable cost lines. As it did in the breakeven chart, breakeven point occurs where the sales revenue and total cost lines intersect, and we can read the corresponding unit volume from the horizontal axis and revenue amount from the vertical axis.

We have just said that the contribution chart in Figures 13.3 and 13.4 does not permit total contribution to be assessed directly. But, since changes in total contribution can provide a useful 'ready reckoner' for management when examining the increase/decrease in profit caused by changes in volume, it may be more useful to present an 'abbreviated' contribution chart which plots total contribution directly against total fixed cost. With this sort of chart, the impact on total contribution (and hence on profit) of volume changes may be more readily appreciated. Figure 13.5 is an 'abbreviated' contribution chart for the bookkeeping service.

The total fixed cost line in Figure 13.5 has been plotted in the same way as before. To plot total contribution, we again need two values (for zero and a volume greater

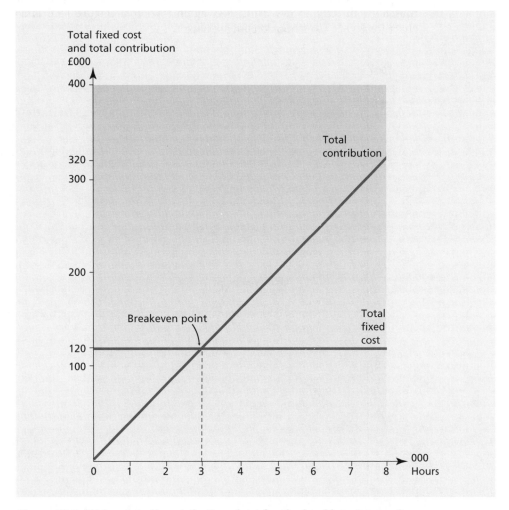

Figure 13.5 'Abbreviated' contribution chart for the bookkeeping service

than zero) joined in a straight line:

zero volume: total contribution	zero
maximum volume: total contribution (8000 @ £40)	£320 000

Breakeven point occurs where the total contribution and total fixed cost lines intersect. Note that in this presentation, it is only possible to read the breakeven volume from the horizontal axis.

As well as permitting quick assessment of profit changes relative to volume changes, our 'abbreviated' contribution chart has two further advantages:

1 only two lines need be plotted, which makes the chart easier to construct and read;
2 it is consistent with the formulaic approach to breakeven calculation – i.e. it highlights the fact that breakeven point occurs where total contribution equals total fixed cost.

3 The profit/volume chart

This approach aims to remedy a weakness of all the previous presentations – namely that none directly shows profit/loss against volume. Figure 13.6 is a profit/volume chart for KD & Co's bookkeeping service.

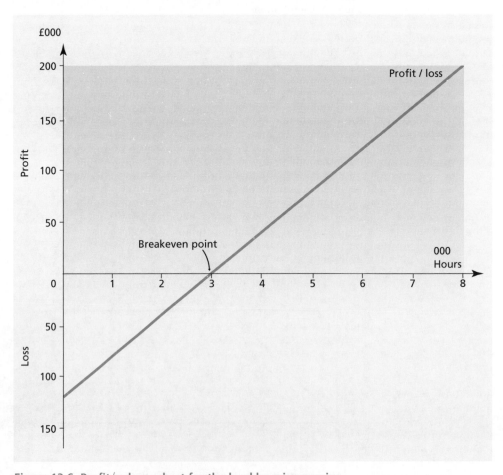

Figure 13.6 Profit/volume chart for the bookkeeping service

Of all presentations, this is probably the easiest to prepare, since only a single line need be plotted. We need two values for profit/loss to enable us to do this; at maximum volume, profit is:

	£
Sales (8000 @ £50)	400 000
Less Total variable cost (8000 @ £10)	80 000
Total contribution	320 000
Less Total fixed cost	120 000
Profit	200 000

 What is the amount of the loss which is incurred at zero volume?

At zero volume, revenue will be zero, as will total variable cost and hence total contribution. However, total fixed cost will still be incurred, so the amount of the loss will be equal to total fixed cost (i.e. £120 000). Joining this point to the profit calculated above provides the profit/loss plot, breakeven point occurring where the profit/loss line intersects the horizontal axis.

SENSITIVITY ANALYSIS

Sensitivity analysis is a 'what-if' technique which allows management to gauge the effect of changing one or more of the variables within the cost/volume/profit model. It permits uncertainty about the value of different variables such as unit variable cost or selling price to be allowed for and can also aid in assessing the financial desirability of different courses of action.

Applying sensitivity analysis to the basic model

Exhibit 13.5 provides some additional information about KD & Co's bookkeeping service next year.

KD & Co: uncertainty over costs

There is some uncertainty within KD & Co about next year's cost levels for the firm's bookkeeping service. The best estimate of variable cost per hour is £10, but this might be as high as £12.50 or as low as £7.50. Total fixed cost could be as much as £131 250 or as little as £106 250, with the most likely amount being £120 000. The charge per hour's work will be £50, and it is expected that 5000 hours' work will be performed. Target profit for the year is £85 000.

Exhibit 13.5 Applying sensitivity analysis to the basic model

Performing a sensitivity analysis of KD & Co's basic data involves using the additional information in Exhibit 13.5 to recalculate the cost/volume/profit model's key indicators: breakeven point, margin of safety and sales required to achieve target profit. One way in which this can be done is to look at three scenarios – the most likely, the best possible and the worst possible; a technique termed **three-level analysis**. The most likely scenario utilises the 'best estimates' of costs, which are the figures we used earlier in the chapter to obtain a breakeven point of 3000 hours, a margin of safety of 40% and sales of 5125 hours to achieve profit of £85 000.

 From Exhibit 13.5, determine the breakeven point in hours for each of the best and worst possible cost combinations.

The best and worst possible scenarios will involve the following cost combinations:

Best possible: £7.50 per hour variable, £106 250 fixed
Worst possible: £12.50 per hour variable, £131 250 fixed.

Combined with a charge per hour of £50, we get the following breakeven points:

$$\text{Best possible } \frac{\text{Total fixed cost}}{\text{Contribution per hour}} = \frac{£106\,250}{(£50 - £7.50)} = 2500 \text{ hours}$$

$$\text{Worst possible: } \frac{\text{Total fixed cost}}{\text{Contribution per hour}} = \frac{£131\,250}{(£50 - £12.50)} = 3500 \text{ hours}$$

Recalculating the margin of safety as a percentage of expected sales along with sales required to earn the target profit gives us the range of values set out in Table 13.1.

Since there will always be uncertainty surrounding business estimates, providing management with a range of potential outcomes is likely to be much more useful than a single point estimate of, e.g. breakeven point. In KD & Co's case, the information in Table 13.1 might suggest that, assuming the estimated volume of work (5000 hours) to be fairly accurate, there is a reasonable expectation of the bookkeeping service comfortably exceeding breakeven point next year. Similarly, management might also conclude from Table 13.1 that, unless some form of action is taken, target profit is unlikely to be achieved.

Our sensitivity analysis of KD & Co's basic data has been limited to changes in two variables, but the technique can easily be extended to deal with changes to the charge per hour, expected sales volume and target profit. The impact of such changes can either be examined in isolation, or in any combination which may be useful in given circumstances.

Table 13.1 Results of sensitivity analysis

Indicator	Best possible	Most likely	Worst possible
Breakeven point (hours)	2500	3000	3500
Margin of safety	50%	40%	30%
Sales to earn target profit	4500	5125	5767

Sensitivity analysis and decision making

Sensitivity analysis can be used to provide management with some indication of the financial viability of alternative courses of action. Exhibit 13.6 will allow us to demonstrate.

KD & Co: alternative bookkeeping software

The firm is considering changing the software package it uses for clients' accounts. If the new package were to be used, total fixed cost would increase to £170 000 next year; however, the variable cost per hour would fall to £7.50. The charge per hour will remain at £50 and it is estimated that 5000 hours of bookkeeping work will be performed. Best estimates of variable cost per hour and total fixed cost using the existing software are £10 and £120 000 respectively.

Exhibit 13.6 Sensitivity analysis and decision making

Based on use of the alternative software, what is the bookkeeping service's breakeven point (in hours), its margin of safety (as a % of estimated sales) and the volume of sales required to earn £85 000 profit?

The contribution per hour for use of the alternative software is $(£50 - £7.50) = £42.50$, giving a breakeven point of:

$$\frac{\text{Total fixed cost}}{\text{Contribution per hour}} = \frac{£170\,000}{£42.50} = 4000 \text{ hours}$$

The margin of safety is:

$$\frac{(\text{Estimated sales} - \text{Breakeven sales})}{\text{Estimated sales}} \times 100\% = \frac{(5000 - 4000)}{5000} \times 100\% = 20\%$$

and the sales volume necessary for £85 000 profit:

$$\frac{(\text{Total fixed cost} + \text{Target Profit})}{\text{Contribution per hour}} = \frac{(£170\,000 + £85\,000)}{£42.50} = 6000 \text{ hours}$$

Table 13.2 compares these three indicative values with the ones we obtained earlier based on the original data:

Using the comparative data in Table 13.2 as the basis, should KD & Co change the software package used for bookkeeping services? Explain your reasoning.

Table 13.2 Key indicators for each software option

Indicator	Original	Alternative
Breakeven point (hours)	3000	4000
Margin of safety	40%	20%
Sales required for target profit (hours)	5125	6000

Financially, using the original software is better: breakeven volume and sales required to earn the target profit are both lower – which means that they should be easier to achieve – and the margin of safety is higher, meaning that profit is less vulnerable to drops in demand. But you should bear in mind that this is based on the very limited information given in Table 13.2. For example, only next year's figures are considered, and changing software package may well offer longer-term benefits which outweigh the shorter-term costs suggested in Table 13.2.

Suppose KD & Co wishes to know at what volume of sales the two software packages yield the same profit (the 'indifference' volume – i.e. the volume at which the firm will be indifferent about which software package is used). This can be determined using some simple algebra. If we convert a summarised marginal costing profit statement into equation form, we get:

$$\text{Sales} - \text{total variable cost} - \text{total fixed cost} = \text{profit}$$

which can be 'tidied up' to read

$$\text{total contribution} - \text{total fixed cost} = \text{profit}$$

If each software package is to yield the same profit, we can say that

total contribution – total fixed cost = total contribution – total fixed cost
[original software]   [alternative software]

Bearing in mind that total contribution is (unit contribution × sales volume), we will call the unknown factor (i.e. sales volume) X and insert the figures which we already know:

$$(\pounds 40 \times X) - \pounds 120\ 000 = (\pounds 42.50 \times X) - \pounds 170\ 000$$
[original]   [alternative]

 Remembering that X has the same value for both original and alternative software packages, determine the sales volume at which each yields the same profit.

Rearranging the equation above gives

$$\pounds 50\ 000 = \pounds 2.5 \times X$$
$$\therefore X = 20\ 000 \text{ hours}$$

In other words, at a sales volume of 20 000 hours, each software package will earn the same profit. We can confirm that this is correct and obtain a value for that profit by preparing a marginal costing profit statement for each option:

	Original Software £	Alternative Software £
Sales (20 000 @ £50)	1 000 000	1 000 000
Less Marginal cost of sales		
(20 000 @ £10/£7.50)	200 000	150 000
Total contribution	800 000	850 000
Less Total fixed cost	120 000	170 000
Profit	680 000	680 000

Alternatively, we could obtain the indifference volume by graphical means. Figure 13.7 is a profit/volume chart showing a profit/loss line for each option across a range of volumes from zero to 25 000 hours. (Note that it has been necessary to increase the assumed maximum volume from the original 8000 in order to accommodate the 'indifference' volume.) Reading down from the point where the two profit/loss lines intersect gives the desired volume.

A graphical presentation of each option's cost/volume/profit consequences clarifies their relative financial desirability at different volumes. From Figure 13.7, we can see that at volumes below the indifference point, using the original software earns a higher profit (or incurs a lower loss below breakeven point); above the indifference point, using the alternative software is financially preferable. So if it were confidently

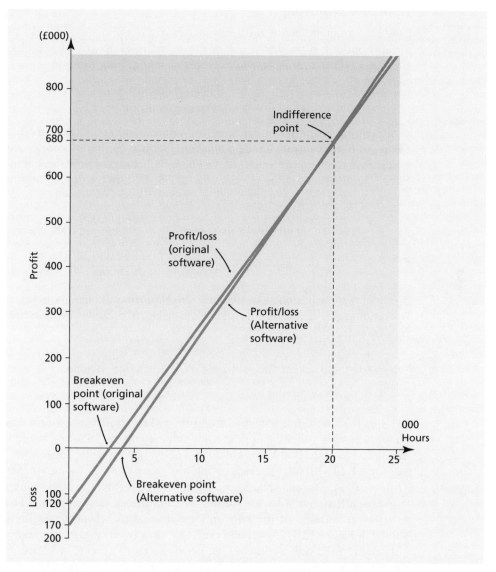

Figure 13.7 Profit/volume chart for two alternative software packages

expected that sales volume might exceed 20 000 hours – which seems very unlikely given an expected volume of 5000 – management may consider changing the software on financial grounds.

For this sort of presentation – i.e. where two or more options are being graphed on the same chart – the profit/volume chart is the best method to use: the cost, contribution and revenue lines variously required by the other charts will make them difficult to plot and interpret.

Calculation of indifference points can also encompass variables other than sales volume. For instance, KD & Co might wish to know, for an expected sales volume of 5000 hours, at what charge per hour both software packages would yield the same profit.

Operational gearing

One important influence on decision making is the degree of risk attaching to the various options. If we define risk as the volatility of returns from each option, we can provide a relevant measure with the **operational gearing ratio**:

$$\frac{\text{Total contribution}}{\text{Operating profit}}$$

'Operating profit' is net profit before interest and tax. Using this measure of profit allows us to concentrate on the *operational* returns from options: i.e. excluding factors extraneous to the options themselves and/or functions of how those options happen to have been financed. Using the data for KD & Co's two software options at the indifference volume, we get operational gearing ratios of:

$$\text{Original software} \qquad \frac{£800\,000}{£680\,000} = 1.18$$

$$\text{Alternative software} \qquad \frac{£850\,000}{£680\,000} = 1.25$$

Since total contribution changes in direct proportion to changes in sales volume, these operational gearing ratios indicate the sensitivity of profit under each option to changes in sales volume.

 Based on these operational gearing ratios, which option appears to be the more risky?

Using the alternative software seems the riskier choice, as profit is more sensitive to changes in sales volume. Suppose sales volume falls by 20% compared to the indifference volume of 20 000 hours calculated above: profit using the existing software will fall by (1.18 × 20%), whereas using the alternative software, profit will fall by (1.25 × 20%). A similar relationship would exist for rises in sales volume, except here, using the alternative software would yield a larger increase in profit. This confirms the relative profitability of the two options above and below the indifference point (as shown in Figure 13.7). Note, however, that the operational gearing ratios we have calculated are valid only for the selling price and cost structure specified in Exhibit 13.6; should any of the data in this exhibit change, then the operational gearing ratios would also change. Management reaction to operational gearing ratios is essentially governed by their attitude to risk: in KD & Co's case, is the 'downside' risk (i.e. of a fall in sales volume) considered to outweigh the 'upside' risk or vice versa?

Sensitivity analysis and computer spreadsheets

As we have seen, sensitivity analysis requires a complete reworking of the cost/volume/profit model to reflect possible changes in its variables. So although it can be a valuable and versatile aid to planning and decision making, it can also be rather cumbersome and time-consuming – especially if several different possible sets of changes to variables are being considered. Where multiple or particularly complex sets of changes are being examined, a computer spreadsheet is of great help, permitting complex combinations of changes to be analysed speedily and without the need for lengthy manual calculation. Once the relationships between a cost/volume/profit model's variables have been specified within the spreadsheet, it is a simple matter to 'interrogate' the computer about the effect of changes to input values.

MULTIPLE PRODUCTS/SERVICES

Our analysis of KD & Co has so far been based on provision of a single service. This might happen in practice, but it is more likely that the firm will offer a range of different services.

KD & Co: range of services

The firm's full range of services next year are detailed below.

	Bookkeeping	Taxation	Auditing	Insolvency
Estimated number of hours' work	5000	6000	7000	2000
Charge per hour's work	£50	£65	£40	£48
Variable cost per hour	£10	£18	£6	£8

KD & Co's total fixed cost for the year will be £460 000.

Exhibit 13.7 KD & Co's sales mix

In order to apply cost/volume/profit analysis to Exhibit 13.7, we need to reflect the **sales mix** detailed there – i.e. the proportion of total sales represented by each of the four services being offered:

	Hours' work	% of total
Bookkeeping	5 000	25
Taxation	6 000	30
Auditing	7 000	35
Insolvency	2 000	10
	20 000	100

We can use these percentages to 'weight' the contribution per hour from each type of work:

	Contribution/hour ×	Weighting =	Weighted average
Bookkeeping	(£50 – £10) = £40	25%	£10.0
Taxation	(£65 – £18) = £47	30%	£14.1
Auditing	(£40 – £ 6) = £34	35%	£11.9
Insolvency	(£48 – £ 8) = £40	10%	£ 4.0
Weighted average contribution per hour			£40.0

This £40 reflects the contribution per hour for KD & Co as a whole assuming every hour consists of the same proportion of each type of service as the overall sales mix.

 What is KD & Co's breakeven point in hours based on the weighted average contribution?

Using the weighted average unit contribution in our breakeven formula, we get

$$\frac{\text{Total fixed cost}}{\text{Weighted average unit contribution}} = \frac{£460\,000}{£40} = 11\,500 \text{ hours}$$

Of this breakeven volume, 25% of the hours will be bookkeeping, 30% taxation, 35% auditing and 10% insolvency. A summarised marginal costing profit statement will verify that profit is zero at this volume and for the specified sales mix:

	£
Total contribution:	
bookkeeping (11 500 hours × 25%) × £40	115 000
taxation (11 500 hours × 30%) × £47	162 150
auditing (11 500 hours × 35%) × £34	136 850
insolvency (11 500 hours × 10%) × £40	46 000
	460 000
Less Total fixed cost	460 000
Profit	nil

 Use the data in Exhibit 13.7 to determine KD & Co's CS ratio based on total contribution and total sales revenue.

By calculating the CS ratio on the basis of total contribution and total sales revenue, we automatically reflect the sales mix – i.e. the resulting ratio is the **weighted average contribution/sales ratio**:

Total sales revenue	£
Bookkeeping (5000 hours @ £50)	250 000
Taxation (6000 hours @ £65)	390 000
Auditing (7000 hours @ £40)	280 000
Insolvency (2000 hours @ £48)	96 000
	1 016 000
Total contribution	
Bookkeeping (5000 hours @ £40)	200 000
Taxation (6000 hours @ £47)	282 000
Auditing (7000 hours @ £34)	238 000
Insolvency (2000 hours @ £40)	80 000
	800 000

The weighted average CS ratio is thus:

$$\frac{\text{Total contribution}}{\text{Total sales revenue}} = \frac{£800\ 000}{£1\ 016\ 000} = 0.7874 \text{ (rounded)}$$

We can now use this as the denominator in our breakeven formula:

$$\frac{\text{Total fixed cost}}{\text{Weighted average CS ratio}} = \frac{£460\ 000}{0.7874} = £584\ 201 \text{ (rounded)}$$

This is the revenue which would be earned from sale of 11 500 hours' work as set out in our summarised profit statement above.

 What sales revenue must KD & Co achieve in order to earn an overall target profit of £400 000?

Again, we can use the weighted average CS ratio as the denominator in our formula:

$$\frac{(\text{Total fixed cost} + \text{Target profit})}{\text{Weighted average CS ratio}} = \frac{(£460\ 000 + £400\ 000)}{0.7874} = £1\ 092\ 202 \text{ (rounded)}$$

Note that the values for breakeven point and sales to earn target profit *only* apply if the sales mix specified in Exhibit 13.7 remains constant. If the sales mix changes, the weighted average contribution per hour and CS ratio will change to reflect the new relative weightings for each type of work, and the cost/volume/profit model's indicators will change in consequence:

KD & Co: revision to sales mix

The firm's full range of services next year are detailed below.

	Bookkeeping	Taxation	Auditing	Insolvency
Estimated number of hours' work	3000	2000	9000	6000
Charge per hour's work	£50	£65	£40	£48
Variable cost per hour	£10	£18	£6	£8

KD & Co's total fixed cost for the year will be £460 000, and the target profit £400 000.

Exhibit 13.8 KD & Co – change in sales mix

The weighted average CS ratio for the revised sales mix in Exhibit 13.8 is:

Total sales revenue	£
Bookkeeping (3000 hours @ £50)	150 000
Taxation (2000 hours @ £65)	130 000
Auditing (9000 hours @ £40)	360 000
Insolvency (6000 hours @ £48)	288 000
	928 000

Total contribution

Bookkeeping (3000 hours @ £40)	120 000
Taxation (2000 hours @ £47)	94 000
Auditing (9000 hours @ £34)	306 000
Insolvency (6000 hours @ £40)	240 000
	760 000

$$\text{CS ratio:} \frac{\text{Total contribution}}{\text{Total sales revenue}} = \frac{£760\,000}{£928\,000} = 0.82 \text{ (rounded)}$$

giving a breakeven point in revenue of:

$$\frac{\text{Total fixed cost}}{\text{Weighted average CS ratio}} = \frac{£460\,000}{0.82} = £560\,976 \text{ (rounded)}$$

To earn profit of £400 000 from the sales mix from Exhibit 13.8, KD & Co. now needs revenue of:

$$\frac{(\text{Total fixed cost} + \text{Target profit})}{\text{Weighted average CS ratio}} = \frac{(£460\,000 + £400\,000)}{0.82} = £1\,048\,780 \text{ (rounded)}$$

We can also obtain the margin of safety for each sales mix, here based on sales revenue:

$$\frac{(\text{Estimated sales revenue} - \text{breakeven sales revenue})}{\text{Estimated sales revenue}} \times 100\%$$

$$\text{Mix in Exhibit 13.7} = \frac{(£1\,016\,000 - £584\,201)}{£1\,016\,000} \times 100\% = 42.5\% \text{ (rounded)}$$

$$\text{Mix in Exhibit 13.8} = \frac{(£928\,000 - £560\,976)}{£928\,000} \times 100\% = 39.6\% \text{ (rounded)}$$

 Why are breakeven point, sales required to earn profit of £400 000 lower and the margin of safety lower for the sales mix in Exhibit 13.8 than they were for that in Exhibit 13.7?

A comparison of Exhibits 13.7 and 13.8 is shown in Table 13.3.

Table 13.3 Analysis of relative profitability of sales mixes

Service	CS ratio	Sales mix (%)	
		Exhibit 13.7	Exhibit 13.8
Bookkeeping	0.80	25	15
Taxation	0.72	30	10
Auditing	0.85	35	45
Insolvency	0.83	10	30

In the revised mix, there has been an increase in the relative weightings of the most profitable types of service (auditing and insolvency) coupled with a reduction in the weightings of the less profitable services (bookkeeping and taxation). The overall effect of this has been to increase the weighted average CS ratio to 0.82 (from 0.7874), thus causing the reduced breakeven point and sales required for target profit. The margin of safety has reduced because estimated revenue from the revised mix is lower in relation to breakeven point. You will appreciate that our calculations for the revised sales mix are simply another application of sensitivity analysis.

Graphing a multi-product/service situation

Graphing a multi-product/service situation is straightforward – providing we bear in mind that the profit/loss lines we plot only hold good for the specified sales mix. Figure 13.8 is a profit/volume chart for KD & Co, showing profit/loss from both sales mixes specified above. You will see that we have scaled the horizontal axis in sales revenue, rather than in hours. This is merely a convenience, as we have already calculated breakeven point for each mix in revenue terms – had both been available in hours, we could equally well have used this measure for the horizontal axis.

The assumed maximum volume in Figure 13.8 is £1 200 000, which is sufficiently high to cover our previously calculated value for sales required to earn £400 000 profit. At sales of £0, the loss equals KD & Co's total fixed cost of £460 000 given in Exhibits 13.7 and 13.8, and this is the same for both sales mixes. We have obviated the

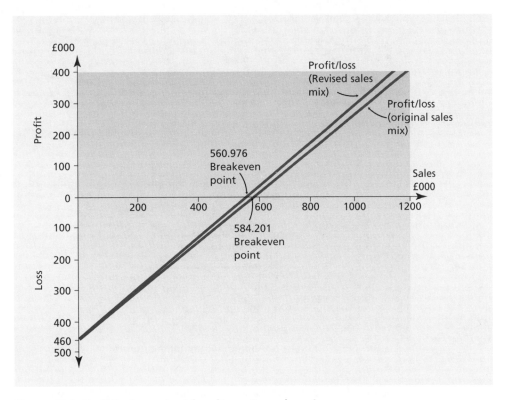

Figure 13.8 Profit/volume chart for alternative sales mixes

need to obtain a profit measure for some sales volume in excess of zero by the simple expedient of taking the breakeven figure for each mix – determined above – as the second point on the profit/loss lines, extending to the left as far as –460 on the vertical axis and to the right as far as the upper limit on the horizontal axis.

Breakeven, contribution and 'abbreviated' contribution charts may also be prepared for multi-product/service situations, but you should bear in mind that a profit/volume chart is preferable for illustration of the impact of sensitivity analysis. Figure 13.9 shows a breakeven, contribution and 'abbreviated' contribution chart for KD & Co's original sales mix only (this is the mix specified in Exhibit 13.7).

As in Figure 13.8, we have used breakeven point (£584 201) to provide a second value when plotting the revenue, total cost and total contribution lines in Figure 13.9. So, in the breakeven and contribution charts, we know that revenue and total cost functions intersect at £584 201 on both horizontal and vertical axes. Similarly, on the abbreviated contribution chart, we know that total contribution and total fixed cost intersect at a horizontal value of £584 201. This is merely a convenience to avoid additional calculation.

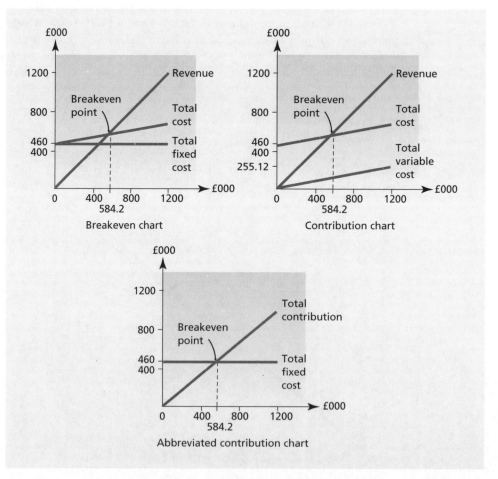

Figure 13.9 Breakeven, contribution and 'abbreviated' contribution charts for KD & Co's original sales mix

However, for the contribution chart, we had to obtain a value of total variable cost for some volume in excess of zero to allow this line to be plotted. From our earlier calculations, we know that the CS ratio is 0.7874; total variable cost as a percentage of sales must therefore be $(1 - 0.7874) = 0.2126$. When sales revenue is £1 200 000, total variable cost will thus be $(0.2126 \times £1\ 200\ 000) = £255\ 120$. But remember that, like total cost, total contribution, revenue and breakeven point, the total variable cost : sales relationship we have just specified will only hold good as long as the sales mix specified in Exhibit 13.7 is unchanged.

ASSUMPTIONS OF COST/VOLUME/PROFIT ANALYSIS

As we have progressed through our example, you will have realised that several assumptions have been made in order to permit analysis. An understanding of these assumptions is vital to correct interpretation and use of the cost/volume/profit model. We discuss these assumptions below before considering whether they can be reconciled with the reality which our model is attempting to reflect.

1 Linear sales revenue function

When we plotted sales revenue against volume in our graphical presentations, we plotted a straight line – in other words we assumed that the unit selling price was constant at all volumes from zero upward. This is unlikely to be the case in reality: it is far more likely that, as sales volume increases, selling price per unit must fall in order to attract additional sales. The revenue function may therefore be **curvilinear**, as illustrated in Figure 13.10.

This type of revenue function reflects what is known as **price elasticity of demand** – i.e. the idea that, if unit selling price increases, quantity demanded decreases and vice versa.

2 Linear cost functions

A linear cost assumption means total fixed cost is constant in amount at all volumes

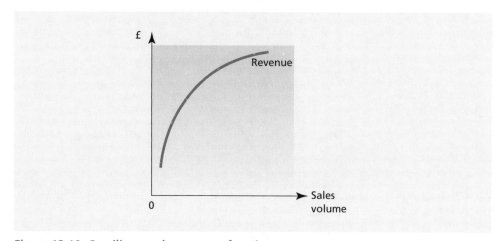

Figure 13.10 Curvilinear sales revenue function

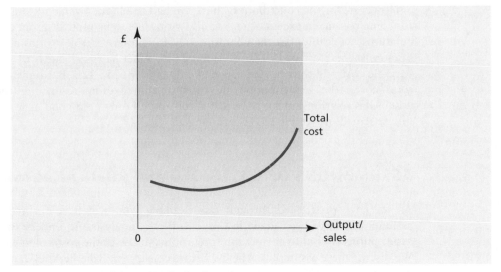

Figure 13.11 Curvilinear total cost function

from zero upward and that the unit variable cost is likewise constant. As we said in Chapter 2, this assumption ignores the possibility of **economies** and **diseconomies of scale** and of **step costs**. Adjusting our cost function to allow for these means that we are more likely to have the kind of curvilinear cost function described in the earlier chapter, an illustration of which is reproduced in Figure 13.11.

If we combine the curvilinear revenue and total cost functions from Figures 13.10 and 13.11 into a breakeven chart, the result is markedly different from Figures 13.1 and 13.2.

Figure 13.12 shows two breakeven points; in fact, this may still be a simplistic view of reality, where cost and revenue behaviour could be extremely complex, resulting in multiple breakeven points.

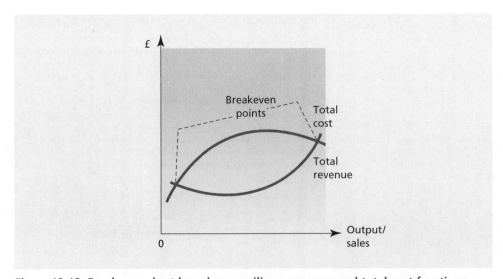

Figure 13.12 Breakeven chart based on curvilinear revenue and total cost functions

3 Single-period model

The cost/volume/profit model treats the period under review as being independent of either the following or previous periods. The implication of this assumption is that (production = sales), or at least that there is no significant change in stocks during the period covered by the model. If, however, a significant part of the current period's sales are being made from stock produced last period, and if the unit variable cost of this stock is markedly different to that of the current period's output, then the results of the model may be seriously distorted if allowance is not made for the fact (e.g. by taking a 'weighted average' approach not unlike that adopted for multi-product situations).

Lack of significant stock changes also suggests that the volume of production/sales is the *only* factor which causes variation in costs. But, if stockholding is important, this could have as great a bearing on cost structure as volume of activity. Fixed costs may be greatly affected by the amount of stock held – storage costs can be high. Unit variable cost may be influenced, not only by the volume of activity, but also by the volume of *purchases*. For example, a business may decide to make a bulk purchase of materials in order to take advantage of quantity discounts being offered by suppliers. It may often be the case that *environmental* factors, such as relationships with suppliers, inflation or exchange rates, play a big part in cost structure.

4 Deterministic model

The model we have been using assumes certainty (is **deterministic**): about unit selling price, unit variable cost and about fixed costs. Such certainty is something of a luxury in practical terms. Sensitivity analysis can help to incorporate uncertainty into the model, but requires the model to be reworked for each different set of component variables which are thought to be possible. And although computer spreadsheets can greatly ease the burden of numerous or complex calculations, sensitivity analysis does nothing to *quantify* uncertainty: e.g. if we are unsure about unit variable cost, it may be helpful to have some idea of how likely the occurrence of a particular possibility might be.

5 Single-product/constant mix

The cost/volume/profit model assumes that a single product/service is sold or that, if more than one product/service is involved, the sales mix is constant at all volumes from zero upward. This assumption is obviously perfectly realistic for single-product/service organisations, but is an unlikely one in multi-product/service situations. In much the same way that it may be necessary to reduce unit selling price in order to increase quantity demanded, it may be necessary to alter sales mix at different volumes of sales so as to increase overall demand. For example, if the total sales volume of 20 000 hours in Exhibit 13.7 were to increase to 25 000, this increase may be due solely to an increase in the number of audit hours worked, in which case the sales mix specified in the exhibit will alter, necessitating recalculation of the model's indicative values.

6 Static model

Our model assumes a static environment: it assumes, for instance, constant technology at all volumes. But as volume increases, the technology involved may well become more sophisticated, with a resultant effect on cost structure.

Cost structure may also be dependent on the *mix* of products/services being produced/sold. Looking again at Exhibit 13.7, we can see that any change to the relative weightings of each type of work will cause cost structure to change – if only because a different mix of variable cost per hour will apply. A change in mix might also affect fixed costs – additional computer hardware and software may be needed to deal with a higher proportion of bookkeeping hours, for example.

7 Only quantitative, financial variables included

The cost/volume/profit model cannot deal with qualitative or non-financial variables. Imagine the operational difficulties faced by KD & Co if relations with key clients suddenly soured, resulting in temporary or permanent loss of business. This would be a serious situation – but it would be almost impossible to incorporate directly into a cost/volume/profit analysis, since the precise effect of reduced goodwill is hard to quantify.

RECONCILING ASSUMPTIONS WITH REALITY

Relevant range

In the forgoing discussion of the model's assumptions the phrase 'at all volumes from zero upward' was repeated several times. But is it reasonable to suppose that management is concerned with *all* possible volumes? Management will be much more concerned with the volume range within which operations are likely to occur in the period under review. Similarly, the time horizon of concern to management will be finite (possibly a year). Given these limitations, what we can say is that management will be principally interested in the **relevant range** – i.e. that range of volumes and time horizon which encompass operational possibilities. We met this concept in Chapter 2 in our discussion about cost behaviour. Figure 13.13 superimposes the relevant range on the curvilinear revenue and cost functions presented in Figures 13.10 and 13.11.

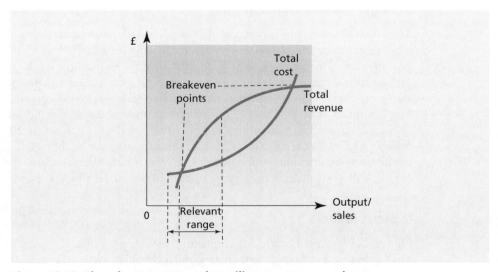

Figure 13.13 The relevant range and curvilinear revenues and costs

Within the relevant range in Figure 13.13, the revenue and total cost lines are similar to those we drew in our breakeven and contribution charts earlier. What we are suggesting is that, **within the relevant range**, the assumptions which underpin the cost/volume/profit model may be acceptable approximations of reality. Outside the relevant range, they are much less realistic and their application may seriously distort the true position. For example, it may be reasonable to assume that, within a volume range of (say) 60–80% of maximum and within a one-year time frame, unit variable cost and selling price are more or less constant; that total fixed cost is unaffected by volume changes; and that sales mix is constant. You should appreciate that restricting the cost/volume/profit model in this way is perfectly consistent with the *short-term* information needs of management. Short-term planning and decision making will be confined to a short time horizon (typically one year) and to the likely range of operational volumes.

However, a warning note needs to be sounded here. From our discussion in Chapter 1, you will recall that a distinction must be drawn between *operational, tactical* and *strategic* considerations – and that assumptions which may hold true in operational and/or tactical terms are unlikely to be reasonable in the long term. For example, the range of possible volumes within a five-year strategic plan may be considerably wider than that within a one-year tactical planning period, with consequent effect on the complexity of cost and revenue functions – step fixed costs, changing unit variable cost and price elasticity of demand may be very much in evidence, meaning that the applicable cost/volume/profit model will be much more like that presented in Figure 13.12.

You should also realise from our discussion in Chapter 3 that accurate separation of fixed and variable costs may be problematic in practice; since the cost/volume/profit model relies on such separation, any significant inaccuracy may have an adverse impact on the model's usefulness.

However, we are not claiming that restricting cost/volume/profit analyses to the relevant range results in a model that is 100% accurate. Since the model is primarily future-oriented, some predictive inaccuracy is inevitable, and, if the importance of the relevant range is borne in mind when constructing and using the model, valuable results may be obtained.

More complex cost functions

Our analysis of KD & Co has been based on the assumption that the cost function is linear – i.e. constant unit variable cost and unchanged total fixed cost. It is possible to amend the basic cost/volume/profit model to incorporate more complex cost behaviour patterns. Consider Exhibit 13.9.

 Bearing in mind the breakeven formula, what will be the effect on breakeven calculations of the information contained in Exhibit 13.9?

Since the breakeven formula is

$$\frac{\text{Total fixed cost}}{\text{Contribution per hour}}$$

KD & Co: cost function for bookkeeping services

Further investigation of the firm's cost structure reveals the following in respect of book-keeping services:

Volume of work performed	Up to 4000 hours	4000 hours and over
Total fixed cost	£120 000	£180 000
Variable cost per hour	£10	£10
Charge per hour	£50	£50

Management estimates that 5000 hours of bookkeeping work will be undertaken in the forthcoming year.

Exhibit 13.9 KD & Co – bookkeeping service's cost structure

and there are two different levels of total fixed cost in Exhibit 13.9, we will have two different breakeven points:

Volume range	Breakeven point
Up to 4000 hours	$\dfrac{£120\,000}{(£50 - £10)} = 3000$ hours
4000 hours and over	$\dfrac{£180\,000}{(£50 - £10)} = 4500$ hours

Figure 13.14 incorporates the revised cost structure into a breakeven chart.

The revenue function in Figure 13.14 is the same as that in Figure 13.2, but the cost functions are radically different and require careful plotting. The total fixed cost line is the easier of the two, having a single step increase of £60 000 at a volume of 4000 hours.

Total cost must be plotted in two segments: one for total cost up to 4000 hours, the other for total cost at 4000 hours and above.

	£
Up to 4000 hours	
Total cost at 0 hours (= total fixed cost)	120 000
Total cost at 3000 hours:	
Variable (3000 × £10)	30 000
Fixed	120 000
	150 000

These two values can be plotted, joined and extended to the right as far as 4000 hours on the horizontal axis, giving the first segment of our total cost function.

	£
4000 hours and above	
Total cost at 4000 hours:	
Variable (4000 × £10)	40 000
Fixed	180 000
	220 000
Total cost at 8000 hours:	
Variable (8000 × £10)	80 000
Fixed	180 000
	260 000

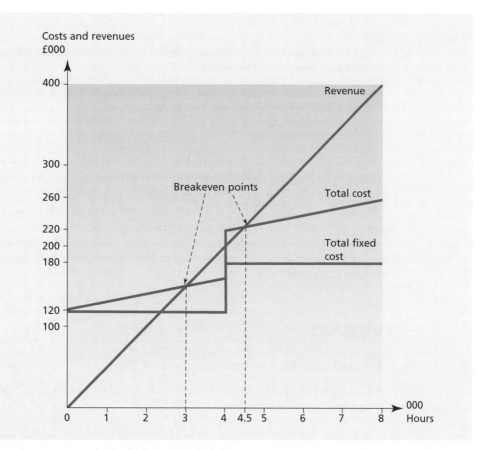

Figure 13.14 Bookkeeping service – revised cost structure

Joining these two values gives us the second segment of the total cost plot.

Figure 13.14 shows the following relationships between volume of work and profit/loss:

Losses incurred	up to 3000 hours
	4000–4500 hours
Profit earned	3000–4000 hours
	above 4500 hours.

Although this is rather less clear-cut than the situation depicted in Figure 13.2, it still provides management with useful information. Since anticipated volume next year is 5000 hours, the higher of the two breakeven points will be of most interest to management. Assuming tolerably accurate estimates, the bookkeeping service ought to break even, though with a margin of safety of only 10% of estimated sales. If there is uncertainty about the volume of work next year, then the relationship between volume and profit/loss below 4500 hours may be of significance to management as part of a sensitivity analysis.

✔ *Figure 13.14 appears to show a third breakeven point at 4000 hours. Is this correct?*

The 'third' breakeven point in Figure 13.14 is spurious and appears on the chart merely as a result of the need to increase total cost by a lump-sum of £60 000: i.e. is an issue of presentation rather than of genuine cost/volume/profit relationship. The true position at a volume of 4000 hours is easily ascertained:

	£	£
Revenue (4000 × £50)		200 000
Variable costs (4000 × £10)	40 000	
Fixed cost	180 000	220 000
Loss		(20 000)

This sort of analysis could be extended to deal with additional complexities in cost behaviour, such as changes in unit variable cost; indeed, price elasticity of demand might also be included. While cost/volume/profit analysis involving complicated cost and revenue functions can be very cumbersome if undertaken manually, use of a computer spreadsheet to model the relationships reduces the burden considerably. Extending the basic model in this way could well provide management with useful operational insights.

SUMMARY

In this chapter, we have seen that

- **Breakeven point** is the sales volume in units or revenue where profit is zero and can be calculated as follows:

  In units: $$\frac{\text{Total fixed cost}}{\text{Contribution per unit}}$$

  In revenue: $$\frac{\text{Total fixed cost}}{\text{CS ratio}}$$

- The **contribution/sales (CS) ratio** is

  $$\frac{\text{Contribution}}{\text{Sales}}$$

  and can be calculated using either total contribution and total sales revenue or unit contribution and unit selling price.

- Sales required to earn a target profit may be calculated as:

  $$\frac{(\text{Total fixed cost} + \text{target profit})}{\text{Contribution per unit [CS ratio]}}$$

- **Margin of safety** is the difference between estimated (or actual) sales and breakeven sales and gives an indication of the vulnerability of profit to reductions in demand; for comparative purposes, it can be expressed as a percentage of estimated (or actual) sales:

  $$\frac{(\text{Estimated or actual sales} - \text{Breakeven sales})}{\text{Estimated sales}} \times 100\%$$

- Cost/volume/profit relationships can be presented graphically, which may have greater impact, but may sacrifice accuracy.
- A **breakeven chart** plots total fixed cost, total cost and sales revenue against volume, breakeven point occurring where total cost and revenue lines intersect.
- A **contribution chart** can take one of two forms:
  - it can plot total variable cost, total cost and revenue against volume, breakeven point occurring where total cost and revenue lines intersect
  or
  - it can plot total fixed cost and total contribution against volume, breakeven point occurring where these two lines intersect.
- A **profit/volume chart** plots profit/loss against volume, breakeven point occurring where the profit/loss line intersects the horizontal axis.
- In situations which involve multiple products/services, breakeven calculations should be based on the **weighted average unit contribution** or on the **weighted average C/S ratio**.
- **Sensitivity analysis** is a 'what-if' technique which can be used to analyse the impact of changing one or more of the variables within the cost/volume/profit model.
- The cost/volume/profit model rests on a number of assumptions:
  - linear revenue function
  - linear cost functions
  - single period model
  - deterministic model
  - single product/constant mix
  - static environment
  - only includes quantitative, financial variables.
- In addition to the above assumptions, the model's accuracy depends on our ability to separate costs into their fixed and variable elements with reasonable accuracy.
- Within the **relevant range**, the above assumptions can be taken as reasonable approximations of reality.
- The basic model can readily be extended to accommodate more complex cost and revenue behaviour patterns.

The financial analysis of decisions introduced in this and in the previous chapter will be further developed in Chapter 14, where we will discuss the important concept of *relevant costs and benefits* in relation to decision making.

FURTHER READING

Hirsch, M., *Advanced Management Accounting*, South-Western Publishing, 1994: Chapter 7 explores extensions to the basic cost/volume/profit model.

Warner, A., *The Bottom Line*, Gower Publishing, 1988: Chapter 11 contains an interesting scenario-based explanation of cost/volume/profit analysis.

SELF-TEST QUESTIONS

13.1 For each of the statements which follows, place a tick in the appropriate box to indicate whether it is true or false.

	True	False
(a) The accountants' cost/volume/profit model assumes that total variable cost is constant at all volumes.	☐	☐
(b) The assumption of linearity is consistent with the existence of price elasticity of demand.	☐	☐
(c) Margin of safety is the difference between budgeted and actual sales.	☐	☐
(d) Other things being equal, there will be as many breakeven points as there are levels of total fixed cost.	☐	☐
(e) Relevant range describes the range of output volumes and time period over which the cost/volume/profit model's assumptions are reasonable approximations of reality.	☐	☐
(f) Other things being equal, a reduction in budgeted sales volume will cause a reduction in breakeven point.	☐	☐
(g) Other things being equal, a reduction in contribution per unit will result in an increase in breakeven point.	☐	☐
(h) The weighted average C/S ratio will change in response to alterations in sales mix.	☐	☐

13.2 Z plc makes a single product which it sells for £16 per unit. Fixed costs are £76 800 per month and the product has a contribution to sales ratio of 40%. In a period when actual sales were £224 000, Z plc's margin of safety, in units, was

    A 2000
    B 6000
    C 8000
    D 12 000
    E 14 000

(CIMA, *Operational Cost Accounting*, November 1998)

13.3 Z plc currently sells products Aye, Bee and Cee in equal quantities and at the same selling price per unit. The contribution to sales ratio for product Aye is 40%; for product Bee it is 50% and the total is 48%. If fixed costs are unaffected by mix and are currently 20% of sales, the effect of changing the product mix to

| Aye 40%   Bee 25%   Cee 35% |

is that the total contribution/total sales ratio changes to

    A 27.4%
    B 45.3%
    C 47.4%
    D 48.4%
    E 68.4%

(CIMA, *Operational Cost Accounting*, May 1997)

13.4 Z plc operates a single retail outlet selling direct to the public. Profit statements for August and September 1996 are as follows:

	August £	*September* £
Sales	80 000	90 000
Cost of sales	50 000	55 000
Gross profit	30 000	35 000
Less:		
Selling and distribution	8 000	9 000
Administration	15 000	15 000
Net profit	7 000	11 000

Requirements

(a) Use the high and low points technique to identify the behaviour of
   (i)   cost of sales,
   (ii) selling and distribution costs,
         and
   (iii) administration costs.   (**4 marks**)

(b) Using the graph paper provided, draw a contribution breakeven chart and identify the monthly breakeven sales value, and area of contribution.   (**10 marks**)

(c) Assuming a margin of safety equal to 30% of the breakeven value, calculate Z plc's annual profit.   (**2 marks**)

(d) Z plc is now considering opening another retail outlet selling the same products. Z plc plans to use the same profit margins in both outlets and has estimated that the specific fixed costs of the second outlet will be £100 000 per annum. Z plc also expects that 10% of its annual sales from its existing outlet would transfer to this second outlet if it were to be opened.
    Calculate the annual value of sales required from the new outlet in order to achieve the same annual profit as previously obtained from the single outlet.   (**5 marks**)

(e) Briefly describe the cost accounting requirements of organisations of this type.
                                                                  (**4 marks**)
                                                          (**Total: 25 marks**)

(CIMA, *Operational Cost Accounting*, November 1996)

13.5 (a) The owners of a chain of retail petrol filling stations are considering opening an additional station. Initially one grade of petrol only would be sold and the normal selling price would be £0.44 per litre. Variable charges – cost of petrol, delivery and Excise Duty – total to £0.40 per litre. The fixed costs for a 4-week period are estimated to be:

	£
Rent	2000
Rates on business premises	1000
Wages – 5 people on shifts	3000
Wage-related costs	400
Electricity for continuous opening (24-hour)	300
Other fixed costs	110

After establishing the site for petrol, it is intended at a later stage to develop on the same site a 'motorists' shop' selling the numerous small sundry items often required by motorists. There would be no increase in staff and one cash till only would be operated. Throughout this question, Value Added Tax is ignored.

Requirements

(i) Calculate the breakeven point in number of litres and also in £s for a four-week period if
  (I) the above costs applied;
  (II) the rent was increased by 75%;
  (III) the rent remained at £2000 but commission of £0.002 was given to the employees as a group bonus for every litre sold;
  (IV) the selling price was reduced to £0.43 and no commission was paid (with the rent at £2000). **(8 marks)**

(ii) State how many litres would need to be sold per four-week period at £0.44 if costs were as in the original data (that is, with rent at £2000) to achieve a profit of £700 per week. **(2 marks)**

(iii) Advise the management about the following proposal, assuming sales for a four-week period at a price of £0.44 per litre are normally
  (I) 275 000 litres, and
  (II) 425 000 litres.
  The possibility of opening from 07.00 to 23.00 hours is being considered. The total savings for a four-week period on the original data would be £120 for electricity and one night-shift person paid £200 per week (wage-related costs £25 per week) would no longer be required. Sales would, however, reduce by 50 000 litres over a four-week period.
  Workings should be shown. **(4 marks)**

(iv) Explain what would be required of the accounting system if the 'motorists' shop' idea was proceeded with. **(5 marks)**

(b) Explain briefly what you understand by the terms 'contribution to sales ratio' and 'margin of safety', illustrating your answer with a diagram or graph (which is not expected to be on graph paper). **(6 marks)**

(Total: 25 marks)

(CIMA, *Cost Accounting*, May 1990)

13.6 HG Ltd has estimated fixed costs of £400 000 next year and requires to sell 5000 units of its only product in order to earn profit of £100 000. Actual sales are anticipated to be 8000 for the year. What is the company's breakeven point in units?

    A   500
    B   1000
    C   3000
    D   4000

13.7 Q owns two newsagents' shops and expects total sales revenue next year to be £200 000, with variable costs amounting to 40% of revenue, and total fixed costs of £61 200. In order to achieve the owner's target profit of £82 800, it has been suggested that a limited line of toys should be sold. If this suggestion is implemented, total sales will rise to £230 000 and the higher profit margin on toys will mean that variable cost will fall to 35% of sales. Total fixed cost will rise by £2250 to cover some extra administrative work if the toys are sold.

Requirement

Determine which, if either, of the two sales patterns (i.e. with or without toys) will achieve the owner's target profit of £82 800.

13.8 SKD Ltd is a courier service which undertakes express delivery of small packages. The charge per delivery is based on a combination of the weight of package and the delivery distance. Next year, the charge per kilogramme per kilometre will be £0.50, with an associated variable cost of £0.10. Estimated fixed costs next year will be £400 000.

Requirements

(a) Prepare a profit/volume chart for SKD Ltd, clearly indicating the company's breakeven point in revenue.

(b) On the same profit/volume chart, indicate the effect of an increase in fixed costs of £100 000.

13.9 Modern Wheelbarrows Ltd produce wheelbarrows for sale to garden centres. The company is operating at less than full capacity and wishes to increase profit.

The business has sales of 45 000 units per annum at £14.15 each. Total fixed costs are £175 000. Variable costs per unit are as follows:

            Labour £3.25   Material £4.50   Overhead £2.40

The directors have produced three separate proposals intended to increase profit.
(i) Reduce selling price by £0.50 per unit thereby increasing sales by 5000 units.
(ii) Undertake an advertising campaign costing £32 400 resulting in additional sales of 5,600 units. Selling price would remain at £14.15 per unit.
(iii) Improve the standard of the product by investing in improved production processes resulting in annual additional fixed costs of £35 000. Under the new processes, variable material cost would rise by £1 per unit. Labour and variable overhead costs would decrease by £0.75 and £0.65 per unit respectively. The improved product would sell for £16.50 per unit with expected sales of 33 300 units per annum.

From the above information:

(a) Calculate the current breakeven point in units and the current profit. **(4 marks)**

(b) Calculate the projected breakeven point and profit resulting from each of the three proposals and state which proposal (if any) you would recommend. **(12 marks)**
(Total: 16 marks)

(CIOBS, *Business Accounting*, May 1996)

13.10 The following statistics have been taken from the information system of PZ Limited for the last five years:

	1990	1991	1992	1993	1994
Activity index	100	98	101	103	106
Cost index	100	105	109	113	115
Total costs (£)	70 000	73 080	76 518	79 778	81 880
Sales (£)	100 000				
Profit (£)	30 000				

Notes:
1 The activity index measures the volume of sales/production.
2 The cost index is representative of the costs incurred by PZ Limited and measures the effects of inflation on costs over the five-year period.
3 The activity index for 1995 is forecast as 110.
4 The cost index for 1995 is forecast as 117.

Requirements

(a) (i) Calculate, using the high and low points method, the forecast fixed and variable costs of PZ Limited for 1995. **(8 marks)**

(ii) Prepare a breakeven chart for 1995, assuming that selling prices will be 20% higher than those of 1990. **(10 marks)**

(b) Comment critically on the use of the high and low points method to separate fixed and variable costs **(7 marks)**
(Total: 25 marks)

(CIMA, *Operational Cost Accounting*, November 1995)

CHAPTER 14

Relevant costs and benefits for decision making

Exhibit 14.1 How would the financial implications of this decision be assessed?

INTRODUCTION

In Chapter 1, we described the alternative choice decision process and stressed that cost accounting information plays a vital decision-support role. If management perceives that a decision about a particular aspect of the organisation is necessary, then the financial implications of that decision – its costs and benefits – must be analysed. The decision taken by Sainsbury's in Exhibit 14.1 would have undergone financial analysis along roughly the following lines. The additional costs of operating a self-billing system would have been weighed against the benefits (in terms of potential cost savings) and, assuming the latter exceeded the former, the decision would be financially worth while. The financial implications of decisions can be substantial and it is essential that the manager or managers who have ultimate responsibility for reaching the decision are fully aware of them. Flawed or incomplete understanding of financial data in the context of decision making can result in incorrect decisions being taken, with possibly disastrous results for the organisation concerned.

In this chapter, we will examine the basic accounting technique for analysing decision-related costs and benefits, illustrate its application, discuss possible pitfalls in its use and finally consider a 'special' application of this technique – the limiting factor decision. In Chapter 15, we will extend our discussion of decision analysis to deal with capital investment decisions; the principles described in this chapter are a necessary foundation for the more complex analyses dealt with in the next chapter.

OBJECTIVES

When you have completed this chapter, you will be able to:

- explain the concepts of relevance, sunk cost, incremental cost, directly attributable fixed cost and opportunity cost;
- use these concepts to analyse the costs/benefits relating to simple decision scenarios;
- discuss the potential problems of a relevant costing approach;
- solve single-constraint limiting factor problems – with and without sub-contract option.

THE CONCEPT OF RELEVANCE

Exhibit 14.2 contains a basic decision situation that we will develop throughout this chapter.

Lasertech Ltd

The company, which specialises in production and sale of CD technology for computers, is considering whether to accept an order from a customer for 1000 50× CD-ROM drives. The estimated variable production cost per unit for a 50× CD-ROM is given below:

	£
Direct materials: from stock	4
other	6
Special packaging	2
Variable production cost	12

Additional information relating to the variable production cost is as follows.

1 Direct materials from stock: the £4 per CD-ROM quoted above reflects the cost paid for these materials some two years ago by Lasertech Ltd. There is a sufficient quantity in store to complete the order and, if not used in this way, the materials concerned have no foreseeable alternative use. 'Other' materials would require to be purchased specially if the order is undertaken.

2 Packaging costs will only be incurred if the order is undertaken.

3 The prospective customer has offered a price of £45 per CD-ROM.

Exhibit 14.2 Relevance – basic scenario

An analysis of the costs and benefits relating to the decision in Exhibit 14.2 is essentially a matter of classification:

> **Costs and benefits used in the financial analysis of a decision should be relevant to the decision to which they relate**

If you are to grasp the meaning of 'relevance' as it is applied to decision-related costs and benefits, you must appreciate two fundamental features of all decisions. As we saw in Chapter 1, one of these features is that decisions involve choice between alternative courses of action, and this must be reflected in the way we interpret 'relevance': relevant costs and benefits must relate to the specific alternatives under consideration. There are two alternatives in Exhibit 14.2: 'accept the order' and 'do not accept the order'.

 List all the costs and benefits (i.e. revenue) of each alternative in Exhibit 14.2, so that you obtain a total cost and a total benefit for each course of action.

The total costs and benefits of each course of action are:

		Accept	*Do not accept*
Costs			
		£	£
Direct materials:	stock (1000 CD-ROMs × £4)	4 000	4 000
	other (1000 CD-ROMs × £6)	6 000	nil
Special packaging (1000 CD-ROMs × £2)		2 000	nil
Total cost		12 000	4 000
Benefits			
Revenue (1000 CD-ROMS × £45)		45 000	nil

 Of the total cost and total benefit listed above for each course of action, how much is relevant to the alternatives under consideration?

The difference in total cost is (£12 000 – £4000) = £8000 and this is the relevant cost of undertaking the order – i.e. this course of action costs £8000 *more* than the alternative. You will notice that cost of materials taken from stock is the same under each alternative: i.e. it is unaffected by the decision made and is therefore irrelevant. The costs of special packaging and other materials arise (or do not arise) solely as a result of the decision reached: thus, these costs are relevant. Applying the same type of reasoning to the benefits of each alternative, then the relevant benefit of undertaking is £45 000 (i.e. the *additional* revenue resulting).

✔ *Is undertaking the project financially desirable?*

To assess the financial desirability of undertaking the project, we can easily determine the net relevant cost or net relevant benefit of this course of action:

	£
Relevant benefit of undertaking	45 000
Less Relevant cost of undertaking	8 000
Net relevant benefit of undertaking	37 000

As this course of action yields a net relevant benefit, it is financially desirable. We could have chosen to analyse the relevant costs and benefits of *not* accepting the order:

	£
Relevant benefit of not accepting (additional costs avoided)	8 000
Less Relevant cost of not accepting (sales revenue lost)	45 000
Net relevant cost of not accepting	37 000

Since only two options are being considered, saying that one is financially undesirable ('do not accept') is exactly the same as saying that the other is financially desirable ('accept'). Where the choice is between two options, we need only evaluate one in order to determine which is financially preferable. Our analysis of the data in Exhibit 14.2 provides us with the first part of a definition of relevance:

Relevant costs and benefits must differ between alternatives

Another way to think about this aspect of relevance is that relevant costs and benefits are **incremental costs and benefits**: i.e. they are the *extra* costs and benefits associated with alternative courses of action. We could therefore say that the **incremental cost** of undertaking the project is £8000; and that the **incremental benefit** of undertaking is £45 000, yielding a net incremental benefit of £37 000. (You will recall that we encountered the concept of incremental costs and benefits in Chapter 10 when we discussed 'sell or process further' decisions for joint products.)

In Chapter 1, we described a second feature of decisions which is important to our definition of relevance. Look again at Exhibit 14.2 and the calculations which follow: we said that the cost of materials in stock was irrelevant to the special order decision because it is not an incremental cost.

 Can you think of another reason why the cost of materials in stock is irrelevant to this decision?

The cost of materials already in stock is irrelevant because these have already been bought. A decision about whether or not to accept the order cannot affect this cost. The key point we are making here is that

Decisions relate to the future

It is simply not possible to take a decision which alters the past; this being the case, all past costs and benefits are irrelevant:

Relevant costs and benefits are future costs and benefits

The irrelevance of past ('historic') costs and benefits can occasionally be hard to come to terms with – especially where the amount involved is large. This difficulty can be compounded by the fact that *financial accounting* is largely based on historic transactions.

Items such as the purchase cost of the materials in Exhibit 14.2 are termed **sunk costs**. A sunk cost is defined as:

A past ('historic') cost   OR
A future cost whose payment is committed as the result of a
different decision from the one under consideration

Sunk costs are always irrelevant because they will never be affected by the particular decision being analysed.

 Suppose Lasertech Ltd had signed a binding contract with its supplier for delivery of the materials designated as 'in stock' but that these had not been delivered at the time the special order decision was being analysed. Would this alter the irrelevant status of this cost?

The answer is 'no': although payment for the materials is a future cost, it is a future cost which the firm is committed to incurring because of another decision – i.e. about purchasing the materials. Assuming there is no way that Lasertech Ltd can withdraw from the contract with its supplier, the material cost is *committed* (i.e. is a sunk cost) and is therefore irrelevant.

Everything we have just said about the irrelevance of sunk costs is equally true of benefits: all past benefits and any future benefits the receipt of which is unrelated to the decision under consideration are irrelevant. Thus, Lasertech Ltd's revenue from routine business while the order is being fulfilled is irrelevant. Although it is a future benefit, it does not arise as a consequence of the decision about the order, but as the result of another decision (or decisions) – i.e. whether/what routine business should be undertaken. Exhibit 14.3 contains some further information about the special order.

Lasertech Ltd: use of owned equipment for special order

Acceptance of the special order for 50× CD-ROMs will require the use of some of the company's equipment, which was bought two years ago for £50 000, has an expected life of five years and is depreciated at £10 000 per year. There is sufficient spare capacity on this equipment to undertake the order without disrupting routine work.

Exhibit 14.3 Use of owned equipment on special order

 What is the relevant cost to Lasertech Ltd of using its equipment on the special order?

The relevant cost of using the equipment is zero. The original cost is historic, hence a sunk cost and irrelevant. Depreciation is likewise irrelevant; in essence, depreciation is merely an apportionment of the equipment's historic cost to each year of its useful life – and if the historic cost is irrelevant, so must apportionment thereof be irrelevant. In addition, being an apportionment, depreciation is not a cash flow: relevant costs and benefits must be **cash flows.** You should be careful to exclude all non-cash items from the financial analysis of decisions; this is particularly important as management accounting abounds in non-cash terminology such as depreciation, absorption and apportionment. The rule is that

> **Cost apportionments, overhead absorbed and depreciation are always irrelevant as they are non-cash items**

We discussed the principles of cost apportionment and overhead absorption procedures in Chapter 5. If you review our earlier discussion of these topics, you will see that even the most logically defensible basis for apportioning or absorbing overhead costs is open to question, and for this reason is unsuitable for use in a decision analysis, which should be based on the most objective figures available. You should never allow yourself to be misled into treating non-cash items as relevant merely because a decision scenario contains a great deal of information about, e.g. the bases used to apportion common costs, or the method used to calculate depreciation. Such information may be readily available, but availability is no guarantee of relevance.

Confusion can sometimes arise in situations where a decision affects the amount of overhead *absorbed*. From our discussion in Chapter 5, you will recall that overhead absorption is essentially a series of cost apportionments with progressively smaller cost objectives, culminating with the cost unit (via the overhead absorption rate). You will also recall that overhead is generally absorbed on a predetermined basis, so the amount of overhead absorbed is unlikely to equate with overhead *incurred* (except by chance). In other words, any increase/decrease in overhead absorbed which may result from a decision cannot automatically be taken to imply an increase in the overhead incurred. If an overhead cost is to be relevant, it must be a future cash flow as must any other relevant cost or benefit.

Lasertech Ltd: overhead implications of special order

Company policy is to absorb both fixed and variable production overhead on the basis of direct labour hours, the absorption rates being, respectively, £20 and £10 per hour. Management has estimated that each of the 1000 50× CD-ROMs will require 0.5 hours of direct labour. For the period during which the order would be undertaken, management expects that fixed production overhead will amount to £30 000 and that the number of direct labour hours worked on routine business will be 1500. Should the order be accepted, £5000 of additional production overhead will be incurred as a result of the need for Lasertech Ltd to hire specialised testing equipment.

Exhibit 14.4 Relevance/irrelevance of overheads

 What is the total production overhead incurred *for each of the 'accept' and 'do not accept' options?*

The total overhead incurred under each option is as follows:

	Accept £	Do not accept £
Fixed overhead:		
Estimate for the period	30 000	30 000
Hire of testing equipment	5 000	nil
Variable overhead:		
Special order		
(1000 CD-ROMs × 0.5 hours × £10 per hour)	5 000	nil
Routine work (1500 hours × £10 per hour)	15 000	15 000
Total production incurred	55 000	45 000

 What is the relevant (or incremental) overhead cost of a decision to accept the proposed order?

The relevant overhead cost of undertaking the proposed project will be (£55 000 – £45 000) = £10 000.

The £20 per direct labour hour for fixed overhead *absorbed* has been totally omitted from the calculation, as it is not a cash flow. Although undertaking the order will increase the fixed overhead absorbed by (500 hours × £20), this will not affect the estimated future cash flow of £30 000 – i.e. the estimate of fixed overhead to be *incurred* for the period.

Inclusion of the variable overhead of £10 per hour may seem odd in light of what we have just said about overhead absorbed; but you should remember that this is a variable cost – if the number of direct labour hours increases, so will the amount of variable overhead *incurred*. Assuming that the rate of £10 per hour is an accurate reflection of the future cash flow, then the extra variable overhead incurred will be the same as the extra variable overhead absorbed. This is merely a feature of variable overhead – it does not invalidate our rule that only future cash flows are relevant.

However, you should be careful not to fall into the trap of treating variable costs as relevant and fixed costs as irrelevant – i.e. you should not confuse cost behaviour with relevance. It is quite possible for a fixed cost to be relevant, always providing it is a future cash flow which differs between alternatives.

For example, the additional £5000 fixed overhead that will be incurred as a result of hiring the testing equipment is relevant (even although it is a fixed cost). Fixed costs of this type are termed **directly attributable fixed costs** – i.e. fixed costs that are incurred as a direct consequence of the decision under consideration.

A FULL DEFINITION OF RELEVANCE

From the forgoing discussion, we can obtain a full definition of relevance:

Relevant costs and benefits are future cash flows which differ between alternatives

In order to qualify as relevant, all three criteria in this definition must be met: i.e. the item being examined must be a future item *and* a cash flow *and* must differ between alternatives. An item which meets only one (or two) of these criteria is irrelevant, such as the extra fixed overhead absorbed by Lasertech Ltd if the project is undertaken. The amount of fixed overhead absorbed undoubtedly differs between alternatives, and is also a future item, but fails the cash flow test and hence is irrelevant.

APPLYING THE DEFINITION IN ANALYSIS

As with so many other aspects of management accounting, there is no 'set' format for presenting analyses of relevant costs and benefits. What *is* required is rigorous application to all financial data of the three criteria contained in the definition above. When we analysed the data from Exhibit 14.4, we extracted the relevant overhead cost by comparing the total overhead cost of each course of action, the difference being the relevant amount. This is perfectly acceptable, providing we list *all* the costs and benefits for *each* alternative.

However, this approach may become cumbersome to operate: irrelevant items (such as the £30 000 fixed overhead cost in Exhibit 14.4) will be listed under each alternative. This could cause confusion and may lead to errors where a great many irrelevant items are concerned, or where more than two options are being considered. In addition, we can argue that this 'total' approach is illogical, since the aim of the exercise is to isolate the relevant items.

It is possible to adopt a much more direct approach to analysis by employing the criteria contained in our definition of relevance to include every item which satisfies all three criteria and to exclude every item which fails one or more. Exhibit 14.5 presents all the data from Exhibits 14.2, 14.3 and 14.4 relating to Lasertech Ltd's decision. At first glance, you may find Exhibit 14.5 rather offputting – but remember that it is just a 'welding together' of the fragmentary information we have already encountered.

Lasertech Ltd: the full scenario

The company, which specialises in production and sale of Cd technology for computers, is considering whether to accept an order from a customer for 1000 50× CD-ROM drives. The estimated variable production cost per unit for a 50× CD-ROM is given below:

		£
Direct materials:	from stock	4
	other	6
Special packaging		2
Variable production cost		12

Additional information relating to the variable production cost is as follows.

1 Direct materials from stock: the £4 per CD-ROM quoted above reflects the cost paid for these materials some two years ago by Lasertech Ltd. There is a sufficient quantity in store to complete the order and, if not used in this way, the materials concerned have no foreseeable alternative use. 'Other' materials would require to be purchased specially if the order is undertaken.
2 Packaging costs will only be incurred if the order is undertaken.
3 The prospective customer has offered a price of £45 per CD-ROM.

Acceptance of the special order will require use of some of the company's equipment, which was bought two years ago for £50 000, has an expected life of five years and is depreciated at £10 000 per year. There is sufficient spare capacity on this equipment to undertake the order without disrupting routine work.

Company policy is to absorb both fixed and variable production overhead on the basis of direct labour hours, the absorption rates being, respectively, £20 and £10 per hour. Management has estimated that each CD-ROM will require 0.5 hours of direct labour. For the period during which the order would be undertaken, management expects that fixed production overhead will amount to £30 000 and that the number of direct labour hours worked on routine business will be 1500. Should the order be accepted, £5000 of additional production overhead will be incurred as a result of the need for Lasertech Ltd to hire specialised testing equipment.

Exhibit 14.5 Relevance – the full scenario thus far

 Apply the three criteria contained in the definition of relevance in order to determine which financial items in Exhibit 14.5 are relevant. You may find it helpful to draw up a table with the following headings:

Item	Future?	Cash?	Differs?	Amount

For every item listed, place a tick in the column for each criterion which that item meets. Only items with a tick in all three columns are relevant.

Table 14.1 Criteria for relevance applied

Item	Future?	Cash?	Differs?	Amount
				£
Direct materials:				
In stock		✓		4 000
Other	✓	✓	✓	6 000
Packaging	✓	✓	✓	2 000
Revenue	✓	✓	✓	45 000
Owned equipment:				
Cost to buy		✓		50 000
Depreciation	✓			10 000
Fixed overhead:				
Period's estimate	✓	✓		30 000
Additional	✓	✓	✓	5 000
Absorbed	✓		✓	
Variable overhead:				
Routine work	✓	✓		15 000
Additional	✓	✓	✓	5 000

Table 14.1 tests each financial item from Exhibit 14.5 against the three criteria contained in the definition of relevance.

It is not absolutely necessary to prepare a table such as 14.1 in order to perform a relevant/irrelevant analysis. However, such an approach should encourage you to apply all three criteria to every item of financial data in a decision scenario.

 Of the financial data identified in Table 14.1, which items are relevant costs and which are relevant benefits of the 'accept' option?

There is only one relevant benefit of undertaking the order, namely the £45 000 receivable from the client. The relevant costs are: 'other' direct materials, special packaging, extra fixed overhead relating to hiring the testing equipment and the additional variable overhead relating to the order.

 Using the information above, and referring to earlier workings if necessary, determine the net relevant cost or net relevant benefit of undertaking the project.

The net relevant benefit of undertaking is:

	£	£
Relevant benefit		
Payment by client		45 000
Relevant costs		
'Other' direct materials	6 000	
Special packaging	2 000	
Additional fixed overhead	5 000	
Additional variable overhead	5 000	18 000
Net relevant benefit		27 000

As this course of action has a net relevant benefit, it is the better on financial grounds.

Had we chosen to analyse the net relevant cost/net relevant benefit of **not** undertaking the project, we would have:

Relevant benefits (costs avoided)	£	£
'Other' direct materials	6 000	
Special packaging	2 000	
Additional fixed overhead	5 000	
Additional variable overhead	5 000	18 000
Relevant cost (revenue lost)		
Payment by client		45 000
Net relevant cost		27 000

As we said earlier, where two courses of action are possible, we need consider the financial implications of only one in order to determine the preferred option.

What does the £27 000 net relevant benefit of accepting represent? It indicates the *extra* profit that Lasertech Ltd will earn if the order is undertaken. This should make sense, since the £27 000 net relevant benefit is calculated as the extra benefit less the extra costs involved in this course of action. Similarly, the net relevant cost of £27 000 associated with not undertaking the order represents the loss of profit or reduction in potential profit resulting from pursuing this course of action.

OPPORTUNITY COST

We must now introduce a final concept associated with financial analysis of decisions – that of **opportunity cost**. So far, all the relevant costs we have encountered have been **out-of-pocket costs**: i.e. additional costs which require to be paid if a particular course of action is pursued. Opportunity costs are different – they are *implicit* in most decision-making situations. What this means is that, if we pursue one course of action, we may be unable to pursue another course of action and this inability may involve a loss of benefit.

Lasertech Ltd: labour requirement for special order

If the special order for 1000 50× CD-ROMs is undertaken, a total of 500 direct labour hours will be required; suitably skilled labour is in very short supply, and, if used on the order, will require to be transferred from routine work, thereby losing Lasertech Ltd contribution of £8 per labour hour thus transferred. The employees concerned are permanently employed by the company and are paid £10 per hour.

Exhibit 14.6 Opportunity cost

 What is the relevant cost to Lasertech Ltd of transferring 500 direct labour hours from routine work to the special order?

The £10 per hour paid to the employees concerned is a sunk cost – Lasertech Ltd is committed to paying this amount per hour, regardless of whether the order is accepted or not – and is thus irrelevant. The potential lost contribution from routine work is a future cash flow and will differ between alternatives – and is therefore a relevant cost of undertaking the proposed project. However, a little care is needed in determining the relevant cost involved. Assuming that the (irrelevant) £10 per hour labour cost has been deducted from selling price in order to arrive at the £8 per hour contribution quoted in Exhibit 14.6, we get:

	£
Lost contribution per hour	8
Add Irrelevant labour cost	10
Relevant cost per hour	18

If we did not add back the £10 per hour labour cost, we would be suggesting, wrongly, that it is relevant. It is essential, in analysing this sort of situation, that we apply the concept of relevance consistently. If we say that the £10 per hour will be paid regardless of the decision (i.e. that it is irrelevant), then we cannot logically treat it as relevant with regard to one of the specific consequences of that decision (i.e. loss of contribution on routine work).

The total loss of benefit resulting from acceptance of the order is (500 hours × £18) = £9000, which is an **opportunity cost** of undertaking the order. Opportunity cost is defined as:

> **The benefit forgone as a result of pursuing one course of action rather than pursuing the best alternative course of action**

Since decisions involve choice between alternatives and since opportunity costs specifically reflect this aspect of decisions, opportunity costs are always relevant.

It may be necessary to determine the 'best alternative course of action' in order to obtain the amount of an opportunity cost.

Lasertech Ltd: direct labour – additional information

The 500 direct labour hours required for the special order could either be used on routine work, earning a contribution of £8 per hour, or could be used to undertake some maintenance work, thereby making a net saving (i.e. after deduction of the labour cost per hour) in payments to an external contractor of £5 per hour.

Exhibit 14.7 Opportunity cost – determining the 'best alternative'

 What is the 'best alternative use' of the 500 direct labour hours compared to the special order?

In this case, both £18 and (£5 + £10) per hour are *potentially* relevant; the best alternative use of the hours is on routine work as this will earn Lasertech Ltd are additional contribution of £9000 (compared to 500 hours × £15 = £7500 cost savings obtained from use on maintenance work). The opportunity cost of using the 500 labour hours on the order is thus £9000. You may have been tempted to suggest an opportunity cost of (£9000 – £7500) = £1500: this is incorrect because inclusion of £9000 and £7500 implies that there are two 'best alternative' courses of action. There is, however, only one 'best alternative', as it is not possible to use the 500 hours on routine work *and* on maintenance.

It can also happen that an opportunity 'benefit' results from a course of action. Suppose direct labour had excessive idle time and if 500 hours were not used on the special order, an employee were to be faced with redundancy. In these circumstances, using the 500 hours on the order could save Lasertech Ltd the cost of a redundancy payment – a benefit of undertaking the order.

A COMPREHENSIVE EXAMPLE

You will realise that the variety of different decisions which an organisation may need to take is potentially extremely wide. For this reason, we have adopted what might be termed a *contingency approach* to the financial analysis of decisions: i.e. the development of a 'general rule' for identification of relevant costs and benefits which can be applied to any decision:

Future cash flows which differ between alternatives

It will therefore be useful at this stage to apply our 'general rule' to a quite different scenario to underline the fact that this approach works regardless of the specifics of a particular decision. The example in Exhibit 14.8 combines all the individual facets of relevance which we have discussed in relation to Lasertech Ltd.

VK Ltd: dust extraction system

VK Ltd operates a timber sawmill in a local town. Following a recent visit by the Health & Safety Inspectorate, the company has been required to install a dust extraction system. This could either be done by VK Ltd's own staff, or by subcontracting the work to BPM Ltd. The following information is available:

1 *Consultants' Report* VK Ltd has employed consultants to advise on the most suitable extraction system. Their report, which has already been received, will form the basis of installation, whether undertaken by VK Ltd's own staff or by the subcontractor. The cost of this report is £4500 and the related invoice will be paid in the near future.

2 *Subcontractor Quotation* BPM Ltd has quoted a firm price of £70 000 which covers supply of the extraction equipment, installation and all associated work.

3 *Cost of Extraction Equipment* If VK Ltd's own staff undertake installation, the extraction equipment and sundry materials needed for installation will need to be purchased at a total cost of £42 000.

4 *VK Ltd Staff Requirement* VK Ltd presently employs staff with the necessary skills to undertake installation. All the staff concerned are employed on long-term contracts and are paid an average rate of £6 per hour. It is estimated that 800 hours' work will be needed by these employees to install the extraction equipment. Of the 800 hours, 200 will be worked in overtime which would not otherwise be necessary; overtime working is paid at an hourly rate of time and one half.

5 *Interruption to Output* Installation of the extraction equipment by VK Ltd's own staff will cause an interruption to normal operation of the sawmill which will result in lost sales of 4000 square metres of timber. The average selling price and unit cost per square metre of timber is:

	£	£
Selling price		10.50
Direct materials	0.90	
Direct labour	0.70	
Fixed overhead	6.20	7.80
Profit		2.70

The direct labour cost per square metre refers to the cost of permanent employees on long-term contracts and the direct materials have still to be bought.

6 *Supervision*   VK Ltd can use one of its own supervisors on the installation work; this individual is presently extremely busy and is paid £8 per hour. If he supervises installation work, VK Ltd will need to employ another supervisor on a temporary basis at a cost of £3000.

Exhibit 14.8 Relevance – a comprehensive example

  Which items of financial data in Exhibit 14.8 are relevant? Adopt the same tabular approach as for Exhibit 14.5.

Table 14.2 is the full analysis of VK Ltd's data into relevant/irrelevant.

Table 14.2 Results of test for relevance

Item	Future?	Cash?	Differs?	Amount
				£
Consultants' report	✓	✓		4 500
Subcontractor quotation	✓	✓	✓	70 000
Cost of extraction equipment	✓	✓	✓	42 000
Labour cost of own staff:				
600 hours (normal time)	✓	✓		3 600
200 hours (overtime)	✓	✓	✓	1 800
Interruption to output:				
Lost revenue	✓	✓	✓	42 000
Direct material costs	✓	✓	✓	3 600
Direct labour costs	✓	✓		2 800
Fixed overhead costs	✓		✓	24 800
Supervision:				
Existing supervisor	✓	✓		6 400
Temporary supervisor	✓	✓	✓	3 000

  Of the items identified in Table 14.2 as being relevant, which are relevant costs and which are relevant benefits of using VK Ltd's own staff to undertake the installation work?

If VK Ltd uses its own staff for installation, there will be two relevant benefits: the subcontractor's quotation (a cost avoided) and the direct materials associated with the lost sales (a cost avoided). The relevant costs are: cost of extraction equipment, overtime working, lost sales due to interruption and the temporary supervisor.

 What is the total opportunity cost associated with the lost sales (i.e. of losing the sales of 4000 square metres)?

Per metre, the opportunity cost of the lost sales is:

	£
Revenue lost	10.50
Less Associated costs saved – direct materials	0.90
Opportunity cost	9.60

giving a total opportunity cost of (4000 @ £9.60) = £38 400.

 Remembering that the direct materials' cost saving associated with the lost sales is included in the total opportunity cost above, what is the net relevant cost or net relevant benefit to VK Ltd of using its own staff to install the extraction equipment? Advise the company on this basis.

The net relevant cost of the identified course of action is:

Relevant benefit	£	£
Payment to subcontractor avoided		70 000
Relevant costs		
Extraction equipment	42 000	
Overtime (200 hours × £6 × 1.5)	1 800	
Opportunity cost of lost sales	38 400	
Temporary supervisor	3 000	85 200
Net relevant cost		15 200

On a financial basis, it would therefore be better to subcontract installation work, as using the company's own staff yields a net relevant cost.

Had we analysed the relevant costs and benefits of subcontracting, the result would have been a net relevant benefit of £15 200. You may wish to check that this is so.

There is one vital point to make about analyses such as that which we have just completed: as a preliminary, it is wise to assure ourselves that we are isolating costs and benefits which are relevant to the *correct decision*. Items which are relevant to one decision will not necessarily be relevant to another – i.e. *relevance is decision-specific*. In the last example, the decision was 'who should undertake installation' *not* 'should installation occur'. If we had incorrectly identified the decision as the latter rather than the former, we would almost certainly have misclassified some costs and benefits, which may have resulted in the wrong decision being taken.

RELEVANT COSTING: POTENTIAL PROBLEMS

We have discussed and illustrated application of the relevance concept at some length and you should appreciate its logic in light of the essential features of decisions which it mirrors. However, a cautionary note must be sounded. Relevant costing is not a 'cure-all' device and possible pitfalls in its application must be appreciated if the technique is to be used to good effect; we discuss these below.

1 Short-term, 'one-off' decisions

If you examine the decision faced by Lasertech Ltd, you will see that it is a 'one-off' decision of a short-term nature and that its financial implications are relatively small. In our analysis, we ignored as irrelevant some substantial costs (e.g. the £30 000 fixed overhead).

 Can you see a potential danger in this approach?

Suppose the decision related to routine business. The danger is that we may be tempted to continue treating items such as the fixed overhead cost as irrelevant, which could result in understatement of costs. Think of the impact of a major understatement of costs on breakeven calculations of the sort we performed in Chapter 13: other things being equal, the breakeven volume will be understated and the margin of safety over-stated. Such a situation may induce a false sense of security about the profitability of the estimated sales volume and may even (in an extreme case) result in sales effort being concentrated on achieving a loss-making volume. In addition, an underestimation of costs may mean artificially low selling prices where these are derived to any significant extent from cost; this may be desirable in certain specific circumstances, but is not consistent with long-term profitability, which requires that all costs be covered.

You may feel that the danger we have just described is so serious as to render our relevant cost/benefit analyses worthless. However, this danger is not an inherent feature of the accounting technique; it stems from a lack of appreciation of the different decisions involved. Decisions like the one about Lasertech Ltd's special order are non-routine and short term, and this is reflected in the associated relevant costs/benefits. A decision about routine business is rather different in nature. It is routine and is likely to have longer-term implications: this difference should be reflected in the associated relevant costs/benefits. For example, the £30 000 fixed overhead which we treated as irrelevant in our earlier analysis would certainly be relevant to a decision about, say, the sales volume required in order to earn a target profit during the period under consideration. This is simply another manifestation of our earlier statement that it is necessary to identify the correct decision before undertaking a classification of costs/benefits into relevant/irrelevant. And, as we shall see in the next chapter, the concept of relevance is equally important in evaluating decisions with long-term implications.

2 Obtaining financial data

In practice, it may be difficult to obtain financial data about alternative courses of action; it may even be difficult to identify the alternatives available. Identifying and quantifying opportunity costs can be particularly problematic. Can we identify the 'best alternative course of action'? And quantify the 'benefit lost' because we may not pursue this best alternative? The danger here is that financial data may degenerate into subjective guesswork by managers – and no analytical technique (relevant costing or any other) is superior to the quality of input data.

However, we must accept that, since decisions are future oriented, related financial data can only be estimated, and an analysis based on such estimates can never be 100% accurate (except by merest chance). This need not prove an insurmountable problem, providing the estimates are as objective and reasonable as possible. If assumptions need to be made, these should be explicit and reasonable and uncertainty about estimates can readily be incorporated into the analysis – as it was in the last chapter when we introduced sensitivity analysis. (For other approaches, see Further Reading at the end of this chapter.)

3 Qualitative factors

The technique we have described in this chapter deals only with a decision's financial implications. These are undoubtedly very important, but it would be rash to base decisions on financial considerations alone. Other, non-financial factors may be equally important as, or more important than, the net relevant cost/benefit of a decision: e.g. qualitative factors such as the timing of a decision, the reaction of competitors, or the skills of the workforce may have a major bearing on the final decision. There may be a conflict between qualitative and financial considerations for the decision-making manager. For example, managerial performance evaluation based on keeping actual costs within budget may pressurise a manager into placing too much emphasis on financial factors and too little on qualitative.

 Suggest some qualitative factors that Lasertech Ltd may need to consider before reaching a final decision about undertaking the special order.

Possible non-financial factors include:

- Can the order be completed on time? what are the penalties for late completion?
- Will the order lead to further work from the same client?
- How will existing clients react if undertaking the order has an adverse impact on their work?

You may have suggested different qualitative factors from those above, you may have thought of a few more; the important point is that factors of this sort are vitally important to the ultimate decision. For example, if undertaking the order would lead to a large volume of future work for the same customer, it might be worth undertaking the project even if it has a net relevant cost, the aim being to gain the additional future work on which a profit will be earned.

4 The 'acceptance' problem

Persuading some managers to accept the business rationale of the relevance concept can cause problems. The 'acceptance' problem for the manager may be due to a combination of two reasons:

- Accounting records are conventionally based on historic (i.e. past) data; this stems from a need for objective evidence of the figures recorded in the form of verifiable transactions. The concept of relevance, with its emphasis on the future, could be viewed as too subjective compared to the accounting status quo and as a concept to be resisted for that reason.

- If, in the past, resources have been committed to a course of action which is currently under review, there may be a feeling among managers that the original course of action must be pursued. This could manifest itself in expression of opinions such as 'we've already spent £2 million on this project, therefore we *must* proceed with it'. Such opinions could arise partly from a misunderstanding about the future orientation of decisions (along with their financial evaluation) and partly from a fear that the concept of relevance represents an attempt to use hindsight to 'fix blame' for wrong decisions taken in the past.

Overcoming the 'acceptance' problem (where it exists) is basically a matter of understanding that the purpose of these analyses is to provide useful information to help managers to manage – in this instance, to provide information which will help managers to reach sound decisions.

5 Financing of decisions

A distinction needs to be drawn between the financial implications of *pursuing* a particular course of action and the method of *financing* that course of action. In Exhibit 14.8, VK Ltd was faced with a decision which involved some quite large cash outlays. Although our analysis demonstrated that, on financial grounds, the company should subcontract installation, it did not indicate where the necessary £70 000 payment to the subcontractor was to be found. How a course of action is to be financed is a different decision with different relevant costs/benefits. You should therefore not assume that the net relevant benefit arising from a course of action also means that financial resources to pursue that course are available.

We will now extend our decision analysis to deal with limiting factors.

LIMITING FACTOR DECISIONS

Skill shortage 'holds back' technology companies

A persistent shortage of skilled staff is holding back the growth of European technology companies, according to research published today.

More than half of all privately owned European technology companies surveyed by PwC, the professional services group, said a shortage of quality staff was the main barrier to planned growth . . .

Pressure to attract and retain staff is forcing companies to offer above-average salary increases. Half of those taking part in the survey had increased average salaries for permanent staff by between 6 and 15% in the past year, while some had awarded increases of more than 20% . . .

Source: Peter Thal Larsen, *Financial Times*, 24 May 1999. Reprinted with permission.

Exhibit 14.9 Shortage of skilled employees – a typical limiting factor

A **limiting factor** – such as the potential shortage of skilled workers referred to in Exhibit 14.9 – is a constraint; these vary from legal and social constraints to financial and resource constraints. We are concerned here with the two latter types, but legal and social constraints should never be ignored in decision making. For example, there is no benefit in undertaking a possibly complex and time-consuming financial analysis if there is only one possible course of action which must be followed in order to comply with legal requirements such as those contained in Health and Safety legislation.

For a commercial organisation, sales demand will almost invariably impose a limit on activity. The situation would be simple enough if limiting factors were restricted to sales demand: sales effort would be channelled into maximising sales of the most profitable product(s)/service(s). As we saw in Chapter 12, contribution analysis can be a useful aid in assessing the relative profitability of different products/services.

The problem is that demand is often not the only limiting factor, and it may not even enter into consideration for non-profit organisations.

 Can you suggest three *financial or resource-related limiting factors other than sales demand which may be faced by an organisation?*

There are many possibilities; you may have thought of some of the following:

1 shortage of suitably skilled staff
2 shortage of appropriate materials
3 lack of available funding
4 insufficient space within premises.

If constraints of the type described above can be overcome, a financial analysis of the options available for overcoming them will be needed, involving assessment of the related relevant costs and benefits. However, it may not be possible – at least in the short term – to recruit more staff, or to raise additional funding. In fact, constraints may be linked so that, for example, additional staff cannot be recruited partly because extra funding cannot be raised. In some cases, the problem may be more than short term: for example, increasingly strict cash limits are a major concern for public sector and non-profit organisations.

Where limiting factors other than demand exist, the implication is that demand will exceed the ability to supply. And if resource constraints cannot be overcome, we must have a technique which allows us to 'make the best of a bad situation' – at least in financial terms. This means using the limited resources available so that demand is satisfied as far as possible and in such a way that profit is maximised (or cost minimised).

We shall now consider a typical limiting factor situation and illustrate a method of financial analysis that attempts to achieve this twofold aim. Exhibit 14.10 contains the basic data.

The problem faced by Lasertech Ltd is that the limitation on the number of direct labour hours next period may mean that potential demand cannot be fully satisfied.

 Determine the number of labour hours required to produce one unit of each product and confirm or refute the suggestion that 7900 labour hours is insufficient to fully satisfy next period's demand.

Labour hours per unit are:

$$\frac{\text{Labour cost per unit}}{\text{£10 per labour hour}}$$

Lasertech Ltd: product range

The company routinely produces a range of four products, for each of which information is provided below in respect of next period.

Product		24× CD-ROM	32× CD-ROM	40× CD-ROM	DVD- ROM
Estimated demand for the period (units)		7000	10 000	8000	6000
Selling price per unit		£45.00	£80.00	£100.00	£120.00
		£	£	£	£
Costs per unit:	direct labour @ £10 per hour	2.50	3.00	5.00	7.50
	direct materials	8.00	15.00	25.00	30.00
	packaging	2.00	2.00	2.00	2.00
	variable production overhead	2.50	3.00	5.00	7.50
	fixed production overhead	5.00	6.00	10.00	15.00
	administration overhead	10.00	10.00	10.00	10.00
	selling overhead	1.00	2.00	2.00	3.00
Total cost		31.00	41.00	59.00	75.00

Notes
1 Direct labour is to be treated as a variable cost.
2 Administration overhead is wholly fixed.
3 Selling overhead is a variable cost.
4 Direct labour is limited to 7900 hours next period.

Exhibit 14.10 A limiting factor problem

This gives 0.25, 0.3, 0.5 and 0.75 hours per unit of 24×, 32×, 40× and DVD CD-ROMs respectively. In order to fully satisfy next period's demand, the total labour hours required are:

24× CD-ROMs	7000 units × 0.25 hours	1 750
32× CD-ROMs	10 000 units × 0.3 hours	3 000
40× CD-ROMs	8000 units × 0.5 hours	4 000
DVD-ROMs	6000 units × 0.75 hours	4 500
		13 250

This confirms that there will be insufficient direct labour hours to fully satisfy next period's demand. If demand cannot be fully satisfied, we need to decide which products should be concentrated on so that the greatest profit can be earned in the circumstances. In other words, we need a criterion to rank the products in order of preference, given the limitation in labour hours.

 Based on the information in Exhibit 14.10, are the fixed overheads relevant to this decision?

The fixed overheads are irrelevant: although they may be future cash flows, in amount they will be unaffected by this decision – i.e. they will not differ between alternatives, thus failing one of the criteria for relevance described earlier in the chapter. Since fixed overheads are irrelevant (the same amount is incurred irrespective of the decision), the higher the amount of total contribution earned, the higher the resultant profit.

 What is the contribution per unit of each of the four products?

Bearing in mind that contribution is (selling price – *all* variable costs), unit contributions for each type of product are:

	24× CD ROM £	32× CD ROM £	40× CD ROM £	DVD-ROM £
Selling price per unit	45.00	80.00	100.00	120.00
Less Variable costs per unit:				
Direct labour	2.50	3.00	5.00	7.50
Direct materials	8.00	15.00	25.00	30.00
Packaging	2.00	2.00	2.00	2.00
Variable production overhead	2.50	3.00	5.00	7.50
Selling overhead	1.00	2.00	2.00	3.00
	16.00	25.00	39.00	50.00
Contribution per unit	29.00	55.00	61.00	70.00

We are now faced with a problem of *ranking*: i.e. which products should be produced and in what quantities in order to obtain the best possible total contribution? It is at this stage that we must make allowance for the limiting factor: we want to obtain maximum total contribution given *the limitation in labour hours*. We should therefore concentrate scarce processing hours on those products having the highest *contribution per labour hour*. Once we have determined each product's contribution per labour hour, we can produce a ranking in terms of financial desirability. Contribution per hour is easily calculated:

$$\frac{\text{Contribution per unit}}{\text{Direct labour hours per unit}}$$

 Determine each product's contribution per labour hour; rank the four products on this basis in descending order.

The contributions per processing hour and product rankings are:

	24× CD ROM	32× CD ROM	40× CD ROM	DVD-ROM
Contribution per unit	£29.00	£55.00	£61.00	£70.00
Labour hours per unit	0.25	0.30	0.50	0.75
Contribution per hour	£116.00	£183.33	£122.00	£93.33
Ranking	III	I	II	IV

Now that we have ranked the four products in order of financial desirability, we can prepare a production plan, remembering that there is no point in producing more of a product than we are able to sell. So the sales maxima in Exhibit 14.10 will place an upper limit on output of each product. The production plan is as follows:

Maximum labour hours	7900
Produce 10 000 32× CD-ROMs – uses (10 000 × 0.3) hours	3000
Hours remaining for other products	4900
Produce 8000 40× CD-ROMs – uses (8000 × 0.5) hours	4000
Hours remaining for other products	900

The 24× CD-ROM is the next best-ranked product; maximum demand next period is estimated at 7000 units, each of which requires 0.25 labour hours. We cannot produce 6600, which requires 1750 hours, and must restrict output of this product to utilise the remaining 900 hours. We will therefore be able to produce

$$\frac{900 \text{ hours}}{0.25 \text{ hours per unit}} = 3600 \text{ units of 24× CD-ROMs}$$

The limited availability of labour hours means that some demand for 24× CD-ROMs will be unsatisfied next period, and no DVD-ROMs will be produced/sold. Given the constraint on labour hours, maximum contribution will be:

	£
3600 24× CD-ROMs @ £29	104 400
10 000 32× CD-ROMs @ £55	550 000
8000 40× CD-ROMs @ £61	488 000
Total contribution	1 142 400

This will fully utilise the available direct labour hours.

 Would it be possible to improve the £1 142 400 contribution above by selling DVD-ROMs and reducing sales of (say) 24× CD-ROMs, assuming no change to the labour hour constraint or to any other factor?

At first glance, increasing sales of DVD-ROMs might appear worth while, since the contribution *per unit* is higher than that earned for 24× CD-ROMs. But this ignores the fact that, in order to sell one additional DVD-ROM, we will lose sales of 24× CD-ROMs:

	£
Extra contribution on one DVD-ROM	70
Contribution lost on sales 24× CD-ROMs	
$\left(\dfrac{0.75}{0.25} \times £29\right)$	87
Net loss of contribution	17

Each additional DVD-ROM requires 0.75 labour hours to be removed from production/sale of 24× CD-ROMs, each of which uses only 0.25 hours (i.e. sales of three 24× CD-ROMs will be lost).

You should note, however, that our analysis is based solely on optimising contribution/profit – i.e. it ignores qualitative factors.

State two qualitative factors which will have a critical bearing on the ultimate decision by Lasertech Ltd.

The company would be extremely ill advised to implement the production plan indicated above without careful consideration of the reaction of both customers and competitors: sales of 24× CD-ROMs will be severely reduced next period, and no DVD-ROMs will be produced/sold. This could result in lost custom which may not be recovered, not only for the two products just mentioned, but also for the other products – especially if Lasertech Ltd's competitors take advantage of the situation by actively trying to expand their own sales.

 Our financial analysis is based on certain assumptions which we encountered in the previous chapter. What are they?

Our analysis rests on five key assumptions:

1 certainty exists: e.g. about sales maxima for products and constraint identification/quantification;
2 revenue is linear: the selling price per unit of each product is the same at all volumes under consideration;
3 costs are linear: variable cost per unit of each product is constant and total fixed costs are unchanged in amount;
4 production = sales; if significant stocks exist at the start of the period under review, it would be possible to reduce (or even eliminate) any shortfall in supply relative to demand – such a situation would require our basic technique to be amended slightly to allow for the reduction in sales maxima which would result from sales being made from stock;
5 sales of different products/services are independent: i.e. restricting output/sales of one or more product(s)/service(s) will not have a 'knock-on' effect on demand elsewhere within the sales mix.

Providing we are working within the *relevant range*, these assumptions may be reasonably acceptable approximations of reality and need not invalidate the analysis. If, however, a limiting factor is likely to have a major effect on volume, possibly over a lengthy time horizon – i.e. if the analysis falls outside the relevant range – then these assumptions may be misleadingly simplistic.

The analysis further assumes that the organisation aims either to maximise profit or to minimise cost; there may be other, non-financial, objectives, which render this assumption questionable; for example, maintaining customer goodwill may militate strongly against limiting supply of particular product(s)/service(s). In such circumstances, it may be desirable to make strenuous efforts to overcome a limiting factor – even if this means a reduction in short-term profit. Subcontracting may be one solution and it is to this aspect of limiting factor situations that we now turn.

The subcontract option

Suppose Lasertech Ltd is able to subcontract production of any products which the constraint on labour hours prevents the company from manufacturing itself. Will this change the optimal production plan arrived at above? Exhibit 14.11 provides details of subcontracting options open to Lasertech Ltd.

Lasertech Ltd: subcontracting

Any shortfall in Lasertech Ltd's production can be made up by subcontracting. An external supplier has quoted the following firm prices to supply any quantity of identical units to those produced by Lasertech Ltd:

	£
24× CD-ROM	30
32× CD-ROM	60
40× CD-ROM	80
DVD-ROM	105

Exhibit 14.11 Overcoming a limiting factor by subcontracting

From our earlier calculations, we know that Lasertech Ltd requires 13 250 labour-hours to produce a volume of output sufficient to fully meet demand for all four products. Since only 7900 hours are available in the period under review, there is a shortage of 5350, which can be made up by subcontracting. Assuming that the company will wish to subcontract (e.g. to protect their market from competitors, or to retain customer goodwill), the problem resolves itself into one of *cost minimisation*. The company will subcontract sufficient production to cover the shortage of labour hours at the least additional cost, since it will almost certainly be more expensive to subcontract than produce in-house.

 What is the relevant cost to Lasertech Ltd of producing one unit of each product in-house?

The relevant cost of producing one unit of each product is:

	24× CD-ROM £	32× CD-ROM £	40× CD-ROM £	DVD-ROM £
Direct labour	2.50	3.00	5.00	7.50
Direct materials	8.00	15.00	25.00	30.00
Packaging	2.00	2.00	2.00	2.00
Variable production overhead	2.50	3.00	5.00	7.50
Relevant cost per unit	15.00	23.00	37.00	47.00

Note that the selling overhead varies with units *sold*, not produced; this cost will therefore be incurred irrespective of who *manufactures* the units and is irrelevant to this decision. Fixed production and administration overhead are also irrelevant, as the amount of each of these costs *incurred* is unaffected by the decision.

 What is the additional cost per unit to subcontract production of each product?

The additional cost per unit of subcontracting is:

	24× CD-ROM £	32× CD-ROM £	40× CD-ROM £	DVD-ROM £
Relevant cost to make	15	23	37	47
Cost to subcontract	30	60	80	105
Additional cost	15	37	43	58

We now need to recognise the impact of the limiting factor. Lasertech Ltd wishes to subcontract sufficient production to cover the shortfall of 5350 labour-hours; there is no need to subcontract more, since 7900 hours are available internally and a total of 13 250 hours will fully meet expected demand for the period. The company needs to rank the four products in terms of their additional cost to subcontract *per labour hour*. In this case, the ranking will be in ascending order, with the lowest-cost option ranking first.

✔ *Determine the extra cost per labour hour of subcontracting one unit of each product and rank the products on this basis.*

We determined the labour hours per unit earlier; the additional cost of subcontracting per hour is simply

$$\frac{\text{Additional cost per unit}}{\text{Labour hours per unit}}$$

Applying this to Lasertech Ltd's data, we get:

	24× CD-ROM	32× CD-ROM	40× CD-ROM	DVD-ROM
Additional cost per unit	£15.00	£37.00	£43.00	£58.00
Processing hours per drum	0.25	0.30	0.50	0.75
Additional cost per hour	£60.00	£123.33	£86.00	£77.33
Ranking	I	IV	III	II

A subcontracting schedule can now be prepared based on these rankings:

Subcontract 7000 24× CD-ROMs:	
releases (7000 × 0.25)	1750 labour hours
Shortfall in hours	5350
Hours still to be covered by subcontracting	3600

DVD-ROM is the second-ranked product; subcontracting 6000 units of this (i.e. sufficient to fully meet next period's demand) will cover (6000 × 0.75) = 4500 labour hours. This is more than is required – it is only necessary to subcontract enough units to cover the remaining shortfall in labour hours (3600 calculated above). Lasertech Ltd should therefore subcontract:

$$\frac{3600 \text{ hours}}{0.75 \text{ hours per unit}} = 4800 \text{ DVD-ROMs}$$

The optimum production/subcontracting plan can now be summarised:

Subcontract:	7000 24× CD-ROMs
	4800 DVD-ROMs

Produce:	10 000 32× CD-ROMs
	8000 40× CD-ROMs
	(6000 – 4800) = 1200 DVD-ROMs

Given the constraint on labour-hours and the subcontracting possibilities available, this plan will minimise Lasertech Ltd's cost, thereby maximising contribution.

As always in decision situations, qualitative factors should be carefully considered.

 State one qualitative factor which will be particularly important in a decision which involves a subcontracting option.

The quality of goods/services being subcontracted is probably the single most important non-financial factor to bear in mind. If quality is questionable, there may be additional costs involved in a decision to subcontract (e.g. inspection of subcontracted items), along with the possibility of dissatisfied customers. There may also be a problem with consistency between goods/services produced in-house and subcontracted. In Lasertech Ltd's case, there may, for example, be minor differences in technical specifications.

Multiple limiting factors

Where an organisation is faced with several constraints, it is not possible to use the approach based on contribution or additional cost per unit of limiting factor that we have just described. Say, for example, that Lasertech Ltd had limited availability of labour hours *and* limitations on direct materials and packaging. Clearly, it would not be feasible to calculate a contribution per unit of limiting factor, as there are now three of these in addition to sales demand. In these circumstances, we must use a technique known as **linear programming**. This is a mathematical approach to maximising or minimising a particular outcome, given the existence of constraints. Constraints are formulated as algebraic expressions and the optimum solution can be found by graphical means. Although the graphical method is fairly straightforward, it will only work where two products/services are involved, as each product/service requires its own axis on the graph. For problems involving more than two products/services, a 'tableau'-based approach known as **simplex** (which normally involves the use of computer software) must be adopted. See Further Reading below for detailed discussion of linear programming.

SUMMARY

In this chapter, we have discussed the basic approach to financial analysis of decisions and have seen that:

- Relevant costs and benefits are **future cash flows which differ between alternatives.**

- Relevant costs and benefits are **incremental costs and benefits**.

- Apportioned costs, overhead absorbed, depreciation and notional costs are all irrelevant, as they are not cash flows.

▶

- Sunk costs are always irrelevant, and are defined as:

  Past costs or future costs which must be incurred as a result of different decisions from the one under consideration

- Directly attributable fixed costs are always relevant and are defined as:

  Fixed costs which arise as a specific consequence of the decision under consideration

- Opportunity costs are always relevant and are defined as:

  The benefit forgone as a result of pursuing one course of action rather than pursuing the best alternative course of action

- Using the concept of relevance may involve certain problems, which can be summarised as:
  - short-term/'one-off' decisions
  - obtaining financial data
  - qualitative factors
  - the 'acceptance' problem
  - financing of decisions

- A **limiting factor** is a constraint placed on the activity of an organisation.

- When an organisation is faced with a sales constraint plus shortage of some other resource, profit will be maximised if products/services are ranked in descending order according to their **contribution per unit of limiting factor**; production/sales should be based on this ranking up to a maximum imposed by demand for each product and this will maximise contribution and hence profit.

- Contribution per unit of limiting factor is calculated as:

$$\frac{\text{Contribution per unit of product/service}}{\text{Units of limiting factor per unit of product/service}}$$

- The 'contribution per unit of limiting factor', approach rests on certain key assumptions:
  - certainty
  - linear cost and revenue behaviour
  - production = sales
  - independence of products/services

- If a subcontract option is available to an organisation faced with a limiting factor, products/services should be ranked in ascending order according to each product/service's **extra cost to buy per unit of limiting factor**; subcontracting/producing according to this ranking will minimise cost.

- Extra cost to buy per unit of limiting factor is calculated as:

$$\frac{\text{Extra cost to buy per unit of product/service}}{\text{Units of limiting factor per unit of product/service}}$$

- Decisions involving multiple products/services and constraints require to be solved by **linear programming**.

- A graphical approach to linear programming is appropriate to two product/service scenarios.
- **Simplex** is a computer-aided technique for solving multi-product/service constraint problems.

FURTHER READING

Amey, L., On opportunity costs and decision making. *Accountancy*, July 1980.

Anderson, D., Sweeney, D. and Williams, T., *An Introduction to Management Science* (7th edition), West Publishing, 1994: see Chapters 5 and 6 for a description of the mathematical procedures underlying simplex.

Dillon, R. and Nash, J., The true relevance of relevant costs, *Accounting Review*, January 1978.

Ezzamel, M. and Hart, H., *Advanced Management Accounting, An Organisational Emphasis*, Cassell, 1987: see Chapter 7 for an interesting discussion of relevant costs and benefits.

Upchurch, A., *Management Accounting Principles and Practice*, Financial Times Pitman Publishing, 1998: see Chapters 8 and 9 for discussion of linear programming and decisions under conditions of uncertainty respectively.

SELF-TEST QUESTIONS

14.1 K Limited manufactures three products, the selling price and cost per unit details of which are given below:

	Product L £	Product M £	Product N £
Selling price	97.50	123.50	123.50
Direct materials	13.00	6.50	19.50
Direct labour	20.80	31.20	26.00
Variable overhead	10.40	15.60	13.00
Fixed overhead	31.20	46.80	39.00

In a period when direct materials are restricted in supply, the most and least profitable uses of direct materials are:

	Most profitable	Least profitable
A	L	N
B	M	N
C	L	M
D	N	M
E	M	L

(CIMA, *Operational Cost Accounting*, November 1998)

14.2 A company is considering accepting a one-year contract which will require four skilled employees. The four skilled employees could be recruited on a one-year contract at a cost of £40 000 per employee. The employees would be supervised by an existing manager who earns £60 000 per annum. It is expected that supervision of the contract would take 10% of the manager's time. Instead of recruiting new employees, the company could retrain some existing employees who currently earn £30 000 per year. The training would cost £15 000 in total. If these employees were used they would need to be replaced at a total cost of £100 000.

The relevant labour cost of the contract is

A £100 000
B £115 000
C £135 000
D £141 000
E £166 000

(CIMA, *Operational Cost Accounting*, November 1997)

14.3 Ealing Limited (Ealing) has received a request to tender for a job involving manufacturing a one-off batch of 2000 valves; similar items are regularly made by Ealing. A standard cost schedule for the batch is set out below.

Standard cost schedule for batch of 2000 valves

		£
Materials:	steel 1000 kg at £26 per kg	26 000
	copper 250 kg at £44 per kg	11 000
Labour	2000 × 0.5 hours at £10 per hour	10 000
Overheads:	Variable 1000 hours at £2.50	2 500
	Fixed 1000 hours at £20.50	20 500
	Total standard cost of batch	70 000

The sales manager knew that a price based on this cost would not be accepted and as work was short he ordered an investigation into the specific costs of this job. The results of this investigation are set out below.

(i)   Steel is ordered twice a week and very low stocks are kept. A price rise to £30 per kg is expected imminently.

(ii) Copper is now rarely used by Ealing and this batch of 250 kg is the last in stock and it had been purchased for £44 per kg. Ealing had been hoping to sell it to another manufacturer for £32 per kg as it foresaw no further use for it.

(iii) Ealing is not working at full capacity at present and this job could be fitted in with other production. However, if the job is taken, maintenance work that the direct labour would have carried out will have to be undertaken by an outside contractor who will charge £15 000.

(iv) Variable overheads for this particular job are estimated at £1.50 per valve.

(v)   Fixed costs in the standard cost schedule are allocated using standard labour hours. The estimated increase in existing fixed costs if this job were taken is £4500.

(vi) The sales department estimate that this job will cause them to incur an additional £2000 to secure the contract.

Requirements

(a) Define and describe what is meant by an 'opportunity cost'.   (**3 marks**)

(b) Prepare a statement showing the minimum price that Ealing could bid to secure this job and not be financially worse off.   (**10 marks**)

(c) Discuss the assumptions that you have made in your answer to part (b).   (**6 marks**)

(d) Discuss the reasons why most companies allocate their overhead costs when calculating product costs for internal and external purposes, and the problems that might result from doing this.   (**6 marks**)
(**Total: 25 marks**)

(ACCA, *Paper D2 Management Accounting*, December 1998)

14.4 (a) Costs may be classified as fixed or variable. This classification method is useful for decision making because variable costs are relevant costs whereas fixed costs are irrelevant. Discuss this statement.   (**5 marks**)

(b) (i) X Limited manufactures four liquids – A, B, C and D. The selling price and unit cost details for these products are as follows:

	A	B	C	D
	£/litre	£/litre	£/litre	£/litre
Selling price	100	110	120	120
Direct materials	24	30	16	21
Direct labour (£6/hour)	18	15	24	27
Direct expenses	–	–	3	–
Variable overhead	12	10	16	18
Fixed overhead (note 1)	24	20	32	36
Profit	22	35	29	18

Note 1:
Fixed overhead is absorbed on the basis of labour hours, based on a budget of 1600 hours per quarter.

During the next three months the number of direct labour hours is expected to be limited to 1345. The same labour is used for all products. The marketing director has identified the maximum demand for each of the four products during the next three months as follows:

A 200 litres
B 150 litres
C 100 litres
D 120 litres

These maximum demand levels include the effects of a contract already made between X Limited and one of its customers, Y Limited, to supply 20 litres each of A, B, C and D during the next three months.

Requirement

Determine the number of litres of products A, B, C and D to be produced/sold in the next three months in order to maximise profits, and calculate the profit that this would yield. Assume that no stock is held at the beginning of the three months which may be used to satisfy demand in this period.   (15 marks)

(ii) After completing the production plan in (i) above, you receive two memos. The first is from the research director:

'New environmental controls on pollution must be introduced with effect from the start of next month to reduce pollution from the manufacture of product D. These will incur fixed costs of £6000 per annum.'

The second memo is from the sales director:

'An overseas supplier has developed a capacity to manufacture products C and D on a sub-contract basis, and has quoted the following prices to X Limited:

C   *£105/litre*
D   *£100/litre'*

Using the information from *both* of these memos, state and quantify the effect (if any) on X Limited's plans.   (10 marks)
                                                                    (Total: 30 marks)

(CIMA, *Operational Cost Accounting*, November 1995)

14.5 Spekobuild plc is in the process of constructing an office block. The highest offer they have so far received for the completed building is £12.5 million. The Construction Manager has produced figures to show that selling at this price will produce a loss, and has therefore proposed that the project be abandoned. His figures are shown below:

			£000
Total costs to date			2400
Estimated costs to completion			
		£000	
Materials:	in stock	1000	
	special order	600	
	to be ordered	1600	3200
Labour			4000
Subcontract work			2500
Overheads			3210

Total cost	15 310
Sales revenue	12 500
Net loss	2 810

He has asked you, the Chief Accountant, for your support for his proposal. Before agreeing, you decide to investigate further, and discover the following: The materials in stock comprise three types, as follows:

	Original cost £000	Resale value £000	Current purchase price £000
X	300	250	350
Y	350	200	380
Z	350	–	380

X is in regular use throughout the company.

Y has been in stock for some time. If not used on this contract, an alternative use on another contract could be found in place of material P, which would cost £280 000 for a similar amount.

Z is perishable, and has no alternative use. If not used on this contract, it will have to be disposed of in an environmentally acceptable manner, which will cost £50 000.

(i) The material on special order has already been made by the supplier, and cannot be cancelled. If the contract does not go ahead, it will have to be sold for its scrap value, £50 000.

(ii) The material to be ordered is shown at current market price.

(iii) Of the labour force represented by the £4m included in the original costing, 60% could be redeployed on other work for which a workforce has not yet been hired. 20% of the cost represents casual workers hired on a weekly basis. The remaining 20% would have to be made redundant. This represents 40 people, at an average annual salary of £20 000. Redundancy payments would average 75% of annual salary.

(v) Some work has already been done by the subcontractors, and if the building is not completed, cancellation payments of 10% of the value of the outstanding work will need to be made.

(vi) There would be site clearance costs of £50 000 if the project is scrapped.

(vii) Overheads specific to this project are as follows:

	£000
Plant hire	750
Site overheads	260

These would be saved if the project did not go ahead, apart from a cancellation charge of 10% on the plant hire.

All remaining overheads included in the original costing are general and fixed.

Requirements

(a) Prepare a report for the Board of Directors of Spekobuild, stating whether or not you support the proposed cancellation, and giving relevant figures to support your case. Your report should clearly explain your reasoning. **(15 marks)**

(b) The Managing Director asks why you have used a different method of costing and pricing in your report in (a) above from that normally used by Spekobuild, and queries whether you will be using this 'new' method for all further contracts. Draft an appropriate answer, giving your reasons. **(4 marks)**

(CIPFA, *Accounting for Decision Making*, June 1996)

QUESTIONS WITHOUT ANSWERS

14.6 Z plc manufactures three products which have the following selling prices and costs per unit:

	Z1	Z2	Z3
	£	£	£
Selling price	15.00	18.00	17.00
Costs per unit:			
Direct materials	4.00	5.00	10.00
Direct labour	2.00	4.00	1.80
Overhead: Variable	1.00	2.00	0.90
Fixed	4.50	3.00	1.35
	11.50	14.00	14.05
Profit per unit	3.50	4.00	2.95

All three products use the same type of labour.

In a period in which labour is in short supply, the rank order of production is:

	Z1	Z2	Z3
A	First	Second	Third
B	Third	Second	First
C	Second	First	Third
D	First	Third	Second
E	Second	Third	First

(CIMA, *Operational Cost Accounting*, November 1997)

14.7 You are the management accountant of a publishing and printing company which has been asked to quote for the production of a programme for the local village fair. The work would be carried out in addition to the normal work of the company. Because of existing commitments, some weekend working would be required to complete the printing of the programme. A trainee accountant has produced the following cost estimate based upon the resources required as specified by the production manager:

			£
Direct materials	– paper (book value)		5 000
	– inks (purchase price)		2 400
Direct labour	– skilled	250 hours @ £4.00	1 000
	– unskilled	100 hours @ £3.50	350
Variable overhead		350 hours @ £4.00	1 400
Printing press depreciation		200 hours @ £2.50	500
Fixed production costs		350 hours @ £6.00	2 100
Estimating department costs			400
			13 150

You are aware that considerable publicity could be obtained for the company if you are able to win this order and the price quoted must be very competitive. The following notes are relevant to the cost estimate above:

1 The paper to be used is currently in stock at a value of £5000. It is of an unusual colour which has not been used for some time. The replacement price of the paper is £8000, whilst the scrap value of that in stock is £2500. The production manager does not foresee any alternative use for the paper if it is not used for the village fair programmes.

2 The inks required are not held in stock. They would have to be purchased in bulk at a cost of £3000. Eighty per cent of the inks purchased would be used in printing the programmes. No other use is foreseen for the remainder.

3 Skilled direct labour is in short supply, and to accommodate the printing of the programmes, 50% of the time required would be worked at weekends for which a premium of 25% above the normal hourly rate is paid. The normal hourly rate is £4.00 per hour.

4 Unskilled labour is presently under-utilised, and at present 200 hours per week are recorded as idle time. If the printing work is carried out at a weekend, 25 unskilled hours would have to occur at this time, but the employees concerned would be given two hours time off (for which they would be paid) in lieu of each hour worked.

5 Variable overhead represents the cost of operating the printing press and binding machines.

6 When not being used by the company, the printing press is hired to outside companies for £6.00 per hour. This earns a contribution of £3.00 per hour. There is unlimited demand for this facility.

7 Fixed production costs are those incurred by and absorbed into production, using an hourly rate based on budgeted activity.

8 The cost of the estimating department represents time spent in discussions with the village fair committee concerning the printing of its programme.

Requirements

(a) Prepare a revised cost estimate using the opportunity cost approach, showing clearly the minimum price that the company should accept for the order. Give reasons for each resource valuation in your cost estimate.   **(16 marks)**

(b) Explain why contribution theory is used as a basis for providing information relevant to decision making.   **(4 marks)**

(c) Explain the relevance of opportunity costs in decision making.   **(5 marks)**

(Total: 25 marks)

(CIMA, *Operational Cost Accounting*, May 1995)

14.8 BVX Limited manufactures three garden furniture products – chairs, benches and tables. The budgeted unit cost and resource requirements of each of these items is detailed below:

	Chair	Bench	Table
	£	£	£
Timber cost	5.00	15.00	10.00
Direct labour cost	4.00	10.00	8.00
Variable overhead cost	3.00	7.50	6.00
Fixed overhead cost	4.50	11.25	9.00
	16.50	43.75	33.00
Budgeted volumes per annum	4000	2000	1500

- These volumes are believed to equal the market demand for these products.
- The fixed overhead costs are attributed to the three products on the basis of direct labour hours.
- The labour rate is £4.00 per hour.
- The cost of the timber is £2.00 per square metre.

The products are made from a specialist timber. A memo from the purchasing manager advises you that because of a problem with the supplier, it is to be assumed that this specialist timber is limited in supply to 20 000 square metres per annum.

The sales director has already accepted an order for 500 chairs, 100 benches and 150 tables which if not supplied would incur a financial penalty of £2000. These quantities are included in the market demand estimates above.

The selling prices of the three products are:

Chair	£20.00
Bench	£50.00
Table	£40.00

Requirements

(a) Determine the optimum production plan *and* state the net profit that this would yield per annum. **(10 marks)**

(b) Calculate *and* explain the maximum prices which should be paid per square metre in order to obtain extra supplies of the timber. **(5 marks)**

(c) The management team has accused the accountant of using too much jargon. Prepare a statement which explains the following terms in a way that a multi-disciplinary team of managers would understand. The accountant will use this statement as a briefing paper at the next management meeting. The terms to be explained are:

- variable costs
- relevant costs
- avoidable costs
- incremental costs
- opportunity costs. **(10 marks)**

(Total: 25 marks)

(CIMA, *Operational Cost Accounting*, May 1997)

CHAPTER 15

Capital investment appraisal

> ### How high a hurdle?
>
> '... Companies generally make their investment decisions by discounting the net cash-flows a project is estimated to generate to their present value. If that net present value is positive, the project should, in theory, make shareholders better off. But the entire decision rests on the accuracy of both the cash-flow forecasts and the discount rate. Set the rate even a sliver too high, and good projects appear bad; set it too low and bad investments look appealing ...
>
> 'Steve Hodge, treasurer of Shell, an Anglo-Dutch oil giant, says that a difference of only one percentage point in the discount rate can change the value of, say, an oil refinery with a 15-year life by hundreds of millions of dollars ... '
>
> *Source*: © *The Economist* Newspaper, London, 8 May 1999. Reprinted with permission.

Exhibit 15.1 A common appraisal technique – and some associated problems

INTRODUCTION

In the previous three chapters, we have discussed and illustrated various cost accounting techniques for analysing the financial implications of *short-term* decisions. We must now turn our attention to decisions of a *strategic* nature. Examples of such decisions are: acquisition of major operating assets, introduction of new products/services, divestment, shutdown and improvement programmes. Every decision has a strategic aspect – e.g. short-term decisions, taken cumulatively, are strategic; capital investment decisions are strategic in their own right and have certain common characteristics:

1 they involve substantial costs and benefits;
2 they have cost/benefit implications which span a number of years; and
3 they are of significance to the entire organisation.

The criteria we use for financial evaluation of such decisions must therefore be capable of reflecting these characteristics. In particular, they must be able to reflect adequately relevant costs and benefits over a capital investment proposal's entire life (which will span a number of years). This is especially important in helping counter 'short-termism' – i.e. emphasising short-term benefits to the exclusion or detriment of long-term and/or strategic considerations. The extent to which short-termism is a problem in the UK is suggested by responses to a questionnaire (Collison, Grinyer and Russell, 1993) in which 66% of the finance directors who responded believed that stock market valuation of companies was based principally on their expected earnings for the current year. Although there is some debate about the source of pressure towards short-termism, the existence of such pressure in many organisations is clear.

As we shall see – and as Exhibit 15.1 suggests – obtaining a wholly satisfactory criterion for appraising capital investment decisions may be difficult.

OBJECTIVES

When you have completed this chapter, you will be able to:

● place capital investment decisions in their strategic perspective;

● evaluate capital investment proposals using:
  – accounting rate of return
  – payback
  – net present value
  – internal rate of return;

● explain the strengths and weaknesses of each of the above criteria;

● appreciate the significance of the time value of money in capital investment appraisal;

● use tables of discount factors for single sums and annuities;

● understand the importance of 'relevance' to DCF calculations;

● identify and employ differential cash flows in net present value calculations;

● compare net present value and internal rate of return as capital investment criteria;

● appreciate the drawbacks common to all financial criteria for evaluating capital investment proposals;

● explain the meaning of project post-audit, along with its advantages and problems.

CAPITAL INVESTMENT APPRAISAL AND ORGANISATIONAL STRATEGY

Given the common characteristics mentioned in the Introduction, it is important that capital investment decisions are consistent with an organisation's overall strategy. Exhibit 15.2 makes quite explicit reference to the strategy being pursued by Bass: 'a five-year drive to quadruple the size of its Inter-Continental and Crowne Plaza luxury hotel brands around the world.'

What should also be clear from Exhibit 15.2 is that a major capital investment should not be made merely because it offers a healthy financial return in the short run. To achieve an organisation's strategic aims, it may be necessary to accept a decision which yields net costs in the short run, but which will prove valuable when a long-term perspective is applied. Capital investment decisions should therefore be viewed not only in the light of financial criteria but also in terms of how well they will help in achieving long-term objectives and the extent to which they 'mesh' with other proposed (or existing) capital investment proposals.

This is not to suggest that financial considerations should be ignored – quite the contrary. What we are suggesting is that, before a financial evaluation is made, the need for major investment should be assessed in the light of the organisation's strategic aims. As

Bass to spend £900m on its luxury hotels

Bass, the brewing and leisure group, is aiming to spend £900m over the next two years in the first part of a five-year drive to quadruple the size of its Inter-Continental and Crowne Plaza luxury hotel brands around the world . . .

At a presentation to analysts in London yesterday, the group said it was aiming for a fourfold increase in Inter-Continental's 42 000 rooms during the next five years. The US – where there are only eight Inter-Continental hotels, representing 10% of the chain's room stock – will be a priority for expansion. Mr Oliver [chief executive of Bass Hotels and Resorts] said there was the potential for at least 100 Inter-Continentals in US cities.

Crowne Plaza, which has 41 000 rooms, will also be expanded to more than 160 000 rooms in five years . . .

The group also aims to double the number of rooms of Holiday Inn and Holiday Inn Express, its budget brand, in the UK, Germany, Italy and China . . .

Source: Scheherazade Daneshkhu, *Financial Times*, 24 June 1999. Reprinted with permission.

Exhibit 15.2 Capital investment programme in pursuit of a growth strategy

we said in Chapter 1, these aims may be varied, so the reason for capital investments will likewise vary: e.g. achieving or improving competitive advantage, improvement in products/services offered, increasing profit, enhancing efficiency, effectiveness and economy, or complying with legal requirements.

Assessing the extent to which capital investment decisions, once taken, achieve their desired objective(s) is a matter of rigorous post-implementation review (**project post-audit**), which we shall discuss later in the chapter: such review is important for all decisions, but is particularly so for strategic decisions.

We therefore need to have a clear objective (or objectives) in mind before prospective courses of action are considered and to use evaluation techniques which adequately reflect the strategic time frame involved. But note that these techniques have a narrow financial focus, and do not, in themselves, assess the *strategy* from which capital investment decisions stem.

ACCOUNTING RATE OF RETURN

This criterion links the key accounting measures of profit and the amount of capital which must be invested in order to earn that profit. You may also see accounting rate of return referred to as **return on capital employed** or **return on investment**. Accounting rate of return can be calculated as:

$$\frac{\text{Average annual profit}}{\text{Initial capital cost}} \times 100\%$$

The numerator in the formula is the total profit generated by the specific proposal during its estimated life divided by the number of years comprising that life. Once a proposal's accounting rate of return has been obtained, it is compared with a **target return** (also termed the **hurdle rate** or **cutoff rate**). The target return may be derived from a variety of sources. Many public sector bodies, for example, have a target return stipulated in regulations governing that body's accounting procedures; commercial organisations might base their target return on an estimate of the minimum return required by investors in the company. If a proposal's return exceeds the target, it is financially viable; if it is lower than the target, the proposal should be rejected.

Exhibit 15.3 contains a scenario involving a capital investment decision; although the amounts involved are small in *absolute* terms (for ease of illustration), they may be substantial from the point of view of the firm concerned.

Sphere Theatre

As part of its profit improvement strategy, management of the Sphere Theatre is considering acquisition of a state-of-the-art ticket/seat booking system. It is hoped that this will result in both a reduction in the costs associated with bookings and extra revenue from additional bookings. Estimates relating to the proposed new system are set out below.

Initial cost of system (payable immediately)		£100 000
Useful life		5 years
		£
Profit increase if bought:	Year 1	5 000
	Year 2	8 000
	Year 3	9 000
	Year 4	10 000
	Year 5	12 000
Resale value of system at the end of Year 5		10 000

The profit increases above are stated after deducting £18 000 per annum depreciation from the proposal's annual net cash inflows.

The Sphere Theatre's required return is 12%.

Exhibit 15.3 Basic data for financial appraisal of a capital investment decision

  What is the average annual profit that will result from purchase of the computer installation?

The average annual profit will be:

$$\frac{\text{Total profit over proposal's life}}{\text{Number of years of proposal's life}}$$

$$= \frac{(£5000 + £8000 + £9000 + £10\ 000 + £12\ 000)}{5 \text{ years}} = £8800$$

  Using the average annual profit just calculated, determine the proposal's accounting rate of return, Compare this with the theatre's target return, and advise whether the proposal is financially viable.

The proposal's accounting rate of return is:

$$\frac{\text{Average annual profit}}{\text{Initial capital cost}} \times 100\% = \frac{£8800}{£100\ 000} \times 100\% = 8.8\%$$

As this is lower than the target return of 12%, the proposal is financially unacceptable using accounting rate of return as the appraisal criterion.

You may feel that basing the numerator on an average profit figure and the denominator on initial capital cost is inconsistent. In order to overcome this, we can amend the denominator and calculate accounting rate of return as:

$$\frac{\text{Average annual profit}}{\text{Average capital cost}} \times 100\%$$

A little care is needed when determining average capital cost. You may be tempted to *deduct* the estimated resale value of £10 000 from the initial cost, but this is incorrect. We are trying to obtain the average capital cost of the proposal over its life: at the start, the capital cost is £100 000 and at the end it is £10 000. In other words, we are looking at the accounting *book values* of the asset concerned at the start and end of its useful life. The average capital cost is a simple arithmetic average of these two values:

$$\frac{(\text{Initial capital cost} + \text{final capital cost})}{2}$$

Since this figure derives from only two measures of cost, we could argue that it is not a true average value, and in this sense is inconsistent with average annual profit as the accounting return's numerator.

Note that there is no change to the numerator in our revised definition of accounting rate of return – it is still average annual profit.

 Recalculate the computer proposal's accounting rate of return using average capital cost as the denominator.

First, we need to determine the proposal's average capital cost:

$$\frac{(\text{Initial capital cost} + \text{final capital cost})}{2} = \frac{(£100\,000 + £10\,000)}{2} = £55\,000$$

This gives a revised accounting rate of return of:

$$\frac{\text{Average annual profit}}{\text{Average capital cost}} \times 100\% = \frac{£8800}{£55\,000} \times 100\% = 16\%$$

As this is higher than the target return of 12%, the proposal is financially acceptable. This assumes that the target rate of 12% is also applicable to the revised method of calculating accounting return. It could well be that the target will be revised upwards to reflect the fact that accounting rate of return on all proposals will be higher using average, rather than initial cost.

Advantages of accounting rate of return

This criterion has two distinct advantages:

1 It is straightforward to calculate.
2 It is readily understood, since it relates two key accounting benchmarks: profit and capital. It is easy to appreciate the significance of a decision criterion which

expresses the profit earned by a proposal in terms of the amount of capital which must be invested in order to earn that amount of profit.

Disadvantages of accounting rate of return

These advantages are offset by a number of disadvantages:

1 At the beginning of this chapter, we said that the 'acid test' we would apply to the various evaluative criteria would be their ability to reflect the strategic time horizon of the decisions being evaluated. Accounting rate of return is only partially successful in this respect: by using average profit (and possibly average capital cost), some recognition is given to the time aspect of proposals. However, this has two drawbacks:

(a) The averaging process may hide the *pattern* of returns each year of a proposal's life and some knowledge of this may be important (e.g. for projecting cash flows or reported profit).

(b) The calculation *implies* that all costs/benefits occur at the same point in time – i.e. now – otherwise we could not validly add and average profit and/or capital cost. In other words, we are implying that £1 spent/received now has the same 'value' as £1 spent/received four years from now. What we can say is that accounting rate of return disregards the **time value of money**. We shall discuss this concept later in the chapter

In terms of strategic orientation, accounting rate of return can therefore be argued to be very weak.

2 Accounting rate of return has no generally accepted definition: we have illustrated two possible versions – other variations exist. Even without these additional versions, we can see from our example just how major can be the effect of changing the basis of calculation:

Using initial capital cost	8.8%
Using average capital cost	16.0%

A substantial difference! In fact, so substantial as to indicate quite different decisions, assuming that the target return remains constant; this is an unsatisfactory situation – a capital expenditure proposal's financial desirability or otherwise should not depend on the definition used in calculation of the appraisal criterion. Consistency of definition may remove anomalies such as this, but it will not remove the potential worry that a viable proposal has been rejected on the basis of how accounting rate of return happens to have been defined.

3 As we have seen, accounting rate of return is based on *profit* – in fact, of all the criteria we shall discuss, it is the *only* profit-based approach. As we observed in Chapter 14, profit is not the best basis for measuring the financial impact of decisions; for example, profit can be affected by the method of depreciation chosen, which is likely to be somewhat subjective. So it is better to use cash flows, which do not contain the same amount of 'informed guesswork'.

4 Accounting rate of return is expressed as a percentage; this gives no indication of the *size* of a proposal, nor does it indicate how much better (or worse) off the organisation will be if a particular proposal is undertaken. This makes the use of accounting

rate of return difficult in situations where a choice must be made between two or more mutually exclusive proposals. Imagine we were faced with the following:

Proposal A	accounting rate of return 15%
Proposal B	accounting rate of return 20%
Target rate of return	10%

If only one of these proposals can be undertaken, Proposal B would seem to be better at first glance. But how much do we need to invest in order to obtain these returns? And what is the *amount* of return from each proposal? These may be critically important questions, answers to which could determine the ultimate decision.

In general, use of percentages is likely to cause difficulty where choice between different proposals exists, and, at the least, some supplementary information should be provided (in the example above, knowing the amount of the initial investment for each of Proposals A and B would have been helpful).

PAYBACK

The **payback period** is the time (usually expressed in years) which is required for a proposal's *cash inflows* to equal its initial cost. A target payback period will be set and proposals that recover their initial cost within this time will be acceptable. When comparing two or more mutually exclusive proposals, shorter paybacks within the target period are preferred to longer. Data relating to the Sphere Theatre's capital investment decision are reproduced in Exhibit 15.4 and will be used to calculate the proposal's payback period.

Sphere Theatre

Estimates relating to the proposed new system are set out below.

Initial cost of system (payable immediately)		£100 000
Useful life		5 years
		£
Profit increase if bought:	Year 1	5 000
	Year 2	8 000
	Year 3	9 000
	Year 4	10 000
	Year 5	12 000
Resale value of system at the end of Year 5		10 000

The profit increases above are stated after deducting £18 000 per annum depreciation from the proposal's annual net cash inflows.
The Sphere Theatre's target payback period is three years.

Exhibit 15.4 Basic data for payback calculation

 What are the annual net cash inflows for each of Years 1–5?

Annual net cash inflows will be (profit increase *plus* depreciation); you should bear in mind that depreciation is not a cash item and it is essential that you distinguish between profit and cash flow: the two are very unlikely to be the same. The net cash inflow each year is:

	£
Year 1 (£5000 + £18 000)	23 000
Year 2 (£8000 + £18 000)	26 000
Year 3 (£9000 + £18 000)	27 000
Year 4 (£10 000 + £18 000)	28 000
Year 5 (£12 000 + £18 000 + £10 000)	40 000

Assuming that the estimated resale value of £10 000 is what the booking system will actually be sold for at the end of Year 5, this amount represents an additional *cash inflow* in that year. The cash inflows for each of Years 1–5 are 'net' because relevant *cash* costs (e.g. cost of operating the new system) have been deducted in their computation.

 Will the proposal pay back its initial cost within the target period of three years?

A simple tabulation allows us to assess the proposal's cumulative cash inflows at the end of each year of its life:

Year	Cash inflow £	Cumulative cash inflow £
1	23 000	23 000
2	26 000	49 000
3	27 000	76 000
4	28 000	104 000
5	40 000	144 000

The proposed system will therefore not recover its initial cost within the target period of three years and is unacceptable using payback as the criterion.

We may wish to ascertain the payback period with more precision. We can say that, by the end of Year 3, the proposal has recovered £76 000 of its initial cost and must recover a further (£100 000 – £76 000) = £24 000 in Year 4.

Assuming cash flows arise evenly during each year, the proportion of Year 4's cash flow needed to gain £24 000 will be:

$$\frac{\text{Cash flow required}}{\text{Total cash flow for year}} = \frac{£24\ 000}{£28\ 000} = 0.86 \text{ of Year 4}$$

So the payback period is 3.86 years.

Advantages of payback

1 Like accounting rate of return, payback is simple to calculate and understand.
2 Compared to accounting rate of return, it has the advantage of concentrating on cash flows, which are more objective than profit.
3 Because it is such a quick, simple method to employ, it may be useful in situations where a great number of competing proposals need to be compared or ranked,

with shorter-than-target payback being one criterion for a proposal being further investigated.

4 Payback may be significant where an organisation has cash flow problems (*liquidity* problems). In these circumstances, it may be important that capital investment proposals cover their initial cost quickly so that proposal cash flows which arise after the (short) payback period will help to alleviate the cash flow problem.

5 If a proposal is considered to be particularly risky, management may prefer that the initial cost be recovered sooner rather than later, feeling that, for an inherently risky proposal, the longer it takes for initial cost to be recovered, the greater is the chance of the related risks adversely affecting the outcome.

Disadvantages of payback

1 Payback (in the form in which we have just calculated it) ignores the **time value of money**. Like accounting rate of return, the implication of this approach is that all proposal cash flows arise at the same point in time. We shall discuss the time value of money shortly.

2 Even if the payback criterion is modified to allow for the time value of money (as it can be), it may still have a serious shortcoming. If you look again at the net cash inflows associated with the Sphere Theatre's new booking system, you will see that, once the payback period has been determined, cash flows which arise *after* that time are effectively removed from the analysis. For the Sphere Theatre proposal, this amounts to:

$$(£4000 \text{ [in Year 4]} + £40\,000 \text{ [in Year 5]}) = £44\,000$$

– i.e. we have excluded cash flows equivalent to 44% of the proposal's initial cost – a substantial omission. What this could mean is that we will accept proposals simply because they have heavy cash inflows in their earlier years (giving a short payback period), but which may not be particularly worthwhile *over their full lives*. At the same time, we might reject proposals which are extremely financially desirable *over their full lives*, but which happen to have heavier cash inflows in later, rather than in earlier years (giving a long payback period).

3 Like accounting rate of return, payback gives no indication of the amount of capital investment required, nor of the overall cost/benefit resulting from acceptance or rejection of a proposal. This, together with the last point regarding omission of some cash flows from the analysis, means that comparison of competing projects on the basis of payback may be dangerously flawed.

Based on the disadvantages above, we can therefore say that payback, as an evaluative criterion for capital investment proposals, is weak in its strategic emphasis.

THE TIME VALUE OF MONEY

We are all aware of the existence of the time value of money, although we may not use this term for it. Phrases such as '£1 today is worth more than £1 in the future' tend to crop up quite often.

> ✔ *Why is it true that £1 today is worth more than £1 in the future?*

There are two reasons why £1 today is worth more than £1 in future:

1 Money which is received now can be invested to earn a return; if receipt is deferred, we will lose this return. For example, if we receive £100 now, we may be able to invest at, say, 10% per annum interest, so that, one year from now, our £100 is worth (£100 × 1.1) = £110. If we had to wait one year to receive the £100, we would lose that year's interest at 10%, so the value to us today of £100 receivable in one year, given the lost interest of 10% per annum, is *less* than £100. (Alternatively, we would need to receive *more* than £100 in one year to compensate for this loss of interest.)

2 Individuals and organisations have a *liquidity preference* – i.e. prefer to have cash available to spend on goods/services now, rather than the chance of having cash to spend in future.

Time value of money

We receive £1000 which we can immediately invest for four years at 8% per annum interest, the annual interest being reinvested, also at 8%.

Exhibit 15.5 Investment over time

 What will be the value of our £1,000 investment at the end of:

- *one year from now*
- *two years from now*
- *three years from now*
- *four years from now?*

(Work to the nearest whole £1)

Remembering that annual interest is reinvested ('compounded'), the original £1000 will be worth:

$$(£1000 \times 1.08) = £1080 \text{ one year from now}$$
$$(£1080 \times 1.08) = £1166 \text{ two years from now}$$
$$(£1166 \times 1.08) = £1259 \text{ three years from now}$$
$$(£1259 \times 1.08) = £1360 \text{ four years from now.}$$

Arithmetically, this is the same as saying that the value of our £1000 is:

$$(£1000 \times 1.08) = £1080 \text{ one year from now}$$
$$(£1000 \times 1.08^2) = £1166 \text{ two years from now}$$
$$(£1000 \times 1.08^3) = £1259 \text{ three years from now}$$
$$(£1000 \times 1.08^4) = £1360 \text{ four years from now.}$$

These calculations provide us with a general expression for compounding:

$$\text{Future value} = \text{present value} \times (1 + r)^n$$

where r is the applicable rate of interest or other return and n is the number of years concerned.

*What is the value in today's terms (the **present value**) of £1259 receivable three years from now if the applicable interest rate is 8% compound?*

From the workings above, we know that £1259 is the future value of £1000 invested at 8% per annum compound interest for three years – i.e. the present value of £1259 at 8% is £1000. Expressing future values in present-day terms is known as **discounting**. Rearrangement of the general formula for compounding yields one for discounting:

$$\text{Future value} = \text{present value} \times (1 + r)^n$$

so

$$\text{Future value} \times \frac{1}{(1 + r)^n} = \text{present value}$$

In discounting calculations, r is referred to as the 'discount rate'.

 Use the discounting formula to confirm that the present value of £1360 received four years from now is £1000 at a discount rate of 8%.

$$\text{Future value} \times \frac{1}{(1 + r)^n} = \text{present value}$$

$$\text{so } £1360 \times \frac{1}{(1 + 0.08)^4} = \text{present value}$$

i.e. £1360 × 0.735 = £1000 (rounded to nearest whole £1)

You may feel that these calculations are rather time-consuming, possibly daunting. However, a short-cut is available: fractions such as the 0.735 above are known as *discount factors* and Appendix B lists such factors for a variety of different discount rates and time horizons. A listing of this sort is available in any book of mathematical tables, so calculation is not usually necessary – we need only refer to tables such as Appendix B and apply the relevant factor to the cash flow which we wish to discount. Examination of the 8% column in Table I of Appendix B shows 0.735 in the '4 years' row.

 Use the discount factors in Table I of Appendix B to obtain discount factors where:

n = 4 years	*r = 18%*
n = 8 years	*r = 5%*
n = 20 years	*r = 10%*

The relevant discount factors are 0.516, 0.677 and 0.149. Looking at the pattern of discount factors in Table I of Appendix B you will notice that, as the time horizon lengthens, the factors for each discount rate decrease. This is a reflection of the time value of money – i.e. the longer the time period involved, the greater the impact of 'lost' interest and liquidity preference and so the lower is the present value of the cash flow.

Where a proposal has equal annual cash flows – an **annuity** – we can take another short-cut. Table II in Appendix B lists *cumulative* discount factors (also known as **annuity factors**), which we can use to discount equal annual cash flows. If you compare the factors in Table II with those in Table I, you will see that Table II factors are the cumulative totals of those in Table I.

 Use Table II in Appendix B to obtain the cumulative discount factors where:

n = 10 years	*r = 12%*
n = 14 years	*r = 6%*
n = 7 years	*r = 18%*

The relevant factors are 5.650, 9.295 and 3.812.

 Both Table I and Table II begin with factors that relate to cash flows which arise one year from now. What is the discount factor for cash flows which arise immediately?

Cash flows which arise immediately have a discount factor of one: the present value of £1 spent/received today is £1. In discounting calculations, 'now' is conventionally referred to as 'Year 0' (or 'Time 0').

DISCOUNTED CASH FLOW (DCF) TECHNIQUES

The appraisal methods we are about to describe are both based on the principle that a proposal's cash flows should all be stated in today's terms before its financial viability is assessed – i.e. they make use of the discounting procedures illustrated above. For this reason, they are known collectively as **discounted cash flow (DCF)** techniques.

Net present value (NPV)

To obtain NPV, we discount a capital investment proposal's cash flows at an appropriate rate. Like the target accounting rate of return, this discount rate may be specified in a public sector body's accounting regulations, or may be based on an estimate of the minimum return required by investors in a commercial organisation. When the latter approach is taken, the discount rate is referred to as the **cost of capital**. While detailed discussion of the cost of capital is beyond the scope of this book, you should note that it is most unlikely that the cost of capital will equate with the interest rate charged on loans. (See *Further Reading* at the end of this chapter for some suggested sources on the cost of capital.)

NPV is the sum of a proposal's cash flows discounted in the manner just described – outflows (i.e. cash payments) plus inflows (i.e. cash receipts or savings). Where the discounted cash inflows exceed the discounted cash outflows, NPV is **positive**; where the discounted cash outflows exceed the discounted cash inflows, NPV is **negative**.

A proposal is acceptable if it has a positive NPV, but should be rejected if it has a negative NPV. When evaluating two or more mutually exclusive proposals, that with the highest positive NPV should be accepted. In certain circumstances, a proposal having a negative NPV may be accepted. For example, where we are evaluating mutually exclusive proposals both of which have a negative NPV, but where we *must* nevertheless choose one or the other; here, we will accept the proposal having the negative

NPV closest to zero. Such a situation may arise, for example, where an organisation is obliged by Health and Safety legislation to choose which of two sprinkler systems to install in its premises. Since the associated cash inflows will either be non-existent or minimal relative to cash outflows, NPVs from the proposals will be negative.

Exhibit 15.6 restates the *undiscounted* cash flows associated with the capital investment decision faced by the Sphere Theatre.

Sphere Theatre: proposal net cash flows

The annual net cash flows resulting from acquisition of the new booking system are:

£	
100 000	Paid now (initial cost – cash outflow)
23 000	Year 1 (net cash inflow)
26 000	Year 2 (net cash inflow)
27 000	Year 3 (net cash inflow)
28 000	Year 4 (net cash inflow)
40 000	Year 5 (net cash inflow)

The theatre's cost of capital is 12%.

Exhibit 15.6 Undiscounted proposal cash flows

 Use the discount factors from Table I of Appendix B and the theatre's cost of capital of 12% to obtain the present value of each year's cash flow; include the Year 0 cash flow in your answer.

The discounted cash flows are as shown in Table 15.1. The Year 0 cash flow in the table has been placed in parentheses to make clear that it is a cash outflow – i.e. a payment, whereas all the other cash flows in this example are inflows – i.e. receipts. Now that we have stated all the proposal's cash flows on a common basis – in today's

Table 15.1 Discounted cash flows for Sphere Theatre's new system

Year	Cash flow	Amount £	Discount factor	Present value £
0	Initial cost	(100 000)	1.000	(100 000)
1	Net cash inflow	23 000	0.893	20 539
2	Net cash inflow	26 000	0.797	20 722
3	Net cash inflow	27 000	0.712	19 224
4	Net cash inflow	28 000	0.636	17 808
5	Net cash inflow	40 000	0.567	12 680

terms – we can validly add them up. Such addition is arguably invalid using undiscounted figures, because they arise at different points in time over the proposal's life and are thus all affected to a different degree by the time value of money.

 Use the discounted cash flows from Table 15.1 to obtain the proposal's net present value (i.e. the sum of its discounted cash flows). Is the proposal acceptable?

The NPV is

$$[(£100\ 000) + £20\ 539 + £20\ 722 + £19\ 224 + £17\ 808 + £22\ 680] = £973$$

(Remember that the Year 0 cash flow is a payment, so it is treated as a negative figure in the NPV calculation.) Since its NPV is positive, the proposal is financially acceptable.

What does a positive NPV of £973 represent? It is the increase in absolute wealth which the Sphere Theatre will obtain if it acquires the new booking system. In other words, even after allowing for 'lost' interest and liquidity preference, the theatre will still be £973 'better off' as a result of acquisition.

Internal rate of return (IRR)

Internal rate of return is another discounted cash flow technique and is defined as

The discount rate yielding a zero NPV

This is the return implicit to a proposal and if it exceeds the organisation's cost of capital, the proposal is acceptable, if it is less than the cost of capital, the proposal should be rejected.

The relationship between NPV and discount rates is as shown in Figure 15.1; the higher the discount rate, the lower the associated NPV.

Note that in the figure the relationship is not linear. The point where the NPV plot intersects the horizontal axis is the internal rate of return – i.e. the discount rate yielding a zero NPV. We could use such a graph ('present value profile') to determine a project's IRR, but this is cumbersome if done manually, as a number of NPVs must be calculated using different discount rates sufficient to permit reasonably accurate plotting of the NPV function.

Where a project's cash inflows consist of equal annual amounts, IRR can be obtained as follows:

(a) Discounting project proposals at the IRR gives NPV of zero – i.e.

(annual cash inflow × appropriate cumulative discount factor)
less
initial cost of proposal
equals
zero

Rearranging this, we get

$$\frac{\text{Initial cost}}{\text{Annual cash in flow}} = \text{appropriate cumulative discount factor}$$

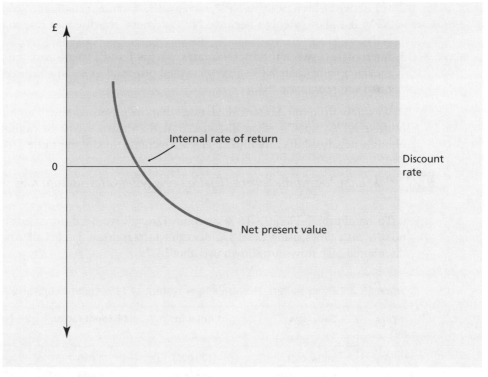

Figure 15.1 NPV and discount rates

(b) Since we know the number of years involved, we can use a table of cumulative factors (Table II in Appendix B) to obtain the IRR.

 A capital investment proposal has an initial cost of £82 000, with an annual cash inflow of £20 000 in each of its five years of life. What is the proposal's IRR?

The appropriate cumulative discount factor is:

$$\frac{\text{Initial cost}}{\text{Annual cash inflow}} = \frac{£82\,000}{£20\,000} = 4.1$$

Reading along the '5-year' row of Table II in Appendix B, we can see that 4.100 is the cumulative factor for a 7% discount rate; the proposal thus has an IRR of 7%. If necessary, we can interpolate between factors in Table II: had our calculation given an answer of, say, 4.0465, then the IRR lies between 7% and 8% – since 4.0465 is the mid-point of the factors for 7% and 8%, we can estimate IRR as 7.5%. Note, however, that IRRs derived from this sort of interpolation are estimates only: the relationship we are approximating is curvilinear, whereas the interpolation is linear.

For capital investment proposals such as the Sphere Theatre's, where the pattern of cash inflows is irregular, determining IRR is a matter of trial and error. The procedures are:

1 Discount the proposal's cash flows at the cost of capital.

2 If 1 above yields a positive NPV, *increase* the discount rate so as to obtain a negative NPV; if 1 above yields a negative NPV, *decrease* the discount rate to give a positive NPV.

3 Interpolate between the discount rates in steps 1 and 2 to estimate the value at which the line joining their NPVs intersects the horizontal axis. This value will be the proposal's approximate IRR.

We know from our earlier calculations that the proposed new booking system has a positive NPV of £973 when discounted at the theatre's cost of capital of 12%. To obtain a negative NPV, we must therefore **increase** the discount rate.

 What is the NPV of the Sphere Theatre's new system at a discount rate of 18%?

To obtain the NPV at a 18% discount rate, all we need do is rediscount the proposal's cash flows using the 18% discount factors from Table I of Appendix B. The discounted cash flows are shown in Table 15.2.

Table 15.2 NPV of Sphere Theatre's new system at 18% cost of capital

Year	Cash flow	Amount £	Discount factor	Present value £
0	Initial cost	(100 000)	1.000	(100 000)
1	Net cash inflow	23 000	0.848	19 504
2	Net cash inflow	26 000	0.718	18 668
3	Net cash inflow	27 000	0.609	16 443
4	Net cash inflow	28 000	0.516	14 448
5	Net cash inflow	40 000	0.437	17 480
			NPV	(13 457)

The proposal's IRR will therefore lie somewhere between 12% and 18%. We can approximate the IRR by interpolating between 12% and 18%:

$$\text{IRR} = 12\% + \left[\frac{£973}{(£973 + £13\ 457)} \times (18\% - 12\%) \right] = 12.4\% \text{ (rounded)}$$

Or alternatively:

$$\text{IRR} = 18\% - \left[\frac{£13\ 457}{(£973 + £13\ 457)} \times (18\% - 12\%) \right] = 12.4\% \text{ (rounded)}$$

Since the proposal's IRR exceeds the 12% cost of capital, it is acceptable using this criterion.

You should note that, for all their seeming complexity, the IRR calculations above are nevertheless approximations. This is because the fractions within the square brackets assume a linear (i.e. straight-line) relationship between NPV and discount rate, whereas, in fact, the relationship is curvilinear, as illustrated in Figure 15.1. Not only this, but the degree of inaccuracy of the approximation resulting from calculations of this sort will be affected by the difference between the two discount rates used: the greater this difference, the greater will be the inaccuracy in our estimate of IRR. Figure 15.2 illustrates this point: the line AB represents the linear approximation of the NPV/discount rate relationship based on the Sphere Theatre proposal's NPVs at rates of 12% and 18% and line AC approximates the same relationship at discount rates of 12% and 50%.

You will see from Figure 15.2 that, as the difference between the two discount rates widens, so the estimate of IRR moves to the right (i.e. increases). Although the resultant change in IRR is fairly small in our example, even such a small change could affect perception about the financial viability of marginal proposals like that being considered by the Sphere Theatre.

Although this trial-and-error approach to determination of IRR can be cumbersome if performed manually, computer spreadsheets greatly reduce the burden of calculation: in fact, many spreadsheet packages contain a preprogrammed facility for calculating IRR.

DCF techniques and the concept of relevance

When appraising the financial desirability of capital investment proposals, it is important not to lose sight of the fact that we are analysing *decisions*. For this reason, the concept of **relevant costs and benefits** needs to be applied in order to determine *which* cash flows to include in a DCF calculation. In Chapter 14, we defined relevant costs and benefits as:

Future cash flows which differ between alternatives

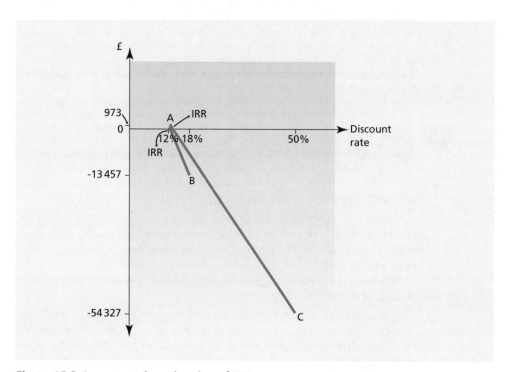

Figure 15.2 Inaccuracy in estimation of IRR

Suppose the Sphere Theatre's capital investment appraisal involved a *choice* of new booking system as detailed in Exhibit 15.7.

Sphere Theatre: choice of new booking system

The theatre has a choice of specification for its new system: System A will meet all basic requirements while System B, although more costly to acquire, is reckoned to have greater potential for profit improvement because of its greater sophistication. Details are as follows:

		System A	System B
Initial cost of hardware and software		£100 000	£150 000
Useful life		5 years	5 years
		£	£
Net cash inflow if bought:	Year 1	23 000	28 000
	Year 2	26 000	30 000
	Year 3	27 000	35 000
	Year 4	28 000	38 000
	Year 5	30 000	42 000
Resale value at the end of Year 5		10 000	14 000

The theatre's existing booking system was bought five years ago for £60 000 and will be sold for £5000 irrespective of which new system is acquired.
The theatre's cost of capital is 12%.

Exhibit 15.7 Mutually exclusive options

We have already calculated System A's net present value (at the theatre's 12% cost of capital) as £973.

 Using the discount factors from Appendix A and the 12% cost of capital, determine System B's net present value. Is System B financially preferable to System A?

System B's NPV is shown in Table 15.3.

The original cost of the existing system is a sunk cost, and the sale proceeds of £5000 will be received irrespective of which new system is bought: both are therefore irrelevant to the decision. The total cash inflow from System B in Year 5 includes the resale value of £14 000.

As System B's NPV is negative, System A (with a positive NPV of £973) is preferable on financial grounds.

By discounting *all* the relevant cash flows of each system, we have arrived at the correct financial evaluation. However, we can shorten the discounting procedures by using **differential cash flows** – i.e. the difference between the relevant cash flows relating to each option.

Table 15.3 NPV of alternative new booking system

Year	Cash flow	Amount £	Discount factor	Present value £
0	Initial cost	(150 000)	1.000	(150 000)
1	Net cash inflow	28 000	0.893	25 004
2	Net cash inflow	30 000	0.797	23 910
3	Net cash inflow	35 000	0.712	24 920
4	Net cash inflow	38 000	0.636	24 168
5	Net cash inflow	56 000	0.567	31 752
			NPV	(20 246)

✔ *What are the differential cash flows associated with purchase of System B?*

The differential cash flows are:

		£
Year 0:	additional purchase cost	(50 000)
Year 1:	additional cash inflow	5 000
Year 2:	additional cash inflow	4 000
Year 3:	additional cash inflow	8 000
Year 4:	additional cash inflow	10 000
Year 5:	additional cash inflow	16 000

✔ *What is the NPV of the differential cash flows at a cost of capital of 12%?*

The differential cash flows' NPV is shown in Table 15.4.

Table 15.4 Systems A and B – NPV of differential cash flows

Year	Cash flow	Amount £	Discount factor	Present value £
0	Initial cost	(50 000)	1.000	(50 000)
1	Net cash inflow	5 000	0.893	4 465
2	Net cash inflow	4 000	0.797	3 188
3	Net cash inflow	8 000	0.712	5 696
4	Net cash inflow	10 000	0.636	6 360
5	Net cash inflow	16 000	0.567	9 072
			NPV	(21 219)

The differential cash flows have a negative NPV, so acquisition of System B is less financially attractive than System A. Alternatively, we could have discounted the differential cash flows associated with purchase of System A, in which case the differential NPV would be £21 219 (positive); you may wish to check that this is so. Our differential NPV is simply the difference between the NPVs we obtained when we discounted all the relevant cash flows for each system:

	£
NPV System B	(20 246)
NPV System A	973
Difference in NPV	(21 219)

Either approach is acceptable, and differential costing can reduce the volume of calculations necessary for the financial appraisal. But caution must be exercised when interpreting the results of differential analysis: a positive *differential* NPV in favour of System A is not the same as saying that System A has a positive NPV. Assume the proposals' NPVs are:

	£
Proposal A	(5000)
Proposal B	(5972)
Difference in NPV	(972)

Here, use of differential NPV unsupported by other information could result in acceptance of a proposal which should, *prima facie*, be rejected.

DCF techniques versus accounting rate of return and payback

Since NPV and IRR not only incorporate all cash flows over a proposal's life, but also make explicit allowance for the time value of money, both appraisal criteria pass our 'acid test' in terms of how well they reflect the nature of the proposal being evaluated. However, there may be some difficulty in determining the most appropriate cost of capital to employ.

It is also worth noting that the mechanics of calculating the present value factors contained in Appendices A and B imply that cash flows arise *at the end* of each year and this is likely to be a simplification of reality. But the effect is, in most cases, unlikely to be sufficiently material to alter the financial standing of a proposal (and it is possible to amend discounting calculations to allow for more complex patterns of cash flows).

It is also possible to argue that the discounting process, by giving greater 'weight' to earlier than later cash flows, could introduce the same kind of short-term bias that we suggested earlier might occur with payback.

A comparative study of appraisal techniques used by the same 100 large UK companies over a period of time (Pike and Wolfe, 1988) seems to suggest that usage of DCF techniques is increasing:

	1975	1981	1986
	%	%	%
Internal rate of return	44	57	75
Net present value	32	39	68
Average accounting rate of return	51	49	56
Payback	73	81	92

These results are echoed by Drury *et al.* (1992), with payback and IRR being the most frequently used techniques. The popularity of payback is interesting – and perhaps worrying – in the light of our earlier comments about short-termism. But it is worth noting that payback is also the dominant approach in Japan and in UK-based Japanese subsidiaries, where a long-term orientation is common (see Bromwich and Inoue, 1994). Problems may therefore lie in the way payback is applied, rather in the technique itself.

NPV versus IRR

If DCF techniques are better in principle than accounting rate of return and payback, which DCF approach is better and why?

Of the two criteria, NPV is technically superior for the reasons we shall discuss below. Where any conflict exists between the two DCF approaches as to the financial desirability of a particular proposal, or the ranking of competing proposals, then 'desirability' as indicated by NPV should be preferred to that indicated by IRR. If NPV conflicts with accounting rate of return and/or payback, then the situation may be less clear: as the only 'wealth-maximising' model, NPV is probably superior.

1 As we have seen, determination of IRR is often a matter of trial and error and the result can thus be much less precise than net present value. Depending on the extent of this imprecision, the acceptability of proposals may be affected.

2 IRR, like accounting rate of return, considers neither the size of the investment required nor the gain/loss which will result from undertaking or not undertaking a particular proposal. It will therefore be difficult to use IRR to make comparisons between competing proposals and it may happen that the two DCF appraisal criteria – IRR and NPV – will give conflicting indications about the financial desirability of a particular proposal.

3 IRR is unable to cope with a change in the cost of capital (i.e. the discount rate) during the life of a proposal. If the cost of capital does change during a proposal's life, it means that there is more than one target return against which to compare IRR. For example:

Proposal's estimated life	10 years
Proposal's IRR	12%
Cost of capital applicable to:	
Years 1–5 of proposal's life	10%
Years 6–10 of proposal's life	14%

Using IRR as the criterion, the proposal seems to be acceptable for Years 1–5, but unacceptable for Years 6–10; is the proposal acceptable over its entire life? IRR does not provide the answer. NPV can easily accommodate such a change: if the cost of capital changes, all we need do is use the present value factors appropriate to the changed cost of capital in our calculations.

4 Where a proposal has annual cash flows which are a mixture of net inflow and net outflow, that proposal may have a single IRR (as did the Sphere Theatre's proposal), it may have no IRR, or it may have more than one. Consider the following pattern of cash flows relating to a capital investment proposal:

		£
Year 0	net cash outflow	100 000
Year 2	net cash outflow	50 000

The pattern of cash flows above will have a negative IRR. Since a discount rate of less than zero is virtually meaningless, implying a reversal of the time value of money, we can effectively say that this proposal has no IRR. You may think that this is rather contrived, but you must remember that a capital investment proposal need not have cash inflows associated with it. For example, the cash flows above might relate to installation of a sprinkler system in an office building – highly desirable on safety grounds, but unlikely to generate any cash inflows. You may also feel that, since the pattern of cash flows above will yield a negative NPV at all discount rates, NPV offers no advantage over IRR. This is true if only one sprinkler system can be installed. But if there are alternatives, we can use NPV to select the least-cost option – i.e. we should install the system with the negative NPV which is closest to zero. Such a comparison is impossible using IRR, as there will be no IRRs to compare. In fact, it can be proved mathematically that a proposal will have as many IRRs as there are changes in the sign attaching to the cash flows (i.e. from net outflow to net inflow or vice versa). In the Sphere Theatre's case, there is an initial outflow followed by a series of inflows – one change of sign – so this proposal has one IRR. Had we been faced with an initial net outflow, followed, say, by net inflows in each of Years 1, 2, 3 and 4, followed by another net outflow in Year 5 – *two* changes in the sign attaching to proposal cash flows – then there would be two IRRs, thus rendering IRR almost meaningless as an evaluative criterion. NPV, on the other hand, can deal with any pattern of cash flows and so does not suffer from this shortcoming.

5 Implicit in the NPV approach is the assumption that project cash inflows are reinvested to earn a return equal to the cost of capital. You may wish to review our earlier description of compounding and discounting to see that this is so. IRR, on the other hand, assumes reinvestment at the project's IRR. The logical flaw in this is not hard to see:

Proposal	A	B
Estimated life	10 years	10 years
IRR	15%	25%

Assuming both proposals to be acceptable and to start at the same point in time, how can it happen that the rate of return on reinvestment of the cash flows from each differs so markedly?

Despite its theoretical shortcomings, surveys of practice, such as those cited earlier, indicate widespread use of IRR. It may be that management finds percentages easier to work with than absolute amounts such as NPV.

GENERAL DIFFICULTIES WITH CAPITAL INVESTMENT CRITERIA

All the criteria we have described in this chapter have some common difficulties.

1 They are all financial measures; for decisions of the type we are considering, non-financial factors may be of major significance, especially for proposals with no associated cash inflows, such as the sprinkler system mentioned earlier, or for many public sector projects where there are large intangible costs and benefits.

2 None of the measures indicates how a proposal is to be funded. Given that the cost

of many capital projects is substantial, their funding must be a major consideration in assessing financial viability.

3 Since the life span of many capital investment projects is long, there may be a problem in producing credible estimates – particularly for the later years. And even if reasonable estimates can be produced, it may be the case – particularly with 'high-tech' assets such as computers – that the proposal's life needs to be artificially shortened to allow for obsolescence. This might be a somewhat arbitrary process which could distort the apparent financial viability of a proposal. Estimation difficulties may somewhat erode the 'simplicity' benefit claimed for accounting rate of return and payback, and could be one reason for the predominance of short target payback periods in practice.

4 Over-reliance on financial criteria for evaluating capital investment decisions may obscure the strategic context. In particular, these criteria may be too internally focused, where strategic assessment requires a much wider perspective. It is also possible that imposition of relatively inflexible financial targets, coupled with their short-term bias, might stifle innovation. For example, adoption of a particular proposal may ultimately pave the way for further developments – a factor unlikely to be shown by financial analysis.

PROJECT POST-AUDIT

Also termed **post-completion audit**, project post-audit reviews the financial impact of a capital expenditure decision on one or more occasions during its life and/or at the end of its life. The main thrust of post-audit is a comparison of a project's actual cash flows with the estimates which were used in its original appraisal; in addition, the 'fit' between a proposal and the strategy which it was adopted in order to support may be assessed.

Benefits and problems of post-audit

Post-auditing capital investment decisions offers a number of benefits:

1 Knowledge that a proposal will be post-audited, if implemented, may result in more rigorous estimation of related costs and benefits at the appraisal stage.

2 Post-audit during a project's life may reveal problems (both with the project itself and on a wider front) which can be corrected, or may indicate problems of such magnitude that project abandonment is required.

3 The post-audit process could suggest hitherto unforeseen opportunities for worthwhile capital investments or strategic improvement.

4 Post-audit results may be incorporated into evaluations of managerial performance.

 Can you suggest any potential problems with post-audit?

Arguably the major danger inherent in post-audit arises from overemphasising its financial control aspect – i.e. the comparison of estimated and actual costs/benefits – which might inhibit managers. Such inhibition could be reflected in a managerial risk-aversion which reinforces pressures towards short-termism. Post-audit can also be a costly, time-consuming exercise, and, given the strategic implications of the audit's subject-matter, we may be committing scarce resources to little or no good effect. Once a capital investment project is underway, its ramifications might be so wide that it is virtually impossible to identify related costs and benefits (let alone quantify them). Similarly, post-audit must recognise the possibility of a lengthy time lapse between project inception and proper appreciation of its consequences.

SUMMARY

In this chapter, we have discussed techniques for financial evaluation of capital investment proposals and have seen that:

- Appraisal of capital investment proposals should be linked to overall organisational strategy

- **Accounting rate of return** is measured as

$$\frac{\text{Average annual profit}}{\text{Initial capital cost}} \times 100\%$$

or

$$\frac{\text{Average annual profit}}{\text{Average capital cost}} \times 100\%$$

- Average capital cost is

$$\frac{(\text{Initial cost} + \text{resale value})}{2}$$

- Accounting rate of return has advantages and disadvantages which can be summarised as

Advantages	Disadvantages
Easy to calculate	Impact of averaging
Easy to understand	Time value of money ignored
	No generally accepted definition
	Based on profit
	Expressed in % terms

- **Payback** is the period, usually expressed in years, taken for a proposal's net cash inflows to equal its initial cost.

- A payback period which is shorter than target is acceptable; one which is longer than target is not.

- Payback has certain advantages and disadvantages which can be summarised as

Advantages	Disadvantages
Easy to calculate and understand	Ignores the time value of money
Based on cash flows	Ignores all cash flows which arise after the payback period
Useful for 'screening'	Ignores the size of investment and its overall cost/benefit
Useful in liquidity crises	
Useful for risky proposals	

- The **time value of money** arises as the result of
  - 'lost' interest
  - liquidity preference

- By **discounting** a proposal's cash flows at the **cost of capital,** we allow for the time value of money and express all cash flows on a common basis – i.e. in today's terms.

- The **present value** of £1 paid/received at the end of n years from now at a cost of capital r is

$$\frac{1}{(1+r)^n}$$

- **Discount factors** for single cash flows and for **annuities** can be obtained from precalculated tables.

- **Net present value** (**NPV**) is the sum of a proposal's discounted cash inflows and outflows. A positive NPV (discounted inflows exceed discounted outflows) is acceptable, a negative NPV (discounted outflows exceed discounted inflows) is not.

- **Internal rate of return** (**IRR**) is the discount rate at which a proposal yields a zero NPV; if IRR exceeds the cost of capital, the proposal is acceptable, if it is less than the cost of capital, the proposal is unacceptable.

- The volume of discounting calculations can be reduced by using **differential cash flows.**

- IRR suffers from a number of problems compared to NPV:
  - calculation is rarely precise
  - expressed in % terms
  - unable to cope with a change in the cost of capital during the proposal's life
  - projects which have either no IRR or have multiple IRRs
  - reinvestment assumed to occur at a project's IRR.

- All the appraisal criteria discussed suffer common difficulties:
  - they are financial criteria
  - they do not indicate how a proposal is to be funded
  - some estimates for later years of a project's life may lack credibility
  - they may obscure strategic considerations.

- **Post-audit** involves comparison of a project's actual outcomes with the estimates used in its appraisal.

- The advantages and problems of post-audit are:

Advantages	*Problems*
More rigorous estimation	Inhibition of managers
May reveal problems	Costly and time-consuming
Suggest opportunities	Identifying/quantifying costs/benefits
Performance evaluation	Time lapse before benefits appear

In the next chapter, we will commence our discussion of another key cost accounting topic: budgetary planning and control.

FURTHER READING

Bromwich, M. and Inoue, S., *Management Practices and Cost Management Problems in Japanese-affiliated Companies in the United Kingdom*, CIMA, 1994: Chapter 7 includes a summary of research findings about capital investment methodology.

Collison, D., Grinyer, J. and Russell, A., *Management's Economic Decisions and Financial Reporting*, ICAS, 1993.

Dixon, R., *Investment Appraisal: A Guide for Managers*, Kogan Page/CIMA, 1994.

Drury, C., Braund, S., Osborne, P. and Tayles, M., *A Survey of Management Accounting Practices in UK Manufacturing Companies*, ACCA, 1992.

Pike, R. and Wolfe, M., *Capital Budgeting for the 1990s*, CIMA, 1988.

Upchurch, A., *Management Accounting Principles and Practice*, Financial Times Pitman Publishing, 1998: Chapter 11 provides an introductory discussion of the cost of capital.

Warner, A., *The Bottom Line*, Gower Publishing, 1988: Chapter 14 discusses capital investment appraisal techniques as part of an extended case study.

SELF-TEST QUESTIONS

15.1 For each of the following statements, tick the appropriate box to indicate whether it is true or false.

	True	False

(a) The higher the cost of capital used to discount a proposal's cash flows, the higher will be that proposal's net present value.

(b) A short payback period indicates quick recovery of a proposal's initial cost.

(c) Use of initial capital cost to determine a proposal's accounting rate of return will yield a lower return than use of average capital cost for the same proposal.

(d) Annual profit arising from a proposal can be determined by adding depreciation to the proposal's cash flows.

(e) Average capital cost can be defined as

$$\frac{(\text{Initial capital cost} - \text{resale value})}{2}$$

(f) £1 received three years from now has a higher present value than £1 received five years from now.

(g) The same cash sum received each year for 15 years is termed an annuity.

(h) A proposal which has several changes from cash inflow to cash outflow over its life will have a single internal rate of return.

15.2 Ash plc is considering investing in new machinery in its factory and has identified three options which are mutually exclusive due to limitations of space within the factory.

Machine 1 has a purchase price of £1.2 million and an expected life of four years, after which its estimated residual value is £200 000. It is expected to bring in net extra cash flows of £350 000 per annum over its life.

Machine 2 costs £2.5 million and will also last four years, after which it will be sold for an estimated £295 000. Its expected net extra cash flows are £725 000 per annum.

Machine 3 costs £2 million and will, again, last for four years, it will then be sold for an estimated £310 000. Its net extra cash flows are estimated at £565 000 per annum.

Ash's current cost of capital is 8%. The company has a policy of evaluating capital projects using its current cost of capital and ignoring the implications of inflation and taxation due to the uncertainty surrounding both.

Requirements

(a) Calculate the net present value of each option, following the company's evaluation policy and the internal rate of return of each option. **(12 marks)**

(b) Based on the results of (a) above state, with reasons, which option you would recommend. **(6 marks)**

(CIPFA, *Accounting for Decision Making*, December 1997)

15.3 The directors of Westwood Ltd regard investment in new plant and equipment as essential to compete with a new product introduced by their main competitor. As the company's banker you are concerned that the project has not been properly costed.

Westwood Ltd has a cost of capital of 10% and a payback period of four years. The project has an estimated initial cost of £360 000 commencing in January 1997. The following net cash flows have been projected.

	£	£
Investment		360 000
Year to 31.12.1997	85 000	
1998	90 500	
1999	87 250	
2000	84 800	
2001	80 600	
2002	74 000	

To assess the project calculate the following:

(a) Payback period. (3 marks)

(b) Net present value. (7 marks)

(c) Internal rate of return. (10 marks)

(Total: 20 marks)

(CIOBS, *Business Accounting*, December 1997)

15.4 The Polygon is a privately-owned theatre on the outskirts of a university city with a population of about half a million people. The theatre seats 600 people: 300 downstairs in the stalls and 300 upstairs in the circle. A typical production opens on a Tuesday, and runs until the following Saturday week, i.e. for eleven working days. (The theatre is not open on Sunday.)

One of Polygon's problems is that, while about 60% of seats are sold during the week, there is frequently excess demand on Fridays and Saturdays, with the result that a lot of potential revenue is lost. Management is considering three options – no change, reorganise the seating, and a major building expansion.

The cash flows (£000) for total costs and total revenue, assuming a five-year plan, have been estimated as follows:

		1997	1998	1999	2000	2001	2002
No change	Costs	1500	1600	1700	1800	1900	2000
	Revenue	1600	1650	1700	1750	1800	1800
Reorganisation	Costs	2000	1900	2000	2000	2100	2200
	Revenue	2000	2000	2000	2000	2000	2000
Expansion	Costs	3000	2000	2000	2500	2500	2500
	Revenue	zero	2500	3000	3500	3500	3500

Requirements:

(a) Use the data on Polygon's expansion plans to evaluate the three options with NPV techniques (assume the cost of capital to be 10%, and year-end cash flows). (10 marks)

(b) Estimate the internal rate of return of your recommendation.   (10 marks)

(c) Comment briefly on the viability of the business.   (5 marks)

(Total: 25 marks)

(CIMA *Management Science Applications*, November 1996)

15.5 Your company is considering investing in its own transport fleet. The present position is that carriage is contracted to an outside organisation. The life of the transport fleet would be five years, after which time the vehicles would have to be disposed of.

The cost to your company of using the outside organisation for its carriage needs is £250 000 for this year. The cost, it is projected, will rise 10% per annum over the life of the project. The initial cost of the transport fleet would be £750 000 and it is estimated that the following costs would be incurred over the next five years:

	Drivers' *costs* £	*Repairs and* *maintenance* £	*Other* *costs* £
Year 1	33 000	8 000	130 000
Year 2	35 000	13 000	135 000
Year 3	36 000	15 000	140 000
Year 4	38 000	16 000	136 000
Year 5	40 000	18 000	142 000

Other costs include depreciation. It is projected that the fleet would be sold for £150 000 at the end of year 5. It has been agreed to depreciate the fleet on a straight-line basis.

To raise funds for the project, your company is proposing to raise a long-term loan at 12% interest rate per annum.

You are told that there is an alternative project that could be invested in using the funds raised, which has the following projected results:

Payback = 3 years
Accounting rate of return = 30%
Net present value = £140 000.

As funds are limited, investment can only be made in one project.

Note: The transport fleet would be purchased at the beginning of the project and all other expenditure would be incurred at the end of the relevant year.

Requirements

(a) Prepare a table showing the net cash savings to be made by the firm over the life of the transport fleet project.   (5 marks)

(b) Calculate the following for the transport fleet project:

(i)   Payback period
(ii) Accounting rate of return
(iii) Net present value.   (13 marks)

(c) Write a short report to the Investment Manager in your company outlining whether investment should be committed to the transport fleet or the alternative project outlined. Clearly state the reasons for your choice.   (7 marks)

(Total: 25 marks)

(AAT, *Cost Accounting and Budgeting*, June 1992)

QUESTIONS WITHOUT ANSWERS

The following information is to be used for 15.6 and 15.7.

A capital investment proposal has the following characteristics:

initial cost	£400 000	scrap value	nil
useful life	4 years	annual depreciation	£100 000

profit per annum (after depreciation): Year 1   £50 000
Year 2 £100 000
Year 3 £100 000
Year 4 £150 000

15.6 What is the proposal's payback period?

A 2.00 years
B 2.25 years
C 3.67 years
D 4.00 years

15.7 What is the proposal's accounting rate of return based on initial investment?

A   12.5%
B   25.0%
C   37.5%
D 100.0%

15.8 Management of Uptown Ltd is aware that it has to invest in new plant to maintain a technical advantage over its competitors. Management is considering applying for a bank loan to fund the purchase of fixed assets which would allow the production of a new range of high technology products. As part of exploratory talks with your bank the business has made available its projections for the project. The cost of capital is 12%.

New plant will cost £140 000 and require an additional £20 000 for building alterations. Additional staffing costs will include £20 000 per annum for a supervisor and £50 000 in total per annum for machine operators, clerical and sales staff. Wage levels are not expected to rise until year three at which point all staffing costs are expected to rise by 5% and remain at that level until the end of the project's life.

Raw material required for the project is expected to cost £95 000 in year one rising by 3% each year thereafter. Projected power costs are as follows:

Year 1 – £28 000   Year 4 – £32 000
Year 2 – £29 000   Year 5 – £34 000
Year 3 – £31 000

The equipment will require an overhaul costing £17 000 in year 3. It is expected that the project will have a life of five years at the end of which the equipment will be sold for £24 000. At this stage projected redundancy costs will be £7000. Projected annual sales income is shown below.

Year	Sales Income
£000	
1	210
2	235
3	260
4	300
5	285

To help assess the project:

(a) Show the annual net cash flow from the project.   (**8 marks**)

(b) Calculate the internal rate of return.   (**10 marks**)

(c) Assess the feasibility of the project.   (**2 marks**)
                                                                 (**Total: 20 marks**)

(CIOBS, *Business Accounting*, May 1997)

15.9 The VWXYZ Company produces a variety of high-quality garden furniture and associated items, mostly in wood and wrought iron. Among its products are speciality garden seats, sheds, gates, summer pavilions, outdoor tables and chairs, barbeque equipment etc. VWXYZ currently sells mostly to the trade but there is a flourishing retail outlet on the same site as the factory at Guildford, in the south of England.

There is potential to expand the business. The directors have identified three main options for a four-year plan:

(a) Expand the retail outlet to include all products.

(b) Branch out into mail order.

(c) Produce greenhouses and conservatories.

These options would require initial expenditures of (a) £75 000, (b) £120 000 or (c) £200 000. The best information on year-end cash flows is:

	Year 1 £000	Year 2 £000	Year 3 £000	Year 4 £000
(a)	40	50	50	50
(b)	50	60	80	100
(c)	50	100	150	150

Requirements:

(a) Using the data on expansion plans, *evaluate* the three investment options using the net present value (NPV) technique, assuming the cost of capital to be 10%, and recommend, with reasons, *one* option.   (**15 marks**)

(b) Find the approximate internal rate of return (IRR) of your choice in (a) above.
                                                                 (**5 marks**)

(c) Interpret your results for management.   (**5 marks**)
                                                                 (**Total: 25 marks**)

(CIMA, *Management Science Applications, Specimen Paper*)

15.10 (a) Essential to an understanding of the investment appraisal techniques of payback, accounting rate of return and net present value is the role of depreciation.

Requirement:

Explain how you would treat depreciation in a computation for each of the above appraisal techniques giving reasons for your decisions.   (**6 marks**)

(b) Company TH Ltd is considering investing in one of two mutually exclusive projects. Both projects would require an investment of £150 000 at the commencement of the project and the profile of returns is as follows:

	Project 1		Project 2	
	Profit	Cash flow	Profit	Cash flow
	£	£	£	£
Year 1	40 000	60 000	30 000	54 000
Year 2	30 000	50 000	20 000	44 000
Year 3	25 000	45 000	15 000	39 000
Year 4	35 000	55 000	25 000	49 000
Year 5			50 000	74 000

You are told that the machinery associated with Project 1 will be sold for £70 000 at the end of year 4 and the machinery associated with Project 2 will be sold for £30 000 at the end of Year 5. The company's cost of capital is 15%.

Requirement

Determine for both projects the:

(i)   Payback period
(ii) Accounting rate of return
(iii) Net present value

and advise which project should be invested in giving your reasons. **(15 marks)**

(c) You have been asked by a manager at TH Ltd why you might need the expected disposal proceeds of the capital investment at the end of the project for any investment appraisal technique as the capital investment has already been depreciated.

Requirement

Clearly answer the manager's query identifying which investment appraisal technique, if any, utilises the disposal proceeds of a capital investment at the end of a project.

(4 marks)
(Total: 25 marks)

(AAT, *Cost Accounting and Budgeting*, June 1993)

CHAPTER 16

Budgetary planning I

Budgetary control – the organisational aspects

Planning and control are major activities of management in all organisations. Budgets are central to the process of planning and control. The involvement with budgets places the management accountant as a key player in the provision of management information. Readers will not be surprised to know that most organisations employ some form of budgeting, those of any size have quite formal mechanisms. A large survey of over 300 companies supported by ACCA, on which the author was engaged, reported recently that almost all respondents used some form of budgeting and budgetary control …

A good starting point is to set budgets within an overall organisational planning and control framework. A common sub-division of the wider planning and control framework in organisations is *strategic planning*, *management control* and *operational or task control*.

Strategic planning is the process of deciding on the goals of the organisation and the formulation of the broad strategies to be used in attaining these goals. It is the responsibility of top management, it is creative and involves identifying a company's strengths and opportunities to grow whilst minimising weaknesses and threats. It has a long-term orientation and looks outside the organisation at customers and competitors.

Management control is the process by which management assures that the organisation carries out its strategies. It is more short-term, is focused on middle managers and is more rhythmic and routine.

Operational or task control is the process of assuring that specific tasks are carried out effectively and efficiently. The timescale here can be very short-term, perhaps daily, and addresses targets of junior management. Often it is based on the use of non-financial measures and may be based on clearly defined input/output relationships …

Source: Mike Tayles, *ACCA Students' Newsletter*, December 1998.

Exhibit 16.1 The importance of budgets

INTRODUCTION

Budgets are a pervasive fact of life and affect us all – directly and indirectly, in both our working and personal environments. Government will set a budget which determines such things as the rate of tax we pay; as individuals, we budget between various forms of spending and saving. The essential difference between the two forms of budget (as suggested in Exhibit 16.1) is the degree of formality involved. Large organisations like the government will have well-developed formal budget systems; small organisations and individuals are likely to be more informal in their approach, but must likewise possess some kind of planning mechanism.

In Chapter 1, we identified planning as one of management's primary functions – and, simply put, budgets represent a statement of managerial plans for the organisation as a whole and for various subsections of the organisation. Since effective planning is so vital to the success of an organisation, an understanding of budgets – a major planning mechanism – is essential, not only for those tasked with the responsibility of preparing, implementing and achieving budgets (i.e. management) but also for those whose operations are governed and influenced by management actions (i.e. the workforce, customers, shareholders, suppliers and possibly society in general).

OBJECTIVES

When you have completed this chapter, you will be able to:

- provide a definition of the term 'budget' and explain the major purposes of budgets, along with their potential shortcomings;
- distinguish between operational, tactical and strategic budgets and appreciate their relationship;
- describe the role of the budget committee, budget officer and budget manual;
- understand the meaning of standard costing, its significance in the budgeting process, its objectives and problems;
- prepare functional budgets for a manufacturing organisation.

'BUDGET': A DEFINITION

Our definition is so straightforward as to seem, perhaps, self-evident: a budget is a *quantified plan targeted at achievement of an objective (or objectives)*. Simple as it may seem, this definition encompasses the three essential elements of a budget. A budget is a plan: i.e. is *future-oriented* – the past is only relevant insofar as it provides a reasonable indicator of the future. We must also be clear that a plan is not an end in itself, but a means to an end – achieving a particular objective (or objectives). In effect, our definition of 'budget' also includes control. We prepare budgets to achieve objectives and then assess how far performance, budgets and objectives are in line with each other (see Chapter 18 for discussion of the control aspects of budgets). In saying this we are, of course, assuming that objectives are clearly defined – which, as we observed in Chapter 1, may not always be the case.

✔ *Why is it important that plans be quantified?*

If they lack quantification, plans can lose much of their value. Suppose a business plans to earn 'some profit' in the forthcoming year. Without knowing how much profit, it is difficult to assess the amount of 'effort' which should be expended in pursuit of the plan – i.e. the required sales and related costs. At the end of the year, how can the business gauge how successful it has been in achieving its plan (and hence its objectives)? In short, the 'plan', having provided neither a meaningful target for future effort nor a benchmark for associated performance, is almost as bad as no plan at all. Quantifying the plan – e.g. 'earn £500 000 profit next year' – helps to remedy these problems.

OBJECTIVES OF BUDGETS

Our definition of 'budget' provides an indication of the major objectives of a system of budgeting. The extent to which budgets succeed in achieving these objectives is, however, questionable.

Compel planning

The existence of a budget forces managers to think ahead, trying to anticipate possible problems and their solution. Although budgets cannot prevent the unforeseen from occurring or remove future difficulties, their formulation can allow some degree of pre-paredness. For example, awareness of a potential future problem with material suppliers would allow contingency arrangements to be made (e.g. finding alternative suppliers) in advance. All of this presupposes that budgets are reasonable estimates of the future; but producing credible estimates, especially in rapidly changing environments, can be extremely difficult. The budget process therefore places great reliance on managerial knowledge and judgement. On the one hand, it might be said that the need to exercise such knowledge and judgement within a formalised budgeting framework will reduce the effect of any overly subjective elements. On the other hand, a formal system might inhibit freedom of management action, thereby adding undue weight to risk-averse courses of action. A further difficulty is that, while budgets may indicate what we should do, they do not necessarily tell us *how* to do it.

Provide a performance benchmark and financial control mechanism

A typical budget system will identify managerial responsibility with particular areas of the budget (**responsibility accounting**), financial control and performance evaluation being frequently based on comparison of budgeted and actual outcomes (**feedback control**) and of budgeted outcomes with objectives (**feedforward control**). It is quite common for managerial salary bonuses to be linked to performance defined in feedback/feedforward terms. We will discuss these topics in Chapters 18 and 19, where we will see that financial measures of control have limitations, possibly even dangers.

Provide motivational impetus

Setting targets may have motivational benefits. If we have a clearly stated and quantified target, it is possible that we will make more effort to achieve it than we might otherwise do. However, the motivational effect of budgetary target-setting is far from clear. Budgeting, and participation in budget-setting *may* be motivationally beneficial, but may also have exactly the opposite effect – especially where budgets are viewed by management as a constraint or as a 'big stick' to punish underachievement. (We will have more to say about this in Chapters 18 and 19.)

Provide a medium of communication

There is no point to having targets, benchmarks and control mechanisms if they are kept secret: people need to know what is expected of them. Budgets provide one means of disseminating such awareness through the organisation. In addition, communication should be enhanced by the budget-setting process where this is undertaken by a combination of 'top-down' and 'bottom-up' procedures: i.e. where budgets are the result of consultation, participation and flow of information from top management downwards (e.g. strategic targets) and from operational management upwards (e.g. detailed estimates – **standard costs** – for individual cost units).

However, the success of budgets as a medium of communication relies on the extent to which the principles and information involved are understood. Thus the criteria governing useful information which we set out in Chapter 1 are especially important. Effective budgetary communication is also predicated on the clarity and openness of formal transmission channels. The extent to which informal channels do/do not predominate over formal could give some indication of the effectiveness of budgetary communication. (You should also bear in mind the barriers to communication which we discussed in Chapter 1.)

It is also possible that the administrative burden associated with budgets could overshadow the purpose of budget preparation, causing the exercise to flounder in bureaucratic 'overkill'.

Enhance co-ordination

In larger organisations particularly, co-ordination between different divisions, departments and managers is of vital importance – especially where these enjoy any significant degree of independence from central control.

 In a manufacturing business, why is it important that the activities of the sales and production departments are co-ordinated?

If there were no co-ordination between these two departments, chaos would almost certainly result. For example, the sales department might promise delivery to customers within unrealistic time limits, or quantities produced might be far in excess of what can be sold, causing an unnecessary build-up in stocks. Formalised budget preparation, by explicitly recognising interrelationships between different organisational segments, should help reduce the chance of such undesirable situations. One of the objectives of budgets is thus to promote **goal congruence**: i.e. to encourage actions by individual employees, managers, sections, departments or divisions which are consistent with overall organisational aims (or at least do not directly conflict with them). Where conflicts of this kind do arise, the results are **suboptimal** (or **dysfunctional**): e.g. promises of impossibly unrealistic delivery dates could well result in lost custom, which is scarcely in the organisation's best interest.

This is a very laudable objective, but it requires that organisational objectives be clearly and unambiguously stated. Not only do we have the problem of diffuse and potentially conflicting organisational objectives (*see* Chapter 1), but we are also faced with the fact that, as Cyert and March (1963) observe, organisations do not have objectives, *people* do. Problems in objective-setting can only hamper proper coordination of diverse activities, and this may be exacerbated by unduly dominant informal communication channels.

Instil financial awareness

Without the existence of budgets, managers may be quite unaware of the financial implications of their actions, or of the need to look for alternatives which are more financially effective. Such a lack of awareness would be detrimental to the organisation as a whole, since there is the danger of scarce resources being carelessly used, as if they were somehow 'free'. But it is also possible to argue that this sort of awareness can (and does) exist independently of any formal budget system – in which case is the formal system redundant? Formalising managerial expectations within a budget system might result in a situation where there is conflict between managerial expectations as expressed in the budget and their *true* expectations. Budgets may instil cost consciousness but may, if used in a 'carrot and stick' manner, inspire feelings almost of fear and loathing among managers. In addition, it is rare for a budget system explicitly to reflect its own cost – i.e. the cost of set-up, maintenance and operation. Not only can these financial costs be substantial, but there is also the question of management time involved in budget-related activities, time which could be more profitably spent in other ways.

So perhaps the sort of cost consciousness instilled by budgets could be organisationally undesirable, focusing managers' attention on annual, financial and internal considerations at the expense of longer-term, non-financial and environmental factors.

Delegation and authorisation

In large organisations, it is common for top management to delegate a certain degree of authority for decision making to lower managerial levels. Budgets provide a mechanism whereby the extent of delegated authority can be defined, as the budget acts as authorisation for lower-level managers to spend. This has the benefit of freeing top management to concentrate on strategic issues, and allows greater flexibility in decision making, as lower-level managers are freed from the need to seek approval for every decision. However, where authority has been delegated, there needs to be an effective control system in place to minimise the incidence of dysfunctional behaviour. One approach adopted by many organisations is to employ a system of **responsibility accounting** (see Chapter 18) where individual managers help set, and are responsible for meeting, their own budgets.

OPERATIONAL, TACTICAL AND STRATEGIC BUDGETS

While achieving budgets can be viewed as a target, budgets themselves must tend towards the achievement of some aim. In Chapter 1, we made the distinction between **strategic**, **tactical** and **operational** planning, control and decision making, contrasting their respective span, scope and level of detail. Thus, the **budget period** (i.e. the length of time to which the budget relates) applicable to strategic budgets will be considerably longer than that applicable to tactical and operational budgets – say, somewhere between 3 and 10 years for the former, one year (or less) for the latter. The scope of strategic budgets will likewise be broader, dealing with major issues of organisational development over the specified time horizon, whereas tactical and operational budgets will be much more limited – dealing, perhaps, with specific aspects of strategic issues.

Would you expect strategic budgets to be more or less detailed than tactical and operational?

Strategic budgets will be considerably less detailed than tactical and operational, being confined to quantifications of strategic aims, such as 'achieving a 25% market share within seven years', 'doubling return on capital over the next five years' or 'achieving world-class status'. Tactical and operational budgets, as we shall see, must contain sufficient detail to guide short-term operations towards attainment of strategic goals and also to provide meaningful information about how to run these operations efficiently, effectively and economically. The key point here is that, not only should budgets encourage goal congruence between individual subunits and the organisational whole, but also between strategic, tactical and operational considerations: i.e. tactical and operational budgets should, over a given strategic time frame, be consistent with achievement of strategic goals, as illustrated in Figure 16.1.

Two aspects of the budgeting process should be clear from Figure 16.1. First, there is the link between strategic, tactical and operational budgeting. Second, there is recognition that budgeting is a two-way process – 'top-down' and 'bottom-up'. In the 'top-down' perspective, strategy regulates operations which influence individual managers, who have a major bearing on actual performance. But equally important is the 'bottom-up' effect, whereby actual performance has an influence on individual managers, operations and strategy: i.e. actual conditions may be such that management activities, along with operational and even strategic objectives, need to be reviewed. (We will describe this **feedback** and **feedforward** mechanism in Chapter 18.) In practice, you should note that the kind of interrelationships illustrated in Figure 16.1 may be less clear-cut: e.g. 'operational' is often used to describe anything which is not strategic.

An example of why close integration of strategic, tactical and operational budgets is important can be seen in the impact of capital expenditure decisions. Strategic objectives will dictate the need for a particular capital expenditure project which will be evaluated using the sort of criteria we discussed in Chapter 15; if acceptable, this project will be incorporated within the strategic budget. This will 'feed through' to tactical level in the form of costs and benefits associated with the project for each year of its life. In the first year, for example, we might expect to see the initial acquisition cost (likely to be a substantial sum) plus current costs and benefits (e.g. annual running costs and increased revenue resulting from acquisition of new plant). At the operational level, the capital expenditure decision could affect work methods, material type and quantity, labour requirements and speed of throughput.

 What dangers might result from failure to recognise the sort of strategic/tactical/ operational relationships we have just described?

There are three potential dangers here:

1 The implications of strategic and tactical budgets may not be appreciated at the operational level; e.g. installation of new plant may require retraining of operatives or respecification of material inputs.
2 The implications of strategic and operational budgets may not be appreciated at the tactical level; e.g. retraining of operatives may be costly and might temporarily depress the rate of output.

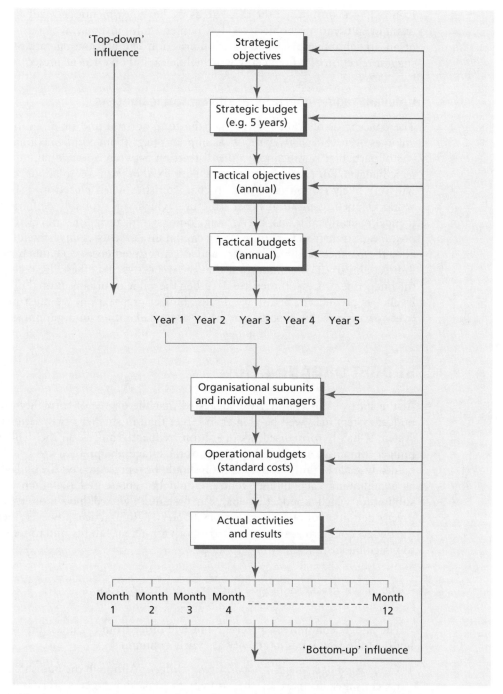

Figure 16.1 Strategic/tactical/operational consistency within the budget process

3 The implications of tactical and operational budgets may not be appreciated at the strategic level; e.g. strategic objectives may need to be revised in the light of tactical and operational constraints.

Failure in one or more of the three areas we have just mentioned will almost certainly result in failure to meet objectives. In Chapter 15, for instance, we saw how application of an arguably inappropriate decision criterion like accounting rate of return might suggest rejection of a financially worthwhile capital investment project.

Relevant range, operational and strategic budgets

The concept of relevant range – i.e. the time horizon and/or range of output/sales volumes over which a given set of assumptions (e.g. about cost behaviour) is reasonable – is of particular significance to the distinction between operational, tactical and strategic budgets. For example, costs which are fixed in terms of an annual tactical budget will very likely exhibit marked step characteristics when placed in a strategic framework. Or the organisation's cost structure, which will probably be fairly immobile in tactical/operational terms, may change quite significantly for strategic budgeting purposes: e.g. strategy may require heavy capital investments/disinvestments, which could alter the balance of direct/indirect and variable/fixed costs very much more towards indirect and fixed. It is important that differences such as these are recognised within the budgeting process. If they are not, then the value of organisational planning – at all levels – is prejudiced. Before we discuss budget preparation, we must provide a brief overview of how this process may be co-ordinated within an organisation.

BUDGET ORGANISATION

At the start of this chapter, we suggested that the degree of formality attaching to a budget system may well be greater in larger than in smaller organisations. Where the system is highly formalised, its operation frequently hinges on the deliberations of a **budget committee** and on the contents of the **budget manual**.

Ideally, each organisational function should be represented on the budget committee; as a minimum, each **budget centre** should be represented (i.e. each organisational subunit for which a budget is separately prepared); we will have more to say about the precise definition of budget centres in Chapter 18. In practice, however, membership of the budget committee is often limited – both for manageability and to reflect the extent to which budget authority is delegated.

 What major functions might a budget committee perform?

The budget committee's precise remit will differ from organisation to organisation, but the following types of activity are fairly common.

1 *Conversion of strategic to operational budgets* Although the budget committee may be consulted as part of the strategy-formulation process, this is ultimately the responsibility of the very top management level (e.g. the board of directors, who could well be represented on the budget committee). What the budget committee needs to decide is how best to translate the strategic budget into a series of tactical (i.e. annual) budgets. In addition, the budget committee will filter, collate and pass on to senior management operational data relevant to strategic planning.

2 *Negotiation of functional budgets* The budget committee will provide a forum in

which managers can negotiate the amount of their budgets; e.g. making a case for substantial increase compared to previous years.

3 *Approval of functional budgets and consolidation into the master budget* Because budget centres often correspond to organisational functions, such as sales or production, these individual budgets are referred to as **functional budgets**. Once they have been approved, functional budgets are consolidated and summarised into a **master** (or **summary**) **budget**, typically consisting of a budgeted profit and loss account, cash budget and probably a budgeted balance sheet. (We will look at the mechanics of budget preparation shortly, and the master budget is the subject of Chapter 17.)

4 *Investigation of significant variances* Since managerial, as well as organisational, performance may be assessed on the basis of comparison between budget and actual, any possibility of personal bias in the investigation process would be highly undesirable. The budget committee may therefore decide what represents a significant difference (**variance**) between budget and actual, which manager should have the responsibility for investigation and what action can be taken as a result of such investigation.

5 *Resolution of disputes* Perhaps one of the most important functions which the budget committee can perform is to resolve any disputes which may arise as a consequence of the budgetary system. For example, there may be areas of budget responsibility which are common to several managers and the budget committee may need to determine the most equitable method of dealing with the cost of these shared areas.

In general, the budget committee will be responsible for budget administration. Liaison between the different functions represented on the committee is often provided by a **budget officer** (typically a management accountant), who can also supply technical advice relating to budgetary matters.

One important role of the budget committee which we have not mentioned is that of preparing and updating the **budget manual**. In essence, this document is a user manual, setting out key aspects of budgetary procedure: e.g. the budget-setting timetable, areas of personal responsibility and details of specific budgets. In large and/or complex organisations, the budget manual can be especially significant, so it is important that the procedures which it documents are described as clearly and comprehensibly as possible.

We will commence our discussion of budget preparation at the operational end of the spectrum before illustrating how tactical budgets for different organisational functions are prepared.

STANDARD COSTS: BUDGETARY BUILDING BLOCKS

Tactical budgets are expressed at a comparatively aggregated level (e.g. functional or organisational) and therefore require to be based on detailed unit-level estimates. **Standard costs** are just such estimates.

✔ *In order to prepare an annual (i.e. tactical) budget for the cost of direct materials used in production, what information would a manufacturing firm require to have?*

We would need to know:

1 the volume of production in units;
2 the material requirement per unit of output; and
3 the cost per unit of material.

Production volume will be obtained from the production budget (a tactical budget), but we need to estimate the material requirement per unit of output and the cost per unit of material. Suppose we know that budgeted production volume is 10 000 units and have estimated that each unit of output requires 6 kg of direct material at a cost of £0.40 per kg. The **standard direct materials' cost** per unit of output will be (6 kg @ £0.40) = £2.40. The budgeted cost of direct materials used in production will thus be (10 000 units produced × £2.40) = £24 000. The standard quantity (i.e. 6 kg per unit of output) and standard price (£0.40 per kg) of direct materials will also be used in construction of the budget for direct materials' purchases.

Similar estimates will be prepared for direct labour – of **standard hours** (labour hours per unit of output) and standard rate (labour rate per hour). Predetermined overhead absorption rates will be developed (see Chapter 5) allowing a standard overhead cost per unit to be calculated. In addition to estimating the input resources necessary per unit of output, a standard selling price will be set and standard profit (or standard contribution) per unit determined.

The detailed estimates which support standard costs (e.g. of materials' usage or labour time per unit) often require considerable expertise to produce. Direct materials' requirements, for example, may result from engineering analysis of inputs and outputs.

Exhibit 16.2 contains some data which we will use to assemble a **standard cost card** per unit of output.

DPA Ltd

One of the company's products is an organic fertiliser which is sold in 5 kg bags. Standard data for next year per 5 kg bag are:

Direct materials	6 kg @ £0.40 per kg
Direct labour	0.2 hours @ £10 per hour
Packing	£0.50
Production overhead	£1.50 per direct labour hour
Selling price	£5.75

Of the 6 kg direct materials' input, 1 kg is expected to be lost under normal operating conditions.

Exhibit 16.2 Data for standard cost card

 From Exhibit 16.2, what is the standard direct labour cost per 5 kg bag?

The standard direct labour cost per bag is (0.2 hours @ £10) = £2. A standard cost card detailing the physical and financial specifications of each 5 kg bag might be as follows:

5 kg bag of fertiliser: standard specification	£
Direct materials (6 kg @ £0.40)	2.40
Direct labour (0.2 hours @ £10)	2.00
Packing	0.50
Standard prime cost	4.90
Production overhead (0.2 hours @ £1.50)	0.30
Standard production cost	5.20
Standard selling price	5.75
Standard gross profit	0.55

Note that the expected direct material loss of 1 kg per bag is incorporated within the standard cost per bag, since it is a consequence of 'normal operating conditions' and should be allowed for in the same way as any other production cost. The standard profit is 'gross' because non-production costs must still be deducted.

Types of standard

When standards are being set, one question which inevitably arises is 'how tight a standard?' In other words, what level of operational efficiency does the standard assume? Three broad categories of standard may be identified.

1 **Ideal** (or **potential**) **standard** An ideal standard assumes optimum efficiency, and would thus make no allowance for items such as the 'normal' materials' loss suffered by DPA Ltd, machine downtime or labour idle time.
2 **Basic standard** Basic standards are derived from efficient operation over a number of years (say, 3–5). The idea is that, by using the same standard for several years, performance can be measured and compared over time against an unchanged benchmark.
3 **Currently attainable** (or **attainable**) **standard** The problem with ideal and basic standards is that they do not really relate to current operating conditions. Attainable standards are based on efficient operation within the current tactical budget period (normally one year). This type of standard, whilst by no means 'easy' to achieve would make allowance for factors like DPA Ltd's 'normal' material loss.

 Which type of standard do you believe is most frequently encountered in practice and why?

Ideal and basic standards may lack credibility: the former because they assume optimum efficiency, the latter because it may be difficult to produce tolerably accurate estimates spanning the requisite time period. And, if the standards lack credibility, then so will any budget which is constructed from them. A 1993 survey by Drury *et al.* indicated that only 4% of the respondent UK manufacturing companies used standards based on maximum efficiency, the remainder employing either currently attainable standards or standards derived from past performance. However, the impact of total quality management, with its 'get it right first time all of the time' approach, coupled with organisations' desire to achieve world-class status, may mean that ideal standards will be more widely used in future. If, for example, current expectation is that performance will be (say) 75% of ideal, then an actual which betters this could indicate a move towards improved quality (although quality might also suffer in a 'push' to exceed standard).

Conversely, standards with an inbuilt allowance for waste – such as the 1 kg material loss in the standard specification of a 5 kg bag of fertiliser above – imply that such waste is acceptable and improvement is not necessary, which could possibly become a self-perpetuating misconception.

We should also point out that currently attainable standards are not without problems. In particular, it is essential that they are updated regularly to keep abreast of current developments. Not only might this be time-consuming and possibly costly, but it is also conceivable that updates could become irregular, or less than thorough – possibly as a result of pressure to produce budgets to tight deadlines.

The standard hour

Rather confusingly, the **standard hour** is a measure of work, not of time: it is the amount of work which should be performed at standard efficiency in one hour.

DPA Ltd: range of organic fertilisers

The company produces its organic fertiliser in four different sizes of bag; details are:

Size of bag	2 kg	5 kg	10 kg	20 kg
Standard labour hours per bag	0.10	0.20	0.40	0.50
Budgeted output (number of bags)	12 000	10 000	8 000	5 000
Actual output (number of bags)	14 000	9 000	6 000	7 000

Exhibit 16.3 Data for calculation of standard hours

As a statement of budgeted and actual output, the information in Exhibit 16.3 is useful, but rather unwieldy: e.g. it is not readily apparent whether actual output *overall* exceeded budget or not. In order to assess this, we need to express output on a common basis, and this common basis is provided by the standard hour. Budgeted output in standard hours is:

2 kg bags (12 000 × 0.10 hours per bag)	1200 standard hours
5 kg bags (10 000 × 0.20 hours per bag)	2000 standard hours
10 kg bags (8000 × 0.40 hours per bag)	3200 standard hours
20 kg bags (5000 × 0.50 hours per bag)	2500 standard hours
	8900 standard hours

We can therefore say that budgeted output, *in total*, represents 8900 standard hours' worth of work.

 Convert DPA Ltd's actual output in Exhibit 16.3 to standard hours and compare this with the budgeted output.

In standard hours, actual output is:

2 kg bags (14 000 × 0.10 hours per bag)	1400 standard hours
5 kg bags (9000 × 0.20 hours per bag)	1800 standard hours
10 kg bags (6000 × 0.40 hours per bag)	2400 standard hours
20 kg bags (7000 × 0.50 hours per bag)	3500 standard hours
	9100 standard hours

Compared to budget, this represents an increase in total output of (9100 − 8900) = 200 standard hours, or approximately 2% of budget. Ability to express output of diverse products/services in a unitary measure may be important for resource planning (e.g. manpower required to achieve budgeted output) and for financial control (as we shall see in Chapter 18).

Advantages of standard costing

Like budgets in general, the formality of a standard costing system will vary from organisation to organisation, and differences in specifics may be particularly marked when we compare manufacturing and service organisations. For tactical budgets to be effective, some degree of estimation at cost unit (i.e. operational) level is necessary, and can offer a number of advantages.

Accuracy of budgets is improved

Building a tactical budget from cost unit estimates should yield a more accurate result than is likely from attempts to estimate on a 'total' basis, especially where a range of different resource inputs and product/service outputs is involved. Consider the problems which would face DPA Ltd in Exhibit 16.3 were the company to attempt to produce a manpower budget based purely on estimated unit output of each product, without the availability of standard unit labour times.

Cost consciousness is instilled

The existence of standard unit specifications, of the type we prepared above for DPA Ltd's 5 kg bag of fertiliser, should help raise awareness of cost-related issues among employees – especially if employees are involved in setting standards and if standard resource and cost information is disseminated by management to those employees principally involved in output of products/services. In addition, the fact that standards comprise not only financial information but also resource quantities (e.g. standard materials' usage quantities) may help to reinforce the role of budgets as targets and performance benchmarks. Employees who might feel 'intimidated' by purely financial information may be more comfortable if this is supported by non-financial data. Standards per unit may also provide a target of greater immediacy to employees 'at the sharp end'. As we have already said, the existence of a target may have beneficial motivational effects.

Methods may be improved

Setting standards for resource inputs such as labour times and material quantities could encourage a search for improved work methods or better materials.

Permits detailed control analysis

As we shall see in Chapter 19, standard costing allows 'global' budget variances to be subdivided into their constituent elements, thereby allowing potential problem areas to be more accurately pinpointed.

Provides a better costing and pricing basis than actual costs

Actual costs and resource inputs per unit are likely to fluctuate, e.g. over a one-year period and between different cost units. Such fluctuations would mean that unit costs would also fluctuate, as would stock values and profit; similarly selling prices, if these are based to any significant extent on cost.

 If selling prices are based on cost, what problem (in addition to fluctuation) would arise from use of actual costs?

As we saw in Chapter 5 (in the context of overhead absorption rates), actuals will not be known until after the event. Producing quotations for work, or price lists, would therefore be difficult – or even impossible – with obvious implications for the organisation's sales effort.

Problems of standard costing

Despite the advantages offered, standard costing may also present some difficulties in operation.

Incorporating inflation into standards

Even where inflation rates are low, this may still be troublesome. Not only is there the difficulty of estimating future rates with tolerable accuracy, but there may also be a problem in comparing budget and actual where the rate of inflation affecting each is materially different (a point we shall return to in Chapter 18). Even where future rates of inflation can be estimated with reasonable confidence and where these estimates are fairly close to reality, the very fact of their inclusion in standards can cause distortions, as we will illustrate using the information in Exhibit 16.4.

DPA Ltd: effect of inflation on standard and actual material costs

For a particular year, the standard material usage quantity and cost per kg of material for each of the company's 5 kg bags of fertiliser is: 6 kg @ £0.40 per kg. The standard cost of £0.40 per kg makes allowance for estimated inflation of 3.5% for the year to which the standard applies. In Month 1 of that year, the actual cost per kg of material was £0.39.

Exhibit 16.4 Standard/actual costs and inflation

On the face of it, the actual material cost per kg in Month 1 was lower than standard, which might be taken to suggest better-than-standard performance in purchasing.

 Why is comparison of the £0.40 per kg standard cost with the Month 1 actual of £0.39 potentially misleading?

The problem is that the £0.40 standard cost incorporates a full year's inflation. Even assuming that the 3.5% inflation estimate for the year is accurate, Month 1 actual costs will not have been affected by a full year's inflation – i.e. the standard is effectively overstated as far as Month 1 is concerned. The apparently 'better-than-standard' purchasing performance may therefore be illusory. We might try to redress this by using, in the standard, an average inflation rate for the year, but even this does not solve the problem. If inflation arises evenly throughout the year and if actual inflation is in line with estimate, then standards for the first half of the year will be overstated whereas those for the second half will be understated. A more sophisticated form of weighting could be employed, but this might complicate the standard setting and budget/actual comparison process so much that its benefits are lost. Alternatively, we might ignore the effect of inflation entirely, in which case any comparison of budget and actual will be distorted by the existence of inflation in the latter figures and its absence from the former. In Chapter 18, we will demonstrate how the potential distortion caused by inflation may be removed from a budget/actual comparison by **deflating** the figures concerned.

Setting an acceptable labour efficiency standard

Where direct labour is a significant element in the output process – as it is in many service industries – setting an appropriate standard for efficiency is important. Adoption of a standard which is too 'tight' could adversely affect labour relations, or be viewed by employees as an impossible target (and thus one which it is pointless to try and achieve). On the other hand, an efficiency standard which is too 'slack' may not motivate employees to improve performance. In either case, the standard, consequent budget and comparison of actual with budget are all likely to be suspect.

Heterogeneous output

Standard costing is well suited to situations where output procedures consist of repetitive processes and where the output itself is fairly standardised. But in job costing and many service industries, where cost units are markedly different to each other, standard costing may work less well. What, for example, should be the standard labour time allowed for settling an insurance claim? Or for repairing a car? It really depends on the specific claim and repair. Attempting to arrive at some kind of 'average' standard based on all estimated output could well result in standards which bear little relationship to the resources and costs involved in particular jobs, thereby cancelling much of the benefit of standard costing.

This is not to suggest that standard costing cannot be applied to output other than mass-produced homogeneous items. The technique is becoming increasingly prevalent in service organisations: e.g. within the UK health service, considerable work is currently underway aimed at producing standard costs for surgical procedures.

Cost of introducing and maintaining system

Standard costing systems can be costly to introduce and to maintain. For example, estimates need to be obtained for resource inputs and their costs and previously set standards will require to be updated periodically – all of which may involve considerable time, effort and cost. The need to review and update standards may incur a less obvious cost. The frequency of this event needs to be handled sensibly, as review which is too frequent or too infrequent may reduce standards' credibility. As a minimum, standards should really be reviewed as part of the annual budget-setting exercise.

May overemphasise operational considerations

Because of their necessarily detailed and precise nature compared to strategy's less-defined approach, there may be a danger that development of workable standards (e.g. on an annual basis) may overshadow the link between operational, tactical and strategic factors, or even entirely mask the need for strategic planning.

Now we have discussed the operational aspect of budgets, we are in a position to demonstrate how the more aggregated tactical budgets are obtained.

PREPARATION OF FUNCTIONAL BUDGETS

Tactical budgets are generally prepared for individual **budget centres**; these can be separate organisational functions like sales or production (hence the term **functional budgets**), or subunits (e.g. departments). Although the precise definition of budget centres will depend on the structure of specific organisations, they will almost always correspond to areas of managerial responsibility. In a manufacturing business, for example, the Production Manager would normally be responsible for achieving (and very likely helping to set) the production budget, which might itself be subdivided into budgets covering narrower areas of managerial responsibility within the production function. Where budget centres reflect managerial responsibility in this way, they are more commonly referred to as **responsibility centres** – a topic we shall discuss in detail in Chapter 18.

For ease of presentation and illustration, the functional budgets we will prepare are based on a fairly simple organisational structure. For the same reason, our functional budgets will employ annual figures. While this may provide a useful tactical overview of the period, effective planning and control require these budgets to be *profiled*. For example, the production budget could show budgeted output and stocks of each product on a month-by-month basis during the year and in total for the year, thus reflecting factors such as seasonal fluctuations and allowing better scheduling of dependent activities such as materials' purchasing. Strategic budgets may also be profiled, e.g. by year within the strategic time-frame. A further reason for profiling the budget is to allow preparation of the cash budget (see the next chapter). Within any budget period, it is essential to be able to identify variations in cash flows, so that the timing of possible shortages and surpluses may be assessed. Profiling budgets in this way can be seen as another illustration of the close link between tactical and operational issues, with the latter having a major bearing on how profiling occurs.

The budgetary 'cycle'

We said earlier that one of the main objectives of budgets is to enhance co-ordination between different organisational functions. This may be seen in the order in which budgets are prepared. Figure 16.2 illustrates how this might occur in DPA Ltd.

 Why does the sequence for preparation of tactical budgets in Figure 16.2 start with the sales budget?

The sales budget is first in sequence because, without an estimate of sales, a meaningful production budget cannot be prepared – and without a meaningful production budget, budgets for material usage, material purchases, manpower and so on will have equally little meaning. The pattern of budgetary interrelationships illustrated in Figure 16.2 appears to be fairly complex, but it is almost certainly an oversimplification of reality. If reality is even more complicated, this merely emphasises the need for effective budget co-ordination. Although the precise budget 'cycle' may vary from one

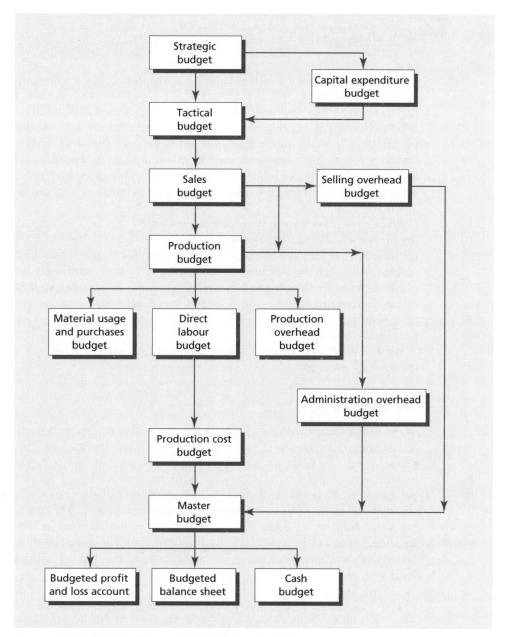

Figure 16.2 DPA Ltd – illustrative budgetary 'cycle'

organisation to the next, the broad principle of a co-ordinated approach applies equally to all and we can say that, in general, the starting-point needs to be an estimate of activity volume.

In practice, it is unlikely that budgets can be prepared in strict sequence from start to finish. In particular, the preparation of budgets may be affected by the existence of **principal budget factors** (i.e. limiting factors of the type we discussed in Chapter 14).

> ✔ *How would the fact that direct materials is a principal budget factor affect DPA Ltd's budget preparation?*

Assuming that this limitation cannot be overcome (e.g. by subcontracting production), then its existence will determine the mix and quantity of products produced, and may mean that the company cannot fully satisfy expected demand in the forthcoming period. In effect, the principal budget factor becomes the starting-point for budget preparation. It could also happen that an unforeseen limitation may emerge during budget preparation; in this case, budgets would need to be revised accordingly. Failure to reflect such a resource limitation – e.g. by undertaking a ranking exercise of the type we described in Chapter 14 – will render budgets pointless at best, seriously misleading at worst.

What all of this means is that budget preparation may be a protracted affair, requiring proper scheduling. Preparation timetables are one area for which the budget committee may have ultimate responsibility, arranging for these to be detailed in the budget manual. Although the administrative effort (and possibly cost) may be significant, it can be justified by the need to have budgets in place prior to the start of the period to which they relate. In some organisations (e.g. local and central government), operations simply cannot proceed without advance preparation and approval of a budget for the relevant period.

We will now consider the functional budgets shown in Figure 16.2 in more detail; the master budget forms the subject of the next chapter.

The sales budget

When preparing the sales budget, management will consider any known internal constraints in conjunction with estimates about conditions within the business's specific market (e.g. possible actions by competitors, or the price sensitivity of the product/service being sold), coupled with an assessment of the wider economic prospects for the period under review (e.g. projected inflation rate or changes in taxation policy). Included in management's assessment will be qualitative factors, such as potential shifts in consumer taste, the impact of proposed changes in product/service specification or in the sales mix. Only after a thorough appraisal of all factors (internal and external to the organisation) which might have an effect on sales should the sales budget be prepared.

We will use the information in Exhibit 16.5 to obtain DPA Ltd's sales budget.

The sales budget is, effectively, contained within Exhibit 16.5 – i.e. the unit selling prices and sales volumes for each product. The only additional information we need to show is the sales revenue for each product and in total:

DPA Ltd: Sales budget	Sales revenue (£)
2 kg bags (15 000 × £4.25)	63 750
5 kg bags (12 000 × £7.10)	85 200
10 kg bags (8200 × £13.50)	110 700
20 kg bags (5400 × £24.75)	133 650
	393 300

Only once the sales budget has been prepared is it possible to give detailed consideration to production and its related budgets. (Had our example involved a principal

DPA Ltd: sales and stock data

After careful consideration of the market for its products and related factors next year, management has produced the following estimates of sales volumes, standard unit selling prices and desired levels of closing stock, along with anticipated stock levels at the end of the current year.

Size of bag	2 kg	5 kg	10 kg	20 kg
Selling price per bag	£4.25	£7.10	£13.50	£24.75
Sales volume (number of bags)	15 000	12 000	8 200	5 400
Stock (number of bags):				
Anticipated at end of current year	4 000	2 500	400	600
Desired at end of next year	1 000	500	200	200

Exhibit 16.5 Data for sales and production budget preparation

budget factor, we would have required to employ our limiting factor techniques from Chapter 14 to determine the optimum mix of products; i.e. the production budget would be prepared first.)

The production budget

The company will aim to produce each product in sufficient quantity to meet the level of demand anticipated in the sales budget *and* to give the desired amount of stock at the end of the year, but after adjusting for the current year's closing stock (which will also be next year's opening stock):

Sales budget	X
Add Closing stock desired at end of budget period	X
	X
Less Opening stock at beginning of budget period	X
= Production required	X

Exhibit 16.6 is DPA Ltd's production budget, completed for 2 kg bags only.

DPA Ltd: production budget

Size of bag	2 kg	5 kg	10 kg	20 kg
Sales budget	15 000			
Add Closing stock desired	1 000			
	16 000			
Less Opening stock	4 000			
Production required	12 000			

Exhibit 16.6 Partly complete production budget

 Use the data from Exhibit 16.5 to complete the production budget in Exhibit 16.6.

DPA Ltd's completed production budget is given in Exhibit 16.7.

DPA Ltd: production budget

Size of bag	2 kg	5 kg	10 kg	20 kg
Sales budget	15 000	12 000	8 200	5 400
Add Closing stock desired	1 000	500	200	200
	16 000	12 500	8 400	5 600
Less Opening stock	4 000	2 500	400	600
Production required	12 000	10 000	8 000	5 000

Exhibit 16.7 Completed production budget

Following our suggested budgetary 'cycle', it is only now that production-related budgets, such as direct labour, materials' usage and materials' purchases can be prepared – a process which could reveal unforeseen limiting factors.

Direct materials' usage and purchases budgets

DPA Ltd: direct materials' standards

The same direct material is used in all the company's products, standard input quantities being as follows for each size of bag produced:

Size of bag	2 kg	5 kg	10 kg	20 kg
kg of material input	2.4	6.0	12.0	24.0

The standard cost per kg of materials is £0.40, and the following amounts of stock are anticipated and desired:

Anticipated stock at the end of the current period	60 000 kg
Desired stock at the end of the budget period	80 000 kg

Exhibit 16.8 Data for preparation of materials' usage and purchases budgets

You will see that the material usage per 5 kg bag, along with the standard cost per kg of materials, are those we gave in Exhibit 16.2 when we built up the standard specification of this product. The materials' usage budget will be determined by output quantities specified in the production budget and by the standard materials' input for each size of bag given in Exhibit 16.8:

DPA Ltd: direct materials' usage budget	kg
2 kg bags (12 000 × 2.4 kg per bag)	28 800
5 kg bags (10 000 × 6.0 kg per bag)	60 000
10 kg bags (8000 × 12 kg per bag)	96 000
20 kg bags (5000 × 24 kg per bag)	120 000
Direct materials' usage	304 800

You will notice that, as with the standard cost card for 5 kg bags which we prepared earlier, the material losses have been incorporated into the usage budget.

Management may wish to show the extent of expected material losses within the usage budget:

Material losses on:	kg
2 kg bags (12 000 × [2.4–2.0])	4 800
5 kg bags (10 000 × [6–5])	10 000
10 kg bags (8000 × [12–10])	16 000
20 kg bags (5000 × [24–20])	20 000
	50 800

Total losses as % of total input (50 800 ÷ 304 800)   16.67%

Inclusion of anticipated material losses will allow management to monitor actual losses and, where these exceed the expected level, to take action to remedy the problem.

The usage budget now forms the starting-point for the materials' purchases budget. We want to purchase sufficient materials to cover the estimated usage in production *and* to leave us with the stock desired at the end of the budget period, but adjusted for anticipated stocks at the start of the budget period (i.e. at the end of the current period):

DPA Ltd: direct materials' purchases budget	kg
Budgeted direct materials' usage	304 800
Add Closing stock desired	_____
Less Opening stock	_____
= Purchases required	_____
	£
Standard cost per kg of material	0.40
Total direct materials' purchases cost	____

 Complete the materials' purchases budget above, using appropriate figures from Exhibit 16.8.

The completed purchases budget is as follows:

DPA Ltd: direct materials' purchases budget	kg
Budgeted direct materials' usage	304 800
Add Closing stock desired	80 000
	384 800
Less Opening stock	60 000
= Purchases required	324 800
	£
Standard cost per kg of material	0.40
Total direct materials' purchases cost	129 920

It is possible to amalgamate the usage and purchases budgets, but this might give an unwieldy statement, especially in situations involving several different direct materials. In addition, purchasing and usage may well occur in different budget centres, so that a combined usage/purchases budget (although offering the benefit of a materials' overview) could create a misleading impression about exactly who, within the management team, is responsible for specific aspects of the budget.

Direct labour budget

Like the materials' budgets which we have just prepared, direct labour requirements will stem from the production budget.

DPA Ltd: standard direct labour requirements

For each of the company's products, standard labour times are:

Size of bag	2 kg	5 kg	10 kg	20 kg
Standard direct labour hours per bag	0.1	0.2	0.4	0.5

After making allowance for idle time, absences through sickness and holidays, management has estimated that 35.6 *productive* hours per worker per week will be available, compared to 44.5 *total* hours per worker per week. The standard weekly wage for direct workers will be £356 during the budget period under consideration and 50 weeks in the year are considered to be working weeks.

Exhibit 16.9 Data for preparation of direct labour budget

Before we prepare the company's direct labour budget, we need to make an adjustment to the standard labour cost to reflect non-productive time:

$$\frac{\text{Standard weekly wage}}{\text{Estimated productive hours per week}} = \frac{£356}{35.6} = £10 \text{ per hour}$$

Again, you will see that the standard labour specification per 5 kg bag is the same as that given in Exhibit 16.2. The £10 per direct labour hour could therefore more accurately be termed the **standard labour charge per productive hour** (to distinguish it from the standard hourly rate of pay, which is [£356 ÷ 44.5] = £8 in this instance).

Based on Exhibit 16.9, DPA Ltd's direct labour budget is as follows:

DPA Ltd: direct labour budget
Productive hours required for budgeted output of:

	Hours
2 kg bags (12 000 × 0.1 hours per bag)	1200
5 kg bags (10 000 × 0.2 hours per bag)	2000
10 kg bags (8000 × 0.4 hours per bag)	3200
20 kg bags (5000 × 0.5 hours per bag)	2500
	8900

	£
Standard charge per productive hour	10
Total direct wages cost	89 000
Productive hours per direct worker per week	35.6
Productive direct worker weeks required (8900 ÷ 35.6)	250
Working weeks per worker per year	50
Number of direct operatives required (250 ÷ 50)	5

✔ *What is the implication for the direct labour budget of a significant inaccuracy in the production budget?*

If the production budget is materially understated, then the company will find itself understaffed (overstaffed if the production budget is markedly overstated). In either case, additional costs will be incurred (e.g. cost of overtime working), which could have repercussions elsewhere (e.g. the need to pay for unforeseen overtime could reduce the amount of cash available for other purposes). Once again, we can see the need for · proper coordination of budget preparation.

An alternative presentation of the direct labour budget could 'gross-up' productive hours to total hours, using the proportion of productive to total hours from Exhibit 16.9:

$$\frac{35.6 \text{ productive hours/worker/week}}{44.5 \text{ total hours/worker/week}} = 0.8$$

Productive hours required for budgeted output (as before)	8 900
Equivalent total hours (8900 ÷ 0.8)	11 125

	£
Standard rate of pay per hour	8
Budgeted direct labour cost	89 000
Total hours per direct worker per week	44.5
Total direct worker weeks required (11 125 ÷ 44.5)	250
Working weeks per worker per year	50
Direct operatives required	5

For monitoring of actual, the direct labour budget may also show the expected number of non-productive hours:

Non-productive hours (11 125 − 8900)	2225
Non-productive hours as % of total hours (2225 ÷ 11 125)	20%

Production overhead budget

The key point to bear in mind about overhead (whether production, selling, distribution or administration overhead) is the fact that the word 'overhead' is generic: i.e. represents the aggregate of different individual costs. For this reason, the factors which influence the amount of overhead will almost certainly be more wide-ranging than those affecting direct production costs. If, for example, the capital expenditure budget indicates the purchase of new production plant, then the related depreciation will be production overhead.

If possible, the overhead budget should distinguish between fixed and variable costs. As we will see in Chapter 18, this could be important in the context of financial control. DPA Ltd's production overhead budget is as follows:

DPA Ltd: production overhead budget (all fixed relative to output)

	£
Apportionment of supervisory costs	4 000
Apportionment of occupancy costs	3 000
Direct-wage related costs	3 400
Indirect materials	2 000
Depreciation of equipment	950
	13 350

Using the direct labour and production overhead budgets, obtain DPA Ltd's overhead absorption rate, assuming this is based on direct labour hours.

As we saw in Chapter 5, a direct labour hour absorption rate is calculated as:

$$\frac{\text{Budgeted overhead cost}}{\text{Budgeted direct labour hours}} = \frac{£13\,350}{8900} = £1.50 \text{ per direct labour hour}$$

Note that productive hours have been used as the denominator and that the company employs a **blanket absorption rate**; in a more complex organisation, primary (and possibly secondary) distribution of overhead may be necessary prior to calculation of **departmental absorption rates** (see Chapter 5).

You will see that the production overhead budget contains apportionments (as do the selling and administration overhead budgets that we will illustrate shortly). In Chapter 5, we suggested that such apportionments may be inappropriate for planning and control because of their potentially arbitrary nature. We will explore this question further in Chapter 18.

Production cost budget

Existence of a production budget also permits preparation of the production cost budget.

DPA Ltd: summary of standard cost data

Standard data per unit for each of the company's products is given below:

Size of bag	2 kg	5 kg	10 kg	20 kg
	£	£	£	£
Direct materials (2.4/6/12/24 kg @ £0.40)	0.96	2.40	4.80	9.60
Direct labour (0.1/0.2/0.4/0.5 hours @ £10)	1.00	2.00	4.00	5.00
Packing	0.45	0.50	0.52	0.55
Standard prime cost	2.41	4.90	9.32	15.15
Production overhead				
(0.1/0.2/0.4/0.5 hours @ £1.50)	0.15	0.30	0.60	0.75
Production cost	2.56	5.20	9.92	15.90
Selling price	4.25	7.10	13.50	24.75

Exhibit 16.10 Data for preparation of production cost budget

The budgeted figure for the separate elements of production cost for each product are calculated as:

$$(\text{budgeted output} \times \text{standard cost per unit})$$

Applying absorption costing principles and using the standard specifications set out in Exhibit 16.10, the production cost budget is as follows:

DPA Ltd: production cost budget

	2 kg	5 kg	10 kg	20 kg	Total
Budgeted output (number of bags)	12 000	10 000	8 000	5 000	
	£	£	£	£	£
Direct material cost	11 520	24 000	38 400	48 000	121 920
Direct labour cost	12 000	20 000	32 000	25 000	89 000
Packing	5 400	5 000	4 160	2 750	17 310
Prime cost	28 920	49 000	74 560	75 750	228 230
Production overhead	1 800	3 000	4 800	3 750	13 350
Production cost	30 720	52 000	79 360	79 500	241 580

✔ *In what respect might the production cost budget above be misleading?*

The production cost budget we have just prepared was based on a standard cost per unit (see Exhibit 16.10) which included a charge in respect of direct labour and production overhead. Within the relevant range, these costs will be either fixed or will exhibit step behaviour. By 'unitising' direct labour and production overhead, we may give the misleading impression that they are variable in nature. If management were considering total production cost over a range of output volumes, or were comparing actual production costs with budget, then inaccurate cost estimates and budget/actual comparisons could result. It may therefore be better to distinguish between variable costs and fixed costs – i.e. to apply marginal costing principles. This would give the following revised production cost budget:

DPA Ltd: production cost budget (marginal costing version)

	2 kg	5 kg	10 kg	20 kg	Total
Budgeted output (number of bags)	12 000	10 000	8 000	5 000	
	£	£	£	£	£
Direct material cost	11 520	24 000	38 400	48 000	121 920
Packing	5 400	5 000	4 160	2 750	17 310
Variable production cost	16 920	29 000	42 560	50 750	139 230
Fixed production costs:					
Direct labour					89 000
Production overhead					13 350
Production cost					241 580

Using the marginal costing format above should help clarify the relationship between volume of output and production cost, which will almost certainly enhance planning and control. We will explore these issues more fully in Chapter 18.

Selling overhead and administration overhead budgets

Budgets for selling and administration overhead, like that for production overhead, will comprise several individual costs. Selling overhead will reflect not only the anticipated volume of sales for the budget period, but also the marketing effort involved (e.g.

advertising and promotion). You should also note that activities such as advertising and promotion are especially strongly linked to the business's strategic aims, since costs will often be incurred within the time frame of a tactical budget with the objective of improving or maintaining market standing in the longer term. The budget for administration overhead will stem from management expectations about the effort and cost of supporting all of the organisation's activities. For DPA Ltd these two budgets are as follows:

DPA Ltd: selling overhead budget	£
Wages and salaries allocated and apportioned	27 000
Depreciation of delivery vans	4 000
Van running and maintenance costs	3 000
Advertising	5 000
Apportionment of occupancy costs	1 000
Sales commission (1% of budgeted revenue)	3 933
	43 933

DPA Ltd: administration overhead budget	£
Wages and salaries allocated and apportioned	22 000
Depreciation of office equipment	2 000
Insurance and stationery	3 000
Apportionment of occupancy costs	1 000
	28 000

 Of the costs listed in the two budgets immediately above, which are likely to vary and which are likely to be fixed relative to the volume of output/sales, given that the budgets are tactical?

Within the relevant range dictated by tactical budgets, only sales commission is variable relative to the volume of sales, rather than of production. Van running and maintenance costs may be semi-variable within the relevant range. The other costs are likely to be fixed.

SUMMARY

In this chapter, we have examined the preparation of functional budgets at the tactical and operational levels. It is worth observing that the budgets we have prepared are not intended to represent an exhaustive classification or listing, but are indicative of the major types of such budget that may be encountered. The precise budgets prepared by an organisation are dictated by that organisation's circumstances; for example by its size, structure and the nature of its output. We shall return to this point in Chapter 17. In this chapter, we have seen that:

- A budget is a quantified plan targeted at achievement of an objective/objectives.
- The objectives of budgets are to:
  - compel planning
  - provide a performance benchmark and financial control mechanism

- provide a motivational impetus
- provide a medium of communication
- promote **goal congruence** (i.e. consistency between the actions of individual managers/organisational sub-units and overall organisational objectives)
- instil financial awareness
- enable delegation by providing authorisation to spend.

● Budgets may suffer from the following problems:
  - producing credible estimates of the future
  - bureaucratic 'overkill'
  - encouraging an ultra-cautious approach by management
  - behavioural implications.

● Strategic objectives and budgets should dictate tactical objectives and budgets which in turn should determine operational aspects.

● Budget preparation and monitoring may be overseen and coordinated by a **budget committee**, with interfunctional liaison being provided by the **budget officer**.

● The **budget manual** is a user guide to the detailed working of the organisation's budget system.

● Budgets are constructed using **standard costs,** which are predetermined costs (or selling prices) expressed at the cost unit level and require estimation of the resource inputs per unit of output along with the associated costs.

● **Ideal standards** are based on maximum efficiency, **basic** standards are medium-term standards and **currently attainable standards** are based on optimum operations under current conditions.

● The **standard hour** measures the amount of work which should be performed in one hour at standard efficiency and is a useful measure of global output in multi-product/service organisations.

● The aims of standard costing are to:
  - improve budgetary accuracy
  - instil cost consciousness
  - encourage the search for improved methods
  - permit detailed control analysis
  - provide a superior costing/pricing basis than actual figures.

● Standard costing may suffer from problems of:
  - incorporating inflation
  - setting an acceptable labour efficiency standard
  - problems where output is heterogeneous
  - cost of introduction and maintenance of system
  - danger of overemphasising operational considerations.

● Tactical budget preparation is sequential, often beginning with the sales budget, or with some estimate of activity volume for the forthcoming budget period, and culminating with the **master budget**.

● Budgets should be revised to reflect the impact of any **principal budget factor**.

▶

- Production (and purchases) budgets should be adjusted to allow for stocks:

Production (purchases) required to meet sales (production) budget	X
Add Desired closing stock	X
	X
Less Stock at end of current period	X
Production (purchases) required	X

- Labour and material usage budgets should be adjusted to allow for expected non-productive time and losses respectively.

In the next chapter, we will extend our discussion of budgeting to deal with the master budget: the cash budget, budgeted profit and loss account and budgeted balance sheet. We will also discuss various different approaches which may be taken in preparation of budgets.

FURTHER READING

Cyert, R. and March, J., *Behavioural Theory of the Firm*, Prentice Hall, 1963.

Drury, C., *Standard Costing*, Academic Press/CIMA, 1992: Chapter 1 provides an overview of the nature and scope of standard costing.

Drury, C., Braund, S., Osborne, P. and Tayles, M., *A Survey of Management Accounting Practices in UK Manufacturing Companies*, CACA, 1993.

Greenall, A., *Finance and Budgeting for Line Managers*, The Industrial Society, 1996: Chapter 5 is a readable management perspective on the budgetary process.

Tayles, M., *Budgetary control – the organisational aspects*, ACCA Students' Newsletter, December 1998.

SELF-TEST QUESTIONS

16.1   A principal budget factor is

A   the highest value item of cost.
B   a factor which limits the activities of an undertaking.
C   a factor common to all budget centres.
D   a factor controllable by the manager of the budget centre.

(CIMA, *Cost Accounting and Quantitative Methods*, November 1998)

16.2   Place a tick in the appropriate box to indicate whether each of the following statements is true or false.

	True	False
(a) The standard hour is a measure of work, not time.	☐	☐
(b) Strategic budgets will show less detail than operational.	☐	☐
(c) Basic standards reflect the current year's operating conditions.	☐	☐
(d) Dysfunctional behaviour exists when individual managers act in the wider organisational interest.	☐	☐
(e) An ideal standard for direct labour will make allowance for idle time.	☐	☐
(f) A principal budget factor is a limiting factor.	☐	☐
(g) The budget officer is responsible for achieving the budget.	☐	☐
(h) Where selling price is based on cost, actual cost is superior to standard.	☐	☐

16.3   X plc manufactures Product X using three different raw materials. The product details are as follows:

Selling price per unit	£250
Material A	3 kg material price £3.50 per kg
Material B	2 kg material price £5.00 per kg
Material C	4 kg material price £4.50 per kg
Direct labour	8 hours labour rate £8.00 per hour

The company is considering its budgets for next year and has made the following estimates of sales demand for Product X for July to October 1999:

July	August	September	October
400 units	300 units	600 units	450 units

It is company policy to hold stocks of finished goods at the end of each month equal to 50% of the following month's sales demand, and it is expected that the stock at the start of the budget period will meet this policy.

At the end of the production process the products are tested: it is usual for 10% of those tested to be faulty. It is not possible to rectify these faulty units. Raw material stocks are expected to be as follows on 1 July 1999:

Material A	1000 kg
Material B	400 kg
Material C	600 kg

Stocks are to be increased by 20% in July 1999, and then remain at their new level for the foreseeable future.

Labour is paid on an hourly rate based on attendance. In addition to the unit direct labour hours shown above, 20% of *attendance time* is spent on tasks which support production activity.

Requirements

(a) Prepare the following budgets for the quarter from July 1999 to September 1999 inclusive:
   (i)   sales budget in quantity and value;
   (ii) production budget in units;
   (iii) raw material usage budget in kg;
   (iv) raw material purchases budget in kg and value;
   (v)   labour requirements budget in hours and value.   **(16 marks)**

(b) Explain the term *'principal budget factor'* and why its identification is an important part of the budget preparation process.   **(3 marks)**

(c) Explain clearly, using data from part (a) above, how you would construct a spreadsheet to produce the labour requirements budget for August 1999. Include a specimen cell layout diagram containing formulae which would illustrate the basis for the spread-sheet.   **(6 marks)**
                (Total: 25 marks)

(CIMA, *Operational Cost Accounting*, November 1998)

QUESTIONS WITHOUT ANSWERS

16.4 When preparing a production budget, the quantity to be produced equals

A sales quantity + opening stock + closing stock
B sales quantity − opening stock + closing stock
C sales quantity − opening stock − closing stock
D sales quantity + opening stock − closing stock
E sales quantity.

(CIMA, *Operational Cost Accounting*, May 1997)

16.5 HJB Ltd, a manufacturer of cardboard boxes, provides the estimated data set out below for one of its products:

	July	August	September
Sales (units)	800	1000	1500

Company policy is that closing stock of this product in any month should be 20% of next month's sales. What is HJB Ltd's budgeted production for August?

A 900 units
B 1000 units
C 1100 units
D 1200 units

QUESTIONS WITHOUT ANSWERS **479**

16.6 An ice cream manufacturer is in the process of preparing budgets for the next few months, and the following draft figures are available:

Sales forecast

June	6000 cases
July	7500 cases
August	8500 cases
September	7000 cases
October	6500 cases

A case has a standard cost of £15 and a standard selling price of £25.

Each case uses $2\frac{1}{2}$ kg of ingredients and it is policy to have stocks of ingredients at the end of each month to cover 50% of next month's production. There are 8500 kg in stock on 1 June.

There are 750 cases of finished ice cream in stock on 1 June and it is policy to have stocks at the end of each month to cover 10% of the next month's sales.

Requirements

(a) Prepare a production budget (in cases) for the months of June, July, August and September. **(5 marks)**

(b) Prepare an ingredients purchase budget (in kgs) for the months of June, July and August. **(3 marks)**

(c) Calculate the budgeted gross profit for the quarter June to August. **(3 marks)**

(d) Describe briefly what advantages there would be for the firm if it adopted a system of flexible budgeting. **(4 marks)**

Total: 15 marks)

(CIMA, *Cost Accounting and Quantitative Methods*, May 1997)

16.7 D Limited is preparing its annual budgets for the year to 31 December 1994. It manufactures and sells one product, which has a selling price of £150. The marketing director believes that the price can be increased to £160 with effect from 1 July 1994 and that at this price the sales volume for each quarter of 1994 will be as follows:

	Sales Volume
Quarter 1	40 000
Quarter 2	50 000
Quarter 3	30 000
Quarter 4	45 000

Sales for each quarter of 1995 are expected to be 40 000 units.

Each unit of the finished product which is manufactured requires four units of component R and three units of component T, together with a body shell S. These items are purchased from an outside supplier. Current prices are:

Component R	£8.00 each
Component T	£5.00 each
Shell S	£30.00 each

The components are expected to increase in price by 10% with effect from 1 April 1994; no change is expected in the price of the shell.

Assembly of the shell and components into the finished product requires 6 labour hours: labour is currently paid £5.00 per hour. A 4% increase in wage costs is anticipated to take effect from 1 October 1994.

Variable overhead costs are expected to be £10 per unit for the whole of 1994; fixed production overhead costs are expected to be £240 000 for the year, and are absorbed on a per unit basis.

Stocks on 31 December 1993 are expected to be as follows:

Finished units	9000 units
Component R	3000 units
Component T	5500 units
Shell S	500 units

Closing stocks at the end of each quarter are to be as follows:

Finished units	10% of next quarter's sales
Component R	20% of next quarter's production requirements
Component T	15% of next quarter's production requirements
Shell S	10% of next quarter's production requirements

Requirement

Prepare the following budgets of D Limited for the year ending 31 December 1994, showing values for each quarter and the year in total:

(i)   sales budget (in £s and units)
(ii)   production budget (in units)
(iii)   material usage budget (in units)
(iv)   production cost budget (in £s).   (**15 marks**)

(CIMA, *Operational Cost Accounting Specimen Examination*)

CHAPTER 17

Budgetary planning II

Financial planning

... Picking up my newspaper on the plane I read about the inability of our own opera house (Covent Garden, London) to produce a financial plan. Despite this it had managed to secure substantial funding from the Arts Council. 'Welcome home!' I thought as the plane touched down at Heathrow.

That evening, my brother-in-law phoned me. He runs a small motor repair business and wants to expand. He's never attended any courses on economics or accountancy but he knows two basic facts which are obvious to any small businessman:

(i) there is a limit to how much money you can raise from other people;

and

(ii) no-one is going to give you any money unless you give them a fairly good idea what you are going to do with it.

So he's decided to produce a business plan, a key component of which will be a financial plan, showing financial projections of profits, cash flow and balance sheets ...

Source: Stewart Maugham, *ACCA Students' Newsletter*, September 1998.

Exhibit 17.1 The importance of budgets

INTRODUCTION

In the previous chapter, we prepared a series of budgets for separate organisational functions like sales, production and purchasing. This chapter demonstrates how these individual budgets are summarised into a master budget. We shall pay particular attention to that element of the master budget dealing with what may be the organisation's most precious resource: cash. The significance of cash planning is clear from Exhibit 17.1. In this respect, it is crucial that management appreciates that cash is not the same as profit. A business may earn high profits, but may nevertheless have insufficient cash to meet its liabilities as they fall due; conversely, a healthy cash balance is no guarantee of profitability. This is not to suggest that profit is unimportant, and we shall also see how budgeted profit and loss accounts and balance sheets are prepared. We will then provide a brief overview of budgeting in service and public sector organisations before concluding the chapter with a discussion of different approaches to budget preparation which may be adopted.

OBJECTIVES

When you have completed this chapter, you will be able to:

- appreciate the importance of the master budget;
- prepare cash budgets;
- outline the particular budgeting problems faced by service and public sector organisations;
- describe the operation, advantages and problems of line item, programme, incremental, zero base, rolling and activity-based budgets.

THE MASTER BUDGET

In most organisations, the **master budget** (or **summary budget**) will comprise three elements:

- a cash budget;
- a budgeted profit and loss account; and
- a budgeted balance sheet.

The functional budgets we prepared in the previous chapter are a valuable planning tool, but they may be inappropriate for certain purposes.

Link between tactical and strategic planning levels

Functional budgets, as we have seen, are very detailed and derive from standard specifications per unit of product or service. As a link between tactical and operational levels of planning, they are therefore ideal. Linking tactical to strategic plans, however, is unlikely to require this level of detail, given that strategic plans are more broad-brush and general in scope. If management were to attempt a tactical–strategic link on the basis of detailed functional budgets, there is a very real danger that evidence of tactical support for strategy could become lost in a welter of unnecessary detail. The result could be uncertainty about whether tactical plans do, in fact, support strategic; and uncertainty about this might call into question the value of the entire planning process.

Information for top management

Implementing, achieving and possibly setting functional budgets is principally the domain of lower levels of management. This is not to say that top management has no concern with tactical and operational plans. But senior managers will be more interested in gaining an overview of tactical and operational matters, so summary information is likely to be more appropriate for their use. In addition, providing tactical and operational information in summary form is likely to free valuable time for senior managers to concentrate on strategic issues.

Information for *ad hoc* purposes

From time to time, organisations may have to prepare budgets for specific purposes. Exhibit 17.1 suggests one important such purpose – seeking additional funding. In such circumstances, providers of extra funds are likely to require certain estimates – and in particular, estimated cash flows and profit projections. The master budget (or an amended version in the form of a 'business plan') may therefore be suitable for many 'one-off' situations of this kind.

Since cash is of great significance to every organisation, we will commence our consideration of the master budget by illustrating how the cash budget is prepared.

THE CASH BUDGET

Cash is such an important resource that the cash budget can almost be considered as a functional budget in its own right, having the following purposes:

- to ensure that sufficient cash is available when required to meet the organisation's commitments; and
- to ensure effective use of surplus cash.

Budgeting the organisation's cash flows allows periods of potential cash shortage and surplus to be anticipated. This permits advance arrangements to be made to overcome the former (e.g. by negotiating an overdraft facility or by attempting to reduce costs) and to take advantage of the latter (e.g. by making short-term investments).

 Unexpectedly running out of cash is obviously not in an organisation's interest, but why might the holding of unnecessarily large cash balances be equally detrimental?

Holding large cash balances in an organisation's bank account is not the best use of this resource: any interest payable on the bank balance will almost invariably be lower than the return which could be earned from short-term investment of the surplus elsewhere. In addition, a large cash surplus may prompt an unwelcome takeover bid. Moreover, defending against a hostile takeover may be extremely costly and possibly damaging to the target.

Exhibit 17.2 contains information about DPA Ltd's budget profiling, along with some additional data relevant to preparation of the company's cash budget. You will see that profiling has occurred on a quarterly basis – this is merely for ease of presentation. In practice, a shorter time-frame would be used – monthly, fortnightly or even weekly – such is the importance of cash.

DPA Ltd: budget profiling and cash-flow data

Management has obtained the following estimated cash flows from the company's profiled functional budgets for next year:

	Quarter I £	Quarter II £	Quarter III £	Quarter IV £
Sales revenue	140 000	105 000	85 000	63 300
Purchases of direct materials	68 920	27 000	20 000	14 000
Direct wages	26 000	23 000	20 000	20 000
Production overhead	3 100	3 100	3 100	3 100
Selling overhead: fixed	8 000	5 000	10 000	13 000
variable	1 400	1 050	850	633
Administration overhead	7 000	7 000	7 000	7 000

▶

Additional information

1   Examination of the capital expenditure budget reveals cash payments of £83 000 and £60 000 in Quarters II and III respectively; in Quarter I, sale of a capital asset will realise £2000 in cash.

2   Corporation tax of £21 000 in respect of last year's profit will be payable in Quarter III.

3   10% of sales are made on a cash basis, the remainder being credit sales; of the credit customers, 80% pay in the quarter after sale, 18% pay two quarters after sale and the balance is irrecoverable bad debts. At the end of the current year, it is estimated that debtors will amount to £142 000, of whom 70% will pay in Quarter I, 26% in Quarter II, the balance being bad debts.

4   Purchases of materials are paid for 50% in the Quarter of purchase, the remainder in the quarter after purchase. At the end of the current year, it is estimated that creditors for purchases will amount to £4000, all of which will be paid in Quarter 1.

5   Direct wages, selling overheads and administration overheads are paid in the quarter in which they are incurred.

6   Depreciation has been excluded from all the overhead figures above *except* that for administration overhead, which includes £500 per quarter depreciation.

7   At the end of the current year, it is expected that the cash balance at the bank will be £3000.

Exhibit 17.2 Data for cash budget preparation

Examination of the detail contained in Exhibit 17.2 provides another illustration of the importance of budget co-ordination. In addition to estimates about the time taken by debtors to pay DPA Ltd and for the company to pay its own creditors, a meaningful cash budget could not be prepared without the prior existence of the functional budgets prepared in the previous chapter. Not only is this an important practical issue, but you should be aware that many exam questions involving preparation of cash budgets also require you to prepare one or more functional budgets (the production budget, for instance) as a prerequisite to completion of the cash budget.

 What adjustment to the overhead costs in Exhibit 17.2 is necessary before the cash budget can be prepared?

Note 6 in Exhibit 17.2 indicates that administration overhead includes £500 per quarter depreciation: since this is not a cash flow, it should not appear in the cash budget. The cash amount of administration overheads is therefore (£7000 – £500) = £6500 per quarter. Other non-cash items, such as the estimated bad debts referred to in note 3 of Exhibit 17.2, or discounts given/received should similarly be omitted from the cash budget.

When preparing a cash budget, it is important to make a distinction between timing of the right to receive (or obligation to pay) cash and of receipt (or payment) itself. The profit and loss account and balance sheet are based on rights and obligations, whereas the cash budget is based on receipts and payments. You should also note that cash budgets, unlike the profit and loss account and balance sheet, make no distinction between *revenue* (profit and loss) and *capital* (balance sheet) items: all cash flows, regardless of their nature, are reflected in the cash budget. We may therefore see cash receipts arising from issue of shares and debentures, or from the sale of fixed assets;

cash payments may be made in respect of loan redemptions, purchase of the company's own shares or of fixed assets.

Exhibit 17.3 shows DPA Ltd's cash budget by quarter and for the year as a whole and involves calculating, for each quarter in sequence:

opening cash balance + cash receipts – cash payments

which will yield the closing cash balance.

 Why is it necessary to calculate the quarterly closing cash balances in sequence?

A sequential approach to calculation of closing cash balances is necessary because each quarter's closing cash balance will provide the following quarter's opening balance. The opening and closing balance for the year as a whole are, respectively, the anticipated balance at the end of the current year (which will be next year's opening balance) and the estimated closing balance for Quarter IV. Cash receipts and payments for the year are simply cross-additions of the quarterly figures.

DPA Ltd: cash budget

	Quarter I	Quarter II	Quarter III	Quarter IV	Year
	£	£	£	£	£
Opening balance	3 000	34 940	13 550	(24 620)	3 000
Add Cash receipts:					
Sale of capital asset	2 000				2 000
Sales					
– cash	14 000	10 500	8 500	6 330	39 330
– credit: 70%/26%					
of debtors at start	99 400	36 920			136 320
80% of credit sales		100 800	75 600	61 200	237 600
18% of credit sales			22 680	17 010	39 690
	118 400	183 160	120 330	59 920	457 940
Less Cash payments:					
Capital expenditure		83 000	60 000		143 000
Corporation tax			21 000		21 000
Purchases:					
creditors at start	4 000				4 000
50% in quarter of purchase	34 460	13 500	10 000	7 000	64 960
50% in quarter after purchase		34 460	13 500	10 000	57 960
Direct wages	26 000	23 000	20 000	20 000	89 000
Production overhead	3 100	3 100	3 100	3 100	12 400
Selling overhead	9 400	6 050	10 850	13 633	39 933
Administration overhead	6 500	6 500	6 500	6 500	26 000
	83 460	169 610	144 950	60 233	458 253
Closing balance	34 940	13 550	(24 620)	(313)	(313)

Exhibit 17.3 Cash budget

The bracketed figures in Exhibit 17.3 reflect the fact that, in Quarters III and IV, cash payments exceed cash receipts – that is, the company's bank account will potentially be overdrawn in those quarters. If expectations come to pass in reality, then the company will suffer a 'liquidity crisis' (i.e. will be unable to meet all of its financial commitments as they fall due) in the quarters concerned, unless management takes action to address the cash flow problem.

 What steps might DPA Ltd's management take in order to meet the cash shortfall anticipated in Quarters III and IV?

Management might try to arrange overdraft facilities with the company's bank, or might try to improve cash flows from sales, or reduce costs. In this latter respect, management may wish to consider the capital expenditures in Quarters II and III, which are largely responsible for the cash deficit. Could these payments be deferred? Or could the assets concerned be financed in a way which does not require such large 'one-off' payments (e.g. by leasing)? An issue of shares or debentures would be no use, since it is unlikely that the cash from such an issue would be received sufficiently early to assist in the periods of predicted cash shortage. It is exactly this sort of vital information about an organisation's liquidity which the cash budget is intended to provide.

In certain situations, the cash budget will not show opening and closing cash balances and it will thus be necessary to amend its format. Where cash inflows and outflows are involved, the latter may be subtracted from the former to give the net cash inflow (or outflow). It is also possible to prepare cash budgets showing simply cash inflows or cash outflows. For example, an organisation with a number of branches in different locations may operate a single central bank account, but may nevertheless wish to prepare cash budgets for each individual branch. Here a 'net cash flow' approach would be used for each branch's cash budget, with these separate budgets being amalgamated by head office to give a company-wide cash budget of the type illustrated in Exhibit 17.3.

THE BUDGETED PROFIT AND LOSS ACCOUNT

The second element of a master budget is the budgeted profit and loss account. To prepare DPA Ltd's budgeted profit and loss account, we need to summarise certain information from the functional budgets completed in the last chapter. This information, along with some supplementary data, is set out in Exhibit 17.4.

Unlike the cash budget, which shows the *proceeds* of sale, the profit and loss account reflects the *profit/loss* arising from sale of the capital asset:

	£
Proceeds of sale	2000
Book value of asset sold	1000
Profit on sale	1000

This will have the effect of increasing budgeted profit for the year.

We also need values for opening and closing stocks of finished goods. Using stock figures and standard unit production costs from Exhibit 17.4 (and assuming that

DPA Ltd: information for budgeted profit and loss account

Summarised information from the company's various functional budgets is as follows:

Budgeted sales revenue	£393 300			
Budgeted production/stock	2 kg bags	5 kg bags	10 kg bags	20 kg bags
Production	12 000	10 000	8000	5000
Opening stock	4 000	2 500	400	600
Closing stock	1 000	500	200	200
Standard unit production cost	£	£	£	£
– variable	1.41	2.90	5.32	10.15
– fixed	1.15	2.30	4.60	5.75
	2.56	5.20	9.92	15.90

Budgeted raw material stocks opening £24 000 closing £32 000
Budgeted total production cost £241 580 (absorption costing), £139 230 (marginal costing)
Budgeted fixed production costs £13 350 (overhead), £89 000 (direct labour)
Budgeted selling overhead £3933 variable, plus £40 000 fixed = £43 933
Budgeted administration overhead (all fixed) £28 000.

The capital asset which is to be sold in Quarter I for £2000 will have a book value of £1000 at the time of sale. Corporation tax on next year's profit is estimated to be £14 000.

Exhibit 17.4 Summary information for budgeted profit and loss account

absorption costing is to be used), budgeted opening stocks are valued at:

	£
2 kg bags (4000 × £2.56)	10 240
5 kg bags (2500 × £5.20)	13 000
10 kg bags (400 × £9.92)	3 968
20 kg bags (600 × £15.90)	9 540
	36 748

 Using absorption costing principles in conjunction with data in Exhibit 17.4, value DPA Ltd's budgeted closing stock.

Closing stock of finished goods will be valued as follows:

	£
2 kg bags (1000 × £2.56)	2 560
5 kg bags (500 × £5.20)	2 600
10 kg bags (200 × £9.92)	1 984
20 kg bags (200 × £15.90)	3 180
	10 324

Exhibit 17.5 shows DPA Ltd's budgeted profit and loss account – here for the year as a whole, but it is perfectly possible to profile this statement in the same way as we did the cash budget.

DPA Ltd: budgeted profit and loss account for the year (absorption costing)

	£	£
Sales revenue		393 300
Less Standard production cost of sales		
Opening stock	36 748	
Cost of production	241 580	
	278 328	
Closing stock	10 324	268 004
Gross profit		125 296
Selling overhead	43 933	
Administration overhead	28 000	
Profit on sale of capital asset	(1 000)	70 933
Net profit before taxation		54 363
Estimated corporation tax		14 000
Net profit after taxation		40 363

Exhibit 17.5 Budgeted profit & loss account (absorption costing)

 Why does Exhibit 17.5 show no adjustment to the profit and loss account for over/underabsorbed overhead?

You will recall from Chapter 5 that over- or underabsorbed overhead is the difference between the amount of overhead absorbed using a predetermined absorption rate and the amount of overhead incurred. Because the statement in Exhibit 17.5 is a *budgeted* profit and loss account (i.e. based on budgeted production overhead cost and budgeted production), no such difference will exist.

As with the production cost budget (see Chapter 16), it is possible to argue that a marginal costing approach to the profit and loss account might be preferable, as it better shows the relationship between volume of sales and profit. Such an approach is presented in Exhibit 17.6.

Budgeted total production cost is taken from Exhibit 17.4, while opening and closing stocks are valued (at variable production cost) as follows:

	Opening £	*Closing* £
2 kg bags (4000/1000 × £1.41)	5 640	1 410
5 kg bags (2500/500 × £2.90)	7 250	1 450
10 kg bags (400/200 × £5.32)	2 128	1 064
20 kg bags (600/200 × £10.15)	6 090	2 030
	21 108	5 954

Because sales volume exceeds production, marginal costing yields the higher profit; you may wish to revise Chapter 12 to remind yourself about why this is the case.

DPA Ltd: budgeted profit and loss account (marginal costing basis)

	£	£
Sales revenue (same as Exhibit 17.5)		393 300
Less Variable production cost of sales		
Opening stock	21 108	
Cost of production	139 230	
	160 338	
Closing stock	5 954	
	154 384	
Variable selling overhead	3 933	158 317
Contribution		234 983
Less Fixed costs		
direct labour	89 000	
production overhead	13 350	
selling overhead	40 000	
administration overhead	28 000	
profit on sale of capital asset	(1 000)	169 350
Net profit before taxation		65 633
Estimated corporation tax		14 000
Net profit after taxation		51 633

Exhibit 17.6 Budgeted profit and loss account (marginal costing)

 Assume that sales volume increases by 20% and that there is no change to the sales/production mix, to the unit selling prices and variable costs or to the total fixed costs; what will be the effect of such a volume increase on net profit before taxation in Exhibit 17.6?

Given our assumptions about sales mix, unit selling price and unit variable cost, a 20% increase in sales volume will result in a 20% increase in contribution:

increase in contribution (20% × £234 983)   £46 996.60

If fixed costs are unaffected by the change in volume, then the increase in contribution is also the increase in net profit before taxation. Use of a marginal costing format may therefore aid management in assessing the impact on profit of different output/sales volumes – a topic we shall return to in the next chapter.

One point to note is that, regardless of whether absorption or marginal costing is employed, the company earns a budgeted profit for the year. Contrast this with the overall cash outflow of £3313 (opening cash balance £3000 – closing cash balance £313 overdrawn) which the cash budget revealed.

 Why will profit and cash flow almost always differ?

The profit and loss account records transactions on the basis of legal right to receive, or obligation to pay, cash. These legal rights and obligations may well arise at quite a different point in time to that at which cash is actually received/paid. Since the cash budget shows receipts and payments of cash, timing differences in recording the associated transactions will frequently arise. In addition, the profit and loss account contains certain non-cash items (depreciation being a major example) – and, being non-cash, such items are excluded from the cash budget.

Therefore profit and cash do *not* equate. If management were to suffer any confusion about this, believing, say, that profit reflected cash availability, then decisions might be taken which could deepen DPA Ltd's potential liquidity crisis in the last two quarters of next year.

THE BUDGETED BALANCE SHEET

A budgeted balance sheet is the final element of the master budget and requires prior preparation, not only of functional budgets but also of the cash budget and profit and loss account. The capital expenditure budget will be explicitly reflected in the balance sheet (via changes to the fixed asset section), as will certain other strategic budgets (e.g. relating to share or debenture issues). Exhibit 17.7 shows DPA Ltd's budgeted balance sheet for next year.

Details of existing fixed assets will be obtained from accounting records, with the capital expenditure budget providing information about acquisitions/disposals. The tax liability is that which is shown in the budgeted profit and loss account, while existing share capital will be extracted from the company's records, any proposed issues and/or

DPA Ltd: budgeted balance sheet			
Fixed assets	Cost	Accumulated depreciation	Net book value
	£	£	£
Premises	80 000	10 000	70 000
Production equipment	46 000	9 000	37 000
Office equipment	72 000	12 000	60 000
Delivery vans	64 000	14 000	50 000
	262 000	45 000	217 000
Current assets			
Stocks: finished goods	10 324		
raw materials	32 000		
Debtors	69 601	111 925	
Current liabilities			
Bank overdraft	313		
Creditors for purchases	7 000		
Taxation	14 000	21 313	90 612
			307 612
Share capital and reserves			
Ordinary shares of £1			220 000
Retained profit: anticipated at end of the current year		47 249	
Add budgeted net profit after taxation		40 363	87 612
			307 612

Exhibit 17.7 Budgeted balance sheet

redemptions being specified in the strategic budget. Anticipated retained profit at the end of the current year will consist of last year's actual retained profit plus an estimate of retained profit for the current year. Since the master budget will be prepared fairly late in the current accounting year, this estimate is likely to be reasonably accurate.

We calculated the value of finished goods' closing stock when we were preparing the budgeted profit and loss account, while budgeted closing raw material stock is given in Exhibit 17.4 (being derived from the material purchases budget in Chapter 16). Note that we have used absorption costing values for closing stocks of finished goods; had the company employed marginal costing for its budgeted profit and loss account, finished goods' stock would be stated at its variable production cost (as per Exhibit 17.6).

 State the source from which the following figures in Exhibit 17.7 have been derived:

   debtors
   bank overdraft
   creditors.

(You do not need to verify the amounts involved.)

The bank overdraft can be obtained directly from the cash budget, where it is the closing bank balance for the year. Debtors and creditors must be determined from the information about payment timings which was used to prepare the cash budget (see Exhibit 17.2):

		£
Debtors	18% of Quarter III's sales	13 770
	90% of Quarter IV's sales	56 970
	Less Bad debts (2% × £56 970)	1 139
	Total outstanding at year-end	69 601
Creditors	50% of Quarter IV's purchases	7 000

It would be unusual for a budgeted balance sheet to be profiled, since it is essentially of a static nature: that is, it is intended to present a 'picture' of the organisation's financial position at a given point in time. Functional budgets, the cash budget and budgeted profit and loss account, however, are all *dynamic*: that is, reflect flows of resources over time – and so will benefit from profiling.

BUDGETING FOR SERVICE INDUSTRIES

The budget preparation example we have just completed is set in an organisation which is producing a tangible output – i.e. DPA Ltd is a manufacturing business.

 Bearing in mind the heterogeneity, simultaneity and intangibility of its output (described in Chapter 11), how would a service business's budgets differ from those we have just prepared for DPA Ltd?

The nature of an organisation's input/output processes has major implications for its budget system. The main differences between service and manufacturing organisations are: that the former cannot store either their output or the majority of their inputs (simultaneity); that output, along with its relationship to input, may be difficult to quantify (intangibility); and that cost units could well be markedly different from each other (heterogeneity). The most visible sign of these differences will be the absence, in service organisations' budgets, of a 'production' budget and of budgeted stock levels for finished goods. Depending on the precise nature of the service being offered, there may or may not be budgets for materials' usage/purchases. A bank, for example, will incur substantial expenditure on materials such as stationery, cheque books, cheque guarantee cards, credit cards and so forth; some of these (e.g. stationery) may be held in stock by the bank, other items (e.g. cheque books) ordered as required. There are two important points which we can make here:

1 Substantial though such expenditures may be, they are unlikely to form the major input to the service provided. In the bank's case, the main input will probably be staff time and expertise.
2 The link between inputs (whether materials, labour or overhead) and outputs can be more difficult to quantify than for many manufacturing businesses – e.g. what labour time is required to service each personal current account?

Unlike manufacturing organisations, standard costing will therefore not always be possible at the cost unit level. A bank could not meaningfully prepare a standard cost card for each personal current account to the same degree of detail as used by DPA Ltd in Exhibit 17.4. At best, standard costing can be only partially implemented. We may, for example, have a standard salary scale for employees at the bank's branches and, based on our expectations about the future volume of business, estimate the number of employees of each grade required during the budget period (along with the related cost). What we cannot readily do, however, is say that each current account in operation during the year requires a given number of staff hours to service. In addition, definition of the cost unit may be problematic – a composite cost unit, such as passenger/kilometre, may be necessary, or there may be some dubiety about the most appropriate cost unit to use (e.g. number of personal bank clients versus number of personal accounts of each different category). We should stress, though, that it is the nature of the service provided, along with our understanding of its inputs, outputs and processes which governs the extent to which we can employ standard costing. A landscape gardener may be well aware of the standard input times, quantities and costs for a particular job, but a firm of solicitors might find this less easy.

What we are describing are really areas of *difference* between service and manufacturing sectors. Yet there is much common ground between the two in budget preparation: for instance, strategic aims and budgets should govern tactical; an estimate of sales (or other volume of activity in a non-profit situation) will be the necessary starting-point for the budget preparation process; functional budgets should stem from this initial volume estimate; principal budget factors must be recognised; and functional budgets will require to be summarised in a master budget. Moreover, budget preparation is every bit as problematic for manufacturing as for service businesses – it is the nature, rather than the scale, of such problems which differs.

PUBLIC SECTOR BUDGETING

Although the general principles of budget preparation apply equally to public sector as to other types of organisation, the influences and constraints operative in the public sector are rather different, and we shall now outline these. At the outset, it must be said that, for many public sector bodies, the budgeting process may be considerably more complex and time-consuming than for others and well-defined procedures are essential. Not only will the budget, once set, represent authority to spend, but, in all probability, it will also represent a maximum amount which can be spent. Such is the significance of budgeting that Jones and Pendlebury (1996) have stated that 'as far as local and central government are concerned, it is probably the single most important financial exercise that they undertake'.

In areas of the public sector which are relatively 'commercialised' – e.g. the quasi-autonomous Direct Service Organisations which provide road maintenance or refuse collection services to many local authorities – budgetary procedures are very similar to those employed in such organisations' commercial equivalents. However, despite their apparent independence from the parent body, and their more commercial outlook, they are subject to the same influences and constraints as more overtly 'public' bodies, although possibly in a more indirect way.

Revenue budgets and capital budgets

Almost every public sector organisation distinguishes between **revenue budgets** and **capital budgets**. Revenue budgets are analogous to tactical budgets in the private sector, with capital budgets having the same strategic orientation in both sectors. Not only is it necessary to recognise the impact of capital on revenue budgets (particularly where capital projects are to be funded from revenue sources such as taxation), but it is also important to recognise that the sources of funding for each category of budget are essentially, but not exclusively, different. Revenue budgets are funded from a combination of taxation and other charges levied (along with central government support in the case of local authorities), whereas capital budgets are funded by other means (e.g. borrowing, again possibly supplemented by grant aid). These different sources of finance are subject to different regulations and, statutory requirements aside, this must largely determine the budgetary framework.

Political influences

As well as the 'budget politics' which will exist in every system (and which we shall discuss in Chapter 18), public sector budgets are subject to party-political influence. For example, a local authority budget which is financially acceptable may fail to gain ultimate approval by elected councillors because its priorities are at odds with those of the majority party, or party political disagreement may disturb the relationship between local and central government. It may therefore be necessary to revise public sector budgets more often than private – not only to reflect unforeseen principal budget factors but also to allow for such political considerations. Scheduling of budget preparation and the need for coordination may thus assume even greater significance in public sector than in other organisations.

High public profile

Public sector budgets are subject to considerable public scrutiny and comment; for private sector organisations, budgeting is primarily an internal affair, with little or no information being made public. This means that in the public sector any shift in spending priority or need for additional finance (e.g. via additional taxation) requires to be justified, not only in financial but also in political and social terms. Failure to justify budget changes in social terms may render a budget politically unacceptable; rejection of proposed changes for such reasons may conceivably result in a budgetary 'philosophy' which is too rigid in a dynamic environment. Some local authorities, for example, might argue that strict limits on their spending and finance-raising powers are inconsistent with the need to provide local services to a desired standard. Although such disagreement may stem from opposing political viewpoints, it might also be seen as evidence of unnecessary rigidity within the budget-setting process. One possible indicator of the extent of such rigidity could be the frequency with which 'virement' is exercised within public sector budgets – i.e. transfer of funds from underspent to overspent budgets.

In the public sector, budgetary difficulties may be compounded by the absence of a charge for the services provided, which removes one output measure common to all commercial enterprises: profit. There is a danger that budgets may stress what is readily measurable ('inputs' – i.e. costs) at the expense of proper consideration of the outputs which result.

APPROACHES TO BUDGET FORMULATION

In the previous chapter, we defined budgets as 'quantified plans' – but *how* are plans quantified? Do we perhaps use current events as a guide, or should we 'wipe the slate clean' before each budget is prepared? How should costs and revenues be categorised within budgets? These issues are discussed below.

Line-item and programme budgets

A **line-item budget** classifies costs according to their nature. A summarised budgeted profit statement prepared using line-item principles might look like the following:

		£	£
Sales revenue			X
Less	Materials' costs	X	
	Labour costs	X	
	Overhead costs	X	X
Profit			X

 Why would a statement such as that above be inadequate for budgetary planning purposes?

The weakness of line-item budgets is that they do not reflect the purpose of expenditure, and if we do not know why costs are being incurred, it is impossible either to plan or to control them in any effective way. **Programme budgets** classify costs according to the reason for their being incurred (e.g. production, selling, administration etc), which allows much more accurate planning of expenditures. If you examine the budgets which we prepared for DPA Ltd, you will be able to see elements of both approaches. The company's production cost budget (see Chapter 16) is a programme budget (the expenditures relate to production) and, within the budget, individual costs are stated on a line-item basis (materials, packing, direct labour and production overhead). This kind of combination approach is predominant in public and private, commercial and non-profit sectors.

Incremental budgets

One possible starting-point for budget formulation is recent experience. **Incremental budgets** start with the current budget, which is then revised to reflect factors such as:

- anticipated events occurring before the end of the current budget period; and
- anticipated data for next budget period, such as the estimated inflation rate, volume of activity, and changes in mix of activity.

Such an approach is undoubtedly straightforward (assuming tolerably accurate estimates) and may be justified on the basis that the focus of budgetary attention should be on *changes* from one budget period to the next, thereby reducing budgetary complexities and narrowing the areas of possible dispute.

 What is the potential weakness inherent in incremental budgeting?

The danger of incremental budgets is that, if they are applied in a mechanistic manner – i.e. 'next year's budget is this year's budget $+x\%$' – then the past will come to dominate the future, with past inefficiencies being carried forward to future periods. Use of incremental budgeting may tempt management to believe that previous levels of expenditure were justified and that the reasons for such expenditure will remain. Such views are not consistent with effective planning. Past experience may *influence* planning, but not to the exclusion of expectations about the future. Carrying forward past inefficiencies to future periods within the budget is one reason for the existence of **budgetary slack**, which is the difference between minimum necessary expenditure and actual/budgeted expenditure. In Chapter 18, we shall discuss other possible reasons for the existence of budgetary slack.

Zero base budgeting (ZBB)

One solution to the problem of budgetary slack is **zero base budgeting** (ZBB). Unlike incremental budgeting, ZBB starts from the position of zero previous expenditure and requires justification of budgeted amounts. Figure 17.1 illustrates how a system of ZBB would operate.

Although the terminology may appear rather daunting, the basic principles being illustrated in Figure 17.1 are quite straightforward:

1 The budget is based on consideration (in **mutually exclusive decision packages**) of alternative ways of achieving objectives.
2 For the best method of achieving their objectives, different levels of expenditure by organisational subunits (**decision units**) are 'justified' with reference to each unit's activities (in **incremental decision packages**): i.e. if a particular functional budget is set at, say, 90% of its current level, how will that function's performance be affected?

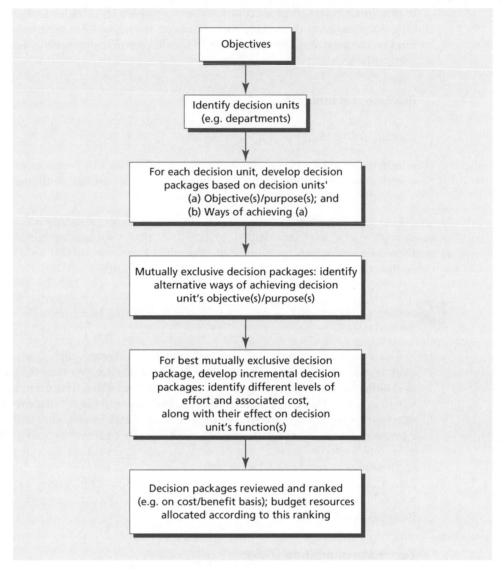

Figure 17.1 A system of zero base budgeting

3 Ranking of competing subunit decision packages in the context of both scarce budget resources and of achieving organisational objectives: e.g. if increasing market share is an objective, then decision packages submitted by the sales department may receive higher ranking than those from some other functions – at least until the specified objective is achievable with the budget resources allocated to sales, at which point other functions may take priority.

As a method of combating budgetary slack, of encouraging managers to examine alternative ways of achieving objectives and in its explicit linking of allocations of scarce budgetary resources to achievement of objectives, ZBB is hard to fault. In addition, ZBB's rationale is (or should be) that which is applied to proposed expenditure in new areas, which should support or encourage systematic use of appraisal techniques like net present value. ZBB may therefore be valuable where organisations are faced with particularly volatile environments.

 What difficulty would you foresee if an organisation were to adopt ZBB for preparation of its tactical budgets?

If the procedures outlined in Figure 17.1 were to be used for tactical budgeting (i.e. on an annual basis), then the system would be extremely cumbersome administratively. Much management time and effort would be required in preparation of mutually exclusive and incremental decision packages, for example. In addition, it may not be possible to define organisational and subunit objectives with sufficient precision to permit their use as the basis of budget allocations, thereby increasing the possibility of dispute. It might also be said that adopting a strict interpretation of 'zero base' is of questionable value. Assuming that the organisation is to continue in existence, some expenditure is absolutely necessary, so it makes more sense to concentrate on what is likely to change between one budget period and the next.

One answer to the administration difficulty might be to subject tactical (and strategic) budgets to periodic **zero base review** (say, every five years); in this way, the chance of carrying forward past inefficiencies might be reduced. Where it is proposed to undertake expenditure in new areas, ZBB *must* be used, as there will be no previous data on which to base the budget. In such cases, the correlation between planning and decision appraisal is particularly evident, with the results of the latter serving as explicit justification for budget inclusion/exclusion.

A variant on ZBB is the **planning, programming and budget system** (PPBS), under which the programmes and programme elements (i.e. subdivisions of programmes) which best meet objectives are selected from the available alternatives on a cost/benefit basis. Unlike zero base budgets, PPBS is not predicated on zero previous expenditure, but still requires consideration of alternative courses of action and allocation of budget resources according to cost/benefit ranking. PPBS is similar to activity-based budgeting in the sense that programmes, like activities, often span traditional departmental boundaries.

Rolling budgets

The problem of uncertainty about the future is one which affects all budgets to a greater or lesser degree – greater for strategic than for tactical budgets and for volatile than stable environments. One way in which the impact of such uncertainty may be reduced is to use **rolling** (or **continuous**) **budgets**. Within a particular strategic or tactical budget period, functional and master budgets will be prepared in the normal manner, but the budget period concerned will be subdivided into a number of shorter periods, for which extremely detailed budgets will be prepared on an ongoing basis. Figure 17.2 illustrates how such a system could be applied to annual budgets.

As you will see from Figure 17.2, the rolling nature of budget preparation applies, not only within a particular budget period but also from one budget period to the next.

 How would the time, effort and expense involved in operation of a rolling budget be justified?

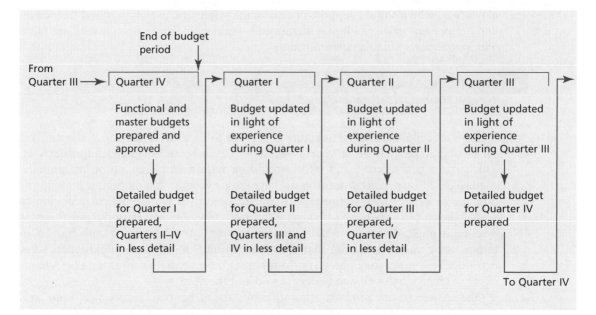

Figure 17.2 Operation of a rolling budget

The time, effort and expense involved in continually updating the budget as suggested in Figure 17.2 is justifiable if the associated cost is exceeded by the benefit derived from additional budget accuracy. This may be particularly true when conditions are volatile and subject to considerable uncertainty.

Activity-based budgeting (ABB)

We discussed the principles of **activity-based costing** (ABC) in Chapter 6, where the main emphasis was on calculation of unit costs. This approach can be extended to produce a system of **activity-based budgeting** (ABB), which in outline is very similar, but with the main aim being planning and control. Once the organisation's major activities have been identified, and a budgeted cost pool assigned to each activity, then the cost driver(s) relating to that cost pool are determined, the budget being constructed on the basis of total budgeted cost for each cost driver and budgeted cost per unit of each cost driver. Morrow and Connolly (1991) have suggested the use of an activity matrix for this purpose. Based on their approach, Exhibit 17.8 illustrates how such a matrix may be constructed for an administration budget.

Four cost drivers have been identified in Exhibit 17.8 as being the main underlying cause of the budgeted administration costs. 'Sustaining costs' are those which cannot meaningfully be related to any specific cost driver and might be thought of as general administration necessary to support the organisation as a whole. Once a system of ABB is in place, management will plan future expenditure by estimating the volume of activity for each cost driver and then work back to determine the cost necessary to support that volume. It is argued that budgeting in this way highlights the cost of activities – e.g. the fact that each employee incurs a £256 administration cost – and knowledge of such figures may encourage management to seek more cost-effective methods of administration. However, the validity of such figures depends on the accuracy with which cost

DPA Ltd: administration activity cost matrix

Cost drivers	No. of employees	No. of customers	Volume of output	Value of sales	Sustaining costs	Total
Administration costs	£	£	£	£	£	£
Management salaries	12 000	16 000	14 000	8 000	20 000	70 000
Clerical salaries	10 000	20 000	6 000	4 000	12 000	52 000
Occupancy costs					15 000	15 000
Computer costs	3 000	2 000	4 000	2 000	6 000	17 000
Bad debts				5 000		5 000
Stationery etc	5 000	7 000	1 000		2 000	15 000
Insurance					9 000	9 000
Sundry costs	2 000	1 000	2 000	1 000	5 000	11 000
Total	32 000	46 000	27 000	20 000	69 000	194 000
Cost driver volume	125	1 150	90 000	1 000 000		
Cost per unit of cost driver	£256	£40	£0.30	£0.20	£69 000	

Exhibit 17.8 Activity-based budgeting

drivers have been identified and on the objectivity with which costs can be related to particular cost drivers.

SUMMARY

In this chapter, we have seen that:

- The cash budget is prepared to help predict periods of possible cash shortage and surplus so that advance measures may be taken to mitigate the effect of the former and to take advantage of the opportunity offered by the latter.

- Because of the importance of cash, the cash budget will be **profiled** (e.g. on a monthly basis) within the budget period.

- Non-cash items such as depreciation and provision for bad debts are omitted from the cash budget, which makes no distinction between capital and revenue items, calculating the periodic closing balance as (opening balance + cash receipts – cash payments) with the opening balance being the previous period's closing balance.

- The budgeted profit and loss account and balance sheet will summarise key information contained in separate functional budgets and in the cash budget.

- Cash flow and profit will not be the same because profit is calculated on the basis of rights to receive/obligations to pay cash and after inclusion of certain non-cash items; cash flows are based solely on cash receipts and payments.

- Depending on the nature of their input, processes and output, service organisations may have difficulty implementing a full system of standard costing because of imprecise input/output relationships and composite cost units.

▶

- Public sector organisations tend to distinguish between **revenue budgets** and **capital budgets**, these budgets being subject to political influences and having a high public profile.

- **Line-item budgets** classify costs according to their nature, **programme budgets** classify costs according to the reason for their being incurred – effective planning requires the use of a combination of both approaches.

- **Incremental budgets** take the current year's adjusted budget as their starting-point but, while simple to operate, may have the effect of perpetuating current inefficiencies into the future.

- **Budget slack** is the difference between minimum necessary expenditure and budgeted/actual expenditure and may arise as a result of incremental budgeting.

- **Zero base budgeting** (ZBB) attempts to address the problem of budgetary slack by requiring justification of all expenditures assuming zero prior expenditure, and may be administratively cumbersome.

- **Rolling** (**continuous**) budgets are produced in detail on an ongoing basis within the budget period and may be a useful device for dealing with uncertainty.

- **Activity-based budgeting** (ABB) extends the principles of activity-based costing (ABC) to deal with budgetary planning, and may produce more useful budgetary information depending on the accuracy of the cost drivers and objectivity of costs assigned to each activity and cost driver.

In the next chapter, we will extend our discussion of budgeting to cover the corollary to planning – control. That is, how do we set about assessing the extent to which we have managed to achieve the plans quantified in our budgets?

FURTHER READING

Drury, C., *Standard Costing*, Academic Press/CIMA, 1992: Chapter 1 provides an overview of the nature and scope of standard costing.

Drury, C., Braund, S., Osborne, P. and Tayles, M., *A Survey of Management Accounting Practices in UK Manufacturing Companies*, CACA, 1993.

Greenall, A., *Finance and Budgeting for Line Managers*, The Industrial Society, 1996: Chapter 5 is a readable management perspective on the budgetary process.

Jones, R. and Pendlebury, M., *Public Sector Accounting* (5th edition), Financial Times Prentice Hall, 2000: Chapters 3, 4 and 5 deal with public sector budgeting.

Maugham, S., Financial planning. *ACCA Students' Newsletter*, September 1998.

Morrow, M. and Connolly, T., The emergence of activity-based budgeting. *Management Accounting*, February 1991, CIMA.

SELF-TEST QUESTIONS

17.1 Of the four costs shown below, which would *not* be included in the cash budget of an insurance firm?

    A Depreciation of fixed assets
    B Commission paid to agents
    C Office salaries
    D Capital cost of a new computer.

(CIMA, *Cost Accounting and Quantitative Methods*, May 1998)

17.2 Place a tick in the appropriate box to indicate whether each of the following statements is true or false.

	True	False
(a) Depreciation should be excluded from the payments recorded in a cash budget.	☐	☐
(b) Discounts received should be included under cash receipts in a cash budget.	☐	☐
(c) Budgetary slack is the difference between budgeted expenditure and actual expenditure.	☐	☐
(d) A line-item budget classifies expenditure according to its nature.	☐	☐
(e) A rolling budget is useful for organisations where estimation is subject to considerable uncertainty.	☐	☐
(f) Incremental budgeting explicitly requires that all future expenditure be justified.	☐	☐
(g) Profit is calculated using the matching concept, which stipulates that transactions be recorded when cash is due for receipt or payment.	☐	☐
(h) In zero base budgeting, mutually exclusive decision packages indicate alternative ways of achieving a particular organisational objective or objectives.	☐	☐

17.3 Rinte plc is considering the possibility of extending its range of products. One proposal is that by adapting existing machinery at a cost of £5000 (which would be paid before the end of the first month of production) a new product, Axot, could be launched.

A selling price of £40 per unit of Axot is considered reasonable, which would reflect a 100% mark-up on the cost of the materials that would be bought in from suppliers. Forecasts are that 750 units would be sold in the first month, which would increase by 20% per month for the first six months.

The policy of Rinte plc is to allow a one-month credit period for debtors, although it is anticipated that one-third of the sales of Axot would be for cash.

Suppliers would allow a one-month credit period before payment is due.

The policy would be to produce enough of Axot in the first month to meet the estimated demand for the first two months, and then from the second month onwards, to produce the forecast demand for the following month.

Wages are estimated to be £3 per unit produced and would be payable in the same month the hours were worked.

Other expenses are estimated at £4 per unit produced. 50% of these expenses would be paid in the month incurred, with the remainder paid in the following month. Promotional costs associated with the launch of Axot are estimated to total £4000, and would be paid in the first month.

Requirements

(a) Prepare a cash budget for the product Axot for the first four months, showing clearly the estimated balance at the end of each month. **(10 marks)**

(b) Using the cash budget prepared in part (a) explain the main purposes of cash budgets.

(5 marks)
(Total: 15 marks)

(CIPFA, *Management Accounting*, June 1998)

17.4 XYZ Limited has the following forecast sales at list price for the nine months to 29 February 1996:

June	£40 000	September	£48 000	December	£44 000
July	£44 000	October	£40 000	January	£42 000
August	£50 000	November	£45 000	February	£50 000

60% of the company's sales are on credit, payable in the month after sale. Cash sales attract a 5% discount off list price.

Purchases amount to 40% of selling price, and these are paid for two months after delivery.

Stock is maintained at a level equal to 50% of the following month's sales except that in November stock is to be increased by £2000 (at cost prices) to ensure that XYZ Limited has a safety stock during the period when its major supplier shuts down. This safety stock will be released in March.

Wages comprise a fixed sum of £2000 per month plus a variable element equal to 10% of sales; these are payable in the month they are incurred.

Fixed costs amount to £7500 per month, payable one month in arrears, of which £1500 is depreciation.

XYZ Limited has capital expenditure/receipts scheduled as follows:

	£
Acquisitions:	
September	15 000
November	10 000
February	4 000
Disposal:	£
October	8 000

Corporation tax, payable in November, amounts to £44 000.
The bank balance on 1 September 1995 is expected to be £5000.

Requirements

(a) Prepare a cashflow forecast for XYZ Limited for *each* of the six months from September 1995 to February 1996, using a row and column format. **(10 marks)**

(b) Explain clearly, using your answer to (a) above, how a spreadsheet may be used to assist in the preparation of cash forecasts. **(10 marks)**

(c) Explain how a cash forecast is an example of both feedforward and feedback control mechanisms. **(5 marks)**

(Total: 25 marks)

(CIMA, *Operational Cost Accounting*, May 1995)

17.5 A small manufacturing firm is to commence operations on 1 July. The following estimates have been prepared:

	July	August	September
Sales (units)	10	36	60
Production (units)	40	50	50
Opening stock (units) NIL			

It is planned to have raw material stocks of £10 000 at the end of July, and to maintain stocks at that level thereafter.

Selling prices, costs and other information:

	Per unit
	£
Selling price	900
Material cost	280
Labour cost	160
Variable overheads	40

Fixed overheads are expected to be £5000 per month, including £1000 depreciation. £60 000 of fixed assets are to be purchased immediately, payable £20 000 per month commencing in August.

Settlement terms:
Sales: 10% cash, the balance payable the month following sale.
Labour is paid in the month incurred, and all other expenditures the following month.

Requirements

(a) Prepare cash budgets for July, August and September, given that the firm started with £20 000 cash on 1 July. **(9 marks)**

(b) Calculate the net working capital at the end of September, making and stating what assumptions you think necessary. The firm values finished goods using absorption costing. **(6 marks)**

(Total: 15 marks)

(CIMA, *Cost Accounting and Quantitative Methods*, November 1998)

QUESTIONS WITHOUT ANSWERS

17.6 A master budget comprises:

  A the budgeted profit and loss account
  B the budgeted cash flow, budgeted profit and loss account and budgeted balance sheet
  C the budgeted cash flow
  D the capital expenditure budget
  E the entire set of budgets prepared

(CIMA, *Operational Cost Accounting*, May 1999)

17.7 The following details have been extracted from the debtor collection records of D Limited:

Invoices paid in the month after sale	70%
Invoices paid in the second month after sale	20%
Invoices paid in the third month after sale	8%
Bad debts	2%

Invoices are issued on the last day of each month.
Customers paying in the month after sale are entitled to deduct a 3% settlement discount.
  Credit sales values for June to September 1999 are budgeted as follows:

June	July	August	September
£52 500	£60 000	£90 000	£67 500

The amount budgeted to be received in September 1999 from credit sales is

  A £74 610
  B £75 960
  C £77 310
  D £77 850
  E £79 200

(CIMA, *Operational Cost Accounting*, November 1998)

17.8 Brian plc produce and sell a single product. They have prepared the following budgeted Profit and Loss Account for the 6 months July to December 1999.

	July £	Aug. £	Sept. £	Oct. £	Nov. £	Dec. £
Sales	18 000	25 200	19 600	21 600	26 000	26 000
Cost of sales:						
Direct materials	12 000	16 800	13 200	14 400	18 000	18 000
Direct wages	2 000	2 800	2 200	2 400	3 000	3 000
Electricity	1 200	1 200	1 200	1 000	800	800
Office expenses	300	340	200	320	360	360
Depreciation	900	900	1 800	1 800	1 800	1 800
Total costs	16 400	22 040	18 600	19 920	23 960	23 960
Profit	1 600	3 160	1 000	1 680	2 040	2 040

Additional information

  (i)   Opening cash balance on 1 July 1999 is expected to be £4000 in hand.
 (ii)   All sales are made on credit. Past experience has shown that 60% of debtors pay
         in the month after sales have been made and 40% pay in the second month
         following the sale. Sales in the months of May 1999 and June 1999 are expected
         to be £16 000 and £18 000 respectively.
(iii)   Material purchases are made on credit; creditors allow one month's credit.
         Purchases for the month of June 1999 are expected to total £12 000.
 (iv)   Wages and office expenses are paid in the month in which they are incurred.
  (v)   Brian will be replacing a piece of equipment in August 1999. The new machine
         costs £44 000 and the old machinery will be sold for a cash scrap value of £2000
         in August. Payment for the new machine is to be made in two equal instalments in
         October and November 1999.
 (vi)   Electricity is paid quarterly, in arrears, in September and December.
(vii)   Tax will have to be paid in December amounting to £1600.

Requirements

(a) Prepare a monthly cash budget for the six month period, July to December 1999.
                                                                     (12 marks)

(b) Advise Brian plc on the possible action they might take to overcome any cash deficit.
    Use the monthly cash budget you have prepared in (a) to illustrate the advice and to
    emphasise the importance of preparing cash budgets.   **(8 marks)**

(c) Briefly explain five differences between Management Accounting and Financial
    Accounting.   **(5 marks)**
                                                                 (Total: 25 marks)

(CIPFA, *Management Accounting*, June 1999)

17.9   A product manager has responsibility for a single product and is in the process of submit-
           ting data to be compiled into budgets for 1999. The manager has performance targets set in
           relation to sales volume, profitability levels and a target cash surplus from the product.
               Shown below are the agreed budgeted sales for the product for December 1998 to May
           1999.

	Dec.	*Jan.*	*Feb.*	*March*	*April*	*May*
Units	14 000	16 000	22 000	17 000	20 000	24 000

The company policy is that, at each month end, the closing stock of finished goods should
be 25% of the following month's forecast sales and the stock of raw material should be sufficient for 10% of the following month's production. Stock levels currently conform to this
policy. One unit of raw material makes one unit of finished stock, there is no wastage. Raw
material purchases are paid for during the month following purchase. All other expenses are
paid for as incurred. All sales are made on credit and the company expects cash receipts for
50% of the sales in the month of sale and 50% in the following month. The company operates an absorption costing system which is computed on a monthly basis. That is, in addition to direct costs it recovers each month's fixed and variable manufacturing overhead
expenses in product costs using the budgeted production and budgeted expenditure in the
month to establish an absorption rate. The cost is used to place a value on the stock holding.
Opening stock is valued at the unit cost which was established in the previous month. At 1
January 1999, finished stock should be assumed at £40 per unit. A flow of cost based on
FIFO is assumed.

Sales are made at a price of £58 per unit.

Estimated costs to be used in the budget preparation for the product are:

Manufacturing costs:	
Material	£10.00 per unit produced
Variable overhead and labour	£16.00 per unit produced
Fixed overhead costs	£210 000 per month
(including depreciation of £54 000 per month)	
Selling costs:	
Variable	£7.00 per unit sold
Fixed	£164 000 per month

Requirements

(a) Compute the monthly budgeted production and material purchases for January to March 1999. **(4 marks)**

(b) Prepare a budgeted profit and loss account and a statement of cash receipts and payments for January 1999. **(7 marks)**

(c) Explain briefly the implications of the company's treatment of fixed manufacturing overheads compared to a predetermined overhead rate prepared annually. **(4 marks)**

(ACCA, *Managerial Finance*, December 1998)

17.10 The following budgeted sales values have been extracted from the budget of AZ Limited for the year ending 31 December 1997:

	£
April	400 000
May	450 000
June	520 000
July	420 000
August	480 000

The contribution/sales ratio is 40%. Fixed costs are budgeted to be £1 200 000 for the year arising at a constant rate per month and including depreciation of £300 000 per annum. 40% of each month's sales are produced in the month prior to sale, and 60% are produced in the month of sale. 50% of the direct materials required for production are purchased in the month prior to their being used in production.

30% of the variable costs are labour costs, which are paid in the month they are incurred. 60% of the variable costs are direct material costs. Suppliers of direct materials are paid in the month after purchase.

The remaining variable costs are variable overhead costs. 40% of the variable overhead costs are paid in the month they are incurred, the balance being paid in the month after they are incurred.

Fixed costs are paid in the month they are incurred.

Capital expenditure expected in June is £190 000.

Sales receipts for the three months of May, June and July are budgeted as follows:

	£
May	401 700
June	450 280
July	425 880

The bank balance on 1 May 1997 is expected to be £40 000.

Requirement

Prepare a cash budget for AZ Limited. Your budget should be in columnar format showing separately the receipts, payments and balances for EACH of the months of May, June and July 1997. **(25 marks)**

(CIMA, *Operational Cost Accounting*, May 1996)

CHAPTER 18

Budgetary control

Flexible budgeting and standard costing: how are they linked?

... The principles of flexible budgeting are straightforward enough. In order to provide meaningful information, a budget statement should take account of activity as well as actual cost related merely to the elapse of time. Thus in simple terms if a budget was established for the production of 1000 units over a year, the quarterly report should reflect the expected expenditure for the output achieved over that period rather than simply 25% of the original budget. After all, the expenditure against which the period budget is compared will be related to units produced.

A further sophistication is to take account of input activity as well as output data. Input activity relates to such items as actual hours worked or materials used. Flexing the budget to take account of input data and output achieved then permits an analysis of volume, efficiency and expenditure variances which will reconcile the budgeted and actual cost or profit ...

Source: Richard Smith, *Management Accounting*, October 1992.

Exhibit 18.1 Principles of flexible budgeting

INTRODUCTION

In the previous two chapters, we discussed the role of budgets as a planning mechanism. However, planning on its own is of limited value – it is necessary to assess the extent to which plans have been achieved (or otherwise) and to take some form of action where it seems that they will not be achieved. In other words, we need to exercise *control*. Comparison of budgeted and actual costs (and revenues) is the most common starting-point for financial control. It is important to appreciate that control cannot be exercised without the existence of some form of plan or objective; similarly, that failure to assess the extent to which plans have been achieved severely curtails the benefit to be derived from the planning process.

In this chapter, we will examine the use of budgets as an aid to financial control, consider managerial responsibility in this context and discuss the potential problems of using budgets in this way.

OBJECTIVES

When you have completed this chapter, you will be able to:

• understand the principles of exceptions reporting;

- distinguish between feedback control and feedforward control;
- appreciate the difference between fixed and flexible budgets and the use of flexible budgets for control purposes;
- prepare flexible budgets and budget control reports, identifying volume and flexible budget variances;
- describe the different approaches which may be adopted in determining the significance of variances;
- describe the features and objectives of a system of responsibility accounting and control reporting;
- explain the use of activity based management, activity based costing and activity based budgeting in a control context;
- appreciate the principles of target costing;
- describe internal and external benchmarking;
- distinguish between cost control and cost reduction, describe the main approaches to cost reduction and the possible problems of cost reduction schemes;
- discuss the potential problem areas of financial control in general and also with particular reference to the philosophy of total quality management.

EXCEPTIONS REPORTING

Exceptions reporting (also termed *management by exception*) forms the basis of financial control and is founded on comparison of budgeted costs and revenues with actual (*feedback control*) or of budgeted costs and revenues with some predetermined objective(s) (*feedforward control*). The two sets of outcomes being compared are most unlikely to be the same (except by chance) and the idea of exceptions reporting is that managerial action should be triggered by any significant differences revealed by this comparison.

 Why should managerial action be triggered only by significant *differences in outcome, rather than by* all *differences?*

Managerial time is an extremely scarce resource. If all differences in outcome were to result in management action – i.e. investigation of cause and/or taking corrective action once cause has been established – then a great deal of valuable time and effort would inevitably be lost in pursuit of trivia, distracting managers from more important concerns. This raises the question of what constitutes a 'significant' difference, an issue which we shall discuss in detail later in the chapter. Differences in outcome of the kind we have been describing are referred to as **variances** and you should not confuse cost accounting variances with the statistical measure of the same name. A *favourable* variance indicates a better-than-expected outcome, whereas an *adverse* (or *unfavourable*) variance reflects a worse-than-expected outcome. When deciding whether a particular variance is favourable or adverse, a distinction needs to be made between costs on the one hand and revenue/profit on the other: e.g. higher-than-expected costs represent an adverse variance, whilst higher-than-expected revenues constitute a favourable variance. It is also important to realise that *all* significant variances should be investigated. There may be a danger of concentrating attention on significant adverse variances, which could result in failure to pursue any potential opportunity offered by significant favourable variances. In addition we need to realise that some variances may arise for reasons which are beyond management's immediate control, so that little or no action may be possible in the short term. We shall explore this issue later in the chapter.

Before we provide a detailed discussion and illustration of budget control reporting, we must consider the basic principles of feedback and feedforward control.

FEEDBACK AND FEEDFORWARD CONTROL

We have said that exceptions reporting is based on a comparison of outcomes; the terms 'feedback' and 'feedforward', in essence, describe *which* outcomes are being compared.

Feedback control compares budgeted and actual results, feedforward control compares desired results (i.e. objectives) and budgeted results. You will see from Figure 18.1 that actual processes and procedures are central to control. Objectives and plans aim to govern actual performance while actual performance governs achievement of objectives and plans. The key to effective control is therefore provision of information to allow managers to ensure not only that actual conforms with plans/objectives but also that plans/objectives remain consistent with actual circumstances.

Because feedback control involves actual results – which will not be known until after the event – it is retrospective. Feedforward control, on the other hand, is forward-looking. This does not mean that the two operate in isolation, as Figure 18.1 shows.

 As one of its short-term objectives, a company wishes to reduce its overdraft by 10% during the forthcoming accounting year. Bearing Figure 18.1 in mind, how might feedforward and feedback control be applied to this situation?

Having determined the objective, the company will prepare functional budgets of the type we described in Chapter 16 (e.g. sales, production, material purchases) and a cash budget will be drawn up based on these functional budgets. If the cash budget suggests that the 10% reduction can be achieved, or will fail by an acceptably small margin, then the functional budgets will be implemented. Should the cash budget suggest a significant failure to achieve the desired reduction, then management may do either or both of the following:

- *amend the objective*: perhaps a 10% reduction in the overdraft next year is too optimistic, and should be revised downward; *and/or*
- *amend the budgets*: management may examine the various functional budgets to see if cash flows can be improved by reducing expenditure or increasing revenue.

When budgets which achieve the desired objective have been agreed and implemented, feedback control will be applied on a regular basis (e.g. monthly) within the budget period to determine the extent to which actual costs and revenues are in line with budget. After the reason for any significant variances has been investigated,

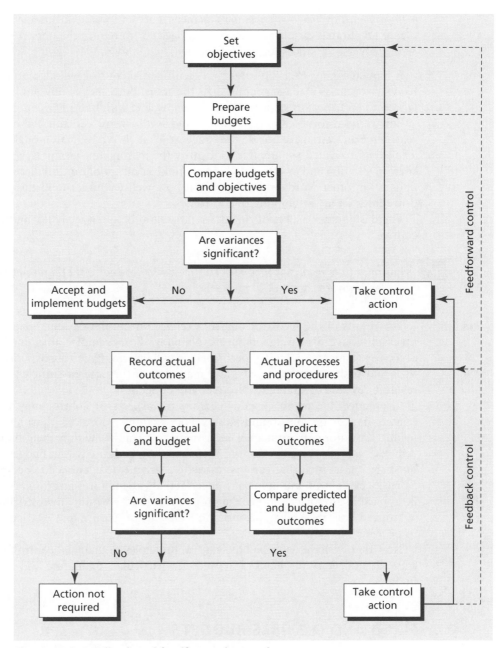

Figure 18.1 Feedback and feedforward control

control action may consist of one or more of the following:

- *amend the objective*: actual operating conditions may be such that the objective requires further amendment; *and/or*
- *amend the budgets*: budgets prepared prior to commencement of the accounting year may need to be revised in light of experiences during the year (e.g. rolling budgets, as described in Chapter 17, may be used); *and/or*

- *improve future performance*: management may act to take advantage of any significant favourable variances (**positive feedback**) or to reduce the impact of any significant adverse variances (**negative feedback**).

A look at Figure 18.1 indicates that feedforward control will also occur within the feedback cycle, as management predicts the actual outcomes of ongoing activities, and, where necessary, takes steps to bring these into line with budget.

But we need to be careful: feedback and feedforward control neither indicate the reason for any variances nor do they suggest what corrective action ought to be taken. The extent to which we are able to identify the reasons for variances, the appropriate corrective action and its efficacy, depend on the accuracy of our 'predictive model' (our budget). In other words, they depend on how well we understand the processes and procedures we are attempting to control.

There is another aspect of the interrelationship between feedback and feedforward control:

 How might the results of feedback control during the current budget period be used in a feedforward context?

The results of the feedback control exercise during the current period will almost invariably have a bearing on future planning. For example, amendments made to objectives, budgets and actual performance will inform the setting of short-term objectives and budgets for next year, and may also (if they are of sufficient significance) result in revision of strategic objectives and budgets.

In practice, the feedback and feedforward aspects of control may be so closely related as to be indistinguishable. For example, local authorities will apply feedback/feedforward principles as a matter of routine within their budgetary procedures. Not only is it important to keep actual expenditure within budget, but budgets must also be set such that various restrictions are met (e.g. council tax capping levels).

Feedback control will monitor budget/actual expenditure; feedforward control will be applied in advance to ensure the proposed budget is within any restrictions and will be applied after the budget has been implemented to ensure that restrictions *continue* to be met.

Now that we have described the general principles of financial control, we can illustrate the budgetary mechanics involved – in particular, the nature and use of flexible budgets.

FIXED AND FLEXIBLE BUDGETS

The basis of a **flexible budget** is the fact that certain financial (and non-financial) items will react to changes in the volume of activity and the budget can be 'flexed' to reflect this.

 What budgeted financial items will react to changes in the volume of activity?

Revenue, wholly variable costs, the variable element of mixed costs and step costs will all react to changes in the volume of activity, and we can incorporate this reaction into budgets as an aid to planning (by preparing a series of budgets based on different volumes of activity) and as part of the control process (to ensure like is being compared to like). These two applications of flexible budgets are illustrated below.

Flexible budgets as a planning aid

Consider the data in Exhibit 18.2, which we shall use to demonstrate how flexible budgets may be used as part of the planning process.

Architrave Partnership: flexible budget for planning

Architrave Partnership provides a variety of architectural services to both private and commercial clients. The following estimates apply to the firm's Commercial Division for next year:

Standard per client-day		£	£
Charge to client			800
Variable costs:	Direct materials	20	
	Direct expenses	70	
	Other	30	120

Fixed costs for the year	£
Direct labour	2 500 000
Overhead attributable to client-based activities	500 000
Administration overhead	400 000
Selling and distribution overhead	200 000

Volume The Partnership's maximum volume is reckoned to be 10 000 client-days in the year under review. Some uncertainty attaches to next year's level of work and management wishes to prepare budgeted profit statements based on 60%, 65% and 70% of maximum volume.

Exhibit 18.2 Data for flexible budget preparation

Since flexible budgets are intended to reflect the reaction of revenue and certain costs to volume changes (i.e. to reflect cost behaviour relative to volume), it seems reasonable that we adopt a marginal costing format for Architrave Partnership's budgeted profit statements, since this format is likewise based on cost behaviour.

 Complete the budgeted profit statements in Exhibit 18.3.

Exhibit 18.4 presents Architrave Partnership's completed flexible budget for the year. You will see that the basis upon which the profit statements have been flexed is the number of cost units, but there are circumstances where an alternative basis is more appropriate (see later). For each budgeted level of activity, totals for those items which react to changes in volume (revenue and variable costs in this case) have been calculated by multiplying the standard unit data in Exhibit 18.2 by the budgeted number of client hours at each level of sales volume. In the absence of additional information, fixed costs are assumed to be unaffected by the volume changes.

Architrave Partnership: flexible budget

Output/sales volume (% of maximum)	60%	65%	70%
Output/sales volume (client-days)	6 000	6 500	7 000
	£	£	£
Revenue			5 600 000
Variable costs: Direct materials			140 000
Direct expenses			490 000
Other			210 000
			840 000
Contribution			4 760 000
Fixed costs: Direct labour			2 500 000
Attributable overhead			500 000
Administration overhead			400 000
Selling and distribution overhead			200 000
			3 600 000
Net profit			1 160 000

Exhibit 18.3 Partly completed flexible budget

Architrave Partnership: flexible budget

Output/sales volume	60%	65%	70%
Output/sales volume (units)	6 000	6 500	7 000
	£	£	£
Revenue	4 800 000	5 200 000	5 600 000
Variable costs: Direct materials	120 000	130 000	140 000
Direct expenses	420 000	455 000	490 000
Other	180 000	195 000	210 000
	720 000	780 000	840 000
Contribution	4 080 000	4 420 000	4 760 000
Fixed costs: Direct labour	2 500 000	2 500 000	2 500 000
Attributable overhead	500 000	500 000	500 000
Administration overhead	400 000	400 000	400 000
Selling and distribution overhead	200 000	200 000	200 000
	3 600 000	3 600 000	3 600 000
Net profit	480 000	820 000	1 160 000

Exhibit 18.4 Completed flexible budget

 What assumption regarding the behaviour of costs and revenue underlies the flexible budget in Exhibit 18.4?

Cost behaviour and revenue are both assumed to have a linear relationship with volume; i.e. the unit selling price and unit variable costs are the same at all volumes and the fixed costs are unaffected by changes in volume. Although this may be rather simplistic in practice, budgets such as that in Exhibit 18.4 can easily accommodate non-linear price and cost functions: e.g. the impact of step costs or of the need to reduce selling price at higher volumes.

A further assumption underlying Exhibit 18.4 is that the variable elements of the budget all vary according to the same measure of activity – units of output/sales in this case. As we shall see later, there may be situations where we need to use more than one basis for flexing a budget. The exhibit also assumes that *volume* is the cause of cost variability – this is not necessarily the case. Changes in factors such as technology or batch size can also cause costs to vary.

The approach taken in Exhibit 18.4 may also be applied to budgets other than the profit statement. For example, budgeted cost may be assessed at different volume levels and the same general principle of distinguishing between variable and fixed items should be applied, the difference here being that revenue, contribution and profit will not be shown. Similarly, budgets such as production, material usage and material purchases may be prepared for different levels of activity.

Flexible budgets provide a useful form of sensitivity analysis in the planning process and will exist to some extent in virtually every budget system, as management will generally consider a range of possible outcomes before finalising the budget.

However, a single budget must ultimately be set – i.e. Architrave Partnership must decide which volume of activity represents the most realistic expectation for next year's operations (and which is most consistent with achieving strategic objectives). It is not possible to implement more than one budget simultaneously (how would managers know which budget to aim to achieve and how could the budget's achievement or otherwise be measured?). The budget which the company finally adopts is known as a **fixed** (or **static**) budget, since it is based on a single volume of activity.

Flexible budgets and control

Exhibit 18.5 contains further information about the Architrave Partnership which we shall use to illustrate the use of flexible budgets as control indicators.

Architrave Partnership: fixed budget and actuals for the year

After consideration of next year's likely operating conditions, the Partnership's management had set the budgeted volume of client days at 65% of maximum; at the end of the year, the fixed budget (based on this volume) and actual results were compared, as shown below.

		Fixed budget	Actual
Volume as % of maximum		65%	72%
Volume (client-days)		6 500	7 200
		£	£
Revenue		5 200 000	5 580 000
Variable costs:	Direct materials	130 000	158 400
	Direct expenses	455 000	482 400
	Other	195 000	208 800
		780 000	849 600

▶

Contribution		4 420 000	4 730 400
Fixed costs:	Direct labour	2 500 000	2 534 000
	Attributable overhead	500 000	491 000
	Administration overhead	400 000	409 000
	Selling and distribution overhead	200 000	177 000
		3 600 000	3 611 000
Net profit		820 000	1 119 400

Although very satisfied by sales and profit that are both well in excess of budget, management is concerned about the extent to which actual costs – and variable costs in particular – exceed budget.

Exhibit 18.5 Fixed budget and actual

 Look at the budgeted and actual figures in Exhibit 18.5. Why might management concern about the adverse variances for variable cost be misplaced?

Management concern may be misplaced because the budget/actual comparison is not altogether valid. A budget based on 6500 client-days is being compared with actuals based on 7200 client-days; this increased volume will be part of the reason for the variable cost variances. A more valid budget/actual comparison would use a budget based on actual volume, so that like is being compared to like – i.e. we should prepare a flexible budget based on actual volume.

Exhibit 18.6 shows the fixed budget (65% of maximum volume), flexible budget

Architrave Partnership: fixed budget, flexible budget and actuals for the year

		Fixed budget	Flexible budget	Actual
Volume as % of maximum		65%	72%	72%
Volume (client-days)		6 500	7 200	7 200
		£	£	£
Revenue		5 200 000	5 760 000	5 580 000
Variable costs:	Direct materials	130 000	144 000	158 400
	Direct expenses	455 000	504 000	482 400
	Other	195 000	216 000	208 800
		780 000	864 000	849 600
Contribution		4 420 000	4 896 000	4 730 400
Fixed costs:	Direct labour	2 500 000	2 500 000	2 534 000
	Attributable overhead	500 000	500 000	491 000
	Administration overhead	400 000	400 000	409 000
	Selling and distribution overhead	200 000	200 000	177 000
		3 600 000	3 600 000	3 611 000
Net profit		820 000	1 296 000	1 119 400

Exhibit 18.6 Fixed budget, flexible budget and actual

based on actual volume (72% of maximum) and actual. The revenue and variable cost figures in the flexible budget have been arrived at by multiplying the standard unit selling price and variable costs in Exhibit 18.2 by the actual volume. As in Exhibit 18.4, fixed costs are assumed to be unaffected by the volume difference between the two budgets.

Comparison of the flexible budget and actuals in Exhibit 18.6 sheds a rather different light on the apparent adverse variable cost variances. When the effect of the volume difference between actual and fixed budget is removed, the adverse variances for direct expenses and for 'other' variable costs become favourable, indicating lower expenditure than would have been expected for the actual volume of work performed. The adverse variance for direct materials is markedly reduced, though still adverse. However, revenue and profit do not emerge so well from such a comparison – both are lower than would be expected from the actual volume of sales.

We are now in a position to extract two sets of variances from our budgeted and actual data:

- *Volume variances*: these are the differences between the fixed and flexible budgets and show the revenue, variable cost, contribution and profit impact of the difference between fixed budget volume and actual volume (there will be no volume variances for fixed costs, since these are assumed not to react to changes in volume and are therefore the same in both fixed and flexible budgets); *and*
- *Flexible budget variances*: these are the differences between the flexible budget and actual, reflecting the impact on revenue, variable cost, contribution, fixed cost and profit of budget/actual differences in factors other than volume – e.g. cost, rate, usage and efficiency.

Exhibit 18.7 shows the full statement of fixed budget, flexible budget and actual, with volume and flexible budget variances identified. Adverse variances are designated 'A' and favourable variances 'F'. Remember that a distinction must be made between revenue, contribution and profit elements and cost elements for the purpose of deciding whether a particular variance is adverse or favourable.

A presentation such as that in Exhibit 18.7 may convey some useful information to management, and might suggest possible areas of performance that merit investigation. For instance, sales volume has been higher than originally budgeted (favourable volume variance for revenue), but selling price has been lower (adverse flexible budget variance for revenue) – possibly, the lower selling price has been the cause of the higher sales volume.

 What conclusions might be drawn from Exhibit 18.7 about budgeted and actual direct materials?

A higher direct materials cost has been incurred than that originally budgeted as the result of a higher-than-budgeted number of client-hours (adverse volume variance for direct materials). The adverse flexible budget variance for direct materials suggests that either or both of the following may have occurred:

1 a difference may have arisen between the standard price of materials and the actual price paid; *and/or*
2 a difference may have arisen between the standard quantity of materials required per unit of output and the actual quantity used.

Architrave Partnership: fixed budget, flexible budget and actuals for the year with volume and flexible budget variances identified

	Fixed budget	Volume variances	Flexible budget	Flexible budget variances	Actual
Volume as % of maximum	65%	7%F	72%	nil	72%
Volume (client-days)	6 500	700F	7 200	nil	7 200
	£	£	£	£	£
Revenue	5 200 000	560 000F	5 760 000	180 000A	5 580 000
Variable costs:					
Direct materials	130 000	14 000A	144 000	14 400A	158 400
Direct expenses	455 000	49 000A	504 000	21 600F	482 400
Other	195 000	21 000A	216 000	7 200F	208 800
	780 000	84 000A	864 000	14 400F	849 600
Contribution	4 420 000	476 000F	4 896 000	165 600A	4 730 400
Fixed costs:					
Direct labour	2 500 000	nil	2 500 000	34 000A	2 534 000
Attributable overhead	500 000	nil	500 000	9 000F	491 000
Administration overhead	400 000	nil	400 000	9 000A	409 000
Selling and distribution overhead	200 000	nil	200 000	23 000F	177 000
	3 600 000	nil	3 600 000	11 000A	3 611 000
Net profit	820 000	476 000F	1 296 000	176 600A	1 119 400

Exhibit 18.7 Fixed and flexible budgets, actual and variances

Further investigation would be required and in the next chapter we will illustrate how flexible budget variances may be subdivided to show the effect of such price and usage differences.

The flexing basis

We said earlier that the basis for flexing the budget will normally be the organisation's cost unit. However, this is only practicable where all cost units are identical. If a budget centre or organisation produces several different types of cost unit, then the budget will require to be flexed in a slightly different way.

Flexing on the basis of standard hours

In Chapter 16, we saw that the **standard hour** is a measure of the work which should be performed in one hour at the specified standard efficiency level and that use of this concept allows output of diverse types of cost unit to be expressed as a single figure. Where different cost units are produced by an organisation or budget centre, a single flexible budget (and fixed budget) can be produced by expressing output in terms of standard hours and flexing variable costs on that basis. Flexible budget revenue is still based on units – in this case, the aggregate of (standard selling price × actual sales volume) for all the individual types of cost unit concerned.

Why is it preferable to flex the budget on the basis of standard, rather than actual hours of output?

If the budget were to be flexed using actual hours, then the flexible budget would be distorted by differences between the standard and actual levels of efficiency, which would result in budget-holding managers being 'penalised' for better-than-standard efficiency and 'rewarded' for lower-than standard efficiency. We will use the information in Exhibit 18.8 to illustrate how this would happen.

Standard versus actual hours as flexing basis

A budget centre which produces several different types of cost unit provides the following data for Periods 7 and 8 of the current accounting year:

	Period 7	Period 8
Standard hours' output achieved	7000	5000
Actual hours worked	8000	4000
Standard variable cost per hour	£6	£6

Exhibit 18.8 Alternative flexing bases

 Calculate the flexible budget variable cost for each of Periods 7 and 8 using:
1 standard hours; and
2 actual hours as the flexing basis.

For each period, the flexible budget variable cost will be:

	Period 7		Period 8
Standard hours (7000 × £6)	£42 000	(5000 × £6)	£30 000
Actual hours (8000 × £6)	£48 000	(4000 × £6)	£24 000

In Period 7, actual efficiency was lower than standard (because 8000 actual hours were required to produce 7000 standard hours' worth of output). Using actual hours as the flexing basis, this is 'rewarded' by a higher flexible budget allowance for variable cost, thereby artificially reducing the flexible budget variance by removing efficiency differences from its calculation. Conversely, in Period 8, use of actual hours as the flexing basis will incur the 'penalty' of a lower flexible budget allowance for variable cost, thereby artificially increasing the flexible budget variance. In both cases, use of actual hours will give an unrealistic view of actual performance against budget and should therefore be avoided.

Multiple flexing bases

Use of standard hours to flex the budget will only be practical where variable costs vary with hours (whether labour or machine hours). If you look again at the data in Exhibit 18.2, you will see that such an approach would not be possible in Architrave Partnership's case where labour is a fixed cost (as is true in many organisations) and where variable costs vary with the number of cost units (i.e. client days). Suppose we were preparing a single budget for the Partnership's Commercial *and* Private divisions; suppose also that the Private division's cost unit was the client-hour (rather than day). In this situation, a unitary flexible (and fixed) budget could only be produced by aggregating the flexible (and fixed) budget allowances for each kind of cost unit.

As an additional complication, variable costs need not necessarily vary in relation to the same measure of activity: e.g. direct materials could vary relative to the number of cost units, with variable overhead varying according to the number of direct labour hours. Here, it would be necessary to ensure that the correct activity measure was used both to prepare the fixed budget and to flex the budget for control purposes. Thus, a degree of care is necessary in selection of the activity measure to be used but, once identified, different activity measures are easily incorporated into fixed and flexible budget calculations.

DETERMINING THE SIGNIFICANCE OF VARIANCES

One of the principles of exceptions reporting is that managerial action is triggered by significant variances from budget and we must now discuss how the significance of variances might be determined.

Absolute amount approach

If this method were adopted, a variance's significance would be measured with reference to a set monetary amount: e.g. Architrave Partnership might stipulate that every variance in excess of £5000 (favourable *and* adverse) should be investigated, which is a simple enough rule to apply.

 What is the weakness of investigating all variances in excess of an absolute monetary amount?

The problem with investigating every variance in excess of (say) £5000 is that such an absolute measure does not, in fact, reflect significance. We may say that £5000 is a large amount of money and that this is sufficient to warrant the time, effort (and possibly cost) involved in investigating variances in excess of £5000; but consider the following:

Budgeted expenditure £	Actual expenditure £	Variance £
4 000	8 000	4 000A
4 000 000	4 006 000	6 000A

Applying our absolute amount rule of investigating every variance in excess of £5000 means that only the second of the above variances will be investigated. A variance of £4000 relative to a budget of £4000 is clearly significant, but £6000 against a budget of £4 million? Application of the absolute amount rule may commit valuable managerial time and resources to investigation of insignificant variances, thereby negating the principle of exceptions reporting. Although it can be argued that elimination of a variance such as the £6000A (even when it relates to a large budgeted/actual amount) will have the effect of improving profit, it is questionable whether this can be achieved without breaching the cost/benefit criterion.

Percentage of budget approach

We can overcome the problem just described by expressing variances *relative* to the budget: i.e. as a percentage of budget, rather than as an absolute amount, so that the criterion for significance may be stated as something like: 'investigate every variance in excess of 5% of flexible budget'. Like the absolute amount approach, this method is easy to apply, but the problem here lies in determining the most appropriate percentage to use. Five per cent is a frequently quoted 'rule-of-thumb', but it has no objective or mathematical justification, and a different percentage (e.g. 10%) could as easily be used and justified, as could use of different percentages for different budget items. Also, if the measure of significance is open to debate, then the credibility of the control process may be questionable.

Statistical definition of significance

Statistics may be able to provide an objective test of the significance of variances. If, say, usage of direct materials is normally distributed, and if the standard cost is the mean value (i.e. average) of this distribution, then it is possible to use statistical theory to set *control limits*. Given the normal distribution referred to, we can predict, e.g. that approximately 95% of output should use direct materials falling within limits of ± two standard deviations of the mean value (i.e. of the standard direct materials usage) and that roughly 99% of output should have direct material usage falling within limits of ±3 standard deviations of the mean value etc. Control limits may then be set at the desired level of statistical tolerance (e.g. ±1 or 2 standard deviations of the mean) and a *statistical control chart* such as Figure 18.2 prepared.

In Figure 18.2, the control limits have been set at mean value ± two standard deviations. All material usage which falls inside these control limits will be deemed to be 'in control', whereas all material usage falling outwith the control limits will be considered

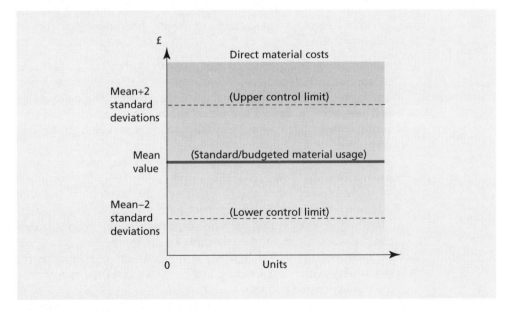

Figure 18.2 Statistical control chart

'out of control' and therefore worthy of investigation. If more than 5% of actual material usage falls outside the control limits, then either there is a problem with material usage and/or the standard needs to be revised. This kind of approach may be useful for repetitive tasks, but is reliant on the accuracy of the mean and standard deviation being used. Since these will be based on past observations, the assumption is being made that the past is a reliable guide to the future. In addition, it will only really be applicable to situations where tolerance levels can be set with reasonable accuracy and where actuals are controllable. This may be true for material usage, but may not hold for material price, which could be determined by external factors not under management's control.

Surveys of practice by Puxty and Lyall (1989) and by Drury *et al.* (1993) strongly suggest that significance appears to be largely a matter of managerial judgement and that many organisations employ more than one criterion in assessing the significance of variances. This same research indicates that statistical approaches are very rare, with the most common methods (listed in decreasing order of frequency) being:

- managerial judgement
- absolute amount method
- percentage approach.

RESPONSIBILITY ACCOUNTING AND CONTROL REPORTING

Responsibility accounting

Operation of a system of budgetary planning and control within a particular organisation will be determined by that organisation's structure, most often following lines of managerial responsibility. In all but the smallest organisations, decision making is delegated and the principle of **responsibility accounting** is that financial control procedures should reflect this delegation of authority. In other words, authority to make decisions confers responsibility for the financial consequences of those decisions on the managers concerned. In broad terms, a system of responsibility accounting possesses the following features.

1 The organisation is divided into **responsibility centres** (i.e. budget centres), of which there are five main types:
  - **cost centre** budgeted and actual costs are recorded and compared
  - **revenue centre** budgeted and actual revenues are recorded and compared
  - **profit centre** budgeted and actual costs, revenues and profit are recorded and compared
  - **investment centres** budgeted and actual costs, revenues and capital expenditure are recorded and compared
  - **strategic business unit** this is effectively an investment centre which has the additional authority to determine its own strategy.

  All five may co-exist within the same organisation, the exact mix depending on the organisation's structure and the nature of its output.
2 An individual manager is delegated the authority and responsibility for running each responsibility centre, for meeting and (in most cases) participating in setting that responsibility centre's budget.
3 **Control reports** comparing budget and actual for each responsibility centre are prepared periodically and passed upwards through the organisational hierarchy.

Responsibility accounting has a twofold objective. First, to enhance planning, control and decision making for a responsibility centre (and for the organisation overall) by delegating these functions to the manager 'at the sharp end', who understands the centre's functions and operations along with their financial consequences. Second, responsibility accounting aims to improve **goal congruence**. Involving managers in planning, control and decision making (via delegation) should reduce the possibility that those managers will act in a manner which is inconsistent with the organisation's overall objectives (i.e. will reduce the incidence of **dysfunctional decisions**).

Control reporting

We have said that control reports for each responsibility centre should be periodically prepared and passed upwards through the organisational hierarchy and it is now necessary to give some consideration to the frequency and content of such reports. Since control reports are supposed to monitor the extent to which budgets are being achieved, their frequency should fit the broader framework of the budget period. We described budget periods in Chapter 16 and saw that, for tactical budgets, this will be one year and for strategic budgets, it may range from three to (say) ten years.

 Exhibit 18.7 could be viewed as a control report for Architrave Partnership covering the tactical budget period of one year. Why would it generally be unwise to prepare control reports only at the end of the budget period?

If an organisation were to wait until the end of the budget period to prepare control reports, then *ongoing* monitoring of the extent to which budgets are being achieved would not be possible. So it is unlikely that any major problems would come to light until the end of the budget period concerned (by which time it will be too late to take any action in response). In extreme circumstances, this could even lead to failure of the business. It is therefore advisable to split each budget period into shorter **control periods**. For tactical budgets, the budget period could be split into 12 calendar months or into 13 periods of four weeks (to prevent any distortion of variances caused by months of differing length). Strategic budgets may be split into annual (or possibly six-monthly) control periods to allow assessment of progress towards strategic objectives. 'Real-time' control statistics (i.e. produced simultaneously with the processes to which they relate) like input/output quantities are an increasingly common feature of automated and computerised production systems.

Control periods of different length from those we have suggested are possible and the frequency of control reporting should ultimately suit the specific circumstances of the organisation. However, care must be exercised in this respect: control periods which are too infrequent may defeat the objective of allowing ongoing monitoring of budget and actual; but too-frequent control periods may run the risk of 'swamping' managers in control data, with the result that reports may not be properly followed up.

The content of control reports also merits careful consideration. The level of detail, for example, may have an important bearing on the extent to which control reports are read, understood and acted on. Exhibit 18.7 may contain sufficient detail for consideration by Architrave Partnership's senior management, but might be insufficiently detailed for managers in charge of individual responsibility centres. In general, the lower the managerial level being reported to, the greater the relevant detail necessary to allow effective response to control reports. The higher the managerial level being reported to, the lower the amount of detail, until, at most senior level, a summarised statement, such as that contained in Exhibit 18.7, will probably suffice. Again, the precise detail contained in control reports to each management level should be governed by specific circumstances, but the principle being followed is the same in all situations: i.e. that 'lower-level' control reports are combined and their key elements summarised in 'higher-level' reports.

In addition to the kind of information shown in Exhibit 18.7, budget control reports may show information such as year-to-date totals for actual and budget, or state variances as a percentage of budget (as well as giving the absolute monetary amount) and where feasible, variable and fixed costs should be distinguished. Items deemed fully controllable by the responsible manager should ideally be separated from those only partly controllable (or uncontrollable) – a vexed issue which we shall discuss in more detail later in the chapter.

ACTIVITY-BASED CONTROL

Our discussion of control has so far concentrated on controlling particular categories of financial item – e.g. cost of direct materials or of direct labour. In Chapters 6 and 17 we described, respectively, activity-based costing (ABC) and activity-based budgeting (ABB). In the earlier chapter, we mentioned the use of activity-based principles as an aid to control, often termed **activity-based management** (ABM) or **activity-based cost management** (ABCM). You will recall from our earlier discussion that the major features of an activity-based approach are:

- identifying key organisational activities;
- setting up a cost pool for each of these activities;
- identifying the **cost driver** for each activity (i.e. the main underlying cause of the associated costs);
- determining unit costs on the basis of each unit's usage of the various cost drivers identified.

ABCM applies these principles to the control (and/or reduction) of costs, regardless of whether unit costs are determined on an activity basis. If key activities and their related cost drivers can be identified, then controlling/reducing the incidence of the cost driver should control/reduce the associated cost. It is also argued that identification, measurement and control of cost drivers (within a system of ABB) will provide additional and valuable control information, thereby attempting to address the possible problem of overemphasising financial control measures (which we shall discuss below). And, by identifying key organisational activities, ABCM should enhance management's ability to 'home in' on activities which are especially important, or which require particular attention. The benefit of ABCM in this context is that it should allow management to distinguish between **value-added activities** and **non-value-added activities** – i.e. between those activities which enhance customer perception of the 'value' of the product/service being offered and those which do not (such as the cost of storing stock of raw materials and finished goods). If non-value-added activities and their cost drivers can be identified, then control of inessential costs and competitiveness may be enhanced through use of activity-based techniques within a cost reduction scheme of the sort we shall describe later in the chapter.

However, the requirement to compare budget and actual, identify variances and take action on the basis of those variances which are significant remains fundamental to ABCM. In addition, the extent to which activity-based approaches (whether ABC, ABB or ABCM) can be successfully applied is heavily dependent on the organisation's ability to correctly identify its main activities and, more problematically (as we saw in Chapter 6), their associated cost drivers. It might also be said that, if a system of 'conventional' responsibility centres has been carefully designed, then these will be a reflection of key activities within the organisation. We could also argue that any attempt to control/reduce costs (irrespective of the use of activity-based methodology) should involve consideration of the underlying cause of the cost(s) concerned. In some circumstances, the 'pooling' of activity-based costs and the identification of a single cost driver for every cost pool may even hamper effective control if the cost driver is not strictly applicable to every cost within that particular pool. As we suggested in Chapter 6, some subjectivity may exist with cost drivers as with apportionment bases.

TARGET COSTING

The financial control mechanisms we have been describing are predominantly driven by concerns internal to the organisation. This may be at odds with the need for an external focus in management accounting information dictated by a strategic perspective or by the existence of a total quality regime (see Chapter 2). Use of **target costing** could alleviate this shortcoming. Target costs are calculated as follows:

Selling price needed to capture desired market share	X
Less Required profit margin	X
= Target cost	X

 Architrave Partnership's management believes that a charge of £800 per client day will obtain the market share required for the Commercial division. The required profit margin is 20% of sales. What is the target cost per client-day?

Target cost per client-day:

	£
Selling price	800
Less Required profit margin (£800 × 20%)	160
= Target cost	640

As you can see, this is somewhat different from the 'traditional' standard costing approach we described in Chapter 16. Here, the target cost derives *explicitly* from external circumstances. Standard costs – at best – are likely to represent a combination of internal and external considerations.

The control aspect of target costing involves comparison of target cost with standard/budgeted cost – i.e. feedforward control. Where there is a significant difference between target and standard/budget, some form of action is needed. Standard/budgeted cost in excess of target may be a particular problem for products/services at very early stages of their life cycle. Closer alignment of the two might be achieved by amending the required profit margin. But, given investor sensitivities about profitability, it would almost certainly be preferable to close the 'cost gap' between standard/budget and target by other means. This can be achieved by application of **cost-reduction** techniques (see below), possibly coupled with some element of product/service redesign. Once standard/budgeted cost and target cost have been brought into line, feedback control may be applied: i.e. actual costs can be compared with a standard/budget which has been revised in the light of target cost. Use of target costing does not necessarily render conventional standard costing irrelevant. Indeed, it can be argued that effective target costing cannot operate without the existence of standard costs because:

- without standard costs, there would be no means of assessing the size of any cost gap;
- the target cost, as calculated above, is insufficiently detailed to permit effective control of individual elements of cost.

BENCHMARKING

Benchmarking is basically the process of target-setting, and can take two forms:

- *Internal benchmarking* Here, targets are generated within the organisation, having reference to what management considers an acceptable and achievable level of performance. Although internal benchmarking may be influenced by external considerations, such influence will often be more implicit than explicit. Many standard costing systems operate along these lines.
- *External benchmarking* Under this approach, targets are set with explicit reference to external conditions and organisations. Where benchmarks are being derived from an external organisation, management will usually seek to use one which is recognised as being 'world class' (see Chapter 2). External benchmarking covers financial issues like cost and selling price, along with market position and market share ('competitive benchmarking'). But it can also extend to how other organisations operate ('process benchmarking'), which should help management to determine the best way of doing things.

Once benchmarks – internal/external, competitive/process – have been obtained, management can use them as a feedback or feedforward yardstick against which to assess revenues, costs, processes and procedures. As with target costing, a cost-reduction scheme might result, or there might be the need for **process re-engineering** (see below).

COST REDUCTION

Cost *control* and cost *reduction* should not be confused. **Cost control**, as should be evident from the preceding discussion, means attempting to keep costs within predetermined limits. **Cost reduction**, on the other hand, involves the reduction of costs from previous levels, *without adverse impact on the quality of product/service being provided*. Although it is often possible to achieve marked cost reductions by taking a common-sense view of the situation or perhaps by application of activity-based cost management, there are other techniques available, the more important of which are described briefly below.

Value analysis (value engineering)

Value analysis is a systematic attempt to remove inessential aspects of a product or service and would normally be undertaken both prior to that product/service being offered for sale (i.e. at the design stage, or possibly as the result of market testing) and at regular intervals throughout the product/service's life cycle. The analysis is normally carried out by a team consisting of technical and accounting personnel, who pose and attempt to answer such questions as:

- Can a product/service's essential function be achieved differently, using less expensive methods/materials etc.?
- Is every proposed product/service function essential, or can some be eliminated without prejudice to quality?
- To what extent is it possible to standardise a new product/service with existing products/services?

If applied thoroughly and on a continuous basis, value analysis should result in a planned, ongoing search for cost reductions.

Variety reduction

As the name suggests, variety reduction involves examination of the range of products/services offered for sale, or of the types and sources of materials/labour/machinery used in provision of these products/services. The objective is to reduce costs by reducing variety – in essence, by standardising wherever possible, again without adversely affecting quality. Variety reduction may be particularly effective in manufacturing organisations, where standardisation may allow longer and less complex production runs involving fewer products, which could significantly reduce costs.

Work study

Slack *et al.* (1995) define work study as 'a generic term for those techniques, particularly method study and work measurement, which are used in the examination of human work in all its contexts, and which lead systematically to investigation of all the factors which affect the efficiency and economy of the situations being reviewed in order to effect improvements'.

The techniques referred to are aimed at determining the most efficient methods of utilising labour, materials and machinery and may be applied across a wide spectrum of organisational activities, ranging from the design of forms, office layout and telephone systems (method study) to the establishment of standard labour times for employees to carry out specified tasks at a predetermined efficiency level (work measurement).

Sensible application of the different specific techniques which fall under the general heading of 'work study' can result in significant cost reductions, especially when applied to major areas of expenditure such as administration.

Business process re-engineering

Although these are more wide-ranging in application than simply as a cost-reduction technique, business process re-engineering is often employed in the context of a cost-reduction programme. Business process re-engineering attempts to improve organisational performance by simplifying/improving procedures, reducing costs and enhancing quality. Business process re-engineering's underlying principle is that operations should be based on the processes which add value to output, rather than on the functions which comprise these processes – a view which is consistent with ABC and ABCM. The move by many manufacturing businesses to a just-in-time basis may be the result of business process re-engineering.

Potential problems with cost reduction schemes

A well-planned cost-reduction scheme is an important tool in the management arsenal, but such schemes are not without their difficulties:

Ombudsman says Whitehall cuts threaten standards

Mr William Reid, the parliamentary ombudsman, yesterday claimed that standards of service to the public were being threatened by large scale reductions in Whitehall funding.

In his annual report to parliament, Mr Reid also said complaints against government bodies – already running at record levels – were likely to go on rising as a result of staff reductions ...

Source: James Blitz, *Financial Times*, 21 March 1996. Reprinted with permission.

Exhibit 18.9 A possible problem with cost reductions?

Exhibit 18.9 highlights the fact that there is a trade-off between cost reduction and the quality of product/service being offered; a narrow or *ad hoc* view of cost reduction may mean that, as with cost control, quality or wider-ranging criteria may suffer (note that the strategic implications of the reductions are indirectly referred to in Exhibit 18.9 – '... likely to go on rising as a result of staff reductions ... ').

 Standardisation of products/services may offer scope for cost reductions. Can you envisage a sales-related problem which may possibly result from a programme of standardisation?

Standardisation of products/services may well yield cost reductions, but there is a danger that these could be more than counterbalanced by loss of sales revenue or customer loyalty – particularly where there is extensive interdependence between sales of different products/services within the range currently offered by the organisation. It can also happen that an organisation deliberately markets a wide range of what are basically similar products, possibly to maintain market share, or to deter would-be entrants to their market. This sort of approach is taken by some manufacturers of soap powders and detergents. The marketing implications of a variety-reduction scheme would thus require careful consideration before being implemented.

Cost reduction schemes may also have undesirable behavioural consequences. Staff may feel threatened or pressurised by cost reduction programmes and could resist their introduction or even attempt to sabotage their effective operation. The need for objectivity in cost reduction schemes means that they may often be devised by external consultants, which might cause resentment among the organisation's own staff, with possibly similar behavioural results. In addition, any cost reduction scheme must itself meet the cost/benefit criterion: design and implementation of cost reduction schemes can be expensive – especially where external consultants are extensively used. So, although an organisation may reap considerable benefit from a cost reduction scheme, such a scheme should not be hurried through in the hope of gaining some narrow or short-term benefit, nor should the behavioural implications be ignored.

FINANCIAL CONTROL: POSSIBLE PROBLEM AREAS

The essence of financial control – budget/actual comparison and investigation/action on the basis of significant variances – may appear to be a straightforward matter. However, there are certain potential problem areas which, if not borne in mind, may utterly defeat attempts at financial control. What we must always remember is that budgetary control does not relate merely to use of financial and physical resources. It also involves people, what they do and how they do it. These two facets of budgetary control could well conflict with one another, giving rise to many (though not necessarily all) of the problems we discuss below.

Cost control versus performance appraisal

Budget/actual comparisons of the type we have been describing are primarily intended as cost control aids. But it is often the case that they are also used to assess managerial performance: there are many instances where management bonuses are linked to their responsibility centre's performance against budget and it is certainly true that variances from budget can provide some indication of performance.

 Can you see any dangers in using only financial budget variances to measure managers' performance?

Using financial budget variances as the sole measure of performance will almost certainly represent a dangerous oversimplification and may result in the problems which are discussed below.

1 Non-financial aspects of performance under-emphasised or ignored

When we described total quality management in Chapter 2, we emphasised the importance of the quality of products/services. If financial measures are the main (or only) measure of performance, then this crucial aspect of organisational activity may be overlooked, with managers concentrating their efforts on achievement of financial targets to the exclusion of virtually everything else.

By taking a more externally oriented view, target costing and benchmarking may help to alleviate the danger of overlooking non-financial aspects of performance and control, but they do not eliminate it entirely. This difficulty might be harder to resolve because of the accounting function's heavy involvement in budgetary procedures. Accountants – either in fact or in the perception of other management disciplines – are concerned above all with financial matters. It is therefore desirable to supplement financially based variances with a range of other indicators. The **balanced scorecard** advocated by Kaplan and Norton (1992, 1993) is aimed at encouraging an holistic view of performance, suggesting that, *in addition* to financial measures, the following areas of performance should be monitored:

1 Customer-focused measures; e.g. complaints as a percentage of total sales volume, average time required to deal with customer enquiries.
2 Internal indicators; e.g. staff turnover, idle time, machine downtime.
3 Indicators of innovation and learning; e.g. research and development activity, proportion of staff attending training courses.

In this way, it is hoped, a more rounded picture of performance may be obtained than that presented by financial indicators alone.

2 Potential irrelevance in a TQM environment

It could be said that budget variances of the type we calculated in Exhibit 18.7 are irrelevant in a total quality management (TQM) context because:

- They do not reflect quality of product/service (although this might be said to be reflected indirectly in sales and contribution variances).
- They do not reflect the cost of attempting to achieve quality (e.g. internal and external failure costs – see Chapter 2).
- They are primarily internal comparisons.

The implication of total quality management is that, if the organisation is 'getting it right first time all of the time', then variances will not arise. But it is debatable whether, even under the most favourable circumstances and given the utmost emphasis on quality, operations will always be 'right first time' – so variances will inevitably rise. As a minimum, it will probably be necessary to monitor the budgeted and actual costs of trying to achieve quality: e.g. by comparing budgeted and actual internal failure costs. And again, target costing and benchmarking can help to address the problem of internal comparisons.

3 The budget may inhibit managers

If the financial control aspect of budgets is overemphasised, managers may come to view budgets as constraints on their activities and as an attempt to 'fix blame', rather than as the aid they are intended to be. While some form of financial constraint is obviously necessary, it should not be so tight that it prevents managers from suggesting new or radical ideas on the grounds that these would 'breach the budget' or 'cost too much' – some freedom to make decisions is necessary within the budget system.

4 Pressure to take panic action

Stemming from the preceding points, overemphasising financial performance against budget may have the effect of 'pressuring' managers into taking precipitate control action. For example, a significant adverse cost variance may result in an attempt to cut costs unnecessarily: variances may indicate the possible existence of a problem, but control action in the form of cost reduction should only follow investigation of the cause of any significant variances. There is a danger that the need to investigate significant variances could be overshadowed by the very existence of what appears to be an adverse performance indicator. But there may be a perfectly valid reason for the existence of an adverse cost variance (e.g. random or uncontrollable factors of the sort we shall describe below). Misplaced control action of this kind may have severe non-financial implications (e.g. for quality), and might adversely affect the strategic dimension.

If financial variances are to be used as performance indicators – and it is perfectly reasonable that they should be used in this way – then it is important that they be used sensibly, and preferably in conjunction with other measures, as suggested by the balanced scorecard.

Random factors

The need for careful investigation of significant variances is underlined by the impact on actual performance of random factors not foreseen at the time the budget was prepared.

In Exhibit 18.7, the flexible budget variance for direct materials was £14 400A. Assuming that the materials concerned are imported, can you suggest two random factors which might underlie this variance (or part of it) and which may not have been foreseen at the time the original budget was prepared?

There are many possible random factors which may have affected the actual direct materials cost: e.g. fluctuations in the exchange rate, unforeseen loosening of import/export regulations, changes in the domestic situation in the country of origin of the materials etc. The point about such random factors is that they will affect the budget variance reported and, because they were neither foreseen when the budget was originally prepared nor were they under managerial control, their effect on the variance concerned should really be eliminated for the purposes of cost control comparison.

Allowing for the impact of inflation

In Chapter 3, we saw the potential impact of inflation on estimates of future costs, and suggested that it would be unwise to omit its effect from such estimates. Clearly, inflation has a bearing on the budgetary planning/control process. Although inflation may have been allowed for in preparation of a budget, it can be argued that any difference between the rate of inflation foreseen when the budget was prepared and that which actually applied within a control period represents a random and uncontrollable factor of the type described above, and that its impact should be allowed for in calculation of variances. Exhibit 18.10 contains further information about Architrave Partnership's actual and budgeted material costs for the year.

Architrave Partnership: inflation and material costs

The budget specifies a standard direct materials cost of £20 per client day, based on an expected average inflation rate of 5% for the year concerned. In the event, the actual inflation rate was only 3%; before adjusting for inflation, comparison of flexible budget and actual revealed the following:

	Flexible budget	Flexible budget variance	Actual
Direct material cost	£144 000	£14 400A	£158 400

Exhibit 18.10 Inflation and financial control

Because of the difference between the anticipated and actual rates of inflation, the flexible budget variance will be distorted because, in essence, we are not comparing like with like.

 In Exhibit 18.10, will the difference between inflation rates cause a favourable or an adverse distortion in the flexible budget variance?

Because we are dealing with a cost and because the actual inflation rate was lower than anticipated, the distortion to the flexible budget variance will be adverse – i.e. the effect is to overstate the budgeted amount against which actual has been compared. To make a true comparison, we can remove this inflationary distortion, by **deflating** the flexible budget:

$$\text{deflated flexible budget: } £144\,000 \times \frac{1.03}{1.05} = £141\,257 \text{ (rounded)}$$

which gives an amended flexible budget variance of:

$$(£141\,257 - £158\,400) = £17\,143A$$

Deflating the budget in this way allows us to compare like with like – i.e. budget and actual both incorporate the same rate of inflation. Had the actual inflation rate been higher than budgeted, then the effect of our adjustment would be to **inflate** the budget. Whether inflating or deflating the budget, the general adjustment to apply is:

$$\frac{1 + \text{actual inflation rate}}{1 + \text{budgeted inflation rate}}$$

Comparison of the deflated variance (£17 143A) with that reported in Exhibit 18.7 (£14 400A) illustrates just how great can be the impact of differences between budgeted and actual inflation.

Controllability of budget items

In an ideal world, control reports submitted to managers in respect of their responsibility centre should reflect only those revenues/costs over which direct and complete control can be exercised at responsibility centre level. Unfortunately, this is rarely the case. Budget control reports will almost invariably contain items for which the locus of control is 'grey', or shared, or items whose genuine controllability in the short term is questionable.

 We said earlier that the flexible budget variance for direct materials reflects differences between standard and actual price and/or usage. How might responsibility for such a variance be unclear?

If purchasing and usage fall within the remit of different responsibility centres (e.g. buying and production) then responsibility for the materials flexible budget variance may be shared between these centres. To complicate matters further, there may well be a link between the price and usage elements of the flexible budget variance: e.g. purchase of cheaper-than-standard materials may result in a favourable price element, but this may be offset by an adverse usage element resulting from poorer-than-standard quality. Problems of this sort may be partly solved by subdividing flexible budget variances in the manner we shall describe in the next chapter – but even this does not solve the difficulties caused by interrelationships between variances and of dual responsibility for those variances.

A second area of possible control difficulty arises in the case of cost **apportionments**: e.g. front-line responsibility centres may receive a 'charge' for central support services (e.g. administration, computer services). While it may occasionally be possible to base such a charge entirely on usage, it is more likely that some element of apportionment will be present. Showing such charges on responsibility centres' control reports (even when based wholly on apportionment) can be justified in terms of providing some indication of the cost of supporting the activities of front-line centres and of making clear that central support services are not 'free'. Even though front-line managers may be unable to directly control support service costs, they may nevertheless be able to exert pressure on support service managers to control costs in the event that apportioned charges appear to be rising to unacceptably high levels. Alternatively, it might be said, particularly by managers of responsibility centres receiving charges of this sort, that their inclusion is unwarranted on the basis that the underlying costs cannot be directly controlled. In which case, serious disputes about controllability versus responsibility may arise to the detriment of working relationships within the organisation and ultimately, of the organisation itself. If apportionments are to be shown on budget control reports, then the fact that certain figures *are* apportionments should be made clear and the apportionment bases should be as objective as practicable, should be applied consistently to all relevant responsibility centres and should not be changed without prior warning.

One final problem area under the general heading of 'controllability' concerns the nature of certain costs being reported on. The fundamental tenet of exceptions reporting, feedback and feedforward control and responsibility accounting is that significant variances, once identified, give rise to management action to control the situation. For those costs which reflect a tangible input/output relationship (**engineered costs**), such as Architrave Partnership's direct material costs, this may be a relatively straightforward matter. But there are two categories of cost which present something of a difficulty where *short-term* control action is required.

Committed costs

We first encountered this term in Chapter 14 when we discussed the concept of relevant costs and revenues for decision making, stating that they were irrelevant to the financial analysis as they would be incurred regardless of the decision under consideration. A similar type of argument may be made in the control context. Once certain strategic decisions have been made (e.g. about the scale of organisational operations), then a certain level of costs will be unavoidable in the short term if the predetermined strategy is to be achieved. This being the case, financial control exercises must attempt to recognise the extent to which some variances (e.g. relating to building occupancy costs, or to certain elements of direct labour) may not be amenable to short-term control measures without prejudice to strategic aims.

Discretionary costs

A **discretionary cost,** as the term implies, is one over the amount of which management has discretion; in an emergency, it would theoretically be possible to reduce such costs to zero without adversely affecting the short-term well-being of the organisation. Much advertising and promotional expenditure, training costs and a certain proportion of legal and accountancy costs, possibly along with items such as the level of staff bonuses, would fall into the category of discretionary costs. The hallmark of discretionary costs is their 'black box' nature – i.e. the fact that there is no definable relationship between input (the amount of expenditure) and output (the benefit derived from that expenditure). This makes discretionary costs very difficult to budget (e.g. what is the 'correct' amount of budgeted expenditure on advertising?) and to control.

 A firm's budget/actual comparison for advertising costs reveals the following:

Flexible budget	Actual
£3 million	*£2 million*

Is the £1 million favourable variance 'good' or 'bad'?

The £1 million favourable variance could be considered a 'good' sign, in that actual expenditure was lower than budgeted by that amount. On the other hand, the same variance could be viewed as 'bad', since it might represent a missed opportunity to improve sales or organisational profile. The point is, we cannot be sure and the result of such uncertainty is often a feeling that budgets for discretionary costs should be 'spent to the hilt', regardless of inability to define the resulting benefits with any precision.

Unclear input/output relationships of this sort can pose a particular problem in service and some non-profit organisations. Given the intangible, heterogeneous and perishable nature of most services which we discussed in Chapter 11, the proportion of discretionary costs may be higher here than in the manufacturing sector, with greater attendant planning and control problems. It may be therefore, that in such organisations, supplementing financial control/performance measures with non-financial indicators may have particular significance. Irrespective of the organisation, planning and control of discretionary costs must be undertaken with care to prevent their spiralling out of control.

Measurement errors

In addition to random factors such as exchange rate fluctuations and the impact of inflation, budgetary control exercises must also attempt to recognise the fact that errors do occur. While most arithmetical errors relating to financial data may be corrected within a computerised accounting system, wide scope still exists for incorrect recording of data such as actual direct labour hours, or usage of materials – a fact which should be borne in mind when interpreting budget control reports.

Tactical versus strategic control

In addition to the dangers discussed above, overemphasising the control aspect of annual operational budgets (e.g. by using budget variances as the main indicator of managerial performance) may have the effect of concentrating managerial attention on a continual 'annual financial firefighting' exercise, in an attempt to keep strictly within tactical budget limits. Where these limits are significantly breached, the result may be the sort of panic cost-cutting reaction we described earlier. Not only might this have implications for quality, but also the tactical benefit of such measures may be more than offset by their adverse impact on achievement of strategic plans. When considering or implementing control action, management must be aware of the potential time lag which could exist between the taking of action and the appearance of its benefits and/or costs, and should beware of the 'ripple effect' of *ad hoc* operational and tactical control into the strategic arena.

Outdated control information

We suggested earlier that control reports should be produced periodically within the budget period to which they relate – say, monthly or four-weekly (or even fortnightly/weekly). For organisations which operate within the sort of advanced manufacturing technology (AMT) framework we described in Chapter 2, reports prepared on this sort of basis might be too infrequent for them to be effective. For example, where automated output processes produce 'real-time' control data, financial measures may be relegated to the position of confirming that which is already known. This may be particularly true where manufacturing processes are heavily oriented towards the just-in-time (JIT) approach. In fact, budget reports based on absorption costing may even conflict with JIT principles. As we illustrated in Chapter 13, unwarranted increases in stocks of finished goods and work in progress may be 'rewarded' by unrealistically high profit figures. In such environments, control reports may therefore be required very much more frequently and sufficiently early than might be necessary in more 'traditional' situations, and the value of absorption costing for internal purposes called even more into question. It is even debatable whether budgetary control has much relevance in AMT environments, where control is likely to be heavily dependent on product/technology design and controllability will reflect management's ability to influence these factors.

Fixed/variable cost analysis

Our flexible budget analysis in Exhibit 18.7 was based on marginal costing principles, but you will recall from Chapters 3 and 12 that there may be problems with this approach both in terms of separating fixed from variable costs and of the predominantly fixed nature of many organisations' cost structures. Although it is true that, in practice, marginal costing in the 'pure' form set out in Exhibit 18.7 is somewhat unlikely, it is important that the principle of flexible budgeting be applied. In other words, to give recognition, as part of the financial control exercise (and as far as practicable, given the cost/benefit criterion), to the fact that certain budget items will react to volume changes. Even if such changes are limited to revenue and step increases in some fixed costs, flexing the budget is still desirable if only as an enhancement of control reports.

Means–end confusion

In the previous chapter, we observed that budget systems may suffer from bureaucratic 'overkill'. One symptom of this can be seen where budgetary control is seen as an end in its own right, rather than as a means to an end (achievement of objectives). This kind of confusion is likely to be seriously at odds with the need for managerial and organisational flexibility and will probably create inconsistencies between operational, tactical and strategic arenas.

SUMMARY

In this chapter, we have examined the principles of financial control and illustrated that, although these principles may be straightforward enough, their application has many potential problem areas. We have seen that:

- Financial control is based on **exceptions reporting** – i.e. the triggering of management action by significant variances between two sets of outcomes.

- **Feedback control** is retrospective: budget is compared with actual and appropriate control action taken (amending budget and/or actual) where significant variances arise.

- **Positive feedback** attempts to maximise the benefit of any favourable variances; **negative feedback** attempts to minimise the adverse impact of any adverse variances.

- **Feedforward control** compares desired outcomes with predicted outcomes and attempts to exert control (amend desired and/or predicted outcomes) in advance to remedy any significant variances.

- Feedback and feedforward control are not mutually exclusive and frequently operate in tandem.

- A **flexible budget** recognises the impact on revenue and certain costs of changes in the volume of activity.

- A **fixed budget** is based on a single volume of activity and cannot therefore accommodate the effects of changes in volume of activity.

- Flexible budgets may be used as a form of sensitivity analysis by preparing budgets based on different volume levels.

- Where actual volume differs from that originally budgeted, the budget should be flexed on the basis of actual volume to permit a valid like-with-like comparison.

- Differences between the fixed and flexible budget are **volume variances**, reflecting the revenue, cost and profit impact of differences between budgeted and actual volume.

- Differences between flexible budget and actual are **flexible budget variances**, reflecting differences between standard and actual price/usage/rate/efficiency.

- The flexing basis may be the cost unit, the number of standard hours produced (for budgets covering multiple products/services) or there may be several flexing bases (where variable items vary with different measures of activity).

- The significance of variances may be stated in terms of their absolute amount, as a percentage of budget, or using statistical theory.

- **Responsibility accounting** is a control framework within which the organisation is divided into a number of **responsibility centres**, in respect of each of which responsibility is delegated to a stated manager and budgets/control reports prepared.

- Control reports should be prepared for each **control period** within a given budget period and should contain adequate detail to permit effective control at the relevant organisational level.

- **Activity-based cost management** (ABCM) attempts to control the cost of activities, rather than control individual costs.

- **Target costing** explicitly incorporates external considerations; target cost is calculated as (selling price needed to capture desired market share *less* required profit margin).

- Target cost can be compared with standard/budget and any significant cost gap closed by means of cost reduction.

- **Benchmarking** is the process of target-setting; benchmarks may be internal or external.

- **Cost reduction** is aimed at reducing costs from their previous level, without adversely affecting the quality of the product/service, some major cost reduction techniques being: value analysis, variety reduction and work study.

- Financial control has several problem areas, which may be summarised under the headings of:
  - cost control versus performance appraisal
  - random factors   allowing for the impact of inflation
  - controllability of budget items   measurement errors
  - tactical versus strategic control   outdated control information
  - fixed/variable cost analysis   means–end confusion

In the next chapter, we will illustrate how budget variances may be further analysed, discuss the benefits which this might offer and the extent to which such analysis could potentially augment the problems of financial control above.

FURTHER READING

Daniel, W. and Terrell, J., *Business Statistics for Management and Economics* (7th edition), Houghton Mifflin Co., 1995: Chapter 17 describes statistical control charts.

Doyle, D., *Cost Control A Strategic Guide*, CIMA, 1994: this comparatively short text places cost control in its strategic context.

Drury, C., Braund, S., Osborne, P. and Tayles, M., *A Survey of Management Accounting Practices in UK Manufacturing Companies*, CACA, 1993.

Kaplan, R. and Norton, D., The balance scorecard – measures that drive performance. *Harvard Business Review*, January–February 1992.

Kaplan, R. and Norton, D., Putting the balanced scorecard to work. *Harvard Business Review*, September–October 1993.

Morrow, M. and Ashworth, G., An evolving framework for activity-based approaches. *Management Accounting*, February 1994, CIMA.

Puxty, A. and Lyall, D., *Cost Control into the 1990s: A Survey of Standard Costing and Budgeting Practices in the UK*, CIMA, 1989.

Slack, N., Chambers, S., Harland, C., Harrison, H. and Johnston, R., *Operations Management*, Financial Times Prentice Hall, 2001: Chapter 9 deals with work study and more general issues of job design.

Smith, R., Flexible budgeting and standard costing: how are they linked? *Management Accounting*, October 1992, CIMA.

Upchurch, A., *Management Accounting Principles and Practice*, Financial Times Pitman Publishing, 1998: Chapters 15 and 16 explore some further issues of performance measurement, and its behavioural implications in particular.

SELF-TEST QUESTIONS

18.1 During Period 4, the following information applied to one of a firm's products:

Budgeted output: 10 000 units   actual output: 9000 units
Standard direct material cost per unit: £40
Actual direct material cost for period: £342 000.

What was the flexible budget variance for direct materials in Period 4?

A £18 000 adverse
B £18 000 favourable
C £58 000 adverse
D £58 000 favourable

18.2 Tick the appropriate box to indicate whether each of the following statements is true or false.

	True	False
(a) Use of actual hours as the flexing basis will distort the budget by incorporating actual inefficiencies.	☐	☐
(b) Investigation of every variance in excess of a given monetary amount will ensure that only significant variances are acted on by management.	☐	☐
(c) Feedforward control is based on comparison of actual and budgeted outcomes.	☐	☐
(d) Discretionary costs display no tangible input/output relationship.	☐	☐
(e) Committed costs are readily controllable in the short term.	☐	☐
(f) Differences between fixed budget and actual are termed volume variances.	☐	☐
(g) A flexible budget may be used as a form of sensitivity analysis during the planning process.	☐	☐

18.3 Solo Limited makes a single product for which the budgeted costs and activity for a typical month are as follows:

Budgeted sales and production	15 000 units
Budgeted unit costs:	£
Direct labour	46
Direct materials	30
Variable overheads	24
Fixed overheads	80
	180

During October, only 13 600 units were produced and sold. At the start of the month, there were unexpected increases of 8% in material prices and 2% in wage rates, but labour efficiency increased by 5%. Variable overheads increased by £1 per unit and fixed overheads increased by a total of £175 000.

The budgeted selling price of £250 was exactly achieved.

Requirements

(a) Produce a columnar statement showing the profit achieved:
    (i)   for the original budget;
    (ii) for a budget flexed on activity alone;
    (iii) for the actual results.   **(12 marks)**

(b) Briefly discuss the figures you have produced in answer to part (a).   **(3 marks)**
                                                                   (Total: 15 marks)

(CIMA, *Cost Accounting and Quantitative Methods*, November 1999)

18.4 The Arcadian Hotel operates a budgeting system and budgets expenditure over eight budget centres as shown below. Analysis of past expenditure patterns indicates that variable costs in some budget centres vary according to Occupied Room Nights (ORN) while in others the variable proportion of costs varies according to the number of visitors (V).

The budgeted expenditures for a period with 2000 ORN and 4300 V were as follows:

Budget centre	Variable costs vary with	Budgeted expenditure	Partial cost analysis
			Budget expenditure includes:
		£	
Cleaning	ORN	13 250	£2.50 per ORN
Laundry	V	15 025	£1.75 per V
Reception	ORN	13 100	£12 100 fixed
Maintenance	ORN	11 100	£0.80 per ORN
Housekeeping	V	19 600	£11 000 fixed
Administration	ORN	7 700	£0.20 per ORN
Catering	V	21 460	£2.20 per V
General overheads	–	11 250	all fixed

In period 9, with 1850 ORN and 4575 V, actual expenditures were as follows:

Budget centre	Actual expenditure
	£
Cleaning	13 292
Laundry	14 574
Reception	13 855
Maintenance	10 462
Housekeeping	19 580
Administration	7 930
Catering	23 053
General overheads	11 325

Requirements

(a) Prepare a flexible budget for period 9.   **(7 marks)**

(b) Show the individual expenditure variance for each budget centre.   **(5 marks)**

(c) Discuss briefly the advantages that a budgeting system brings to the Arcadian Hotel.
                                                                   (3 marks)
                                                                   (Total: 15 marks)

(CIMA, *Cost Accounting and Quantitative Methods*, November 1997)

18.5 (a) Explain briefly the differences between fixed and flexible budgets. (5 marks)

(b) Prepare a report, addressed to the Board of Directors, clearly explaining the advantages/disadvantages of using fixed/flexible budgets as part of a budgetary control system. (10 marks)

(c) Spreadsheets are often used by accountants to assist in the preparation of budgets. Describe how a spreadsheet may be used to prepare a sales budget AND explain the advantages of using spreadsheets to assist in this task. (Your answer should refer to input, use of formulae, and output reports). (10 marks)

(Total: 25 marks)

(CIMA, *Operational Cost Accounting*, November 1996)

QUESTIONS WITHOUT ANSWERS

18.6 A flexible budget is

A A budget comprising variable production costs only.
B A budget which is updated with actual costs and revenues as they occur during the budget period.
C A budget which shows the costs and revenues at different levels of activity.
D A budget which is prepared using a computer spreadsheet model.
E A budget which is prepared for a period of six months and reviewed monthly. Following such review a further one month's budget is prepared.

(CIMA, *Operational Cost Accounting*, May 1999)

18.7 A fixed budget is

A A budget for a single level of activity.
B Used when the mix of products is fixed in advance of the budget period.
C A budget which ignores inflation.
D Used only for fixed costs.
E An overhead cost budget.

(CIMA, *Operational Cost Accounting*, May 1997)

18.8 (a) 'Spreadsheets are suited to the development of planning tools such as budgets and standard costs, but databases are appropriate for recording actual data and converting it into useful information.'

Requirement

Compare and contrast spreadsheets and databases, using examples to illustrate how each might be used. (10 marks)

(b) The following cost per unit data has been extracted from the weekly flexible budgets of the MAZ hotel:

Number of guests	100	150	200
Cost per guest	£	£	£
Food costs	20.00	20.00	20.00
Heating, lighting, power	6.50	6.00	5.75
Cleaning	11.00	10.67	10.50
Administration	30.00	20.00	15.00

During week 38, there were 120 guests at the MAZ hotel and the costs incurred were as follows:

	£
Food costs	2490
Heating, lighting, power	710
Cleaning	1440
Administration	2850

Requirement

Prepare a budgetary control statement for the MAZ hotel for week 38. **(15 marks)**

(Total: 25 marks)

(CIMA, *Operational Cost Accounting*, May 1999)

18.9 The local authority in which you are a CIPFA student moved to devolved budgets over two years ago. At the end of the first full year there was a budget surplus, and budget holders were urged to 'spend it or lose it'. Your Director of Finance was unhappy with that outcome, and the next year urged her management accountants to encourage budget holders to be more proactive with their budget spends.

Unfortunately, the outcome was a general *overspend* in the Council budgets which required further year-end work to be done to bring the whole back in balance.

This year she is determined to have a more orderly approach, and has asked for your help in determining a new set of procedures. In particular, the Director wonders about the possible benefits that feedforward control might bring.

Requirements

Write a Briefing Note for your Director of Finance setting out the following:

(a) A summary of the theory of feedforward control, with the help of a diagram.

(10 marks)

(b) A summary of the practical benefits and difficulties that may be encountered should a feedforward control system be implemented in practice. **(10 marks)**

(Total: 20 marks)

(CIPFA, *Information Management and Control*, June 1998)

18.10 The following report has been prepared relating to one product for March 1997. This has been sent to the appropriate product manager as part of PDC Limited's monitoring procedures.

Monthly variance report – March 1997

	Actual	Budget	Variance	%
Production volume (units)	9 905	10 000	95A	0.95A
Sales volume (units)	9 500	10 000	500A	5.00A
Sales revenue (£)	27 700	30 000	2300A	7.67A
Direct material (kg)	9 800	10 000	200F	2.00F
Direct material (£)	9 600	10 000	400F	4.00F
Direct labour (hours)	2 500	2 400	100A	4.17A
Direct labour (£)	8 500	8 400	100A	1.19A
Contribution	9 600	11 600	2000A	17.24A

The product manager has complained that the report ignores the principle of flexible budgeting and is unfair.

Requirements

(a) Prepare a report to the management team which comments critically on the monthly variance report. Include as an appendix to your report the layout of a revised monthly variance report which will be more useful to the product manager. Include row and column headings, but do *not* calculate the contents of the report. **(15 marks)**

(b) Explain the differences between budgetary control and standard costing/variance analysis. In what circumstances would an organisation find it beneficial to operate both of these cost control systems? **(5 marks)**

(c) Explain briefly how a database may be used to collect the information required to prepare a report such as that illustrated in part (a) above. **(5 marks)**

(Total: 25 marks)

(CIMA, *Operational Cost Accounting*, May 1997)

CHAPTER 19

Analysis of variances

Standard costing – a status check

Standard costing and variance analysis has been in use since the early twentieth century. Since then, its methodology and scope has expanded and evolved to accommodate changing views about its relevance as a useful aspect of a management accounting information system. In recent years, the role of standard costing and variance analysis ... has been increasingly questioned. More and more a philosophy of continuous improvement is being seen as the way forward for the achievement of improved levels of business profitability and efficiency ...

Standards may be viewed as a static base against which to measure actual events. The main objective may be seen as its use as a control device, with conformance to standards and the elimination of any variances which occur. This may be seen as restrictive and inhibiting action likely to lead to progress in business profitability and efficiency. However, it may be argued that standard costing may be used in other ways as part of the management accounting tool kit ...

Source: George Brown, *ACCA Students' Newsletter*, March 1999.

Exhibit 19.1 The relevance of variance analysis under debate

INTRODUCTION

When we introduced the concept of standard costing in Chapter 16, we said that one of its purposes was to permit more detailed analysis of variances. In the previous chapter, we suggested that flexible budget variances, while of considerable use for control purposes, may still be too aggregated to permit effective pinpointing of problems and of managerial responsibility. In this chapter, we will demonstrate how the 'global' budget variances can be analysed into their constituent elements and how this may enhance financial control. We will also illustrate how these variances can be presented so as to reconcile budgeted and actual profit and discuss the extent to which detailed variance analysis might aggravate the argued weaknesses of standard costing and 'conventional' budgetary control.

OBJECTIVES

When you have completed this chapter, you will be able to:

- appreciate the potential enhancement of financial control which may result from availability of detailed variance information;

- for each element of cost and for sales, calculate budget variances by formula and subdivide these into their constituent elements;
- prepare an operating statement reconciling budgeted and actual costs;
- prepare an operating statement incorporating variances and reconciling budgeted and actual profit;
- calculate and explain the purpose and meaning of standard costing control ratios;
- appreciate how a system of detailed variance analysis may exacerbate the argued 'general' shortcomings of standard costing and budget variance analysis, along with arguments about the relevance of such systems in modern operating environments.

WHY ANALYSE BUDGET VARIANCES?

You will recall from the previous chapter that our flexible budget/actual comparison revealed variances such as:

materials   £5000 adverse.

This undoubtedly indicates that actual spending on materials was £5000 higher than the budget based on an identical output volume, but does it tell us anything about what aspect of material cost may be causing problems, or about where, within a responsibility accounting system, the locus of managerial responsibility might lie?

 State two general reasons why actual and budgeted material cost might differ.

In general, actual and budgeted materials costs may differ because either or both of the purchase cost and/or usage differ, and it is these differences which a 'global' flexible budget variance such as '£5000 adverse' cannot reflect. Suppose, in addition, that, within a responsibility accounting system, purchase of materials is the responsibility of the Buyer whereas usage is the responsibility of (say) the Operations Manager. In this sort of situation, subdivision of the flexible budget variance into price and usage elements may help to decide to whom the respective variances should be reported. But, as we shall discover later, this is not the same as suggesting that the Buyer and Operations Manager are responsible, respectively, for the price and usage elements of the budget variance. This is an important point. Variances (regardless of their level of detail) are merely indicative of possible problem areas, but without further investigation, do not constitute conclusive evidence of personal responsibility or of anything else. What we are suggesting is that reporting detailed variances may help identify the individual who is in the best position to investigate and perhaps to suggest or initiate corrective action. It is worth repeating the point made in the previous chapter that a budget system which is used (or thought to be used) as some form of managerial witchhunt is unlikely to find much support amongst managers and, as a consequence, is unlikely to work particularly well.

SUBDIVIDING BUDGET VARIANCES

If, as we have just suggested, there may be a case for further analysis of budget variances, how can this be achieved? The prerequisite is existence, within the budget system, of standard costing data such as the estimated material usage per unit of output and the estimated cost per unit of material. Without the existence of such information in a reasonably formal way, it is hard to see how meaningful budgets can be prepared let alone analysis of budget variances undertaken. We shall use the data in Exhibit 19.2 to illustrate how an organisation's budget variances may be analysed in detail.

OV Management Skills Ltd

OV Ltd is a privately owned training company, specialising in provision of management skills courses. Standard, budgeted and actual data relating to a two-day course run regularly by the company throughout the year are given below.

	£
Standard per student per course	
Direct materials: 2 course manuals @ £5	10
Direct labour: 20 hours @ £15 per hour	300
Variable course overhead: 20 hours @ £0.75	15
Fixed course overhead: 20 hours @ £1.25	25
Variable selling cost	5
Standard cost per student per course	355
Fee per student per course	450
Budgeted data for the year	
Number of students attending the course	3500
Fixed course overhead	£87 500
Administration overheads	£100 000
Actual data for the year	
Number of students attending the course	3100
	£
Total revenue	1 534 500
Direct materials' cost (6375 course manuals used)	30 600
Direct labour cost (59 000 hours)	1 062 000
Variable course overhead	46 300
Fixed course overhead	82 000
Variable selling cost	17 800
Administration overhead	104 000

Exhibit 19.2 Data for variance analysis

Before commencing our detailed analysis of OV Ltd's variances, it might be useful to present a statement of the company's fixed and flexible budgets for the month, along with actuals and variances; this is done in Exhibit 19.3, the format and construction being those used in the last chapter.

OV Ltd: fixed and flexible budgets, actuals and variances for the month

	Fixed budget	Volume variances	Flexible budget	Flexible budget variances	Actual
Sales volume (students)	3500	400A	3100	nil	3100
	£	£	£	£	£
Sales revenue	1 575 000	180 000A	1 395 000	139 500F	1 534 500
Variable costs:					
Direct material	35 000	4 000F	31 000	400F	30 600
Direct labour	1 050 000	120 000F	930 000	132 000A	1 062 000
Course overhead	52 500	6 000F	46 500	200F	46 300
Selling costs	17 500	2 000F	15 500	2 300A	17 800
	1 155 000	132 000F	1 023 000	133 700A	1 156 700
Contribution	420 000	48 000A	372 000	5 800F	377 800
Fixed costs:					
Course overhead	87 500	nil	87 500	5 500F	82 000
Administration	100 000	nil	100 000	4 000A	104 000
	187 500	nil	187 500	1 500F	186 000
Net profit	232 500	48 000A	184 500	7 300F	191 800

Exhibit 19.3 Fixed and flexible budgets, actual and variances

Looking at Exhibit 19.3 provides us with some information about OV Ltd's performance, but there may be areas of particular strength or weakness which are 'masked' by the aggregate nature of the variances being reported. Before proceeding, it is also worth stating that the extent (if any) to which budget variances are analysed should depend on the precise circumstances: e.g. if materials form a small proportion of total cost, further analysis of budget variances may not be worth while in cost/benefit terms.

Materials' variances

Flexible budget (total) material variance

In the previous chapter and in Exhibit 19.3, we computed this variance by comparing flexible budget and actual figures:

Actual number of students *should* have a material cost of

    (3100 students × £10)   £31 000   (AO × SMCU)

Actual number of students *did*

    have a direct materials' cost of   £30 600   (TAMC)

Flexible budget variance   £400F

F representing a favourable variance, since actual cost is lower than flexible budget.

It is possible to compress the variance calculation into a formula:

$$([AO \times SMCU] - TAMC)$$

where AO   represents actual output

     SMCU is the standard materials' cost per unit of output and

     TAMC is the total actual materials' cost.

$[AO \times SMCU]$ is the flexible budget cost, and you will see that the formulaic version is merely an alternative presentation of the 'narrative' calculation, with both methods being equally acceptable.

 Insert the appropriate data from Exhibit 19.2 into the formula and obtain the flexible budget variance for materials.

The formula gives:

$$([3100 \times £10] - £30\ 600) = £400F$$

The flexible budget variance for materials can be subdivided as follows:

flexible budget variance
(total material variance)
$([AO \times SMCU] - TAMC)$

materials' price variance   materials' usage variance
$(SP - AP) \times AQ$ $(SQ - AQ) \times SP$

We will explain the formulae for price and usage variances below.

Material price variance

This shows the extent to which the flexible budget variance is due to differences between the actual and standard cost of materials. The actual cost per course manual (i.e. per unit of direct material) is not given in Exhibit 19.2, but can easily be determined as:

$$\frac{\text{Total actual materials' cost}}{\text{Actual manuals used}} = \frac{£30\ 600}{6375} = £4.80$$

One unit of direct material *should* cost	£5.00	(SP)
One unit of direct material *did* cost	£4.80	(AP)
Difference per unit of material	£0.20F	
Actual units of material purchased were	6375	(AQ)
So material price variance is	£1275F	

Since the actual cost per unit of material is less than standard, we have a favourable price variance. As a formula, the price variance can be expressed as:

$$(SP - AP) \times AQ$$

where SP represents the standard purchase price per unit of material

   AP is the actual purchase price per unit of material and

   AQ is the actual purchase quantity of materials

Insert OV Ltd's data from Exhibit 19.2 into the price variance formula and compute the variance.

Using the formula, we have:

$$(£5 - £4.80) \times 6375 \text{ units} = £1275F$$

In this particular example, purchase and usage quantities have been assumed to be identical; had they been different, we would have based the price variance on the *purchase* quantity. Determining variances at the earliest identifiable point in the business cycle is necessary to enable effective control action to be taken if needed. If material purchases are placed in store prior to use, there may be a marked time lag between purchase and usage. Waiting until materials are used before extracting the price variance could mean that action cannot be taken to avoid future adverse variances or to perpetuate favourable ones (e.g. because firm orders have already been placed).

 Can you suggest two possible reasons for the price variance calculated?

One possibility is that inferior quality (and cheaper) manuals have been purchased; or OV Ltd may have changed to a cheaper supplier, or might have negotiated a quantity discount from the existing supplier; perhaps there has been a slump in demand for this type of work, resulting in a lowering of the market price. In the absence of additional information, however, we can only speculate – hence the need for further investigation if the variance is significant enough to warrant it.

Material usage variance

This measures the extent to which the flexible budget variance is due to differences between actual and standard usage of materials – i.e. the extent to which we have used more or less materials for the output achieved than envisaged in the standard. The usage variance is:

Actual number of students *should* use		
(3100 students × 2)	6200 manuals	(SQ)
Actual number of students *did* use	6375 manuals	(AQ)
Difference in units used	175 manuals A	
Per unit, this difference should have cost	£5.00	(SP)
So material usage variance is	£875A	

'A' indicating that the variance is adverse: actual output required more direct materials than the standard allowed.

As a formula, the usage variance is:

$$(SQ - AQ) \times SP$$

where SQ represents the standard quantity of materials allowed *for actual output*
       AQ is the actual quantity of materials used and
       SP is the standard purchase price per unit of material.

Standard price is employed in the usage variance because, had actual price been substituted, the resulting variance would have been due partly to usage and partly to price factors – giving an unclear control 'signal' to management.

Use the data in Exhibit 19.2 to determine OV Ltd's material usage variance by formula.

OV Ltd's usage variance is:

$$([3100 \times 2 \text{ manuals}] - 6375 \text{ manuals}) \times £5 = £875\text{A}$$

Since the price and usage variances represent subdivisions of the flexible budget variance, we can check the arithmetic integrity of our calculations:

	£
Price variance	1275F
Usage variance	875A
Flexible budget variance	400F

 Can you suggest two possible reasons for the usage variance?

Since actual usage exceeded standard, it may be that there has been some laxity in handling of manuals by either the company's employees or by students. Alternatively, it may be that purchase of inferior manuals or purchase from a different supplier has caused problems in their use: pages may be missing, for instance. You will see that the last two reasons we have suggested were also suggested in respect of the price variance – i.e. there may be a link between the favourable price variance arising from (say) purchase of inferior, cheaper manuals and resultant problems in their usage. We shall return to the problem of *interdependence of variances* later in the chapter.

Labour variances

Flexible budget (total) variance

This is determined as follows:

	£	
Actual number of students *should* have a direct labour cost of (3100 students × £300)	930 000	(AO × SLCU)
Actual number of students *did* have a direct labour cost of	1 062 000	(TALC)
Flexible budget variance	132 000A	

As a formula, the total variance is:

$$([\text{AO} \times \text{SLCU}] - \text{TALC})$$

where AO represents actual output
SLCU is the standard labour cost per unit of output and
TALC is the total actual labour cost.

 Use the formula to determine OV Ltd's flexible budget variance for direct labour.

Using the formula gives:

$$([3100 \text{ students} \times £300] - £1\,062\,000) = £132\,000\text{A}$$

The flexible budget variance for direct labour can be subdivided in a manner very similar to that adopted with the material budget variance:

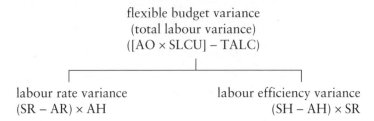

flexible budget variance
(total labour variance)
([AO × SLCU] – TALC)

labour rate variance
(SR – AR) × AH

labour efficiency variance
(SH – AH) × SR

Labour rate variance

This variance assesses the extent to which the flexible budget variance arises because of differences between standard and actual rates of pay per hour. As with the actual direct material cost, we need to calculate the actual labour rate per hour from Exhibit 19.2:

$$\frac{\text{Actual direct labour cost}}{\text{Actual direct labour hours}} = \frac{\pounds 1\,062\,000}{59\,000} = \pounds 18$$

Direct labour rate per hour *should* have been	£15.00	(SR)
Direct labour rate per hour *was*	£18.00	(AR)
Difference per hour	£ 3.00A	
Actual hours paid for were	59 000	(AH)
so labour rate variance is	£177 000A	

Converting the rate variance to a formula:

$$(SR – AR) \times AH$$

where   SR   represents the standard rate of pay per hour
        AR is the actual hourly rate of pay and
        AH is the actual number of hours.

The adverse rate variance might have arisen because a different, more highly paid, grade of labour has been employed from that which was incorporated into the standard. However, a more probable explanation is that a pay rise anticipated when the standard was set turned out to be lower than the pay rise actually awarded.

Labour efficiency variance

This variance reflects the extent to which the flexible budget labour variance arises because of differences between standard and actual labour efficiency:

Actual number of students *should* take		
(3100 students × 20 hours)	62 000 hours	(SH)
Actual number of students *did* take	59 000 hours	(AH)
Difference in hours	3 000F	
Standard rate per hour	£15	(SR)
Labour efficiency variance	£45 000F	

As a formula, the efficiency variance is:

$$(SH - AH) \times SR$$

where SH represents the standard hours allowed *for actual output*
  AH is the actual hours and
  SR is the standard rate of pay per hour.

The standard rate per hour is used in the efficiency variance for the same reason that standard price was used in the material usage variance – i.e. to prevent distortion of the efficiency variance by rate differences.

Using the data from Exhibit 19.2 gives an efficiency variance of:

$$([3100 \text{ students} \times 20 \text{ hours}] - 59\,000 \text{ hours}) \times £15 = £45\,000F$$

Again, we can check the arithmetic accuracy of our labour variance calculations:

Labour rate variance	£177 000A
Efficiency variance	£ 45 000F
Labour flexible budget variance	£132 000A

 Can you see a possible interrelationship between the rate and efficiency variances above?

We suggested earlier that the adverse rate variance may have arisen because an actual pay rise awarded might have been higher than that anticipated in the standard. This may have had a bearing on better-than-expected efficiency. Perhaps making the higher-than-anticipated pay award has had some effect on worker motivation. Once more, we are faced with the possibility of interdependence between variances – but beware the danger of leaping to quickfire cause/effect conclusions.

Variable overhead variances

Flexible budget (total) variance

The important computational aspect of all variable overhead variances is to remember that we are dealing with a *variable* cost (which also happens to be indirect).

 Use the data in Exhibit 19.2 to complete the calculation below.

Actual number of students *should* have incurred variable course overhead of (.........@.........)	£..........
Actual number of students *did* incur variable course overhead of	£..........
Flexible budget variance	£..........

The completed variance calculation is:

Actual number of students *should* have incurred variable course overhead of

	£	
(3100 students @ £15)	46 500	(AO × SVOU)
Actual number of students *did* incur variable course overhead of	46 300	(AVO)
Flexible budget variance	200F	

As a formula, we have:

$$([AO \times SVOU] - AVO)$$

where   AO   represents actual output
           SVOU is standard variable overhead per unit of output and
           AVO   is the actual variable overhead cost.

Applying the formula gives:

$$([3100 \text{ students} \times £15] - £46\,300) = £200F$$

The flexible budget variable overhead variance can be split into an expenditure variance and, where the overhead varies with labour hours, into an efficiency variance:

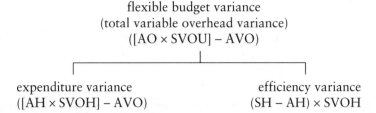

flexible budget variance
(total variable overhead variance)
$$([AO \times SVOU] - AVO)$$

expenditure variance   efficiency variance
$$([AH \times SVOH] - AVO) \qquad (SH - AH) \times SVOH$$

Variable overhead expenditure variance

This shows the extent to which the total variance is due to differences between budgeted and actual expenditure. In OV Ltd's case, variable overhead varies with the number of direct labour hours, which form the basis for calculating the standard cost allowed; where variable overhead varies with the number of units of output, this will replace actual hours in the variance calculation.

	£	
Actual labour hours *should* incur variable course overhead of		
(59 000 @ £0.75)	44 250	(AH × SVOH)
Actual labour hours *did* incur variable course overhead of	46 300	(AVO)
So variable overhead expenditure variance is	2 050A	

As a formula:

$$([AH \times SVOH] - AVO)$$

where   AH   is the actual hours
           SVOH is the standard variable overhead rate per hour and
           AVO   is the actual variable overhead cost.

✔   *Use the formula to confirm OV Ltd's variable overhead expenditure variance.*

The expenditure variance is:

$$([59\,000 \text{ hours} \times £0.75] - £46\,300) = £2050A$$

Variable overhead efficiency variance

Where variable overhead varies with labour hours, part of the flexible budget variance may arise because of differences between standard and actual efficiency:

Actual number of students *should* take		
(3100 students × 20 hours)	62 000 hours	(SH)
Actual number of students *did* take	59 000 hours	(AH)
Difference in hours	3 000F	
Standard variable course overhead per hour	£0.75	(SVOH)
Variable overhead efficiency variance	£ 2 250F	

You will see that the variance is essentially the same as that for direct labour efficiency, the only difference being that the standard variable overhead rate per hour replaces the standard labour rate.

In formulaic layout:

$$(SH - AH) \times SVOH$$

where SH represents the standard hours allowed for actual output
  AH is the actual hours worked and
  SVOH is the standard variable overhead rate per hour.

Application of the formula gives a variance of:

$$([3100 \text{ students} \times 20 \text{ hours}] - 59\,000 \text{ hours}) \times £0.75 = £2250F$$

In situations where variable overhead varies with the number of units of output, an efficiency variance will not be calculated and the expenditure variance will equal the flexible budget variance.

 Is there a possible link between the variable overhead efficiency and labour rate variances?

Since, in this example, variable overhead varies with direct labour hours, any factors which affect labour efficiency will also affect variable overhead efficiency. This variance, like the labour efficiency variance, may be linked to the adverse labour rate variance – i.e. a higher-than-anticipated pay award may have had a beneficial effect on efficiency. It is quite possible for interdependence to affect different elements of cost as well as separate subvariances of the same cost element.

 Reconcile the variable overhead expenditure and efficiency variances with the flexible budget variance.

The variances reconcile as follows:

	£
Variable overhead expenditure variance	2050A
Variable overhead efficiency variance	2250F
Flexible budget variance	200F

Fixed overhead variances

As a service business, OV Ltd does not have production overhead; the equivalent here being fixed and variable course overhead. You will recall from Chapter 12 that fixed overhead of this type receives different treatment in absorption costing (where it is included in unit costs) and marginal costing (where it is not included in unit costs, but is written off in full to the relevant period's profit statement). In describing the variances relating to fixed course ('production') overhead, we must therefore distinguish between marginal and absorption costing.

Marginal costing

Fixed overhead expenditure variance

In a marginal costing system, the only variance for fixed overhead is an expenditure variance reflecting the difference between budgeted and actual cost:

	£	
Budgeted fixed overhead cost was	87 500	(BFO)
Actual fixed overhead cost was	82 000	(AFO)
Expenditure variance	5 500F	

As a formula, the fixed overhead expenditure variance is thus:

$$(BFO - AFO)$$

where   BFO   is the budgeted fixed overhead cost and
           AFO   is the actual fixed overhead cost

A glance at Exhibit 19.3 shows that the expenditure variance is also, in marginal costing, the flexible budget variance.

 Why might expenditure variances such as the £5500F for fixed overhead and £200F for variable overhead prove unsatisfactory for cost control purposes?

The expenditure variance is likely to be of limited value since, in most cases, the terms 'fixed overhead' and 'variable overhead' are generic descriptions of several costs sharing the same behaviour pattern relative to volume of output. Before any control action can be taken, it will normally be necessary to investigate budget and actual for each individual cost which, in total, comprise 'fixed overhead' or 'variable overhead'. If such investigation reveals some (or possibly all) of the overheads to be committed costs then, as we said in the last chapter, they may not be susceptible to short-term control action by management.

Absorption costing

Here, variances for fixed production overhead are complicated by their absorption into the cost per unit of output, and it is important to realise that the additional variances we are about to discuss all derive from the process of absorption.

Fixed overhead total variance

Exhibit 19.2 indicates that OV Ltd absorbs fixed course ('production') overhead at £1.25 per *standard* direct labour-hour. In Chapter 16, we saw that the standard labour-hour is a measure of work (i.e. output) and we know (from Chapter 5) that overhead is absorbed on the basis of actual output. A distinction must therefore be drawn between actual *input hours* (59 000 in Exhibit 19.2) and the output which actually resulted from this number of hours:

(3100 students × 20 standard hours per student) = 62 000 standard hours.

Fixed overhead absorbed for the month will therefore be:

(62 000 standard hours × £1.25 per standard hour) = £77 500

Since each unit of OV Ltd's output requires the same input of standard hours, we can obtain the identical result by using actual unit output (i.e. number of students) and the fixed overhead absorbed per student:

(3100 students × £25 per student) = £77 500

£25 per student being equivalent to (20 standard hours per student × £1.25 per hour). The fixed overhead total variance measures the difference between the amount absorbed and the amount incurred:

	£	
Fixed overhead absorbed by actual output	77 500	(AO × FOPU)
Actual fixed overhead	82 000	(AFO)
Total variance	4 500A	

Stated as a formula:

$$([AO \times FOPU] - AFO)$$

where AO   is actual output in units
FOPU   is the fixed overhead per unit of output and
AFO   is the actual fixed overhead cost.

You should be careful, when calculating the total fixed overhead variance, that the overhead rate employed is a rate per cost unit. In situations like OV Ltd's, where overhead is absorbed other than by a cost unit rate, it is easy to fall into the error of using the wrong rate – OV Ltd's unit rate is (20 standard hours × £1.25) = £25.

 What does the fixed overhead total variance represent?

Calculation of the total variance involves comparison of overhead absorbed with overhead incurred, so we are indicating overabsorption (favourable total variance) and underabsorption (adverse total variance).

The total variance may be subdivided as follows:

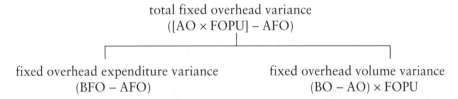

total fixed overhead variance
$([AO \times FOPU] - AFO)$

fixed overhead expenditure variance
$(BFO - AFO)$

fixed overhead volume variance
$(BO - AO) \times FOPU$

The expenditure variance is exactly the same as that which we calculated for marginal costing, but the total and volume variances *do not exist in marginal costing*, as they derive from absorption of fixed overhead (which does not occur in marginal costing). In Chapter 6, we saw that a predetermined overhead absorption rate derives from estimates of overhead expenditure and of volume, over- and underabsorption occurring because either or both of these estimates differ from actual – and it is the impact of such differences which the expenditure and volume variances represent.

Fixed overhead volume variance

This variance indicates the extent to which the total variance is due to differences between budgeted and actual volumes of output:

Budgeted number of students was	3500	(BO)
Actual number of students was	3100	(AO)
Difference	400 studentsA	
Fixed overhead per student	£25	(FOPU)
Fixed overhead volume variance	£10 000A	

As a formula:

$$(BO - AO) \times FOPU$$

where BO   represents budgeted output in units
AO   is actual output in units and
FOPU   is the fixed overhead absorption rate per cost unit.

OV Ltd's volume variance for the month by formula is:

$$(3500 \text{ students} - 3100 \text{ students}) \times £25 = £10\,000A$$

 Why is the volume variance of £10 000 adverse?

The volume variance is adverse because actual output was 400 students lower than budget and to this extent, an underabsorption of fixed overhead has arisen.

The volume variance may be of particular interest to management of organisations where there is a heavy investment in technology, with high related fixed costs. In these circumstances, volume, and the extent to which it does/does not recover fixed costs, can be a major consideration in judging whether or not resources are being effectively and efficiently used. Where absorbing fixed overhead through volume is especially important (e.g. in high-technology set-ups, with a large proportion of fixed costs), the volume variance may be subdivided into a fixed overhead efficiency variance and a fixed overhead capacity variance. The efficiency variance reflects the extent to which differences between budgeted and actual volume are due to labour efficiency, while the capacity variance reflects the impact on volume of other factors (e.g. unexpected machine downtime).

Fixed overhead efficiency variance

This variance is calculated in exactly the same manner as the efficiency variances for direct labour and variable overhead, except here, the overhead absorption rate *per direct labour hour* is used:

Actual number of students *should* use		
(3100 × 20 hours)	62 000 hours	(SH)
Actual number of students *did* use	59 000 hours	(AH)
Difference in hours	3 000F	
Fixed overhead rate per hour	£1.25	(FOPH)
Fixed overhead efficiency variance	£ 3 750F	

Convert the overhead efficiency variance into a formula and confirm the result above.

As a formula, the fixed overhead efficiency variance is:

$$(SH - AH) \times FOPH$$

where   SH   is the standard hours allowed for *actual output*
         AH   is the actual hours taken and
         FOPH   is the fixed overhead rate per labour-hour.

Using OV Ltd's data gives:

$$([3100 \text{ students} \times 20 \text{ hours}] - 59\,000 \text{ hours}) \times £1.25 = £3750F$$

The fixed overhead efficiency variance is attributable to the same causes as are the direct labour and variable overhead efficiency variances.

Fixed overhead capacity variance

We can assess the extent to which the fixed overhead volume variance arose because of factors other than labour efficiency as follows:

Budgeted direct labour hours (3500 students × 20 hours)	70 000	(BH)
Actual direct labour hours	59 000	(AH)
Difference in hours	11 000A	
Fixed overhead rate per hour	£1.25	(FOPH)
Fixed overhead capacity variance	£13 750A	

Like the fixed overhead volume variance, the capacity variance here is adverse because it reflects an underabsorption of fixed overhead. As a formula, the variance is:

$$(BH - AH) \times FOPH$$

where   BH   is the number of direct labour-hours required for output in the *fixed budget* (i.e. for 3500 students in OV Ltd's case)
         AH   is the actual direct labour hours and
         FOPH   is the fixed overhead rate per direct labour hour.

Using the formula to confirm our earlier calculation:

$$([3500 \text{ students} \times 20 \text{ hours}] - 59\,000 \text{ hours}) \times £1.25 = £13\,750A$$

Since the fixed overhead efficiency and capacity variances attempt to explain why the fixed overhead volume variance has arisen, the three variances can be reconciled:

	£
Fixed overhead efficiency variance	3 750F
Fixed overhead capacity variance	13 750A
Fixed overhead volume variance	10 000A

However, care is needed in use of the volume variance and its subvariances, as there is a danger that they might wrongly be thought to reflect expenditure (rather than over- or underabsorption of overhead) and could thus mislead managers into taking inappropriate control action. It is very arguable, for example, whether reporting fixed overhead efficiency and capacity variances would offer any real benefit to OV Ltd's management.

Reconciling the expenditure and volume variances with the total variance, we get:

	£
Fixed overhead expenditure variance	5 500 F
Fixed overhead volume variance	10 000A
Total fixed overhead variance	4 500A

Variances for selling and administration costs

Because of the discretionary nature of many of the costs that fall under this general heading, close monitoring of actual expenditure against budget is particularly important. However, it will rarely be possible to calculate more than the flexible budget or expenditure variance, given the nature of the costs concerned.

From Exhibit 19.2, we can determine variances for OV Ltd's selling and administration costs.

Variable selling cost variance

The flexible budget variance is:

	£	
Actual sales *should* have a selling cost of (3100 students × £5)	15 500	(FBC)
Actual sales *did* have a selling cost of	17 800	(AC)
Flexible budget variance	2 300A	

By formula:

$$(FBC - AC)$$

where FBC is the flexible budget cost and
       AC   is the actual cost.

Where output and sales volumes differ, you should be careful to flex the budget on the correct volume, i.e. sales.

 Why might the adverse variance for selling costs cause concern to management?

The concern is likely to be twofold: first, actual selling costs have exceeded budget and second, in spite of higher-than-budgeted selling costs, sales volume is still lower than budget. However, had the variance been favourable, management might still have cause for concern: i.e. spending less on selling costs might have had an adverse impact on sales volume. The moral – as with all variances – is that investigation of the circumstances is needed.

Fixed administration overhead variance

We can compute an expenditure variance for this cost:

	£	
Budgeted administration overhead was	100 000	(BC)
Actual administration overhead was	104 000	(AC)
Expenditure variance	4 000A	

As a formula, the variance is:

$$(BC - AC)$$

where BC is the budgeted cost and
           AC is the actual cost.

 Even in an absorption costing system, a total and volume variance for fixed administration overhead are unlikely. Why is this?

Fixed overheads which are not related to output, such as administration, selling and distribution, are not normally absorbed into unit costs (see Chapter 5), except for specific purposes such as setting selling prices; calculation of a total or a volume variance (both deriving from overhead absorption) would therefore be irrelevant.

Sales variances

Selling price variance

This measures the difference between the standard and the actual selling price per unit. Actual selling price per course must be calculated from the information in Exhibit 19.2:

$$\frac{\text{Actual sales revenue}}{\text{Actual sales volume}} = \frac{£1\ 534\ 500}{3100\ \text{students}} = £495$$

The selling price variance is:

Selling price per student/course *should* have been	£450	(SSP)
Selling price per student/course *was*	£495	(ASP)
Difference in selling price per student/course	£ 45F	
Actual sales volume	3100 students	(AS)
So selling price variance	£139 500F	

As a formula, the variance is:

$$(SSP - ASP) \times AS$$

where SSP is the standard selling price per unit
           ASP is the actual selling price per unit and
           AS   is the actual sales volume in units.

Remember that, for sales, an actual in excess of budget/standard is a favourable variance.

Sales volume variance

This variance indicates the effect on budgeted contribution/gross profit/revenue of differences between the budgeted and actual sales volumes. Before computing this variance for OV Ltd, we must determine the standard contribution and gross profit per student attending the course:

	£	£
Fee per student		450
Direct materials	10	
Direct labour	300	

Variable course overhead	15	
Variable selling overhead	5	330
Contribution per student		120

 What will the standard gross profit per student be?

Gross profit per student is:

	£	£
Fee per student		450
Direct materials	10	
Direct labour	300	
Variable course overhead	15	
Fixed course overhead	25	350
Gross profit per student		100

We can now compute the sales volume variance. Using marginal costing principles, we get:

Budgeted sales volume was	3500 students	(BS)
Actual sales volume was	3100 students	(AS)
Difference in sales volume	400 studentsA	
Standard contribution per student	£120	(SCU)
So sales volume variance	£48 000A	

 What is the sales volume variance based on absorption costing?

In the absorption costing variance, standard gross profit per student replaces standard contribution:

Budgeted sales volume was	3500 students	(BS)
Actual sales volume was	3100 students	(AS)
Difference in sales volume	400 students A	
Standard gross profit per student	£100	(SΠ)
So sales volume variance is	£40 000A	

A third variant of the sales volume variance uses standard selling price per unit:

Budgeted sales volume was	3500 students	(BS)
Actual sales volume was	3100 students	(AS)
Difference in sales volume	400 students A	
Standard selling price per student/course	£450	(SSP)
So sales volume variance is	£180 000A	

You will notice that each version is valued in standard terms: this prevents distortion of the sales volume variance by other variances, i.e. for costs and selling prices.

As a formula, the sales volume variance is:

$$(BS - AS) \times SCU/SΠ/SSP$$

where BS is the budgeted sales volume in units
AS is the actual sales volume in units and

SCU is standard contribution per unit
SΠ   is the standard gross profit per unit and
SSP   is standard selling price per unit.

Of these three approaches, the absorption costing basis is consistent with external reporting requirements for many organisations, but is somewhat distorted by absorption of fixed overheads. The marginal costing basis comes closest to reflecting the cash impact of additional/reduced sales against budget and may be the best approximation of the opportunity cost attaching to lost sales (or opportunity 'benefit' resulting from additional sales). Although the revenue-based sales volume variance excludes all costs in its calculation, it may nevertheless be of great interest to management in assessing factors such as lost/gained market share, or relative competitiveness.

 How might interdependence present a particular problem in relation to the sales volume and selling price variances?

The problem here is **price elasticity of demand** – i.e. the notion that the higher the selling price, the lower the quantity demanded and the lower the selling price, the higher the quantity demanded. In OV Ltd's case, the actual selling price per student/course (£495) exceeds the standard selling price by £45 and it is possible that this may account for the lower-than-budgeted sales volume. So the problem of interdependence may make selling price and sales volume variances especially difficult to interpret.

RECONCILING BUDGETED AND ACTUAL COSTS AND PROFIT

In order to summarise financial control information for the period under review, it is possible to prepare statements ('operating statements') that reconcile budgeted with actual cost, budgeted with actual contribution and budgeted with actual profit. When undertaking such reconciliations, it is necessary to distinguish between marginal costing and absorption costing systems, as the reconciliation statement's format, and the variances to be included, differ between the two. It is also essential that we do not double-count variances: for example, we have calculated total, price and usage variances for materials, and must bear in mind that (price + usage = total) – adding *all three* in our reconciliation would therefore be incorrect.

Cost reconciliation

A statement reconciling OV Ltd's budgeted and actual costs, and prepared using marginal costing principles, is given below:

OV Ltd Reconciliation of budgeted and actual cost	£
Flexible budget variable cost (3100 students × £330)	1 023 000
Flexible budget fixed cost (from Exhibit 20.3)	187 500
Flexible budget total cost	1 210 500

Variances	£F	£A	
Material price	1 275		
Material usage		875	
Labour rate		177 000	
Labour efficiency	45 000		
Variable overhead expenditure		2 050	
Variable overhead efficiency	2 250		
Fixed overhead expenditure	5 500		
Selling cost expenditure		2 300	
Administration cost expenditure		4 000	
	54 025	186 225	132 200A
Actual total cost			1 342 700

The arithmetic accuracy of our reconciliation can be checked using actual costs presented in Exhibit 19.3:

	£
Actual total variable cost	1 156 700
Actual total fixed cost	186 000
Total actual cost	1 342 700

In similar fashion, we can derive the overall variance for total cost given in our reconciliation (£132 200A) from the 'Flexible Budget Variances' column in Exhibit 19.3:

	£
Total flexible budget variance for variable costs	133 700A
Total flexible budget variance for fixed costs	1 500F
Overall variance for total cost	132 200A

In order to reconcile actual and budgeted costs using absorption costing, we need to recognise two key facts about the unit cost (i.e. cost per student for OV Ltd):

1 selling costs are omitted (i.e. 'non-production' costs); and
2 fixed course overhead ('production overhead') is included.

The cost per student is therefore:

Variable 'production' cost per student:

	£
Direct materials	10
Direct labour	300
Course overhead	15
	325
Fixed course overhead per student	25
Cost per student	350

Detailed cost variances are identical to those presented in the marginal costing reconciliation above; for brevity, we have merely shown the totals. However, the absorption costing reconciliation also contains the fixed overhead volume variance:

OV Ltd Reconciliation of budgeted and actual costs

	£
Flexible budget total 'production' cost (3100 students × £350)	1 085 000
Flexible budget total 'non-production' cost (Exhibit 19.3)*	115 500
Flexible budget total cost	1 200 500

Variances	£F	£A	
Total of cost variances from marginal costing reconciliation	54 025	186 225	
Fixed overhead volume variance		10 000	
	54 025	196 225	142 200A
Total actual cost (as before)			1 342 700

*The flexible budget for 'non-production' costs comprises the variable selling cost (£15 500) plus the fixed administration cost (£100 000).

Profit reconciliation

We can undertake the same sort of procedure for budgeted and actual profit, again taking care to distinguish between marginal and absorption costing and ensuring that variances are not double-counted. We also need to remember to include the sales variances. Using marginal costing, the profit reconciliation is as follows:

OV Ltd Reconciliation of budgeted and actual profit

		£
Original (fixed) budget contribution (3500 students @ £120)		420 000
Sales volume variance		48 000A
Flexible budget contribution (3100 students @ £120)		372 000

	£	
Budgeted fixed costs: course overhead	87 500	
administration	100 000	187 500
Flexible budget profit		184 500

Variances	£F	£A	
Selling price	139 500		
Direct material price	1 275		
Direct material usage		875	
Direct labour rate		177 000	
Direct labour efficiency	45 000		
Variable overhead expenditure		2 050	
Variable overhead efficiency	2 250		
Fixed overhead expenditure	5 500		
Selling cost expenditure		2 300	
Administration cost expenditure		4 000	
	193 525	186 225	7 300F
Actual profit (as per Exhibit 19.3)			191 800

Had absorption costing been used, some minor amendment to the presentation above would be necessary:

OV Ltd Reconciliation of budgeted and actual profit

		£
Original (fixed) budget gross profit (3500 students @ £100)		350 000
Sales volume variance		40 000A
Flexible budget gross profit (3100 students @ £95)	£	310 000
Flexible budget selling cost (3100 students @ £5)	15 500	
Budgeted administration overhead	£100 000	115 500
Flexible budget net profit		194 500

Variances	£F	£A
(As in the statement above, *except* the fixed overhead volume variance of £10 000A is included)		
	193 525	196 225	2 700A
Actual profit			191 800

In this particular example, output and sales are the same, so absorption and marginal costing will report the same net profit; but you should bear in mind that, where stock increases or decreases occur during a period, the two systems will yield different net profit figures (see Chapter 12). Changes in stock level can pose something of a problem when reconciling budgeted profit or cost to actual. Look at the additional information presented in Exhibit 19.4.

OV Ltd: purchase and usage of course manuals

Each student on the company's management skills course should be issued with two course manuals; in line with the budgeted number of students (3500), OV Ltd has purchased 7000 manuals. In the event, only 6375 of these were actually used. It is company policy to calculate the materials' price variance on the basis of purchase quantity rather than usage. The standard cost per manual is £5, whilst the actual cost was £4.80. There was no stock of course manuals at the start of the period.

Exhibit 19.4 Additional information about OV Ltd's materials

 Using the formulaic approach, calculate OV Ltd's materials' price variance based on purchase quantity.

Using the purchase quantity, we have a price variance of:

$$(SP - AP) \times AQ$$
$$= (£5.00 - £4.80) \times 7000 = £1400F$$

Inserting this value into the marginal costing version of the profit reconciliation (the absorption costing could equally well have been used), we get:

OV Ltd Reconciliation of budgeted and actual profit

	£	£
Original (fixed) budget contribution (3500 students @ £120)		420 000
Sales volume variance		48 000A
Flexible budget contribution (3100 students @ £120)		372 000
Budgeted fixed costs: course overhead	87 500	
administration	100 000	187 500
Flexible budget profit		184 500

Variances	£F	£A	
Selling price	139 500		
Direct material price	1 400		
Direct material usage		875	
Direct labour rate		177 000	
Direct labour efficiency	45 000		
Variable overhead expenditure		2 050	
Variable overhead efficiency	2 250		
Fixed overhead expenditure	5 500		
Selling cost expenditure		2 300	
Administration cost expenditure		4 000	
	193 650	186 225	7 425F
'Actual profit'			191 925

But we know from Exhibit 19.3 that actual profit was £191 800.

 Can you explain the £125 discrepancy in actual profit in the reconciliation statement above?

The £125 discrepancy arises because of the increase in stock of materials in conjunction with the fact that the price variance has been calculated on purchase quantity. There were no course manuals in stock at the start of the period, but $(7000 - 6375) = 625$ at the end. If you look at Exhibit 19.3, you will see that actual profit is determined after deduction of the actual cost of manuals *used* in the period; the cost of closing stock is carried forward to next period – normal accounting practice. However, some of the price variance we just calculated (and wrote off against profit in our reconciliation statement) relates to the closing stock. In order to arrive at a true reconciliation of budgeted and actual profit, we must eliminate that element of the price variance which relates to the increase in stock:

$$(SP - AP) \times \text{stock increase} = (£5.00 - £4.80) \times 625 = £125F$$

£125F being the profit discrepancy noted above. Thus, sound cost control dictates purchases as the basis of the price variance, whereas for profit reconciliation purposes, we are effectively forced to employ quantity used. This process of apportioning variances between cost of sales and stocks is termed **pro-ration of variances**. For OV Ltd, it was a fairly straightforward matter, being limited to materials only. For a manufacturing business, which is likely to have stocks of work-in-progress and finished goods in addition to materials, pro-ration is likely to be rather more complex. Not only would the material price variance need to be pro-rated between cost of sales and stock (as with OV Ltd), but all the other cost variances would require pro-ration between cost of sales, units in finished goods stock and equivalent units in work-in-progress.

But the potential complication posed by the need to pro-rate variances need not automatically invalidate their value as a financial control device. Use of computer spreadsheets will greatly ease the associated burden of computation and, with the increasing use of just-in-time (JIT) systems involving zero or minimal stock-holdings, there is likely to be a corresponding decrease in the need for pro-ration.

STANDARD COSTING CONTROL RATIOS

Management may wish to make comparisons of performance – say over time, or between different departments, cost centres, products and services. Although variances of the sort we have been calculating might be used for this purpose, such use could also result in misleading information being given to managers.

 Why might performance comparisons based on variances be misleading?

As we saw in the previous chapter, one problem with variances – whether they be budget variances or the more detailed variety encountered in this chapter – is assessing how material they are: i.e. is a particular variance sufficiently large to warrant investigation? This question cannot be answered without reference to some benchmark – typically the flexible budget. Making performance comparisons based on variances unsupported by other information would therefore be fraught with difficulty. Standard costing control ratios aim to address this difficulty in the areas of volume, efficiency and capacity. And, since they are all based on hours, rather than units, standard costing control ratios can provide a useful 'global' performance measure for organisations that produce multiple products/services. Certain data relating to OV Ltd's operations is reproduced in Exhibit 19.5 in order to allow us to calculate these ratios.

OV Ltd: standard costing control ratios

For the company's management skills course, budgeted, standard and actual information is as follows:

Budgeted number of students taking the course	3500
Actual number of students taking the course	3100
Standard direct labour time per student	20 hours
Actual direct labour-hours worked	59 000

Exhibit 19.5 Data for calculation of standard costing control ratios

Volume ratio

This ratio is roughly equivalent to the fixed overhead volume variance, and expresses actual output as a percentage of budgeted output. The difference between the ratio and the variance is that the ratio expresses output in *standard hours*, rather than in units. You will recall from Chapter 16 that the standard hour is a measure of the work that should be performed in one hour at standard efficiency; it is not a measure of time.

The volume ratio is calculated as:

$$\frac{\text{Standard hours produced}}{\text{Budgeted standard hours}} \times 100\%$$

 Bearing in mind that standard hours produced is (actual output × standard hours per unit of output), determine OV Ltd's volume ratio from the data in Exhibit 19.5.

OV Ltd's volume ratio is:

$$\frac{(3100 \text{ students} \times 20 \text{ hours per student})}{(3500 \text{ students} \times 20 \text{ hours per student})} \times 100\%$$

$$= \frac{62\,000 \text{ standard hours}}{70\,000 \text{ standard hours}} \times 100\% = 88.57\%$$

In other words, the actual volume of courses provided represents 88.57% of the budgeted volume.

Capacity ratio

This ratio is somewhat similar to the fixed overhead capacity variance, and reflects the extent to which budgeted capacity was actually used. It is calculated as:

$$\frac{\text{Actual hours worked}}{\text{Budgeted standard hours}} \times 100\%$$

For OV Ltd, we get:

$$\frac{59\,000 \text{ hours}}{(3500 \text{ students} \times 20 \text{ hours per student})} \times 100\% = \frac{59\,000}{70\,000} \times 100\% = 84.29\%$$

Thus, 84.29% of budgeted capacity was used during the period. You should note that the capacity ratio assumes budgeted capacity to be the same as maximum capacity. In practice, this is unlikely to be strictly correct. Budgeted capacity is typically what management believes to be attainable during the budget period, and is unlikely to be the same as theoretical maximum capacity.

Efficiency ratio

Also referred to as the **productivity ratio**, this reflects the efficiency of actual hours worked, and is calculated as:

$$\frac{\text{Standard hours produced}}{\text{Actual hours worked}} \times 100\%$$

From Exhibit 19.5, OV Ltd's efficiency ratio is

$$\frac{(3100 \text{ students} \times 20 \text{ hours per student})}{59\,000 \text{ hours}} \times 100\% = \frac{62\,000}{59\,000} \times 100\% = 105.08\%$$

 What does the productivity ratio of 105.08% indicate?

Since it exceeds 100%, OV Ltd's productivity ratio indicates that labour efficiency for the period was better than standard, and this is consistent with the favourable efficiency variances we calculated earlier.

Like the fixed overhead volume, capacity and efficiency variances, there is an arithmetical relationship between the ratios which approximate to them:

$$\text{volume ratio} = (\text{capacity ratio} \times \text{efficiency ratio})$$

Checking OV Ltd's ratios in this way gives:

$$88.57\% = (84.29\% \times 105.08\%)$$

OV Ltd's control ratios therefore paint the same picture of performance as their equivalent variances, except here, the information is presented in non-financial terms: while efficiency was better than standard, volume of output and usage of capacity were both below budget.

Though they can provide useful information, you will appreciate that the control ratios we have examined deal with performance in a much narrower way than our analysis of budget variances.

VARIANCE ANALYSIS: REINFORCING SOME GENERAL PROBLEMS?

Potential for dysfunctional decisions

The main reason for undertaking the kind of detailed variance analysis which we have been describing is to help pinpoint potential problem areas in order to enhance control action and possibly identify managerial 'responsibility'. While this may work perfectly well, there might be a risk that overemphasising the 'responsibility' aspect of budget subvariances could backfire in the form of dysfunctional decisions by managers.

Suppose, for example, that OV Ltd's Administration Department has responsibility for the material price variance (i.e. for purchase of course manuals) and that the Course Leader has responsibility for the usage variance. We have already seen that these two variances may be interdependent – i.e. that purchase of cheaper-than-standard materials (resulting in a favourable price variance) may result in an adverse usage variance (due, e.g. to poorer quality materials). The problem with linking detailed variances to managerial responsibility is that this may encourage (or may 'pressure') managers into taking decisions which optimise the variance(s) for which they are 'responsible' but which have an adverse effect on other managers' areas of responsibility, and on the organisation as a whole. Thus OV Ltd's Administration Department may purchase cheaper-than-standard course manuals as a matter of optimising the price variance, but at the expense of an adverse usage variance when these same manuals come to be issued to students attending the course.

Problems of this sort may be addressed by ensuring that managers are aware of the wider implications of their actions (as would be the case with a total quality management philosophy), or by placing less emphasis on the 'control' and 'responsibility' aspects of variances and more on their role as an *aid* to management. In some cases, interdependencies between budget subvariances may be so intricate that their report and investigation fails the cost/benefit test.

Interpretation and investigation of variances

As we mentioned at the start of this chapter, variances are indicative, but not conclusive; as a minimum, all significant variances should be investigated to establish likely cause and/or learn lessons. As well as the question of interdependence, this raises several issues which we discussed in detail in the previous chapter, but which are important enough to warrant repetition in summary here:

1 defining what constitutes a 'significant' variance;
2 assessing the impact on variances of random factors;
3 making allowance for the effect of inflation, especially in volatile areas, such as some raw material markets;
4 controllability of certain budget lines and their associated variances;
5 impact of measurement errors;
6 risk of stressing financial performance and control to the detriment or even exclusion of non-financial considerations;
7 means–end confusion.

All the concerns listed above are relevant to any form of variance analysis regardless of level of detail, but the last two difficulties may be aggravated by reporting budget subvariances. The potential danger is that detailed calculations of the type we have just been undertaking may imply a spurious degree of controllability (e.g. overhead expenditure variances) and in no way reflect important factors such as quality of product/service. You will recall that we made this point in Chapter 18 when we compared an inwardly focused financial control system with an outward-looking, market-oriented **target costing** approach.

You should also bear in mind the potential weaknesses of standard costing which we discussed in Chapter 16 (all of which have a bearing on variance analysis). In particular, there is always the possibility of error in the standards themselves giving rise to some or all of the variances reported. Where this happens to any significant extent, managers may waste valuable time investigating variances which are due to planning error, rather than to operational factors. In some cases, incorrect control action may result from reporting such variances. This problem could be overcome by further analysing budget variances into those which arise due to error/inaccuracy in the standards ('planning variances') and those which are caused by operational factors ('operational variances'). The rationale for this further analysis is that management should concentrate their immediate control activities on the latter category of variance, with the former being used to improve future planning efforts. One danger of this approach is that the system could become unduly complex, and cause confusion to those whom it is intended to help. (See Further Reading for additional discussion of this topic).

Misdirected emphasis?

When analysing OV Ltd's budget variances, we calculated labour rate and efficiency variances; reporting these variances might be appropriate in OV's situation, where labour costs form a significant part of the budget, but for many organisations, labour costs are of far less importance relative to materials, machine and technology costs. Reporting detailed variances for labour or for any other costs which are comparatively immaterial could attach a 'weight' to them which they do not possess. This may, in turn, result in cost control or cost reduction effort which is misplaced in the context of organisations which are highly automated and which operate in highly competitive and increasingly 'global' markets. For example, adverse labour variances could be seen as suggestive of a 'quick fix' for cost problems, whereas a better solution in strategic terms may lie elsewhere. As Doyle (1994) puts it:

Many corporate experts watching the events of the past decade are now convinced that the effort expended in appraising activities, devising downsizing plans and implementing them is misdirected. Their main fear is that company heads are being distracted by direct labour costs and in-house efficiencies to the detriment of what it really takes to be competitive in today's markets.

Standard costs and budget subvariances may have the effect of concentrating managerial attention on immediate and internal concerns (at the expense of strategic and external), simply because of their level of detail and 'demand' for speedy response. For example, highlighting comparison of actual costs with internally generated standards may obscure the need to compete in cost terms with external organisations operating in the same market.

As we suggested in the previous chapter, a strict interpretation of total quality management, with its emphasis on customer satisfaction, 'getting it right first time' and continuous improvement, would view the very existence of a standard costing and variance analysis system having an inbuilt allowance for anticipated inefficiencies as irrelevant (at best) or harmful (at worst).

Variance analysis has the potential to misdirect managerial attention in another way. Being essentially retrospective in nature, it could be detrimental to control at the design stage of products/services – encouraging the belief that design errors can somehow be rectified by addressing resultant variances. This may be of especial significance in organisations which employ advanced manufacturing technology (AMT): in this sort of environment, the major 'standard' is technological specification. Similarly, we suggested in Chapter 16 that one advantage of setting standards might be use of improved methods/materials; but the opposite may equally be true – that standard setting, with its 'after-the-event' control philosophy could induce an unhealthy rigidity in planning and design of products/services. For example, substitutability and flexibility of resource inputs might be subordinated to the short-term need for a minimum-cost solution.

Responsiveness to sudden change

Sudden and unforeseen changes in an organisation's operational environment may cause difficulty in the operation of a system of standard costing and variance analysis, and may increase pressure on managers to react to financial control measures in a dysfunctional manner. Suppose, for example, that volume of output must be increased to meet a quite unexpected upsurge in demand: meeting such an increase in demand may be in the long-term interest of the organisation (if sustained), but may give rise to adverse variances in the short term.

 How might a sudden, unexpected increase in demand give rise to adverse variances?

If the rise in demand is sufficiently large, additional resources will be required, almost certainly at short notice: e.g. labour may need to work overtime and emergency orders for materials placed with suppliers. There is a strong likelihood that acquiring resources at short notice will attract a penalty such as premium payments for overtime working and increased material purchase costs. Such penalties will not have been included in the determination of standards for labour and materials, thus giving rise to adverse variances. In other words, the very need to respond to a dynamic environment may give rise to adverse variances; reporting variances which arise due to this kind of situation raises two issues:

1 to what extent are the variances genuinely controllable? and
2 what is the likelihood of such variances prompting inappropriate responses from management (e.g. failure to react to a change in demand because of adverse short-term consequences)?

If there is a danger that detailed variance analysis might inhibit managerial action, then we have another argument either for a more flexible approach or for a more radical solution, such as adoption of the planning/operational variance methodology or even complete abandonment.

SUMMARY

Our discussion of variance analysis suggests that it may be a useful tool, but that it may also aggravate certain potential weaknesses of 'conventional' financial control mechanisms; care is therefore needed if its use is to enhance, rather than hinder, managerial and organisational activity. We have seen that:

- Budget variances, because of their 'global' nature, may mask important aspects of performance which merit investigation.

- Analysis of budget variances requires the existence of a standard costing system.

- A formulaic approach to variance analysis gives the following:

Materials	Flexible budget variance	$([AO \times SMCU] - TAMC)$
	Price variance	$(SP - AP) \times AQ$
	Usage variance	$(SQ - AQ) \times SP$
Labour	Flexible budget variance	$([AO \times SLCU] - TALC)$
	Rate variance	$(SR - AR) \times AH$
	Efficiency variance	$(SH - AH) \times SR$
Variable overhead	Flexible budget variance	$([AO \times SVOU] - AVO)$
	Expenditure variance	$([AH \times SVOH] - AVO)$
	Efficiency variance	$(SH - AH) \times SVOH$
Fixed overhead	Total variance	$([AO \times FOPU] - AFO)$
	Expenditure variance	$(BFO - AFO)$
	Volume variance	$(BO - AO) \times FOPU$
	Efficiency variance	$(SH - AH) \times FOPH$
	Capacity variance	$(BH - AH) \times FOPH$
Sales	Selling price variance	$(SSP - ASP) \times AS$
	Sales volume variance	$(BS - AS) \times S\Pi/SCU/SSP$

- Operating statements can be prepared to reconcile budgeted and actual cost and profit based on marginal or absorption costing principles.

- In a marginal costing system, there are no variances for total fixed overhead or fixed overhead volume, and the sales volume variance is based on standard unit contribution.

▶

- Standard costing control ratios may be useful for making performance comparisons.
- The volume ratio is

$$\frac{\text{Standard hours produced}}{\text{Budgeted standard hours}} \times 100\%$$

- The capacity ratio is

$$\frac{\text{Actual hours worked}}{\text{Budgeted hours}} \times 100\%$$

- The efficiency (productivity) ratio is

$$\frac{\text{Standard hours produced}}{\text{Actual hours worked}} \times 100\%$$

- In addition to the potential weaknesses of standard costing and budget variances described in Chapters 16 and 18, detailed variance analysis may

  - increase the chance of dysfunctional decisions by managers
  - have a large element of interdependence and pose problems in interpretation and investigation
  - misdirect managerial attention, especially in the context of a total quality environment
  - cause problems in a dynamic environment.

In the next chapter, we will discuss standard cost bookkeeping systems, illustrating the accounting disposition of the different variances we have been calculating.

FURTHER READING

Brown, G., Standard costing – a status check. *ACCA Students' Newsletter*, March 1999.

Doyle, D., *Cost Control A Strategic Guide*, CIMA, 1994: this book places cost control in its strategic perspective.

Ezzamel, M. and Hart, H., *Advanced Management Accounting, An Organisational Emphasis*, Cassell, 1992: Chapter 14 contains a discussion of more advanced aspects of standard costing and variance analysis.

Upchurch, A., *Management Accounting Principles and Practice*, Financial Times Pitman Publishing, 1998: see Chapter 14 for further discussion of planning and operational variances.

SELF-TEST QUESTIONS

19.1 For each of the following statements, tick the appropriate box to indicate whether it is true or false.

	True	False
(a) If actual output is lower than budgeted output, the fixed overhead volume variance will be favourable.	☐	☐
(b) Where variable overhead varies with direct labour hours, an efficiency variance may be calculated for this cost.	☐	☐
(c) An adverse fixed overhead total variance indicates an underabsorption of overhead.	☐	☐
(d) Expressing the sales volume variance in revenue terms provides the best approximation to the cash effect involved.	☐	☐
(e) In a marginal costing system, only the fixed overhead expenditure variance is calculated.	☐	☐
(f) Actual material losses which are unexpected will have a favourable impact on the usage variance.	☐	☐

19.2 APF Ltd's standard absorption costing system reported the following fixed overhead variances last month:

 total variance £16 000 A volume variance £7000F

What was the company's fixed overhead expenditure variance for the month?

A £9000A
B £9000F
C £23 000F
D £23 000A

19.3 The Alternative Burger chain operates a group of burger restaurants specialising in unusual tastes and flavours. One of their best-selling lines is the Upside-Down burger containing kangaroo meat. Because of the high volumes and closely specified recipes and procedures, they are considering the use of standard costing and variance analysis.

Contents of a cooked, ready-to-eat Upside-Down Burger:

 1 bun
 110 grams meat and herb mix
 55 grams buffalo cheese
 25 grams relish

It is company policy to guarantee the cooked weight of meat to be a minimum of 110 grams. There is a 20% loss of meat weight during cooking. Losses due to accidental damage, dropped burgers etc. are estimated to be 3% of completed burgers.

Anticipated prices of raw materials for the next period are:

Buns	4.5p each
Meat and herb mix	£2.80 per kg
Buffalo cheese	£4.00 per kg
Relish	£1.40 per kg

Requirements:

(a) Prepare the standard material cost of one Upside-Down Burger. **(8 marks)**

(b) As an experiment, it has been decided to calculate the variances relating to the main ingredient (the kangaroo meat and herb mix) for one of the branches. The following data are available:

49 725 burgers sold.
Usage of meat and herb mix: 7368 kg at a cost of £20 262
There were no opening or closing stocks.

Calculate the price and usage variances for the meat and herb mix. What information do these variances convey? **(7 marks)**
(Total: 15 marks)

(CIMA, *Cost Accounting and Quantitative Methods*, May 1998)

19.4 T Rubble plc manufactures a cat basket which sells for £30. A standard costing system is in operation and the standard cost card for one basket is given below:

STANDARD COST CARD

Direct materials:	Wicker	0.4 kg at £2 per kg
	Padding	0.5 kg at £3 per kg
Direct labour:	Assembly	2 hours at £6.50 per hour
	Finishing	1 hour at £5.00 per hour

T Rubble expected output to be 5000 baskets for a month, and profit on each basket is expected to be £5 (after taking into account the overhead costs).

The following table shows actual results for the month:

Actual output	5100 baskets	
Direct materials:	Wicker	2070 kg (costing £4200)
	Padding	2500 kg (costing £7400)
Direct labour:	Assembly	10 250 hours at £6.60 per hour
	Finishing	5050 hours at £4.90 per hour

The actual selling price of each basket was £32.

Requirements:

(a) Calculate the materials, labour and sales variances. **(15 marks)**

(b) Suggest possible reasons for the variances found in part (a). **(5 marks)**
(Total: 20 marks)

(CIPFA, *Management Accounting*, December 1996)

19.5 Goblin Limited manufactures a variety of garden ornaments which are made from resin in a moulding machine and coloured with special paint. The machine is semi-automated and it can make different ornaments in batches which each take half a day to process. Goblin Limited has a reporting system of thirteen four-week periods; 40 batches are scheduled for each period. Two workers are required to operate the machine. They work a standard 40-hour week with occasional Saturday working at double rates of pay.

The standard cost of a batch is set out below.

		£
Direct materials	resin – 25 litres	100
	paint – 1 litre	18
Direct labour	8 hours	28
Variable overheads	8 hours*	36
Fixed overheads	8 hours*	160
Total standard cost		342

* All overheads are allocated to production using standard labour hours. Forty-four batches were produced during period five, and the actual costs incurred are set out below.

		£
Direct materials	resin – 1130 litres	4 463.50
	paint – 46 litres	920.00
Direct labour	352 hours	1 344.00
Variable overheads		1 660.00
Fixed overheads		6 200.00
		14 587.50

Requirements:

(a) An operating statement for Goblin Limited for period five which reconciles budgeted cost with actual cost, and shows appropriate cost variances for operations management.

(15 marks)

(a) Comment on the performance of Goblin Limited in period five. **(10 marks)**

(Total: 25 marks)

(ACCA, *Paper D2 Management Accounting*, June 1998)

QUESTIONS WITHOUT ANSWERS

19.6 The following details relate to product T, which has a selling price of £44.00:

	£/unit
Direct materials	15.00
Direct labour (3 hours)	12.00
Variable overhead	6.00
Fixed overhead	4.00
	37.00

During April 1996, the actual production of T was 800 units, which was 100 units fewer than budgeted. The budget shows an annual production target of 10 800, with fixed costs accruing at a constant rate throughout the year.

Actual overhead expenditure totalled £8500 for April 1996.

The overhead variances for April 1996 were:

	Expenditure	Volume
	£	£
A	367A	1000A
B	500A	400A
C	100A	1000A
D	367A	400A
E	100A	400A

(CIMA, *Operational Cost Accounting*, May 1996)

19.7 Demeo plc produces and sells one product, Testers. The following sales and direct costs have been budgeted, based on standard costs, for a period as shown below:

		£
Sales	50 000 units at £10 per unit	500 000
Direct labour	10 000 hours at £3 per hour	30 000
Direct materials	55 000 units at £4 per unit	220 000
Sales – direct costs		250 000

There was no increase or decrease in stocks in the period.

In the actual period, 55 000 units of Testers were sold for a total of £522 500. This was explained by the Sales Manager as being the result of a successful strategy to increase net contribution by increasing sales and reducing sales price.

Actual total costs of labour rose to £38 700. This included 1500 hours extra overtime paid at a premium rate and worked at a cost of £7200, and there were no variations in basic labour hours. The Production Manager has alleged that the extra production is the only reason for the increase in labour cost over the standard.

Actual materials used in the period were 3000 units higher than budgeted at a total cost of £237 800. The Production Manager has alleged that the difference from standard is due to higher costs of purchase of raw materials.

Requirements:

(a) Calculate all the sales, labour and material variances for the period.   **(12 marks)**

(b) Comment on the plausibility of the explanations and statements offered in respect of the variances.   **(8 marks)**
     (Total: 20 marks)

(CIPFA, *Management Accounting*, December 1997)

19.8 One of the departments of Leather Limited manufactures leather briefcases. The standard cost schedule applicable for April 1998 is set out below.

Standard cost schedule per briefcase
(assuming monthly production of 640 items)

		£
Leather	0.7 square metres at £30 per square metre	21.00
Set of buckles etc.		2.50
Labour	2 hours at £16 per hour	32.00
Variable overheads*	2 hours at £2 per hour	4.00
Fixed overheads*	2 hours at £6 per hour	12.00
Total standard cost		71.50
Margin		23.50
Selling price		95.00

* Overheads are allocated on the basis of standard labour hours.

The actual figures for April 1998 are set out below. There were no changes in stock levels.

		£	£
Sales	700 briefcases		63 000
	Less expenses		
	Leather: 525 square metres	16 800	
	Buckles etc.: 710 sets	1 420	

Labour: 1350 hours	22 275	
Variable overheads	2 600	
Fixed overheads	8 000	51 095
Profit for April		11 905

Requirements:

(a) Prepare an operating statement for the briefcase department for April 1998 showing two variances for each category. **(15 marks)**

(a) Submit a report to the plant manager assessing the performance of the briefcase department, noting where further information is needed to complete this assessment of performance. **(10 marks)**

(Total: 25 marks)

(ACCA, *Paper D2 Management Accounting*, December 1998)

19.9 The following profit reconciliation statement summarises the performance of one of SEW's products for March 1997:

	£
Budgeted profit	4250
Sales volume variance	850A
Standard profit on actual sales	3400
Selling price variance	4000A
	(600)

Cost variances:	Adverse	Favourable	
	£	£	
Direct material price		1000	
Direct material usage	150		
Direct labour rate	200		
Direct labour efficiency	150		
Variable overhead expenditure	600		
Variable overhead efficiency	75		
Fixed overhead expenditure		2500	
Fixed overhead volume		150	
	1175	3650	2475F
Actual profit			1875

The budget for the same period contained the following data:

Sales volume		1500 units
Sales revenue	£20 000	
Production volume		1500 units
Direct materials purchased		750 kg
Direct materials used		750 kg
Direct material cost	£4500	
Direct labour-hours		1125
Direct labour cost	£4500	
Variable overhead cost	£2250	
Fixed overhead cost	£4500	

Additional information:

- stocks of raw materials and finished goods are valued at standard cost;

● during the month the actual number of units produced was 1550;
● the actual sales revenue was £12 000; and
● the direct materials purchased were 1000 kg.

Requirements:

(a) Calculate

(i)   the actual sales volume
(ii)   the actual quantity of materials used;
(iii) the actual direct material cost;
(iv) the actual direct labour hours;
(v)   the actual direct labour cost;
(vi) the actual variable overhead cost;
(vii) the actual fixed overhead cost.   **(19 marks)**

(b) Explain the possible causes of the direct materials usage variance, direct labour rate variance, and sales volume variance.   **(6 marks)**
                                                                        (Total: 25 marks)

(CIMA, *Operational Cost Accounting*, May 1997)

19.10   A labour-intensive production unit operating a standard absorption cost accounting system provides the following information for period 10:

Normal capacity, in direct labour hours	9600
Budgeted variable production overhead	£3 per direct labour-hour
Budgeted fixed production overhead per four-week financial period	£120 000

To produce one unit takes two hours of working.
Actual figures for the four-week period 10 were:

Production, in units	5000
Variable production overhead incurred	£28 900
Fixed production overhead incurred	£118 000
Actual direct labour hours worked	9300

Requirements:

(a) To calculate the variances for

(i)   variable production overhead expenditure;
(ii)   variable production overhead efficiency;
(iii) fixed production overhead expenditure;
(iv) fixed production overhead volume;   **(8 marks)**

(b) Subdivide your volume variance for (a)(iv) above into two subvariances and explain the meaning of these in the form of a brief report to management.   **(7 marks)**
                                                                        (Total: 15 marks)

(CIMA, *Cost Accounting*, November 1992)

CHAPTER 20

Standard cost bookkeeping

Backflush cost accounting

The following CIMA Terminology definition is developed by Hammer *et al.* (1994). They emphasise that it is a workable way of cost accumulation in a very fast moving manufacturing environment.

'A method of costing, associated with a JIT (Just in Time) production system, which applies cost to the output of a process. Costs do not mirror the flow of products through the production process, but are attached to output produced i.e. finished goods stock and cost of sales, on the assumption that such backflushed costs are a realistic measure of the actual costs incurred.'

... This method is in marked contrast to traditional product cost accounting, which starts with the raw material and works forward, adding and absorbing costs as the process progresses ...

Advocates of this method argue that it reflects the reality of the production process rather than relying on a financial accounting/score keeping driven system. By eliminating the extensive yet repetitive exercises of cost allocation, apportionment and absorption, the score keeping system is simplified. A further advantage is that the resultant accounting system is more attention directing and as such, more useful in decision making and control ...

Source: Mark Lee Inman, *ACCA Students' Newsletter*, November 1997.

Exhibit 20.1 An attempt to simplify bookkeeping procedures?

INTRODUCTION

In the previous chapter, we saw how budget variances may be subdivided as an aid to more effective financial control. We now combine this material with that presented in Chapter 7 to illustrate how such information may be incorporated within an organisation's accounting ledger. We will also examine the application of standard costing techniques to process costing and see that this requires some amendment to the procedures used in an actual costing situation, (discussed in Chapter 9). Finally, we will look at the backflush costing approach described in Exhibit 20.1, and discover how this method could simplify our bookkeeping.

OBJECTIVES

When you have completed this chapter, you will be able to:

- post the accounts within an integrated system, incorporating standard costs and variances for materials, labour and overhead;
- post the accounts within an interlocking system, incorporating the same information as above;
- prepare journal entries for a standard cost bookkeeping system;
- calculate variances and post the WIP account within a standard process costing system;
- appreciate the principles of backflush costing and apply these to simple scenarios;
- explain the strengths and weaknesses of backflush costing.

STANDARD COST BOOKKEEPING

Before working through the example that follows, you might like to review the basic cost bookkeeping procedures we described in Chapter 7. Regardless of whether an integrated or interlocking system is in use, introduction of standard costs and variances basically involves grafting an additional set of double-entries onto those recording actual costs which we encountered in the earlier chapter. We will use the information in Exhibit 20.2 to illustrate how this is achieved – initially within an integrated ledger, then within an interlocking system.

Integrated standard cost ledger

You will remember (from Chapter 7) that, in an integrated ledger, cost accounting and financial accounting information is recorded within a single, unified system.

NCS Ltd: integrated standard cost ledger

The company manufactures UPVC mouldings for double-glazing units. These mouldings are produced and sold in batches of 10 10-metre lengths, which NCS Ltd's customers (manufacturers of double-glazing units) then cut to size as required for individual windows, doors etc. The following standard information applies to NCS Ltd's operations in March:

Standard per batch		£	£
Selling price			120
Direct materials	105 metres @ £0.20	21	
Direct labour	2 hours @ £7.00	14	
Variable overhead	2 hours @ £7.50	15	
Fixed overhead		20	70
Gross profit			50

The fixed overhead absorption rate is based on budgeted production volume of 4500 batches for the month.

Budgeted sales for March: 4200 batches.
   Actual transactions for March
   Direct materials: purchased, 500 000 metres, total cost £90 000; issued to production
                      466 000 metres

Gross direct wages   9600 hours, total cost £69 120
Gross indirect wages   £14 200 (fixed overhead)
PAYE tax £18 200   Employees' NI contributions £5200
                       Employers' NI contributions £5400 (fixed overhead)
Variable overhead expenses (all credit) £64 000
Fixed overhead: expenses (credit) £57 400; depreciation £16 000.
Payments made to creditors for materials £105 000
Sales (all credit) 4000 batches, total revenue £500 000   Production 4700 batches
Completed output transferred to Finished Goods 4300 batches

At the beginning of March, the following balances existed in the company's accounts:

Raw materials	£12 000	Creditors' control	£42 000
WIP	£35 000		
Finished goods	£70 000		

It is company policy to value all stocks at standard cost.

Exhibit 20.2 Data for posting integrated ledger

As a simplification, we will work at Control Account level, though you will remember from Chapter 7 that these accounts represent the sum of transactions posted to individual accounts within different areas of the ledger. However, this simplification in no way affects the basic double-entries involved. Similarly, we will omit some accounts that are not affected by the variances and which will appear exactly as they did in Chapter 7. Before we can post the ledger for March, we need to calculate the appropriate variances following the method described in the previous chapter (which you might wish to review at this point).

 From Exhibit 20.2, what is the appropriate 'actual quantity' to use in calculation of the material price variance?

As we saw in the previous chapter, the material price variance should be based on the purchase quantity, so that the price variance can be identified at the earliest point in the trading cycle, thus enabling timely control action should a significant variance emerge. There may be a time lag between purchase and use – identification of the price variance at the latter time may mean that it is too late to take any sort of effective control action in response to the variance. NCS Ltd's variances for March are:

Material price variance $(SP - AP) \times AQ$

$$\left(£0.20 - \frac{£90\,000}{500\,000}\right) \times 500\,000 \text{ metres} = £10\,000\text{F}$$

Material usage variance $(SQ - AQ) \times SP$
Remember that 'standard quantity' is the standard quantity allowed for actual production.

$$([4700 \text{ batches} \times 105 \text{ metres}] - 466\,000 \text{ metres}) \times £0.20 = £5500\text{F}$$

Labour rate variance (SR – AR) × AH

$$\left(£7.00 - \frac{£69\,120}{9600}\right) \times 9600 \text{ hours} = £1920\text{A}$$

Labour efficiency variance (SH – AH) × SR
'Standard hours' should be the hours allowed for actual output.

$$([4700 \text{ batches} \times 2 \text{ hours}] - 9600 \text{ hours}) \times £7.00 = £1400\text{A}$$

Variable overhead expenditure variance ([AH × SVOH] – AVO)

$$([9600 \times £7.50] - £64\,000) = £8000\text{F}$$

Variable overhead efficiency variance (SH – AH) × SVOH

$$([4700 \text{ batches} \times 2 \text{ hours}] - 9600 \text{ hours}) \times £7.50 = £1500\text{A}$$

Fixed overhead expenditure variance (BFO – AFO)

 Determine the amount of budgeted fixed overhead for March.

Budgeted fixed overhead is: (budgeted production × fixed overhead per batch)

$$= (4500 \text{ batches} \times £20) = £90\,000$$

Actual fixed overhead (from Exhibit 20.2):

	£
Expenses	57 400
Depreciation	16 000
Indirect wages	14 200
Employers' NI contributions	5 400
	93 000

This gives an expenditure variance of:

$$(£90\,000 - £93\,000) = £3000\text{A}$$

Fixed overhead volume variance (BO – AO) × FOPU

$$(4500 \text{ batches} - 4700 \text{ batches}) \times £20 = £4000\text{F}$$

Bear in mind that this variance is favourable when actual exceeds budget.

 We have not calculated flexible budget (total) variances for materials, labour and variable overhead, nor a total variance for fixed overhead. Why?

As we saw in the previous chapter, the total variances are merely aggregates of the subvariances for each cost element. Calculating total variances in addition to the subvariances would therefore mean that we are double-counting.

When posting the ledger, the fundamental rules of double-entry apply, as they did when we dealt with actual cost ledgers in Chapter 7. In addition, we will need to open an account for each variance calculated above. Within the ledger, variances are dealt with as follows:

- Adverse variances: credit the account of origin, debit the variance account.
- Favourable variances: debit the account of origin, credit the variance account.
- At the end of the accounting period, transfer the balance on variance accounts to the profit and loss account. Since these accounting records are for internal use, the relevant accounting period is the budgetary control period (see Chapter 18) – typically four weeks or one calendar month.

We will start our posting for NCS Ltd with raw materials.

Raw materials

As we saw in Chapter 7, purchases are credited to the appropriate creditor account (Creditors' Control in this case), with the payment made during March being a debit.

Creditors' Control Account

	£		£
Bank	105 000	Balance b/fwd	42 000
Balance c/fwd	27 000	Raw Materials' Control (purchases)	90 000
	132 000		132 000
		Balance b/fwd	27 000

The Raw Materials' Control Account is debited with the actual cost of purchases and also with the material price variance (favourable). The effect of these two debits is that the Materials' Control Account has now been charged with the standard cost of actual purchases: (500 000 metres @ £0.20). Issues of materials to Work-in-Progress are credited to the Raw Materials Control Account at (actual quantity × standard cost per metre).

Raw Materials' Control Account

	£		£
Balance b/fwd	12 000	WIP Control	
Creditors' Control (purchases)	90 000	(466 000 metres @ £0.20)	93 200
Material price variance	10 000	Balance c/fwd	18 800
	112 000		112 000
Balance b/fwd	18 800		

The closing balance of £18 800 is thus stated at standard cost. Finally, we credit the Material Price Variance Account and, at the end of the period, transfer its balance to the Profit and Loss Account.

Material Price Variance Account

	£		£
Profit and Loss Account	10 000	Raw Materials' Control	10 000

Valuing stocks at standard cost avoids the need for stores valuation methods like First-in–First-out, Last-in–First-out or Average Cost (see Chapter 4), which might simplify costing procedures, especially where numerous materials are involved. Use of standard cost also means that fluctuations in actual material cost are not reflected in the cost of output, which could ease decisions like external price-setting (if price is based on cost). However, in the UK, standard cost is not a permissible method of stock valuation for published accounts; so where a company uses standard cost for internal purposes, this will need to be adjusted to actual for published accounts. Such an adjustment might be effected through a Stock Adjustment Account; while not of itself a particularly difficult procedure, it does add extra steps to the bookkeeping, which might increase the possibility of error. A further potential drawback of standard cost as a stock valuation basis occurs where material prices are especially volatile. Here, there is a danger that the standard may become seriously out of line with reality, causing material stocks and issues to production to be significantly over- or undercosted.

Wages

The Wages Control Account is debited with actual net wages paid plus all wage deductions; the account is credited with the labour rate variance and with actual direct labour hours at standard rate per hour (see Chapter 7). Gross indirect wages are credited at actual cost: any difference between this and standard will be reflected in the fixed overhead variances (extracted in the Fixed Overhead Control Account).

Net wages paid in March are:

		£	£
Gross:	direct wages		69 120
	indirect wages		14 200
			83 320
Less:	PAYE tax	18 200	
	Employees' NI	5 200	23 400
	Net wages paid		59 920

Remember that Employers' NI contributions do not pass through the Wages Control Account – they are treated as overhead (fixed overhead in this example).

Wages Control Account

	£		£
PAYE tax	18 200	Labour rate variance	1 920
Employees' NI contributions	5 200	WIP Control (9600 hours @ £7)	67 200
Bank (net wages paid)	59 920	Fixed Overhead Control	14 200
	83 320		83 320

The Labour Rate Variance Account (including the month-end transfer of the variance to Profit and Loss) is:

Labour Rate Variance Account

	£		£
Wages Control Account	1 920	Profit and Loss Account	1 920

Variable overhead

The Variable Overhead Control Account is debited with the actual cost and with the expenditure variance (favourable); WIP is charged with (actual hours × standard variable overhead rate per hour).

✔ *Should we credit the Variable Overhead Control Account with the adverse variable overhead efficiency variance?*

The variable overhead efficiency variance is extracted in the WIP account. In our example, variable overhead varies in relation to direct labour hours and labour efficiency is principally related to production. The Control and Variance Accounts are set out below; we will deal with the WIP Control Account shortly.

Variable Overhead Control Account

	£		£
Expense creditor	64 000	WIP Control (9600 hours @ £7.50)	72 000
Variable Overhead Expenditure			
Variance	8 000		
	72 000		72 000

Variable Overhead Expenditure Variance Account

	£		£
Profit and Loss Account	8000	Variable Overhead Control	8000

Fixed overhead

The Fixed Overhead Control, Fixed Overhead Expenditure Variance and Fixed Overhead Volume Variance Accounts are as follows:

Fixed Overhead Control Account

	£		£
Wages Control (indirect wages)	14 200	WIP Control (4700 batches @ £20)	94 000
Employers' NI contributions	5 400	Fixed Overhead Expenditure	
Expense creditor	57 400	Variance	3 000
Depreciation	16 000		
Fixed Overhead Volume Variance	4 000		
	97 000		97 000

The charge to WIP is (actual batches produced × absorption rate per batch) – i.e. the amount of fixed overhead *absorbed* in March.

Fixed Overhead Expenditure Variance Account

	£		£
Fixed Overhead Control	3000	Profit and Loss Account	3000

Fixed Overhead Volume Variance Account

	£		£
Profit and Loss Account	4000	Fixed Overhead Control	4000

In this particular example, fixed overhead is being absorbed on a cost unit basis and both expenditure and volume variances are extracted from the Fixed Overhead Control Account. In this way, the total fixed overhead variance passes through the control account.

✔ *What does the total fixed overhead variance represent?*

As we discovered in the previous chapter, the total fixed overhead variance represents the amount of over- or underabsorbed overhead. In March, NCS Ltd had a total fixed overhead variance of:

$$£3000A \text{ (expenditure)} + £4000F \text{ (volume)} = £1000F$$

In other words, there was an overabsorption of £1000:

	£
Fixed overhead absorbed (4700 batches × £20)	94 000
Fixed overhead incurred	93 000
Overabsorption	1 000

Suppose fixed overhead were absorbed on the basis of 2 standard labour hours @ £10 per hour, rather than on the existing cost unit basis. How would this affect the Fixed Overhead Control Account? The only difference would be that the charge to WIP is calculated as:

$$(4700 \text{ batches} × 2 \text{ standard hours}) × £10 \text{ per standard hour} = £94\,000$$

However if – as is quite likely – fixed overhead is absorbed on the basis of *actual* labour hours, we need to amend our bookkeeping entries. What we need to reflect is the fact that actual hours worked are essentially connected with production, so the volume variance is extracted from the WIP Control Account. In these circumstances, it might be more useful to think of the volume variance as the sum of the fixed overhead efficiency and capacity variances (see previous chapter). The capacity variance will be extracted from the Fixed Overhead Control Account, whilst the efficiency variance passes through WIP Control. A revised Fixed Overhead Control Account will charge WIP with absorbed fixed overhead of:

$$(\text{actual hours} × \text{standard rate per hour})$$

The Fixed Overhead Control Account would now be:

Fixed Overhead Control Account

	£		£
Wages Control (indirect wages)	14 200	WIP Control (9600 hours @ £10)	96 000
Employers' NI contributions	5 400	Fixed Overhead Expenditure	
Expense creditor	57 400	Variance	3 000
Depreciation	16 000		
Fixed Overhead Capacity Variance	6 000		
	99 000		99 000

The capacity variance is calculated as (BH – AH) × FOPH.

✔ *From Exhibit 20.2, determine the budgeted direct labour hours for March.*

Budgeted direct labour hours:

(budgeted production × standard hours per batch) = (4500 × 2) = 9000

So the fixed overhead capacity variance is:

(9000 hours – 9600 hours) × £10 = £6000F

Remember that the capacity variance (like the volume variance) is favourable when actual exceeds budget. If you look at the revised control account above, you will see that the full overabsorption (£3000) is still reflected in the double-entry. In effect, the capacity variance acts as a 'proxy' volume variance.

The fixed overhead efficiency variance is:

(SH – AH) × FOPH = ([4700 batches × 2 hours] – 9600 hours) × £10 = £2000A

We will see how this affects the WIP Control Account in the next section.

Work-in-progress

The WIP Control Account is debited with labour, materials and overhead on the basis of actual quantity/hours/output valued at standard cost in each case. Usage and efficiency variances are extracted, so that WIP stock and transfers from WIP to Finished Goods are valued at standard cost. From Exhibit 20.2, the standard cost per batch is £70 and 4300 batches were transferred to Finished Goods during March.

Work-in-Progress Control Account

	£		£
Balance b/fwd	35 000	Labour efficiency variance	1 400
Raw Materials' Control		Variable overhead efficiency	
(466 000 metres @ £0.20)	93 200	variance	1 500
Wages Control (9600 hours @ £7)	67 200	Finished Goods Control	
Variable Overhead Control		(4300 batches @£70)	301 000
(9600 hours @ £7.50)	72 000	Balance c/fwd	63 000
Fixed Overhead Control			
(4700 batches @ £20)	94 000		
Material usage variance	5 500		
	366 900		366 900
Balance b/fwd	63 000		

The related variance accounts are:

Material Usage Variance Account

	£		£
Profit and Loss Account	5500	WIP Control	5500

Labour Efficiency Variance Account

	£		£
WIP Control	1400	Profit and Loss Account	1400

Variable Overhead Efficiency Variance Account

	£		£
WIP Control	1500	Profit and Loss Account	1500

If fixed overhead were absorbed using actual labour hours, the WIP Control Account would change slightly (changes are highlighted in bold):

Work-in-Progress Control Account

	£		£
Balance b/fwd	35 000	Labour efficiency variance	1 400
Raw Materials' Control		Variable overhead efficiency	
(466 000 metres @ £0.20)	93 200	variance	1 500
Wages Control (9600 hours @ £7)	67 200	**Fixed overhead efficiency variance**	**2 000**
Variable Overhead Control		Finished Goods Control	
(9600 hours @ £7.50)	72 000	(4300 batches @ £70)	301 000
Fixed Overhead Control		Balance c/fwd	63 000
(9600 hours @ £10)	**96 000**		
Material usage variance	5 500		
	368 900		368 900
Balance b/fwd	63 000		

So although WIP absorbs £2000 of additional fixed overhead compared to the amount using standard hours and cost units as the absorption basis, this extra is exactly balanced by the fixed overhead efficiency variance (calculated earlier as £2000A). Thus, the value of WIP stock and of transfers to Finished Goods are unaffected. This should make sense, because the fixed overhead absorbed *per batch* (i.e. per unit of output) remains £20.

Finished goods, cost of sales, sales

All postings in the Finished Goods Control Account will be stated in standard cost terms: opening and closing balances, transfers from WIP and transfers to cost of sales. We know from Exhibit 20.2 that 4000 batches were sold during March, which allows us to value the transfer from Finished Goods to Cost of Sales.

Finished Goods Control Account

	£		£
Balance b/fwd (from Exhibit 20.2)	70 000	Cost of sales (4000 batches @ £70)	280 000
WIP Control (4300 batches @ £70)	301 000	Balance c/fwd	91 000
	371 000		371 000
Balance b/fwd	91 000		

Cost of Sales Account

	£		£
Finished Goods Control	<u>280 000</u>	Profit and Loss Account	<u>280 000</u>

You may have wondered why we did not calculate either the selling price variance or the sales volume variance. The reason is that these variances are not normally recorded in the ledger; management may feel that sales price and volume are insufficiently under their genuine control to warrant such treatment. The Sales Account is therefore credited with actual revenue (from Exhibit 20.2), which is the amount transferred to Profit and Loss – exactly as happened in Chapter 7.

Sales Account

	£		£
Profit and Loss Account	<u>500 000</u>	Debtors' Control	<u>500 000</u>

Profit and Loss Account

Now that we have posted the individual ledger accounts, we are in a position to prepare the Profit and Loss Account. For consistency, we show this in double-entry format, though a vertical presentation is more usual.

NCS Ltd
Profit and Loss Account for the month ending 31 March

	£		£
Cost of sales	280 000	Sales	500 000
Labour rate variance	1 920	Material price variance	10 000
Labour efficiency variance	1 400	Material usage variance	5 500
Variable overhead efficiency		Variable overhead expenditure	
variance	1 500	variance	8 000
Fixed overhead expenditure		Fixed overhead volume	
variance	3 000	variance	4 000
Actual gross profit c/fwd	<u>239 680</u>		
	<u>527 500</u>		<u>527 500</u>

Interlocking standard cost ledger

We saw in Chapter 7 that an interlocking system maintains a separate ledger for each of cost and financial accounting purposes. 'Interlocking' and reconciliation of the two ledgers is achieved by means of a Memorandum Control Account in the financial accounting ledger and a Cost (or Financial) Ledger Control Account in the cost accounting ledger. The purpose of these two accounts is to record, as equal but opposite double-entries, transactions that are common to both financial and cost ledgers.

✔ *What is the implication of an interlocking system for the bookkeeping entries used to record variances?*

Variances, being produced entirely for internal purposes, will be posted only to the cost ledger. That being so, the double-entries required to record variances are exactly the same in an interlocking as in an integrated system. The Cost Ledger Control Account is relevant solely to those transactions and items common to both ledgers. In our example, sales, purchases, depreciation (possibly), net wages, wage deductions and profit would all require one 'leg' of their double-entry to be in the Cost Ledger Control Account because the cost ledger does not contain creditor, debtor, and bank accounts. In an interlocking system, the Wages Control Account would be:

Wages Control Account

	£		£
Cost Ledger Control (PAYE tax)	18 200	Labour rate variance	1 920
Cost Ledger Control		WIP Control (9600 hours @ £7)	67 200
(Employees' NI Contributions)	5 200	Fixed Overhead Control	14 200
Cost Ledger Control			
(net wages paid)	59 920		
	83 320		83 320

Differences in profit recorded in the two ledgers due, e.g. to different stock valuation methods (actual cost in the financial ledger, standard cost in the cost ledger) will be reconciled using the approach illustrated in Chapter 7.

Journal entries

Once we know which accounts are to be debited and which credited, preparing journal entries for a standard cost ledger is straightforward. As ever, you should take care to include an appropriate narrative with your journal entries. Exhibit 20.3 restates some information about NCS Ltd's raw materials and variable overhead for March.

NCS Ltd: raw materials and variable overhead, March

Purchases (credit) £90 000	Standard variable overhead per hour £7.50
Issues to production 466 000 metres	Variable overhead expenditure variance
Standard cost per metre £0.20	£8000F
Material price variance £10 000F	Variable overhead efficiency variance
Material usage variance £5500F	£1500A
Variable overhead expenses incurred	Actual hours 9600
(all credit) £64 000	

Exhibit 20.3 Data for journal entries

The journal entries for variable overhead are:

	Dr £	Cr £
Variable Overhead Control Account	72 000	
Expense Creditor Control Account		64 000
Variable Overhead Expenditure Variance Account		8 000
Variable overhead expenses incurred and related expenditure variance isolated		
WIP Control Account (9600 hours @ £7.50)	72 000	
Variable Overhead Control Account		72 000
Absorption of variable overhead by production		
Variable Overhead Efficiency Variance Account	1500	
WIP Control Account		1500
Isolation of variable overhead efficiency variance		

You will see that the total debited to the Variable Overhead Control Account in the first journal entry comprises the actual cost (£64 000) plus the favourable expenditure variance (£8000). The journal entry recording purchase of raw materials follows the same pattern.

 Use Exhibit 20.3 to prepare journal entries recording purchase and issue of raw materials, along with the related variances.

The journal entries are:

	Dr £	Cr £
Raw Materials' Control Account	100 000	
Creditor Control Account		90 000
Material Price Variance Account		10 000
Purchase of materials and isolation of price variance		
WIP Control Account (466 000 metres @ £0.20)	93 200	
Raw Materials' Control Account		93 200
Issue of raw materials to production		
WIP Control Account	5500	
Material Usage Variance Account		5500
Isolation of usage variance		

The WIP Control Account in our example presented little problem. However, we must now examine a type of WIP account that requires slightly more complex treatment in a standard cost system: the process account.

STANDARD PROCESS COSTING

With its mass production of identical output and input/output relationships that can generally be fairly accurately defined, process costing readily lends itself to application of standard costing. We will use Exhibit 20.4 to illustrate how this is achieved. (At this stage, you may wish to revise our earlier discussion of actual process costing systems in Chapter 9: in particular the sections on process costing terminology, equivalent units and the FIFO approach to work-in-progress valuation.)

SPC Ltd: distillation process

The company, which produces an epoxy bonding agent, uses standard costing within its integrated ledger. The standard and actual information below relates to the Distillation Process for August.

Standard
Normal loss: 10% of input. This is due to evaporation, being waste.

Standard cost of inputs per litre of finished product		£
Transfer from Mixing Process	1 litre @ £4.00	4.00
Added material Z	2 grams @ £3.00	6.00
Direct labour	0.1 hours @ £10	1.00
Variable overhead	0.1 hours @ £2	0.20
Fixed overhead	0.1 hours @ £8	0.80
		12.00

Material Z is input at the start of the process; all other costs are incurred evenly throughout the process.
Overhead absorption rates are based on a budgeted monthly output of 90 000 equivalent units.

Actual for August
Opening WIP 20 000 litres, 20% complete, standard cost £208 000
Completed output transferred to Finished Goods 90 000 litres
Closing WIP 15 000 litres, 40% complete
Transfers from Mixing Process 95 000 litres

Actual cost of Distillation Process for August
Added material Z 186 000 grams @ £2.95
Direct labour 10 700 hours @ £10.40
Variable overhead £2400
Fixed overhead £93 000

It is company policy to identify variances at the earliest feasible stage of each month's production cycle.

Exhibit 20.4 Standard process costing

When we discussed process costing in Chapter 9, we said that the principle governing treatment of normal losses is that, being expected under normal conditions, their cost should be borne by all the other units in the process. This remains the case in a standard costing system, with the standard cost per unit of output being uplifted to allow for the normal loss.

> ✔ *Using the data in Exhibit 20.4, uplift the standard input cost per litre to allow for the specified normal loss.*

Standard *output* cost per litre of finished product:

		£
Transfers from Mixing Process (1.1 litres @ £4.00)		4.40
Added material Z (2.2 grams @ £3.00)		6.60
Direct labour (0.11 hours @ £10)		1.10
Variable overhead (0.11 hours @ £2)		0.22
Fixed overhead (0.11 hours × £0.80)		0.88
		13.20

You will see that all the input resources (hence the associated standard cost also) have been increased by 10% to allow for the normal loss. But note that we need to adjust the standard quantity of each input resource individually: this information will be required when we calculate usage and efficiency variances for August. When the normal loss has a scrap value, this is deducted from the standard cost.

Here, adjusting standard cost to reflect normal loss is straightforward, as both standard and loss are expressed in terms of input. However, if the normal loss were 10% of completed output, the adjustment would be:

		£
Transfers from Mixing Process (1.11 litres @ £4.00)		4.44
Added material Z (2.22 grams @ £3.00)		6.66
Direct labour (0.11 hours @ £10)		1.10
Variable overhead (0.11 hours @ £2)		0.22
Fixed overhead (0.11 × £0.80)		0.88
Standard output cost per litre		13.30 (rounded)

Since standard input represents 90% of standard output, standard input resources have each been increased by 1/0.9 to allow for the normal loss.

Careful reading of questions is thus needed to determine which approach is required.

Equivalent production is calculated using the First-In–First-Out method we described in Chapter 9. We use this method because it excludes opening WIP from the calculation – any variances relating to opening WIP would have been reported in the last accounting period (July in our example). Table 20.1 illustrates.

Since direct labour, variable overhead and fixed overhead are all incurred evenly, we have followed the procedure described in Appendix 9A and simplified the table by aggregating these three costs under the heading 'conversion cost'.

Table 20.1 Equivalent units produced

	Transfers from Mixing Process	Added material Z	Conversion cost
Completed output *less* **Opening WIP equivalent units**	(100% × 90 000) – (100% × 20 000) 70 000	(100% × 90 000) – (100% × 20 000) 70 000	(100% × 90 000) – (20% × 20 000) 86 000
Closing WIP	(100% × 15 000) 15 000	(100% × 15 000) 15 000	(40% × 15 000) 6000
Total equivalent units	85 000	85 000	92 000

Table 20.1 does not give a cost per equivalent unit for each element of cost. Why is this?

We do not need to calculate a cost per equivalent unit for each cost element because the standard costs (adjusted for normal loss) are used. Transfers to Finished Goods are therefore valued at £13.20 per litre. You will also see that we have omitted any mention of abnormal gain or abnormal loss from Table 20.1; these will be reflected in the labour and variable overhead efficiency, material usage and fixed overhead volume variances. We can now use the equivalent units from Table 20.1 in conjunction with the formulas from the last chapter to determine the appropriate variances to allow us to post the Distillation Process Account.

Material usage variance (SQ − AQ) × SP
Transfers from Mixing Process
([85 000 equivalent units × 1.1 litres] − 95 000 litres) × £4.00 = £6000A
Added material Z
([85 000 equivalent units × 2.2 grams] − 186 000 grams) × £3.00 = £3000F
Labour efficiency variance (SH − AH) × SR
([92 000 equivalent units × 0.11 hours] − 10 700 hours) × £10 = £5800A
Variable overhead efficiency variance (SH − AH) × SVOH
([92 000 equivalent units × 0.11 hours] − 10 700 hours) × £2 = £1160A

Although it does not appear in the Distillation Process Account, the fixed overhead volume variance also derives from the equivalent units in Table 20.1:

(BP − AP) × FOPU = (90 000 equivalent units − 92 000 equivalent units) × £0.80

= £1600F

Finally, we can post the Distillation Account, where we follow the procedures for a standard cost WIP Account described earlier in the chapter. Input resources and transfers to Finished Goods are valued at (actual quantity × standard cost).

Distillation Process Account

	£		£
Opening WIP (from Exhibit 20.4)	208 000	Usage variance, transfers	
Mixing Process		from Mixing	6 000
(95 000 litres @ £4.00)	380 000	Labour efficiency variance	5 800
Material Z (186 000 grams @ £3)	558 000	Variable overhead efficiency	
Direct labour		variance	1 160
(10 700 hours @ £10)	107 000	Finished goods	
Variable overhead		(90 000 litres @ £13.20)	1 188 000
(10 700 hours @ £2)	21 400	Closing WIP c/fwd (balance)	157 400
Fixed overhead			
(92 000 equivalent units			
@ £0.88)	80 960		
Usage variance, Material Z	3 000		
	1 358 360		1 358 360
Balance b/fwd	162 040		

The process account above differs slightly from those we presented in Chapter 9, as no 'units' columns are shown within the account. They are omitted here because normal losses, abnormal losses and abnormal gains are included within the variances, rather than being shown separately in the account. So it would not be possible to reconcile physical inputs and outputs, although this might be done as a separate exercise and might even be performed by the production equipment on a 'real-time' basis.

 If you examine the debit side of the Distillation Process Account, you will see that the standard cost of inputs has not been adjusted to reflect normal loss. Why is this?

The normal loss adjustment to standard which we preformed earlier relates to *outputs* from the process, which is why transfers to Finished Goods are valued at the adjusted standard cost of £13.20. Resource costs debited to the account represent *inputs* to the process, which must be valued at the standard input cost – i.e. before any normal loss adjustment.

In the final section of the chapter, we examine a technique that aims, among other things, to simplify the standard cost bookkeeping procedures we have been illustrating.

BACKFLUSH COSTING

When we described Just-in-Time (JIT) systems in Chapter 2, we said that one of their basic principles was elimination or significant reduction of the non-value-added costs associated with stockholding. According to the JIT view, stocks should thus be zero or minimal, in which case, there is no justification for expending large amounts of time and effort assigning costs to stock. This is the basic tenet of the **backflush costing** approach described in Exhibit 20.1.

If you review the two bookkeeping examples we have just completed, you will see that the Work-in-Progress Account is central to both. This reflects the traditional accounting view that 'value' is obtained by the creation of the asset known as stock. In a backflush system, no separate WIP account is kept, the view being that production occurs on a 'demand-pull' basis – i.e. production occurs in response to demand, rather than from a desire to accumulate stocks. Sale of output is therefore the 'trigger point' in backflush costing, the key accounts being Finished Goods and Cost of Sales. In essence, bookkeeping could operate along the following lines:

- Total production cost is charged to Finished Goods.
- Cost of sales is transferred from Finished Goods to the Cost of Sales Account.
- The balance remaining on the Finished Goods Account is 'backflushed' to a combined Raw Materials/WIP Account.

Exhibit 20.5 will illustrate.

For ease of illustration, in Exhibit 20.5 we have chosen to group labour and overhead together under the heading 'conversion cost'; the bookkeeping principles illustrated below can easily accommodate separate labour and overhead accounts. Since there are two trigger points in this system, the ledger will need to contain an account that accommodates each of them. These accounts are:

- A composite account for raw materials and work-in-progress; and
- A finished goods account.

CFB Ltd: backflush system

Standard data per unit of the company's only product, a high-density computer disk drive, is:

	£
Selling price	200
Direct materials	70
Conversion cost (labour & overhead)	40
	110

In August, 4500 disk drives were sold. At the beginning of the month, there were no stocks of raw material, work-in-progress or finished goods.

During August, £362 000 of raw materials were purchased on credit and conversion costs amounted to £192 000. After a physical stock-count, it was discovered that, of the units in stock at the end of August, 200 were fully complete. The company employs backflush principles in its ledger, and there are two trigger points: purchase of raw materials and completion of output.

Exhibit 20.5 Backflush costing

In order to highlight the sequence of ledger postings, we have used journal entries to record the occurrences in Exhibit 20.5.

	Dr £	Cr £
Raw Material/WIP Account	362 000	
Creditor Account		362 000
Purchase of raw materials		
Finished Goods Account	554 000	
Raw Materials/WIP Account		362 000
Conversion Cost Account		192 000
Raw materials and conversion cost charged to production		
Cost of Sales Account (4500 units @ £110)	495 000	
Finished Goods Account		495 000
Cost of goods sold transferred out of Finished Goods		
Raw Materials/WIP Account	37 000	
Finished Goods Account		37 000
Materials' and WIP cost backflushed to composite stock account		

The amount backflushed to the Raw Materials/WIP Account is calculated as:

Cost incurred in August: material purchases		362 000
conversion costs		192 000
		554 000
Less Charged to cost of sales	495 000	
Finished Goods stock		
(200 units @ £110)	22 000	517 000
Therefore raw materials/WIP stock =		37 000

What should be clear from our example is that it is sales which form the focal point of the bookkeeping, rather than production. Proponents of backflush costing would argue that not only is this a better reflection of reality, but also that it greatly simplifies bookkeeping procedures. A further argument in favour of backflush costing is related to our discussion of absorption costing in Chapter 12, where we demonstrated how it is possible to increase profit simply by building up stocks. By switching the accounting emphasis away from production onto sales, backflush costing may reduce the possibility of unnecessary and costly stock build-ups.

 Exhibit 20.5 contains both standard and actual costs, yet the journal entries contain no variances. Can you determine from the journal entries which account/figure will include any variances that have arisen?

The charge to cost of sales and valuation of finished goods stock were both made at standard cost. By process of elimination, therefore, such variances as exist will all be contained within the figure backflushed to the Raw Materials/WIP Account. This might be quite acceptable providing closing stocks are minimal and providing actual cost does not differ markedly from standard. Such a view – especially for material – is entirely consistent with the JIT philosophy reflected in backflush costing. One of the hallmarks of a successful JIT system is the existence of stable relationships with suppliers of materials. It is thus very likely that material prices will be pretty constant in the short term, possibly as a consequence of contractual agreement. In any case, our ledger postings can easily be amended to allow for the material price variance. Suppose a price variance of £2000A arose in August; our initial journal entry recording purchase of raw materials would become:

	Dr £	Cr £
Raw Material/WIP Account (£362 000 – £2000)	360 000	
Material Price Variance Account	2 000	
Creditor Account		362 000
Purchase of raw materials and isolation of price variance		

The remaining journal entries are exactly as shown earlier. What about variances related to production – usage and efficiency? In our (admittedly simple) illustration, they cannot readily be dealt with, because we do not have a global 'production' figure for August. In order to obtain one, we would need to undertake an equivalent-units type calculation of the type performed earlier with standard process costing. Doing so could be seen as somewhat contradicting the basic principle of backflush costing – i.e. that costs are not attributed in detail to WIP. And while such equivalent unit calculations may well be less involved than those for a traditional WIP valuation approach, the inherent contradiction with the backflush rationale might strike at the credibility of backflush costing.

It would therefore seem that use of backflush costing can only be justified when stock levels are very low, and where its use does not prejudice effective control of costs and resources.

SUMMARY

In this chapter, we have discussed standard cost bookkeeping in general, standard process costing and backflush costing. We have seen that:

- Actual transactions are recorded as normal within the accounts.
- Favourable variances are debited to the originating account, credited to the appropriate variance account; adverse variances are credited to the originating account, debited to the appropriate variance account.
- At the end of the accounting (control) period, the balance on variance accounts is transferred to the Profit and Loss Account.
- The material price variance is based on purchase quantity and is extracted from the Raw Materials' Control Account at the time of purchase.
- Issues from Raw Materials to WIP are valued at (actual quantity × standard cost per unit).
- The labour rate variance is extracted from the Wages Control Account, with direct wages being charged to WIP at (actual hours × standard rate per hour).
- Indirect wages are charged to the Fixed (or Variable) Overhead Account at their actual cost.
- The variable overhead expenditure variance is extracted from the Variable Overhead Control Account, with WIP being charged (actual hours × standard rate per hour).
- The fixed overhead volume and expenditure variances are both extracted from the Fixed Overhead Account, so that WIP is charged with fixed overhead absorbed.
- Where fixed overhead is absorbed on the basis of actual direct labour hours, fixed overhead expenditure and capacity variances are extracted from the Fixed Overhead Account, with the fixed overhead efficiency variance being extracted from WIP.
- Variances for material usage, labour efficiency and variable overhead efficiency are extracted from the WIP Account; stock of WIP is thus valued at standard cost.
- Selling price and sales volume variances are not normally posted to the ledger.
- The bookkeeping disposition of variances within an interlocking ledger is exactly the same as it is within an integrated ledger.
- In a standard process account, normal losses are not shown on the face of the account, but are incorporated into the standard cost.
- Abnormal losses and abnormal gains are reflected in material usage, labour efficiency and overhead efficiency variances.
- Standard process costing determines equivalent units on a FIFO basis, with the appropriate number of equivalent units from this calculation being taken as the basis of usage, efficiency and fixed overhead volume variances.
- Backflush costing does not trace costs to WIP, but to completed output, 'backflushing' a residual cost to a composite Raw Materials/WIP Account.

- Backflush costing may simplify accounting records, may provide a better reflection of reality and might discourage unnecessary stock build-ups.
- Where stocks are significant and/or where effective control might be prejudiced, use of backflush costing may be difficult to justify.

FURTHER READING

Inman, M. L., Backflush cost accounting. *Students' Newsletter*, November 1997 (ACCA).

Bromwich, M. and Bhimani, A., *Management Accounting: Pathways to Progress*, CIMA, 1994: see Chapter 4 for further discussion of backflush costing.

SELF-TEST QUESTIONS

20.1 The bookkeeping entries in a standard cost system when the actual price for raw materials is less than the standard price are:

A DR Raw materials control account
   CR Raw material price variance account
B DR WIP control account
   CR Raw materials control account
C DR Raw materials price variance account
   CR Raw materials control account
D DR WIP control account
   CR Raw materials price variance account.

(CIMA, *Cost Accounting and Quantitative Methods*, May 1997)

20.2 Place a tick in the appropriate box to indicate whether each of the following statements is true or false.

	True	False
(a) The originating account for the fixed overhead volume variance is WIP.	☐	☐
(b) In order to value raw material stocks at standard cost, the material price variance should be extracted from the WIP account and calculated on the basis of purchase quantity.	☐	☐
(c) In standard process costing, equivalent units are determined on a FIFO basis.	☐	☐
(d) The bookkeeping disposition of variances is the same in an interlocking as in an integrated ledger.	☐	☐
(e) Backflush costing allocates cost to WIP and cost of sales, treating finished goods stock as the residual value.	☐	☐
(f) Backflush costing is argued to reflect the reality of a JIT environment.	☐	☐
(g) In standard process costing, abnormal gains are credited to the process account at standard cost.	☐	☐

20.3 (a) Show by journal entries (narrations are *not* required) how the following transactions would be accounted for within the integrated accounting system of E Ltd which uses standard prices for materials. The price variance is isolated on purchase.

October
1 E Ltd bought and received 1000 kg of raw Material AB from D Ltd for £5500. The standard price of Material AB was £5 per kg.
2 400 kg of Material AB were issued to production.
6 20 kg of Material AB were accidentally knocked off a shelf in the stores, the spilled contents were unusable and had no scrap value.
8 200 of the 400 kg issued to production on 3 October were found to be substandard and returned to the stores with a materials returns note. These 200 kg were immediately returned to D Ltd. Replacements were issued to production with additional requirements against a requisition note for 300 kg. **(12 marks)**

(b) 'An integrated accounting system is superior to a non-integrated system.'

Requirement

Comment on the above statement, demonstrating that you understand the difference between the two systems, and explain **two** advantages and **two** limitations of an integrated system.

(**13 marks**)

(**Total: 25 marks**)

(CIMA, *Cost Accounting*, November 1987)

20.4 The following uncompleted accounts appear in the ledger of MDX plc for March 2000. The company operates a standard costing system, values stock at standard cost, and uses a single plant-wide standard labour rate of £6 per hour for all employees.

Raw Materials

	£		£
Balance b/fwd	240	Price variance	460
Creditors	?	Work-in-progress	6000
		Balance c/fwd	180

Wages Control

	£		£
Gross wages	?	Wage rate variance	618
		Work-in-progress	?

Work-in-progress

	£		£
Raw materials	6000	Labour efficiency variance	900
Wages control	?	Finished goods	34 720
Material usage variance	1440		
Production overhead control	?		

Production Overhead Control

	£		£
Expenses – creditors	?	Balance b/fwd	345
Provision for depreciation	800	Work-in-progress	?
Volume variance	2400	Expenditure variance	980
Balance c/fwd	260		

Data extracted from the standard cost card for MDX plc's only product is as follows:

		£ per unit
Direct materials	5 kg @ £2.40 per kg	12.00
Direct labour	4 hours @ £6.00 per hour	24.00
Fixed overhead		20.00

Budgeted fixed overhead costs are £10 000 per month.

Note: All relevant transactions affecting the above accounts have been identified.

Requirements

(a) Calculate

    (i)   the actual price paid per kg of materials

    (ii)   the actual output

    (iii) the production overhead absorbed

    (iv) the actual direct labour hours

    (v)   the cost incurred in respect of expense creditors

    (vi) the actual labour rate paid per hour.   **(18 marks)**

(b) Integrated accounting systems are usually considered to be more efficient than inter-locking systems. Explain the difference between these systems and discuss their relative advantages and usefulness.   **(7 marks)**

                                     (Total: 25 marks)

(CIMA, *Operational Cost Accounting*, May 2000)

20.5 CU Ltd employs a standard costing system. One of the company's products is produced by means of a chemical process, whereby a specially purchased chemical compound is intro-duced at the start of the process and subjected to various operations to produce the finished product.

The following standard and actual data relate to August:

Standard input data per unit of output
Chemical compound: 1.8 kg @£4 per kg
Labour: 5.4 hours @ £6 per hour
Variable overhead: 5.4 hours @ £3 per hour
Normal loss is 10% of output.

Actual data
Opening WIP: 2000 units, 40% complete
Completed output: 5000 units
Closing WIP: 1500 units, 50% complete
Chemical compound: purchased   11 500 kg @£3.80 per kg
                        used   10 200 kg
Labour: 31 000 hours @ £5.90 per hour
Variable overhead: £98 000

Additional information
Labour and variable overhead are incurred evenly throughout the process.
There are no fixed overheads.
The costing system is such that materials are issued to production at standard cost.

Requirement

Write up the process account for August, showing all relevant variances.

QUESTIONS WITHOUT ANSWERS

20.6 A standard marginal costing system

  (i)   calculates fixed overhead variances using the budgeted absorption rate per unit
  (ii) records adverse variances as debit entries in variance accounts within the ledger
  (iii) values finished goods stock at the standard variable cost of production.

Which of the above statements is/are correct?

  A (i) and (iii) only
  B (ii) only
  C (ii) and (iii) only
  D (i) and (ii) only
  E All of them.

(CIMA, *Operational Cost Accounting*, May 1997)

20.7 JC Ltd produces and sells one product only, Product J, the standard cost for which is as follows for one unit.

	£
Direct Material X – 10 kg @ £20	200
Direct Material Y – 5 litres @ £6	30
Direct wages – 5 hours @ £6	30
Fixed production overhead	50
Total standard cost	310
Standard gross profit	90
Standard selling price	400

The fixed production overhead is based on an expected annual output of 10 800 units produced at an even flow throughout the year; assume each calendar month is equal. Fixed production overhead is absorbed on direct labour hours.

During April, the first month of the 1989/90 financial year, the following were the actual results for an actual production of 800 units.

	£	£
Sales on credit: 800 units @ £400		320 000
Direct materials: X 7800 kg	159 900	
Y 4300 litres	23 650	
Direct wages: 4200 hours	24 150	
Fixed production overhead	47 000	254 700
Gross profit		65 300

The material price variance is extracted at the time of receipt and the raw materials stores control is maintained at standard prices. The purchases, bought on credit, during the month of April were:

  X   9000 kg at £20.50 per kg from K Ltd
  Y   5000 litres at £5.50 per litre from C plc

Assume no opening stocks.

Wages owing for March brought forward were £6000. Wages paid during April (net) £20 150. Deductions from wages owing to the Inland Revenue for PAYE and NI were £5000 and the wages accrued for April were £5000.

The fixed production overhead of £47 000 was made up of expense creditors of £33 000, none of which was paid in April, and depreciation of £14 000. The company operates an integrated accounting system.

Requirements

(a) (i) calculate price and usage variances for each material
(ii) calculate labour rate and efficiency variances
(iii) calculate fixed production overhead expenditure and volume variances.

(9 marks)

(b) Show all the accounting entries in T accounts for the month of April – the work-in-progress account should be maintained at standard cost and each balance on the separate variance accounts is to be transferred to a profit and loss account which you are also required to show. (18 marks)

(c) Explain the reason for the difference between the actual gross profit given in the question and the profit shown in your profit and loss account. (3 marks)

(Total: 30 marks)

(CIMA, *Cost Accounting*, May 1989)

20.8 STD Limited operates a standard costing system for its single product. During a period the following details were recorded:

Opening trial balance	£	£
Financial ledger control account		52 950
Finished goods control account (at standard cost)	42 600	
Materials control account (at standard cost)	10 350	
	52 950	52 950

There was no opening work-in-progress.
The standard cost for the product was:

	£ per unit
Materials	40
Labour	35
Overheads	25
	100

Standard selling price was £160 each.

During the period the following details were recorded:

	£
Purchase of materials	102 450
Wages paid	91 855
Overheads paid	72 490
Materials issued to production (at standard cost)	106 075

2700 units were completed during the period and 2675 units were sold at the standard selling price.

The following variances have been calculated:

	FAV £	ADV £
Material price		3710
Material usage	9016	
Labour rate		1200
Labour efficiency	490	
Total overhead expenditure		2780

Requirements

(a) Prepare *all* cost and variance accounts. (11 marks)

(b) Prepare a closing trial balance, given that the profit for the period was £162 316.

(4 marks)

(Total: 15 marks)

(CIMA, *Cost Accounting and Quantitative Methods*, May 1997)

20.9 A light engineering company has a forming process in which standard lengths of titanium are pre-formed prior to use in production. Standard and actual data for April in respect of this process are given below.

Standard per length of pre-formed titanium

Titanium:	3 metres^2 @ £40 per metre^2
Labour:	2 hours @ £10 per hour
Variable overhead:	2 hours @ £20 per hour
Fixed overhead:	£10 per standard length introduced into the process.
Normal loss:	10% of input.

Actual for the month

Opening WIP:	100 lengths, 20% complete, cost £15 976
Completed output:	1200 lengths
Closing WIP:	140 lengths, 40% complete
Titanium:	purchased – 4400 metres^2 @ £38
	used – 4100 metres^2
Labour:	2950 hours @ £10 per hour
Variable overhead:	£61 000
Fixed overhead:	£18 000

The company's policy is to value stocks of raw materials, WIP and finished goods at standard cost. Materials are introduced at the start of the forming process, whilst conversion costs are incurred evenly throughout the process.

Requirement

Prepare the forming process account for April, showing all relevant variances.

20.10 SP Ltd commenced production of a new hand-held games console at the beginning of the month. Standard data per console are:

	£	£
Selling price		75
Materials	15	
Conversion cost	40	55
Gross profit		20

Actual costs and other information for the month:

Materials purchased	£40 000
Conversion costs	£86 000
Production (units)	2000
Sales (units)	1200
Completed output not sold (units)	300

Requirements

(a) Assuming that SP Ltd operates a backflush system, prepare journal entries recording the transactions above. Use two trigger points: purchase of materials and completion of output.

(b) Discuss the suitability of a backflush system for SP Ltd.

GLOSSARY

ABC classification material cost control approach that concentrates on those materials that represent the majority of annual purchase cost ('category A')

abnormal gain excess of normal loss over actual loss

abnormal loss loss in excess of what is expected under normal conditions

absorption costing costing system which includes fixed and variable overhead in cost per unit

accounting rate of return appraisal criterion for capital investment proposals:

$$\frac{\text{Average annual profit}}{\text{Initial capital cost}} \times 100\% \quad or \quad \frac{\text{Average annual profit}}{\text{Average capital cost}} \times 100\%$$

activity-based budgeting budget system based on activities and cost drivers

activity-based cost management approach to financial control aimed at controlling cost of activities, rather than amount of individual costs

activity-based costing (ABC) absorption of overhead based on activities' consumption of resources and output's consumption of activities

actual absorption rate overhead absorption rate derived from actual overhead cost and actual activity measure

allocation attribution of cost to a single cost objective

AMT advanced manufacturing technology

annual budgeted volume volume of activity (e.g. output) upon which annual budget is based

annuity equal annual cash flow over life of an investment

apportionment splitting a common cost between the cost objectives to which it relates

apportionment basis basis of apportioning a common cost between the cost objectives to which it relates

appraisal cost cost incurred to ensure desired quality is achieved

attention-directing provision of reports on key aspects of operations

average capital cost possible definition of cost for use in accounting rate of return:

$$\frac{(\text{Initial cost} + \text{resale value})}{2}$$

backflush costing costing system attributing costs firstly to completed output, then assigning the residual between this and total cost to a composite raw materials/WIP account

barriers to communication factors which prevent effective communication of information

basic standard standard that represents efficient operation over the medium term

batch costing costing methodology for batches of identical/similar items which may/may not be produced to customer specification

batch-level activities activities performed every time a batch of cost units is produced

benchmarking identification of performance target by reference to either internal or external criteria

bin card record of quantity kept at physical location of stocks, updated as receipts/ issues occur

blanket absorption rate *see* **plantwide absorption rate**

breakeven chart graphical representation of relationship between volume, revenue, total fixed cost and total cost, from which breakeven point can be determined

breakeven point sales volume (units or revenue) at which profit is exactly zero:

$$\text{in units} \frac{\text{Total fixed costs}}{\text{Contribution per unit}}$$

$$\text{in revenue} \frac{\text{Total fixed costs}}{\text{CS ratio}}$$

budget a quantified plan aimed at achieving objective(s)

budget centre organisational subunit for which a budget is prepared

budget committee management group which deals with issues of budget implementation

budget manual document containing procedural guidance on budget preparation

budget officer provides budgetary liaison between different organisational functions

budget period period to which budget is to apply

budget slack difference between minimum necessary expenditure and actual/budgeted expenditure

buffer stock *see* **safety stock**

by-product incidental outcome of producing main products

capacity ratio

$$\frac{\text{Actual hours worked}}{\text{Budgeted hours}} \times 100\%$$

capital budget budget detailing capital expenditure proposals

coefficient of determination indicates proportion of variation (e.g. in cost) predictable relative to changes in selected activity measure and is the correlation coefficient squared

committed cost cost which must be incurred if the organisation is to continue in existence

composite cost unit cost unit that reflects two/more key aspects of output

continuous allotment *see* **repeated distribution**

continuous budget *see* **rolling budget**

continuous inventory updating of stores ledger as each receipt/issue occurs

continuous operation costing group of costing methodologies applicable to output of identical/similar products/services

continuous stocktaking physical verification of stock quantities on a rolling basis

contract costing costing methodology for dissimilar cost units produced to customer requirements, where output designedly spans two/more accounting periods

contract provision account used to make prudence-based adjustment to notional contract profit

contribution sales revenue (or unit selling price) less total (unit) variable costs

contribution analysis determination of product/department/division contribution to general costs

contribution chart graphical representation of relationship between volume, revenue, total variable cost and total cost, from which breakeven point can be determined

contribution : sales ratio total (or unit) contribution as a percentage of sales revenue (or unit selling price)

control account summary account reflecting total of similar, but separate, items

control period subdivision of budget period for control purposes

correlation coefficient measures the strength of linear relationship between two variables:

$$r = \frac{\Sigma \, (x - \bar{x})(y - \bar{y})}{\sqrt{\Sigma \, (x - \bar{x})^2 \, \Sigma \, (y - \bar{y})^2}}$$

cost accounting process of determining the cost of an organisation's activities, being integral to both financial and management accounting

cost attribution process of associating costs with cost objective(s)

cost/benefit analysis evaluation of capital investment proposal based on quantification of monetary and non-monetary outcomes

cost/benefit criterion need for the benefit of an action to exceed the associated cost

cost centre organisational subunit to which costs are attributed

cost classification grouping together costs that share the same attribute(s) in relation to a stated cost objective

cost driver underlying cause of cost

cost/effectiveness analysis evaluation of capital investment proposal based on quantification of monetary outcomes and assessment of unquantified non-monetary outcomes

cost ledger control account within an interlocking system, provides locus for bookkeeping entries relating to accounts that do not exist within the cost accounting ledger

cost objective target or purpose of a cost attribution exercise

cost reduction reduction of cost from previous level without adverse effect on quality

cost unit unit of product/service to which costs are attributed

cost/volume/profit (CVP) analysis marginal costing technique analysing relationship between costs, volume and profit

CS ratio *see* **contribution/sales ratio**

currently attainable standard cost/performance standard based on efficient operation under current conditions

curvilinear cost total cost exhibits concave or convex pattern because unit cost is not constant

cutoff rate target rate of return

data unprocessed information

DCF yield *see* **internal rate of return**

deflating removing inflation from series of costs/revenues so as to state them on a common basis

delivery note document included with supplier's consignment specifying its contents

departmental absorption rate overhead absorption rate based on cost centre overhead and activity measure

deterministic model model which assumes certainty/perfect knowledge

differential cost/benefit difference in relevant cost/benefit between alternative courses of action

direct cost cost which can be unambiguously and quantifiably associated with a single cost objective

direct costing *see* **marginal costing**

direct expenses non-labour, non-materials cost allocable to a single cost unit

direct labour cost/hours labour cost/hours allocable to a single cost unit

direct material cost/quantity material cost/quantity allocable to a single cost unit

direct reapportionment method of secondary overhead distribution which ignores reciprocal services

discounted cash flow (DCF) future cash flow stated in today's terms after allowing for the time value of money; for £1 received at the end of n years from now at a cost of capital r, this is

$$\frac{1}{(1+r)^n}$$

discretionary cost cost incurred at management's discretion

dysfunctional conflict between aims of individual managers/sub-units and those of organisation overall

economic order quantity (EOG) order size that minimises the total cost of ordering plus holding stock:

$$\sqrt{\frac{2DO}{H}}$$

efficiency ratio

$$\frac{\text{Standard hours produced}}{\text{Budgeted standard hours}} \times 100\%$$

engineered cost cost having a definable input/output relationship

engineering cost estimation technical methods of cost estimation

equivalent unit partly complete output expressed as notional fully-complete equivalent

exceptions reporting *see* **management by exception**

external failure cost cost incurred as result of quality failure after output has reached end-user

facility-sustaining activities activities that occur in order to permit the whole organisation to function

feedback control control exercised by retrospective comparison of standard/budget with actual

feedforward control future-oriented control exercised by comparison of desired and budgeted outcomes

final sales value sales value after further processing

financial accounting records monetary transactions of the organisation with principal aim of satisfying external users and requirements

financial ledger control account memorandum account within the financial accounting ledger of an interlocking system, equal but opposite to the cost ledger control account

first-in–first-out (FIFO) stock valuation method that applies the oldest available purchase cost to stores' issues

fixed budget budget prepared on basis of single volume prediction

fixed cost cost whose total amount is unaffected by increases/decreases in the volume of activity

fixed overhead capacity variance difference between fixed budget labour hours and actual, multiplied by fixed overhead absorption rate per hour

fixed overhead efficiency variance difference between standard hours allowed for actual output and actual hours, multiplied by fixed overhead absorption rate per hour

fixed overhead expenditure variance difference between budgeted and actual fixed overhead cost

fixed overhead volume variance difference between budgeted and actual unit output, multiplied by the unit fixed overhead absorption rate

flexible budget budget which recognises impact of volume change on costs/revenues

flexible budget variance difference between flexible budget and actual amount

free stock amount of stock notionally available to users: (on hand + ordered) − (allocated but not issued)

full-time equivalent (FTE) part-time staff expressed as a notional number of equivalent full-time staff

functional budget budget relating to an individual organisational function (e.g. production)

general ledger control account *see* **cost ledger control account**

goal congruence convergence of individual managers' and subunits' aims with those of the organisation overall

goods received note document raised when supplier delivery received, detailing items delivered

heterogeneity descriptive of output/activities which are non-uniform

high–low analysis cost estimation technique which takes the variable cost per unit of activity to be:

$$\frac{\text{(Difference between total cost of high activity and total cost of low activity)}}{\text{(Difference between high and low volumes of activity)}}$$

fixed cost being determined by substitution of this result into either of the high or low volume total cost

homogeneity descriptive of output/activities which are identical/very similar

hurdle rate *see* **cutoff rate**

ideal standard performance/cost standard based on maximum efficiency

idle time unproductive time (expected or unexpected) for which employees are paid

idle time variance difference between hours paid for and hours worked, multiplied by the standard rate per hour

incremental budget budget prepared by adjusting previous period's budget for expected future changes in conditions

incremental cost/benefit additional cost/benefit resulting from an action

incremental profit/loss additional profit/loss resulting from an action

indirect cost cost which is common to two or more cost objectives

inflating adding inflation to a series of costs/revenues to restate them on a common basis

information data which has been processed into a useful form

inspection of accounts estimation technique based on inspection of past accounting records

intangibility descriptive of output having no physical form

integrated system bookkeeping system where cost accounting and financial accounting records are kept within the same ledger

interest on capital opportunity cost of using capital in a particular way (often a notional cost)

interlocking system bookkeeping system where cost accounting and financial accounting records are kept in separate ledgers

intermediate sales value sales value at split-off point

internal failure cost cost resulting from quality failure before output reaches end-user

internal rate of return discount rate yielding zero net present value

investment centre organisational subunit to which costs, revenues and capital investment are attributed

job costing costing methodology relevant to output of dissimilar units to customer requirement, units being smaller than for contract costing

job card (/sheet) document detailing estimated and actual resources used on a job

joint cost cost attributable to two/more cost objectives

joint process process producing two/more main products

joint products two/more main products which result from the same production process

journal narrative record of accounting entries

just-in-time (JIT) system that aims to reduce lead times between purchase/production and use/sale

key factor *see* **limiting factor**

labour efficiency variance difference between standard labour hours allowed for actual output and actual hours worked, multiplied by standard rate per hour

labour rate variance difference between standard labour rate per hour and actual rate per hour, multiplied by number of hours actually paid for

last-in–first-out (LIFO) stock valuation method that applies the most recent available purchase cost to stores' issues

limiting factor constraint on organisational activity

line item budget budget which classifies costs according to their nature

linear costs cost behaviour pattern where the variable cost per unit of activity is constant at all volumes and/or the total fixed cost is the same for all volumes

linear programming mathematical technique for optimising a given outcome subject to constraints

linear regression mathematical technique used to formulate the equation of a straight line, $y = a + bx$ where

$$b = \frac{n \sum xy - \sum x \sum y}{n \sum x^2 - (\sum x)^2} \quad \text{and} \quad a = \frac{\sum y}{n} - \frac{b \sum x}{n}$$

management accounting provision of useful information to help management in their planning, control and decision-making activities

management by exception control principle whereby management action is triggered by exceptions to plan

management information system (MIS) set of interrelated subsystems which processes and filters data from internal and external sources

manufacturing resource planning (MRPII) system that integrates material requirement planning, production scheduling and cost accounting

margin of safety difference between budgeted/actual and breakeven sales in units, revenue, or as a percentage:

$$\frac{(\text{Budgeted or actual sales} - \text{breakeven sales})}{\text{Budgeted or actual sales}} \times 100\%$$

marginal costing costing system which attributes marginal/variable costs to units of output

mark-up profit expressed in terms of cost

master budget summary of functional and cash budgets

material price variance difference between standard and actual purchase price of materials multiplied by actual purchase quantity

material requirement planning (MRPI) system that links material requirements to the pattern of output

material usage variance difference between standard material usage allowed for actual output and actual usage, multiplied by standard price per unit of material

maximum level stock indicator warning of lower-than-expected usage: (reorder level + EOQ) – (minimum usage × minimum lead time)

memorandum account account produced for reference purposes only, and not part of the double-entry system

minimum level stock indicator warning of higher-than-expected usage: (reorder level – [average usage × average lead time])

mission statement statement of an organisation's desired economic/social role over the long term

mixed cost *see* **semi-variable cost**

multiple regression analysis analytical technique which recognises impact on target variable of several factors

negative feedback seeking to minimise the unfavourable impact of adverse variances

net present value (NPV) sum of a capital investment proposal's discounted relevant cash inflows and outflows over its lifespan

net sales value *see* **notional sales value**

net realisable value amount for which a product may be sold

noise irrelevant/distracting information within communication system

non-integrated system *see* **interlocking system**

non-programmed decision non-routine/non-recurrent decision – variables/outcomes subject to considerable uncertainty

non-value added activity activity which adds no worth to output in perceptions of its end-user

normal loss loss expected under normal operating conditions

normal volume medium-term average volume

notional contract profit hypothetical contract profit before prudence-based adjustment

notional cost hypothetical costs intended to reflect potential loss of benefit

notional rent hypothetical rent that could be levied/paid for owned premises

notional sales value final sales value less further processing cost

objective classification linkage between subjective classification and cost objective

operational gearing

$$\frac{\text{Contribution}}{\text{Profit}}$$

operational information plans and resources which translate tactics into action

opportunity cost benefit forgone as result of pursuing one course of action rather than the best alternative course of action

overabsorption arises where overhead absorbed using predetermined rate exceeds overhead incurred

overhead sum of all indirect costs

overhead absorption practice of including overhead in unit cost

overhead absorption rate mechanism for determining overhead cost per unit, taking the general form:

$$\frac{\text{Estimated overhead cost}}{\text{Estimated activity measure}} \quad or \quad \frac{\text{Estimated overhead cost}}{\text{Estimated units of cost driver}}$$

overhead analysis sheet presentation of primary and secondary distribution of overhead

overhead application *see* **overhead absorption**

overhead cost pool collection point for overheads relating to an activity

overhead recovery *see* **overhead absorption**

overtime premium extra payment in addition to normal pay rate in respect of overtime working

payback period (usually expressed in years) required for capital investment proposal's net cash inflows to equal its initial cost

periodic stock-taking physical verification of stocks once per period

perishability descriptive of output that cannot be stored

plantwide absorption rate overhead absorption rate based on total, rather than departmental, overhead and activity measure

positive feedback seeking to maximise the benefit of favourable variances

post-audit comparison of a project's actual outcomes with estimates used in its appraisal

practical capacity volume measure based on maximum operational capability

predetermined absorption rate overhead absorption rate based on estimated figures

prevention cost cost incurred to prevent inferior quality

price elasticity of demand relationship between selling price and quantity demanded

primary distribution of overhead allocation and apportionment of overhead to cost centres

prime cost sum of all direct costs

principal budget factor *see* **limiting factor**

problem-solving quantification of costs/benefits of actions, often coupled with recommendation based thereon

process costing costing methodology for output of identical/similar items by means of single process/sequence of processes

product-sustaining activities activities that occur in order to permit production/sale of particular products/services

productivity ratio *see* **efficiency ratio**

profit centre organisational subunit to which costs and revenues are attributed

profit margin profit expressed relative to sales value

profit/volume chart graphical representation of relationship between volume and profit, from which breakeven point can be determined

profit : volume ratio *see* **contribution : sales ratio**

programme budget budget which classifies costs according to the reason for their being incurred

programmed decision routine decision with fairly predictable outcomes

progress payment periodic payments in respect of contract in progress, made at agreed stages during progress

purchase order document sent to an organisation's suppliers specifying materials/services to be supplied

purchase requisition document raised by internal users requesting that a supplier order be placed for materials/services

quantitative information information expressed in numerical form

qualitative information information which is not (or which cannot be) expressed in numerical form

relevant cost/revenue future cash flow arising as result of a decision under consideration

relevant range range of activity volumes and/or time horizon over which a particular assumption/set of assumptions is a reasonable approximation of reality

reorder level stock level at which new supplier order placed: (maximum usage × maximum lead time)

repeated distribution method of secondary overhead distribution which fully recognises reciprocal services

responsibility accounting planning/control system based on assigning budget responsibility to individual managers

responsibility centre budget centre within responsibility accounting system

retention agreed proportion of contract price withheld by client pending satisfactory completion of work

revenue budget annual budget of routine operational transactions

rolling budget budget which is updated on a continuous basis

safety stock stock held as precaution against incorrect estimation of usage/lead time

sales required for target profit key cost/volume/profit indicator, calculated in units (revenue) as:

$$\frac{\text{Total fixed costs} + \text{Target profit}}{\text{Contribution per unit (\emph{or} CS ratio)}}$$

sales price variance difference between standard and actual unit selling prices, multiplied by actual unit sales volume

sales volume variance difference between budgeted and actual sales volumes, multiplied by standard profit/contribution per unit

scattergraph graphical cost estimation technique using a number of past costs plotted against volume of activity

scorekeeping keeping tally of financial data as basis of provision of useful information

secondary distribution of overhead reapportionment of service/support cost centres' overhead to production/front-line cost centres

scrap discarded substances with some value

semi-fixed cost *see* **semi-variable cost**

semi-variable cost cost which is partly variable, partly fixed

sensitivity analysis 'what-if' technique examining the effect of changing one or more variables in a model

separation point *see* **split-off point**

service costing costing methodology for provision of service, rather than tangible output

simplex technique for solving problems involving multiple constraints and products

simultaneity descriptive of output that is consumed at/very near the point of its production

specific order costing group of costing methodologies appropriate where work is carried out to customers' requirements

specified order of closing *see* **step reapportionment**

split-off point stage of production at which joint products become separately identifiable

staff turnover ratio

$$\frac{\text{Number of staff replaced during period}}{\text{Total number of staff employed during period}}$$

stakeholders those who have an interest in, or who are affected by, organisational activity

standard cost predetermined unit specifications of resource inputs and associated costs

standard hour amount of work which should be performed in one hour at standard efficiency

step cost cost whose total amount is fixed within a range of activity volumes, increasing/decreasing by a lump-sum amount above/below this range

step reapportionment method of secondary overhead distribution which partially recognises reciprocal services

stochastic model model which allows for impact of uncertainty

stocktaking physical verification of materials' quantities

stores ledger record of receipts, issues and costs for all materials

stores requisition document raised by internal users requesting and detailing an issue from stores

strategic information relates to organisational objectives and the policies/resources required to achieve them

subjective classification classification according to specific attribute(s)

suboptimal(ity) *see* **dysfunctional**

summary budget *see* **master budget**

tactical information relates to objectives, plans and resources by which strategy is translated into action

target cost(ing) selling price/revenue less desired profit

three-level analysis analyses uncertainty by considering three possible outcomes of a decision – the best possible, the worst possible and the most likely (often combined with probabilistic analysis)

time value of money phenomenon of £1 paid/received today having greater value than £1 paid/received at some point in future

time sheet document detailing an employee's activity during period

total quality management (TQM) management philosophy based on 'getting it right first time all of the time'

underabsorption arises where overhead absorbed using predetermined rate is less than overhead incurred

unit-level activities activities that occur every time a cost unit is produced

value-added activity activity which adds worth to output in perception of its end-user

value analysis cost-reduction method aimed at elimination of inessential aspects of products/services/procedures

value for money (VFM) economic, efficient and effective operation

variable cost cost whose total amount increases/decreases in line with increases/decreases in the volume of activity

variable costing *see* **marginal costing**

variable overhead efficiency variance difference between standard hours allowed for actual output and actual hours worked, multiplied by variable overhead rate per hour

variable overhead expenditure variance difference between flexible budget variable overhead and actual variable overhead

variance difference between standard/budgeted and actual outcome

volume ratio

$$\frac{\text{Standard hours produced}}{\text{Budgeted standard hours}} \times 100\%$$

volume variance difference between fixed budget and flexible budget amounts

waste discarded substances of no value

weighted average contribution unit contributions (c/s ratios) weighted by each individual product/service's proportion of overall sales mix

weighted average cost (AVCO) stock valuation method that applies an average cost to stores' issues, this cost being recalculated after each receipt

whole-time equivalent *see* **full-time equivalent**

work certified proportion of contract work certified on client's behalf as being satisfactorily completed

world class manufacturing (WCM) response to global and competitive markets which emphasises quality, lead time, adaptability and cost

zero base budgeting (ZBB) approach to budget preparation which assumes zero prior expenditure, with justification of budgeted costs required

APPENDIX A

Solutions to self-test questions

CHAPTER 1

1.1 (a) T (b) F (c) T (d) F (e) F (f) F (g) T

1.2 The three elements of the scenario are:

- *strategic*: decision to enter into a joint venture to expand range of productions
- *tactical*: decision to produce two costume dramas and one documentary during first year of joint venture
- *operational*: seeking locations for first costume drama.

1.3 C III only

Published accounting information will not be sufficiently timely for management purposes, typically being produced on an annual basis. If management has to wait until some time after the end of the current accounting year before receiving financial information about operations, then effective action based on this information will not be possible. Costs may therefore spiral out of control, unknown to management, and opportunities may be missed through lack of information.

1.4 D II and III only

The information generated will incur costs which are both explicit, such as stationery, and which are recorded in the accounts, plus costs which are implicit, and which are therefore not recorded in the accounts. The fact that managers must spend time gathering and interpreting the information (when they might be more gainfully employed on other tasks) is an example of the latter kind of cost.

1.5 MEMORANDUM

TO: Chairman, Telec plc

FROM:

New management accounting system

The aim of management accounting is to provide useful information to help management to plan, control and make decisions. Although these activities could be said to constitute the fundamentals of management, it is doubtful whether management accounting can (or should) attempt to 'tell managers everything they need to know'. The reasons for this are as follows:

- Management accounting's main medium of communication is quantitative, with the majority of the information being financial; managers need more than this – e.g. possible action by competitors is an important consideration which may not be readily incorporated into management accounting reports.
- Attempting to tell managers everything may seriously breach the cost/benefit criterion, even if it is possible to determine what constitutes 'everything' and obtain relevant data.
- Attempting to be comprehensive in provision could cause information overload.

- Management accounting is not intended to act as a surrogate, but as a support for managerial judgement; ability to 'hide behind' figures could erode this judgement, and might be encouraged by overprovision.

What the company requires is an effective management information system, with management accounting forming one part of a wider, integrated whole.

Signed

CHAPTER 2

2.1 D   £400 000
Prime cost refers to the total of all direct costs; in TG's case, this is:

	£
Direct labour	150 000
Direct expenses	250 000
Prime cost	400 000

2.2 (a) F   (b) F   (c) T   (d) F   (e) T   (f) F

2.3 B   Job costing
The firm will undertake jobs to customer specification and each will be different; relative to contract costing, the size of job will be small. Job costing is therefore appropriate. Had the firm specialised in industrial (rather than domestic) work, where the jobs could be very large, then contract costing might have been appropriate.

2.4 B   Can be economically identified with the item being costed.

2.5 (a) *Payment to insurance company* Figure 2.9(c): this is a variable cost relative to volume of policies sold, but the cost per policy is not constant. The fact that the slope of the total cost line in Figure 2.9(c) has three progressively less steep gradients indicates that there are three levels of cost per unit.
Payments to sales staff Figure 2.9(a): up to a certain volume, this cost is fixed (the annual salary of £10 000, which is paid irrespective of volume). Once this volume is exceeded, the cost becomes semi-variable, the variable element representing the £20 per policy commission on all sales above the target number.
Administration costs Figure 2.9(b): administration costs are semi-variable at all volumes: at zero volume £60 000 will still require to be paid in respect of premises and full-time staff (assuming PP remains in business); on top of this amount, £5 per policy is payable, meaning that the total cost will increase above £60 000 in line with the volume of sales.

(b) Figure A2.1 illustrates the revised behaviour of each cost.
Figure A2.1(a) represents the payment to the insurance company, which is now a linear variable cost, being a flat-rate £3 per policy sold. Payments to sales staff is shown in Figure A2.1(b): since commission is now payable on *all* policies sold, the variable element of this cost commences immediately volume exceeds zero. Within a one-year time span, the administration cost is wholly fixed for all foreseeable volumes, as illustrated in Figure A2.1(c); outside the relevant range – one year and 'foreseeable volume' in this instance – administration cost will probably exhibit step behaviour

(c) Preparation of tolerably realistic budgets requires some knowledge about how costs are

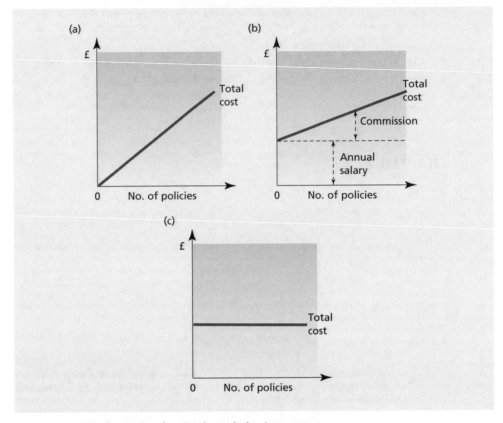

Figure A2.1 Sketch graphs of revised cost behaviour patterns

likely to be affected by the volume of activity upon which the budget is based. Budgets may be prepared for a variety of different volumes, the purpose of this being primarily to assess the impact of different volumes on costs/revenues/profit.

Financial control is typically exercised by comparing budgeted and actual costs; if these two sets of costs are based on different volumes of activity, part of the difference may arise because of this difference in volume, rather than because of efficiency/cost factors. For a more meaningful control exercise, the impact on budgeted/actual costs of such volume differences must be appreciated.

Decisions involve choice between alternatives; analysing the financial implications of different alternatives requires an awareness of how costs are likely to react to each course of action being considered. This will be particularly true when the decision concerned affects volume of activity – e.g. should a component be made in-house or subcontracted to an external supplier?

CHAPTER 3

3.1 B £14 700

High-low analysis yields the following variable cost per unit:

$$\frac{(£12\,900 - £11\,100)}{(6000 - 4000)} = \frac{£1800}{2000} = £0.90$$

Substituting into the total cost of 4000 units:

	£
Total cost	11 100
Less Variable element (4000 × £0.90)	3 600
= Fixed element	7 500

Budget cost allowance for 8000 units:

Variable cost (8000 × £0.90)	7 200
Fixed cost	7 500
Total cost	14 700

3.2   (a) F   (b) T   (c) T   (d) F   (e) T   (f) F   (g) F

3.3   Bearing in mind the cumulative nature of inflation, we get:

19X6: (£4 000 000 × 1.028)	£4 112 000
19X5: (£3 400 000 × 1.035 × 1.028)	£3 617 532
19X4: (£3 200 000 × 1.047 × 1.035 × 1.028)	£3 564 759

Note that the inflation applicable to each year is already contained within the actual cost stated for that year, so there is no need to adjust, say, the 19X6 cost for 19X6 inflation.

3.4   (a) *High-low*

High and low volumes occur, respectively, in April and January:

	Units 000	Costs £000
High volume	60	580
Low volume	21	380
Difference	39	200

Variable cost/unit: $\dfrac{£200\ 000}{39\ 000} = £5.13\text{(rounded)}$.

Substitute into total cost of 60 000 units:

	£
Total cost	580 000
Less Variable element (60 000 × £5.13)	307 800
= Fixed element	272 200

Regression analysis (figures in 000s and £000s)

x	y	xy	x^2
21	380	7 980	441
40	462	18 480	1 600
50	558	27 900	2 500
60	580	34 800	3 600
42	486	20 412	1 764
33	396	13 068	1 089
Σ246	Σ2862	Σ122 640	Σ10 994

Variable cost per unit:

$$b = \frac{n\sum xy - \sum x \sum y}{n\sum x^2 - (\sum x)^2} = \frac{6(122\ 640) - (246 \times 2862)}{6(10\ 994) - 246^2} = \frac{735\ 840 - 704\ 052}{65\ 964 - 60\ 516} = £5.83$$

Fixed cost:

$$\frac{\sum y}{n} - \frac{b \sum x}{n} = \frac{2862}{6} - \frac{5.83(246)}{6} = 477 - 239.03 = 237.97$$

Bearing in mind that the figures are stated in £000, fixed cost is thus £237 970.

(b) Using high–low, the total cost is:

	£
July (70 000 × £5.13 variable) + £272 200 fixed	631 300
August (45 000 × £5.13 variable) + £272 200 fixed	503 050
September (65 000 × £5.13 variable) + £272 200 fixed	605 650
	1 740 000

Using the regression estimates gives:

	£
July (70 000 × £5.83 variable) + £237 970 fixed	646 070
August (45 000 × £5.83 variable) + £237 970 fixed	500 320
September (65 000 × £5.83 variable) + £237 970 fixed	616 920
	1 763 310

(c) The difference between the two estimates for July–September is very small, which might call into question whether the additional complexity of regression analysis is warranted here. Of the two estimates, that produced by regression analysis is, however, the more statistically reliable – but this does not mean that it is a more accurate estimate. Both techniques rely on past data, and this might not be a reasonable guide to the future, especially for July, where the volume of output exceeds any recorded in the last six months. What this might mean is that the July cost structure could be markedly different to that in other months, so that both techniques could produce misleading and inaccurate estimates. Further, it has been assumed in (a) and (b) that costs have been adjusted for any inflationary effects: if this is incorrect, then both estimates are likely to be incorrect.

3.5 (a) The past costs are inflated as follows:

Year	Adjustment	Inflated amount
		£
19X3	(£133 000 × 1.07 × 1.05 × 1.06 × 1.04 × 1.05)	172 963
19X4	(£150 000 × 1.05 × 1.06 × 1.04 × 1.05)	182 309
19X5	(£120 000 × 1.06 × 1.04 × 1.05)	138 902
19X6	(£163 000 × 1.04 × 1.05)	177 996
19X7	(£170 000 × 1.05)	178 500

(b) The high and low volumes occur in 19X7 and 19X5 respectively, giving differences in total cost and volume of:

	Volume of work (hours' processing time)	Total cost £
High volume	63 680	178 500
Low volume	32 000	138 902
Difference	31 680	39 598

The variable cost per hour of processing time is:

$$\frac{\text{Difference in total cost}}{\text{Difference in activity}} = \frac{£39\ 598}{31\ 680} = £1.25 \text{ (rounded)}$$

Substituting into either the high or low volume total cost gives the fixed cost; using the high volume gives:

	£
Total cost	178 500
Less Variable element (63 680 @ £1.25)	79 600
So fixed element is	98 900

(c) The estimated total cost for 19X8 is:

	£
Variable cost (68 000 hours @ £1.25)	85 000
Fixed cost	98 900
Total cost	183 900

The charge to be made to each user department will therefore be:

$$(1/10 \times £98\ 900) + £1.25 \text{ per processing hour}$$

i.e. £9890 + £1.25 per processing hour.

(d) Two factors which may have a bearing on the Computer Services Department's 19X8 costs are:

- Changes in technology: these occur very rapidly and might mean that new hardware and/or software must be bought, so that the department's costs are likely to change as a result.
- Type of work performed: this will not necessarily be the same in 19X8 as it has been in the past, which could be reflected in the 19X8 costs.

CHAPTER 4

4.1 C 10 820

Maximum level: (re-order level + EOQ) – (minimum usage × minimum lead time)

$$= (6300 + 6500) - (180 \times 11 \text{ days}) = 12\ 800 - 1980 = 10\ 820$$

Note: the question does not refer to 'EOQ' but to 're-order quantity'.

4.2 D 1750

Buffer stock is the minimum stock level:

$$\text{reorder level} - (\text{average usage} \times \text{average lead time})$$

Average usage is given in the question; average lead time is:

$$\frac{\text{Minimum lead time} + \text{maximum lead time}}{2} = \frac{11 + 15}{2} = 13 \text{ days}$$

Minimum stock level:

$$6300 - (350 \times 13) = 1750$$

4.3 (a) F (b) T (c) F (d) T (e) F (f) F (g) T (h) F

4.4 (a) The stock ledger cards in Tables A4.1–A4.3 set out the cost of issues to production and the stock value at 31 May.

Table A4.1 FIFO

Material code						Description: Drum 4	
	Receipts			**Issues**		**Balance**	
Date	Quantity	Cost per unit £	Amount £	Quantity	Amount £	Quantity	Amount £
1 May						80 @£20	1600
2 May	100	22	2200			180	3800
6 May				80 @£20	1600		
				70 @£22	1540		
				150	3140	30	660
13 May	300	25	7500			330	8160
19 May				30 @£22	660		
				170 @£25	4250		
				200	4910	130	3250
21 May	120	30	3600			250	6850
30 May				130 @£25	3250		
				20 @£30	600		
				150	3850	100	3000

Table A4.2 LIFO

Material code						Description: Drum 4	
	Receipts			**Issues**		**Balance**	
Date	Quantity	Cost per unit £	Amount £	Quantity	Amount £	Quantity	Amount £
1 May						80 @£20	1600
2 May	100	22	2200			180	3800
6 May				100 @£22	2200		
				50 @£20	1000		
				150	3200	30	600
13 May	300	25	7500			330	8100
19 May				200 @£25	5000	130	3100
21 May	120	30	3600			250	6700
30 May				120 @£30	3600		
				30 @£25	750		
				150	4350	100	2350

Table A4.3 AVCO

Material code						Description: Drum 4		
	Receipts			**Issues**		**Balance**		
Date	Quantity	Cost per unit £	Amount £	Quantity	Amount £	Quantity	Amount £	
1 May						80 @£20	1600	
2 May	100	22	2200			180	3800	
6 May				150 @£21.11	3167	30	633	
13 May	300	25	7500			330	8133	
19 May				200 @£24.65	4930	130	3203	
21 May	120	30	3600			250	6803	
30 May				150 @£27.21	4082	100	2721	

Weighted average cost after each receipt:

$$2 \text{ May} \quad (£3800 \div 180) = £21.11 \text{ (rounded)}$$
$$13 \text{ May} \quad (£8133 \div 330) = £24.65 \text{ (rounded)}$$
$$19 \text{ May} \quad (£6803 \div 250) = £27.21 \text{ (rounded)}$$

(b) Perpetual inventory describes a system that updates stock records as receipts and issues occur. The advantages of this compared to a system of periodically updating stock records stem from the fact that, under a perpetual inventory approach, records are kept up to date.

- Stocktaking should be facilitated, as records will reflect the quantity that ought to be on hand at the time the stocktake occurs.
- Receipts are recorded as they occur: this may be useful for assessing lead times, indicators like EOQ and possibly holding cost.
- Issues are recorded as they occur: the materials' cost of units can therefore be calculated without any delay that could occur with periodic updating of records.
- If records are automatically updated after each receipt/issue (e.g. by computer), then there is less chance of accidentally omitting or double-counting a receipt/issue.

4.5 (a) Gross hours per annum: (52 weeks × 40 hours) = 2080. To obtain productive hours, we need to deduct employees' holiday entitlement from gross annual hours: (52 − [5 + 2] weeks) × 40 hours = 1800 productive hours per annum. Total pay per employee per annum: (2080 hours × £4) = £8320. Charge per productive hour is thus: (£8320 ÷ 1800 hours) = £4.62 (rounded).

(i) Labour cost charged = (2 hours × £4.62) = £9.24.

(ii)

	£
Overtime hours at normal rate (2000 hours × £4.62)	9 240
Overtime premium at time and a half (80% × 2000 hours × [0.5 × £4.62])	3 696
Overtime premium at double time (20% × 2000 hours × £4.62)	1 848
Total labour cost	14 784

(b) Assuming 2 hours per week to be idle, productive hours (i.e. 'time taken') are (40 − 2) = 38. Standard time allowed for 184 units: (184 × 0.25 hour) = 46 hours.

    (i) *Halsey system*

Bonus: ($\frac{1}{2}$ time saved against standard × standard rate per hour)
$$= \tfrac{1}{2}(46 - 38) \times £4 = £16$$

	£
Full pay: Normal wage (40 hours × £4)	160
Bonus	16
	176

    (ii) *Rowan scheme*

Bonus: $\dfrac{\text{Time taken}}{\text{Time allowed}}$ × time saved × standard rate per hour

$$= \frac{38 \text{ hours}}{46 \text{ hours}} \times (46 - 38 \text{ hours}) \times £4 = £26.43$$

	£
Full pay: Normal wage (40 hours × £4)	160.00
Bonus	26.43
	186.43

(c) *Advantages of time-based system*

- Fairly straightforward to administer and understand.
- May be the only practical method – e.g. for some indirect workers where output is difficult to define/quantify, or where volume of output is not under employees' control.
- May encourage quality rather than quantity of output.

Disadvantages of time-based system

- The same rate applies to all, regardless of productivity; more productive workers may feel aggrieved.
- Following from the previous point, more supervision may be needed, to prevent less productive employees taking advantage of the fact that they will be paid the same irrespective of productivity.
- Does not encourage a high rate of output.

CHAPTER 5

5.1 D £600 000

	£
Overhead absorbed (11 000 client/hours × £50)	550 000
Add Underabsorption	50 000
Actual overhead	600 000

5.2 (a) F (b) T (c) T (d) F (e) T

5.3 Examination of the data in the question suggests that Production is heavily machine-intensive and that Installation is labour-intensive, so a machine-hour and direct labour-hour rate would be appropriate, respectively, for the cost centres. A unit rate is inappropriate here, because the question states that a *range* of decoders is produced and installed – i.e. cost units are not uniform (which would be the implication of using a unit rate). The absorption rates are:

$$Production \quad \frac{\text{Estimated overhead cost}}{\text{Estimated machine hours}} = \frac{£240\,000}{48\,000} = £5 \text{ per machine-hour}$$

$$Installation \quad \frac{\text{Estimated overhead cost}}{\text{Estimated direct labour hours}} = \frac{£330\,000}{15\,000} = £22 \text{ per direct labour-hour}$$

5.4 (a) (i) *Continuous allotment*

Table A5.1 Secondary distribution by continuous allotment

	Amount £	Reapportionment percentages	Machining £	Finishing £	Assembly £	Handling £	Inspection £
TOTALS	850 000		400 000	200 000	100 000	100 000	50 000
Inspection overhead reapportioned		20%, 30%, 45%, 5%	10 000	15 000	22 500	2 500	(50 000)
						102 500	
Handling overhead reapportioned		30%, 25%, 35%, 10%	30 750	25 625	35 875	(102 500)	10 250
Inspection overhead reapportioned		20%, 30%, 45%, 5%	2 050	3 075	4 613	512	(10 250)
Handling overhead reapportioned		30%, 25%, 35%, 10%	154	128	179	(512)	51
Inspection overhead reapportioned		Arbitrary allocation	17	17	17	–	(51)
TOTALS			442 971	243 845	163 184		

(ii) *Algebraic method*

Let M represent total handling overhead (including share of Inspection) and I represent total Inspection overhead (including share of Handling):

$$M = £100\,000 + 0.05I \quad (1)$$

$$I = £50\,000 + 0.1M \quad (2)$$

Rearranging (1): $M - 0.05I = £100\,000$ (3)
Rearranging (2): $I - 0.1M = £50\,000$ (4)
Multiplying (4) by 10: $10I - M = £500\,000$ (5)
Adding (3) and (5): $M - 0.05I = £100\,000$
                $+ 10I - M = £500\,000$
                $= 9.95I = £600\,000$

I is therefore (£600 000 ÷ 9.95) = £60 302 (rounded).
Substituting this value into (1) gives a value for M of:

$$M = £100\,000 + 0.05(£60\,302) = £103\,015$$

Table A5.2 apportions these values for M and I to the three production departments.

Table A5.2 Algebraic reapportionment

	Amount £	Reapportionment percentages	Machining £	Finishing £	Assembly £
TOTALS			400 000	200 000	100 000
Handling overhead reapportioned	103 015	30%, 25%, 35%	30 905	25 754	36 055
Inspection overhead reapportioned	60 302	20%, 30%, 45%	12 060	18 091	27 136
TOTALS			442 965	243 845	163 191

(b) Reapportioning service cost centre costs is worthwhile if:

- It provides useful information (e.g. more accurate unit costs).
- It meets the cost/benefit criterion.

Alternative treatments might be:

- To employ a blanket absorption rate, which avoids the need for cost centre overhead figures.
- To use activity based costing (ABC – see Chapter 6). This allocates and apportions overhead to activities, rather than to cost centres.

5.5 High–low analysis must be applied to the costs/hours in the question to obtain the answers to (a) and (b):

(a)

	Total overheads	Labour-hours
	£	
High	356 375	16 500
Low	338 875	14 500
Difference	17 500	2 000

Variable overhead per hour:

$$\frac{£17\,500}{2000} = £8.75$$

(b) Substituting the answer from (a) into the total overhead for 16 500 hours:

	£
Total overhead	356 375
Less Variable element (16 500 hours × £8.75)	144 375
= Fixed overhead	212 000

(c) Composite absorption rate = £22/hour. The fixed overhead absorption rate is therefore (£22 – £8.75) = £13.25 per hour. This rate is calculated as:

$$\frac{\text{Budgeted overhead cost}}{\text{Budgeted labour-hours}}$$

Inserting what we know gives:

$$\frac{£212\,000}{\text{Budgeted labour-hours}} = £13.25$$

Budgeted labour hours must therefore be (£212 000 ÷ £13.25) = 16 000.

(d)

	£
Overhead absorbed (15 850 hours × £22)	348 700
Actual overhead	355 050
Under recovery	6 350

(e) A departmental rate may provide a more accurate absorption basis where processes differ between departments (e.g. machine intensive in one, labour intensive in another) and/or where output is not uniform. However, use of departmental rates requires both primary and secondary distribution of overhead. This could involve time, effort and cost in determining suitable apportionment/reapportionment bases. And, as some of these bases may be subjective, the quality of information may not be greatly improved. (In other words, departmental rates could fail the cost/benefit test).

CHAPTER 6

6.1 C Cost pools

In an ABC system, a cost pool is created for each major activity, to which costs are allocated and apportioned, with the related cost driver being used as the basis for each pool's absorption rate.

6.2 (a) T (b) T (c) F (d) F (e) T (f) F (g) F

6.3 (a) Current absorption rates are based on direct labour hours. Total budgeted hours is the sum of (budgeted output × hours/unit) for the three products:

$$(2000 \times 24/60 \text{ hours}) \text{ [Product X]} + (1500 \times 40/60 \text{ hours}) \text{ [Product Y]}$$
$$+ (800 \times 60/60 \text{ hours}) \text{ [Product Z]} = 2600$$

Absorption rates:

$$\text{Receipt and inspection:} \quad \frac{£15\,600}{2600} = £6 \text{ per labour hour}$$

$$\text{Power:} \quad \frac{£19\,500}{2600} = £7.50 \text{ per labour hour}$$

$$\text{Material handling:} \quad \frac{£13\,650}{2600} = £5.25 \text{ per labour hour}$$

Overhead absorbed per unit of	Product X £	Product Y £	Product Z £
Receipt and inspection: £6 × 24/60, 40/60, 60/60 hours	2.40	4.00	6.00
Power: £7.50 × 24/60, 40/60, 60/60 hours	3.00	5.00	7.50
Material handling: £5.25 × 24/60, 40/60, 60/60 hours	2.10	3.50	5.25

The ABC absorption rates are as follows.

Receipt and inspection:

$$\frac{\text{Budgeted overhead cost}}{\text{Number of batches}} = \frac{15\,600}{(10 + 5 + 16)} = £503.23 \text{ (rounded) per batch}$$

Power: $\dfrac{\text{Budgeted overhead cost}}{\text{Number of drill operations}} = \dfrac{£19\,500}{18\,100} = £1.08$ (rounded) per operation

Number of drill operations is the sum of (budgeted output × operations per unit) for the three products: (2000 × 6) [Product X] + (1500 × 3) [Product Y] + (800 × 2) [Product Z] = 18 100.

Material handling:

$\dfrac{\text{Budgeted overhead cost}}{\text{Square metres of material}} = \dfrac{£13\,650}{19\,400} = £0.70$ (rounded) per square metre

Number of square metres of material handled is the sum of: (budgeted output × square metres per unit) for the three products: (2000 × 4) [Product X] + (1500 × 6) [Product Y] + (800 × 3) [Product Z] = 19 400.

Overhead absorbed per unit of	Product X £	Product Y £	Product Z £
Receipt and inspection:			
£503.23 per batch × 10, 5, 16 batches	5032.30	2516.15	8051.68
÷ 2000, 1500, 800 units	2.52	1.68	10.06
Power:			
£1.08 per operation × 6, 3, 2 operations	6.48	3.24	2.16
Material handling:			
£0.70 per square metre × 4, 6, 3 square metres	2.80	4.20	2.10

Comparative product costs are presented in Table A6.1.

Table A6.1 Budgeted product costs

	Product X		Product Y		Product Z	
	Existing £	ABC £	Existing £	ABC £	Existing £	ABC £
Direct material	5.00	5.00	3.00	3.00	6.00	6.00
Direct labour*	1.60	1.60	2.67	2.67	4.00	4.00
Prime cost	6.60	6.60	5.67	5.67	10.00	10.00
Overhead:						
Receipt and inspection	2.40	2.52	4.00	1.68	6.00	10.06
Power	3.00	6.48	5.00	3.24	7.50	2.16
Material handling	2.10	2.80	3.50	4.20	5.25	2.10
Product cost	14.10	18.40	18.17	14.79	28.75	24.32

* Direct labour cost/unit: £4 per hour × 24/60, 40/60, 60/60 hours.

(b) Cost drivers are the main underlying causes of costs; e.g. for Hensau Ltd, the main cause of Power costs is the number of power drill operations that occur. As demonstrated in (a), cost drivers are used to absorb overhead into unit cost. It is argued that by doing so, unit costs more accurately reflect resources consumed in production. For example, a unit of Product X requires twice as many drill operations as one of Product Y, so we would expect to see X being charged twice the amount of Y for the related cost. Using ABC this is what happens (£6.48/unit compared to £3.24); under the existing method, X is charged less than Y for power – use of a labour-hour absorption rate masks the different pattern of resource consumption and, to that extent, produces distorted unit costs.

It is further argued that identification of cost drivers aids cost control. If we know, for example, that receipt and inspection costs are driven by the number of batches of material, any action to reduce the number of batches should also reduce the associated cost. In addition, knowledge of an organisation's major activities can help pinpoint those which relate to non-value-added activities like material handling. In a cost reduction exercise, reduction of such costs should be the first priority.

However, all this depends upon our ability to correctly identify and quantify cost drivers.

6.4 (a) Cost per unit using conventional methods:

	Product X £	Product Y £	Product Z £
Direct labour ($\frac{1}{2}$, $1\frac{1}{2}$, 1 hours × £6)	3.00	9.00	6.00
Direct materials	20.00	12.00	25.00
Prime cost	23.00	21.00	31.00
Overhead ($1\frac{1}{2}$, 1, 3 hours × £28)	42.00	28.00	84.00
Cost per unit	65.00	49.00	115.00

(b) Total overhead to be apportioned to activities: (total machine hours × absorption rate per hour). Machine hours: $(750 \times 1\frac{1}{2})$ [Product X] + (1250 × 1) [Product Y] + (7000 × 3) [Product Z] = 23 375. Total overhead is therefore (23 375 × £28) = £654 500. This is apportioned to activities using the percentages given:

Activity	%	Apportionment (£)	Cost driver
Set-ups	35	229 075	Set-ups
Machinery	20	130 900	Machine hours
Materials handling	15	98 175	Movements
Inspection	30	196 350	Inspections
		654 500	

The relevant cost driver for each activity is taken from the question.

Absorption rate per set-up: $\dfrac{\text{Budgeted set-up cost}}{\text{Number of set-ups}} = \dfrac{£229\ 075}{670} = £341.90$ (rounded)

Absorption rate per machine-hour: $\dfrac{\text{Budgeted machine cost}}{\text{Number of machine hours}} = \dfrac{£130\ 900}{23\ 375} = £5.60$

Absorption rate per movement: $\dfrac{\text{Budgeted handling cost}}{\text{Number of movements}} = \dfrac{£98\ 175}{120} = £818.13$ (rounded)

Absorption rate per inspection: $\dfrac{\text{Budgeted inspection cost}}{\text{Number of inspections}} = \dfrac{£196\ 350}{1000} = £196.35$

Absorbed per unit of:	Product X £	Product Y £	Product Z £
Set-up costs:			
75, 115, 480 set-ups × £341.90	25 642.50	39 318.50	164 112.00
÷ 750, 1250, 7000 units	34.19	31.45	23.44
Machine costs: $1\frac{1}{2}$, 1, 3 hours × £5.60	8.40	5.60	16.80
Materials handling costs:			
12, 21, 87 movements × £818.13	9 817.56	17 180.73	71 177.31
÷750, 1250, 7000 units	13.09	13.74	10.17
Inspection costs:			
150, 180, 670 inspections × £196.35	29 452.50	35 343.00	131 554.50
÷ 750, 1250, 7000 units	39.27	28.27	18.79

Cost per unit		Product X	Product Y	Product Z
		£	£	£
Prime cost (from (a))		23.00	21.00	31.00
Overhead:	Set-up cost	34.19	31.45	23.44
	Machine cost	8.40	5.60	16.80
	Handling cost	13.09	13.74	10.17
	Inspection cost	39.27	28.27	18.79
Cost per unit		117.95	100.06	100.20

(c)

Comparative cost per unit	Product X	Product Y	Product Z
	£	£	£
Using machine hour rate	65.00	49.00	115.00
Using ABC	117.95	100.06	100.20
Difference	52.95	51.06	(14.80)

These are very significant differences. If the cost driver information is reasonably accurate, then the existing absorption rate causes the high-volume product (Z) to heavily subsidise the other two, which have lower volumes. Product costs may therefore be inaccurate, with implications for stock valuation and profit. Also, to the extent that they are based on cost, selling prices may be too low for X and Y, while being too high for Z. X and Y may thus be selling at a loss, whereas Z's sales volume may be depressed by an artificially high price.

6.5 (a) (i) Packing materials weighted to reflect relative fragility: (30 000 cubic metres × 1) + (45 000 cubic metres × 2) + (25 000 cubic metres × 3) = 195 000. Packing materials per cubic metre (£1 950 000 ÷ 195 000) = £10. Weighted for each customer, the average packing material cost per cubic metre is: John Ltd (£10 × 1) = £10, George Ltd (£10 × 2) = £20, Paul Ltd (£10 × 3) = £30.

Charge per cubic metre for other costs:

$$\frac{(£350\ 000 + £30\ 000 + £500\ 000 + £60\ 000)}{(30\ 000 + 45\ 000 + 25\ 000)} = £9.40$$

Average cost per cubic metre	John Ltd	George Ltd	Paul Ltd
	£	£	£
Packing materials	10.00	20.00	30.00
Other costs	9.40	9.40	9.40
Cost per cubic metre	19.40	29.40	39.40

(ii) Cost apportionment to each of the three activities is undertaken using the percentages given in the question:

		Receipt and Inspection	Storage	Packing	Total
		£	£	£	£
Labour:	basic	52 500	35 000	262 500	350 000
	overtime	15 000	4 500	10 500	30 000
Occupancy		100 000	300 000	100 000	500 000
Admin. and management		24 000	6 000	30 000	60 000
Total		191 500	345 500	403 000	940 000

Total receipt and inspection time is the sum of (cubic metres handled × minutes/cubic metre) for each customer: (30 000 × 5) [John Ltd] + (45 000 × 9) [George Ltd] + (25 000 × 15) [Paul Ltd] = 930 000 minutes. Charge per receipt and inspection minute:

$$\frac{£191\ 500}{930\ 000} = £0.21 \text{ (rounded)}$$

Total square metres of storage is the sum of (cubic metres handled × square metres of storage/cubic metre) for each customer: $(30\ 000 \times 0.3)$ [John Ltd] + $(45\ 000 \times 0.3)$ [George Ltd] + $(25\ 000 \times 0.2)$ [Paul Ltd] = 27 500. Charge per square metre of storage:

$$\frac{£345\ 500}{27\ 500} = £12.56 \text{ (rounded)}$$

Total packing time is the sum of (cubic metres handled × minutes per cubic metre) for each customer: $(30\ 000 \times 36)$ [John Ltd] + $(45\ 000 \times 45)$ [George Ltd] + $(25\ 000 \times 60)$ [Paul Ltd] = 4 605 000 minutes. Charge per minute of packing time:

$$\frac{£403\ 000}{4\ 605\ 000} = £0.09 \text{ (rounded)}$$

Average cost per cubic metre	John Ltd £	George Ltd £	Paul Ltd £
Packing materials (from (a)(i))	10.00	20.00	30.00
Other costs:			
Receipt and inspection: £0.21 per minute			
× 5, 9, 15 minutes	1.05	1.89	3.15
Storage: £12.56 per square metre			
× 0.3, 0.3, 0.2 square metres	3.77	3.77	2.51
Packing: £0.09 per minute			
× 36, 45, 60 minutes	3.24	4.05	5.40
Cost per cubic metre	18.06	29.71	41.06

(b) The activities are the major activities undertaken by Repak Ltd, and the cost drivers are the main underlying cause of the cost associated with each activity. The principle being applied is that activities incur costs and products consume activities, so costs should be charged to products in a way that recognises this fact – i.e. on the basis of cost drivers.

Assuming that activity and cost driver information is reasonably accurate, cost driver charges should produce unit costs that more accurately reflect the resources used for each product. For example, each cubic metre handled for John Ltd and George Ltd requires the same storage space, so each ought to be charged the same for the related cost – which ABC achieves, both customers being charged £3.77 per cubic metre handled. Differences of this sort are very likely to be obscured or even distorted using the method in (a)(i), where each cubic metre is charged a blanket rate of £9.40. Such treatment implies that all cubic metres handled have the same requirements for receipt and inspection, storage and packing, which is clearly not the case. Any distortion in unit cost could have a knock-on effect on profit, and possibly on selling prices; it is possible that high-volume products may subsidise the cost of low-volume products.

Cost control may be enhanced if cost drivers are known: control the incidence of the cost driver and the associated cost can be controlled. Thus, if Repak Ltd can reduce receipt and inspection times, the related cost is likely to fall. Identification of major activities may also aid cost reduction schemes by allowing management to focus on the cost of non-value-added activities.

CHAPTER 7

7.1 D DR Work-in-progress control account
CR Overhead control account

7.2 (a) T (b) F (c) T (d) T (e) F (f) T (g) F

7.3 A The financial accounting profit is £300 greater than the cost accounting profit.

The difference in opening and closing stock between the two ledgers is:

		Financial £	*Cost* £
Opening stock:	materials	5 000	6 400
	finished goods	9 800	9 600
		14 800	16 000

Higher opening stock means lower profit, so financial accounting profit is (£16 000 – £14 800) = £1200 higher as a result of this difference.

		Financial £	*Cost* £
Closing stock:	materials	4 000	5 200
	finished goods	7 900	7 600
		11 900	12 800

Higher closing stock means higher profit, so cost accounting profit is higher by (£12 800 – £11 900) = £900 as a result of this difference.

The overall profit difference is thus:

	£
Higher financial profit due to opening stock difference	1200
Higher costing profit due to closing stock difference	900
Overall higher financial profit	300

7.4 (i)

Work-in progress control account

	£		£
Balance b/d	125 750	Finished goods control (given)	1 241 500
Wages control: direct wages	173 400	Balance c/d	147 000
Stores control: material issues	598 050		
Production overhead control:			
overhead absorbed	491 300		
	1 388 500		1 388 500
Balance b/d	147 000		

Direct material stores control account

	£		£
Balance b/d	48 250	Work-in-progress control	598 050
Cost ledger control: purchases	617 300	Balance b/d	67 500
	665 550		665 550
Balance b/d	67 500		

Finished goods control account

	£		£
Balance b/d	94 500	Cost of sales (given)	1 310 750
Work-in-progress control	1 241 500	Balance c/d	25 250
	1 336 000		1 336 000
Balance b/d	25 250		

Production overhead control account

	£		£
Cost ledger control:		Work-in-progress control:	
overhead incurred	392 525	overhead absorbed (balance)	491 300
Additional depreciation	35 000		
Costing profit and loss account:			
overabsorption (given)	63 775		
	491 300		491 300

(b) Overhead absorbed (£491 300) = (hours worked × £17); therefore, hours worked = (£491 300 ÷ £17) = 28 900. The overabsorption has arisen because actual cost differs from budgeted and/or because actual hours differ from budgeted. It may be that budgeted overhead cost over-estimated inflation, or that the budgeted labour-hours did not allow for receipt of some unanticipated customer orders.

7.5 (a) Overheads are absorbed on a machine hour basis:

$$\frac{\text{Budgeted overhead cost}}{\text{Budgeted machine hours}} = \frac{£500\,000}{50\,000} = £10 \text{ per machine hour}$$

Overhead absorbed: (actual machine hours × £10) = (44 000 × £10) = £440 000.

Raw materials control account

	£		£
Balance b/d	72 000	Work-in-progress control	392 000
Creditor control (purchases)	450 000	Production overhead control	15 000
Work-in-progress control (returns)	4 000	Creditor control (returns)	24 000
		Balance c/d	95 000
	526 000		526 000
Balance b/d	95 000		

Production overhead control account

	£		£
Raw materials control	15 000	Work-in-progress control (overhead	
Creditor control	465 000	absorbed	440 000
		Profit and loss account	
		(underabsorption) [balance]	40 000
	480 000		480 000

Work-in-progress control account

	£		£
Balance b/d	132 000	Raw materials control (returns)	4 000
Raw materials control	392 000	Finished goods control (balance)	1 205 000
Production overhead control	440 000	Balance c/d (given)	180 000
Wages control (direct labour)	425 000		
	1 389 000		1 389 000
Balance b/d	180 000		

Finished goods control account

	£		£
Balance b/d	82 000	Cost of sales (balance)	1 035 000
Work-in-progress control	1 205 000	Balance c/d (given)	252 000
	1 287 000		1 287 000
Balance b/d	252 000		

Rontree: Profit and loss account for the six months ended 31 May 1997

	£	£
Sales		1 800 000
Cost of sales		1 035 000
Gross profit		765 000
General overheads	375 000	
Underabsorbed overhead	40 000	415 000
Net profit		350 000

(b) Pre-determined recovery (absorption) rates might be used because:

- Actual costs and volume of absorption base (e.g. machine-hours) will not be known until the end of the period. Estimated unit costs would therefore not be available for purposes such as price-setting.
- Actual costs and volume of absorption base are likely to fluctuate over time, so that unit cost could be as much a function of when it happens to be calculated as it is of the resources consumed to produce output.

(c) Direct production cost ('prime cost') can be unambiguously and quantifiably associated with a unit of output. We can therefore state the quantity of direct materials (and the associated cost) required to produce one unit of output. Indirect costs ('overheads') cannot be attributed to individual cost units in this way, and require to undergo primary and secondary distribution before being absorbed into unit cost.

CHAPTER 8

8.1 E (ii) only: customer-driven production.

8.2 (a) F   (b) T   (c) T   (d) T   (e) T   (f) F   (g) F

8.3 (a) The cost of each job is presented in Table A8.1. Note that selling, distribution and administration costs are only absorbed into the cost of complete jobs (X123, X124 and X125 here).

Table A8.1 Job costs for December

	Job X123 £	Job X124 £	Job X125 £	Job X127 £	Job X128 £
Direct labour @ £5/hour: at 30 November	820	600			
For December	260	390	1560	755	290
Direct materials: at 30 November	1250	722			
For December	420	698	1900	1221	516
Returned to stores	(120)		(70)	(217)	
Transferred	(100)		100		
Factory overhead @200% of direct labour					
At 30 November	1640	1200			
For December	520	780	3120	1510	580
Total factory production cost	4690	4390	6610	3269	1386
Selling, distribution and admin. costs @					
20% of total factory cost	938	878	1322	——	——
	5628	5268	7932	3269	1386

(b) **Profit/loss on jobs invoiced to customers in December**

	Job X123 £	Job X124 £	Job X125 £
Amount invoiced	6250	6000	7900
Less Job cost (from (a))	5628	5268	7932
Profit/(loss)	622	732	(32)

(c) **Enquiry: total cost and price**

	£
Direct materials (given)	4500
Direct labour (125 hours × £5)	625
Production overhead (200% of labour cost)	1250
	6375
Selling, distribution and admin overhead (20% × £6375)	1275
Total cost of job	7650
Profit at 30% of total cost	2295
Price to be quoted	9945

8.4 (a) (i) Works Orders 488 and 517 are both substantial in respect of the monetary amounts involved and also with reference to their time-span. Contract costing is therefore appropriate. Works Orders 518 and 519 are both of comparatively short duration and small as regards monetary amount. The fact that their completion spans two accounting periods is likely to be purely accidental, whereas with Works Orders 488 and 517, it is inherent to the nature of the work. Job costing is appropriate for Works Orders 518 and 519.

(ii) Company policy is to recognise profit on contracts only when they are at least 50% complete. At 30 April 1997, Works Order 517 has not reached this degree of completion (regardless of whether this is judged on the basis of sales value or cost) – so no profit will be recognised on this contract. Because they are being dealt with as jobs, no profit is recognised on Works Orders 518 and 519. The cost for each contract/job is given below:

Works Order	488	517	518	519
	£000	£000	£000	£000
Costs to date				
Direct labour	105	10	5	2.0
Direct materials	86	7	4	2.0
Overhead (40% × direct labour cost)	42	4	2	0.8
	233	21	11	4.8

Estimated costs to complete	
Direct labour	40
Direct materials	10
Overhead (40% × direct labour cost)	16
	66

Notional profit	
Contract sales value	450
Less Costs to date	233
Estimated costs to complete	66
	151

Profit recognised on Works Order 488:

$$\frac{\text{Value certified to date}}{\text{Total contract value}} \times \text{notional profit} = \frac{350}{450} \times 151 = 117.45$$

Alternatively, using a cost basis, profit recognised is:

$$\frac{\text{Costs to date}}{\text{Total contract costs}} \times \text{notional profit} = \frac{233}{(233 + 66)} \times 151 = 117.6$$

The balance sheet valuation for Works Orders 517, 518 and 519 is their cost to date, as calculated above. For Works Order 488, we need to obtain a figure for the cost of work not certified:

	£
Value of work certified to date	350.00
Less Profit recognised	117.45 (117.6)
= Cost of sales	232.55 (232.4)
Costs to date	233.00
So cost of work not certified is	0.45 (0.6)

(The figures in parentheses show the results if profit recognised is based on cost to date.)
Balance sheet entries for work-in-progress:

	£000
Works Order 488	0.45 (0.6)
Works Order 517	21.00
Works Order 518	11.00
Works Order 519	4.80
	37.25 (37.4)

(iii) Use of direct labour cost to attribute overhead suggests that overhead costs are mostly driven by direct labour cost. This may be true where the majority of overheads comprise items like employers' National Insurance contributions (which are based on direct labour cost). However, where overhead bears little relation to labour cost, unit costs may be distorted, as the method of output could be ignored and the amount of overhead absorbed could vary according to how much employees happen to be paid.

(b) Main features of process costing:

- Output is homogeneous and typically mass-produced.
- Cost units are rarely separately identifiable until they emerge from the process.
- Process costs are averaged to obtain a cost per unit.

The choice between job and process costing will depend on:

- The nature of the production process.
- The nature of the product.
- The extent to which costs can readily be traced to individual cost units.
- The extent to which output is produced to customer specification.

8.5 (a) The contract commenced at the start of January; since the contractor's accounting year ends on 30 September, the contract will have been underway for 9/12 of an accounting year by 30 September 19X2. The contract account will therefore be charged with 9/12 of a year's depreciation of plant – i.e. (9/12 × £20 000) = £15 000. The book value of plant on site at 30 September 19X2 is thus (£49 000 – £15 000) = £34 000.

Refrigerated Store Contract Account

	£		£
Wages: paid	140 660	Materials returned to stores	630
Accrued c/d	2 300	Materials transferred	1 580
Materials purchased	166 320	Expenses prepaid c/d	1 500
Materials from stores	5 780	Plant on site at 30 September c/d	34 000
Plant: book value at 3 January	49 000	Materials on site at 30 Sept. c/d	16 200
Subcontract work	64 000	Cost of work not certified c/d	31 000
Site expenses	22 000	Cost of work certified c/d	
Architects' fees	40 000	(balance)	405 150
	490 060		490 060
Cost of work certified b/d	405 150		
Contract provision (balance)	36 928	Cost of sales (from (b))	442 078
	442 078		442 078
Expenses prepaid b/d	1 500	Wages accrued b/d	2 300
Plant on site b/d	34 000		
Materials on site b/d	16 200		
Cost of work not certified b/d	31 000		

Notional contract profit:

	£
Sales value of contract	1 000 000
Costs to date: work certified	405 150
work not certified	31 000
Estimated cost to complete	414 000
Notional profit	149 850

Profit to be recognised:

$$\frac{\text{Invoice value to date}}{\text{Total contract value}} \times \text{notional profit} = \frac{£520\,000}{£1\,000\,000} \times £149\,850 = £77\,922$$

Profit to be recognised could also be based on:

$$\frac{\text{Cost to date}}{\text{Total contract cost}} \times \text{notional profit} = \frac{£436\,150}{£850\,150} \times £149\,850 = £76\,877$$

(b) *Profit and loss account extract*

	£
Sales	520 000
Less Cost of sales (balance to contract account)	442 078
Profit (from (a))	77 922

Balance sheet extract

		£	£
Fixed assets	Plant on site		34 000
Current assets	Stock: materials on site	16 200	
	Debtors: amounts recoverable on contracts	110 000*	
	prepayment	1 500	

Creditors: amounts falling due within one year
Provisions for liabilities and charges:

	£
Accrued wages	(2 300)
Contract provision	(5 928)**

* Debtors:	£
Invoice value of work certified	520 000
Less Cash received	410 000
	110 000

(This figure includes retentions of 15% of invoice value.)

** Contract balances (cost of work not certified)	31 000
Contract provision	36 928
Net provision per balance sheet	5 928

CHAPTER 9

9.1 (a) T (b) F (c) F (d) F (e) T (f) T (g) T

9.2 A *Materials*   *Conversion*
                7290   7230

In order to answer the question, we need to assume that the normal loss was the same as the actual loss during April. Table A9.1 shows the equivalent unit calculation.

Table A9.1 FIFO equivalent unit calculation

	Materials	Conversion
Completed output *Less* Opening WIP equivalent units	(100% × 7250) −(80% × 300) 7010	(100% × 7250) −(60% × 300) 7070
Closing WIP	(70% × 400) 280	(40% × 400) 160
Total equivalent units	7290	7230

9.3 C   *Materials*   *Conversion*
          21 600   21 150

A check on the process's inputs and outputs reveals the following:

		Litres	*Litres*
Inputs	Opening WIP		2 000
	Material input		24 000
			26 000
Outputs	Normal loss (10% × 24 000)	2 400	
	Output to Process 2	19 500	
	Closing WIP	3 000	24 900
Abnormal loss			1 100

Assuming the abnormal loss to be 100% complete, the equivalent unit calculation is in Table A9.2.

Table A9.2 FIFO equivalent unit calculation

	Materials	Conversion
Abnormal loss	(100% × 1100) 1100	(100% × 1100) 1100
Completed output *Less* Opening WIP equivalent units	(100% × 19 500) −(100% × 2 000) 17 500	(100% × 19 500) −(40% × 2 000) 18 700
Closing WIP	(100% × 3000) 3000	(45% × 3000) 1350
Total equivalent units	21 600	21 150

9.4 (a) Comparison of each process's inputs and outputs shows that there were no losses or gains during period 10, that neither process had opening WIP and that only Process 1 has closing WIP. For simplicity, labour and production overhead are combined as 'conversion costs' in Table A9.3, with the total associated cost being the sum of direct labour plus production overhead in Process 1 (£2260 + [100% × £2260]) = £4520.

Table A9.3 Cost per equivalent unit for Process 1

	Materials	Conversion
Completed output	(100% × 2200) 2200	(100% × 2200) 2200
Closing WIP	(100% × 200) 200	(30% × 200) 60
Total equivalent units	2400	2260
Cost	£5280	£4520
Cost/equivalent unit	£2.20	£2.00

Cost of completed output transferred to Process 2: 2200 units × (£2.20 + £2.00) = £9240. Cost of closing stock:

	£
Materials (200 equivalent units × £2.20)	440
Conversion (60 equivalent units × £2.00)	120
Closing stock	560

(b) Since Process 2 does not have opening WIP, closing WIP, or any losses/gains during the period, the cost of transfers to finished goods is the same as the process's total input cost:

	£
Transfers from Process 1	9 240
Material	9 460
Direct labour	10 560
Production overhead (2/3 of direct labour cost)	7 040
Cost of transfers to Finished Goods	36 300
Units transferred	2 200
Cost per unit	£16.50

(c) Scrap proceeds are debited to bank/cash and credited to either the normal loss or abnormal loss account.

(d) Abnormal losses are credited to the process account at cost, and debited to the abnormal loss account. Any associated scrap value is credited to the abnormal loss account, with the balance on the abnormal loss account being debited to the profit and loss account at the period end.

(e) Abnormal gains are debited to the process account at cost and credited to the abnormal gain account. Any associated scrap value is debited to the abnormal gain account and credited to the normal loss account. The abnormal gain account balance is credited to the profit and loss account at the end of the period.

9.5 (a) As a first step to determining any loss/gain for the period, we need to obtain a figure for completed output (including losses, as these are 100% complete):

	kg
Input from mixing	36 000
Less Closing WIP	8 000
Completed output (including losses)	28 000

Completed output excluding losses (i.e. the number of kg transferred to finished goods) is (28 000 − 3600) = 24 400 kg.

Comparison of normal and actual loss gives:

	kg
Normal loss (10% × 28 000)	2800
Actual loss (given)	3600
Therefore abnormal loss is	800

(b) Since closing WIP has reached the same stage of completion for both labour and overheads, these are combined in Table A9.4; the associated cost is (£43 800 + £29 200) = £73 000. It has been assumed that the abnormal loss is 100% complete and that the units concerned are scrapped (as with the normal loss).

Table A9.4 Cost per equivalent unit for Distillation Process

	Materials	Conversion
Abnormal loss	(100% × 800)	(100% × 800)
	800	800
Completed output	(100% × 24 400)	(100% × 24 400)
	24 400	24 400
Closing WIP	(100% × 8000)	(50% × 8000)
	8000	4000
Total equivalent units	33 200	29 200
Cost	£166 000	£73 000
Cost/equivalent unit	£5.00	£2.50

Cost of abnormal loss: (800 × [£5.00 + £2.50]) = £6000.
Cost of completed output: (24 400 × [£5.00 + £2.50]) = £183 000.

Distillation Process Account

	kg	£		kg	£
Mixing process (material)	36 000	166 000	Normal loss	2 800	–
Direct labour		43 800	Abnormal loss	800	6 000
Overhead		29 200	Finished goods	24 400	183 000
			Balance c/d	8 000	50 000
	36 000	239 000		36 000	239 000
Balance b/d	8 000	50 000			

(a) The process account will be credited with the scrap value of the normal loss, the corresponding debit being to the normal loss account. Proceeds of scrap sale are debited to cash/bank and credited to the normal loss and/or abnormal loss account.

CHAPTER 10

10.1 (a) F (b) T (c) T (d) F (e) T (f) F (g) T (h) T

10.2 (a) Process loss for the period is 10% of inputs: $(10\% \times 3200 \text{ litres}) = 320$ litres. The joint process cost to be apportioned is:

	£
Direct materials	24 000
Direct labour	48 000
Prime cost	72 000
Overhead (120% × prime cost)	86 400
	158 400
Less Scrap value of loss (320 × £16.20)	5 184
Joint cost to apportion	153 216

(i)

Table A10.1 Joint cost apportionment using relative sales value

Product	Output (litres)	Sales value of output £	% of total sales value	Joint cost apportioned £
Chemical X	1440	(1440 × 100) = 144 000	58.14	89 080
Chemical Y	864	(864 × 80) = 69 120	27.91	42 763
Chemical Z	576	(576 × 60) = 34 560	13.95	21 373
		247 680		153 216

(ii)

Table A10.2 Joint cost apportionment using volume

Product	Output (litres)	% of total output	Joint cost apportioned £
Chemical X	1440	50.00	76 608
Chemical Y	864	30.00	45 965
Chemical Z	576	20.00	30 643
	2880		153 216

(b)

Joint Process Account

	Litres	£		Litres	£
Direct materials	3200	24 000	Normal loss	320	5 184
Direct labour		48 000	Finished goods: X	1440	89 080
Overhead		86 400	Y	864	42 763
			Z	576	21 373
	3200	158 400		3200	158 400

(c) Assuming that the loss is expressed as a percentage of input, then 200 litres of good output represents 90% of inputs. Inputs are therefore 200/0.9 = 222.22 litres. Conversion cost (i.e. labour plus overhead) for this volume of inputs is:

	£
Labour (222.22 × £50)	11 111
Overhead (222.22 × £40)	8 889
	20 000

10.3 (a) (i) Joint costs (£40 000 from the question) are apportioned on the basis of volume.

Table A10.3 Joint cost apportionment using volume

Product	Output (litres)	% of total output	Joint cost apportioned £
Product B	3500	43.75	17 500
Product K	2500	31.25	12 500
Product C	2000	25.00	10 000
	8000		40 000

Estimated profit/loss for June

	Product B £	Product K £	Product C £	Total £
Revenue (3500 × £10), (2500 × £20), (2000 × £30)	35 000	50 000	60 000	145 000
Share of joint costs	17 500	12 500	10 000	40 000
Further processing costs	20 000	10 000	22 500	52 500
Profit/(loss)	(2 500)	27 500	27 500	52 500

(ii) The further processing decision is based on comparison of incremental revenue and incremental costs:

		£
Product B	Incremental revenue (3500 litres × [£10 – £6])	14 000
	Incremental cost	20 000
	Incremental loss	(6 000)
Product K	Incremental revenue (2500 litres × [£20 – £8])	30 000
	Incremental cost	10 000
	Incremental profit	20 000
Product C	Incremental revenue (2000 litres × [£30 – £9])	42 000
	Incremental cost	22 500
	Incremental profit	19 500

Therefore B should be sold at the split-off point while K and C should be further processed.

Revised profit:

		£
Sales:	B (3500 × £6)	21 000
	K (2500 × £20)	50 000
	C (2000 × £30)	60 000
		131 000

			£	
Costs:	Joint process		40 000	
	Further processing:	K	10 000	
		C	22 500	72 500
Profit				58 500

This represents a £6000 increase on the profit earned if all three products are processed further.

(b) (i) If the joint process were treated as a profit centre, then it would be credited with the intermediate sales value of the joint products, rather than with their cost. The balance on the joint process account represents profit or loss.

(ii) Profit is (intermediate sales value of joint products *less* joint process costs):

	£
B (3500 × £6)	21 000
K (2500 × £8)	20 000
C (2000 × £9)	18 000
	59 000
Joint process costs	40 000
Profit	19 000

(iii) Two advantages of treating the joint process as a profit centre:
- The need for arbitrary cost apportionments is removed.
- It is consistent with the principles of responsibility accounting (see Chapter 18) – i.e. it treats the joint process almost as if it were a commercial enterprise in its own right, with process managers taking responsibility for meeting process budgets/targets etc.

(c) The problem with cost apportionments is that they do not represent cash flows and may be somewhat arbitrary. If they are used for planning, control and decision making purposes, there is a danger that management may believe that they represent cash costs – which could result in unrealistic plans, inappropriate control action and incorrect decisions. For planning and control, it is preferable to use estimated and actual costs incurred (rather than apportionments thereof); for decision making, we should use relevant costs (see Chapter 14).

CHAPTER 11

11.1 B (i) and (ii) only.

11.2 (a) F (b) T (c) T (d) F (e) F (f) F (g) T

11.3 C £1984
Total cost for the year: (£20 000 general expenses + £30 000 salary) = £50 000. Total chargeable hours: 75% × ([52 – 4 weeks] × 35 hours) = 1260. Per chargeable hour, this amounts to: £50 000/1260 = £39.68. For a job lasting 50 hours, the charge will be (50 × £39.68) = £1984.

11.4 The first stage is to allocate and apportion costs to each of the hospital's eight departments. This is done in Table A11.1. Table A11.2 reapportions the support department costs to each of surgical and medical wards and out-patients. Note that direct reapportionment is used (see Chapter 5). You may have chosen different reapportionment bases from those shown in Table A11.2 – this is acceptable, providing the bases selected are reasonable given the nature of the cost and the limited information available.

Table A11.1 Allocation and apportionment to departments

Cost item	Amount £000	Basis	Proportion	Surgical	Medical	Out-patients	Laundry	Porterage and cleaning	X-ray dept	Surgical supplies	Labora-tories
Doctors' sal.	2950	Allocated	N/a	1000	1500	450	–	–	–	–	–
Nurses' sal.	4650	Allocated	N/a	1650	2100	900	–	–	–	–	–
Equipment	400	Allocated	N/a	400	–	–	–	–	–	–	–
Mainten'ce	320	Allocated	N/a	120	200	–	–	–	–	–	–
Op theatre	800	Allocated	N/a	800	–	–	–	–	–	–	–
Medicine	1870	Allocated	N/a	600	820	450	–	–	–	–	–
Reception	90	Allocated	N/a	–	–	90	–	–	–	–	–
Support	3690	Allocated	N/a	–	–	–	300	410	900	880	1200
Occupancy	1300	Given %	30%,40%,10%,5%, 5%,2%,3%,5%	390	520	130	65	65	26	39	65
Admin.	1200	Given %	30%,30%,20%,5%, 5%,2%,3%,5%,	360	360	240	60	60	24	36	60
Canteen	500	Given %	30%,45%,5%,5%,5%, 5%,2%,3%,5%	150	225	25	25	25	10	15	25
TOTALS				5470	5725	2285	450	560	960	970	1350

Table A11.2 Reapportionment of support department costs

	Amount £000	Basis	Proportion	Surgical	Medical	Out-patients	Laundry	Porterage and cleaning	X-ray dept	Surgical supplies	Laboratories
Total from Table A11.1				5470	5725	2285	450	560	960	970	1350
Laundry reapportioned	450	Number of beds†	25/57, 30/57, 2/57	197	237	16	(450)				
Porterage reapportioned	560	Area	4/15, 6/15, 5/15	149	224	187		(560)			
X-ray reapportioned	960	Number of patients*	8%, 12%, 80%*	77	115	768			(960)		
Supplies reapportioned	970	Number of requisitions	33/90, 36/90, 21/90	356	388	226				(970)	
Labs reapportioned	1350	Number of patients*	8%, 12%, 80%*	108	162	1080					(1350)
TOTALS				6357	6851	4562					

* For surgical and medical wards, the number of patients is calculated as:

(wards × beds per ward × 365 days × occupancy %) ÷ average patient stay

Surgical: (10 × 25 × 365 × 90%) ÷ 10 days	8 212.5	8%
Medical: (12 × 25 × 365 × 85%) ÷ 7 days	13 296.4	12%
Out-patients (given)	86 000.0	80%
Total	107 508.9	100%

Patient bed-days are (wards × beds per ward × 365 days × occupancy %):

Surgical (10 × 25 × 365 × 90%)   82 125
Medical (12 × 25 × 365 × 85%)   93 075

(i) Cost per patient bed-day in surgical wards:

$$\frac{£6\ 357\ 000}{82\ 125} = £77.41$$

(ii) Cost per patient bed-day in medical wards:

$$\frac{£6\ 851\ 000}{93\ 075} = £73.61$$

(iii) Cost per patient in out-patients:

$$\frac{£4\ 562\ 000}{86\ 000} = £53.00$$

† Number of beds:

Surgical: (10 wards × 25 beds)	250
Medical: (12 wards × 25 beds)	300
Out-patients (given)	20
	570

11.5 (a) Annual depreciation on the two cars is:

$$\frac{(2 \times £13\,000) - (2 \times £4000)}{3 \text{ years}} = £6000$$

Available hours per year: 2 partners × 8 hours × 5 days × 45 weeks	3600
Hours spent on administration (25% × 3600)	900
Idle time (22.5% × 3600)	810
Total chargeable hours	1890
Travelling time (25% × 1890)	472.5 hours
Professional services (75% × 1890)	1417.5 hours

Travelling time is to be charged at 1/3 of the full rate; this means that total chargeable hours amount to 1417.5 + (1/3 × 472.5) = 1575; this is the number of hours to be used in determination of the hourly rate for productive client work.

Classification of annual costs	Professional services £	Vehicle costs £
Salaries (2 × £20 000)	40 000	
Vehicle depreciation		6 000
Electricity	1 200	
Professional liability and office insurance	600	
Fuel		1 800
Vehicle insurance		800
Mobile telephones	1 200	
Office occupancy	8 400	
Office telephone/fax	1 800	
Postage/stationery	500	
Secretarial costs	8 400	
Vehicle servicing/repair		1 200
Road tax		280
	62 100	10 080

Rate/hour for productive client work:

$$\frac{£62\,100}{1575} = £39.43$$

Rate/hour for travelling (1/3 of full rate): (£39.43 ÷ 3) = £13.14.

Rate per mile:

$$\frac{£10\,080}{18\,000 \text{ miles}} = £0.56$$

(b) The partners should set a budget for income and costs for the year and monitor actual income and costs against this budget regularly (say every month) as the year progresses. Where significant differences between budget and actual emerge, these should be investigated with a view to taking appropriate control action. In order for this to be effective, time spent on various activities needs to be accurately recorded, as do the related costs.

(c) Since the work undertaken by the partners is done to client specification, and since it is likely to be of fairly short duration, job costing would be appropriate. A unique identification number will be assigned to each job, and the hours spent on it (both productive and travelling) are recorded, along with costs charged. Possibly, job records may show both budgeted and actual information about hours and costs, which could help assess performance and control costs.

CHAPTER 12

12.1 (a) T   (b) F   (c) F   (d) T   (e) F   (f) T

12.2 E   There are insufficient data to calculate the difference between reported profits.

In order to determine the profit difference, we need to know (or be able to determine) how much fixed production overhead has been absorbed into opening and closing stock values. This is not possible here, as we are only given the actual and target [absorption] cost per unit, with no detail about the fixed overhead.

12.3 (a) Closing stock in each period:

	Period I	Period II
Opening stock	nil	2 000
Add Production	20 000	20 000
	20 000	22 000
Less Sales	18 000	22 000
= Closing stock	2 000	nil

The marginal cost per unit is (direct materials + direct wages) = (£7 + £10) = £17, while the absorption cost per unit is £17 + £3 for fixed production overhead = £20.

There is no over- or underabsorption of fixed overhead in either period because:

- No information is given about actual fixed overhead incurred, we need to assume that it is the same as the budgeted figure used to obtain the £3 per unit absorption rate; and
- Actual production volume equals the normal level used in the absorption rate calculation.

The amount of fixed overhead in each period is (production × £3) = (20 000 × £3) = £60 000).

(i) *Marginal costing operating statements*

	Period I £	Period I £	Period II £	Period II £
Sales (18 000/22 000 × £30)		540 000		660 000
Opening stock (nil/2000 × £17)	nil		34 000	
Cost of production				
(20 000/20 000 × £17)	340 000		340 000	
	340 000		374 000	
Closing stock (2000/nil × £17)	34 000	306 000	nil	374 000
Contribution		234 000		286 000
Fixed production overhead		60 000		60 000
Profit		174 000		226 000

(ii) *Absorption costing operating statements*

	Period I £	Period I £	Period II £	Period II £
Sales (18 000/22 000 × £30)		540 000		660 000
Opening stock (nil/2000 × £20)	nil		40 000	
Cost of production				
(20 000/20 000 × £20)	400 000		400 000	
	400 000		440 000	
Closing stock (2000/nil × £20)	40 000	360 000	nil	440 000
Gross Profit		180 000		220 000

(b) The difference in profit is due to the absorption of fixed overhead into stock values under absorption costing, compared to its being charged in full each period under marginal costing.

Reconciliation of profit differences	Period I £	Period II £
Absorption costing profit	180 000	220 000
Marginal costing profit	174 000	226 000
Difference	6 000	(6 000)
Fixed overhead absorbed by stock increase/ (decrease) (2000/(2000) × £3)	6 000	(6 000)

(c) Marginal costing is more appropriate for planning, control and decision-making purposes and avoids the potential confusion caused by treating fixed costs as if they were variable. However, it does rely on our ability to separate fixed from variable costs with reasonable accuracy, and it is not permissible in the published accounts of companies subject to the requirements of Statement of Standard Accounting Practice No. 9.

12.4 In the answer that follows, direct wages are assumed to be variable, though it is also possible to treat them as fixed.

J Docherty: marginal costing statement

	Product X £	Product Y £	Product Z £	Total £
Revenue	262 400	140 800	295 000	698 200
Variable costs				
Direct material	37 200	45 100	69 000	151 300
Direct wages	82 400	94 600	110 000	287 000
Sales and admin (Note 1)	4 680	5 800	6 640	17 120
Production overhead (Note 2)	17 720	22 480	24 760	64 960
Total variable costs	142 000	167 980	210 400	520 380
Contribution	120 400	(27 180)	84 600	177 820
Fixed costs				
Sales and admin (*Note 1*)				68 480
Production overhead (*Note 2*)				97 440
Profit				11 900

On purely financial grounds, Product Y should be dropped. By removing Y's negative contribution this will improve overall profit by £27 180 to £39 080. (The analysis assumes that fixed costs will be unaffected by a decision to drop Y.) However, before such a decision is taken, its other implications should be considered. In particular, management should investigate any possible impact on sales of the remaining two products, along with the potential reactions of competitors.

Notes
1 20% of selling and admin costs given in the question for each product are variable. Total selling and admin cost is (£23 400 + £29 000 + £33 200) = £85 600, of which 80% is fixed – and is assumed to be a general company cost.
2 40% of production overhead costs given in the question for each product are variable. Total production overhead cost is (£44 300 + £56 200 + £61 900) = £162 400, of which 60% is fixed – and is assumed to be a general company cost.

12.5 (a) Before preparing the marginal costing statement, we can separate wages and selling costs into their specific and general elements.

			£
Wages	General:	(40% of £112 000)	44 800
	Specific:	house insurance (60% of £28 000)	16 800
		car insurance (60% of £50 000)	30 000
		commercial insurance (60% of £34 000)	20 400

Selling costs			
	General:	(70% of £56 000)	39 200
	Specific:	house insurance (30% of £12 000)	3 600
		car insurance (30% of £30 000)	9 000
		commercial insurance (30% of £14 000)	4 200

MP & Co: contribution analysis of business

		House insurance £	Car insurance £	Commercial insurance £	Total £
Revenue		80 000	220 000	105 000	405 000
Specific costs:	variable	16 000	90 000	40 000	146 000
	wages	16 800	30 000	20 400	67 200
	selling	3 600	9 000	4 200	16 800
		36 400	129 000	64 600	230 000
Contribution to general costs		43 600	91 000	40 400	175 000
General costs:	administration				24 000
	wages				44 800
	selling costs				39 200
Net profit					67 000

(b) Comparison of the additional revenue and costs relating to the proposed sales campaign will permit assessment of the proposal's financial viability:

	£
Additional revenue (30% × £80 000)	24 000
Less Additional variable costs (15% × £16 000)	2 400
Additional specific selling costs	10 000
Additional contribution to general costs	11 600

Since the proposal offers an increase in house insurance's contribution to the firm's general costs (hence in overall profit), it is financially worth while and the sales campaign should be undertaken.

CHAPTER 13

13.1 (a) F   (b) F   (c) F   (d) T   (e) T   (f) F   (g) T   (h) T

13.2 A 2000 units.
Contribution per unit: (CS ratio × selling price per unit) = (0.4 × £16) = £6.40. Breakeven point: £76 800/£6.40 = 12 000 units. At a unit selling price of £16, revenue of £224 000 represents a sales volume of £224 000/£16 = 14 000 units. Margin of safety: (actual sales volume – breakeven sales volume) = (14 000 – 12 000) = 2000 units.

13.3 C 47.4%

The weighted average CS based on selling equal quantities of Aye, Bee and Cee is 48%. This comprises one-third Aye's CS ratio (i.e. 1/3 × 40% = 13.33%) plus one-third Bee's CS ratio (i.e. 1/3 50% = 16.67%) plus one-third Cee's CS ratio (not given). Cee's share of the weighted average CS ratio is therefore (48% − [13.33% + 16.67%]) = 18%. Bearing in mind that the weighted average CS ratio comprises one-third of each product's individual CS ratio, then Cee's CS ratio is (18% × 3) = 54%. Revised weighted average CS ratio: (40% × 40%) [Aye] + (25% × 50%) [Bee] + (35% × 54%)[Cee] = 47.4%.

13.4   (i)   Variable cost of sales as percentage of revenue:

$$\frac{(£55\,000 - £50\,000)}{(£90\,000 - £80\,000)} = 0.5$$

Substituting into August figures:	£
Cost of sales	50 000
Less Variable element (£80 000 × 0.5)	40 000
So fixed element is	10 000

(ii) Variable selling and distribution cost as percentage of revenue:

$$\frac{(£9000 - £8000)}{(£90\,000 - £80\,000)} = 0.1$$

Substituting into August figures:	£
Selling and distribution cost	8000
Less Variable element (£80 000 × 0.1)	8000
So fixed element is	nil

(iii) Despite the different sales volume, administration cost is the same in both months, and is therefore wholly fixed.

(a) Before preparing the chart, it is useful to check breakeven point by formula:

$$\frac{(£10\,000 + £15\,000)}{0.4} = £62\,500$$

Total fixed cost is the sum of fixed cost of sales (£10 000) and administration cost (£15 000) – calculated in (a). We also know from (a) that 50% of revenue is variable cost of sales and a further 10% is variable selling and distribution cost – i.e. variable costs represent 60% of revenue; contribution is therefore 40% of revenue.

Breakeven point occurs where the revenue and total cost lines intersect; contribution is represented by the vertical distance between the revenue and total variable cost lines.

Note that because there is no unit information, the horizontal axis must be scaled in £s. Figure A13.1 is based on an assumed maximum sales revenue of £100 000 – you may have selected another value. The following values have been used to plot the chart:

			£
Total cost	volume 0 (total fixed cost only)		25 000
	volume £100 000	fixed cost	25 000
		variable cost (£100 000 × 0.6)	60 000
			85 000
Total variable cost		volume 0	0
		volume £100 000	60 000
Revenue		volume 0	0
		volume £100 000	100 000

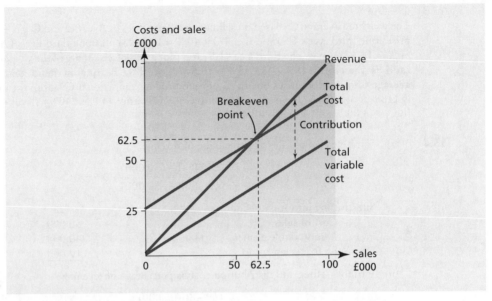

Figure A13.1 Z plc contribution chart

(c) Assuming that the monthly breakeven value can be extended to an annual basis, annual breakeven revenue is (12 months × £62 500) = £750 000. If margin of safety is 30% of breakeven value, then margin of safety is (30% × £750 000) = £225 000, meaning that annual sales are (£750 000 + £225 000) = £975 000.

Annual profit	£
Total contribution (40% × £975 000)	390 000
Fixed costs (12 months × £25 000)	300 000
Annual profit	90 000

(d) Sales required to earn target profit of £90 000:

$$\frac{£300\ 000 + £100\ 000 + £90\ 000}{0.4} = £1\ 225\ 000$$

The numerator in our calculation comprises the existing outlet's annual fixed cost plus the fixed cost of the new outlet plus the existing profit level.

If 10% of the existing outlet's customers move to the new outlet, then the existing outlet's revenue will be (90% × £975 000) = £877 500. The new outlet will therefore need revenue as follows:

	£
Revenue to achieve target profit	1 225 000
Revenue from existing outlet	877 500
Revenue required from new outlet	347 500

(e) Since the key asset of a retail organisation is likely to be stock, then its cost accounting system must be able to track stock costs from point of order through receipt to sale. Where a number of suppliers are supplying a range of different items, and/or where different departments operate within a store, then the system should ideally be able to trace sales and cost of sales to these different items/departments. For more expensive items there should also be a rigorous system of (perhaps continuous) stocktaking, possibly based on an ABC analysis of purchase costs (see Chapter 4).

13.5 (a) (i) Total fixed cost per 4-week period: (£2000 + £1000 + £3000 + £400 + £300 + £110)
= £6810.

$$\text{I Breakeven point: } \frac{£6810}{(£0.44 - £0.40)}$$

$$= 170\,250 \text{ litres or } (170\,250 \times £0.44) = £74\,910$$

$$\text{II Breakeven point: } \frac{£6810 + (75\% \times £2000)}{(£0.44 - £0.40)}$$

$$= 207\,750 \text{ litres or } (207\,750 \times £0.44) = £91\,410$$

$$\text{III Breakeven point: } \frac{£6810}{(£0.44 - £0.40 - 0.002)}$$

$$= 179\,210.52 \text{ litres or } (179\,210.52 \times £0.44) = £78\,852.63$$

$$\text{IV Breakeven point: } \frac{£6810}{(£0.43 - £0.40)}$$

$$= 227\,000 \text{ litres or } (227\,000 \times £0.43) = £97\,610$$

(ii) Litres to be sold: $\dfrac{(£6810 + [4 \times £700])}{(£0.44 - £0.40)} = 240\,250$ litres

(iii) The costs and benefits of the proposal are:

		£
Savings	Electricity	120
	Wages (4 weeks × £200)	800
	Wage-related costs (4 weeks × £25)	100
		1020
Costs	Contribution lost	
	(50 000 litres × [£0.44 – £0.40])	2000
	Net cost of proposal	980

The proposal is therefore not financially viable, as it results in a net loss of £980 per 4-week period. This loss will occur regardless of whether the volume of sales is 275 000 or 425 000 litres: the relevant factor is the sales that are lost as a consequence of the decision. (See Chapter 14 for further discussion of relevant costs for decisions.)

(iv) The system would need to separately identify costs and revenues associated with sale of petrol etc. and those relating to the motorists' shop. It would be preferable if actual and budgeted figures were available. Profitability and cost control for each part of the venture could then be implemented.

(b) The CS ratio is contribution expressed relative to sales value (either per unit or in total). The ratio has an inverse relationship with breakeven point: i.e. the higher the CS ratio, the lower the breakeven point and vice versa. On the profit/volume chart in Figure A13.2, this is reflected in the slope of the profit/loss line: the higher the CS ratio, the steeper the slope.

Margin of safety is the difference between estimated/actual sales and breakeven sales – expressed in units, in revenue, or as a percentage of estimated/actual sales. It is a measure of the extent to which sales can fall before losses are incurred, and is indicated on Figure A13.2 by the distance between breakeven volume and an assumed actual sales volume x.

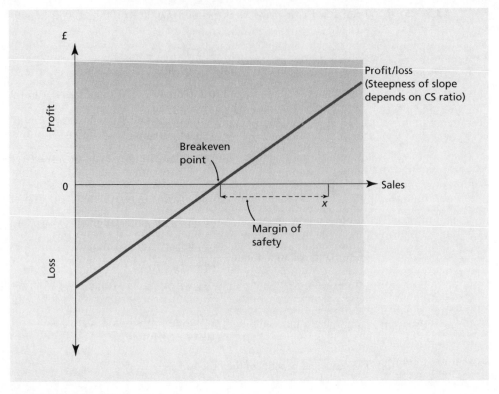

Figure A13.2 Profit/volume chart

CHAPTER 14

14.1 B   *Most profitable*   *Least profitable*
                 M   N

Since we cannot determine material quantities from the question, we need to calculate contribution per £1 of direct material cost:

	Product L £	Product M £	Product N £
Selling price	97.50	123.50	123.50
Variable costs			
Direct materials	13.00	6.50	19.50
Direct labour	20.80	31.20	26.00
Variable overhead	10.40	15.60	13.00
Contribution/unit	53.30	70.20	65.00
Contribution/£1 materials	4.10	10.80	3.33
Ranking	II	I	III

14.2 B £115 000

The cost of supervision is a sunk cost, hence irrelevant. The options are either to recruit 4 skilled employees at £40 000 each (i.e. £160 000 in total) or to retrain existing employees. Relevant cost of the latter option:

	£
Cost of replacements	100 000
Cost of training	15 000
	115 000

Note that the salaries of existing employees are sunk, so irrelevant. As retraining is the cheaper option, this would be chosen.

14.3 *Note: in this, and the answers which follow, we have adopted the tabular approach to analysis used in Chapter 14; you need not have done this, providing you have tested all financial items against each criterion for relevance.*

(a) Opportunity cost is the benefit forgone as a result of undertaking one course of action rather than the best alternative course of action. Since decisions involve choice between alternatives, opportunity cost is always relevant in their financial evaluation.

(b) Table A14.1 tests all the financial data from the question against each of the criteria for relevance – relevant items having a tick in each of the three 'criteria' columns.

Note that the variable overhead as stated in the standard schedule is not relevant. It is an estimate – which, in this instance, happens to be wrong.

Ealing should charge sufficient to at least cover the relevant cost of the job:

Proposed contract: minimum price/relevant cost

	£
Steel	30 000
Copper	8 000
Variable overhead	3 000
Maintenance	15 000
Increase in fixed costs	4 500
Extra selling costs	2 000
	62 500

The minimum price that Ealing can charge is therefore £62 500.

Table A14.1 Relevance test

Item	Future?	Cash?	Differs?	Amount £
Steel: original cost		✓		26 000
Replacement cost	✓	✓	✓	30 000
Copper: original cost		✓		11 000
Sales value	✓	✓	✓	8 000
Labour cost	✓	✓		10 000
Variable overheads:				
per standard schedule	✓		✓	2 500
per estimate for the job	✓	✓	✓	3 000
Fixed overheads			✓	20 500
Maintenance	✓	✓	✓	15 000
Increase in existing fixed costs	✓	✓	✓	4 500
Sales department extra costs	✓	✓	✓	2 000

(c) Assumptions underlying (a) include:

- All the estimates are accurate, and there are no additional costs.
- All costs listed as relevant are cash items: any non-cash costs need to be excluded.
- The maintenance work cannot be delayed until after completion of the job; if it could be delayed, then the £15 000 payable to external contractors is irrelevant.

(d) Overhead costs are included in unit costs for two main reasons:

1. To comply with accounting regulations governing the valuation of stock in published accounts.
2. To provide an estimate of average long-run cost. This may be useful for price-setting purposes to ensure that prices cover all costs in the long run.

However, overheads absorbed in this way are not cash costs. Also 'unitising' fixed overheads may give the misleading impression that they are variable in nature. And, where absorption is based on estimates of cost and activity level, over- or underabsorption of overhead will almost always arise. Finally, the absorption process involves a certain amount of subjectivity, and the resultant unit costs are suspect for decision making purposes. (See Chapters 5 and 6 for further discussion of overhead absorption.)

14.4 (a) The statement confuses two different cost classifications. Relevant costs are future cash flows which differ between alternatives. Any cost which satisfies this definition is relevant – regardless of its behaviour pattern. Thus, variable costs may be irrelevant (e.g. non-cash costs), and fixed costs relevant (specifically attributable fixed costs). In certain situations, variable cost may provide a reasonable approximation to relevant cost, providing fixed costs are unaffected by the decision. This may be true, for example, in some decisions concerning volume or product mix.

(b) (i) Labour hours per unit of each product:

$$\frac{\text{Labour cost per litre}}{\text{£6 per hour}}$$

$$\text{Product A: } \frac{£18}{£6} = 3 \qquad \text{Product B: } \frac{£15}{£6} = 2.5$$

$$\text{Product C: } \frac{£24}{£6} = 4 \qquad \text{Product D: } \frac{£27}{£6} = 4.5$$

Assuming the direct labour cost to be variable, then contribution per labour hour and associated product rankings are:

	Product A £	Product B £	Product C £	Product D £
Selling price	100	110	120	120
Variable costs				
Direct materials	24	30	16	21
Direct labour	18	15	24	27
Direct expenses			3	
Variable overhead	12	10	16	18
Contribution/litre	46	55	61	54
Hours/litre	3	2.5	4	4.5
Contribution/hour	15.33	22.00	15.25	12.00
Ranking	II	I	III	IV

Remembering that maximum production is determined by demand for each product, and also that we need to make allowance for the 20 litres of each product the company is contracted to supply, we get the following production/sales schedule:

Hours available		1345
Less hours required for contracted sales:		
A: (20 litres × 3)	60	
B: (20 litres × 2.5)	50	
C: (20 litres × 4)	80	
D: (20 litres × 4.5)	90	280
Remaining		1065
Make (150 − 20) litres of B, using (130 × 2.5)		325
Remaining		740
Make (200 − 20) litres of A, using (180 × 3)		540
Remaining		200
Make (200/4) = 50 litres of C, using		200

Fixed overhead absorption rate:

$$\frac{\text{Fixed overhead per litre}}{\text{Labour-hours per litre}}$$

Using Product A, we get: £24/3 = £8 per labour-hour. Budgeted fixed overhead is therefore (1600 hours × £8) = £12 800 for the quarter.

Profit statement		£
Contribution:	A (200 litres × £46)	9 200
	B (150 litres × £55)	8 250
	C (70 litres × £61)	4 270
	D (20 litres × £54)	1 080
		22 800
Fixed overhead		12 800
Profit		10 000

(ii) If C is made in-house, the contribution per unit is £46, as calculated in (i). If this product is subcontracted, the contribution per unit is:

	£
Selling price	120
less Purchase cost	105
Contribution	15

Since a contribution is still earned on litres subcontracted, any C that cannot be produced in-house should be subcontracted.

For Product D, we need to consider the specific fixed cost that is avoided if we subcontract:

	£
Cost/litre to make (sum of variable costs in (i))	66
Cost/litre to sub-contract	100
Extra cost per litre	34

If all production of D is subcontracted next quarter:

	£
Extra cost (120 litres × £34)	4080
Fixed cost avoided	6000
Benefit of subcontracting	1920

Therefore, all D should be subcontracted next quarter. Looking at the production schedule in (i), subcontracting D will release 90 hours next quarter, which can be used to produce an additional (90/4) = 22.5 litres of C. In-house production of C is now 70 litres (from (i)) plus 22.5 = 92.5. Remaining demand for C (100 – 92.5) = 7.5 litres can be subcontracted. The revised profit is given below:

		£
Total contribution:	A (from (i))	9 200.00
	B (from (i))	8 250.00
	C: in-house (92.5 litres × £61)	5 642.50
	subcontracted (7.5 litres × £15)	112.50
	D (120 litres × [£120 – £100])	2 400.00
		25 605.00
Fixed costs (as in (i))		12 800.00
Profit		12 805.00

Compared with the profit in (i) above, this represents an increase of £2805.

14.5 (a) **REPORT**
TO: Directors, Spekobuild plc
FROM: Chief accountant
RE: Abandonment of office block project.
On financial grounds, I do not recommend cancellation of the project, as this incurs a net relevant cost of £3 735 000. (See Appendix to Report for calculations.) This assessment is based on consideration solely of those costs and benefits that relate specifically to completion of the project. All historic, non-cash, committed and general items have been excluded as being irrelevant. Note, however, that there may be non-financial factors that suggest a different course of action to continuation. Also, estimates involved are assumed to be accurate, and it has been further assumed that there are no additional costs associated with completion of the project.

Signed............

APPENDIX TO REPORT

Table A14.2 Relevance test (figures in £000)

Item	Future?	Cash?	Differs?	Amount £
Total costs to date		✓		2 400
Materials: stock value		✓	✓	1 000
X: Current purchase price	✓	✓	✓	350
Y: opportunity cost in place of P	✓	✓	✓	280
Z: disposal cost	✓	✓		50
Special order: cost	✓	✓		600
Sale proceeds	✓	✓	✓	50
Still to be ordered	✓	✓	✓	1 600
Labour: Redeployed	✓	✓	✓	2 400
Casual	✓	✓	✓	800
Redundancy	✓	✓	✓	200
Subcontract work	✓	✓	✓	2 250
Site clearance costs	✓	✓	✓	50
Overheads: general	✓	✓		2 200
Plant hire	✓	✓	✓	675
Site overheads	✓	✓	✓	260
Sales revenue	✓	✓	✓	12 500

Relevant costs and benefits of abandoning project (£000)

Benefits	£	£
Purchase of material X avoided	350	
Saving in purchase of Material P	280	
Sale proceeds of special materials' order	50	
Materials still to be ordered: cost avoided	1 600	
Saving through redeployment	2 400	
Saving in casual labour	800	
Saving through redundancy of labour	200	
Saving in subcontract work	2 250	
Saving in plant hire costs	675	
Saving in site overheads	260	8 865
Costs		
Material Z: disposal cost	50	
Site clearance costs	50	
Sales revenue lost	12 500	12 600
Net relevant cost		3 735

Notes

1 The original cost of materials in stock is historic, therefore irrelevant.
2 Resale values of materials in stock are irrelevant. X would not be resold, as it is in regular use. Y would not be resold for £200 000, because it can be used in place of Material P, which would cost £280 000 to acquire.
3 Of the labour costs, all the payments to casual workers (20% × £4 000 000) will be saved if work ceases. Wages of the 60% who are redeployed represent a saving of (60% × £4 000 000) as this amount would need to be paid to newly engaged workers if the office contract proceeds. For the workers made redundant, 75% of annual salary will be paid regardless of whether the project proceeds or not, so this amount is irrelevant.
4 For subcontractors and plant hire, an amount at least equal to the cancellation charge will be paid regardless of whether or not work proceeds, so this element is irrelevant.

(b) The costing method adopted identifies the relevant costs and benefits of a 'one-off' decision. The company's normal costing methodology is very probably absorption costing. For routine purposes (e.g. setting selling prices or valuing work-in-progress), this method will continue to be used. For stock valuation purposes, it may well be required in published accounts. And for regular pricing decisions absorption costing helps to recognise the fact that, in the long run, all costs need to be covered (by providing an approximation of long-run average cost). If the method adopted in (a) were applied to every situation, then the business would incur serious losses, as substantial costs would not be covered.

CHAPTER 15

Note: in those questions involving calculation of IRR, you may have used a different second trial discount rate from that in the solution, meaning that your IRR will also differ slightly from that shown below. This is perfectly acceptable, being merely a consequence of the trial-and-error approach to calculation.

15.1 (a) F (b) T (c) T (d) F (e) F (f) T (g) T (h) F

15.2 (a) Since discounting the three proposals' cash flows at the 8% cost of capital yields a positive NPV, we need to increase the discount rate in order to obtain a negative NPV.

Table A15.1 NPV of Machine 1 (£000)

Year	Cash flow	Amount £	Discount factor (8%)	Discount factor (15%)	Present value (8%) £	Present value (15%) £
0	Initial cost	(1200)	1.000	1.000	(1200.0)	(1200.0)
1–4	Net cash inflow	350	3.312	2.855	1159.2	999.3
4	Resale value	200	0.735	0.572	147.0	114.4
				NPV	106.2	(86.3)

$$\text{IRR: } 8\% + \left[\frac{106.2}{(106.2 + 86.3)} \times (15\% - 8\%) \right] = 11.86\%$$

Table A15.2 NPV of Machine 2 (£000)

Year	Cash flow	Amount £	Discount factor (8%)	Discount factor (15%)	Present value (8%) £	Present value (15%) £
0	Initial cost	(2500)	1.000	1.000	(2500.0)	(2500.0)
1–4	Net cash inflow	725	3.312	2.855	2401.2	2069.9
4	Resale value	295	0.735	0.572	216.8	168.7
				NPV	118.0	(261.4)

$$\text{IRR: } 8\% + \left[\frac{118.0}{(118.0 + 261.4)} \times (15\% - 8\%) \right] = 10.18\%$$

Table A15.3 NPV of Machine 3 (£000)

Year	Cash flow	Amount £	Discount factor (8%)	Discount factor (15%)	Present value (8%) £	Present value (15%) £
0	Initial cost	(2000)	1.000	1.000	(2000.0)	(2000.0)
1–4	Net cash inflow	565	3.312	2.855	1871.3	1613.1
4	Resale value	310	0.735	0.572	227.9	177.3
				NPV	99.2	(209.6)

$$\text{IRR: } 8\% + \left[\frac{99.2}{(99.2 + 209.6)} \times (15\% - 8\%) \right] = 10.25\%$$

(a) All three proposals have a positive NPV at the company's cost of capital and an IRR in excess of this rate; so all three proposals are financially acceptable. On financial grounds, Machine 2 should be purchased, as it yields the highest NPV at the company's current cost of capital. This means that it is the option which offers the greatest increase in the company's absolute wealth (hence in that of its shareholders). IRR gives no indication of the amounts involved (being a relative measure), so is suspect when comparing mutually exclusive proposals. The fact that Machine 2's IRR is marginally the lowest is therefore not a significant consideration here.

15.3 (a) Payback:

Year	Cash flow £	Cumulative cash flow £
1997	85 000	85 000
1998	90 500	175 500
1999	87 250	262 750
2000	84 800	347 550
2001	80 600	428 150

The proposal's payback therefore occurs in the fifth year. More precisely, by the end of 2000, the project still requires (£360 000 – £347 550) = £12 450 to achieve payback. Assuming cash flows arise evenly throughout the year, this will take £12 450/ £80 600 = 0.15 of 2001. Payback therefore occurs in 4.15 years. Since this exceeds the company's 4-year payback target, the proposal is financially unacceptable using this criterion.

(b)/(c) Since discounting at 10% yields a positive NPV, we need to increase the discount rate to obtain a negative result.

Table A15.4 Project NPV (£000)

Year	Cash flow	Amount £	Discount factor (10%)	Discount factor (15%)	Present value (10%) £	Present value (15%) £
0	Initial cost	(360.00)	1.000	1.000	(360.00)	(360.00)
1	Net cash inflow	85.00	0.909	0.870	77.27	73.95
2	Net cash inflow	90.50	0.826	0.756	74.75	68.42
3	Net cash inflow	87.25	0.751	0.658	65.52	57.41
4	Net cash inflow	84.80	0.683	0.572	57.92	48.51
5	Net cash inflow	80.60	0.621	0.497	50.05	40.06
6	Net cash inflow	74.00	0.565	0.432	41.81	31.97
				NPV	7.32	(39.68)

$$\text{IRR: } 10\% + \left[\frac{7.32}{(7.32 + 39.68)} \times (15\% - 10\%) \right] = 10.77\%$$

The proposal has a positive NPV at the company's cost of capital, along with an IRR in excess of this rate. Based on these criteria, it is therefore financially acceptable. Of the three criteria applied, NPV is superior, and the proposal should be accepted on the basis of its positive NPV. However, management would be advised to check the accuracy of their estimates, as only a relatively small error would be needed to render the proposal financially unacceptable using NPV/IRR.

15.4 (a)/(b) The annual net cash flow from the proposals is (revenue – costs) from the table given in the question. Note that 1997 is assumed to be Year 1 for discounting purposes.

Table A15.5 NPV of 'no change' option (£000)

Year	Cash flow	Amount £	Discount factor (10%)	Present value (10%) £
1997	Net cash inflow	100	0.909	90.90
1998	Net cash inflow	50	0.826	41.30
1999	Net cash inflow	0	0.751	0.00
2000	Net cash outflow	(50)	0.683	(34.15)
2001	Net cash outflow	(100)	0.621	(62.10)
2002	Net cash outflow	(200)	0.565	(113.00)
			NVP	(77.05)

Table A15.6 NPV of 'reorganisation' option (£000)

Year	Cash flow	Amount £	Discount factor (10%)	Present value (10%) £
1997	Net cash inflow	0	0.909	0.00
1998	Net cash inflow	100	0.826	82.60
1999	Net cash inflow	0	0.751	0.00
2000	Net cash inflow	0	0.683	0.00
2001	Net cash outflow	(100)	0.621	(62.10)
2002	Net cash outflow	(200)	0.565	(113.00)
			NVP	(92.50)

Table A15.7 NPV of 'expansion' option (£000)

Year	Cash flow	Amount £	Discount factor (10%)	Present value (10%) £
1997	Net cash outflow	(3000)	0.909	(2727)
1998	Net cash inflow	500	0.826	413
1999	Net cash inflow	1000	0.751	751
2000	Net cash inflow	1000	0.683	683
2001	Net cash inflow	1000	0.621	621
2002	Net cash inflow	1000	0.565	565
			NVP	306

As the 'expansion' option is the only one to offer a positive NPV at the 10% cost of capital, it is the only option that is financially acceptable.

(b) Since the proposal has a positive NPV at a 10% discount rate, we must increase the rate to obtain a negative result.

Table A15.8 NPV of 'expansion' option at 15% (£000)

Year	Cash flow	Amount £	Discount factor (15%)	Present value (15%) £
1997	Net cash outflow	(3000)	0.870	(2610)
1998	Net cash inflow	500	0.756	378
1999	Net cash inflow	1000	0.658	658
2000	Net cash inflow	1000	0.572	572
2001	Net cash inflow	1000	0.497	497
2002	Net cash inflow	1000	0.432	432
			NVP	(73)

$$\text{IRR: } 10\% + \left[\frac{306}{(306 + 73)} \times (15\% - 10\%)\right] = 14.04\%$$

(c) Assuming that the revenue and cost estimates are reasonably accurate, then the business appears to be in a very precarious state. Without the expansion scheme, it is questionable whether it would be able to survive. However, even if this scheme proceeds, there may still be question marks. For example, where is the theatre to obtain the £3 million needed in 1997 for the expansion scheme? In conjunction with expansion, management may need urgently to review costs (with a view to possible reduction), along with possible methods for increasing revenue during the week (e.g. offering discounts to students?). The fact that the theatre is located in a university town may also create problems. In particular, students may not have sufficient disposable income to attend theatre performances, and the non-student population may not be large enough to sustain a theatre financially.

15.5 (a) The total annual operating cost of the transport fleet each year is the sum of drivers' costs plus repairs and maintenance plus other costs given in the question. However, to obtain the cash saving, depreciation must be excluded from 'other costs'.
On a straight-line basis, annual depreciation is:

$$\frac{(\text{Initial cost} - \text{residual value})}{5 \text{ years}} = \frac{(£750\,000 - £150\,000)}{5} = £120\,000$$

Note that the present cost of outside provision rises by 10% per annum from its Year 0 value of £250 000.

Net cash savings

	Year 0 £000	Year 1 £000	Year 2 £000	Year 3 £000	Year 4 £000	Year 5 £000	Total £000
Own fleet							
Initial cost	750						750
Sale proceeds						(150)	
Drivers		33	35	36	38	40	182
Repairs		8	13	15	16	18	70
Other		10	15	20	16	22	83
	750	51	63	71	70	(70)	935
Outside provision	nil	275	303	333	366	403	1680
Saving	(750)	224	240	262	296	473	745

Note that, in Year 5, the 'own fleet' cost is reduced by £150 000 to reflect the anticipated sales proceeds.

(b) (i) Payback:

Year	Cash flow £	Cumulative cash flow £
1	224	224
2	240	464
3	262	726
4	296	1022

By the end of Year 3, the proposal still needs to recover (£750 000 – £726 000) = £24 000. Assuming even cash flows, this will take 24 000/296 000 = 0.08 of the fourth year. Payback therefore occurs in 3.08 years.

(ii) Accounting rate of return will be based on average savings after depreciation. Total depreciation over the fleet's life is (£750 000 – £150 000) = £600 000. Total cash savings in Years 1–5 are: (£224 000 + £240 000 + £262 000 + £296 000 + £323 000) = £1 345 000. (Note that sale proceeds have been omitted from the Year 5 saving, as depreciation has already been reduced to allow for this.) Savings after depreciation are therefore (£1 345 000 – £600 000) = £745 000. Average annual savings are (£745 000 ÷ 5 years) = £149 000. In relation to an initial investment of £750 000, this yields an accounting rate of return of:

$$\frac{£149\ 000}{£750\ 000} \times 100\% = 19.9\%$$

(iii) In the absence of a cost of capital figure, it is necessary to discount the proposal's cash savings at the 12% interest rate associated with the loan that will be raised to finance the project.

Table A15.9 NPV of fleet proposal's cash savings (£000)

Year	Cash flow	Amount £	Discount factor (12%)	Present value £
0	Initial cost	(750)	1.000	(750)
1	Cash cost saving	224	0.893	200
2	Cash cost saving	240	0.797	191
3	Cash cost saving	262	0.712	187
4	Cash cost saving	296	0.636	188
5	Cash cost saving	473	0.567	268
			NVP	**284**

(c) **REPORT**

TO: Investment Manager
FROM: Management Accountant
RE: Capital investment proposals

Proposed acquisition of our own fleet markedly outperforms the alternative option for use of the funds raised by the loan. Its NPV is twice that offered by the alternative, although its accounting rate of return is lower and payback is marginally longer. Based on the substantial benefit in NPV terms, I would recommend acquisition of the fleet – this will increase the company's absolute wealth by more than twice the best alternative.

Signed............

CHAPTER 16

16.1 B A factor which limits the activities of an undertaking.

16.2 (a) T   (b) T   (c) F   (d) F   (e) F   (f) T   (g) F   (h) F

16.3 (a) (i) **Sales budget**

	July	Aug.	Sept.	Total
Unit sales	400	300	600	1300
Selling price/unit	£250	£250	£250	
Revenue	£100 000	£75 000	£150 000	£325 000

(ii) **Production budget**

Required for sales	1300
Add desired closing stock[1]	225
	1525
Less opening stock[1]	200
Good output required	1325
Normal loss[2]	147
Production required[2]	1472

Notes

1 The question states that closing stock of finished goods is to be 50% of next month's sales requirement. Thus, at the end of September, desired closing stock is 50% of October sales (= 50% × 450). We can apply the same approach to obtain the quarter's opening stock. Closing stock at the end of June (which is July's opening stock) equals 50% of July sales (= 50% × 400).

2 Output is tested at the end of production, at which point, 10% of units are faulty. Normal loss is therefore 10% of completed output. Good output is therefore 90% of completed output; if we require good output of 1325 units, then we need to produce (1325 ÷ 0.9) units in total.

(iii) **Raw materials usage budget**

	Material A	Material B	Material C
Required for production:			
1472 units × 3 kg/2 kg/4 kg	4416 kg	2944 kg	5888 kg

(iv) **Raw material purchases budget**

	Material A kg	Material B kg	Material C kg
Required for production	4416	2944	5888
Add Desired closing stock*	1200	480	720
	5616	3424	6608
Less opening stock (given)	1000	400	600
Purchases required	4616	3024	6008
Purchase cost/kg	£3.50	£5.00	£4.50
Purchase cost	£16 156	£15 120	£27 036
Total purchase cost		£58 312	

* Stocks are to be increased by 20% in July and maintained at this level for the foreseeable future.

(v) **Labour requirements budget**

Hours required for production (1472 × 8)	11 776
Add time on support tasks*	2 944
Attendance time*	14 720
Rate per hour	£8.00
Total labour cost	£117 760

* 20% of attendance time is spent on support tasks. Therefore productive hours are 80% of attendance time, meaning that attendance time is (productive hours ÷ 0.8).

(b) The principal budget factor is a constraint on organisational activity (i.e. a limiting factor). Thus, if the limiting factor is sales demand, then the sales budget will be the key determinant of other budgets (e.g. production). Failure to allow for limiting factors in budget preparation could result in unachievable and unrealistic budgets – say, production levels that are too low in relation to demand.

(c) The working area of a spreadsheet might be something as in Table A16.1.

Table A16.1 Spreadsheet working area

	A	B
1	**Labour requirements budget**	
2	Budgeted production (units)	1 472
3	Hours per unit produced	8
4	Hours required for production	11 776
5	Time on support tasks	2 944
6	Attendance time	14 720
7	Rate per hour	£8
8	Total labour cost	£117 760

The number of units produced may be imported from another spreadsheet containing the production budget, or from another section of the same spreadsheet. Typical formulas might be:

For Cell B4	= B2*B3
For Cell B5	= B4*0.25
For Cell B6	= B4+B5
For Cell B8	= B6*B7

It is possible that the spreadsheet's output may be exported to a special output section where information is presented in a manner likely to prove most useful to managers.

CHAPTER 17

17.1 A Depreciation of fixed assets.

17.2 (a) T (b) F (c) F (d) T (e) T (f) F (g) F (h) T

17.3 (a) Before preparing the cash budget, we need budgets for sales, production, purchases and labour.

Sales budget	Month 1	Month 2	Month 3	Month 4
Units	750	900	1080	1296
Price/unit	£40	£40	£40	£40
Revenue	£30 000	£36 000	£43 200	£51 840
Cash receipts	£	£	£	£
1/3 this month's sales	10 000	12 000	14 400	17 280
2/3 last month's sales	nil	20 000	24 000	28 800
	10 000	32 000	38 800	46 080
Production budget (units)	1650^1	1080	1296	1556^2

Notes

1 Production in Month 1 is sufficient to meet demand for Months 1 plus 2.
2 Month 4 production must cover Month 5 demand, which is (Month 4 + 20%) = (1296 + 20%).

Material purchases budget	Month 1	Month 2	Month 3
Production × £20*/unit	£33 000	£21 600	£25 920

(These amounts are paid in the month following purchase.)

* The selling price of £40 is stated to be sufficient to allow a 100% mark-up on the cost of materials, so materials per unit = (1/2 × £40) = £20.

Wages budget	Month 1	Month 2	Month 3	Month 4
Production × £3/unit	£4950	£3240	£3888	£4668

(These amounts are paid in the month they are incurred.)

Other expenses	Month 1	Month 2	Month 3	Month 4
	£	£	£	£
Production × £4/unit	6600	4320	5184	6224
Paid:				
50% in month incurred	3300	2160	2592	3112
50% in month after	nil	3300	2160	2592
	3300	5460	4752	5704

Axot: cash budget for first four months

	Month 1	Month 2	Month 3	Month 4
	£	£	£	£
Opening balance	nil	(7250)	(16 950)	(8390)
Cash receipts				
Sales	10 000	32 000	38 800	46 080
	10 000	24 750	21 850	37 690
Cash payments				
Machinery	5 000			
Promotional	4 000			
Materials		33 000	21 600	25 920
Wages	4 950	3 240	3 888	4 668
Other costs	3 300	5 460	4 752	5 704
	17 250	41 700	30 240	36 292
Closing balance	(7 250)	(16 950)	(8 390)	1 398

(b) By estimating cash inflows and outflows, the cash budget allows management to predict potential cash shortages in advance, thus allowing them to take appropriate steps. Here, for example, the new product has a projected cash deficit until Month 4. This will either need to be reduced (e.g. by controlling costs more rigorously) and/or by using existing cash resources and/or by arranging overdraft facilities. Cash budgets also allow management to predict periods of potential cash surplus, thereby allowing it to be used more effectively (e.g. placed on short-term deposit to earn interest).

17.4 (a) Before preparing the cash budget, we need to determine the cost of purchases. We are told in the question that the cost of purchases equals 40% of selling price and also that stock is maintained at 50% of next month's sales (excepting the increase applicable from November). To determine closing stock values, we therefore need to take: 40% × (50% × next month's sales value). Opening stock each month is the previous month's closing stock carried forward. July's opening stock is therefore the same as June's closing stock – i.e. (40% × 50% × July's sales). Because we are attempting to obtain a figure for purchases, we need to work backwards from cost of sales, to which we *add* closing stock and from which we *deduct* opening stock, as shown in Table A17.1. Note that, since purchases are paid for two months after purchase, we need only work as far as December.

Sales are made 40% for cash (therefore receivable in the month of sale) – less a 5% discount; and 60% on credit, receivable in the month after sale.

Table A17.1 Determination of monthly purchases

	July	August	September	October	November	December
	£	£	£	£	£	£
Cost of sales (40% of sales)	17 600	20 000	19 200	16 000	18 000	17 600
Add closing stock	10 000	9 600	8 000	9 000	10 800[1]	10 400[1]
	27 600	29 600	27 200	25 000	28 800	28 000
Less opening stock	8 800	10 000	9 600	8 000	9 000	10 800
= Purchases	18 800	19 600	17 600	17 000	19 800	17 200

1 (40% × 50% × next month's sales) + £2000 increase.

Table A17.2 Determination of cash sales receipts

	September	October	November	December	January	February
	£	£	£	£	£	£
Cash sales (40% of this month's sales)	19 200	16 000	18 000	17 600	16 800	20 000
Less 5% discount	960	800	900	880	840	1 000
	18 240	15 200	17 100	16 720	15 960	19 000
Credit sales (60% of last month's sales)	30 000	28 800	24 000	27 000	26 400	25 200
	48 240	44 000	41 100	43 720	42 360	44 200

Table A17.3 Cash budget September–February

	September £	October £	November £	December £	January £	February £
Opening balance	5 000	6 640	27 040	(15 960)	(1 640)	8 720
Cash receipts						
Capital disposal		8 000				
Sales	48 240	44 000	41 100	43 720	42 360	44 200
	53 240	58 640	68 140	27 760	40 720	52 920
Cash payments						
Capital acquisitions	15 000		10 000			4 000
Corporation tax			44 000			
Purchases	18 800	19 600	17 600	17 000	19 800	17 200
Wages[1]	6 800	6 000	6 500	6 400	6 200	7 000
Fixed costs[2]	6 000	6 000	6 000	6 000	6 000	6 000
	46 600	31 600	84 100	29 400	32 000	34 200
Closing balance	6 640	27 040	(15 960)	(1 640)	8 720	18 720

Notes
1 £2000 fixed per month plus 10% of each month's sales.
2 £7500 *less* £1500 depreciation.

(b) The spreadsheet will specify first, whether the content of each cell is descriptive or numeric; second any mathematical relationships between different cells. Thus, for example, cells in the first row and first column of Table A17.3 would be designated as being descriptive, whilst the remaining cells would be designated numeric. Similarly, cells containing, say, total cash payments each month would be shown being the sum of cells containing individual cash payments. Supporting detail, such as that shown in Tables A17.1 and A17.2 can be stored in a separate area of the spreadsheet, as can the underlying mathematical relationships. The great strength of spreadsheets is their flexibility – and in particular their ability to perform complex sensitivity analyses.

(c) Feedback control involves comparing budgeted outcomes with actual – in this case budgeted cash flows with actual – and taking action in response to significant differences between the two. Feedforward control involves comparing budgeted outcomes with objectives or desired outcomes and taking action to reduce any significant difference between the two. Thus, if actual cash outflows are higher than budgeted, management might take action to reduce cash costs (feedback control). If the aim is, say, to reduce the need for an overdraft, the budget can be used to assess whether or not this is likely to happen. If it is not, then management may seek to improve cash flows, or may amend their objective. (See Chapter 18 for full discussion of feedback and feedforward control.)

17.5 (a) Raw materials purchases budget:

	July £	August £	September £
Required for production (@ £280 per unit)	11 200	14 000	14 000
Add Desired closing stock	10 000	10 000	10 000
	21 200	24 000	24 000
Less Opening stock	nil	10 000	10 000
Purchases	21 200	14 000	14 000

(Purchases are paid for in the month after purchase)

Cash receipts from sales:	July £	August £	September £
Revenue (@ £900/unit)	9000	32 400	54 000
Cash sales (10% of this month's sales)	900	3 240	5 400
Credit sales (90% of last month's sales)	nil	8 100	29 160
	900	11 340	34 560

Cash budget, July–September

	July £	August £	September £
Opening balance	20 000	14 500	(7 760)
Cash receipts			
Sales	900	11 340	34 560
	20 900	25 840	26 800
Cash payments			
Fixed assets		20 000	20 000
Fixed overheads[1]		4 000	4 000
Variable overhead[2]		1 600	2 000
Labour[3]	6 400	8 000	8 000
	6 400	33 600	34 000
Closing balance	14 500	(7 760)	(7 200)

Notes
1 £5000 per month less £1000 depreciation, payable in the month after it is incurred.
2 £40 per unit produced, payable in the month after it is incurred.
3 £160 per unit produced, payable in the month it is incurred.

(b) Net working capital is: (stock + debtors) *less* (bank overdraft + creditors). Closing stock of finished goods at the end of September:

	July	August	September
Opening stock	nil	30	44
Production	40	50	50
	40	80	94
Sales	10	36	60
Closing stock	30	44	34

Finished goods stocks are valued using absorption costing, so we need an absorption rate:

$$\frac{\text{Budgeted overhead}}{\text{Budgeted production}} = \frac{£5000}{50} = £100 \text{ per unit}$$

Cost per unit of finished goods:

	£
Materials	280
Labour	160
Variable overhead	40
Fixed overhead	100
	580

September's closing stock of finished goods is therefore valued at (34 units × £580) = £19 720. Debtors at the end of September will be in respect of 90% of September sales = (90% × [60 × £900]) = £48 600. Creditors will consist of £20 000 (fixed assets) + £14 000 (September purchases) + £4000 (September fixed overhead) + £2000 (September variable overhead) – i.e. £40 000 in total.

Net working capital as at 30 September

		£	£
Stock:	raw material (given)		10 000
	finished goods		19 720
Debtors			48 600
			78 320
Bank overdraft (from (a))		7 200	
Creditors		40 000	47 200
			31 120

CHAPTER 18

18.1 B £18 000 favourable

The flexible budget cost for direct material is

$$(\text{actual output} \times \text{standard direct material cost per unit})$$
$$= (9000 \text{ units} \times £40) = £360\,000$$

Thus, the flexible budget variance is

$$(\text{flexible budget direct material cost} - \text{actual material cost})$$
$$= (£360\,000 - £342\,000) = £18\,000\text{F}$$

18.2 (a) T (b) F (c) F (d) T (e) F (f) F (g) T

18.3 (a) Total budgeted fixed overheads: (budgeted production × overhead per unit) = (15 000 × £80) = £1 200 000. Actual fixed overheads were therefore (£1 200 000 + £175 000) = £1 375 000.

Table A18.1 Solo Ltd budget statement

	Original budget	Flexible budget	Actual
Sales/production (units)	15 000	13 600	13 600
	£	£	£
Revenue (@ £250/unit)	3 750 000	3 400 000	3 400 000
Variable costs			
Direct labour	690 000	625 600	606 206[1]
Direct materials	450 000	408 000	440 640[2]
Variable overheads	360 000	326 400	340 000[3]
	1 500 000	1 360 000	1 386 846
Contribution	2 250 000	2 040 000	2 013 154
Fixed overheads	1 200 000	1 200 000	1 375 000
Profit	1 050 000	840 000	638 154

Notes

1 (£46 per unit + 2% increase) × 13 600 units = £638 112; adjusted for improved efficiency = (£638 112 × 95%) = £606 206.

2 (£30 per unit + 8% increase) × 13 600 units.

3 (£24 per unit + £1 per unit increase) × 13 600 units.

(b) Comparing the original budget with actual provides little useful information for financial control purposes, as such a comparison does not compare like with like. However, the original budget can still provide useful information – for example, here it indicates that actual output/sales is lower than expected. This could prompt questions about the accuracy of the planning process and/or about sales and market conditions. Price, rate, usage and efficiency differences are indicated by the variances between flexible budget and actual.

18.4 (a)/(b) Before preparing the flexible budget, we need to separate the budgeted expenditure into its fixed and variable elements.

		£
Cleaning	Budgeted total cost	13 250
	Less Variable element (2000 ORN × £2.50)	5 000
	Fixed element	8 250

Flexible budget allowance: £8250 + (1850 ORN × £2.50) = £12 875.

		£
Laundry	Budgeted total cost	15 025
	Less Variable element (4300 V × £1.75)	7 525
	Fixed element	7 500

Flexible budget allowance: £7500 + (4575 V × £1.75) = £15 506.

		£
Reception	Budgeted total cost	13 100
	Less fixed element (given)	12 100
	Variable cost of 2000 ORN	1 000 = £0.50/ORN

Flexible budget allowance: £12 100 + (1850 ORN × £0.50) = £13 025.

		£
Maintenance	Budgeted total cost	11 100
	Less variable element (2000 ORN × £0.80)	1 600
	Fixed element	9 500

Flexible budget allowance: £9500 + (1850 ORN × £0.80) = £10 980.

		£
Housekeeping	Budgeted total cost	19 600
	Less fixed element (given)	11 000
	Variable cost of 4300 V	8 600 = £2/V

Flexible budget allowance: £11 000 + (4575 V × £2) = £20 150.

		£
Administration	Budgeted total cost	7700
	Less variable element (2000 ORN × £0.20)	400
	Fixed element	7300

Flexible budget allowance: £7300 + (1850 ORN × £0.20) = £7670.

		£
Catering	Budgeted total cost	21 460
	Less variable element (4300 V × £2.20)	9 460
	Fixed element	12 000

Flexible budget allowance: £12 000 + (4575 V × £2.20) = £22 065.

Table A18.2 Arcadian Hotel: flexible budget statement

	Flexible budget £	Actual £	Variance £
Cleaning	12 875	13 292	417A
Laundry	15 506	14 574	932F
Reception	13 025	13 855	830A
Maintenance	10 980	10 462	518F
Housekeeping	20 150	19 580	570F
Administration	7 670	7 930	260A
Catering	22 065	23 053	988A
General overheads	11 250	11 325	75A
	113 521	114 071	550A

(c) Advantages of a budgeting system include:

- it provides a basis for financial control
- it compels planning
- it may motivate managers
- it may enhance communication and departmental co-ordination.

(See Chapter 16 for full discussion of these points.)

18.5 (a) Fixed budgets are based on a single volume of activity/output and, as such, cannot reflect the impact on revenue and costs of changes to this volume. Flexible budgets, on the other hand, recognise that revenue and variable costs will react to changes in volume. Flexible budgets can be used as a form of sensitivity analysis in the planning process and and are an inherent part of effective financial control, as they allow like-with-like comparison between actual and budget based on actual volume.

(b) **REPORT**
TO: Board of Directors
FROM:
RE: Fixed and flexible budgets
A fixed budget is predicated on a single volume level and is the principal financial planning mechanism. The master budget is an example of a fixed budget. Advantages include:

- provision of a performance target, which might have motivational benefits;
- enhancement of inter-departmental co-ordination;
- enhancement of communicaiton between departments and across the organisation generally;
- provision of a benchmark for control and performance evaluation.

Disadvantages include:

- producing credible estimates in a volatile environment;
- overemphasising control may inhibit management action;
- possibility that budget is rendered out-dated by events.

Flexible budgets recognise the impact on revenue and variable cost of changes in volume, Main advantage:

- allow for like-with-like comparison between actual and budget based on actual – this makes for valid control variances.

Disadvantages:

- may not always be easy in practice to separate costs into variable and fixed elements;
- detailed financial control may distract management from important, external, developments.

In addition, both types of budgets, as numerical statements, may imply a degree of accuracy which is spurious.

Signed............

(c) A spreadsheet contains three elements:

- an input area for input of raw data like sales volumes, prices, discounts;
- a working area where formulas are used to specify mathematical relationships between input variables – e.g. that revenue equals (selling price × sales volume); it is within this area that calculations occur and raw input data are transformed into output;
- an output area containing the sales budget classified according to management needs – e.g. by product, or by region.

Once it has been set up, a spreadsheet's main advantages are:

- ability to quickly perform repetitive and complex calculations;
- ability to undertake complex sensitivity analysis; and
- flexibility in output format produced.

These advantages should mean that, after expending time and effort on initial set-up of the spreadsheet, staff time will then be freed for other purposes.

CHAPTER 19

Note: in the answers which follow, we have adopted the formulaic approach to calculation; you may have used the narrative method, which is equally acceptable. Both methods yield the same answers.

19.1 (a) F (b) T (c) T (d) F (e) T (f) F

19.2 D £23 000A
We can obtain the expenditure variance by working backwards from the variances given: volume + expenditure variances = total variance:

$$£7000F + \text{expenditure variance} = £16\ 000A$$
i.e. $$£7000F + £23\ 000A = £16\ 000A$$

19.3 (a) The standard cost per burger produced must be adjusted to allow for expected losses. There is a 20% loss of meat weight during cooking, so, in order to produce a burger with a 110 gram meat content, $110/(1 - 0.2) = 137.5$ need to be cooked. There is also a loss of 3% of completed burgers; the standard cost per completed burger must therefore be:

$$\frac{\text{Standard input cost per burger}}{(1 - 0.03)}$$

Upside-Down Burger: standard cost	£
1 bun	0.045
137.5 grams meat and herb mix @ £2.80 per kg	0.385
55 grams buffalo cheese @ £4.00per kg	0.220
25 grams relish @ £1.40 per kg	0.035
Standard input cost	0.685
Standard loss (£0.706 – £0.685)	0.021
Standard cost per burger (£0.685 ÷ [1 – 0.03])	0.706

(b) Price variance: (SP – AP) × AQ

$$= (£2.80 – [£20\ 262/7368\ kg]) × 7368\ kg \qquad = £368.40F$$

Usage variance: (SQ – AQ) × SP

The standard quantity must be adjusted to allow for the 3% loss of completed burgers: i.e. to produce 49 725 saleable burgers, (49 725 ÷ [1 – 0.03]) in total must be produced = 51 263.

$$= ([51\ 263 × 0.1375\ kg] – 7368\ kg) × £2.80 \qquad = £894.15A$$

The price variance indicates that the actual price per kg was lower than standard (£2.75 as opposed to £2.80). However, usage of the mix was greater than the standard allowed to produce 49 725 burgers. It is possible that the two variance might be linked: a cheaper mix may be of lower quality, resulting in a higher-than-expected rate of usage/waste.

19.4 (a) Material price variance (SP – AP) × AQ

Wicker: (£2 – £4200/2070 kg) × 2070 kg	= £ 60A
Padding: (£3 – £7400/2500 kg) × 7500 kg	= £300F

Material usage variance (SQ – AQ) × SP

Wicker: ([5100 × 0.4 kg] – 2070 kg) × £2	= £ 60A
Padding: ([5100 × 0.5 kg] – 2500 kg) × £3	= £150F

Labour rate variance (SR – AR) × AH

Assembly: (£6.50 – £6.60) × 10 250 hours	= £1025A
Finishing: (£5.00 – £4.90) × 5050 hours	= £ 505F

Labour efficiency variance (SH – AH)

Assembly: ([5100 × 2 hours] – 10 250 hours) × £6.50	= £325A
Finishing: ([5100 × 1 hour] – 5050 hours) × £5.00	= £250F

Selling price variance (SSP – ASP) × AS

(£30 – £32) × 5100	= £10 200F

Sales volume variance (BS – AS) × SΠ

(5000 – 5100) × £5	= £500F

(b) Possible reasons for the variances might be:

- *Material price variance* Unexpected changes in supplier(s) of wicker and padding.
- *Material usage variance* Changes to the method of production or in the quality of materials.
- *Labour rate variance* Use of a different grade of labour from that incorporated into the standard.

- *Labour efficiency variance* Change in production methods, use of different grade labour.
- *Sales price and volume variances* Unexpected increase in market demand; exit of a competitor from the market.

19.5 (a) Material price variance (SP – AP) × AQ

Resin	The standard price per litre is £100/25 litres (from the standard cost specification per batch).	= £4
	(£4 – £4463.50/1130 litres) × 1130 litres	= £56.50F
Paint	(£18 – £920/46 litres) × 46 litres	= £92.00A

Material usage variance (SQ – AQ) × SP

Resin	([44 × 25 litres] – 1130 litres) × £4	= £120.00A
Paint	([44 × 1 litre] – 46 litres) × £18	= £ 36.00A

Labour rate variance (SR – AR) × AH

The standard rate per hour (from the standard batch specification) is (£28 ÷ 8 hours) = £3.50, giving a variance of: (£3.50 – £1344/352 hours) × 352 hours = £112.00A

Labour efficiency variance (SH – AH) × SR

([44 × 8 hours] – 352 hours) × £3.50   = £nil

Variable overhead expenditure variance ([AH × SVOH] – AVO)

Standard variable overhead per hour (from standard batch specification) is (£36 ÷ 8 hours) = £4.50, giving a variance of: ([352 hours × £4.50] – £1660)   = £76.00A

Variable overhead efficiency variance (SH – AH) × SVOH

([44 × 8 hours] – 352 hours) × £4.50   = £nil

Fixed overhead expenditure variance (BFO – AFO)

Budgeted fixed overhead per period is (budgeted output × fixed overhead per batch) = (40 × £160) = £6400, giving a variance of: (£6400 – £6200)   = £200.00F

Fixed overhead volume variance (BP – AP) × FOPU

(40 – 44) × £160   = £640.00F

Reconciliation of budgeted and actual cost

			£
Budgeted cost of actual production (44 batches × £342)			15 048.00

		F	*A*	
Variances		£	£	
Material price:	resin	56.50		
	paint		92.00	
Material usage:	resin		120.00	
	paint		36.00	
Labour rate variance			112.00	
Variable overhead expenditure variance			76.00	
Fixed overhead expenditure variance		200.00		
Fixed overhead volume variance		640.00		
		896.50	436.00	460.50F
Actual cost				14 587.50

(b) Although Goblin Ltd's actual cost is lower than budget for the actual volume of output, this is largely due to the favourable fixed overhead volume variance, which has arisen solely as a result of the higher-than-budgeted output. There has been a saving against budget in fixed overhead expenditure and in the purchase cost of resin. However, all the other variances are adverse (albeit by relatively small amounts). It may be that additional volume has been achieved at the expense of operational efficiency and that the saving in the purchase cost of resin has resulted in poorer quality material (hence the adverse usage variance for resin). Management would therefore be advised to investigate the reasons for all variances considered significant, with a view to taking advantage of any opportunity offered by favourable variances, and to minimising the likelihood of future adverse variances.

CHAPTER 20

20.1 A DR Raw materials control account
CR Raw material price variance account

20.2 (a) F (b) F (c) T (d) T (e) F (f) T (g) F

20.3 (a) The material price variance is: $(£5 - £5500/1000 \text{ kg}) \times 1000 \text{ kg} = £500\text{A}$.

	Dr £	Cr £
Material AB account (1000 kg × standard cost)	5000	
Material price variance account	500	
D Ltd (creditor) account		5500
WIP control account (400 kg × £5)	2000	
Material AB account		2000
Stock loss account (20 kg × £5)	100	
Material AB account		100
Material AB account (200 kg × £5)	1000	
WIP control account		1000
D Ltd (creditor) account (200 kg × £5.50)	1100	
Material AB account		1000
Material price variance account (see Note)		100
WIP control account (300 kg × £5)	1500	
Material AB account		1500

Note
The portion of the price variance relating to the substandard materials needs to be reinstated, since the company will seek credit from the supplier to the extent of these items' actual cost.

(b) In an integrated system, cost accounting and financial accounting records are kept within the same ('integrated') ledger. In a non-integrated ('interlocking') system, separate ledgers are kept to record cost accounting and financial accounting transactions. The two ledgers within a non-integrated system are 'interlocked' by means of a cost ledger control account within the costing ledger, and a general ledger control account within the financial ledger. If the system has been properly maintained, the balance on these two accounts should always be equal and opposite. However, there may be valid reasons for the two ledgers to differ in certain respects – e.g. stock valuation, which may be at standard within the costing ledger, but at actual within the financial ledger. Where such differences arise, it is necessary to periodically reconcile the two ledgers.

Integrated systems may be superior because:

- They are simpler to operate – hence cheaper and with less likelihood of error.
- The potential confusion that could result from having two valuations, say, for stock, does not exist.

However, integrated systems use a single ledger to meet both internal and external accounting requirements, which may give rise to problems:

- The need to meet statutory and other requirements for external (financial) reporting may dominate the system, resulting in inadequate attention being paid to internal reporting needs.
- Information produced for external purposes may be totally inappropriate for planning, control and decision making (i.e. internal) purposes.

(See Chapter 7 for further discussion of integrated and interlocking systems.)

20.4 (a) (i) Assuming that opening raw materials stock is valued at £2.40 per kg, along with issues to WIP and closing stock, then we have 100 kg, 2500 kg, 75 kg respectively. To balance the physical quantities on the raw materials account, purchases must therefore be: (issues to WIP + closing stock – opening stock) = 2475 kg. The actual cost of these purchases is the missing amount due to creditors on the raw materials account – i.e. the balancing monetary amount of £6400. Actual cost of materials purchased is therefore (£6400 ÷ 2475 kg) = £2.59 (rounded).

(ii) From the WIP account, we know that the standard cost of completed output was £34 720. The standard cost per unit is:

	£
Direct materials	12
Direct labour	24
Fixed overhead	20
	56

Completed output is thus (£34 720 ÷ £56) = 620 units.

(iii) Overhead absorbed: (actual output × standard overhead per unit) = (620 × £20) = £12 400.

(iv) Inserting information from the question into the labour efficiency variance calculation, we get: £900A = ([620 × 4 hours] – AH) × £6

i.e.   150A = (2480 – AH), so AH = 2630

(v) The amount transferred from production overhead control to WIP is the overhead absorbed, which was £12 400 (from (iii)). The amount owing to expense creditors is therefore the balancing figure on this account – i.e. £10 265.

(vi)

	£
Standard labour cost of actual output (620 × £24)	14 880
Add Adverse rate variance	618
Adverse efficiency variance	900
= Actual wages cost	16 398
Actual labour-hours (from (iv))	2 630
Actual rate per hour	£6.24 (rounded)

(b) See solution to Question 20.3(b) above.

20.5 Standard cost per unit must be adjusted to allow for normal loss. Since normal loss is 10% of output, standard input costs need to be uplifted by 1/0.9:

	£
Chemical compound (1.8 kg × 1/0.9) = 2 kg @ £4	8
Labour (5.4 hours × 1/0.9) = 6 hours @ £6	36
Variable overhead (5.4 hours × 1/0.9) = 6 hours @ £3	18
Standard cost per unit of output	62

In the equivalent unit calculation that follows, labour and variable overhead are treated together as 'conversion cost'.

Table A20.1 Equivalent unit calculation for August

	Chemical compound	Conversion cost
Completed output *less* opening WIP equivalent units	(100% × 5000) − (100% × 2000) = 3000	(100% × 5000) − (40% × 2000) = 4200
Closing WIP	(1500 × 100%) = 1500	(1500 × 50%) = 750
Total equivalent units	4500	4950

Variances

Note that the material price, labour rate and variable overhead expenditure variances need not be calculated as they do not appear in the process account.

Material usage variance (SQ − AQ) × SP

([4500 × 2 kg] − 10 200 kg) × £4 £4800A

Labour efficiency variance (SH − AH) × SR

([4950 × 6 hours] − 31 000 hours) × £6 £7800A

Variable overhead efficiency variance (SH − AH) × SVOH

([4950 × 6 hours] − 31 000 hours) × £3 £3900A

Before posting the process account, we need the cost of opening WIP:

	£
Opening WIP	
Chemical compound (2000 units × 100%) × 2 kg × £4/kg	16 000
Labour (2000 units × 40%) × 6 hours × £6/hour	28 800
Variable overhead (2000 units × 40%) × 6 hours × £3/hour	14 400
	59 200

For labour and variable overhead, the process account is debited with (actual hours × standard rate per hour): (31 000 × £6) for labour, and (31 000 × £3) for variable overhead. For chemical compound, the debit is (actual quantity × standard cost/kg) – i.e. (10 200 × £4). Finally, the transfer to finished goods is (completed output × standard cost per unit of output).

Process Account

	£		£
Opening WIP	59 200	Material usage variance	4 800
Chemical compound	40 800	Labour efficiency variance	7 800
Labour	186 000	Variable overhead efficiency	
Variable overhead	93 000	variance	3 900
		Finished goods (5000 × £62)	310 000
		Closing WIP c/d (balance)	52 500
	379 000		379 000
Opening WIP b/d	52 500		

APPENDIX B

Present value tables

Table I Present value of a single payment/receipt of £1 at the end of *n* years from now, discounted at *r*%

Years	1%	2%	3%	4%	5%	6%	7%	8%	9%	10%	11%	12%	13%	14%
1	0.990	0.980	0.971	0.962	0.952	0.943	0.935	0.926	0.917	0.909	0.901	0.893	0.885	0.877
2	0.980	0.961	0.943	0.943	0.907	0.890	0.873	0.857	0.842	0.826	0.812	0.797	0.783	0.770
3	0.971	0.942	0.915	0.889	0.864	0.840	0.816	0.794	0.772	0.751	0.731	0.712	0.693	0.675
4	0.961	0.924	0.889	0.855	0.823	0.792	0.763	0.735	0.708	0.683	0.659	0.636	0.613	0.592
5	0.952	0.906	0.863	0.822	0.784	0.747	0.713	0.681	0.650	0.621	0.594	0.567	0.543	0.519
6	0.942	0.888	0.838	0.790	0.746	0.705	0.666	0.630	0.596	0.565	0.535	0.507	0.480	0.456
7	0.933	0.871	0.813	0.760	0.711	0.665	0.623	0.584	0.547	0.513	0.482	0.452	0.425	0.400
8	0.924	0.854	0.789	0.731	0.677	0.627	0.582	0.540	0.502	0.467	0.434	0.404	0.376	0.351
9	0.914	0.837	0.766	0.703	0.645	0.592	0.544	0.500	0.460	0.424	0.391	0.361	0.333	0.308
10	0.905	0.820	0.744	0.676	0.614	0.558	0.508	0.463	0.422	0.386	0.352	0.322	0.295	0.270
11	0.896	0.804	0.722	0.650	0.585	0.527	0.475	0.429	0.388	0.351	0.317	0.288	0.261	0.237
12	0.887	0.789	0.701	0.625	0.557	0.497	0.444	0.397	0.356	0.319	0.286	0.257	0.231	0.208
13	0.879	0.773	0.681	0.601	0.530	0.469	0.415	0.368	0.326	0.290	0.258	0.229	0.204	0.182
14	0.870	0.758	0.661	0.578	0.505	0.442	0.388	0.341	0.299	0.263	0.232	0.205	0.181	0.160
15	0.861	0.743	0.642	0.555	0.481	0.417	0.362	0.315	0.275	0.239	0.209	0.183	0.160	0.140
16	0.853	0.728	0.623	0.534	0.458	0.394	0.339	0.292	0.252	0.218	0.188	0.163	0.142	0.123
17	0.844	0.714	0.605	0.513	0.436	0.371	0.317	0.270	0.231	0.198	0.170	0.146	0.125	0.108
18	0.836	0.700	0.587	0.494	0.416	0.350	0.296	0.250	0.212	0.180	0.153	0.130	0.111	0.095
19	0.828	0.686	0.570	0.475	0.396	0.331	0.277	0.232	0.195	0.164	0.138	0.116	0.098	0.083
20	0.820	0.673	0.554	0.456	0.377	0.312	0.258	0.215	0.178	0.149	0.124	0.104	0.087	0.073

Years	15%	16%	17%	18%	19%	20%	21%	22%	23%	24%	25%	30%	35%	40%
1	0.870	0.862	0.855	0.848	0.840	0.833	0.826	0.820	0.813	0.807	0.800	0.769	0.741	0.714
2	0.756	0.743	0.731	0.718	0.706	0.694	0.683	0.672	0.661	0.650	0.640	0.592	0.549	0.510
3	0.658	0.641	0.624	0.609	0.593	0.579	0.565	0.551	0.537	0.525	0.512	0.455	0.406	0.364
4	0.572	0.552	0.534	0.516	0.499	0.482	0.467	0.451	0.437	0.423	0.410	0.350	0.301	0.260
5	0.497	0.476	0.456	0.437	0.419	0.402	0.386	0.370	0.355	0.341	0.328	0.269	0.223	0.186
6	0.432	0.410	0.390	0.370	0.352	0.335	0.319	0.303	0.289	0.275	0.262	0.207	0.165	0.133
7	0.376	0.354	0.333	0.314	0.296	0.279	0.263	0.249	0.235	0.222	0.210	0.159	0.122	0.095
8	0.327	0.305	0.285	0.266	0.249	0.233	0.218	0.204	0.191	0.179	0.168	0.123	0.091	0.068
9	0.284	0.263	0.243	0.226	0.209	0.194	0.180	0.167	0.155	0.144	0.134	0.094	0.067	0.048
10	0.247	0.227	0.208	0.191	0.176	0.162	0.149	0.137	0.126	0.116	0.107	0.073	0.050	0.035
11	0.215	0.195	0.178	0.162	0.148	0.135	0.123	0.112	0.103	0.094	0.086	0.056	0.037	0.025
12	0.187	0.169	0.152	0.137	0.124	0.112	0.102	0.092	0.083	0.076	0.069	0.043	0.027	0.018
13	0.163	0.145	0.130	0.116	0.104	0.094	0.084	0.075	0.068	0.061	0.055	0.033	0.020	0.013
14	0.141	0.125	0.111	0.099	0.088	0.078	0.069	0.062	0.055	0.049	0.044	0.025	0.015	0.009
15	0.123	0.108	0.095	0.084	0.074	0.065	0.057	0.051	0.045	0.040	0.035	0.020	0.011	0.006
16	0.107	0.093	0.081	0.071	0.062	0.054	0.047	0.042	0.036	0.032	0.028	0.015	0.008	0.005
17	0.093	0.080	0.069	0.060	0.052	0.045	0.039	0.034	0.030	0.026	0.023	0.012	0.006	0.003
18	0.081	0.069	0.059	0.051	0.044	0.038	0.032	0.028	0.024	0.021	0.018	0.009	0.005	0.002
19	0.070	0.060	0.051	0.043	0.037	0.031	0.027	0.023	0.020	0.017	0.014	0.007	0.003	0.002
20	0.061	0.051	0.043	0.037	0.031	0.026	0.022	0.019	0.016	0.014	0.012	0.005	0.003	0.001

Table II Present value of £1 paid/received at the end of each of n years from now, discounted at r%

Years	1%	2%	3%	4%	5%	6%	7%	8%	9%	10%	11%	12%	13%	14%
1	0.990	0.980	0.971	0.962	0.952	0.943	0.935	0.926	0.917	0.909	0.901	0.893	0.885	0.877
2	1.970	1.942	1.913	1.886	1.859	1.833	1.808	1.783	1.759	1.736	1.713	1.690	1.668	1.647
3	2.941	2.884	2.829	2.775	2.723	2.673	2.624	2.577	2.531	2.487	2.444	2.402	2.361	2.322
4	3.902	3.808	3.717	3.630	3.546	3.465	3.387	3.312	3.240	3.170	3.102	3.037	2.974	2.914
5	4.853	4.713	4.580	4.452	4.329	4.212	4.100	3.993	3.890	3.791	3.696	3.605	3.517	3.433
6	5.795	5.601	5.417	5.242	5.076	4.917	4.767	4.623	4.486	4.355	4.231	4.111	3.998	3.889
7	6.728	6.472	6.230	6.002	5.786	5.582	5.389	5.206	5.033	4.868	4.712	4.564	4.423	4.288
8	7.652	7.325	7.020	6.733	6.463	6.210	5.971	5.747	5.535	5.335	5.146	4.968	4.799	4.639
9	8.566	8.162	7.786	7.435	7.108	6.802	6.515	6.247	5.995	5.759	5.537	5.328	5.132	4.946
10	9.471	8.983	8.530	8.111	7.722	7.360	7.024	6.710	6.418	6.145	5.889	5.650	5.426	5.216
11	10.368	9.787	9.253	8.760	8.306	7.887	7.499	7.139	6.805	6.495	6.207	5.938	5.687	5.453
12	11.255	10.575	9.954	9.385	8.863	8.384	7.943	7.536	7.161	6.814	6.492	6.194	5.918	5.660
13	12.134	11.348	10.635	9.986	9.394	8.853	8.358	7.904	7.487	7.103	6.750	6.424	6.122	5.842
14	13.004	12.106	11.296	10.563	9.899	9.295	8.745	8.244	7.786	7.367	6.982	6.628	6.302	6.002
15	13.865	12.849	11.938	11.118	10.380	9.712	9.108	8.559	8.061	7.606	7.191	6.811	6.462	6.142
16	14.718	13.578	12.561	11.652	10.838	10.106	9.447	8.851	8.313	7.824	7.379	6.974	6.604	6.265
17	15.562	14.292	13.166	12.166	11.274	10.477	9.763	9.122	8.544	8.022	7.549	7.120	6.729	6.373
18	16.398	14.992	13.754	12.659	11.690	10.828	10.059	9.372	8.756	8.201	7.702	7.250	6.840	6.467
19	17.226	15.678	14.324	13.134	12.085	11.158	10.336	9.604	8.950	8.365	7.839	7.366	6.938	6.550
20	18.046	16.351	14.877	13.590	12.462	11.470	10.594	9.818	9.129	8.514	7.963	7.469	7.025	6.623

Years	15%	16%	17%	18%	19%	20%	21%	22%	23%	24%	25%	30%	35%	40%
1	0.870	0.862	0.855	0.847	0.840	0.833	0.826	0.820	0.813	0.806	0.800	0.769	0.741	0.714
2	1.626	1.605	1.585	1.566	1.547	1.528	1.509	1.492	1.474	1.457	1.440	1.361	1.289	1.224
3	2.283	2.246	2.210	2.174	2.140	2.106	2.074	2.042	2.011	1.981	1.952	1.816	1.696	1.589
4	2.855	2.798	2.743	2.690	2.639	2.589	2.540	2.494	2.448	2.404	2.362	2.166	1.997	1.849
5	3.352	3.274	3.199	3.127	3.058	2.991	2.926	2.864	2.803	2.745	2.689	2.436	2.220	2.035
6	3.784	3.685	3.589	3.498	3.410	3.326	3.245	3.167	3.092	3.020	2.951	2.643	2.385	2.168
7	4.160	4.039	3.922	3.812	3.706	3.605	3.508	3.416	3.327	3.242	3.161	2.802	2.508	2.263
8	4.487	4.344	4.207	4.078	3.954	3.837	3.726	3.619	3.518	3.421	3.329	2.925	2.598	2.331
9	4.772	4.607	4.451	4.303	4.163	4.031	3.905	3.786	3.673	3.566	3.463	3.019	2.665	2.379
10	5.019	4.833	4.659	4.494	4.339	4.192	4.054	3.923	3.799	3.682	3.571	3.092	2.715	2.414
11	5.234	5.029	4.836	4.656	4.486	4.327	4.177	4.035	3.902	3.776	3.656	3.147	2.752	2.438
12	5.421	5.197	4.988	4.793	4.611	4.439	4.278	4.127	3.985	3.851	3.725	3.190	2.779	2.456
13	5.583	5.342	5.118	4.910	4.715	4.533	4.362	4.203	4.053	3.912	3.780	3.223	2.799	2.469
14	5.724	5.468	5.229	5.008	4.802	4.611	4.432	4.265	4.108	3.962	3.824	3.249	2.814	2.478
15	5.847	5.575	5.324	5.092	4.876	4.675	4.489	4.315	4.153	4.001	3.859	3.268	2.825	2.484
16	5.954	5.668	5.405	5.162	4.938	4.730	4.536	4.357	4.189	4.033	3.887	3.283	2.834	2.489
17	6.047	5.749	5.475	5.222	4.990	4.775	4.576	4.391	4.219	4.059	3.910	3.295	2.840	2.492
18	6.128	5.818	5.534	5.273	5.033	4.812	4.608	4.419	4.243	4.080	3.928	3.304	2.844	2.494
19	6.198	5.877	5.584	5.316	5.070	4.843	4.635	4.442	4.263	4.097	3.942	3.311	2.848	2.496
20	6.259	5.929	5.628	5.353	5.101	4.870	4.657	4.460	4.279	4.110	3.954	3.316	2.850	2.497

INDEX